"How Much Can I Make?"

Actual Sales and Profit Potential for Your Small Business

3rd Edition

(Originally titled *Franchising: The Bottom Line*)

Robert E. Bond
Publisher

Nicole Thompson
Editor

Amy Lau
Editorial Assistant

Source Book Publications
Serving the Franchising Industry

P.O. Box 12488
Oakland, CA 94604
510/839-5471

ISBN 1-887137-10-6

DISCLAIMER

The Earnings Claim Statements in *"How Much Can I Make?"* are based on data submitted by the franchisors themselves to various state and/or federal regulatory agencies. The franchisor profiles are based on information submitted to Source Book Publications by the franchisors themselves. Every reasonable effort has been made to ensure that the information presented accurately reflects the original data submitted. Although the author and Source Book Publications feel confident that the information submitted is accurate and complete, they have not independently verified or corroborated the information. Accordingly, neither the author nor Source Book Publications assumes any responsibility for errors or omissions. They strongly encourage any prospective franchisee to conduct an aggressive independent investigation into the sales and income potential of the franchises being considered. Readers should keep in mind that some of the franchisors may have terminated their franchising efforts since the submission of the original data. Others may have superseded the information contained herein with more current earnings claim statements.

It is the intent of the author and publisher to periodically update *"How Much Can I Make?"* To the extent that any franchisor making an Earnings Claim Statement wishes to be included in subsequent editions, please forward a current copy of your offering circular or Item XIX to Source Book Publications, P. O. Box 12488, Oakland, CA 96404.

Cover Design by Joyce Coffland, Artistic Concepts.

ISBN 1-887137-20-3

Printed in the United States of America.
10 9 8 7 6 5 4 3 2 1

"How Much Can I Make?" is available at special discounts for bulk purchase. Special editions or book excerpts can also be created to specifications. For details, contact Source Book Publications, P. O. Box 12488, Oakland, CA 94604. Phone: (510) 839-5471; Fax: (510) 547-3245.

To Pat Curran —

A wonderful friend and comrade in arms throughout many of life's most challenging and rewarding experiences.

Preface

As a prospective franchisee, the **single most important task ahead of you is to get an accurate and reliable sense of a business's potential sales, expenses and profits.** Without this analysis, you will have only a faint idea of how much you are going to earn as a result of your investment and considerable efforts.

Keep in mind that, in acquiring a franchise, or any business for that matter, you are making an investment that has long-term responsibilities and consequences that are potentially far reaching. If you find out 12 months after starting your business that you didn't properly project the negative cash flows that would occur during the start-up phase, or didn't appreciate the magnitude of advertising/promotion costs or assumed that revenues would be 30% higher than they actually are, then shame on you. At that point, you can't re-negotiate your franchise contract. If you can't make the business work financially, the fact that you really enjoy being your own boss, really like the franchisor's management team and its vision and really believe in the product/service is of secondary importance. If, six months after starting the business, you find yourself financially strapped, your options are severely limited. You can continue to limp along operating the business, working even harder, and most likely hating what you are doing. You can borrow more money in the hopes of generating increased revenues. Or you can sell the business, most likely for substantially less than you invested.

Do yourself a favor. Take whatever time is necessary to do your homework. You will no doubt be under an inordinate amount of pressure to start your new business as soon as possible. Resist the temptation to do so until you are completely conversant with all facets of the particular business in which you are investing and the dynamics of the industry itself. Spend the extra time and money to ensure that no stones are left unturned. In addition to the required due diligence, make sure you fully understand what cash flow statements are about, the distinction between fixed and variable costs and what industry operating standards are. Know where to go to get industry data. Call as many existing (and former) franchisees as are required to corroborate your projections. They will be able to tell you if your assumptions are either too optimistic or too pessimistic. Keep in mind that the existing franchisee base represents your best source of information on the business. You will only get one chance to perform your due diligence.

Given these alarmist warnings as a preamble, it is incumbent on you to thoroughly research all aspects of the industry you are considering prior to making an irreversible investment. The risks are high. Your failure could well result in the loss of your investment, as well as any other property you may have pledged, your marriage (to the extent that your spouse was not equally committed to franchising and the inherent risks involved) and, possibly most important, your self-esteem. Contrary to much of the hype surrounding the industry, there are no guarantees. To think that you can simply pay a franchise fee and automatically step into a guaranteed money machine is naive at best and fatal at worst. There is **absolutely no substitute for extensive due diligence.** The burden is on you to do your homework and ensure that the choice is fully researched. Only you can maximize the chances of success and minimize the chances of failure or unfulfilled expectations.

"How Much Can I Make?" contains over 160 earnings claims statements from 46 distinct industry categories. The roster of franchisors runs from large, well-established operations like Burger King and McDonald's to newer, smaller franchises with only a handful of operating units. Keep in mind that the financial data presented below is based on actual, verifiable operating results that the franchisors must be able to document. Understanding these financial statements is only one step in a long and tedious process. They nevertheless provide an invaluable source of critical background information that you will not find in any other source.

One of the most important exercises you can do is to rigorously determine what the **net earnings** from your investment will be. Realize that you have an "opportunity cost" associated with your investment in the business. If you invest $100,000 of equity, that money could probably earn a minimum of 8% if deployed elsewhere and with considerably less risk. Accordingly, the first $8,000 earned is not really a profit, but a return on your investment. Does the remaining "adjusted net cash flow" adequately reward you for the stress and strain of running your own business: putting in long, hard hours at work, wearing 10 hats at a time, living with financial uncertainty and giving up much of your discretionary time? On the other side of the ledger are the advantages of owning your own business: the pride and independence of running your own show, the chance to start something from scratch and sell it 5–10 years later at a multiple of your original investment, and the opportunity to take full advantage of your management, sales and people skills. Clearly there is a balance, but make sure that you have a strong sense of how realistic your expectations are and if they have a solid chance of being achieved.

Although the level of detail and applicability to your own investment differs substantially among the various earnings claims statements, you can, nevertheless, learn a great deal by reviewing the data presented. Just because an earnings claims statement is not in the same industry you are considering, don't assume that you shouldn't read it. Reviewing a wide range of actual operating results provides an invaluable chance to become acquainted with basic accounting practices — how to get from gross sales to net income, how to differentiate between fixed expenses (such as rent, equipment rental and utilities) and variable expenses (direct labor, shipping and percentage rent) and how to determine a break-even point. Consider how various aspects of a totally different type of business might apply to your business. This is a great chance to avoid saying six months from now, "why wasn't I aware of that expense?" Devoting even a minimal amount of time and energy will provide invaluable insights.

Presuming that you are committed to maximizing your chances for success, you have a great deal of work ahead of you. Because it is tedious, many people will opt for the easy way out and do only a modest amount of homework. Many of these will ultimately regret their slothfulness and, accordingly, their investment decision. Others will be happy with the decision to enter franchising, but will wish they had joined another franchise system. Still others will go out of business. I strongly recommend that you commit the next several months to learn everything you can about the franchising industry in general, the specific industry you are considering in particular, all of the franchise opportunities within that industry and, most importantly, the individual franchise you ultimately select.

You have a great deal at risk, and you don't get a second chance. Your cheapest form of insurance is the time you put in investigating a business before you invest. Take full advantage of the tools available to you. Do your homework.

Good luck and Godspeed.

Table of contents

Section Three — Index

30 minute overview

There are three stages to the franchise selection process: the investigation, the evaluation and the negotiation stages. This book is intended to assist the reader in the first two stages by providing a framework for developing reasonable financial guidelines upon which to make a well-researched and properly-documented investment decision.

Understand at the outset that the entire franchise selection process should take many months and can involve a great deal of frustration. I suggest that you set up a realistic timeline for signing a franchise agreement and that you stick to that schedule. There will be a lot of pressure on you to prematurely complete the selection and negotiation phases. Resist the temptation. The penalties are too severe for a seat-of-the-pants attitude. A decision of this magnitude clearly deserves careful consideration.

Before starting the selection process, briefly review the areas covered below.

Franchise Industry Structure

The franchising industry is made up of two distinct types of franchises. The first, and by far the larger, includes product and trade name franchising. Included in this group are automotive and truck dealers, soft drink bottlers and gasoline service stations. For the most part, these are essentially distributorships.

The second group encompasses business format franchisors. This book only includes information on this latter category.

Layman's Definition of Franchising

Business format franchising is a method of market expansion by which one business entity expands the distribution of its products and/or services through independent, third-party operators. Franchising occurs when the operator of a concept or system (the franchisor) grants an independent businessperson (the franchisee) the right to duplicate its entire business format at a particular location and for a specified period, under terms and conditions set forth in the contract (franchise agreement). The franchisee has full access to all of the trademarks, logos, marketing techniques, controls, and systems that have made the franchisor successful. In effect, the franchisee acts as a surrogate for a company-owned store in the distribution of the franchisor's goods and/or services. It is important to keep in mind that the franchisor and the franchisee are separate legal entities.

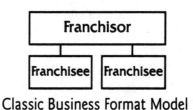

Classic Business Format Model

In return for a front-end franchise fee — which usually ranges from $15,000–35,000 — the franchisor is obligated to "set up" the franchisee in business. This generally includes assistance in selecting a location, negotiating a lease, obtaining financing, building and equipping a site and providing the necessary training, operating manuals and start-up assistance. Once the training is completed and the store is open, the new franchisee should have a carbon copy of other units in the system and enjoy the same benefits they do, whether they are company-owned or not.

Business format franchising is unique because it is a long-term relationship characterized by an on-going, mutually beneficial partnership. On-going services include research and development, marketing strategies, advertising campaigns, group buying, periodic field visits, training updates, and whatever else is required to make the franchisee competitive and profitable. In effect, the franchisor acts as the franchisee's "back office" support organization. To reimburse the franchisor for this support, the franchisee pays the franchisor an on-going royalty fee, generally 4–8 % of gross sales. In many cases, franchisees also contribute an advertising fee to reimburse the franchisor for expenses incurred in maintaining a national or regional advertising campaign.

To work to maximum advantage, both the franchisor and the franchisees should share common objectives and goals. Both parties must accept the premise that their fortunes are mutually intertwined and that they are each better off working in a co-operative effort rather than toward self-serving goals. Unlike the parent/child relationship that has dominated franchising over the past 30 years, franchising is now becoming a true relationship of partners.

The Players

Franchisors

Source Book Publications routinely tracks approximately 2,300 U.S. and Canadian franchisors. We believe this represents the number of legitimate, active franchisors in North America at any point in time. Profiles of these franchisors can be found in

Bond's Franchise Guide, published annually by Source Book Publications. Copies of this 550+ page directory, which is considered the definitive directory in the field, are available for $29.95 plus $4.00 for shipping and handling ($42.75 + $5.75 in Canada). Call (510) 839-5471 or fax (510) 839-2104 to place a credit card order, or send a check to Source Book Publications, P.O. Box 12488, Oakland, CA 94604. There is an order form at the end of this book.

While you may already have your sights on a particular franchise opportunity, it would be short-sighted not to find out as much as you can about both the direct and indirect competition. You might discover that other franchises have similar products or services, but offer superior training and support, a reduced royalty fee or vastly superior financing options. I strongly encourage you to read either *Bond's Franchise Guide* or one of the other franchise directories to fully explore the options open to you.

The Regulatory Agencies

The offer and sale of franchises are regulated at both the federal and state levels. Federal requirements cover all 50 states. In addition, certain states have adopted their own requirements.

In 1979, after many years of debate, the Federal Trade Commission (FTC) implemented Rule 436. This Rule requires that franchisors provide prospective franchisees with a disclosure statement (called an offering circular) containing specific information about a company's franchise offering. The Rule has two objectives: to ensure that potential franchisees have sufficient background information to make an educated investment decision and to provide them with adequate time to do so.

Certain "registration states" require additional safeguards to protect potential franchisees. Their requirements are generally more stringent than the FTC's requirements. These states include California, Florida, Hawaii, Illinois, Indiana, Maryland, Michigan, Minnesota, New York, North Dakota, Oregon, Rhode Island, South Dakota, Virginia, Washington and Wisconsin. Separate registration is also required in the province of Alberta.

For the most part, these registration states require a disclosure format known as the Uniform Franchise Offering Circular (UFOC). The state requirements are generally more demanding than the federal requirements. As a matter of convenience, most franchisors have adopted the UFOC format. This format requires that the franchisor provides a prospective franchisee with the required information at their first face-to-face meeting or at least 10 business days prior to the signing of the franchise agreement, whichever is earlier. Required information includes:

1. The franchisor and any predecessors.
2. Identity and business experience of persons affiliated with the franchisor.
3. Litigation.
4. Bankruptcy.
5. Franchisee's initial fee or other initial payments.
6. Other fees.
7. Franchisee's initial investment.
8. Obligations of franchisee to purchase or lease from designated sources.
9. Obligations of franchisee to purchase or lease in accordance with specifications or from approved suppliers.
10. Financing arrangements.
11. Obligations of the franchisor; other supervision, assistance or services.
12. Exclusive area or territory.
13. Trademarks, service marks, trade names, logotypes and commercial symbols.
14. Patents and copyrights.
15. Obligations of the participate in the actual operation of the franchise business.
16. Restrictions on goods and services offered by franchisee.
17. Renewal, termination, repurchase, modification and assignment of the franchise agreement and related information.
18. Arrangements with public figures.
19. Actual, average, projected or forecasted franchise sales, profits or earnings.
20. Information regarding franchises of the franchisor.
21. Financial statements.
22. Contracts.
23. Acknowledgment of receipt by respective franchisee.

If you live in a registration state, make sure that the franchisor you are evaluating is, in fact, registered to sell franchises there. If not, and the franchisor has no near-term plans to register in your state, you should consider other options.

Keep in mind that neither the FTC nor any of the states has reviewed the offering circular to determine whether the information submitted is true and accurate or not. They merely require that the franchisor make representations based upon a prescribed format. If the information provided is false, franchisors are subject to civil penalties. You should also be aware of the reality that neither the FTC nor the individual states has the staff or budget necessary to pursue a lengthy battle over possible misrepresentations. If you run into problems, your only real option is to retain an attorney and battle a franchisor who may have an in-house legal staff and a bottomless war chest. While you might win the battle, you would most likely lose the war.

It is up to you to read and thoroughly understand all elements of the offering circular and to take full advantage of the documentation that is available to you. Know exactly what you can expect from the franchisor and what your own obligations are. Under what circumstances can the relationship be unilaterally terminated by the franchisor? What is your protected territory? What are the terms of a renewal? Can you expand within your territory? While there is no question that the UFOC is tedious reading, it, nevertheless, provides invaluable information. The penalties for not doing your homework are severe. You will have no one to blame but yourself. Hedge your bet by having a professional also review the UFOC.

The Trade Associations

The **International Franchise Association** (IFA) was established in 1960 as a non-profit trade association to promote franchising as a responsible method of doing business. The IFA currently represents over 600 franchisors in the U.S. and around the world. It is recognized as the leading spokesperson for the industry. For most of its 30+ years, the IFA has represented the interests of franchisors only. In recent years, however, it has initiated an aggressive campaign to recruit franchisees into its membership and to represent their interests as well. The IFA's offices are located at 1350 New York Avenue, NW, Suite 900, Washington, DC 20005. (202) 628-8000; FAX (202) 628-0812.

The **Canadian Franchise Association** (CFA), which has some 250+ members, is the Canadian equivalent of the IFA. Information on the CFA can be obtained by writing the group at 5045 Orbit Drive, Suite 401, Building 9, Mississauga, ON L4W 4Y4, Canada. (905) 625-2896; FAX (905) 625-9076.

What Makes a Winning Franchise

Virtually every writer on the subject of franchising has his or her own idea of what determines a winning franchise. I believe there are five primary factors.

1. A product or service with clear advantages over the competition. These advantages may include brand recognition, a unique, proprietary product or service, or 30 years of proven experience.

2. A standardized franchise system that has been time-tested. A company that has operated numerous units, both company-owned and franchised, has usually worked out most of the bugs in the system. By the time a system has 30 or more operating units, it should be thoroughly tested.

3. Exceptional franchisor support. This includes not only the initial training program, but the on-going support (Research & Development, refresher training, [800] help-lines, field representatives who provide on-site training, annual meetings, advertising and promotion, central purchasing, etc.).

4. The financial wherewithal and management experience to carry out any announced growth plans without short-changing its franchisees. Sufficient depth of management is often lacking in younger, high-growth franchises.

5. A strong mutuality of interest between franchisor and franchisees. Unless both parties realize that their relationship is one of long-term partners, the system will probably never achieve its full potential. A few telephone calls to existing and former franchisees can easily determine whether the necessary rapport between franchisor and franchisees exists.

The Negotiation Process

Once you have narrowed your options down to your two or three top choices, you now have to negotiate the best deal you can with the franchisor. In most cases, the franchisor will tell you that the franchise agreement cannot be changed. Think twice before you accept the statement that the contract is non-negotiable. Notwithstanding the legal requirement that all of a franchisor's agreements be substantially the same at any point in time, there are usually a number of variables that are flexible. If the franchisor truly wants you as a franchisee, it may be willing to make concessions not available to the next applicant.

Will the franchisor take a short-term note for all or part of the franchise fee? Can you expand from your initial unit after you have proven yourself? If so, can the franchise fee on a second unit be eliminated or reduced? Can you get a right of first refusal on adjacent territories? Can the term of the agreement be extended from 10 to 15 years? Can you include a franchise cancellation right if the training and/or initial support don't meet your expectations or the franchisor's promises? The list goes on ad infinitum.

To successfully negotiate, you must have a thorough knowledge of the industry, the franchise agreement you are negotiating (and agreements of competitive franchise opportunities) and access to experienced professional advice. This can be a lawyer, an accountant or a franchise consultant. Above all else, he or she should have proven experience in negotiating franchise agreements. Franchising is a unique method of doing business. Don't pay someone $100+ per hour to learn the industry. Make him or her demonstrate that he or she has been through the process several times before. Negotiating a long-term agreement of this type is extremely tricky and fraught with pitfalls. The risks are extremely high. Don't think that you can handle the negotiations yourself, or that you can't afford outside counsel. In point of fact, you can't afford not to employ an experienced professional advisor.

The 4 R'S of Franchising

At a young age we're taught that the three R's of reading, 'riting, and 'rithmatic are critical to our scholastic success. Success in franchising depends on four R's — realism, research, reserves and resolve.

Realism

At the outset of your investigation, be realistic about your strengths, weaknesses, goals and capabilities. I strongly recommend you take the time necessary to do a personal audit — possibly with the help of outside professionals — before investing your life's savings in a franchise.

Franchising is not a money machine. It involves hard work, dedication, set-backs and long hours. Be realistic about the nature of the business you are buying. What traits will ultimately determine your success? Do you have them? If it is a service-oriented business, will you be able to keep smiling when you know the client is a fool? If it is a fast-food business, will you be able to properly manage a minimum-wage staff? How well will you handle the uncertainties that will invariably arise? Can you make day-to-day decisions based on imperfect information? Can you count on the support of your spouse after you have gone through all of your working capital reserves and the future looks increasingly cloudy?

Be equally realistic about your franchise selection process. Have you thoroughly evaluated all of the alternatives? Have you talked with everyone you can, leaving no stone unturned? Have you carefully and realistically assessed the advantages and disadvantages of the system offered, the unique demographics of your territory, near-term market trends and the financial projections? The selection process is tiring. It is easy to convince yourself that the franchise opportunity in your hand is really the best one for you before you've done all your homework. The penalties for such slothfulness so, however, are extreme.

Research

There is no substitute for exhaustive research!

Bond's Franchise Guide contains over 2,000 franchise listings, broken into 45 distinct business categories. This represents a substantial number of options from which to choose. Other directories also cover the industry in varying degrees of thoroughness and accuracy. Spend the time required to come up with an optimal selection. At a minimum, you will probably be in the business for five years. More likely, you will be in it for 10 years or more. Given the long-term commitment, allow yourself the necessary time to ensure you won't regret your decision. Research is a tedious, boring process, but doing it carefully and thoroughly can greatly reduce your risk and exposure. The benefits are measurable.

First, determine which industry groups hold your interest. Don't arbitrarily limit yourself to a particular industry in which you have first-hand experience. Next, request information from all of the companies that participate in those industries. The incremental cost of mailing (or calling) an additional 15 or 20 companies for information is insignificant in the big picture. Based on personal experience, you may feel you already know the best franchise. Step back. Assume there is a competing franchise out there with a comparable product or service, comparable management, etc., but which charges a royalty fee 2% of sales less than your intuitive choice. Over a 10-year period, that could add up to a great deal of money. It certainly justifies your requesting initial information.

A thorough analysis of the literature you receive should allow you to reduce the list of prime candidates to six or eight companies. Aggressively evaluate each firm. Talking with current and former franchisees is the single best source of information you can get. Where possible, visit franchise sites. My experience is that franchisees tend to be candid in their level of satisfaction with the franchisor. However, since they don't know you, they may be less candid about their sales, expenses and income. *"How Much Can I Make?"* should be of some assistance in filling this void. Go to the library and get studies that forecast industry growth, market saturation, industry problems, technical break-throughs, etc. Don't find out a year after becoming a franchisee of a coffee company that readily available reports suggested that the coffee market was over-saturated or that coffee was linked to some obscure form of colon cancer in rats.

Reserves

Like any new business, franchising is replete with uncertainty, uneven cash flows and unforeseen problems. It is an imperfect world that might not bear any relation to the clean pro formas you prepared to justify getting into the business. Any one of these unforeseen contingencies could cause a severe drain on your cash reserves. At the same time, you will have fixed and/or contractual payments that must be met on a current basis regardless of sales: rent, employee salaries, insurance, etc.

Adequate back-up reserves may be in the form of savings, commitments from relatives, bank loans, etc. Just make certain that the funds are available when, and if, you need them. To be absolutely safe, I suggest that you double the level of reserves recommended by the franchisor.

Keep in mind that the most common cause of business failure is inadequate working capital. Plan properly so you don't become a statistic.

Resolve

Let's assume for the time being that you have demonstrated exceptional levels of realism, thoroughly researched your options and lined up ample capital reserves. You have picked an optimal franchise that takes full advantage of your strengths. You are in business and bringing in enough money to achieve a positive cash flow. The future looks bright.
Now the fourth R — resolve — comes into play. Remember why you chose franchising in the first place: to take full advantage of a system that had been time-tested in the marketplace. Remember also what makes franchising work so well: that the franchisor and franchisees maximize their respective success by working within the system for the common good. Invariably, two obstacles arise.

The first is the physical pain associated with writing that monthly royalty check. Annual sales of $250,000 and a 6% royalty fee result in a monthly royalty check of $1,250 that must be sent to the franchisor. Every month. As a franchisee, you may look for any justification to reduce this sizable monthly outflow. Resist the temptation. Accept the fact that royalty fees are simply another cost of doing business. They are also a legal obligation that you willingly agreed to pay when you signed the franchise agreement. In effect, they are the dues you agreed to pay to belong to the club.

Although there may be an incentive, don't look for loopholes in the contract that might allow you to sue the franchisor or get out of the relationship. Don't report lower sales than actual in an effort to reduce royalties. If you have received the support that you were promised, continue to play by the rules. Honor your commitment. Let the franchisor enjoy the rewards it has earned from your success.

The second obstacle is the desire to change the system. You need to honor your commitment to be a "franchisee" and to live within the franchise system. What makes franchising successful as far as your customers are concerned is uniformity and consistency of appearance, product/service quality and corporate image. The most damaging thing an individual franchisee can do is suddenly and unilaterally introduce changes into a proven system. While these modifications may work in one market, they only serve to diminish the value of the system as a whole. Imagine what would happen to the national perception of your franchise if every franchisee had the latitude to make unilateral changes in his or her operations. Accordingly, any ideas you have on improving the system should be submitted directly to the franchisor for its evaluation. Accept the franchisor's decision on whether or not to pursue an idea.

If you suspect that you have a penchant for being an entrepreneur, for unrestrained experimenting and tinkering, you are probably not cut out to be a good franchisee. Seriously consider this question before you get into a relationship, instead of waiting until you are locked into an untenable situation.

Summary

I hope that I have been clear in suggesting that the selection of an optimal franchise is both time and energy-consuming. Done properly, the process may take six to nine months and involve the expenditure of several thousand dollars. The difference between a hasty, gut-feel investigation and an exhaustive, well-thought-out investigation may mean the difference between finding a poorly-conceived, or even fraudulent, franchise and an exceptional one.

There is a strong correlation between the efforts put into the investigative process and the ultimate degree of success you enjoy as a franchisee. The process is to investigate, evaluate and negotiate. Don't try to bypass any one of these elements.

Earnings claims statements

The harsh reality is that no one can tell (much less guarantee) you how much you might make in a specific investment. If someone does, don't believe him or her. Even the most successful business model, whether a franchise or not, simply cannot be replicated by someone who isn't prepared to run the business the way it should be run. Area demographics (population, disposable per capita income, education, etc.) are critical. For a retail business, having a heavily-trafficked location is critical. Adequate capital is critical. Management skill and decision-making ability are critical. Hard work is critical. The list goes on. It is up to you to ensure that all of these factors are optimized to the extent possible. If any one of these critical factors is missing or marginal, the chances are that the business will not meet your expectations.

This compendium of earnings claims statements is meant to provide prospective franchisees with a better sense of what they **might** earn as a result of their efforts. Without a sure understanding of potential sales, expenses and profits, an investor is inviting disappointment at best and failure at worst. I strongly encourage you to take whatever time is required to carefully review the earnings claims statements following. Some are easy reading, some are extremely tedious and detail-oriented. The better versed you are on the actual, historical operating results of the over 150 different companies included, however, the better positioned you will be to make an optimal selection of a franchise.

You will be able to ask intelligent, penetrating questions of franchisors when you evaluate them. You will be better prepared to compare franchising options in the same industry. You will have more credibility with existing franchisees when you seek their insights and experience. If you take the time to develop your own financial projections, you will not have to rely so heavily on expensive outside accountants and financial advisors. Most importantly, you will have a real understanding of the business before you commit your financial resources and several years of your life to it. If your objective is to maximize your bottom line, taking full advantage of the earnings claims statements below is an important start.

The Average Franchisee

The only in-depth study of actual franchisee earnings and satisfaction is conducted annually by *Franchise Times Magazine*. In their Second Annual Franchisee Survey, *Franchise Times* surveyed more than 1,000 franchisees. The results show that the **average franchisee** owned 3.5 units, had been in franchising for 8.9 years and enjoyed net pre-tax earnings of $171,000 (or roughly $50,000 per unit). Total annual household income before taxes averaged $118,000 for all franchisees. The median income, however, was $81,000. The initial start-up cost was $151,000 and the average loan size was $196,000 (median $88,000). 75% of those surveyed answered that they were either "very" or "somewhat" satisfied with franchising. 15.2% were "not

16

too" satisfied, while only 9.8% were "not at all" satisfied. If you think that franchising is an automatic pot of gold, you should temper your enthusiasm with the facts of life as brought out in the survey.

Depending on your viewpoint, you may be satisfied or alarmed at the above averages. Most prospective franchisees will probably be surprised to learn that, even after 8+ years in the business, the average franchisee has pre-tax earnings of less than $50,000 per unit. Keep in mind, however, that the above statistics are only that — statistics. How well you compare with the average franchisee is what counts. If you hope to make $100,000 per year with your initial unit, however, you will have to be markedly more successful than the average franchisee. Picking up the right franchise in the right market is the first step.

The Market Void

The single most important factor in buying a franchise — or any business for that matter — is determining a realistic and supportable projection of sales, expenses and profits. Specifically, how much can you expect to earn after working 65 hours a week for 52 weeks a year? A prospective franchisee clearly does not have the experience to sit down and project what his or her sales and profits will be over the next five years. This is especially true if he or she has no applied experience in that particular business. The only source in a position to supply accurate information (subject to caveats) about a franchise opportunity is the franchisor itself.

It is unfortunate that all franchisors are not required to supply prospective franchisees with the results of their own operating experience. At a very minimum, the franchisors have the information on net sales of all franchised units. Clearly they have complete accounting information on the operation of their company-owned units. Similarly, if they have any sophistication, they must have developed computer models for outlets in various geographic and retail environments.

The sad reality, however, is that the franchisors are not required to share this information and accord-

ingly, 80% don't. The likelihood that any such requirement will be implemented within the next 2 or so years is slim. Accordingly, the franchisee is left to his or her own devices.

Less than 20% of all franchisors currently supply earnings claims statements to prospective franchisees. *"How Much Can I Make?"* has attempted to locate and publish over 150 of these documents for your review. Nowhere else can a potential franchisee find such a wealth of financial information on the industry.

I strongly encourage you to read through the various earnings claims statements.

General Disclosure Background

In 1979, the Federal Trade Commission adopted the "FTC Rule," which regulates the franchising industry. Titled "Disclosure Requirements and Prohibitions Concerning Franchising and Business Opportunities Ventures," it specifically required that a disclosure document or Offering Circular, prepared in accordance with the FTC Rule format, be delivered to a prospective purchaser of a franchise at the earlier of either 1) the first personal meeting or 2) at least ten business days prior to the signing of any contract or the payment of any consideration. In addition, 15 states have adopted their own disclosure laws that are generally more demanding than the FTC's requirements. Chapter 1 provides more information about the requirements of both the FTC and "registration" states.

Earnings claims statements are covered under Item XIX of both the FTC and the state Uniform Franchise Offering Circular (UFOC) requirements. Whether a franchisor provides an earnings claim statement or not is entirely voluntary. The actual format and level of detail are also left to the company's discretion. If the franchisor decides to include an earnings claim statement in its offering circular, however, the only requirement of Item XIX is that the franchisor have a "reasonable basis" for making the earnings claim at the time the statement was prepared. In theory, the burden of proof is placed on the franchisor to justify the claims made.

Earnings Claims Defined

In their broadest sense, earnings claims are defined as estimates or other representations made and substantiated by franchisors about the level of sales, expenses and/or income a prospective franchisee might realize as a result of an investment in a particular franchise.

As defined by the FTC Rule, an earnings claim is "any oral, written or visual representation to a prospective franchisee or for general dissemination in the media which states or suggests a specific level or range of potential or actual sales, income, gross or net profits."

Alternatively, the UFOC definition is "information given to a prospective franchisee by, on behalf of or at the direction of the franchisor or its agent, from which a specific level or range of actual or potential sales, costs, income or profit from franchised or non-franchised units may be easily ascertained. A chart, table or mathematical calculation presented to demonstrate possible results based upon a combination of variables (such as multiples of price and quantity to reflect gross sales) is an earnings claim subject to this item."

FTC Boilerplate

The Federal Trade Commission requires that all offering circulars start with the following disclaimer.

INFORMATION FOR PROSPECTIVE FRANCHISEES REQUIRED BY THE FEDERAL TRADE COMMISSION.

&

TO PROTECT YOU, WE'VE REQUIRED YOUR FRANCHISOR TO GIVE YOU THIS INFORMATION. WE HAVEN'T CHECKED IT , AND DON'T KNOW IF IT'S CORRECT. IT SHOULD HELP YOU MAKE UP YOUR MIND. STUDY IT CAREFULLY. WHILE IT INCLUDES SOME INFORMATION ABOUT YOUR CONTRACT, DON'T RELY ON IT ALONE TO UNDERSTAND YOUR CONTRACT. READ ALL OF YOUR CONTRACT CAREFULLY. BUYING A FRANCHISE IS A COMPLICATED INVESTMENT. TAKE YOUR TIME TO DECIDE. IF POSSIBLE, SHOW YOUR CONTRACT AND THIS INFORMATION TO AN ADVISOR, LIKE A LAWYER OR AN ACCOUNTANT. IF YOU FIND ANYTHING YOU THINK MAY BE WRONG OR ANYTHING IMPORTANT THAT'S BEEN LEFT OUT, YOU SHOULD LET US KNOW ABOUT IT. IT MAY BE AGAINST THE LAW.

THERE MAY ALSO BE LAWS ON FRANCHISING IN YOUR STATE. ASK YOUR STATE AGENCIES ABOUT THEM.

FEDERAL TRADE COMMISSION
WASHINGTON, D.C. 20580

The important point to keep in mind is that neither the FTC, nor the state regulatory agencies, has checked the document for accuracy or completeness. They merely require that the document be delivered to them before the franchise can be sold. Although they suggest that you should let them know if something is amiss, they do not mention that they do not have the manpower or budget to pursue any but the most flagrant and obvious violations. For the most part, you are on your own. Don't assume that Uncle Sam will come to your assistance if you subsequently find that you have been misled or that fraud on the part of the franchisor was involved.

Recommendations Regarding Mandatory Earnings Claims Statements

Virtually everyone agrees that the information included in an earnings claim statement can be exceedingly helpful to a potential franchisee. Unfortunately, there are many reasons why franchisors don't willingly make their actual results available to the public. Many franchisors feel that prospective investors will be turned off if they have access to actual operating results. In this case, it would be better to let them draw their own conclusions.

Other franchisors are legitimately afraid of being sued for "misrepresentation." There is considerable risk to a franchisor if a published earnings claim statement is interpreted in any way as a "guarantee" of sales or income for new units. Given today's highly litigious society and the propensity of courts to award large settlements to the "little guy," it's not surprising that so few franchisors provide the information.

Notwithstanding all the potential problems (and they are not insignificant), I feel strongly that franchisors should be required to provide prospective franchisees with some form of earnings claims. To the extent that they are able to substantiate their claims, franchisors should be protected from frivolous and potentially devastating lawsuits that might otherwise follow from franchisees who fail and blame it on the earnings claims. Everyone should realize that the historical data used as the basis for the claims do not apply to every geographic region, individual location or franchisee whose experience and/or business acumen may vary. Clearly, there is no universal methodology that covers the broad range of variables. All involved parties — the franchisors, the franchisees, the regulatory agencies and the legal system — should rely on common business sense.

As it now stands, the franchisor is liable if it misrepresents its earnings claims (or any of the other items in the offering circular). Normally, one would interpret this to mean that someone goes to jail if it is proven that he or she intentionally misled the prospective investor or misrepresented the facts. Unfortunately, neither the FTC nor any of the registration states has the budget, the manpower or the technical expertise to enforce any such misrepresentation. If a franchisor wants to mislead, unless it is a flagrant violation, there is little chance it will be severely penalized. Accordingly, you should not assume that anyone is going to protect you or support you if, after the fact, you determine that you have been misled.

If there are going to be mandatory requirements, however, there must be some corresponding penalties for fraudulent earnings claims. Specifically there must be a "right of action" on the part of franchisees that would give the various regulatory bodies the muscle to move against fraud and deception. This would involve some form of budget and staff to aggressively police the industry. My sense is that this funding should come from the franchisors themselves in the form of a registration fee. Alternatively, a portion of the initial franchise fee paid by the franchisee could go towards the super agency's budget.

At some point, the various registration states and the FTC (or its successor) will find a common ground upon which to merge their efforts and require the filing of a single offering circular acceptable to all parties involved. This will go a long way toward significantly reducing the expense, effort and frustration required as part of the current, highly redundant registration process. At that time, mandatory earnings claims statements should be instituted, along with general, common-sense guidelines for their preparation, substantiation and presentation. Equally important is a standard set of rules for documenting and penalizing fraud and deception.

Other Resources

A. Without doubt, the most meaningful information that you can obtain on a particular franchise is from the existing base of franchisees. My experience is that franchisees tend to be very candid about their level of satisfaction with the franchisor, but less candid about their sales, expenses and income. If you put yourself in their position, you would most likely be reluctant to share confidential information with a total stranger, notwithstanding his or her proclaimed motivations.

The better prepared you are to ask them knowledgeable, well-thought out questions, the more likely existing franchisees will respond with meaningful answers and insights. Depending on how well you have done your homework and your ability to ask questions that show a solid understanding of the basic business and its underlying economics, they should be willing to respond to your questions about: the major cost elements of the cash flow statement; the biggest surprises they encountered when they started their business; whether to buy supplies from the franchisor or from a third-party supplier; potential lenders; negotiable points in the franchise agreement; etc. In reviewing the financials, pay particular attention to the major expense items. See if there are any expense categories that you might have left out. At the early stages, even a $1,000 non-recurring expense can have a dramatic impact.

You should be very aggressive about pursuing existing franchisees as a source of insights that are not available elsewhere. If possible, visit them at their business. This not only shows your commitment, but allows you to see them in their working environment. Don't call only the franchisees specifically recommended by the franchisor. Current franchisees are listed in the offering circular. Contact as many as you can until you feel comfortable that you are hearing a consensus. Past offering circulars list franchisees that may no longer be in the system. To the extent that you can find them, you should also talk with as many former franchisees as you can. It is up to you to separate the truth from the fiction as to why they left the system. Too many disenchanted former franchisees should be a strong warning to be exceedingly cautious in your investigation and analysis.

B. *Bond's Franchise Guide* provides detailed profiles of over 1,100 North American franchisors and more general information on an additional 1,200 franchisors. The profiles note whether or not the franchisor includes an earnings claim statement with its offering circular. Of the U.S. franchisors who responded to the question (98%) for the 1995 Edition, roughly 20% said that they provide an earning claim statement to prospective franchisees. Assuming that there are currently 1,900 active U.S. franchisors, this suggests that there are roughly 380 earnings claims statements at one or more of the various regulatory bodies. This book contains some 153 earnings claims statements.

C. If you live in one of the registration states (see the section on Regulatory Agencies in Chapter 1), you can contact them to request a copy of the earnings claim statement from any of the franchisors who are registered to do business in the state. Unfortunately, most such state agencies are not set up to accommodate you unless you are physically

at their offices. The best bet is to call them and see what your options are. Some states, such as Maryland, are clearly more helpful than others in providing access to their library of offering circulars.

D. The next best source of information is provided by various publications that compile general operating statistics on industries broken down by SIC codes. Three of the best-known annual industry surveys are 1) the *RMA Annual Statement Studies*, published by Robert Morris Associates of Philadelphia, PA, 2) the *Almanac of Business and Industrial Financial Ratios*, edited by Leo Troy and published by Prentice Hall and 3) the *Industry Norms and Key Business Rations*, published by Dun & Bradstreet Information Services.

Although none of these publications provides detailed expense data, each is extremely helpful in determining industry averages/norms and key financial ratios. Based on actual tax returns for the entire spectrum of business categories (manufacturing, wholesaling, agriculture, service, and retailing), the composite financial data reflect actual operating results for major SIC code industries.

As an example, the *RMA 1999 Annual Statement Studies* lists 2 pages of detailed statistics on Restaurant/Lodging — Restaurants: Fast Foods (SIC #5812). The data is sorted both by Total Assets and by Annual Sales. Assets are broken down into the following categories $0–500,000, $500,001–2,000,000, $2,000,000–10,000,000, $10,000,000–50,000,000, $50,000,000–100,000,000 and $100,000,000– 250,000,000. Similarly, Annual Sales are broken down into the following ranges: $1–1,000,000, $1,000,000–3,000,000, $3,000,000–5,000,000, $5,000,000–10,000,000, $10,000,000–25,000,000 and over $25,000,000. A total of 659 separate companies are included in the composite results.

Within the overall fast food industry analysis, the survey lists 109 companies that had annual sales between $1 million and $3 million. Among other statistics provided, the following would be of interest to a prospective franchisee in the fast food business:

Restaurant/Lodging — Restaurants: Fast Foods (Sic #5812)

	%		
ASSETS:		Gross Profit	64.1
Cash & Equivalents	19.0	Operating Expenses	<u>56.6</u>
Trade Receivables (Net)	2.5	Operating Profit	7.5
Inventory	4.8	All Other Expenses (Net)	<u>2.2</u>
Other Current Assets	<u>2.7</u>	Profit Before Taxes	5.3
Total Current	29.0		
Fixed Assets	50.2	**RATIOS (MEDIAN):**	
Intangibles	11.9	Current	0.9
All Other Non-Current	<u>8.9</u>	Quick	0.6
Total Assets	100.0	Sales/Receivables	UND
		Cost of Sales/Inventory	42.7
		Cost of Sales/Payables	22.4
LIABILITIES:		Sales/Working Capital	-91.9
Notes Payable - Short-Term	4.6	EBIT/Interest	3.5
Cur. Mat. - L/T/D	6.7	Net Profit + Depr., Dep.,	
Trade Payables	9.3	Amort. Cur. Mat. L/T/D	3.1
Income Taxes Payable	0.1	Fixed/Worth	3.6
All Other Current	<u>15.6</u>	Debt/Worth	4.7
Total Current	36.3	% Profit Before Taxes	
Long-Term Debt	35.3	Tangible Net Worth	57.2
Deferred Taxes	0.0	% Profit before Taxes/	
All Other Non-Current	5.0	Total Assets	14.2
Net Worth	<u>23.3</u>	Sales/Net Fixed Assets	8.2
Total Liabilities/Net Worth	100.0	Sales/Total Assets	3.7
		% Depr., Dep., Amort./Sales	2.9
INCOME DATA:		% Officers', Directors', Owners'	
Net Sales	100.0	Comp./Sales	3.6

Source: RMA Annual Statement Studies (1999), Published by Robert Morris Associates, One Liberty Place, Philadelphia, PA.

Unfortunately, not all of the 33 specific industries covered in this publication are covered in the above industry surveys. The *RMA Annual Statement Studies* (1999) covers the following specific retail SIC codes: auto and home supplies; books, stationery and office supplies; cameras and photographic supplies; computers and software; cut flowers and growing plants; bakeries; convenience food stores; health food and vitamin stores; ice cream and yogurt shops; fast food restaurants; floor coverings; furniture; hobby, toy and game shops; jewelry; and optical goods. Service industries covered include: accounting, auditing and bookkeeping; adjustment and collection services; auto repair services (exhaust systems, general, and top, body and upholstery repair and paint shops); cleaning

and maintenance — building; car washes; day care — child; direct mail advertising; disinfecting and pest control services; employment agencies; hair stylists; health care — home; help supply services; laundry and drycleaners; motels, hotels and tourist courts; photocopying and duplicating; physical fitness facilities; security systems; training and vocational rehabilitation; travel agencies; and video tape rentals.

While you may not feel entirely comfortable with many of the ratios and their significance, you should have someone who is well versed in accounting compare the industry statistics with figures that you have generated in your own pro formas. It is critical to ensure that you haven't made some fatal leap in logic that, for example, allows you to spend 10% less on cost of goods sold than the industry norm and thereby generate an operating profit that is 30% above the norm. Any such discrepancies should be carefully analyzed and justified.

E. Industry trade associations publish composite financial statistics, usually on an annual basis. Consult the Directory of Trade Associations at your local business library for the address of the relevant trade association(s). Be prepared to pay reasonable fees to obtain as much industry-specific information as possible. Keep in mind that these statistics are made up solely of like-minded businesses that have similar expenses and competitive pressures. To not take advantage of this potential source would be very short-sighted.

F. Most industries are covered by one or more research houses that sell studies pertaining to the future of that industry. These cover new technology, industry trends, competitive trends, financial projections for various sales levels, etc. Even if these studies are somewhat outdated, it may be a worthwhile investment to get the best possible industry information before risking your life savings based on incomplete information.

Given this wealth of industry-specific information, I strongly encourage you to visit a library that has one or more of these invaluable reference books.

Your Own Cash Flow Projections

Armed with earnings claim statements, industry operating statistics and the information gathered from your conversations with existing and former franchisees, as well as input from your trusted colleagues and consultants, you are now in a position to prepare your own financial projections. I cannot overemphasize the importance of thinking of this as the most critical step in the entire franchise evaluation and selection process. Without a solid understanding of the financial aspects of the business, you may well be throwing your investment away. Investors who says they don't understand an income statement or that they aren't a "numbers person" may soon regret their lack of motivation and homework.

A number of well-written books on the subject of preparing financial projections are available. Most are written for the layman who has little or no formal understanding of the process. (Some are even written by laymen with little or no formal understanding of the process themselves.) Purchase a few of these books and spend the time necessary to become proficient in the rudiments of accounting and finance. Remember, you are playing with your own money and your livelihood. Don't put yourself in a position where you have to pay your accountant $100+ per hour every time you have a question. Learn the distinction between income statements and cash flow statements. Realize that you have an "opportunity cost" associated with your investment, and that you must receive an annual return on this investment (as well as the return of the investment itself) before a true net profit from the business can be determined. Put a value on the psychic income you will derive from being your own boss. This is especially important when comparing your near-term income on an hourly basis with what you might otherwise earn working for someone else. Ask yourself objectively if you would invest in the business if you were an investor rather than an owner/operator. Alternatively, would you loan money to the business if you were a banker?

If you don't know how to develop a pro forma cash flow model on a computer, have someone help you. Perform "what if" calculations to see what would happen under best case and worst case scenarios. This represents the cheapest insurance you can buy to fully understand the dynamics of your new business. You will probably be sorely handicapped in the operation of your business unless you are "computerized." To the extent this is true, learn the basics of operating a computer before, rather than after, you have made your investment. Your discretionary free time is likely to be minimal during the start-up phase of your new business.

Although the process of generating realistic cash flow statements may seem daunting without any prior business management experience, it is easier than you think. With a little common sense and sequential thinking, you can learn it quickly.

TABLE I		
FRONT-END INVESTMENT REQUIREMENTS		
	Franchisor's Item IX.	Actual in Your Area
Initial Franchise Fee	$	$
Land & Improvements		
Leasehold Improvements		
Architectural/Engineering Fees		
Furniture & Fixtures		
Vehicles Purchased		
Initial Inventory		
Initial Signage		
Initial Advertising Commitment		
Initial Training Fees		
Travel/Lodging/Etc. for Initial Training		
Rent Deposits		
Utility Deposits		
Telephone Deposits		
Initial Insurance		
In-Store Graphics		
Yellow Page Advertising		
Initial Office Supplies		
Prepaid Sales Taxes		
Initial Business Permits/Fees		
Office Equipment:		
Computer Hardware		
Computer Software		
Computer Installation		
Computer Training		
Point-of-Sale Computer		
Answering Machine		
Fax Machine		
Postage Meter		
Telephone System (Including Installation)		
Copier		
Security System		
Initial Loan Fees		
Due Diligence Expenses:		
Attorney Fees		
Accounting Fees		
Consultant Fees		
Books Purchases/Courses/Etc.		
Travel Expenses		
Telephone/Mailing Expenses		
Total Non-Recurring Expenses	$	$
Working Capital Requirements		
FRONT-END INVESTMENT REQUIREMENTS	$	$

	Month 1	Month 2	Month 3	Month 4	Month - - - - >	Total 12 Months
TABLE 2						
PRO FORMA CASH FLOW STATEMENT						
Gross Sales	$	$	$	$	$	$
Less Returns and Allowances						
Net Sales						
Less Cost of Goods Sold						
Gross Profit						
Gross Profit As A % Of Sales	%	%	%	%	%	%
Operating Expenses:						
Payroll:						
Direct Labor						
Indirect Labor						
Employee Benefits						
Payroll Taxes						
Owner Salary & Benefits						
Rent & Common Area Maintenance						
Equipment Rental/Lease Payments						
Advertising Fund Payments To Franchisor						
Yellow Page & Local Advertising						
Insurance						
Utilities:						
Telephone/Fax						
Gas & Electric						
Water						
Janitorial Expense						
Trash Removal						
Security						
Travel & Lodging						
Meals & Entertainment						
Delivery Charges						
Printing Expense						
Postage						
Operating Supplies						
Office Supplies						
Vehicle Expense						
Equipment Maintenance						
Uniforms & Laundry						
Professional Fees:						
Accounting						
Legal						
Consulting						
Repairs & Maintenance						
Business Licenses/Fees/Permits						
Dues & Subscriptions						

Property Taxes						
Business Taxes						
Bad Debt/Theft						
Bank Charges & Credit Card Fees						
Royalties To Franchisor						
Interest Expense						
Total Operating Expenses						
Pre-Tax Operating Cash Flow	$	$	$	$	$	$
Operating Cash Flow As A % Of Sales	%	%	%	%	%	%

ADJUSTMENT TO PRE-TAX NET CASH FLOW						
Pre-Tax Operating Cash Flow	$	$	$	$	$	$
Less Depreciation/Amortization						
Pre-Tax Income						
Plus Depreciation/Amortization						
Less Principal Payments						
Less Capital Expenditures						
Pre-Tax Net Cash Flow	$	$	$	$	$	$

ADJUSTMENT TO "REAL" CASH FLOW						
Pre-Tax Net Cash Flow						
Less Return on Invested Capital @ x%						
Pre-Tax "Real" Cash Flow						

In an attempt to provide a framework for starting your own financial projections, I have prepared the following tables. They are by no means complete and do not purport to represent all possible scenarios. They are only a starting point. Each industry will have its own unique investment requirements and related operating expenses.

Table 1 lists Total Investment Requirements. In the second column, you should place the appropriate expenses listed by the franchisor in Item IX of the offering circular. In the third column, you should place your own well-researched estimate of what that expense or service will cost in your market. The sum of these various expenses represents the non-recurring expenses you will incur in starting the business. Some of the expenses, such as land and improvements, may not be appropriate if you can lease your space at an acceptable market rate over the term of your investment. Consult with your financial advisor as to the appropriate figures to include if you lease rather than purchase various expense items.

Table 2 is a Pro Forma Cash Flow Statement. The objective is to rigorously project monthly and annual sales over the next five years, then deduct the corresponding operating expenses. The end result is the pre-tax operating cash flow. From this number, you should deduct the non-cash items (depreciation and amortization) to arrive at a pre-tax income. Further additions and subtractions determine net cash flow before tax.

Again, I would strongly recommend that you (with the help of outside assistance if necessary) construct a computer model that includes all of the items that will impact your business.

Hopefully, when the time comes, you can negotiate an agreement with the franchisor that allows you to extend the contract for successive 5–15 year periods, presuming you have performed satisfactorily. If you have done a good job in selecting and managing the franchise, the real pay-off will most likely come when you sell the business. Over the next 7–15 years, you will attempt to build your business to its maximum potential. At some point, you will want to retire or try something else. The market value of your business will be a function of how much cash flow the business generates. Based on the current earnings potential, the prospective buyer will most likely use one of two valuation models. The first, and more simplistic, simply involves multiplying the current cash flow by some multiple (say 3 to 5 times) to arrive at a purchase price. The more sophisticated buyer will develop a 5–10 year cash flow statement, put in his or her own liquidation value and discount the annual cash flows at a rate that properly reflects the inherent risk of achieving those cash flows. As an example, if your business generates a legitimate cash flow of $150,000 after 10 years, you should be able to sell the business for $450,000–750,000 based on the above scenario.

The Franchisor Profiles

The information contained in the franchisor profiles was submitted to Source Book Publica-tions by the franchisors for inclusion in one or more of its various publications on franchising. Franchisors were given the opportunity to update the information as they saw fit, as well as to submit their logo for inclusion with their profile. The majority did so.

Where we were unable to contact the management of the franchise or if the franchisor is no longer actively franchising, that status was noted below the profile.

For the most part, the franchisor profiles are self-explanatory. Noted below is a brief description of the various fields in the profile, as well as some observations as to their interpretation. AAMCO has been selected to illustrate how the data might be interpreted.

1. Description of Business: The questionnaire provided franchisors with adequate room to differentiate their franchise from the competition. In a minor number of cases, some editing was required. **Observation:** In instances where franchisors show no initiative or imagination in describing their operations, you must decide whether this is symptomatic of the company or simply a reflection of the individual who responded to the questionnaire.

AAMCO TRANSMISSIONS

One Presidential Blvd.
Bala Cynwyd, PA 19004
Mr. Bob Castellani, Director Franchise Development
Tel: (800) 523-0402 (610) 668-2900
FAX: (610) 617-9532
AAMCO is the world's largest chain of transmission specialists with 35 year's experience as the undisputed industry leader. An American icon, AAMCO's trademark is recognized by 90% of the driving public. Transmission repair is a $2.9 billion business in the United States and is projected to be a $3.6 billion business by 2001.

Franchise Units:	712
Company-Owned Units:	2
Total Units:	714
Founded:	1963
First Franchise:	1963
Franchise Fee:	$30,000
On-Going Royalty:	7%
Advertising Fee:	4–5%
Avg. Total Investment:	$175,000
Financial Assistance Provided:	Yes — Indirect
Site Selection Assistance:	Yes
Lease Negotiation Assistance:	Yes
Contract Terms (Init./Renew):	15/15 Yrs.

Initial Training Provided: 5 Weeks Home Office, Philadelphia, PA.

2. Franchise Units: 712. AAMCO currently has 712 franchisee-owned and operated units.

3. Company-Owned Units: 2. AAMCO currently has 2 Company-owned and operated units.

Observation: As a general rule, a younger franchise should prove that its concept has worked successfully in one or more company-owned units before it markets its "system" to an inexperienced franchisee. Without company-owned proto-type stores, the new franchisee may well end up being the "testing kitchen" for the franchise concept itself.

4. Total Units: 714. AAMCO has a total of 714 franchisee-owned and company-owned units.

Observation: Like a franchisor's years in business, its experience in successfully operating multiple units offers considerable comfort. Those franchisors with over 15–25 operating units have proven that their system works and have probably encountered and overcome most of the problems that plague a new operation. Alternatively, the management of franchises with less than 15 operating units may have gained considerable industry experience before joining the current franchise. It is up to the franchisor to convince you that it is providing you with as risk-free an operation as possible. You don't want to be providing a company with its basic experience in the business.

5. Founded: 1963. AAMCO was founded in 1963, and, accordingly, has over 30 years of experience in its primary business. It should be intuitively obvious that a firm that has been in existence for over 5 years has a greater likelihood of being around 5 years from now than a firm that was founded only last year.

6. First Franchise: 1963. 1963 was also the year that AAMCO's first franchised unit(s) were established.

Observation: The number of years a franchisor has been in business is one of the key variables to consider in choosing a franchise. 30+ years of continuous operation, both as an operator and as a franchisor, is compelling evidence that the firm has staying power. This is not to say, however, that a new franchise should not receive your full attention. Every company has to start from scratch. Ultimately, a prospective franchisee has to be convinced that the franchise has either 1) been in operation long enough, or 2) that its key management personnel have adequate industry experience to have worked out the bugs normally associated with a new business. In most cases, this knowledge can only be gained through on-the-job experience. Again, don't be the guinea pig that provides the franchisor with the experience it needs to develop a smoothly running operation.

7. Franchise Fee: $30,000. AAMCO requires a front-end, one-time-only payment of $30,000 to grant a franchise for a single location. As noted in Chapter 1, the franchise fee is a payment to reimburse the franchisor for the costs incurred for setting the franchisee up in business — from recruiting through training and manuals. The fee usually ranges from $15,000–35,000 and is a function of competitive franchise fees, the actual out-of-pocket costs incurred by the franchisor, and whether outside brokers were used in the recruiting process.

Depending upon the franchisee's particular circumstances and how well the franchisor thinks he or she might fit into the system, the franchisor may finance all or part of the franchise fee. (See below if a franchisor provides any direct or indirect financial assistance.)

Observation: Ideally, the franchisor should do no more than recover its costs on the initial franchise fee. Profits come later in the form of royalty fees, which are a function of the franchisee's sales and, presumably, profits. Whether the franchise fee is $5,000 or $45,000, the total should be carefully evaluated. What are competitive fees and are they financed? How much training will you actually receive? Are the fees reflective of the franchisor's expenses? If the fees appear to be non-competitive, don't hesitate to address your concerns with the franchisor.

Realize that a $5,000 differential in the one-time franchise fee is a secondary consideration in the overall scheme of things. You are in the relationship for the long-term.

By the same token, don't get suckered in by an extremely low franchise fee if there is any doubt about the franchisor's ability to follow through. Franchisors need to collect reasonable fees to recover their actual costs. If they don't recoup these costs, they cannot recruit and train new franchisees on whom your own future success partially depends.

8. On-Going Royalty: 7% means that 7% of gross sales (or other measure, as defined in the franchise agreement) must be periodically paid directly to the franchisor in the form of royalties.

This on-going expense is your cost for being part of the larger franchise system and for all of the "back-office" support you will receive. In a few cases, the amount of the royalty fee is fixed rather than variable. In others, the percentage fee decreases as the volume of sales (or other measure) increases (i.e., 6% on the first $200,000 of sales, 5% on the next $100,000 and so on). In others, the fee is held at artificially low levels during the start-up phase of the franchisee's business, then increases once the franchisee is better able to afford it.

Observation: Royalty fees represent the mechanism by which the franchisor finally recoups the costs it has incurred in developing its business. It may take many years and many operating units before the franchisor is able to make a true operating profit. Alternatively, evaluate what it would cost you, as a sole proprietor, to provide the myriad services included in the royalty payment.

In assessing various alternative investments, the amount of the royalty percentage is a major on-going expense. Assuming average annual sales of $500,000 per annum over a 15 year period, the total royalties at 5% would be $375,000. At 6%, the cumulative fees would be $450,000. You have to be fully convinced that the $75,000 differential is justified. While this is clearly a meaningful number, what you are really evaluating is the quality of management and the unique competitive advantages of the goods and/or services offered by the franchisor.

9. Advertising Fee: 4–5%. Most national or regional franchisors require their franchisees to contribute a certain percentage of their sales (or other measure, as determined in the franchise agreement) into a corporate advertising fund. These individual advertising fees are pooled to develop a corporate advertising/marketing effort that produces significant economies of scale. The end result is a national or regional advertising program that promotes the franchisor's products and services. Depending upon the nature of the business, this percentage usually ranges from 2% to 6% and is in addition to the royalty fee.

Observation: One of the greatest advantages of a franchised system is its ability to promote its products and services on a national or regional basis. The promotions may be through television, radio, print medias or direct mail. The objective is name recognition and, over time, the assumption that the product and/or service has been "time-tested." An individual business owner could never justify the expense of mounting a major advertising program at the local level. For a smaller franchise that may not yet have an advertising program or fee, it is important to know when an advertising program will start, how it will be monitored and its expected cost.

10. Average Total Investment: $175,000. On average, AAMCO franchisees will invest a total of $175,000, including both cash and debt, by the time the franchise opens its doors.

Observation: The total investment should be the cash investment noted above plus any debt that you will incur in starting up the new business. Debt could be in the form of a note to the franchisor for all or part of the franchise fee, an equipment lease, building and facilities leases, etc. Make sure that the total includes all of the obligations that you assume, especially any long-term lease obligations.

Be conservative in assessing what your real exposure is. Table 1 above is provided to help you determine the real costs of getting into the business. If you are leasing highly-specialized equipment or if you are leasing a single-purpose building, it is naive to think that you will recoup your investment if you have to sell or sub-lease those assets in a buyer's market. If there is any specialized equipment that may have been manufactured to the franchisor's specifications, determine if the franchisor has any form of buy-back provision.

It is critically important that you be realistic about the amount of cash you can comfortably invest in a business. Stretching beyond your means can have grave and far-reaching consequences. Assume that you will encounter periodic set-backs and that you will have to draw down on your reserves. The demands of starting a new business are harsh enough without adding the uncertainties associated with inadequate working capital. Temper the franchisor's recommendations regarding the suggested minimum cash investment with your own results in Table 1. If anything, there will be an incentive for the franchisor to set the recommended level of investment too low, rather than too high. It may not include the expenses related to the due diligence process, or of fully outfitting an electronic office system, or of a lawyer's time, etc.

Keep in mind that you will probably not achieve a positive cash flow from the business prior to six months or more of operation. Be absolutely certain that your calculations include an adequate working capital reserve. Be conservative and leave enough margin to cover the unforeseen contingencies that will almost certainly present themselves.

11. Financial Assistance Provided: Yes (Indirect) notes that AAMCO is indirectly involved in providing financial assistance. Indirect assistance might include making introductions to the franchisor's financial contacts, providing financial templates for preparing a business plan or actually assisting in the loan application process. In some cases, the franchisor becomes a co-signer on a financial obligation (equipment lease, space lease, etc.). Other franchisors are directly (Direct) involved in the process. In this case, the assistance may include a lease or loan made directly by the franchisor. Any loan would generally be secured by some form of collateral. A very common form of assistance is a note for all or part of the initial franchise fee. The level of assistance will generally depend upon the relative strengths of the franchisee.

Observation: The best of all possible worlds is one in which the franchisor has enough confidence in the business and in you to co-sign notes on the building and equipment leases and allow you to pay off the franchise fee over a specified period of time. Depending upon your qualifications, this could happen. Most likely, however, the franchisor will only give you some assistance in raising the necessary capital to start the business. Increasingly, franchisors are testing a franchisee's business acumen by letting him or her assume an increasing level of personal responsibility in securing financing. The objective is to find out early in the process how resourceful a franchisee really is.

12. Site Selection Assistance: Yes means that AAMCO will assist the franchisee in selecting a site location. While the phrase "location, location, location" may be hackneyed, its importance should not be discounted, especially when a business depends upon retail traffic counts and accessibility. If a business is home- or warehouse-based, assistance in this area is of negligible or minor importance.

Observation: Since you will be locked into a lease for a minimum of three, and probably five, years, optimal site selection is absolutely essential. Even if you were somehow able to sub-lease and extricate yourself from a bad lease or bad location, the franchise agreement may not allow you to move to another location. Accordingly, it is imperative that you get it right the first time.

If a franchisor is truly interested in your success, it should treat your choice of a site with the same care it would use in choosing a company-owned site. Keep in mind that many third-party firms provide excellent demographic data on existing locations at a very reasonable cost.

13. Lease Negotiation Assistance: Yes. Once a site is selected, AAMCO will be actively involved in negotiating the terms of the lease.

Observation: Given the complexity of negotiating a lease, an increasing number of franchisors are taking an active role in lease negotiations. There are far too many trade-offs that must be considered — terms, percentage rents, tenant improvements, pass-throughs, kick-out clauses, etc. This responsibility is best left to the professionals. If the franchisor doesn't have the capacity to support you directly, enlist the help of a well-recommended broker. The penalties for signing a bad long-term lease are very severe.

14. Contract Terms (Initial/Renew): 15/15. AAMCO's initial franchise period runs for 15 years. The first renewal period runs for an additional 15 years. Assuming that the franchisee operates within the terms of the franchise agreement, he or she has

30 years within which to develop and, ultimately, sell the business.

Observation: The potential (discounted) value of any business (or investment) is the sum of the cash flows that are generated each year plus the value of the business upon liquidation. Given this truth, the length of the franchise agreement and any renewals are extremely important to the franchisee. It is essential that he or she has adequate time to develop the business to its full potential. At that time, he or she will have maximized the value of the business as an on-going concern. The value of the business to a potential buyer, however, is largely a function of how long the franchise agreement runs. If there are only two years remaining before the agreement expires, or if the terms of an extension(s) are vague, the business will be worth only a fraction of the value assigned to a business with 15 years to go. For the most part, the longer the agreement and the subsequent extension, the better. (The same logic applies to a lease. If your sales are largely a function of your location and traffic count, then it is important that you have options to extend the lease under known terms. The term of your lease should never be longer than the remaining term of your franchise agreement, however.)

Assuming the term of the franchise agreement is acceptable, be clear under what circumstances renewals might not be granted. Similarly, know the circumstances under which a franchise agreement might be prematurely and unilaterally canceled by the franchisor. I strongly recommend you have an experienced lawyer review this section of the franchise agreement. It would be devastating if, after spending years developing your business, there were a loophole in the contract that allowed the franchisor to arbitrarily cancel the relationship.

15. Initial Training Provided: 5 Weeks Home Office, Philadelphia, PA.

Observation: Assuming that the underlying business concept is sound and competitive, adequate training and on-going support are among the most important determinants of your success as a franchisee. The initial training should be as lengthy and as "hands-on" as necessary to allow the franchisee to operate alone and with confidence. Obviously, every potential situation cannot be covered in any training program. The franchisee should come away with a basic understanding of how the business operates and where to go to resolve problems when they come up. Depending on the business, there should be operating manuals, procedures manuals, company policies, training videos, (800) help-lines, etc. It may be helpful at the outset to establish how satisfied recent franchisees are with a company's training. I would also recommend having a clear understanding about how often the company updates its manuals and training programs, the cost of sending additional employees through training, etc.

Remember, you are part of an organization that you are paying (in the form of a franchise fee and on-going royalties) to support you. Training is the first step. On-going support is the second step. If you project royalties of $15,000 per year throughout the term of the franchise agreement, be fully confident that you will receive a corresponding value in the form of franchisor-supplied services.

Methodology

90+% of the earnings claim statements presented were received directly from the franchisors themselves. In the remaining cases, we received the Item 19 data from various state agencies or groups that had the missing data in their libraries. Once the earnings claim information was scanned and proofed 2 times, a draft was sent to the franchisors for their own proofing and review. Any changes were incorporated in the final edition. For many companies, the underlying UFOC had been updated, in which case an entirely new earning claim statement was substituted. Similarly, the profile data was proofed and modified by the franchisors themselves.

In almost all cases, we have presented the verbatim information that was supplied to us in the Item 19 statement. Unfortunately, the original data sometimes includes periodic punctuation errors, incomplete sentences and other grammatical errors that slipped both our proofers and the franchisor's proofers, we apologize.

There are a few instances where we have provided information that is more than 18 months old. Generally, this occurred when the franchisor had stopped supplying an earnings claim statement in its UFOC and we determined that the reader would benefit from another example of historical data even though somewhat dated.

31

Recommended Reading

My strong sense is that every potential franchisee should be well-versed in the underlying fundamentals of the franchising industry before he or she commits to the way of life it involves. The better you understand the industry, the better prepared you will be to take maximum advantage of the relationship with your franchisor. There is no doubt that it will also place you in a better position to negotiate the franchise agreement — the conditions of which will dictate every facet of your life as a franchisee for the term of the agreement. The few extra dollars spent on educating yourself could well translate into tens of thousand of dollars to the bottom line in the years ahead.

With the 2000 Edition, we have taken the liberty of limiting the number of franchising-only books included in the bibliography. In addition to general franchising publications, we have included several special interest books that relate to specific, but critical, parts of the start-up and on-going management process — site selection, hiring and managing minimum wage employees, preparing accurate cash flow projections, developing comprehensive business and/or marketing plans, etc. Also included are several audio tapes and software packages that we feel represent good values.

We have also attempted to make the purchasing process easier by allowing readers to purchase the books directly from Source Book Publications, either via our 800-line or our website. All of the books are currently available in inventory and are generally sent the same day an order is received. A 15% discount is available on all orders over $100.00. See page 41 for an order form. Your complete satisfaction is 100% guaranteed on all books.

Background/Evaluation

Buying a Franchise: How To Make the Right Choice, Kezios, Women in Franchising. 1996. Audio cassettes. $49.95. *Item #4.*

Dynamic advice on selecting a franchisor, the advantages and potential pitfalls of owning a franchise and protecting your investment. Includes legal and financial considerations, as well as insider's tips about franchising. Two audio cassettes and companion workbook are well-presented and packed with nuts-and-bolts information. Excellent industry overview.

Franchise Bible: A Comprehensive Guide, 3rd Edit., Keup, Oasis Press. 1996. 314 pp. $24.95. *Item #6.*

This recently updated classic is equally useful for prospective franchisees and franchisors alike. The comprehensive guide and workbook explain in

detail what the franchise system entails and the precise benefits it offers. The book features the new franchise laws that became effective January, 1995. To assist the prospective franchisee in rating a potential franchisor, Keup provides necessary checklists and forms. Also noted are the franchisor's contractual obligations to the franchisee and what the franchisee should expect from the franchisor in the way of services and support.

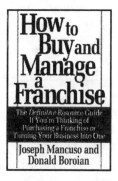

How to Buy and Manage a Franchise, Mancuso and Boroian, Simon & Schuster. 1993. 287 pp. $11.00. *Item #12.* If your objective is to either be your own boss or to expand a business you already own, you should seriously consider franchising. The authors share their expert advice on purchasing, owning and operating a franchise. Keen insights into the mechanics and advantages of franchising. Good starter book.

Tips & Traps When Buying a Franchise, Revised 2nd Edition, Tomzack, Source Book Publications. 1999. 236 pp. $19.95. *Item #19.*

Many a green franchisee is shocked to discover that the road to success in franchising is full of hidden costs, inflated revenue promises, reneged marketing support and worse. In this candid, hard-hitting book, Tomzack steers potential franchisees around the pitfalls and guides them in making a smart, lucrative purchase. Topics include: matching a franchise with personal finances and lifestyle, avoiding the 5 most common pitfalls, choosing a prime location, asking the right questions, etc.

Franchising 101, Dugan, Upstart Publishing Company. 1998. 267 pp. $22.95. *Item #10.*

A thoughtful, thorough guide that offers indispensable advice on everything you need to know about evaluating, buying and growing a franchise — from choosing the right franchise to handling taxes and banks to keep records. It will help you evaluate your needs and your personality in order to determine the type of franchise that will make you happy — and prosperous — for the long term. You'll also learn how to scout for a franchise company that is a leader within the strong, vibrant and growing franchise industry. This book offers valuable guidance and support from respected professionals in the franchising industry.

Understanding an Offering Circular and Negotiating a Franchise Agreement, Kanouse, Professional Press. 1995. 159 pp. $21.95. *Item #20.*

Allows you to better understand and evaluate the information in the franchisor's Uniform Franchise Offering Circular (UFOC). Discusses 62 legal and business issues which should be "negotiated" in a franchise agreement to make it fairer from a franchisee's standpoint. With an understanding of the key underlying issues, you will be better able to communicate with your own franchise attorney.

Databases

Franchisor Database, Source Book Publications. (800) 841-0873/(510) 839-5471. *Item #21.*

Listing of over 2,500 active North American franchisors. 23 fields of information per company: full address, telephone/800/fax numbers, Internet address, contact/title/salutation, president/title/salutation, # of franchised units, # of company-owned units, # total units, IFA/CFA Member, etc. 54 industry categories. Unlimited use. Guaranteed deliverability — $0.50 rebate for any returned mail. $550 for initial database, $75 per quarter for updates. See page 186 for details.

Directories

Bond's Franchise Guide — 1999 Edition, Bond, Source Book Publications, 1999. 496 pp. $29.95. *Item #1.*

The definitive and most comprehensive franchising directory available. Over 2,150 listings, including over 1,050 detailed franchisor profiles resulting from an exhaustive 40-point questionnaire. 51 distinct business categories. Excellent industry overview.

Bond's Minority Franchise Guide — 2000 Edition, Bond, Source Book Publications, 2000. 272 pp. $19.95. *Item # 22*

The only minority franchising directory! Contains detailed profiles and company logos of over 400 forward-looking franchisors that encourage and actively support the inclusion of minority franchisees. It also includes a listing of resources available to prospecitve minority franchisees.

Financing Your Franchise

Financing Your Franchise, Whittemore/Sherman/Hotch, McGraw-Hill. 1993. 275 pp. $16.95. *Item #5.*

This book is an easy-to-understand guide on how to locate money for a franchise. It offers information on steps and techniques for raising capital, including how to write a loan proposal, how to deal with bankers, what is in a purchasing agreement, financing tips for women and minorities, interpreting disclosure documents and how to cut through the sales hype. In addition, the book provides directories of franchise lenders, sample forms, checklists and business plans. Lists of franchisors who offer financing assistance, those who target women and minorities and helpful federal agencies are also included.

General

Guide to Selecting the Best Entity to Own and Operate Your Business, Kanouse, Professional Press. 1995. 139 pp. $15.95. *Item #17.*

Clearly explains the differences between joint ventures, sole proprietorships, general partnerships, "C" corps, "S" corps, etc. Learn the advantages and disadvantages of these and many more organizational forms from a formation, tax, liability adn management perspective. Understand complex financial, business and legal words and phrases. Extremely valuable in forming your business.

How to Really Create a Successful Marketing Plan, Gumpert, Inc., Business Resources. 319 pp. $19.95. *Item #14.*

By examining the actual marketing plans of many "hot" companies, you'll learn practical steps for developing a winning plan, including the wisdom of: targeting the right market, staying current with your competition, communicating with your market, developing and executing your budget, linking your marketing plan to your business plan and maximizing your marketing efforts. Real experience-based advice.

How to Really Start Your Own Business, Gumpert, Inc., Business Resources. 278 pp. $19.95. *Item #15.*

Takes you step-by-step through the launch process, exploring questions like: where do the best, most viable launch ideas come from; what kind of legal protection do entrepreneurs need; how to attract the best employees on start-up budgets; and how to create cash flow projections that are on target. Packed with eye-opening detailed worksheets that allow you to assess launch ideas, evaluate market potential, determine needs, projections, financing. Includes worksheets/forms.

International Franchising

The International Herald Tribune International Franchise Guide, Bond/Thompson, Source Book Publications. 1999. 192 pp. $34.95. *Item #3.*

This annual publication, sponsored by the International Herald Tribune, is the definitive guide to international franchising. It lists comprehensive, in-depth profiles of major franchisors who are committed (not just the usual lip service) to promote and support overseas expansion. Details specific geographic areas of desired expansion for each company, country by country — as well as the number of units in each foreign country as of the date of publication. Geared specifically to the needs and requirements of prospective international area developers, master franchisees and investors. Investors must be prepared to assume responsibility for the development of large geographic areas. Also listed are international franchise consultants, attorneys and service providers. Covers 32 distinct business categories.

Legal

Franchising Law & Practice Forms, Fern, Costello, Asbill & Scott, STP Specialty Technical Publishers. 3 volumes in loose-leaf manual. Individual volumes are $275. $480 for full set. Annual subscription includes quarterly updates at no extra cost. *Not eligible for 15% volume discount. Item #11.*

The definitive word on franchising law for franchisors, franchisees and legal counsel. This definitive 3-volume set, fully updated, is an essential resource containing practical legal advice about every facet of franchising. Separate sections on *The Franchisor; The Franchisee/Source Materials;* and *Forms.* The work provides quick-reference, practical advice on the legal and business aspects of franchising, with clause-by-clause analysis of agreements, precedent cases and advice on how to minimize potentially devastating disputes (and liabilities), as well as the significant costs of complying with federal and state regulations. 30-day risk-free trial. Choose any combination of the 3 volumes.

Site Selection

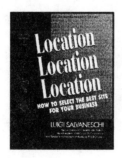

Location, Location, Location: How to Select the Best Site for Your Business, Salvaneschi, Oasis Press. 1996. 280 pp. $19.95. *Item #16.*

Whether you are searching for a new business site or relocating an existing business, you have the power to dramatically increase your profits by choosing the right location. For any business that depends on a customer's ability to find it, location is the most important ingredient for success. Learn how to: spot the essential characteristics of the best location; understand why and how people move from one point to another; analyze and learn from your competitor's business; and learn about the retail trading zone and how to use it to capture the most customers.

Other Franchise Publications

Franchise Times, Restaurant Finance Corp., 2500 Cleveland Ave., North, # D-South, Roseville, MN 55113; (651) 631-3132; FAX (651) 633-8749.

Published 10 times per year, *Franchise Times* magazine focuses on the issues multi-unit franchisees and franchisors need to take their businesses to the next level. Issues such as financing (where is it; who's doing it), real estate (tips for site selection, leases, etc.) and legal issues are tackled. The magazine also highlights successful franchisees and franchisors. In these profiles, the reveal how they have grown their companies to be large franchise businesses and discuss the problems they have conquered along the way. Along with those profiles, *Franchise Times* covers the constantly changing relationship between franchisors and franchisees; how they offer support to each other and conversely the never-ending legal battles that sometimes ensue. The franchise owner survey and the top 200 franchise businesses are eagerly anticipated issues.

The Franchise Bookstore
Order Form

Call (800) 841-0873 or (510) 839-5471; or FAX (510) 839-2104

Item #	Title	Price	Qty.	Total

Basic postage (1 Book)	$4.00
Each additional book add $3.00	
California tax @ 8.25% (if CA resident)	
Total due in U.S. dollars	
Deduct 15% if total due is over $100.00	
Net amount due in U.S. dollars	

Please include credit card number and expiration date for all charge card orders! Checks should be made payable to Source Book Publications. All prices are in U.S. dollars.

Mailing Information: All books shipped by USPS Priority Mail (2nd Day Air). Please print clearly and include your phone number in case we need to contact you. Postage and handling rates are for shipping within the U.S. Please call for international rates.

Name: _____

Company: _____

Address: _____

City: _____

❏ Check enclosed or

Charge my:
❏ MasterCard   ❏ VISA

Card #: _____

Expiration Date: _____

Signature: _____

Title: _____

Telephone No.: (____) _____

State/Prov.: _____ Zip: _____

Special Offer — Save 15%

If your total order above exceeds $100.00, deduct 15% from your bill.

Please send order to:
Source Book Publications
P.O. Box 12488, Oakland, CA 94604
Satisfaction Guaranteed. If not fully satisfied, return for a prompt, 100% refund.

Automotive Products & Services

AAMCO TRANSMISSIONS
One Presidential Blvd.
Bala Cynwyd, PA 19004
Tel: (800) 523-0402 (610) 668-2900
Fax: (610) 617-9532
E-Mail: rcastellani@aamco.com
Internet Address: www.aamcotransmissions.com
Contact: Mr. Bob Castellani, Director Franchise Development

Description: AAMCO is the world's largest chain of transmission specialists with 35 years' experience as the undisputed industry leader. An American icon, AAMCO's trademark is recognized by 90% of the driving public. Transmission repair is a $2.9 billion business in the United States and is projected to be a $3.6 billion business by the year 2001.

# Franchised Units:	712 Units
# Company-Owned Units:	2 Units
Total # Units:	714 Units
Founded In:	1963
1st Franchised In:	1963
Average Total Investment:	175K
Franchise Fee:	30K
On-Going Royalty:	7%
Advertising Fee:	4-5%
Financial Assistance:	Yes(I)
Site Selection Assistance:	Yes
Lease Negotiation Assistance:	Yes
Contract Terms (Init./Renew):	15/15
Initial Training Provided:	5 Weeks Home Office, Philadelphia, PA.

In 1998, in the Central Region, which is composed of centers in the States of Colorado, Illinois, Indiana, Iowa, Kansas, Michigan, Minnesota, Missouri, Montana, Nebraska, New Mexico, North Dakota, Oklahoma, South Dakota, Texas, Wisconsin, Wyoming and the Provinces of Alberta, Manitoba, Saskatchewan and Ontario, AAMCO had 162 centers. Listed in the table that follows this page are the TOTAL ACTUAL GROSS SALES for the Central Region of each of those centers for the years 1995 through 1998.

Of the centers in the Central Region, 125 have been in business for more than ten years; 9 have been in business less than ten years but more than five years; 19 have been in business less than five years but more than two years; and 9 have been in business less than two years but more than one year. During the calendar year 1998, 162 centers were in operation for the full 12-month period. The average gross sales of those 162 centers was $585,593. Seventy or 43% of the centers attained or surpassed this gross sales level.

The following figures were obtained from Weekly Business Reports of franchisees for the period January 2, 1995 through week ending January 2, 1999, which reports are required to be filed with AAMCO. These reports are prepared by each franchisee. Substantiation of the data used in preparing the earnings claim is available for inspection to prospective franchisees upon reasonable request. Some of the centers listed were not in existence all four years; thus, there are blanks in some of the columns. Additionally, you should be aware that some centers may not have been open for a full 12 months in their first year of operation; therefore, the gross sales reported are only for part of a year.

It should be emphasized that while the sales figures are actual sales figures, they are determined, to a large extent, by the quality of the management of the centers. Among the determinant factors are the hours the centers keep, the energy and dedication of the center owners and the quality of the work performed. For you to assume that you will achieve similar results, you must realize that similar dedication to managing the business is required.

CAUTION: THERE IS NO ASSURANCE YOU'LL DO AS WELL AS THESE CENTERS. IF YOU RELY UPON THESE FIGURES, YOU MUST ACCEPT THE RISK OF NOT DOING AS WELL.

Central Region

Center	1998	1997	1996	1995
1	595,963	332,728	312,276	288,516
2	419,350	377,981	438,512	462,990
3	567,078	641,867	499,731	370,410
4	471,039	459,590	497,906	473,647
5	886,097	816,712	762,124	632,330
6	504,020	581,786	550,737	382,873
7	639,595	616,448	583,407	472,893
8	647,250	661,812	511,202	450,671
9	490,380	470,444	404,499	454,159
10	491,749	513,704	375,128	58,080
11	835,666	745,960	771,429	709,917
12	518,537	496,293	561,896	514,202
13	512,261	442,534	473,715	349,227
14	1,110,007	1,475,018	1,537,541	1,491,152
15	357,424	394,384	339,745	362,829
16	347,914	332,366	350,199	409,319
17	504,790	548,805	402,847	380,720
18	459,689	458,032	404,434	318,211
19	460,084	427,099	433,360	186,221
20	710,597	848,680	644,298	482,525
21	266,011	304,245	306,742	300,442
22	1,516,614	1,428,605	1,411,159	1,384,032
23	1,486,660	1,323,070	1,174,013	1,084,963
24	495,437	361,477	361,216	390,048
25	569,455	718,024	512,083	547,871
26	930,567	947,685	797,862	687,250

Center	1998	1997	1996	1995
27	721,548	390,263	448,343	391,971
28	554,824	536,993	476,526	486,362
29	704,693	648,155	696,750	642,394
30	593,986	559,303	513,669	451,632
31	152,864	150,876	182,775	151,844
32	1,473,424	1,219,092	1,181,273	1,065,645
33	1,176,363	1,375,608	1,160,302	861,815
34	1,620,532	1,518,091	1,244,318	475,251
35	719,449	701,901	625,185	569,246
36	400,320	390,110	370,521	427,200
37	267,050	297,279	311,759	57,856
38	763,839	705,081	658,743	606,907
39	418,388	441,707	424,344	394,281
40	852,403	1,108,395	1,229,297	1,257,370
41	649,848	632,634	546,114	500,662
42	622,100	570,965	558,815	531,396
43	841,797	658,931	702,758	680,356
44	454,126	289,011	261,506	221,326
45	690,058	636,172	584,003	519,284
46	199,495	154,576	125,337	191,438
47	400,223	132,408	339,867	102,550
48	517,703	504,233	453,383	424,037
49	727,826	829,463	913,097	514,957
50	412,652	412,187	387,032	348,618
51	505,891	499,124	541,462	411,716
52	332,380	291,699	294,802	281,520
53	419,351	478,139	449,295	388,359
54	497,404	476,107	435,990	381,673
55	258,459	310,135	235,585	245,830
56	485,403	466,337	472,822	421,273
57	419,356	411,116	391,693	362,036
58	510,104	517,662	617,826	463,947
59	464,625	452,373	414,430	351,105
60	306,876	164,906	244,926	287,090
61	228,896	268,903	421,000	350,167
62	659,062	602,538	467,251	514,314
63	646,921	587,950	518,124	510,906
64	703,145	721,426	596,279	626,111
65	585,787	594,062	693,552	610,779
66	519,722	535,374	471,731	471,916

Center	1998	1997	1996	1995
67	419,914	426,416	390,020	310,111
68	690,664	664,919	701,832	569,792
69	759,824	714,107	736,334	670,530
70	508,628	517,804	500,245	490,052
71	308,511	297,277	258,660	271,451
72	480,365	512,860	450,342	405,946
73	447,316	440,151	420,965	410,917
74	332,381	343,265	346,669	320,063
75	767,281	960,393	944,643	875,604
76	685,135	648,180	662,570	697,682
77	920,814	888,843	856,551	1,119,756
78	685,524	755,572	748,273	719,184
79	563,403	609,817	662,293	604,188
80	839,749	786,081	771,307	66,326
81	466,025	385,158	364,101	290,523
82	670,332	561,938	594,749	582,252
83	677,662	658,702	595,435	590,489
84	623,129	617,396	460,232	340,863
85	614,486	541,155	657,456	499,283
86	572,489	548,176	563,111	637,821
87	310,536	404,655	317,869	304,739
88	454,831	548,762	446,641	377,205
89	155,202	267,887	221,464	192,674
90	280,471	310,073	297,177	295,130
91	701,836	641,563	554,158	595,199
92	288,109	384,658	267,370	380,513
93	789,002	772,747	662,517	477,973
94	350,813	322,454	325,235	339,805
95	841,609	558,730	528,931	453,747
96	730,349	804,138	755,431	653,603
97	548,201	584,207	614,822	399,441
98	396,313	376,743	432,828	377,045
99	975,730	999,173	899,643	779,945
100	482,164	451,321	355,579	73,785
101	464,371	646,854	486,738	453,254
102	353,012	411,117	301,255	439,446
103	378,282	448,165	354,444	363,637
104	559,191	642,399	559,359	473,289
105	593,127	572,242	503,641	401,347
106	614,749	597,547	563,577	484,497

Center	1998	1997	1996	1995
107	716,392	828,582	367,136	281,942
108	476,924	527,058	574,089	511,599
109	471,649	454,888	506,255	513,328
110	735,012	750,380	663,773	643,215
111	58,809	55,687	55,654	55,212
112	453,718	536,348	582,353	345,919
113	374,833	343,292	380,528	173,657
114	420,568	435,076	427,292	278,829
115	538,855	515,874	476,982	405,103
116	964,073	995,773	858,943	764,615
117	552,310	499,698	435,521	330,608
118	627,272	710,085	572,856	415,038
119	556,746	610,964	462,990	359,915
120	464,422	589,830	404,838	341,606
121	564,699	613,363	456,857	344,354
122	819,833	825,420	655,785	586,539
123	616,263	704,099	648,593	666,018
124	375,371	423,767	371,415	387,807
125	808,244	795,713	774,368	740,436
126	630,502	750,480	691,766	605,957
127	496,528	493,525	539,536	524,526
128	839,732	936,068	821,669	580,701
129	473,293	450,236	424,155	383,076
130	383,735	394,013	396,614	394,557
131	790,201	780,381	749,589	627,465
132	503,794	560,470	599,765	436,551
133	425,077	403,011	453,155	383,678
134	618,122	587,646	525,980	490,235
135	671,044	624,175	501,045	586,819
136	455,885	451,307	518,876	465,929
137	436,148	372,497	407,707	391,363
138	336,858	299,165	197,471	44,726
139	754,600	589,818	560,220	492,182
140	774,702	683,628	684,761	737,651
141	905,898	906,955	802,992	751,633
142	585,729	559,296	571,175	558,974
143	426,884	400,867	337,356	343,474
144	421,487	452,464	469,952	438,428
145	333,148	369,622	221,428	
146	886,730	864,358	232,648	

Center	1998	1997	1996	1995
147	494,950	354,723	235,881	
148	579,941	423,124	298,850	
149	573,326	511,373	174,213	
150	420,207	397,773	49,023	
151	636,034	407,017	97,065	
152	470,552	428,740	88,557	
153	497,990	462,973	343,141	
154	830,599	266,917		
155	677,298	41,208		
156	662,433	150,598		
157	715,053	355,870		
158	721,127	451,340		
159	720,064	165,954		
160	576,887	40,916		
161	499,842	118,928		
162	464,123.54	181,971.38		

Franchisees agree to share local advertising costs with other franchisees in their local area. The composition of the local advertising pool is determined by AAMCO using Neilsen, a recognized industry guide, and its Designated Market Areas. There are thirteen advertising pools in the Central Region with four or more centers. The 1998 and 1997 average weekly gross sales for these advertising pools are as follows:

Ad Pool Name   **1998**   **1997**

Denver, CO

1st Qtr.	$12,790	$13,921
2nd Qtr.	12,638	12,963
3rd Qtr.	15,142	14,372
4th Qtr.	14,029	13,091
Yearly Average:	$13,653	$13,571

Number of centers in Pool:
(12)   (12)
Number of centers which attained or surpassed average: 7 or 58%   5 or 42%

Chicago, IL

1st Qtr.	$9,561	$9,596
2nd Qtr.	9,122	9,625
3rd Qtr.	9,437	9,913
4th Qtr.	9,369	9,197
Yearly Average:	$9,372	$9,579

Number of centers in Pool:
(26)   (26)
Number of centers which attained or surpassed average: 12 or 46%   11 or 42%

Indianapolis, IN

1st Qtr.	$12,509	$15,574
2nd Qtr.	13,611	14,282
3rd Qtr.	14,917	14,487
4th Qtr.	13,488	13,281
Yearly Average:	$13,631	$14,339

Number of centers in Pool:
(7)   (7)
Number of centers which attained or surpassed average: 3 or 43%   3 or 43%

Kansas City, MO

1st Qtr.	$8,123	$7,558
2nd Qtr.	8,178	7,711
3rd Qtr.	10,131	8,165
4th Qtr.	8,733	7,513

Yearly Average:	$8,791	$7,733

Number of centers in Pool:

	(7)	(7)

Number of centers which attained or surpassed

average:	3 or 43%	3 or 43%

Saint Louis, MO

1st Qtr.	$7,353	$7,657
2nd Qtr.	7,147	7,757
3rd Qtr.	8,668	8,404
4th Qtr.	8,179	7,475

Yearly Average:	$7,856	$7,817

Number of centers in Pool:

	(4)	(4)

Number of centers which attained or surpassed

average:	2 or 50%	2 or 50%

Minneapolis, MN

1st Qtr.	$8,806	$10,167
2nd Qtr.	9,430	9,688
3rd Qtr.	9,873	9,963
4th Qtr.	9,568	9,311

Yearly Average:	$9,419	$9,773

Number of centers in Pool:

	(8)	(8)

Number of centers which attained or surpassed

average:	5 or 63%	4 or 50%

Omaha, NE

1st Qtr.	$13,291	$11,281
2nd Qtr.	13,384	11,349
3rd Qtr.	13,356	11,741
4th Qtr.	11,420	10,503

Yearly Average:	$12,877	$11,205

Number of centers in Pool:

	(4)	(4)

Number of centers which attained or surpassed

average:	1 or 25%	2 or 50%

Tulsa, OK

1st Qtr.	$11,779	$11,008
2nd Qtr.	13,342	9,977
3rd Qtr.	11,943	12,338
4th Qtr.	10,799	11,098

Yearly Average:	$11,966	$11,105

Number of centers in Pool:

	(4)	(4)

Number of centers which attained or surpassed

average:	2 or 50%	2 or 50%

Toronto, ON

1st Qtr.	$15,213	$20,156
2nd Qtr.	16,195	25,254
3rd Qtr.	15,970	17,046
4th Qtr.	14,227	14,098

Yearly Average:	$15,328	$17,733

Number of centers in Pool:

	(5)	(5)

Number of centers which attained or surpassed

average:	3 or 60%	1 or 20%

Austin, TX

1st Qtr.	$10,822	$10,674
2nd Qtr.	12,856	10,339
3rd Qtr.	13,537	10,483
4th Qtr.	13,145	9,971

Yearly Average:	$12,590	$10,359

Number of centers in Pool:

	(4)	(4)

Number of centers which attained or surpassed

average:	2 or 50%	3 or 75%

Dallas/Ft. Worth, TX

1st Qtr.	$14,603	$13,934
2nd Qtr.	16,891	13,972
3rd Qtr.	19,211	15,475
4th Qtr.	17,031	14,243

Yearly Average:	$16,934	$14,404

Number of centers in Pool:

	(9)	(9)

Number of centers which attained or surpassed

average:	3 or 33%	3 or 33%

Houston, TX

1st Qtr.	$ 9,997	$ 9,600
2nd Qtr.	10,337	9,832
3rd Qtr.	11,112	9,917
4th Qtr.	9,300	9,228

Yearly Average: $10,187 $9,637

Number of centers in Pool:
     (13)   (13)

Number of centers which attained or surpassed
   average: 7 or 54%   6 or 50%

San Antonio, TX

1st Qtr.	$11,912	$10,761
2nd Qtr.	13,218	12,000
3rd Qtr.	12,376	12,013
4th Qtr.	11,579	10,943

Yearly Average: $12,271 $11,420

Number of centers in Pool:
     (6)   (6)

Number of centers which attained or surpassed
   average: 3 or 50%   3 or 50%

Centers in the Chain:	**1998**	**1997**
1st Qtr.	$11,228	$11,105
2nd Qtr.	11,345	10,956
3rd Qtr.	12,028	11,606
4th Qtr.	11,196	10,481

Yearly Average: $11,449 $11,025

Number of centers in Chain:
     (724)   (714)

Number of centers which attained or surpassed
   average: 322 or 44%   313 or 44%

ALTRACOLOR SYSTEMS

111 Phlox Ave.
Metairie, LA 70001
Tel: (800) 678-5220 (504) 454-7233
Fax: (504) 455-8025
E-Mail: altra@home.com
Internet Address: www.altracolor.com
Contact: Mr. James A. Richards, President

Description: Low-cost, home-based, automotive paint and plastic repair franchise, very low overhead, fixed royalties, mobile business, no leases to sign. Turn key operation includes everything you need, including business cards.

# Franchised Units:	80 Units
# Company-Owned Units:	<u>90</u> Units
Total # Units:	170 Units
Founded In:	1988
1st Franchised In:	1991
Average Total Investment:	34-49K
Franchise Fee:	9.95K
On-Going Royalty:	$95/Wk.
Advertising Fee:	0
Financial Assistance:	Yes(D)
Site Selection Assistance:	Yes
Lease Negotiation Assistance:	N/A
Contract Terms (Init./Renew):	15/5/5

Initial Training Provided: 4 Days in New Orleans, 1 Week Franchisee's Home Territory.

The data contained in the following chart are based on monthly reports generated in the field by Altracolor franchisees covering 1998. Every report received has been used in the compilation of this earnings claim. There have been no omissions for any reason. The information contained in the monthly reports received has not been subject to audit and may contain inaccuracies. Verification of the data used in the preparation of this report will be made available upon request.

The information used in this report, while not audited, is believed to be an accurate assessment of production from our franchisees. Weekly service fees are not dependent on sales, so there is no incentive to report sales incorrectly.

The data in the chart in no way represents what any new franchisee may or may not do. **A new franchisee's individual sales figures are likely**

to differ from the average sales figure reported below.

Any prospective franchisee must proceed carefully when setting up his or her operating plan for an Altracolor franchise. We recommend that you contact as many operating franchisees listed in this offering circular as you would like. You may visit several franchisees to observe the system. You may wish to consult with an accountant or an attorney or any other competent business analyst to help you with your decision to purchase an Altracolor franchise.

In the calendar year 1998, we received 507 monthly production reports from operating franchisees. The average sales figure reported was $6,920 per unit per month. Our records show a total of 63 units reporting which is approximately 79% saturation. The following table gives a breakdown of the information.

Monthly Sales Level	Franchisee Reports	PCT.
$12,001 or above	28	6%
$10,001 to $12,000	43	9%
$8,001 to $10,000	61	13%
$6,001 to $8,000	141	32%
$5,001 to $6,000	59	13%
$4,001 to $5,000	45	10%
$3,001 to $4,000	32	7%
0 to $3,000	28	6%
At or above average ($6,920)	196	38%
At $5,000 avg. or above	374	74%
At $4,000 avg. or above	443	87%

Altracolor does not know the sales figures for the approximately 21% of non-reporting franchisees. Altracolor has no reason to believe that their sales figures would average less than the average for the reporting franchisees.

BATTERIES PLUS
925 Walnut Ridge Dr., # 100
Hartland, WI 53029
Tel: (800) 274-9155 (262) 369-0690
Fax: (262) 369-0680
E-Mail: batplus@batteriesplus.com
Internet Address: www.batteriesplus.com
Contact: Mr. Richard Zimmerman, Director of Franchise Sales

Description: BATTERIES PLUS is America's Battery Store, providing 1,000's of batteries for 1,000's of items, serving both retail and commercial customers. The $17 billion battery market, growing 6% annually, is driven by technology and lifestyles.

BATTERIES PLUS is a unique opportunity in this growth industry not yet saturated with competitors. Our turn-key program includes a unique store design, graphics, signage and product brands and proven operating methods.

# Franchised Units:	191 Units
# Company-Owned Units:	20 Units
Total # Units:	211 Units
Founded In:	1988
1st Franchised In:	1992
Average Total Investment:	185-225K
Franchise Fee:	25K
On-Going Royalty:	4%
Advertising Fee:	1%
Financial Assistance:	Yes(I)
Site Selection Assistance:	Yes
Lease Negotiation Assistance:	Yes
Contract Terms (Init./Renew):	15
Initial Training Provided:	4 Weeks Corporate Training Center; 2 Weeks On-Site Franchisee's Store.

Exhibit G is a statement of actual gross sales and expenses for BATTERIES PLUS STORES operated by BATTERIES. Except as set forth

in Exhibit G, BATTERIES does not furnish or authorize its salespersons to furnish any oral or written information or representations or statements of actual sales, costs, income or profits of a BATTERIES PLUS STORE. Actual results vary from unit to unit and BATTERIES cannot estimate the results of any particular Franchisee. You must execute a disclosure acknowledgment statement (Exhibit J), whereby you acknowledge that no earnings claims other than those set forth in Exhibit G have been made to you.

ACTUAL RESULTS VARY FROM STORE TO STORE AND BATTERIES CANNOT ESTIMATE THE RESULTS OF ANY PARTICULAR FRANCHISEE. A NEW FRANCHISEE'S FINANCIAL RESULTS MAY DIFFER FROM THE FIGURES PRESENTED IN EXHIBIT G. YOU SHOULD MAKE YOUR OWN INVESTIGATION AND DETERMINE WHETHER YOUR FRANCHISE BATTERIES PLUS STORE WILL BE PROFITABLE.

Exhibit G
Statement of Actual Gross Sales for Batteries Plus Stores
As of December 31, 1998, there are nineteen (19) Batteries Plus Stores in operation, owned by BATTERIES. All of the retail stores are comparable to the franchises being offered.

The Batteries Plus store located in Green Bay, Wisconsin opened in November 1988; the Batteries Plus store in Appleton, Wisconsin opened in April 1989; the Batteries Plus store in Wausau, Wisconsin opened in April 1990; the Batteries Plus store in Oshkosh, Wisconsin opened in December 1990; the Batteries Plus store in Waukesha, Wisconsin opened in March 1992; the Batteries Plus store in Sheboygan, Wisconsin opened in September 1992; the Batteries Plus store in Racine, Wisconsin opened in November 1992; the Batteries Plus store in Janesville, Wisconsin opened in April, 1993; the Batteries Plus store in Madison, Wisconsin opened in June, 1994; the Batteries Plus store in Menomonee Falls, Wisconsin opened in June, 1994; the Batteries Plus store in Loves Park, Illinois opened in September, 1994; the Batteries Plus store on N. 76th Street in Milwaukee, Wisconsin opened in January, 1995; the Batteries Plus store on S. 27th Street in Milwaukee, Wisconsin opened in February, 1995; the Batteries Plus store in Lake Zurich, Illinois opened in June, 1995; the Batteries Plus store in Oaklawn, Illinois opened in October, 1995; the Batteries Plus store in Fond Du Lac, Wisconsin opened in December, 1995; the Batteries Plus store in Lombard, Illinois opened in January, 1996; the Batteries Plus store in West Allis, Wisconsin opened in March, 1996; and the Batteries Plus store in Rockford, Illinois opened January 2, 1998.

Set forth below are the actual gross sales and cost of sales figures for the period January 1, 1998 through December 31, 1998, for the nineteen (19) Batteries Plus stores owned and operated by BATTERIES.

Store	Gross Sales	Cost of Sales	Gross Profit
Appleton, WI	694,459	361,416	333,043
*Fond Du Lac, WI	364,444	201,077	163,367
Green Bay, WI	1,185,539	704,872	480,667
Janesville, WI	565,232	330,293	234,940
Lake Zurich, IL	545,731	305,330	240,400
Lombard, IL	379,333	231,967	147,366
Loves Park, IL	499,335	277,520	221,815
Madison, WI	729,225	371,896	357,330
Menomonee Falls, WI	599,150	351,562	247,587
S. 27th St., Milwaukee, WI	674,076	339,015	335,061
N. 76th St., Milwaukee, WI	533,408	308,260	225,148
Oaklawn, IL	448,145	251,737	196,408
Oshkosh, WI	457,947	235,657	222,290

Store	Gross Sales	Cost of Sales	Gross Profit
Racine, WI	613,668	325,672	287,996
**Rockford, IL	332,520	172,659	159,861
Sheboygan, WI	587,083	328,880	258,203
Waukesha, WI	854,191	454,348	399,843
*Wausau WI	350,896	215,643	135,253
West Allis, WI	738,043	347,755	390,288

*Small Market Stores
**Open Less Than 2 Years

Expenses of a Batteries Plus Store

Variable Expenses

You incur certain variable expenses in the operation of a Batteries Plus store. The variable expenses include:

    Direct labor
    Royalty and service fees
    Advertising
    Supplies and services

The royalty fees are set forth in the Franchise Agreement and are four percent (4%) of Franchisee's total net revenues.

Fixed Expenses

A Batteries Plus store incurs certain fixed expenses. The following explanations assist in compiling a full profile of expenses:

1. Occupancy Expenses. Included in this item are rent, real estate taxes, insurance, repair and maintenance and building licenses expenses. Depending on the area and location of the proposed Batteries Plus store, these expenses vary.

2. Utilities. Included in this item are telephone, electricity and heating expenses.

3. Professional Fees. Included in this item are expenses for accounting and legal fees.

4. Yellow Pages and Local Advertising. Included in this item are expenses for all Yellow Page advertising and expenses for any local advertising and public relations you elect to do in addition to the contribution to the National Marketing and Promotional Fund. Presently, you must spend four percent (4%) of gross sales on Yellow Page and local advertising, marketing and public relations. Yellow Page fees vary depending on size, placement and number of ads, number of Batteries Plus stores in the market, number of directories, etc.

5. Debt Requirement. Included in this item are expenses for loan principal repayment and applicable interest charges. This expense category varies depending upon loan amount, amortization schedule and interest rates.

6. Owner's Salary. Included in this item are expenses for the owner's salary. This expense varies depending upon owner's desires.

Substantiation of the data used in preparing this statement are available to you upon reasonable request.

YOUR INDIVIDUAL FINANCIAL RESULTS ARE LIKELY TO DIFFER FROM THE RESULTS STATED.

CAR-X MUFFLER & BRAKE
8430 W. Bryn Mawr Ave., # 400
Chicago, IL 60631
Tel: (800) 359-2359 (773) 693-1000
Fax: (773) 693-0309
E-Mail: dmaltzma@carx.com
Internet Address: www.carx.com.
Contact: Mr. David Maltzman, Franchise
Development Manager

Description: Retail automotive specialists providing service in brakes, exhaust, road handling, steering systems, air conditioning, and oil changes for all makes of cars and light trucks.

# Franchised Units:	132 Units
# Company-Owned Units:	<u>53</u> Units
Total # Units:	185 Units
Founded In:	1971
1st Franchised In:	1973
Average Total Investment:	225-285K
Franchise Fee:	20K
On-Going Royalty:	5%
Advertising Fee:	5-7%
Financial Assistance:	Yes(I)
Site Selection Assistance:	Yes
Lease Negotiation Assistance:	Yes
Contract Terms (Init./Renew):	15/5

Initial Training Provided: 5 Weeks Headquarters; 2 Weeks at Franchisee's Shop.

Attached as Exhibit B-1 is a statement of actual gross sales for Car-X Centers. Attached as Exhibit B-2 is a statement of net sales, gross profit and specified operating expenses of affiliated Car-X Centers. Except as set forth in Exhibits B-1 and B-2, Car-X does not furnish or authorize its salespersons to furnish any oral or written information concerning the actual or potential sales, costs, income or profits of a Car-X Center. Actual results vary from unit to unit and you cannot estimate the results of any particular franchise. You must execute a Disclosure Acknowledgement Statement, a copy of which is attached as Exhibit E-11, acknowledging that no earnings claims other than those set forth in Exhibits B-1 and B-2 have been made to you. The representations made in the disclosure acknowledgement statement are not intended to and do not act as a release, estoppel or waiver of any liability Car-X may incur under state franchise law.

Exhibit B-1
Statement of Actual Gross Sales for Car-X Centers
As of January 2, 1999, there were 182 Car-X Centers in operation. 53 of these were owned and operated by Discoverer Services, Inc., an affiliate of Car-X and 129 are franchised Centers. 176 of these Centers were owned and operated for at least one year. All of the Centers except for one Center in South Florida are located in metropolitan areas in the Midwest. All of the Centers are comparable to the franchises being offered.

Set forth below are ranges of the actual gross sales figures of franchised Centers for the year ending January 2, 1999 and of the affiliate-owned Centers for the last fiscal year period commencing January 4, 1998 and ending January 2, 1999 for the Centers in operation for more than one year and less than two years. The average actual gross sales of these Centers was $533,269. All of these Centers are franchised. Of these 6 Centers in operation for more than one year and less than two years, 3 had gross sales in excess of $533,269.

Range of Sales	Number of Centers	Percentage
$0–349,000	1	16.66%
$350,000–399,999	0	0.00%
$400,000–449,999	1	16.66%
$450,000–499,999	1	16.66%
$500,000–549,999	0	0.00%
$550,000–599,999	1	16.66%
$600,000–649,999	1	16.66%
$650,000–699,999	0	0.00%
$700,000–749,999	1	16.66%
Total	6	100.00%

Set forth below are the ranges of the actual gross sales figures of franchised Centers for the year ending January 2, 1999 and of the affiliate-owned Centers for the last fiscal year period commencing January 4, 1998 and ending January 2, 1999 for the Centers in operation for more than two years. The average actual gross sales of these Centers was $698,082. 117 of these Centers are franchised. Of these 117, 71 Centers or 61% of the franchised Centers in operation for more than two years had gross sales in excess of $698,082.

Range of Sales	Number of Centers	Percentage
$1,900,000–1,949,999	0	0.00%
$1,950,000–1,999,999	0	0.00%
$2,000,000–2,149,999	1	0.59%
Total	170	100.00%

Range of Sales	Number of Centers	Percentage
$300,000–349,999	2	1.18%
$350,000–399,999	2	1.18%
$400,000–449,999	15	8.82%
$450,000–499,999	18	10.59%
$500,000–549,999	14	8.23%
$550,000–599,999	14	8.23%
$600,000–649,999	14	8.23%
$650,000–699,999	20	11.77%
$700,000–749,999	15	8.82%
$750,000–799,999	9	5.30%
$800,000–849,999	11	6.47%
$850,000–899,999	6	3.53%
$900,000–949,999	10	5.88%
$950,000–999,999	3	1.76%
$1,000,000–1,149,999	10	5.88%
$1,150,000–1,199,999	2	1.18%
$1,200,000–1,249,999	2	1.18%
$1,250,000–1,299,999	0	0.00%
$1,300,000–1,349,999	0	0.00%
$1,350,000–1,399,999	1	0.59%
$1,400,000–1,449,999	0	0.00%
$1,450,000–1,499,999	1	0.59%
$1,500,000–1,549,999	0	0.00%
$1,550,000–1,599,999	0	0.00%
$1,600,000–1,649,999	0	0.00%
$1,650,000–1,699,999	0	0.00%
$1,700,000–1,749,999	0	0.00%
$1,750,000–1,799,999	0	0.00%
$1,800,000–1,849,999	0	0.00%
$1,850,000–1,899,999	0	0.00%

The sales figures set forth in this Statement have not been audited by the Franchisor. The sales figures used in this Statement are gross sales figures. Net income will vary from Center to Center depending upon such factors as rental or real estate costs, costs of goods sold, labor costs and other costs relating to the operation of the Center.

The sales figures set forth in this Statement have not been audited by the Franchisor. The sales figures used in this Statement are gross sales figures. Net income will vary from Center to Center depending upon such factors as rental or real estate costs, costs of goods sold, labor costs and other costs relating to the operation of the Center.

Car-X offered substantially the same services to all of the Centers described in this Statement. These Centers offered substantially the same products and services to the public.

All of the Centers report gross sales information to Car-X based upon a uniform reporting system. Car-X believes that this Statement is consistent with generally accepted accounting principles, to the extent applicable.

Substantiation of the data used to prepare this Statement will be made available to a prospective franchisee on reasonable request.

SUCH ACTUAL SALES ARE OF FRAN-CHISED AND COMPANY-OWNED AND OPERATED UNITS AND SHOULD NOT BE CONSIDERED AS THE ACTUAL OR PROB-ABLE SALES THAT WILL BE REALIZED BY ANY FRANCHISEE. THE FRANCHISOR DOES NOT REPRESENT THAT ANY FRAN-CHISEE CAN ATTAIN SUCH SALES. A NEW FRANCHISEE'S INDIVIDUAL FINANCIAL

RESULTS ARE LIKELY TO DIFFER FROM THE RESULTS STATED HEREIN.

Exhibit B-2
Statement of Net Sales, Gross Profit and Specified Operating Expenses of Affiliated Car-X Centers

The net sales, gross profit and operating expenses set forth below are based on actual results of the fifty-three (53) Car-X Centers owned by an affiliate of Car-X which were in operation for the last full fiscal year ended January 2, 1999. These Centers were operated in three (3) states and offer substantially the same products and services that are provided by the franchised Centers. The majority of these Centers are free-standing buildings located in metropolitan areas. These figures are not audited; however, these Centers utilize a uniform accounting method which is consistent with generally accepted accounting principles. There are no material economic or market differences, such as lower cost of goods, services and operating expenses, between the affiliate-owned Centers and the franchised Centers.

			% of Sales (Based on Average)
Net Sales (1)	Range	$328,585–1,227,933	
	Average	$638,942	100.00%
Gross Profit (2)	Range	$218,862–836,441	
	Average	$442,888	69.31%
Wages (3)	Range	$130,577–378,992	
	Average	$200,501	31.38%
Occupancy	Range	$24,188–113,206	
	Average	$57,059	8.93%
Variable Supplies (4)	Range	$11,023–34,293	
	Average	$19,423	3.03%
Fixed Supplies (5)	Range	$12,227–24,749	
	Average	$18,338	2.87%

1. *Net Sales:* Included in this Item are all retail sales associated with the Center, less applicable taxes.

2. *Gross Profit:* This item is achieved by reducing net sales by the following expenses: product costs, warranty costs, inventory adjustments and freight.

3. *Wages:* Included in this item are expenses for direct labor, management salaries and benefits costs.

4. *Variable Supplies:* Included in this item are Center supplies, charge card and bank charges.

5. *Fixed Supplies:* Included in this item are utility costs, general maintenance insurance, postage and tool replacement costs.

A franchisee will incur certain other operating expenses. These include royalty and service fees (5%), yellow page and advertising expenditures. The minimum advertising contribution payable by the franchisee at this time is 5% of the monthly gross sales of the Center. Presently the fee varies depending upon the market with a majority of markets being assessed at six percent 6%. The expenses specified do not include provision for debt service which may be incurred in connection with a franchisee's financing of the acquisition of his Center.

Substantiation of the data used in preparing this statement will be made available to a prospective franchisee upon reasonable request.

THESE RANGES OF ACTUAL SALES AND GROSS PROFITS ARE OF UNITS OWNED BY

AFFILIATES OF THE FRANCHISOR AND SHOULD NOT BE CONSIDERED AS THE ACTUAL OR PROBABLE SALES OR GROSS PROFITS THAT WILL BE REALIZED BY ANY FRANCHISEE. THE FRANCHISOR DOES NOT REPRESENT THAT ANY FRAN- CHISEE CAN EXPECT TO ATTAIN SUCH SALES OR GROSS PROFITS. A NEW FRANCHISEE'S INDIVIDUAL FINANCIAL RESULTS ARE LIKELY TO DIFFER FROM THE RESULTS STATED HEREIN.

COTTMAN TRANSMISSION
240 New York Dr.
Fort Washington, PA 19034
Tel: (888) 4COTTMAN (215) 643-5885
Fax: (215) 643-2519
E-Mail:
Internet Address: www.cottman.com
Contact: Mr. Barry Auchenbach, Manager Franchise Development

Description: Automotive transmission service franchise with centers nationwide. A market leader with new opportunities available in major markets as a result of our expansion plans. A highly-supportive company that offers intensive training, outstanding advertising and on-site support.

# Franchised Units:	260 Units
# Company-Owned Units:	4 Units
Total # Units:	264 Units
Founded In:	1962
1st Franchised In:	1964
Average Total Investment:	130-160K
Franchise Fee:	25K
On-Going Royalty:	7.5%
Advertising Fee:	$605/Wk.
Financial Assistance:	Yes(I)
Site Selection Assistance:	Yes
Lease Negotiation Assistance:	Yes
Contract Terms (Init./Renew):	15/15
Initial Training Provided:	3 Weeks Ft. Washington, PA; 1 Week On-Site.

Attached as Exhibit "E" is an Earnings Claim based on average sales and expenses of 52 Cottman franchises operating in the Mid-Atlantic Region, composed of Connecticut, Delaware, Maryland, New Jersey, New York, Pennsylvania , Virginia and West Virginia, of the United States from January 1, 1996 through December 31, 1996. The Centers are either free standing or located in auto malls. 57 Centers who operated in the Mid-Atlantic Region during this period, with no change in ownership, were sent a questionnaire, in the format of the Earnings Claim (Exhibit "E"), to obtain their sales and expenses. 52 or 91% of those Centers responded, a list of these franchised locations, in the Mid-Atlantic Region, number of years of operation, and whether the franchise is owner manager, is attached as Exhibit "F."

The type of franchised business currently offered by us is substantially the same as the franchised business utilized in the survey and has been sub- stantially the same since the start of our business. In addition, all franchisees have received substan- tially the same services from us, and those in the survey have not received any services generally not available to any franchisee. The franchised loca- tions that participated in the survey opened under the new, elite or super elite programs.

All of our franchisees offer substantially the same services to the public as those described in this Offering Circular. Accordingly, the Earnings Claim directly relates to franchisees operating in the Mid-Atlantic Region.

The $504,177 gross sales figure on Exhibit "E" is the average gross sales figure of all Cottman Transmission Centers in the Mid-Atlantic Region, from January through December 1996, who par- ticipated in the survey. 19 or 37% of the participat- ing Centers actually achieved or surpassed this sales level.

The estimated annual gross sales to "break-even" for franchisees in the Mid-Atlantic region is $317,615. The "break-even" point is defined as the point at which there is no profit or loss demonstrated by the business and depreciation, bank loan interest and any salaries or other benefits taken by operator are not included. 46 or 88% of all Cottman Transmission Centers in the Mid-Atlantic Region who participated in the survey actually achieved or surpassed the "break-even" gross sales level.

Attached as Exhibit "E.1" is a schedule showing the total actual gross sales for the Mid-Atlantic Region for the years 1996, 1997, and 1998. During the one year period ending December 31, 1998, 94 Centers operated in the Mid-Atlantic Region. The average gross sales of the 75 Centers that were open the entire period is $482,661. 31 or 41% of the 75 Centers attained or surpassed this gross sales level. The Earnings Claims reported in Exhibit "E" and "E.1" were prepared on a basis consistent with generally accepted accounting principles. The gross sales were obtained from licensees reports as sent to us throughout our fiscal year and were audited by the Certified Public Accounting firm of BDO Seidman, Philadelphia, Pennsylvania. However, while each licensee must report his gross sales to us on a weekly basis, there is no requirement that said sales reports be audited by the individual licensees. We did not audit the costs, profits or earnings reported by the franchisees on the questionnaire.

All licensees who responded to the survey provided the sales, costs and earnings information which was then compiled into the average figures No special considerations or provisions were made for affiliate or company-owned locations. The Earning Claim does not include the expenses of depreciation, bank loan interest and any salaries or any other benefits paid to or incurred for the benefit of the franchisee because these expenses vary greatly for each individual Cottman Center. In addition, cost and earnings may vary due to material differences in wages, rents, insurance premiums and/or taxes in different geographic locations.

Upon reasonable demand made by you we will make available the substantiating information, supplied by franchisees, used to prepare the Earnings Claim, Exhibit "E" and "E.1."

CAUTION: THESE SALES, PROFITS, OR EARNINGS ARE AVERAGES OF SPECIFIC FRANCHISES AND SHOULD NOT BE CONSIDERED AS THE ACTUAL OR POTENTIAL SALES, PROFITS, OR EARNINGS THAT WILL BE REALIZED BY ANY OTHER FRANCHISE. WE DO NOT REPRESENT THAT YOU CAN EXPECT TO ATTAIN THESE SALES, PROFITS, OR EARNINGS.

CAUTION: SOME CENTERS HAVE EARNED THIS AMOUNT. THERE IS NO ASSURANCE YOU'LL DO AS WELL. IF YOU RELY UPON OUR FIGURES, YOU MUST ACCEPT THE RISK OF NOT DOING AS WELL.

Exhibit "E" Earnings Claim
Statement of Actual Average Sales
and Earnings for the Mid-Atlantic Region
January 1996 through December 1996

	Sales	Percentage
Retail	$377,124	74.8%
Outside	127,053	25.2%
Total Sales	504,177	100.0%
Cost of Sales		
Parts	93,263	18.5%
Laundry	2,458	0.5%
Shop Supplies	8,655	1.7%
Towing	5,758	1.1%
Wages	94,818	18.8%
Total Cost of Sales	204,952	40.7%
Gross Profit on Sales	299,225	59.3%
Selling Expenses		
Salary — Manager	34,986	6.9%
O/S Sales Commissions	3,003	0.6%
O/S Sales — Auto	454	0.1%
Sign Rental	249	0.0%
Advertising	29,063	5.8%
Total Selling Exp.	67,755	13.4%
Net Profit On Sales	231,470	45.9%

	Sales	Percentage
Overhead Expenses		
Service Fees	37,716	7.5%
Bank Charges	3,561	0.7%
Employee Benefits	4,156	0.8%
Heat, Light & Power	5,886	1.2%
Insurance	8,742	1.7%
Repairs & Maintenance	1,634	0.3%
Office Supplies	1,589	0.3%
Travel & Entertainment	243	0.0%
Payroll Taxes	12,100	2.4%
Professional Fees	2,047	0.4%
Local Taxes	284	0.1%
Telephone	3,116	0.6%
Rent	31,921	6.3%
Total Overhead Expenses	112,995	22.4%
Net Income Before Income Taxes	$118.475	23.5%

THIS INCOME STATEMENT DOES NOT INCLUDE THE EXPENSES OF DEPRECIATION, BANK LOAN INTEREST AND ANY SALARIES OR ANY OTHER BENEFITS PAID TO OR INCURRED FOR THE BENEFIT OF THE FRANCHISEE, BECAUSE THESE AMOUNTS MAY VARY GREATLY FOR EACH INDIVIDUAL FRANCHISEE.

CAUTION: THESE SALES, PROFITS OR EARNINGS ARE AVERAGES OF SPECIFIC FRANCHISES AND SHOULD NOT BE CONSIDERED AS THE ACTUAL OR POTENTIAL SALES, PROFITS OR EARNINGS THAT WILL BE REALIZED BY ANY OTHER FRANCHISE. WE DO NOT REPRESENT THAT YOU CAN EXPECT TO ATTAIN THESE SALES, PROFITS OR EARNINGS.

SOME FRANCHISES HAVE EARNED THIS AMOUNT. THERE IS NO ASSURANCE YOU'LL DO AS WELL. IF YOU RELY UPON OUR FIGURES, YOU MUST ACCEPT THE RISK OF NOT DOING AS WELL.

Exhibit "E.1"
Gross Sales Figures for Centers Operating in the Mid-Atlantic
Region January 1, 1996 through December 31, 1998

Center	1996	1997	1998
0106	$634,319.00	$450,679.00	$529,297.00
0108	$456,071.00	$470,934.00	$438,084.00
0109	$598,296.00	$491,019.00	$506,029.00
2038			$395,523.00
1713	$361,631.00	$302,192.00	$297,470.00
1544	$499,146.00	$538,770.00	$549,874.00
1369	$619,676.00	$706,059.00	$711,502.00
2039			$478,898.00
1960	$535,588.00	$525,165.00	$623,933.00
2228	$412,455.00	$313,263.00	$252,106.00
2037			$296,942.00
1451	$443,575.00	$465,053.00	$450,130.00
2113	$479,690.00	$338,351.00	$291,541.00
2196	$469,442.00	$356,121.00	$320,195.00
1884	$469,982.00	$491,678.00	$578,503.00
2097			$221,132.00

Center	1996	1997	1998
0876	$472,379.00	$491,277.00	$354,406.00
1511	$476,116.00	$601,114.00	$611,745.00
0180	$362,767.00	$378,134.00	$415,079.00
2141	$463,722.00	$392,474.00	$303,940.00
0181	$583,229.00	$677,708.00	$708,470.00
0790	$480,145.00	$473,953.00	$435,473.00
1405	$640,748.00	$651,207.00	$647,404.00
1554	$438,968.00	$441,378.00	$457,698.00
2052			$211,940.00
2133	$434,650.00	$385,392.00	$396,842.00
0187	$348,201.00	$333,313.00	$448,727.00
0189	$526,280.00	$521,269.00	$525,569.00
1684	$435,651.00	$499,311.00	$484,046.00
1835	$328,203.00	$371,233.00	$338,262.00
0190	$417,316.00	$358,497.00	$312,326.00
2230	$216,103.00	$209,930.00	$177,958.00
1304	$370,768.00	$369,476.00	$389,922.00
2054			$308,658.00
1847	$392,708.00	$375,450.00	$421,660.00
1694	$697,956.00	$628,214.00	$576,996.00
1545	$161,600.00	$158,297.00	
2177	$359,168.00	$340,392.00	$340,628.00
2049	$379,446.00	$484,433.00	$556,112.00
2224	$446,988.00	$358,036.00	$289,721.00
2217			$324,513.00
0211	$274,638.00	$249,975.00	$210,080.00
2064		$374,641.00	$537,676.00
2195	$617,335.00	$337,151.00	$383,789.00
0213	$380,839.00	$396,044.00	$337,120.00
1538	$529,906.00	$449,752.00	$409,142.00
2001		$414,456.00	$466,060.00
1956	$424,602.00	$306,579.00	$301,930.00
1563	$677,452.00	$678,047.00	$642,989.00
0218	$495,096.00	$426,559.00	$387,805.00
0220	$750,159.00	$718,185.00	$675,238.00
1090	$680,811.00	$710,679.00	$692,532.00
0483	$400,175.00	$468,326.00	$541,487.00
0205	$1,188,131.00	$1,395,771.00	$1,375,920.00
0581	$485,869.00	$500,702.00	$518,447.00
1793	$514,086.00	$531,814.00	$589,187.00

Center	1996	1997	1998
1972	$523,533.00	$557,588.00	$499,457.00
2071	$484,838.00	$429,392.00	$435,640.00
1780	$480,879.00	$536,793.00	$610,321.00
0222	$1,458,574.00	$1,556,513.00	$1,718,668.00
1190	$504,643.00	$460,624.00	$486,056.00
2032	$536,204.00	$521,263.00	$466,746.00
1966	$724,074.00	$689,781.00	$664,774.00
1415	$493,114.00	$390,464.00	$440,564.00
2050	$363,988.00	$446,304.00	$597,925.00
2069	$304,578.00		
2068			$208,836.00
0232	$591,634.00	$583,964.00	$669,255.00
0231	$308,931.00	$302,835.00	$295,811.00
0233	$259,299.00	$228,116.00	$268,242.00
0234	$395,454.00	$407,911.00	$388,273.00
2010	$329,182.00	$397,748.00	$437,301.00
2131	$384,169.00	$425,453.00	$440,469.00
1733	$356,982.00	$400,941.00	$462,723.00
2016	$812,916.00	$662,195.00	$671,277.00
2015	$789,977.00	$736,410.00	$820,709.00
1945	$406,645.00	$492,027.00	$567,875.00
Average	$497,637.00	$487,276.00*	$482,661.00*

*Without Co-Brand Centers

CAUTION: THESE SALES ARE OF SPECIFIC FRANCHISES AND SHOULD NOT BE CONSIDERED AS THE ACTUAL OR POTENTIAL SALES THAT WILL BE REALIZED BY ANY OTHER FRANCHISE. WE DO NOT REPRESENT THAT YOU CAN EXPECT TO ATTAIN THESE SALES.

SOME FRANCHISES HAVE ATTAINED THESE SALES. THERE IS NO ASSURANCE YOU'LL DO AS WELL. IF YOU RELY ON OUR FIGURES, YOU MUST ACCEPT THE RISK OF NOT DOING AS WELL.

GLASS DOCTOR
P. O. Box 3146, 1010 N. University Parks Dr.
Waco, TX 76707

Tel: (800) 490-7501 (254) 745-2400
Fax: (254) 745-2590
Internet Address: www.dwyer.com
Contact: Ms. Mollie Eisenman, Marketing Coor.

# Franchised Units:	25 Units
# Company-Owned Units:	0 Units
Total # Units:	25 Units

Representations Regarding Earnings Capability

These sales or earnings are of specific franchises and should not be considered as the actual or potential sales or earnings that will be realized by any other franchise. We do not represent that You can expect to attain these sales or earnings. We encourage You to review this material with Your attorney and/or accountant.

Glass Doctor Franchisees Annual Sales, Expenses and Operating Income[1]
Fiscal Year Ended December 31, 1998 (Dollars in Thousands)

	Store #1	Store #2	Store #3	Store #4	Store #5	Store #6	Store #7	Store #8
Net Revenues	$1,420	$1,808	$2,279	$ 597	$ 786	$1296	$2,764	$2,816
Cost of Sales	311	531	572	220	269	341	660	749
Gross Profit	1,109	1,277	1,707	377	517	955	2,104	2,067
Expenses								
Operating	345	736	870	113	314	457	411	450
Selling & Marketing	264	126	310	22	75	133	292	218
Gen. & Administrative	251	325	428	156	102	228	529	908
Total Expenses	860	1,187	1,608	291	491	818	1,232	1,576
Operating Income[2]	$249	$90	$99	$86	$26	$137	$872	$491

[1]THIS FINANCIAL INFORMATION IS PREPARED WITHOUT AN AUDIT. PROSPECTIVE FRANCHISEES OR SELLERS OF FRANCHISES SHOULD BE ADVISED THAT NO CERTIFIED PUBLIC ACCOUNTANT HAS AUDITED THESE FIGURES OR EXPRESSED HIS/HER OPINION WITH REGARD TO THE CONTENT OR FORM

[2]Operating Income before: a) consulting and rental charges of affiliated companies, b) owner's compensation; C) depreciation and amortization; and (d) profit sharing.

Notes:

The 8 franchises, whose reported sales, expenses and operating income are shown above, represent approximately 27% of all Glass Doctor® franchises in operation for a full calendar year or more as of the 1998 fiscal year end. We do not have income statements from all franchisees; therefore, We do not know exactly what percentage of franchisees have equaled or exceeded the data presented for the 8 franchises. We do not believe that the results of remaining franchisees would materially alter the data presented above.

The franchisee income statements upon which the Table is based are available for inspection upon request.

We prepared this Table based upon unaudited income statements submitted by the respective franchisees, which were not prepared according to generally accepted accounting principles. We believe those income statements to be accurate but We have not conducted an independent audit to verify the figures.

The franchises listed in the Table operate and service markets from 3 to 14 territories.

Sales, expenses and operating income will vary from franchisee to franchisee and market to market. We do not represent that the sales, expenses and operating income of the 8 franchises shown on the Table for the year indicated will accurately predict the future results for those franchises or any potential franchisee. Factors that may affect sales, expenses and operating income should be considered carefully in evaluating this information and in making any decision to purchase a franchise. These factors include: business skills; motivation and effort of the individual franchisee; income and demographic characteristics of a particular market area; number of franchised territories serviced by a service center; expense variable in a particular market, e.g., rent, yellow page expense, insurance, labor costs; competition; number of years in operation; as well as conditions generally prevailing in the local and national economy.

YOUR FINANCIAL RESULTS ARE LIKELY TO DIFFER FROM THOSE LISTED AND THERE IS NO ASSURANCE THAT YOU WILL DO AS WELL. IF YOU RELY UPON THESE FIGURES, YOU MUST ACCEPT THE RISK OF NOT DOING AS WELL.

GREASE MONKEY INTERNATIONAL
633 17th St., # 400
Denver, CO 80202
Tel: (800) 364-0352 (303) 308-1660
Fax: (303) 308-5908
E-Mail: greasemonkey@rmi.net
Internet Address:
Contact: Mr. Michael Brunetti, VP Franchise Sales

Description: GREASE MONKEY INTERNATIONAL (GMI) ranks fourth in size among all independently-owned quick-lube operations. GMI's sole business is providing convenient preventative maintenance services for motor vehicles. The benefit to owning a GREASE MONKEY franchise is an attention to you're the customer as you would provide to your customer. This is enhanced because we are not in the oil business, but rather the service business. We offer assistance in literally every aspect of the business.

# Franchised Units:	179 Units
# Company-Owned Units:	35 Units
Total # Units:	214 Units
Founded In:	1978
1st Franchised In:	1979
Average Total Investment:	222.5-999K
Franchise Fee:	28K
On-Going Royalty:	5%
Advertising Fee:	6%
Financial Assistance:	Yes(I)
Site Selection Assistance:	Yes
Lease Negotiation Assistance:	Yes
Contract Terms (Init./Renew):	15/15

Initial Training Provided: 1 Week Corporate Headquarters, Denver, CO; 1 Week Market Center.

Attached to this Offering Circular as *Exhibit K* is a Pro Forma Annual Statement of Operations. Other than as specifically set forth in *Exhibit K*, no representations or statements of actual, average, projected, forecasted or potential sales, costs, income or profits are made to franchisees by us. We do not furnish, or make, or authorize our sales personnel to furnish or make, any oral or written information concerning the actual, average, projected, forecasted or potential sales, costs, income or profits of a franchise or prospects or chances of success that any franchisee can expect or that present or past franchisees have had, other than as set forth in *Exhibit K*. **A new franchisee's financial results are likely to differ from the figures presented in Exhibit K.** We recommend that you make your own investigation and determine whether your GREASE MONKEY Center will be profitable. We are not bound by allegations of any unauthorized representations as to earnings, sales, profits, prospects or chances of success. Substantiation of the data used in preparing *Exhibit K* will be made available to you on reasonable request.

Grease Monkey Centers — Operational Results Based on Car Counts

CAUTION: THE FOLLOWING RESULTS OF OPERATIONS AT VARIOUS AVERAGE DAILY AND ANNUAL VEHICLE COUNT LEVELS SHOULD NOT BE CONSIDERED AS THE ACTUAL OR POTENTIAL INCOME OR RESULTS OF OPERATIONS OF ANY PARTICULAR FRANCHISE. THE FRANCHISOR DOES NOT REPRESENT THAT THE FRANCHISEE CAN EXPECT TO ATTAIN THESE VOLUMES.

Average Vehicles per Day (Note 1)	35	50	65
Average Sale per Vehicle (Note 2)	$39.80	$39.80	$39,80
Sales (Net of coupons and discounts)	$429,044	$612,920	$796,796
Cost of Sales (Note 3)	111,551	159,359	207,167
Gross Profit	317,493	453,561	589,629
Salaries, Wages and Benefits (Note 4)	133,004	183,876	231,071
Operating Expenses (Note 5)	38,614	55,163	71,712
Insurance (Note 6)	3,600	3,600	3,600
Marketing Materials Fee (0.5%) (Note 8)	2,145	3,065	3,984
Other Marketing Allocation (5%) (Note 8)	21,452	30,646	39,840
Royalty Fee (5%) (Note 8)	21,452	30,646	39,840
General and Administrative Expenses (Note 7)	12,871	18,388	23,904
Earnings before Interest, Taxes, Depreciation, Amortization and Occupancy Costs	$84,355	$128,178	$175,679

CAUTION: A FRANCHISEE'S FINANCIAL RESULTS ARE LIKELY TO DIFFER FROM THE FIGURES PRESENTED. SEE ATTACHED NOTES.

Grease Monkey International, Inc. Summary of Factual Basis for Statement

This Statement ("Statement") is based on costs, expenses, and selling prices existing during 1998. The Statement is based on (1) our experience in operating an average of 31 company-owned Centers during 198 and (2) certain national contract prices which have been negotiated by us and made available to all franchisees.

The Statement does not include the average results of our franchised Grease Monkey Centers because the system wide average includes many older Centers that do not offer the full range of services which a new franchisee is trained to provide and generally will offer. These services generally consist of higher end services. As a result, those Centers have a lower average sales per vehicle than a Center which offers those services. Since our company-owned Centers offer the same full range of services a new franchisee is trained to provide and generally will offer, we believe the results of our company-owned Centers more accurately depict the results of a full service Center. HOWEVER, WE MAKE NO ASSURANCES OR GUARANTEES THAT YOU WILL REALIZE THE RESULTS SET FORTH IN THE STATEMENT. The Centers upon which the Statement is based offered substantially the same products and services to the public.

At January 31, 1999, 181 Centers were open at least one year in the United States and Mexico. During the month of January, 1999, these Centers achieved the following average daily vehicle counts:

Number of Vehicles Serviced: 204,275, January, 1999		
Center Averages Per Day	Percent	Number
90 or greater	0.6%	1
75 to 89	4.4%	8
60 to 74	13.3%	24
45 to 59	25.4%	46
30 to 44	33.1%	60
13 to 29	23.2%	42
	100%	181

Sites are preferably located on major commercial thoroughfares with average daily traffic counts of greater than 20,000 vehicles in a 24-hour period and with a maximum speed limit of 40 miles per hour. Demographic parameters of sites include 50,000 people, 26,000 registered vehicles and an average household income of greater than $25,000 within a three mile radius. Other than these demographics, we know of no geographic factors which might materially affect a franchisee's vehicle count volumes in relation to that set forth in this Statement.

The vehicle counts include all vehicles entering a Grease Monkey Center. Approximately 95 percent of a Center's customers purchase the Center's full service oil, filter and lubrication. Customers also purchase air filters, wiper blades, transmission, radiator, differential and other services. We require Centers to follow a particular method for reporting vehicle counts which is consistent system-wide.

Notes to Pro Forma Monthly Statement of Operations at Various Average Daily Vehicle Count Levels

1. Average vehicles per day are calculated for a 6 day week, based on a 26 day month. Grease Monkey Centers are normally open between 8:00 am. and 6:00 p.m., Monday through Saturday. Some Centers are open 10:00 a.m. to 4:00 p.m. on Sunday, which, for purposes of calculating the average per day for a 7 day week, is counted as 0.6 of a day, or a 28.4 day month.

2. The average sales per vehicle is based on the actual average for the year 1998 for 31 company-owned Centers. The system wide average for Centers in the United States in 1998 was $33.65. We se the average of our company-owned Centers in the Statement because the system wide average includes many older Centers that do not offer the full range of services which a new franchisee is trained to provide and generally will offer. As a result, those Centers have a lower average sales per vehicle. Since our company-owned Centers offer the same full range of services a franchisee is trained to provide and generally will offer,

we believe the results of our company-owned Centers more accurately depict the results of a full service Center. HOWEVER, WE MAKE NO ASSURANCES OR GUARANTEES THAT YOU WILL REALIZE THE AVERAGE SALES PER VEHICLE SET FORTH IN THE STATEMENT.

3. Cost of sales is calculated at 26% of sales and includes only inventory items (oil, filters, greases, fluids, etc.). Cost of sales does not include any salaries or wages. The percentage is based on the Center purchasing oil products at national account prices and purchasing in sufficient quantities to earn volume discounts (approximately one month's supply).

4. Hourly wages are based on an average hourly rate of approximately $7.41 per employee for all employees including the manager. Manager's salary is based on $27,000 per year. No overtime wages are included. Wages can vary significantly depending on local and regional employment conditions and the availability of labor. Total average number of employees on duty at all times, excluding the manager are: 3 at 500 vehicles per month, 4 at 1,000 vehicles per month, 6 at 1,500 vehicles per month, 8 at 2,000 vehicles per month, and 9 at 2,500 vehicles per month.

5. Operating expenses include the following items: trash hauling, uniforms and laundry, repairs and maintenance, operating supplies, small tools, utilities, warranties, equipment rental and material disposal.

6. Insurance premiums are for liability and property damage only.

7. General and administrative expenses include the following items: telephone, bank charges and fees, accounting, postage, office supplies, beverage service and travel and meeting expenses.

8. These items and percentages are required under the Franchise Agreement. A company-owned Center does not pay a royalty fee. We

have included royalties fees, however, to more accurately set forth a franchisee's results.

THE ABOVE NOTES CONSTITUTE THE MATERIAL ASSUMPTIONS AND SIGNIFICANT MATTERS UPON WHICH A FRANCHISEE'S FUTURE RESULTS ARE EXPECTED TO DEPEND.

CAUTION: SOME CENTERS HAVE INCURRED THE COSTS AS DESCRIBED ABOVE. THERE IS NO ASSURANCE YOU WILL DO AS WELL. IF YOU RELY UPON OUR FIGURES, YOU MUST ACCEPT THE RISK OF NOT DOING AS WELL.

SUBSTANTIATING MATERIAL PERTAINING TO THIS STATEMENT IS AVAILABLE FOR INSPECTION AT OUR HEADQUARTERS AND WILL BE PROVIDED UPON REASONABLE REQUEST.

THE STATEMENT IS BASED UPON OUR RECORDS AND FINANCIAL STATEMENTS AND HAVE BEEN COMPILED TO THE EXTENT POSSIBLE IN A MANNER WHICH IS CONSISTENT WITH GENERALLY ACCEPTED ACCOUNTING PRINCIPLES. YOU ARE ADVISED THAT CERTAIN UNDERLYING DATA ON WHICH THE STATEMENT IS BASED, HOWEVER, ARE NOT PREPARED IN ACCORDANCE WITH GENERALLY ACCEPTED ACCOUNTING PRINCIPLES.

meineke® Discount Mufflers

MEINEKE DISCOUNT MUFFLERS
128 S. Tryon St., # 900
Charlotte, NC 28202
Tel: (800) 275-5200 (704) 377-8855
Fax: (704) 358-4706
E-Mail: Alice_Griffin@meineke.com
Internet Address: www.meineke.com
Contact: Ms. Alice Griffin, Franchise Develop. Coord.

Description: MEINEKE DISCOUNT MUFFLERS is the nation's largest discount muffler and brake repair specialist with more than 860 shops across the nation. They have been offering great service at discount prices for more than 25 years. Their franchisees come from all walks of life and represent many nationalities.

# Franchised Units:	859 Units
# Company-Owned Units:	8 Units
Total # Units:	867 Units
Founded In:	1972
1st Franchised In:	1973
Average Total Investment:	140-250K
Franchise Fee:	25K
On-Going Royalty:	2.5-7%
Advertising Fee:	1.5-10%
Financial Assistance:	Yes(I)
Site Selection Assistance:	No
Lease Negotiation Assistance:	Yes
Contract Terms (Init./Renew):	15/15
Initial Training Provided:	4 Weeks Charlotte, NC.

Meineke Shop Average Gross Revenues for 1998

Shops Open More Than 2 Years	Shops Open Less Than 2 Years
$419,425	$281,975

THIS CHART REFLECTS THE MEAN AVERAGE GROSS REVENUES FOR 1998 OF CERTAIN MEINEKE FRANCHISEES, AND SHOULD NOT BE CONSIDERED AS THE ACTUAL OR PROBABLE RESULTS THAT WILL BE REALIZED BY YOU OR ANY OTHER FRANCHISEE. WE DO NOT REPRESENT THAT ANY FRANCHISEE CAN EXPECT TO ATTAIN THESE RESULTS. A NEW FRANCHISEE'S RESULTS ARE LIKELY TO DIFFER FROM THESE RESULTS.

The first column in the Meineke Shop Average Gross Revenues for 1998 statement ("Average Revenues Statement") reflects the mean average gross revenues for 1998 reported by all 805 franchised Meineke Shops that had been open and operating for more than 2 years as of December 31, 1998. The second column reflects the mean average gross revenues for 1998 reported by all 52 franchised Meineke Shops that had been open and operating for less than 2 years as of December 31, 1998. The Average Revenues Statement does not include any Meineke Shops we own. The Average Revenues Statement is based on weekly sales reports submitted by Meineke franchisees for the purpose of computing royalty fees. These reports have not been audited by certified public accountants nor have we sought to independently verify their accuracy for purposes of the Average Revenues Statement.

As of December 31, 1998, there were 884 Meineke franchises. Of those, 857 shops were already opened, 11 had locations and were awaiting openings, 5 had approved locations that had not yet been secured, and 11 had not yet secured locations. There are 3 company franchise outlets, which are not included in this statement.

Of the 857 open shops, 20 have been open less than one year, 32 have been open more than one year but less than two years, and 805 have been open more than two years.

The following chart breaks down into ranges of gross revenues the information on which the average revenue statement is based.

Annual Gross Revenues	Shops Open More Than 2 Years		Shops Open 1 to 2 Years	
	Number	Percentage	Number	Percentage
$0–200,000	79	10%	2	6%
$200,001–400,000	345	43%	22	59%
$400,001–600,000	259	32%	7	22%
$600,001–800,000	86	11%	1	3%
$800,001–1,000,000	25	3%	0	0%
>$1,000,000	11	1%	0	0%

Exhibit X-I, Part 1 to this document is a list of the franchises together with their geographic locations from which Meineke compiled these figures. All of these franchises are substantially similar to the franchises Meineke offers in that (1) all shops offer essentially the same services and products as described in Item 1 of this Offering Circular, and (2) all franchises are located in buildings that contain between two and twelve automobile services lifts. Meineke makes available the same support to all franchisees.

Attached as Exhibit W is a breakdown of the Average Revenues Statement by geographic region, as well as certain typical expenses and other pertinent information relating to Meineke Shops. The listing of expenses is not all-inclusive and Meineke franchisees will incur additional expenses in the operation of their Meineke Shops, including, for example, federal and state taxes, interest payments,

royalty fees, MAF contributions, and salary or draw of the owner of the franchise.

Meineke obtained the expense information listed in Exhibit W from responses to a 1996 chainwide franchisee survey, and the other information was obtained from our own records based on information reported by franchisees in the ordinary course of business. Not all franchisees participated in the survey, and in some cases, less than 50% of the franchisees responded to questions in the survey. Furthermore, in some cases we did not have information in our own records regarding certain questions.

Note that expenses vary for Meineke Shops depending on many factors, including local and regional variations in real estate values or rental rates, construction costs and building specifications, financing terms which the franchisee was able to obtain, local and regional variations in utility and telephone rates, insurance rates, local and state taxes and wage rates, degree of skilled labor, cost of parts and supplies used, services offered and the efficiency and managerial skills of the franchisee, local economic factors, the density of vehicle ownership and the number of other automotive aftermarket outlets in a particular market area.

THE EXPENSES LISTED IN EXHIBIT W ARE BASED ON RESPONSES PROVIDED BY MEINEKE FRANCHISEES AND YOU SHOULD NOT CONSIDER THESE AS THE ACTUAL OR POTENTIAL SALES OR OPERATING EXPENSES THAT WILL BE REALIZED BY YOU OR ANY OTHER FRANCHISEE. WE DO NOT REPRESENT THAT ANY FRANCHISEE CAN EXPECT TO ATTAIN THESE RESULTS. A NEW FRANCHISEE'S RESULTS ARE LIKELY TO DIFFER FROM THOSE CONTAINED IN EXHIBIT W.

Substantiation of the date used in preparing the Average Revenues Statement will be made available to you on reasonable request, provided we will not disclose data that identifies specific locations. Our sales representatives are prohibited from providing you with any further information about actual, average or potential sales, operating expenses, income, profits or earnings, and are prohibited from commenting on the likelihood of success of any Meineke Shop or the business potential of any territory. Any such unauthorized information is inherently unreliable, and you should not rely on it.

Exhibit W
Midwest Notes:

1. For the purposes of this exhibit Midwest includes Meineke shops located in the following states: Iowa, Illinois, Indiana, Missouri, Minnesota, Montana, Nebraska, Ohio, South Dakota and Wisconsin. As of December 31, 1996, Meineke had 148 Meineke shops operating in the Midwest which had been operating for a year. The information in this chart was accumulated from Meineke's records as well as from information provided by Meineke's fran-

chisees located in Midwest for the 148 shops that had been operating for a year or more as of December 31, 1996 The information regarding gross sales figures, number of bays, type of building, type of area, number of traffic lanes, type of traffic flow and number of competitors was provided from Meineke's own business records. Unless otherwise indicated, all other information was provided to Meineke from its franchisees in response to a chainwide survey sent by Meineke to its franchisees. Where 'No Response" is indicated, the shop failed to provide Meineke with information regarding that category or Meineke did not have this information available.

2. Based on the unaudited gross sales figures as reported to Meineke Discount Muffler Shops, Inc. by its franchise shops for the year ending December 31, 1996.

3. Includes average of all inventory purchased for all services offered at each particular Meineke. Core services include exhaust and brakes.

4. 45 of the Midwest shops indicated that the shops were managed by the owner of the franchise. 49 shops indicated that they had an outside manager. 54 shops did not respond. "Average weekly pay" includes salary, commission and bonus.

5. Average weekly pay includes salary, commissions and bonus.

6. "Part-time" is defined as working less than 40 hours per week. Average hours worked on a weekly basis for the 23 shops that reported that they had part-time mechanics.

7. Average weekly pay includes salary, commissions and bonus.

8. These population figures are based on the 1990 Consensus Statistical Date provided by the U.S. Department of Commerce Bureau of Consensus. Some small towns will be listed as the urban area with which they are associated.

9. Competitors include national, regional, local and independent retailers which specialize in automotive parts, service and repair. Competitors do not include other licensed Meineke shops.

10. In some instances, a bay may contain more than one automotive lift.

11. 53 Midwest Meineke shops indicated that they lease the premises from which they operate from a third party. 39 shops indicated that they did not lease from a third party. While 56 shops did not respond. "Rental" payments include base rent, common area maintenance charges, triple net charges and any other additional rents or payments made to the landlord on a regular basis pursuant to the terms of the lease agreement.

Midwest
(Note 1)

Amount of Sales (Note 2)	Number of Shops	Percent			
$0–400,000	93	62.8%			
$400,000–800,000	52	35.1%			
$800,000 or more	3	2.0%			
Cost of Goods Sold Percentage (Note 3)	Number of Shops	Percent	Average Weekly Pay of Non- Owner Manager (Note 4)	Number of Shops	Percent
17–19%	2	1.4%	Less than $349	1	2.0%
20–22%	8	5.4%	$350–499	13	26.5%
23–25%	23	15.5%	$500–649	18	36.7%
26–28%	26	17.6%	$650–799	5	10.2%
29–30%	13	8.8%	$800–949	5	10.2%
30–35%	5	3.4%	$950–1,099	0	0.0%
More than 35%	1	0.7%	No Response	7	14.3%
No Response	70	47.3%			
Number of Full-Time Mechanics	Number of Shops	Percent	Average Weekly Pay of Full-Time Mechanics (Note 5)	Number of Shops	Percent
0	0	0.0%	$0–199	0	0.0%
1	6	4.1%	$200–349	10	6.8%
2	16	10.8%	$350–499	49	33.1%
3	34	23.0%	$500–649	15	10.1%
4	14	9.5%	$650–799	3	2.0%
5	7	4.7%	$800–949	1	0.7%
6	1	0.7%	$950–1,099	0	0.0%
7	0	0.0%	$1,100–1,249	0	0.0%
8	1	0.7%	$1,350–1,499	0	0.0%
9	0	0.0%	$1,500 or more	0	0.0%
No Response	69	46.6%	No Response	70	47.3%

Number of Part-Time Mechanics	Number of Shops	Percent	Average Hours for Part Time Mechanics (Note 6)	Number of Shops	Percent
0	57	38.5%	1–9	2	8.7%
1	18	12.2%	10–19	10	43.5%
2	4	2.7%	20–29	9	39.1%
3	0	0.0%	30–39	1	4.3%
4	1	0.7%	40–49	0	0.0%
No Response	68	45.9%	No Response	1	4.3%
Average Weekly Pay for Part-Time Mechanics (Note 7)	Number of Shops	Percent	Number of Full-Time Counter Clerks	Number of Shops	Percent
$99 or less	2	8.7%	0	46	31.1%
$100–199	12	52.2%	1	26	17.6%
$200–299	8	34.8%	2	5	3.4%
$300–399	0	0.0%	3	1	0.7%
$400–499	0	0.0%	4	0	0.0%
$500–599	0	0.0%	No Response	70	47.3%
No Response	1	4.3%			
Number of Part Time Counter Clerks	Number of Shops	Percent	Population of Location (Note 8)	Number of Shops	Percent
0	68	45.9%	Under 300,000	105	70.9%
1	8	5.4%	300,000–600,000	16	10.8%
2	2	1.4%	600,000–900,000	16	10.8%
3	0	0.0%	900,000–1,200,000	0	0.0%
4	0	0.0%	1,200,000–1,500,000	0	0.0%
No Response	70	47.3%	Over 1,500,000	9	6.2%
			No Response	2	1.4%

Type of Area	Number of Shops	Percent	Number of Competitors within 2 Mile Radius (Note 9)	Number of Shops	Percent
Commercial	68	45.9%	0	7	4.7%
Residential	16	10.8%	1	0	0.0%
Industrial	1	0.7%	2	14	9.5%
No Response	63	42.6%	3	17	11.5%
			4	19	12.8%
			5	9	6.1%
			6	7	4.7%
			7	0	0.0%
			8 or more	19	12.8%
			No Response	56	37.8%
Number of Street Traffic Lanes	Number of Shops	Percent	Type of Traffic Flow	Number of Shops	Percent
2	14	9.5%	One way	1	0.7%
3	1	0.7%	Two way	90	60.8%
4	70	47.6%	No Response	57	38.5%
5	0	0.0%			
6	5	3.4%			
7	0	0.0%			
8	1	0.7%			
No Response	56	38.1%			
Type of Building	Number of Shops	Percent	Number of Bays (Note 10)	Number of Shops	Percent
Auto Mall	10	6.8%	2	1	0.7%
Stand Alone	82	55.4%	3	46	31.1%
No Response	56	37.8%	4	61	41.2%
			5	21	14.2%
			6	14	9.5%
			7	2	1.4%
			8	1	0.7%
			9	0	0.0%
			10 or more	0	0.0%
			No response	2	1.4%

Average Monthly Rental (Note 11)	Number of Shops	Percent	Average Monthly Utility Bill	Number of Shops	Percent
Less than $1,500	4	7.5%	Less than $100	0	0.0%
$1,500–2,499	23	43.4%	$100–199	4	2.7%
$2,500–3,499	17	32.1%	$200–299	31	20.9%
$3,500–4,499	4	7.5%	$300–399	26	17.6%
$4,500–5,499	0	0.0%	$400–499	9	6.1%
$5,500–6,499	0	0.0%	$500–599	2	1.4%
$6,500–7,499	0	0.0%	$600–699	2	1.4%
No Response	5	9.4%	$700–799	1	0.7%
			$800–899	1	0.7%
			$900–999	0	0.0%
			$1,000–1,099	0	0.0%
			No Response	72	48.6%
Number of Phone Lines	Number of Shops	Percent	Average Monthly Phone Bill	Number of Shops	Percent
2	53	35.8%	Less than $100	7	4.7%
3	17	11.5%	$100–199	48	32.4%
4	9	6.1%	$200–299	22	14.9%
5	0	0.0%	$300–399	1	0.7%
6 or more	0	0.0%	$400–499	0	0.0%
No Response	69	46.6%	$500–599	0	0.0%
			$600–699	0	0.0%
			$700–799	0	0.0%
			$800–899	0	0.0%
			No Response	70	47.3%

MIGHTY DISTRIBUTING SYSTEM OF AMERICA
650 Engineering Dr.
Norcross, GA 30092
Tel: (800) 829-3900 (770) 448-3900
Fax: (770) 446-8627
E-Mail: tracy.brown@mightyautoparts.com
Internet Address: www.mightyautoparts.com

Contact: Ms. Tracy Brown, Franchise Marketing Manager

Description: Wholesale distribution of original equipment-quality, MIGHTY-branded auto parts. Franchisees operate in exclusive territories, supplying automotive maintenance and repair facilities with undercar and underhood products, such as filters, belts, tune-up and brake parts.

# Franchised Units:	142 Units
# Company-Owned Units:	5 Units
Total # Units:	147 Units
Founded In:	1963
1st Franchised In:	1970

Average Total Investment:	84-190K	Site Selection Assistance:	No
Franchise Fee:	5K+ $.035/Vcl	Lease Negotiation Assistance:	No
On-Going Royalty:	5%	Contract Terms (Init./Renew):	10
Advertising Fee:	0.5%	Initial Training Provided: 1 Week Home Office; 1	
Financial Assistance:	Yes(I)	Week On-The-Job Training.	

The following 1998 Sales Volume Analysis is based upon historical sales volume reports filed by 135 Mighty franchisees operating franchise territories throughout the entirety of calendar year 1998. A total of 139 franchise territories were in operation at year-end; however, five (5) new franchisees entered the system in 1998, of which 4 were in operation less than 12 months of 1998.

Gross sales figures were derived from unaudited sales volume reports submitted by these franchisees for the purpose of computing royalties. Such data was accumulated using a uniform method which included direct reports these franchisees made to Mighty. Mighty franchisees must pay royalties on gross sales and, accordingly, all franchisees in operation during all months of calendar year 1998 are represented in the Sales Volume Analysis.

Of the 134 franchisees that reported gross sales and were in operation for all months of 1997, 105 (78%) also reported operating statistics for a twelve month period which included all months of 1997.

Operating expense detail is based on financial reports filed by 105 Mighty franchisees which submitted operating results for the twelve calendar months beginning January, 1997 and ending December, 1997 regardless of their fiscal year end.

Mighty believes that the following financial data has been compiled on the basis of generally accepted accounting principles, but the data is unaudited, and no assurance can be offered that the data does not contain inaccuracies which an audit might disclose.

The average of reported operating expenses has been organized in a uniform chart of accounts for comparative purposes. No assurances can be given, and Mighty does not represent, that any franchisee achieves financial results similar to the averages reported here. The low-high range of individual franchise performance indicates a wide variation in expenses among reporting franchisees. Operating expenses vary substantially between reporting franchisees due both to individual franchisee business discretion and local economic factors including the geographic dispersion of franchisees' customers, the density of vehicle ownership and the number of independent automotive aftermarket service outlets in any particular franchised territory.

No provision has been made for state and federal income taxes, interest payments, or owner salary/draw. The success of Mighty franchises is substantially reliant upon direct, personal sales and service calls that each franchisee performs. Mighty's internal studies suggest that new franchisees operating in previously undeveloped territories should allocate working capital sufficient to cover normal living expenses for the period before operating at a "break even" point

All of the franchises represented in the following schedules are substantially similar to the franchise offered in this offering circular except that there are substantial variations in territorial size. Since all franchisees must offer the products and services currently required by Mighty, and only the products that Mighty approves as meeting our uniform quality standards and specifications, all reporting franchisees offered substantially the same products and services to their customers. Mighty offered substantially the same services to all of the reporting franchisees included in the schedules.

Substantiation of the data used in preparing the following schedules will be made available to you upon reasonable request.

EXCEPT FOR THE INFORMATION APPEARING IN THIS ITEM 19, ALL SALES REPRESENTATIVES OF MIGHTY ARE STRICTLY PROHIBITED FROM SUPPLYING YOU WITH ANY INFORMATION UNDER

ACTUAL, AVERAGE, PROJECTED OR FORE-CASTED PROFITS OR EARNINGS, NOR ARE THEY AUTHORIZED TO COMMENT AS TO THE LIKELIHOOD OF SUCCESS OR FAIL-URE OF A MIGHTY FRANCHISE TERRI-TORY. ANY SUCH INFORMATION WHICH YOU MAY RECEIVE IS UNAUTHORIZED AND SHOULD NOT BE RELIED UPON.

THE FOLLOWING SALES, GROSS PROFITS AND EXPENSES ARE HISTORICAL AVER-AGES OF SPECIFIC FRANCHISES DURING THE SAMPLE PERIOD AND SHOULD NOT BE CONSIDERED AS THE ACTUAL OR PROBABLE SALES, GROSS PROFITS OR EXPENSES THAT YOU REALIZE. MIGHTY DOES NOT REPRESENT THAT YOU CAN EXPECT TO ATTAIN SUCH SALES, GROSS PROFITS OR EXPENSES.

1998 Sales Volume Analysis

Sales Volume Category	Number of Franchisees	Percentage of Total	Total Gross Sales	Franchisee Sales Average	Number Exceeding Sales Average
Up to $125,000	14	10.4%	$1,066,268	$76,162	8
$125,001–250,000	40	29.6%	7,614,481	190,362	18
$250,001–500,000	32	23.7%	11,277,228	352,413	15
$500,001–750,000	17	12.6%	10,726,307	630,959	8
$750,001–1,000,000	8	5.9%	6,536,712	817,089	3
$1,000,001–1,500,000	15	11.1%	18,155,092	1,210,339	7
$1,500,001–2,000,000	4	3.0%	6,879,976	1,719,994	2
Over $2,000,000	5	3.7%	12,387,448	2,477,490	1
Total	135	100.0%	$74,643,512	$552,915	46

Figures exclude Company-Owned Operations and franchisees not in the system for an entire twelve months of the reporting period.

1997 Operating Analysis Up to $125,000 Volume Group

		Number	Gross Total Sales	Average Sales/9 Territories
Franchisees Reporting Expense Detail		9	$761,935	$84,659
Percentage Reporting Expense Detail		56%		
Dollars and Percentages of Annual Gross Sales				
	Average Territory		Range in Individual Franchisee Performance**	
	$	%	Low	High
Annual Gross Sales	$84,659	100.0%		
Cost of Goods Sold	45,865	54.2%		
Gross Profit	38,795	45.8%	33.9–56.2%	
Operating Expenses*	$24,768	29.3%	14.8–52.6%	
Net Operating Income	$14,027	16.6%	-5.9–34.6%	
Operating Expense Detail				
Employee Salary	$3,154	3.7%	0.0–27.0%	
Employee Benefits	1,393	1.6%	0.0–7.1%	
Payroll Taxes	620	0.7%	0.0–2.1%	

Dollars and Percentages of Annual Gross Sales				
	Average Territory		Range in Individual Franchisee Performance**	
	$	%	Low	High
Royalties	4,151	4.9%	4.2–5.2%	
Business Insurance	740	0.9%	0.0–2.2%	
Truck Expense/Freight	4,791	5.7%	2.7–11.3%	
Depreciation	774	0.9%	0.0–4.5%	
Warehouse/Storage	2,794	3.3%	0.0–6.1%	
Office	1,717	2.0%	0.2–6.5%	
Promotional/Advertising	1,355	1.6%	0.5–3.3%	
Outside Services	1,750	2.1%	0.0–14.9%	
Miscellaneous	1,198	1.4%	0.0–2.5%	
Business Taxes/Licenses	551	0.7%	0.0–3.1%	
Other Income/(Expense)	220	0.3%	-0.2–1.4%	

*No provision has been made for state and federal income taxes, interest payments or owner salary/draw.

**Specific territory reporting the high and low percentages vary by operating expense category. Therefore, these two columns are not additive.

Selected Asset Values	Average/Franchisee	Range in Individual Franchisee Performance
Accounts Receivable Trade	$3,816	$173–7,033
Inventory/Merchandise	$18,366	$4,135–45,154

THESE SCHEDULES HAVE BEEN PREPARED WITHOUT AN AUDIT. PROSPECTIVE FRAN-CHISEES SHOULD BE ADVISED THAT NO CERTIFIED PUBLIC ACCOUNTANT HAS AUDITED THESE FIGURES OR EXPRESSED AN OPINION WITH REGARD TO THEIR CONTENT OR FORM.

1997 Operating Analysis $125,001–250,000 Volume Group

	Number	Gross Total Sales	Average Sales/29 Territories
Franchisees Reporting Expense Detail	29	$5,418,970	$186,861
Percentage Reporting Expense Detail	76%		

Dollars and Percentages of Annual Gross Sales				
	Average Territory		Range in Individual Franchisee Performance**	
	$	%	Low	High
Annual Gross Sales	$186,861	100.0%		
Cost of Goods Sold	106,119	56.8%		
Gross Profit	80,742	43.2%	34.0–54.1%	
Operating Expenses*	$54,590	29.2%	11.9–54.8%	
Net Operating Income	$26,152	14.0%	-8.0–34.7%	
Operating Expense Detail				
Employee Salary	$8,592	4.6%	0.0–16.6%	

Dollars and Percentages of Annual Gross Sales				
	Average Territory		Range in Individual Franchisee Performance**	
	$	%	Low	High
Employee Benefits	1,994	1.1%	0.0–4.0%	
Payroll Taxes	1,614	0.9%	0.0–2.0%	
Royalties	9,330	5.0%	3.7–6.8%	
Business Insurance	2,720	1.5%	0.3–3.7%	
Truck Expense/Freight	8,212	4.4%	1.3–11.6%	
Depreciation	3,311	1.8%	0.0–10.2%	
Warehouse/Storage	7,387	4.0%	0.0–18.7%	
Office	4,168	2.2%	0.2–5.1%	
Promotional/Advertising	3,071	1.6%	0.5–6.0%	
Outside Services	1,220	0.7%	0.1–2.2%	
Miscellaneous	2,583	1.4%	0.0–5.0%	
Business Taxes/Licenses	407	0.2%	0.0–1.1%	
Other Income/(Expense)	19	0.0%	-0.4–0.4%	

*No provision has been made for state and federal income taxes, interest payments or owner salary/draw.

**Specific territory reporting the high and low percentages vary by operating expense category. Therefore, these two columns are not additive.

Selected Asset Values	Average/Franchisee	Range in Individual Franchisee Performance
Accounts Receivable Trade	$10,233	$0–33,534
Inventory/Merchandise	$26,559	$300–65,359

THESE SCHEDULES HAVE BEEN PREPARED WITHOUT AN AUDIT. PROSPECTIVE FRANCHISEES SHOULD BE ADVISED THAT NO CERTIFIED PUBLIC ACCOUNTANT HAS AUDITED THESE FIGURES OR EXPRESSED AN OPINION WITH REGARD TO THEIR CONTENT OR FORM.

1997 Operating Analysis $250,001–500,000 Volume Group

	Number	Gross Total Sales	Average Sales/23 Territories
Franchisees Reporting Expense Detail	23	$7,986,503	$347,239
Percentage Reporting Expense Detail	70%		

Dollars and Percentages of Annual Gross Sales				
	Average Territory		Range in Individual Franchisee Performance**	
	$	%	Low	High
Annual Gross Sales	$347,239	100.0%		
Cost of Goods Sold	197,374	56.8%		
Gross Profit	149,865	43.2%	35.7–57.8%	
Operating Expenses*	$119,645	34.5%	21.2–52.0%	
Net Operating Income	$30,220	8.7%	-13.4–22.8%	

Dollars and Percentages of Annual Gross Sales				
	Average Territory		Range in Individual Franchisee Performance**	
	$	%	Low	High
Operating Expense Detail				
Employee Salary	$39,976	11.5%	0.0–29.0%	
Employee Benefits	5,289	1.5%	0.0–4.2%	
Payroll Taxes	5,360	1.5%	0.1–4.1%	
Royalties	17,348	5.0%	4.6–5.5%	
Business Insurance	3,786	1.1%	0.0–2.2%	
Truck Expense/Freight	12,354	3.6%	1.5–13.3%	
Depreciation	4,172	1.2%	0.0–3.6%	
Warehouse/Storage	12,136	3.5%	0.0–7.1%	
Office	7,310	2.1%	0.5–5.0%	
Promotional/Advertising	4,901	1.4%	0.5–3.2%	
Outside Services	2,365	0.7%	0.1–2.9%	
Miscellaneous	5,049	1.5%	0.1–5.2%	
Business Taxes/Licenses	665	0.2%	0.0–1.2%	
Other Income/(Expense)	1,066	0.3%	-0.2–2.0%	

*No provision has been made for state and federal income taxes, interest payments or owner salary/draw.

**Specific territory reporting the high and low percentages vary by operating expense category. Therefore, these two columns are not additive.

Selected Asset Values	Average/Franchisee	Range in Individual Franchisee Performance
Accounts Receivable Trade	$21,034	$0–42,553
Inventory/Merchandise	$45,182	$8,816–100,941

THESE SCHEDULES HAVE BEEN PREPARED WITHOUT AN AUDIT. PROSPECTIVE FRAN-CHISEES SHOULD BE ADVISED THAT NO CERTIFIED PUBLIC ACCOUNTANT HAS AUDITED THESE FIGURES OR EXPRESSED AN OPINION WITH REGARD TO THEIR CONTENT OR FORM.

1997 Operating Analysis $500,001–750,000 Volume Group

	Number	Gross Total Sales	Average Sales/16 Territories
Franchisees Reporting Expense Detail	16	$10,277,450	$642,341
Percentage Reporting Expense Detail	84%		

Dollars and Percentages of Annual Gross Sales				
	Average Territory		Range in Individual Franchisee Performance**	
	$	%	Low	High
Annual Gross Sales	$642,341	100.0%		
Cost of Goods Sold	361,630	56.3%		
Gross Profit	280,711	43.7%	32.1–52.4%	

Dollars and Percentages of Annual Gross Sales				
	Average Territory		Range in Individual Franchisee Performance**	
	$	%	Low	High
Operating Expenses*	$223,229	34.8%	23.6–42.4%	
Net Operating Income	$57,482	8.9%	-0.2–18.2%	
Operating Expense Detail				
Employee Salary	$98,501	15.3%	8.2–21.9%	
Employee Benefits	8,940	1.4%	0.0–2.1%	
Payroll Taxes	12,523	1.9%	1.0–3.1%	
Royalties	31,329	4.9%	4.2–5.4%	
Business Insurance	6,704	1.0%	0.4–2.0%	
Truck Expense/Freight	17,506	2.7%	1.0–7.4%	
Depreciation	7,971	1.2%	0.0–2.8%	
Warehouse/Storage	14,574	2.3%	0.1–5.3%	
Office	7,583	1.2%	0.4–2.5%	
Promotional/Advertising	7,350	1.1%	0.5–2.4%	
Outside Services	4,368	0.7%	0.0–4.6%	
Miscellaneous	5,161	0.8%	-0.8–2.4%	
Business Taxes/Licenses	2,076	0.3%	0.0–1.5%	
Other Income/(Expense)	1,357	0.2%	0.0–0.9%	

*No provision has been made for state and federal income taxes, interest payments or owner salary/draw.

**Specific territory reporting the high and low percentages vary by operating expense category. Therefore, these two columns are not additive.

Selected Asset Values	Average/Franchisee	Range in Individual Franchisee Performance
Accounts Receivable Trade	$43,398	$0–96,660
Inventory/Merchandise	$85,319	$18,127–152,608

THESE SCHEDULES HAVE BEEN PREPARED WITHOUT AN AUDIT. PROSPECTIVE FRANCHISEES SHOULD BE ADVISED THAT NO CERTIFIED PUBLIC ACCOUNTANT HAS AUDITED THESE FIGURES OR EXPRESSED AN OPINION WITH REGARD TO THEIR CONTENT OR FORM.

1997 Operating Analysis $750,001–1,000,000 Volume Group

	Number	Gross Total Sales	Average Sales/8 Territories
Franchisees Reporting Expense Detail	8	$6,700,146	$837,518
Percentage Reporting Expense Detail	100%		
Dollars and Percentages of Annual Gross Sales			
	Average Territory		Range in Individual Franchisee Performance**
	$	%	Low	High
Annual Gross Sales	$837,518	100.0%		
Cost of Goods Sold	476,254	56.9%		

Dollars and Percentages of Annual Gross Sales				
	Average Territory		Range in Individual Franchisee Performance**	
	$	%	Low	High
Gross Profit	361,264	43.1%	37.9–46.6%	
Operating Expenses*	$309,903	37.0%	32.5–42.0%	
Net Operating Income	$51,361	6.1%	1.3–10.7%	
Operating Expense Detail				
Employee Salary	$126,838	15.1%	8.3–20.0%	
Employee Benefits	10,967	1.3%	0.1–2.8%	
Payroll Taxes	14,974	1.8%	0.3–2.4%	
Royalties	40,782	4.9%	4.6–5.1%	
Business Insurance	8,129	1.0%	0.5–1.6%	
Truck Expense/Freight	22,924	2.7%	1.4–4.6%	
Depreciation	9,563	1.1%	0.4–2.5%	
Warehouse/Storage	36,770	4.4%	2.0–9.8%	
Office	17,001	2.0%	1.4–2.5%	
Promotional/Advertising	10,963	1.3%	0.6–3.3%	
Outside Services	4,940	0.6%	0.2–1.0%	
Miscellaneous	7,508	0.9%	0.0–1.7%	
Business Taxes/Licenses	1,662	0.2%	0.0–0.5%	
Other Income/(Expense)	3,118	0.4%	0.0–1.2%	

*No provision has been made for state and federal income taxes, interest payments or owner salary/draw.

**Specific territory reporting the high and low percentages vary by operating expense category. Therefore, these two columns are not additive.

Selected Asset Values	Average/Franchise	Range in Individual Franchisee Performance
Accounts Receivable Trade	$78,970	$35,340–161,267
Inventory/Merchandise	$82,797	$0–151,843

THESE SCHEDULES HAVE BEEN PREPARED WITHOUT AN AUDIT. PROSPECTIVE FRANCHISEES SHOULD BE ADVISED THAT NO CERTIFIED PUBLIC ACCOUNTANT HAS AUDITED THESE FIGURES OR EXPRESSED AN OPINION WITH REGARD TO THEIR CONTENT OR FORM.

1997 Operating Analysis $1,000,001–1,500,000 Volume Group

	Number	Gross Total Sales	Average Sales/13 Territories
Franchisees Reporting Expense Detail	13	$16,290,226	$1,253,094
Percentage Reporting Expense Detail	100%		

Dollars and Percentages of Annual Gross Sales				
	Average Territory		Range in Individual Franchisee Performance**	
	$	%	Low	High
Annual Gross Sales	$1,253,094	100.0%		
Cost of Goods Sold	690,793	55.1%		
Gross Profit	562,301	44.9%	40.6–47.8%	
Operating Expenses*	$468,777	37.4%	25.6–44.3%	
Net Operating Income	$93,524	7.5%	1.6–16.1%	
Operating Expense Detail				
Employee Salary	$200,755	16.0%	5.7–23.0%	
Employee Benefits	23,353	1.9%	0.4–5.4%	
Payroll Taxes	21,796	1.7%	1.2–2.4%	
Royalties	62,904	5.0%	4.8–5.4%	
Business Insurance	12,378	1.0%	0.0–2.2%	
Truck Expense/Freight	39,389	3.1%	1.3–6.4%	
Depreciation	17,776	1.4%	0.2–3.0%	
Warehouse/Storage	33,882	2.7%	1.0–5.6%	
Office	21,436	1.7%	0.6–3.6%	
Promotional/Advertising	19,413	1.5%	0.9–2.7%	
Outside Services	4,582	0.4%	0.0–0.7%	
Miscellaneous	15,258	1.2%	0.3–3.4%	
Business Taxes/Licenses	3,216	0.3%	0.0–0.6%	
Other Income/(Expense)	7,361	0.6%	0.0–4.3%	

*No provision has been made for state and federal income taxes, interest payments or owner salary/draw.
**Specific territory reporting the high and low percentages vary by operating expense category. Therefore, these two columns are not additive.

Selected Asset Values	Average/Franchisee	Range in Individual Franchisee Performance
Accounts Receivable Trade	$89,698	$45,018–133,530
Inventory/Merchandise	$138,206	$71,758–228,975

THESE SCHEDULES HAVE BEEN PREPARED WITHOUT AN AUDIT. PROSPECTIVE FRAN-CHISEES SHOULD BE ADVISED THAT NO CERTIFIED PUBLIC ACCOUNTANT HAS AUDITED THESE FIGURES OR EXPRESSED AN OPINION WITH REGARD TO THEIR CONTENT OR FORM.

1997 Operating Analysis $1,500,001–3,000,000 Volume Group

	Number	Gross Total Sales	Average Sales/7 Territories
Franchisees Reporting Expense Detail	7	$12,892,984	$1,841,855
Percentage Reporting Expense Detail	100%		

Dollars and Percentages of Annual Gross Sales				
	Average Territory		Range in Individual Franchisee Performance**	
	$	%	Low	High
Annual Gross Sales	$1,841,855	100.0%		
Cost of Goods Sold	1,004,912	54.6%		
Gross Profit	836,943	45.4%	40.2–51.8%	
Operating Expenses*	$686,414	37.3%	34.4–42.5%	
Net Operating Income	$150,529	8.2%	3.0–16.7%	
Operating Expense Detail				
Employee Salary	$318,623	17.3%	13.1–22.5%	
Employee Benefits	19,894	1.1%	0.4–2.0%	
Payroll Taxes	35,463	1.9%	1.3–2.8%	
Royalties	86,644	4.7%	4.4–5.1%	
Business Insurance	17,685	1.0%	0.6–1.6%	
Truck Expense/Freight	47,464	2.6%	1.6–4.0%	
Depreciation	19,035	1.0%	0.1–2.3%	
Warehouse/Storage	49,772	2.7%	1.6–3.6%	
Office	29,884	1.6%	0.6–3.0%	
Promotional/Advertising	30,267	1.6%	1.0–3.1%	
Outside Services	11,796	0.6%	0.2–1.9%	
Miscellaneous	21,696	1.2%	0.6–2.6%	
Business Taxes/Licenses	3,890	0.2%	0.0–0.5%	
Other Income/(Expense)	5,699	0.3%	-0.1–0.6%	

*No provision has been made for state and federal income taxes, interest payments or owner salary/draw.

**Specific territory reporting the high and low percentages vary by operating expense category. Therefore, these two columns are not additive.

Selected Asset Values	Average/Franchisee	Range in Individual Franchisee Performance
Accounts Receivable Trade	$148,732	$121,983–174,610
Inventory/Merchandise	$224,275	$147,867–343,565

THESE SCHEDULES HAVE BEEN PREPARED WITHOUT AN AUDIT. PROSPECTIVE FRANCHISEES SHOULD BE ADVISED THAT NO CERTIFIED PUBLIC ACCOUNTANT HAS AUDITED THESE FIGURES OR EXPRESSED AN OPINION WITH REGARD TO THEIR CONTENT OR FORM.

MR. TRANSMISSION
4444 W. 147th St.
Midlothian, IL 60445
Tel: (800) 377-9247 (708) 389-5922
Fax: (708) 389-9882
E-Mail: vsmithson@moranindustries.com
Internet Address: www.moranindustries.com
Contact: Ms. Virginia Smithson, Qualifications Specialist

Description: MR. TRANSMISSION, a division of Moran Industries, franchises transmission service centers throughout the US. We offer our franchisees a superior business system, strong brand name, customized marketing and a service that is in strong demand. In addition, comprehensive training and continuous support help to ensure our franchisees maximaize their potential. Our exclusive business system, along with the skills of our franchisees, create customer experiences that result in satisfaction and loyalty.

# Franchised Units:	86 Units
# Company-Owned Units:	1 Units
Total # Units:	87 Units
Founded In:	1956
1st Franchised In:	1990
Average Total Investment:	149K
Franchise Fee:	27.5K
On-Going Royalty:	7%
Advertising Fee:	$100/Mo.
Financial Assistance:	Yes(I)
Site Selection Assistance:	Yes
Lease Negotiation Assistance:	Yes
Contract Terms (Init./Renew):	20/20
Initial Training Provided:	Yes

Actual, Average, Projected or Forecasted Franchisees Sales, Profits or Earnings.
Attached hereto as Exhibit A is the statement of "AVERAGE OPERATING CASH FLOW OF THE TRANSMISSION USA, MIDLOTHIAN, IL MR. TRANSMISSION CENTER." Attached hereto as Exhibit B is the statement of "AVERAGE SALES OF OPERATING FRANCHISED TRANSMISSION USA CENTERS." Attached hereto as Exhibit C is TRANSMISSION USA SUGGESTED BUSINESS GUIDELINE, which is used by its Franchisees. The Franchisor will substantiate information set forth in Exhibit A, Exhibit B and Exhibit C to prospective Franchisees upon reasonable demand, provided, however, that this shall not be construed to require disclosure of the identity of a specific Franchisee to require the release of data without the consent of the specific Franchisee, except to any applicable state registration authorities.

Other than as described in Exhibit A, Exhibit B and Exhibit C, no representations or statement of actual, average, projected or forecasted sales, profits or earnings are made to prospective Franchisees with respect to Transmission USA centers. Neither the Franchisors sales personnel nor any employee or officer of the Franchisor is authorized to make any claims or statements as to the earnings, sales or profits or prospects or chances of success that any Franchisee can expect or that have been experienced by present or past Franchisees. The Franchisor has specifically instructed sales personnel, agents, employees and officers that they are not permitted to make such claims or statements as to the earnings, sales or profits or the prospects or chances of success, nor are they authorized to represent or to estimate dollar figures as to any given Transmission USA center. The prospective Franchisee should not rely on any unauthorized representations as to earnings, sales, profits or prospects or chances of success

A prospective Franchisee is urged to consult with appropriate financial and legal advisors in connection with using the information set forth in this claim.

Exhibit A
Average Operating Cash Flow of Certain Transmission USA Centers.

General Information
The following statement (herein referred to as the "Operating Cash Flow Statement"), consists of the average sales of Transmission USA centers and

operating cash flow of the Transmission USA, Midlothian, IL Mr. Transmission center. Although the Company requires all Franchisees to follow particular accounting methods, such methods have not been uniformly and substantially implemented by many existing Franchisees. Furthermore, the cost information which the Company has received from most existing Franchisees is not considered to be sufficiently reliable to accurately evaluate their levels of net income. Accordingly, while the Operating Cash Flow Statement is based upon the Transmission USA Midlothian, IL Mr. Transmission center open more than two years as of June 30, 1998, it is not indicative of general net income levels.

During the twelve month period ending June 30, 1998 the center from which the Operating Cash Flow Statement is based used a uniform accounting method, which was consistent with generally accepted accounting principles. The Company is unable to state the percentage of existing Franchisees who have actually attained or surpassed the operating cash flow level shown in the Operating Cash Flow Statement.

Sales volume may vary considerably due to a variety of factors, such as the demographics of the area (including age, income level, population density and population turnover) and the business abilities and efforts of the person managing the center. Actual sales volumes range between $106,000 and $1.4 million per year.

Operating Cash Flow Statement
THESE OPERATING CASH FLOWS ARE THE AVERAGE RESULTS OF OPERATIONS FOR THE TWELVE MONTHS ENDING JUNE 30, 1998, OF THE TRANSMISSION USA, MIDLOTHIAN, IL MR. TRANSMISSION CENTER AND SHOULD NOT BE CONSIDERED AS THE ACTUAL OR PROBABLE OPERATING CASH FLOW THAT WILL BE REALIZED BY ANY FRANCHISEE. THE COMPANY DOES NOT REPRESENT THAT ANY FRANCHISEE CAN EXPECT TO ATTAIN SUCH OPERATING CASH FLOW. A NEW FRANCHISEE'S FINANCIAL RESULTS ARE LIKELY TO DIFFER FROM THE RESULTS ASSISTED HEREIN.

Gross Revenues (1)	$553,124.15
Expenses:	
Labor (2)	177,309.50
Occupancy (Lease) (3)	54,000.00
Parts (4)	134,445.98
Royalties (5)	37,419.65
Advertising Fund (6)	26,168.99
Other (7)	85,705.78
Total Expenses	$515,049.90
Operating Cash Flow	$38,074.25
Operating Cash Flow as a percentage of revenues	6.9%

Notes and Assumptions
1. Services Revenue:
   This figure represents the average actual service gross revenue for the Transmission USA, Midlothian, IL Mr. Transmission center open more than two years as of June 30, 1998. This center is indicative of an above average center in the Chicago Metro market.
2. Labor:
   This figure represents the average manager and employee expenses for the Transmission USA, Midlothian, IL Mr. Transmission center open more than two years as of June 30, 1998. Labor expenses included in this figure include: salaries of shop personnel and center manager's salary.
3. Occupancy:
   This figure represents the average rental and common area maintenance expenses for the Transmission USA, Midlothian, IL Mr. Transmission center open more than two years as of June 30, 1998. This figure includes the annual minimum rent plus estimated rent, if any. This figure also includes other lease charges, including expenses paid to the landlord in addition to rent, such as charges for common area maintenance, security, trash removal, merchants association dues, shopping center promotional expenses, insurance and real estate taxes.
4. Parts and Fluid Costs:
   This figure represents the average cost to purchase parts and fluid for resale for the Trans-

mission USA, Midlothian, IL Mr. Transmission center open more than two years as of June 30, 1998. This figure includes the cost to purchase the products from outside, unrelated third party vendors plus product commissions paid to shop employees, if any.

5. Royalties:
    This figure was calculated based upon the Company's current royalty fee of 7% on service and product sales revenue, which would be paid by Franchisees.

6. Advertising Fund:
    This figure was calculated based upon Advertising at a rate of 4% on service sales revenue and includes newspaper, TV, radio, yellow pages and miscellaneous organization dues and donations. In addition, this figure includes a monthly contribution of $100 to the Transmission USA Creative Marketing Fund which is utilized to develop creative advertising campaigns for TV, radio, print and point of sale.

7. Other:
    This category comprised all other expense items not previously identified elsewhere and would include such items as travel, shop and office supplies, dues and subscriptions, telephone, utilities, repairs and maintenance, insurance, postage freight and courier, bad debts, taxes and fees, cash over/short, recruitment expense, etc. The figure shown is the average annual expense for the Transmission USA, Midlothian, IL Mr. Transmission center open more than two years as of June 30, 1998.

Exhibit B
Average Sales of Franchised Mr. Transmission Centers
The Franchisor provides prospective Franchisees with information regarding the average sales of all franchised Transmission USA centers of the Transmission USA system (hereinafter referred to as the "TRANSMISSION USA SYSTEM") in operation for a full twelve month period.

THESE AVERAGE SALES FIGURES ARE COMPILED BY THE FRANCHISOR FROM INFORMATION SUPPLIED BY THE FRANCHISEES OF THE TRANSMISSION USA SYSTEM AND SHOULD NOT BE CONSIDERED AS THE ACTUAL OR POTENTIAL SALES THAT WILL BE REALIZED BY ANY OTHER FRANCHISEE. THE FRANCHISOR DOES NOT REPRESENT THAT ANY FRANCHISEE CAN EXPECT TO ATTAIN THESE SALES. A NEW FRANCHISEE'S INDIVIDUAL FINANCIAL RESULTS ARE LIKELY TO DIFFER FROM THE AVERAGE FIGURES PRESENTED BELOW.

The average sales figures of the Transmission USA System were obtained from the information submitted to the Franchisor by its Franchisees from the sales reports required by the Franchisor. Neither the Franchisor nor its independent certified public accountant has independently audited or verified the sales reports. Although the Franchisor does not require certified or audited financial information from its Franchisees, to the best of the Franchisor's knowledge, the sales information received from all stores was prepared in accordance with generally accepted accounting principles.

All Transmission USA centers offer substantially the same products and services to the public. None of the franchised centers have received any services not generally available to other Franchisees and substantially the same services will be offered to new Franchisees

The Franchisor does not provide prospective Franchisees with projections or forecasts of sales, profits or earnings. There is no guarantee that any new Franchisee will attain the average sales levels attained by any existing Franchisees. Substantiation of the average sales of the Transmission USA System will be provided to prospective Franchisees upon reasonable request.

Transmission USA System's Average Sales

Region	Average Annual Sales/Ctr.	% of Centers Exceeding Avg.	# of Centers Calculations
Chicago Metro	$433,218	52%	17
Nashville Metro	$495,924	28%	7
Atlanta Metro	$547,526	27%	11
All Stores	$445,224	42%	145

Exhibit C to Item 19

Actual cash flow, expenses and parts cost will differ for each franchisee. A new franchisee's financial results are likely to differ from percentage herein.

Suggested Business Guideline

Profit and Loss	Weekly	Monthly	Yearly
Sales			
Parts			
Labor			
Cost of Goods			
Gross Profit Margin			
Center Manager			
Payroll Tax			
Rent			
Advertising			
Yellow Pages			
Telephone			

Profit and Loss	Weekly	Monthly	Yearly
Insurance			
Card Fees			
Franchise Fees			
Utilities			
Laundry			
Towing			
Accounting			
Shop Supplies			
Repairs			
Subscriptions			
Health Insurance			
Miscellaneous			
Total Expenses			
Profit			
Debt Service			
Net			

OIL CAN HENRY'S INTERNATIONAL
1200 NW Naito Pkwy., # 690
Portland, OR 97209
Tel: (800) 765-6244 (503) 243-6311
Fax: (503) 228-5227
E-Mail:
Internet Address: www.oilcanhenry.com
Contact: Ms. Kaye Branche, Director of Franchising

Description: Automotive lubrication and filter specialist. Our concept blends old-fashioned American service values with high technology. Staff wear striped shirts, bow ties and Gatsby caps. Customers remain in the car and watch service on the monitors. We offer a high-profile building design and impeccably clean facilities and state-of-the-art point-of-sale computers.

# Franchised Units:	37 Units
# Company-Owned Units:	1 Units
Total # Units:	38 Units
Founded In:	1978
1st Franchised In:	1989
Average Total Investment:	150-800K
Franchise Fee:	35K
On-Going Royalty:	5.5%
Advertising Fee:	1%
Financial Assistance:	Yes(I)
Site Selection Assistance:	Yes
Lease Negotiation Assistance:	Yes
Contract Terms (Init./Renew):	10/5+
Initial Training Provided:	5 Weeks Portland, OR.

Except as outlined below, We do not provide nor do We authorize Our salespersons to furnish any oral or written information concerning the actual or potential sales, costs, income or profits of an "Oil Can Henry's" Service Center. Actual results vary from unit to unit and We cannot estimate the results of any particular Franchise.

The following composite of a cash flow breakeven analysis and pre-tax cash flow were prepared by taking an average of the expenses incurred by our Franchisees during the operation of our Centers which have been opened for at least one full year. It reflects an average based on Our experience and the experience of Our franchisees in operating Oil Can Henry's Service Centers, not on the actual operating experience of any one particular Center. The expenses projected in the cash flow breakeven analysis are those which, on average, can be expected to occur when Our operating systems and procedures are followed as outlined in the training We provide and the Operations Manuals. The analysis is followed by notes explaining the material assumptions Used in the preparation of this item.

Information concerning the actual operating results of Our franchised and company-owned

Centers open and operating for the period covered by this item follows.

The following breakeven and pre-tax cash flow analysis are examples only and should not be considered the actual costs, expenses, sales, revenues and earnings that will be realized by any specific franchisee. Be aware that the sales, profits, expenses and earnings of an individual Franchise may vary greatly depending on a wide variety of factors, including the location of the Franchise, lease/purchase terms, structure and composition of the Center, population demography, competition in the area, the franchisee's business and management expertise, economic and market conditions, labor and product costs, etc.

We will provide substantiation of the data used in preparing this item to the prospective franchisee on reasonable request.

Oil Can Henry's Breakeven Analysis
(Example)

	Variable Expenses	Fixed Expenses
Cost of Goods Sold	25.0%	
Labor*	20.0%	$30,000 (Manager)
Controllables	7.0%	
Occupancy:(1)		
Royalties	5.5%	
Advertising	1.0%	
Local Center	7.0%	
Accounting		$3,600
Other	0.5%	
Totals:	66.0%	$105,600

Cash Flow Breakeven $310,588
Average Ticket (2) $36.80
Cars per day (3) 25.45
*At revenues of $400,000 and above, crew wages drop to 16% of gross revenue.

Notes:
1. This rental rate is based on a leased project with real property and improvement costs (land and building) of $500,000 and a capitalization return for the developer of 12% on

a ten-year lease. The Common Area Maintenance (CAM), Taxes and Insurance are computed as 20% of the rent.

2. See System Average Ticket below.

3. Our Centers are open 6.5 days a Week (open for half a day on Sundays) and 51 Weeks a year (closed for the seven major holidays).

Pre-Tax Cash Flow*

Revenue	$$	% of Revenue
$310,588	0	0
$400,000	$47,080	12%
$500,000	$85,250	17%
$600,000	$123,420	21%
$800,000	$199,760	25%
$1,000,000	$276,100	28%

*Before taxes, amortization, depreciation, debt service and interest.

The following actual gross sales, ticket average and daily car count information is for system centers (franchised and company-owned) open the full year of 1998:

	Gross Sales	Daily Car Counts	Average Ticket
Average	$534,821	43.84	$36.86
Median	$662,573	48.55	$37.15
Range	$237,983–1,087,164	17.01–80.09	$32.12–42.18

Of these Centers, 44% met or exceeded the average gross sales, 44% met or exceeded the average ticket, and 51% met or exceeded the average daily car count.

TOP VALUE MUFFLER AND BRAKE SHOPS

36887 Schoolcraft
Livonia, MI 48150
Tel: (800) 860-8258 (734) 462-3633 x.16
Fax: (734) 462-1088
E-Mail: franchiseinfo@top_value.com
Internet Address: www.top_value.com
Contact: Mr. Richard E. Zimmer, Dir. of Franchise Development

Description: Our reputation of high quality, courteous service and competitive prices sets us apart. Our motto: Top Quality + Service + Price = TOP VALUE. We are the 'Undercar Specialist.'

TOP VALUE is offering franchise opportunities in MI, OH, IN, and N. KY. As an owner of a TOP VALUE MUFFLER & BRAKE SHOP, you can start enjoying the benefits of a franchise while keeping the freedom of private ownership. Plus, you get one of the best-recognized logos in the undercar industry.

# Franchised Units:	31 Units
# Company-Owned Units:	5 Units
Total # Units:	36 Units
Founded In:	1977
1st Franchised In:	1980
Average Total Investment:	125K
Franchise Fee:	15K
On-Going Royalty:	2-5%
Advertising Fee:	3%
Financial Assistance:	Yes(I)
Site Selection Assistance:	Yes
Lease Negotiation Assistance:	Yes
Contract Terms (Init./Renew):	10/5
Initial Training Provided:	3 Weeks in Livonia, MI; 1 Week On-Site.

The table below lists Gross Sales, Cost of Sales, Gross Profits, Costs and Expenses, and Net Earnings (Losses) from operations for six (6) company-owned Top Value Muffler & Brake Shop locations for the twelve month period of January 1, 1998–December 31, 1998 and the average of all six (6) locations for each category.

In referring to the information in the table, you must understand that the results of the Company-Owned locations may differ from a franchised location for several reasons, including: varying building occupancy rates (rent); differences in market penetration and its effect on advertising budgets and market presence; and differences in wage rates and taxes, depending on the state or city in which the franchise store is located and differences in product costs. ALSO, YOU MUST PAY A WEEKLY ROYALTY OF BETWEEN FIVE (5%) PERCENT TO TWO (2%) PERCENT OF GROSS SALES (SEE ITEM 6) WHICH IS NOT REFLECTED IN THE TABLE SINCE COMPANY-OWNED STORES DO NOT PAY A ROYALTY. General economic conditions beyond Top Value's control and its franchisees' control are also important: inflationary pressures, unemployment, energy shortfalls and related or similar conditions, depending on their existence and degree, may adversely affect the market for a franchisee's business with a corresponding adverse affect on earnings. Other factors that will affect a Top Value Muffler & Brake Shop's performance include labor costs, reinvestment, special location, a franchisee's operational and management methods, legal and accounting fees, insurance expense, depreciation expenses, interest expense and miscellaneous non-controllables.

International Top Value Automotive, LLC Company Store
Operations January 1, 1998–December 31, 1998

	Store 1		Store 2		Store 3		Store 4		Store 5		Store 6		Average	
	YTD	% Sales	YTD	% Sales	YTD	% Sales	YTD	% Sales	YTD	% Sales	YTD	% Sales	YTD Avg.	% Sales Avg.
Total Revenue:	423,047.67	100.00%	474,835.87	100.00%	398,542.63	100.00%	432,173.73	100.00%	417,537.09	100.00	678,944.80	100.00	470,846.97	100.00
Total Cost of Sales:	139,026.68	32.86%	118,225.96	24.90%	117,795.89	29.56%	109,520.73	25.34%	113,587.14	27.20%	167,603.22	24.69%	127,626.60	27.11%
Gross Profit:	284,020.99	67.14%	356,609.91	75.10%	280,746.74	70.44%	322,653.00	74.66%	303,949.95	72.80%	511,341.58	75.31%	343,220.36	72.89%
Cost and Expenses:														
Direct Labor	78,832.39	18.63%	80,448.34	16.94%	66,243.60	16.62%	75,025.80	17.36%	61,234.76	14.67%	113,701.24	16.75%	79,247.69	16.83%
Managers' Pay	41,424.42	9.79%	37,542.64	7.91%	40,299.29	10.11%	39,615.14	9.17%	47,361.58	11.34%	48,414.05	7.13%	42,442.85	9.01%
Deferred Managers' Pay	–	–	2,132.32	0.45%	1,649.16	0.41%	2,395.83	0.55%	829.98	0.20%	6,112.10	0.90%	2,186.57	0.46%
Payroll Tax Expense	10,976.21	2.59%	10,647.16	2.24%	10,154.15	2.55%	9,784.39	2.26%	9,927.09	2.38%	13,877.62	2.04%	10,894.44	2.31%
Insurance — Health	11,374.00	2.69%	14,520.00	3.06%	12,436.00	3.12%	11,553.00	2.67%	11,959.00	2.86%	17,284.00	2.55%	13,187.67	2.80%
Insurance — Life	280.20	0.07%	379.00	0.08%	256.20	0.06%	328.00	0.08%	224.20	0.05%	354.20	0.05%	303.63	0.06%
Insurance — Worker's Comp.	3,581.84	0.85%	3,689.22	0.78%	3,676.28	0.92%	3,604.94	0.83%	3,454.02	0.83%	5,149.50	0.76%	3,859.30	0.82%
Employee Relations	592.54	0.14%	400.00	0.08%	309.03	0.08%	400.00	0.09%	405.51	0.10%	500.00	0.07%	434.51	0.09%
Uniforms	1,614.34	0.38%	2,174.68	0.46%	1,718.95	0.43%	2,182.74	0.51%	2,087.97	0.50%	1,683.87	0.25%	1,910.43	0.41%
Training	–	–	–	–	–	–	–	–	–	–	–	–	–	–
Outside Services	3,215.78	0.76%	3,352.89	0.71%	3,103.40	0.78%	3,101.70	0.72%	2,888.44	0.69%	4,183.98	0.62%	3,307.70	0.70%
Meals/Entertainment	76.90	0.02%	572.21	0.12%	77.95	0.02%	133.28	0.03%	168.03	0.04%	1,019.31	0.15%	341.28	0.07%
Postage	360.00	0.09%	360.00	0.08%	360.00	0.09%	360.00	0.08%	360.00	0.09%	360.00	0.05%	360.00	0.08%
Office Supplies	956.48	0.23%	1,491.05	0.31%	1,768.71	0.44%	1,333.52	0.31%	1,343.56	0.32%	1,934.62	0.28%	1,471.32	0.31%
Shop Supplies	6,864.72	1.62%	1,116.08	0.24%	2,656.76	0.67%	1,545.05	0.36%	1,976.65	0.47%	1,483.20	0.22%	2,607.08	0.55%
Welding Supplies	1,172.22	0.28%	1,764.59	0.37%	1,604.52	0.40%	1,434.08	0.33%	1,411.11	0.34%	3,245.10	0.48%	1,771.94	0.38%
Maint. & Rep. Bldg.*	15,409.72	3.64%	45,033.49	9.48%	8,265.96	2.07%	27,190.81	6.29%	7,881.12	1.89%	22,779.57	3.36%	21,093.45	4.48%
Maint. & Rep. Equip.	2,146.89	0.51%	1,744.75	0.37%	1,430.73	0.36%	2,625.44	0.61%	2,877.51	0.69%	1,494.86	0.22%	2,053.36	0.44%
Maint. & Rep. Cust. Car	1,601.61	0.38%	–	–	320.04	0.08%	200.00	0.05%	62.68	0.02%	–	–	364.06	0.08%
Towing	1,500.00	0.00%	–	–	239.45	0.00%	–	–	35.00	–	–	–	295.74	0.06%
Alarm — Security	1,056.54	0.25%	789.00	0.17%	670.77	0.17%	672.78	0.16%	833.44	0.20%	937.50	0.14%	826.67	0.18%
Rent	54,000.00	12.76%	52,800.00	11.12%	33,000.00	8.28%	33,000.00	7.64%	36,000.00	8.62%	39,600.00	5.83%	41,400.00	8.79%

	Store 1		Store 2		Store 3		Store 4		Store 5		Store 6		Average	
	YTD	% Sales	YTD	% Sales	YTD	% Sales	YTD	% Sales	YTD	% Sales	YTD	% Sales	YTD Avg.	% Sales Avg.
Property Taxes	4,781.48	1.13%	5,763.60	1.21%	4,328.77	1.09%	5,997.31	1.39%	4,121.43	0.99%	5,359.40	0.79%	5,058.67	1.07%
Insurance — General	2,983.20	0.71%	2,983.20	0.63%	2,983.20	0.75%	3,013.20	0.70%	2,983.20	0.71%	2,983.20	0.44%	2,988.20	0.63%
Trash & Waste Oil Removal	282.04	0.07%	460.25	0.10%	272.00	0.07%	316.75	0.07%	276.25	0.07%	312.25	0.05%	319.92	0.07%
Utilities — Electric	4,544.78	1.07%	2,666.54	0.56%	3,578.30	0.90%	4,814.75	1.11%	4,397.43	1.05%	2,970.06	0.44%	3,828.64	0.81%
Utilities — Gas	2,632.76	0.62%	2,277.96	0.48%	1,529.22	0.38%	1,731.80	0.40%	1,601.01	0.38%	1,658.95	0.24%	1,905.28	0.40%
Water & Sewage	1,244.11	0.29%	127.38	0.03%	233.34	0.06%	388.00	0.09%	966.53	0.23%	960.16	0.14%	653.25	0.14%
Telephone	3,649.18	0.86%	2,644.08	0.56%	2,085.12	0.52%	1,728.32	0.40%	2,425.19	0.58%	2,097.91	0.31%	2,438.30	0.52%
Advertising**	21,152.38	5.00%	23,741.79	5.00%	19,927.13	5.00%	21,608.69	5.00%	20,876.85	5.00%	33,947.24	5.00%	23,542.35	5.00%
Promotions	–		–		–		168.62	0.04%	109.50	0.03%	25.00	–	50.52	0.01%
Vehicle Fuel/License	682.82	0.16%	288.75	0.06%	966.14	0.24%	112.30	0.03%	391.87	0.09%	967.90	0.14%	568.30	0.12%
License & Dues	541.67	0.13%	736.67	0.16%	500.00	0.13%	655.00	0.15%	676.65	0.16%	525.00	0.08%	605.83	0.13%
Depreciation	8,086.86	1.91%	8,086.86	1.70%	8,849.19	2.22%	8,086.86	1.87%	8,086.86	1.94%	8,086.86	1.19%	8,213.92	1.74%
Equipment Lease Expense	10,900.64	2.58%	10,827.64	2.28%	5,100.00	1.28%	5,100.00	1.18%	5,100.00	1.22%	5,100.00	0.75%	7,021.38	1.49%
Freight	–		–		–		–		–		–		–	
Miscellaneous	14,761.61	3.49%	-52.48	-0.01%	-242.99	-0.06%	9.89	–	-1,040.54	-0.25%	-151.06	-0.02%	2,214.07	0.47%
Bank Charges	629.74	0.15%	703.21	0.15%	589.64	0.15%	630.51	0.15%	603.08	0.14%	1,001.31	0.15%	692.92	0.15%
Credit Card Charges	3,329.86	0.79%	3,077.93	0.65%	3,444.29	0.86%	3,268.22	0.76%	3,726.34	0.89%	5,099.97	0.75%	3,657.77	0.78%
Total Cost & Expenses	317,239.93	74.99%	325,290.80	68.51%	244,384.30	61.32%	274,116.72	63.43%	248,623.30	59.55%	355,058.87	52.30%	294,118.99	62.47%
Earnings (loss) from operations:	-33,218.94	-7.85%	31,319.11	6.60%	36,362.44	9.12%	48,536.28	11.23%	55,326.65	13.25%	156,282.71	23.02%	49,101.38	10.43%

* The company-owned stores underwent a major refurbishment program during this 12-month period. You can expect to pay approximately $2,000–3,500 per year.

**This item includes the Yellow Page Advertising for the company-owned locations. You would pay 3% into the advertising fund, which is spent for local marketing in your area, and pay for any Yellow Pages separately.

The information in the table is based on six (6) company-owned locations open for 9 to 21 years which are similar to comparable franchises operating in Michigan. There are three (3) additional locations, owned and operated by Top Value, not included in the table. They are not included because they were not company-owned for this full twelve-month period. The locations were company-owned for 3 weeks, 2 months, and 25 months, respectively. The data set forth in the table was received from locations using a uniform accounting system, whose operating statements were prepared internally on a basis consistent with generally accepted accounting principals, but were not audited. Both Top Value's company-owned locations and independent franchises are similar with respect to their operations and operating results and receive similar services from Top Value. A NEW FRANCHISEE'S INDI-VIDUAL FINANCIAL RESULTS ARE LIKELY TO DIFFER FROM THE RESULTS REPRESENTED IN THE TABLE. As noted above, you must pay a royalty which is not reflected in the table.

Substantiation of the data used in preparing the earnings claim will be made available to the prospective franchisee on reasonable request.

THESE GROSS SALES, COST OF SALES, GROSS PROFITS, COSTS AND EXPENSES, AND NET EARNINGS (LOSSES) REPRESENT SPECIFIC DESIGNATED COMPANY-OWNED LOCATIONS AND SHOULD NOT BE CONSIDERED AS THE ACTUAL OR POTENTIAL SALES, PROFITS OR EARNINGS THAT WILL BE REALIZED BY ANY OTHER FRANCHISEE THE FRANCHISOR

DOES NOT REPRESENT THAT ANY FRANCHISEE CAN EXPECT TO ATTAIN THESE SALES, PROFITS OR EARNINGS.

Other than this listing, we do not furnish or authorize others to furnish any oral or written information concerning the actual or potential sales, costs, income or profits of a franchised business.

CARS. WE KNOW 'EM. WE LOVE 'EM.™

VALVOLINE INSTANT OIL CHANGE
3499 Blazer Pkwy.
Lexington, KY 40509
Tel: (800) 622-6846 (606) 357-7070
Fax: (606) 357-7049
E-Mail:
Internet Address: www.vioc.com
Contact: Mr. Rich Tammany, Manager Franchise Sales/Dev.

Description: Offers licenses and development agreements for the establishment and operation of a business which provides a quick oil change, chassis lubrication and routine maintenance checks on automobiles. The licensor and/or its affiliates will offer (to qualified prospects) leasing programs for equipment, signage, POS systems and mortgage based financing for land, building.

# Franchised Units:	217 Units
# Company-Owned Units:	357 Units
Total # Units:	596 Units
Founded In:	1988
1st Franchised In:	1988
Average Total Investment:	96-201.8K
Franchise Fee:	30K
On-Going Royalty:	6%
Advertising Fee:	2%
Financial Assistance:	Yes(I)
Site Selection Assistance:	Yes
Lease Negotiation Assistance:	Yes
Contract Terms (Init./Renew):	15/5/5

Initial Training Provided:2 Days Real Estate and Construction Training in Lexington, KY; 4 Weeks Operational Train.

The following summary of average cars per day, monthly sales, monthly cost of goods, monthly labor costs, and certain monthly operating costs is based in pan upon VIOC's actual results at 367 Centers ("Company Centers") which are company-operated by VIOC, and which had been open for at least one year as of September 30, 1998. The time period covered is October 1, 1997, through and including September 30, 1998, and is the most recently available data as of October 1, 1998. All Company Centers that had been open for at least one year on September 30, 1998, are included in the summary. Company Centers that had been operating less than one year on September 30, 1998, are not included in the summary. Company Centers in their first months of operation use discount coupons, price promotions and other promotions that may increase the number of cars per day, but may also affect the ratio of cars per day to sales and costs. In addition, Company Centers open less than one year generally have higher percentage of labor costs than those open for longer periods, due to training wages and related expenses. For these reasons, you should expect to have lower total sales and higher costs during the first year of your Center's operation than the numbers shown in the summary

The Company Centers' cost of advertising was not included in the summary because the amount of each Center's advertising costs has varied over the time period covered in the summary. However, your minimum total of advertising expenses and contributions are stated in ITEM 6 of this Offering Circular under the headings "Advertising" and "Initial Advertising Contribution."

Company Centers do not pay royalties, so the summary does not reflect the payment of royalties. However, you will pay royalties as stated in ITEM 6 of this Offering Circular under the heading Royalties.'

Company Centers are covered by Ashland Inc.'s corporate insurance program. The types, amounts and costs of coverage provided by the Ashland program may not reflect your cost for the types and amounts of insurance required under the License Agreement. The summary does not reflect Company Centers' insurance costs. However, ITEM 7 of this Offering Circular contains an estimate of initial insurance costs for a Licensee-operated Center.

The cost of purchasing or leasing land, buildings, other improvements and operating equipment and depreciation, taxes, utilities, maintenance, repairs,

and other occupancy costs, are not included in the summary. These costs vary greatly across the country and in various circumstances. VIOC acquired several already established businesses and other locations have been constructed or remodeled on land already owned by Ashland. Information as to occupancy costs at Company Centers has not been included in the summary for these reasons. You may pay higher occupancy costs than VIOC pays on the average for the Centers covered in the summary.

Labor Costs also will vary widely depending on location, and may be somewhat higher than the labor costs shown in the summary, particularly in the Northeast and California and in some urban and suburban areas of the U.S.

Average Cars Per Day (Note 2)	Up to 19	20–29	30–39	40–49	50–59	60–69	70+
No. of Units (Note 3)	18	33	126	94	53	31	12
Actual							
Net Sales (Note 4)	$8,832	$20,407	$27,107	$34,416	$42,354	$49,962	$58,240
Net Sales %	100.0%	100.0%	100.0%	100.0%	100.0%	100.0%	100.0%
Actual							
Cost of Goods Sold (Note 5)	$2,323	$4,590	$6,114	$7,680	$9,227	$10,729	$12,421
Cost of Goods Sold %	26.3%	22.5%	22.6%	22.3%	21.8%	21.5%	21.3%
Actual							
Total Labor (Note 6)	$5,828	$7,746	$9,064	$10,817	$12,561	$14,133	$15,699
Total Labor %	66.0%	38.0%	33.4%	31.4%	29.7%	28.3%	27.0%
Actual							
Operating Costs (Note 7)	$1,099	$2,020	$2,236	$2,431	$2,539	$3,172	$3,386
Operating Costs %	12.4%	9.9%	8.2%	7.1%	6.0%	6.3%	5.8%

*These figures are unaudited.

1. VIOCF's assumption is that a well-managed, Licensee-operated Center experiencing similar car counts ("cars per day") will experience sales, costs and operating cash flows similar to those experienced by Company Centers. All actual figures in the summary reflect fiscal year to date experience; twelve months with a fiscal year end of September 30, 1998, and were the latest figures available at the time this summary was prepared. All Company Centers used to compile the actual figures shown were open

and operating for at least one year as of September 30, 1998.

2. These figures show the average number of cars or customers for any product or service offered at a Company Center, each day over the twelve-month period covered by the summary.

3. These figures show the number of Company Centers that experienced the indicated "average

actual cars per day" range for the twelve-month period ending September 30, 1998.

4. These amounts show the average actual monthly sales (also shown as percentage of sales) excluding any sales or similar taxes collected and discounts for the Company Centers shown in each grouping for the twelve-month period ending September 30, 1998

5. These numbers reflect the average actual monthly costs of goods sold (also shown as a percentage of sales) by the Company Centers shown in each grouping for the twelve-month period ending September 30, 1998. The pricing is based upon a Transfer Price Formula then applicable on certain products (bulk oil, packaged oil, air filters, oil filters and lubricants). This Transfer Price Formula is available to you if you elect to purchase those products from or through VIOCF or its designee. If you elect to purchase VALVOLINE Products from sources other than VIOCF, you may experience greater costs of goods sold because of the Transfer Price Formula offered by VIOCF. The average actual costs experienced by the Company Centers for bulk oil was $2.40/gallon, air filters — $3.38/each, and oil filters — $1.35/each for the twelve-month period ending September 30, 1998.

6. These numbers represent the average actual monthly labor cost (excluding contract, temporary, or outside labor, all of which are included in operating costs at note 7 below) experienced by Company Centers in each grouping.

   Note: The management and staffing guidelines used by Company Centers will be made available to you.

7. These numbers represent the average of certain actual monthly operating costs experienced by units in each grouping, and fairly represent what you will pay for similar services. This category of expenses includes maintenance, janitorial and cleaning services and supplies, cash overages and shortages, and miscellaneous, one-time costs. You may experience

lower claims costs than VIOC since VIOC seldom collects from an insurance carrier and you may be able to recover more from your insurance carrier.

In addition to the categories listed in the preceding "Summary of Actual Average Monthly Sales and Certain Costs for Certain Categories of Centers." you must also take into consideration other types of costs, including the following

1. *Advertising Costs* — This includes your monthly expense calculated on the basis of the required contribution, as stated in this Offering Circular (See ITEM 6), applied to the actual Adjusted Gross Revenue at each Center.

2. *Royalties* — This includes your monthly expense calculated on the basis of the percentage royalty payment required of you as stated in this Offering Circular (see ITEM 6) applied to the actual Adjusted Gross Revenue at each Center.

3. *Occupancy Costs* — This includes occupancy costs specific to a given property, including rent or mortgage payments, depreciation, utilities, taxes, operating fees. and similar charges. Prediction of your occupancy costs is very difficult because of the very wide range of these costs.

4. *Insurance Costs* — This includes the cost of business and property insurance required of you (see ITEM 7 of this Offering Circular).

5. *Administrative Costs* — This includes the sum of administrative expenses and costs. reflecting the unpredictable items like salaries, general office and clerical expenses, training and hiring costs, and all other costs, fees and expenses of operating a Center not expressly covered in the summary

YOUR INDIVIDUAL FINANCIAL RESULTS ARE LIKELY TO DIFFER FROM THE RESULTS STATED IN THIS ITEM 19.

THE DATA USED IN PREPARING THIS ITEM 19 WILL BE MADE AVAILABLE TO YOU UPON REASONABLE REQUEST.

ZIEBART

1290 E. Maple Rd., P. O. Box 1290
Troy, MI 48007-1290
Tel: (800) 877-1312 (248) 588-4100
Fax: (248) 588-0718
E-Mail: rbass@ziebart.com
Internet Address: www.ziebart.com
Contact: Mr. Dick Bass, Director Franchise
Development

Description: Business format consists of auto-mobile detailing, accessories and protection services. Ultra-modern showrooms maximize the exposure for the services offered by the franchisee. The customer base consists of retail, wholesale and fleet — making ZIEBART TIDYCAR #1 in the world.

# Franchised Units:	427 Units
# Company-Owned Units:	22 Units
Total # Units:	449 Units
Founded In:	1954
1st Franchised In:	1962
Average Total Investment:	100-161K
Franchise Fee:	24K
On-Going Royalty:	5-8%
Advertising Fee:	5%
Financial Assistance:	Yes(I)
Site Selection Assistance:	Yes
Lease Negotiation Assistance:	Yes
Contract Terms (Init./Renew):	10/10

Initial Training Provided: 3-6 Weeks
Sales, Management and Technical Training at Home Office.

The franchise being offered is ZIEBART. In the past, we offered ZIEBART or ZIEBART-ARTECH franchises and had converted all but 8 of them in the expanded format. The remaining 8 ZIEBART stores generally did not include the full range of products and services offered as the expanded format. You are encouraged to contact Ziebart franchisees in order to obtain the most pertinent information about the franchise being offered.

The following chart shows the number of Ziebart Company-owned, Ziebart Expanded Franchised and Ziebart Limited Franchised stores open for the entire year in each of three geographical areas that achieved sales in each of three categories during fiscal year ending 10/31/98. These stores have been open from one to thirty-three years with the average being eleven years. Exhibit K of this Offering Circular is a list of all three types of stores. Those whose sales are included in the chart are designated in Exhibit J as Ziebart Company-owned — 3 asterisks; Ziebart Expanded Franchised — 2 asterisks; ZIEBART Limited Line — 1 asterisk.

	Over $400,000	$250,000 to 400,000	Up To $250,000	Total	Average 1998 Sales
		(Number of Stores)			($)
Region 1 (West) AZ, IA, IL, KS, MN, MO, NE, WI					
Company-Owned	5	2	0	7	485,061
Expanded Franchised	12	21	21	54	297,879
Ziebart Limited	0	0	0	0	
Region 2 (East) CT, FL, MD, MA, ME, NC, NH, NJ, NY, PA, VA, WV					
Company-Owned	1	0	0	1	385,258
Expanded Franchised	11	11	30	52	268,487
Ziebart Limited	0	0	5	5	58,451

	Over $400,000	$250,000 to 400,000	Up To $250,000	Total	Average 1998 Sales
		(Number of Stores)			($)
Region 3 (Central) IN, KY, MI, OH, TN, TX					
Company-Owned	6	4	1	11	467,534
Expanded Franchised	28	21	38	87	390,233
Ziebart Limited	0	0	3	3	89,928
Total					
ZTC Company-Owned	63%	12***	32%	6***	5%	1	19	
ZTC Franchised	26%	51	28%	51	46%	89	193	
Ziebart Franchised	0%	0	8%	0	100%	8	8	

***Gross profit calculations for these stores are shown on page 2 of this Section.
*Does not offer expanded products/services.

The chart below shows gross profit calculations based on actual sales and cost of sales of the 15 Ziebart Company-Owned stores open during the entire fiscal year ending 10/31/98.

Each gross profit calculation uses average sales and average cost of sales of stores in the three categories shown. Actual sales and cost of sales of individual stores in each category were combined to reach the average shown.

THE FINANCIAL INFORMATION SHOULD NOT BE VIEWED AS AN ASSURANCE THAT ANY FRANCHISEE WILL ACHIEVE THE SAME RESULTS. The sales volume of a Ziebart store is directly affected by the local and national economic conditions, new car sales, status of competitive businesses, length of time a store has been open, and the diligence and experience of the Franchisee. Expenses vary greatly in different parts of the country. Support data for information shown here is available upon request.

Ziebart Company Stores — F.Y.E. 10/31/98

	Over $400,000 in Sales 9 Stores		$325,000–400,000 in Sales 5 Stores		Below $325,000 1 Stores	
	Average $	% of Total Sales	Average $	% of Total Sales	Average $	% of Total Sales
Sales						
Protection/Cleaning	347,410	60.2%	252,934	69.4%	129,465	56.3%
Accessories	212,037	36.8%	102,732	28.2%	87,838	38.2%
Other	17,173	3.0%	8,917	2.4%	12,608	5.5%
Total Sales	576,621	100.0%	364,583	100.0%	229,911	100.0%
Cost of Sales Materials						
Protection/Cleaning	28,343	4.9%	17,827	4.9%	6,420	2.8%
Accessories	72,456	12.6%	39,023	10.7%	37,808	16.4%
Royalty	41,732	7.2%	26,730	7.3%	16,435	7.1%
Direct Labor	98,459	17.1%	54,741	15.0%	48,395	21.0%
Other	14,207	2.5%	9,639	2.6%	7,412	3.2%
Total Cost of Sales	255,197	44.3%	147,960	40.6%	116,470	50.7%
Gross Profit	321,424	55.7%	216,623	59.4%	113,441	49.3%

THESE FINANCIAL STATEMENTS ARE PREPARED WITHOUT AN AUDIT. PROSPECTIVE FRANCHISEES OR SELLERS OF FRANCHISES SHOULD BE ADVISED THAT NO CERTIFIED PUBLIC ACCOUNTANT HAS AUDITED THESE FIGURES OR EXPRESSED HIS/HER OPINION WITH REGARD TO THE CONTENT OR FORM.

To determine potential net profit, anticipated operating expenses, manager's compensation and/or owner's compensation and income taxes must be deducted from the gross profit. Standard operating expense categories are shown below.

Standard Operating Expense Categories
Variable Expenses:
Utilities
Laundry
Insurance — Employees
Payroll Taxes
Insurance — Workman's Compensation
Office Supplies/Forms
Telephone
Repairs — Customer's Property

Fixed Expenses:
Maintenance — Land and Building
Rent
Depreciation — Equipment, Furniture & Fixtures
Amortization — Leasehold Improvements
Property Taxes
Insurance — General
Legal and Accounting Fees

In addition to the above standard operating expenses, three categories are peculiar to the franchise being offered: (1) you can expect to spend approximately 2% of gross sales on shop supplies needed to perform the licensed services, including such items as buffing pads, scrub brushes and electrical connectors; (2) you can expect to spend approximately 1% of gross sales on expenses for repairs or maintenance connected with work done for warranted services; and (3) you can expect to spend approximately 8% of gross sales for advertising expenses consisting of production fees, local media costs and Yellow Pages ads (The license agreement requires that 5% of gross sales be spent on advertising, but 8% as stated here is highly recommended. For purposes of compliance, cost of Yellow Pages ads may not be included in the 5% requirement.).

In the event you have secured outside financing in connection with the establishment of the licensed business, interest expense should also be included as an expense.

Building & Remodeling/Furniture/ Appliance Repair

BATH FITTER
27 Berard Dr., # 2701
South Burlington, VT 05403-5810
Tel: (800) 892-2847 (802) 860-2919
Fax: (802) 862-7976
E-Mail: bathfitter@videotron.ca
Internet Address: www.bathfitter.com
Contact: Ms. Linda F. Brakel, VP Franchise Operations

Description: BATH FITTER® franchisees sell and install custom-molded acrylic bathtub liners, one-piece wall surrounds, shower bases and walls, and accessories.

# Franchised Units:	80 Units
# Company-Owned Units:	3 Units
Total # Units:	83 Units
Founded In:	1984
1st Franchised In:	1992
Average Total Investment:	60-100K
Franchise Fee:	24.5K
On-Going Royalty:	N/A
Advertising Fee:	N/A
Financial Assistance:	No
Site Selection Assistance:	N/A
Lease Negotiation Assistance:	N/A
Contract Terms (Init./Renew):	5/5
Initial Training Provided:	5 Days Headquarters; 5 Days Franchisee Site.

Statement of Average Gross Profit Margin of 22 Responding U.S. Bath Fitter® Franchises (Polled in September 1998)

Revenue	100%
Cost of Materials (includes freight)	37.97%
Gross Profit	62.03%

A NEW FRANCHISEE'S GROSS PROFIT MARGIN MAY DIFFER FROM THE AVERAGE NOTED ABOVE. BATH FITTER® DOES NOT REPRESENT THAT ANY FRANCHISEE WILL ACHIEVE THIS MARGIN. THE FOREGOING STATEMENT OF AVERAGE GROSS PROFIT DOES NOT ACCOUNT FOR CERTAIN COSTS AND EXPENSES FRANCHISEES MAY INCUR REGULARLY SUCH AS LEASE PAYMENTS, LABOR COSTS, ADVERTISING EXPENDITURES, INSURANCE AND ADMINISTRATIVE EXPENSES.

This Statement of Average Gross Profit Margin comprises the average gross profit margin reported by 22 of 27 operating U.S. Bath Fitter® franchisees in September 1998 who have been in business for between one and six years. The franchisees reported their results by compiling the figures developed through a systematic job costing procedure. The franchisor has not undertaken to independently verify the accuracy of this information. The overall average gross profit percentage was achieved by adding all reported percentages and dividing by the number of reporting territories. Eight (8) franchisees (36% of those reporting) attained or surpassed 62.03% gross profit.

The gross profit margin experienced by Bath Fitter® franchisees varies relatively little from one territory to another. However, the total sales revenue, costs, and/or expenses associated with individual franchisee's may vary more significantly due to several factors, including the franchisee's management ability, franchisees salary or draw, and other local factors. For example, labor costs at franchised locations will vary significantly depending on whether or not employees are hired to perform Bath Fitter® services or the franchisees perform the services themselves. In addition, franchisees may experience different results because they establish their own prices for Bath Fitter® products and services. Finally, they contribute varying degrees of efficiency in product installation.

Bath Fitter® will, upon reasonable demand, provide prospective franchisees with substantiation of the data reported. Prospective franchisees are encouraged to obtain further financial and operating information from existing Bath Fitter® franchisees and other industry sources.

Certa ProPainters®

CERTA PROPAINTERS
1140 Valley Forge Rd., Valley Forge, PA 19482
Tel: (800) 452-3782 (770) 455-4300

Fax: (770) 455-4422
Internet Address: www.gocerta.com4
Contact: Mr. Tom Wood, VP Franchise Dev.

# Franchised Units:	163 Units
# Company-Owned Units:	1 Units
Total # Units:	164 Units

The following table presents the average gross sales realized by Certa Pro's franchisees as of December 31, 1998. Certa Pro is providing you with this information to help you make a more informed decision about our franchises. You should not use this information as an indication of how well your franchise will do. A number of factors will effect the success of your Certa Pro franchise. These factors include the current market conditions, the type of market in your franchise area, the location of your franchise area, the competition and your ability to operate the franchise. Certa Pro will provide you with the information we used to prepare the following table upon reasonable request.

Average Gross Sales of Certa Pro Franchisees as of December 31, 1998[1]

Type of Franchisee	Total Franchisees	Total Franchisees Reporting	% of Franchisees Reporting	Average Gross Sales[2]	% of Franchisees at or above Average Gross Sales
Franchisees Operating for More Than 12 Months, But Less than 24 Months	30	30	100%	$267,168	47%
Franchisees Operating for More Than 24 Months	55	55	100%	$385,759	36%
All Franchisees (Totals)	85	85	100%	$343,904	44%

Note 1: All figures are based upon information provided to Certa Pro by franchisees who operated a Certa Pro franchise for at least 12 months as of December 31, 1998. The information is for

the period January 1, 1998 through December 31, 1998. Certa Pro has confirmed these figures, however, they have not been audited by an independent certified public accountant.

Note 2: The term "Gross Sales means all revenues, whether collected or not, derived from the operation of the franchise. The formula used to compute the Average Gross Sales is as follows: (total gross sales) + (total number of franchisees).

Note 3: The results described in the table are for the franchisees who have reported this information to Certa Pro. They should not be used as a projection of your potential earnings. The financial results of your franchise are likely to differ from the results stated in this table.

CREATIVE COLORS INTERNATIONAL
5550 W. 175th St.
Tinley Park, IL 60477
Tel: (800) 933-2656 (708) 614-7786
Fax: (708) 614-9685
E-Mail: mark@creativecolorsintl.com
Internet Address: www.creativecolorsintl.com
Contact: Mr. Mark Bollman, Senior Vice President

Description: Mobile units providing repair and restoration in all markets that have leather, vinyl, fabric, velour, plastics and fiberglass. These markets include car dealerships (new and used), furniture retailers and manufactures, hotels, airports, car rental agencies and company fleet cars.

# Franchised Units:	38 Units
# Company-Owned Units:	2 Units
Total # Units:	40 Units
Founded In:	1980
1st Franchised In:	1991
Average Total Investment:	19.5K+
Franchise Fee:	27.5K
On-Going Royalty:	6%/$173.33/Mo.
Advertising Fee:	0%
Financial Assistance:	Yes(D)
Site Selection Assistance:	Yes
Lease Negotiation Assistance:	N/A
Contract Terms (Init./Renew):	10
Initial Training Provided:	3 Weeks Headquarters, Tinley Park, IL; 1 Week in Franchisee's Territory.

Statement of Actual Sales
For the Year Ended December 31, 1998

Franchisee Sales
The Information included herein represents the sales experience, subject to the assumptions outlined below, of franchisee owned businesses for the period of January 1 through December 31, 1998. The figures reflect the annual and average weekly sales per franchise for thirty-five (35) franchises that were in operation from January 1, 1998 through December 31, 1998.

SUCH ACTUAL SALES, INCOME, GROSS OR NET PROFITS ARE OF FRANCHISEE OPERATED BUSINESSES AND SHOULD NOT BE CONSIDERED AS THE ACTUAL OR PROBABLE SALES, INCOME, GROSS OR NET PROFITS THAT WILL BE REALIZED BY ANY FRANCHISEE. THE FRANCHISOR DOES NOT REPRESENT THAT ANY FRANCHISEE CAN EXPECT TO ATTAIN THESE SALES, INCOME, GROSS OR NET PROFITS.

Of the thirty-five (35) franchises operating for the twelve (12) month period from January 1 through December 31, 1998, there were nine (9) franchises that operated a 100+ Auto Dealership Territory and twenty-eight (28) franchises that operated a 50 Auto Dealership Territory. Your franchise will contain approximately 50 automobile dealerships. The franchises with 100+ automobile dealerships in their territory were granted prior to the Franchisor's restructuring of the size of territories.

The average annual sales per franchise with 100+ Auto Dealership Territory was Two Hundred Four Thousand Nine Hundred Eighty-Six Dollars and Thirteen Cents ($204,986.13). For the twelve (12) months ending December 31, 1998, four (4) of the CREATIVE COLORS INTERNATIONAL franchises exceeded the average and five (5) of the CREATIVE COLORS INTERNATIONAL franchises had annual sales below the average. The lowest and highest annual sales for the twelve (12) months were Twenty-Four Thousand Five Hundred Thirty Dollars and no cents ($24,530.00) and Six Hundred Ninety-One Thousand Two Hundred Twenty-Seven Dollars and no cents ($691,227.00), respectively.

The average annual sales per franchise with a 50 Auto Dealership Territory was One Hundred Five Thousand, Three Hundred Fifty-One Dollars and Fifty-Eight Cents ($105,351.58). For the twelve (12) months ending December 31, 1998, seven (7) of the CREATIVE COLORS INTERNATIONAL franchises exceeded the average and nineteen (19) of the CREATIVE COLORS INTERNATIONAL franchises had annual sales below the average. The lowest and highest annual sales for the twelve (12) months were Twenty-Five Thousand Seven Hundred Sixty-Five Dollars and no cents ($25,765.00) and Three Hundred Twenty-Nine Thousand Five Hundred Twenty-Six Dollars and Fifty-Five Cents ($329,526.55), respectively.

The following information should be carefully-considered in reviewing the accompanying Statement of Actual Sales and Expenses. A NEW FRANCHISEE'S INDIVIDUAL FINANCIAL RESULTS ARE LIKELY TO DIFFER FROM THE RESULTS STATED IN THE STATEMENT.

Basis of Compilation

The accompanying statement of average weekly sales per franchisee includes thirty-five (35) franchises located in Alabama, Arkansas, Arizona, Colorado, Georgia, Florida, Illinois, Indiana, Kentucky, Louisiana, Michigan, Mississippi, Missouri, New Jersey, North Carolina, Ohio, Pennsylvania, Texas, and Canada, and have been in operation for the period of twelve (12) months from January 1, 1998 through December 31, 1998. The thirty-five franchises represent all the franchises that were in operation throughout calendar 1998.

The accompanying statement has been compiled from figures that have been reported from CREATIVE COLORS INTERNATIONAL franchises for the twelve (12) months ending December 31, 1998. The accompanying statement does not include any expenses related to the operation of the business.

The franchises included in the statement use a uniform system for reporting their sales to us. Specific assumptions used in the presentation of the statement are indicated below.

Franchisee Owned Businesses for the Period of January 1 through December 31, 1998
100+ Auto Dealership Territory

Franchisee	Date Started	Number of Trucks	Total Annual Sales	Average Weekly Sales
Streamwood, IL—Northern Illinois	July, 1991	Six One P/T	$691,227.00	$13,292.83
South Bend, IN—Northern Indiana	July, 1991	Four	$353,100.53	$6,790.39
Tinley Park, IL—North East Illinois	August, 1991	Three	$110,722.00	$2,129.27
Bremen, IN—Southern Indiana	December,1991	Four	$239,964.00	$4,614.69
Lansing, IL—Northern Indiana	February,1992	One	$24,530.00	$471.73
Oak Forest, IL—Northwest Illinois	April, 1992	Two	$69,963.00	$1,345.44
Union, MO—East Central Missouri	August, 1992	One	$64,875.00	$1,247.60
Gobles, MI—Southwest Michigan	October,1992	Two	$66,569.10	$1,280.18
Union, KY—Northern Kentucky	November,1992	Four	$223,924.60	$4,306.24

50 Auto Dealership Territory

Franchisee	Date Started	Number of Trucks	Total Annual Sales	Average Weekly Sales
Grayslake, IL—Northern Illinois	October, 1991	One	$55,430.00	$1,065.96
Vermillion, OH—North Central Ohio	April, 1994	One	$75,895.00	$1,459.52
Middleburg Heights, OH—Northeast Ohio	September 1994	Three	$231,100.91	$4,444.25
Elkmont, AL—North Alabama	October, 1994	Two	$99,214.00	$1,907.96
Akron, OH—Central Ohio	November, 1994	Two	$116,666.00	$2,243.58
Toms River, NJ—Southern New Jersey	January, 1995	One	$93,093.00	$1,790.25
Destrehan, LA—Southern Louisiana	January, 1995	One	$56,191.00	$1,080.60
Sheridan, IL—Southern Illinois	May, 1995	Three	$253,401.75	$4,873.11
Waynesville, NC—Western North Carolina	May, 1995	Two	$98,875.00	$1,901.44
Ontario, Canada—London, Canada	July, 1995	Three	$116,747.36	$2,245.14
Tempe, AZ—South Central Arizona	August, 1995	Four	$329,526.55	$6,337.05
Jacksonville, FL—Northeast Florida	October, 1995	One	$50,927.00	$979.37
Wernersville, PA—Southeast Pennsylvania	November, 1995	One	$25,765.00	$495.48
Bedford, IN—Southern Indiana	May, 1996	Two	$89,432.50	$1,719.86
Washington, IA—East Central Iowa	July, 1996	Two	$63,687.00	$1,224.75
Poplarville, MS—Southern Mississippi	July, 1996	Two	$138,944.52	$2,672.01
San Antonio, TX—Southern Texas	July, 1996	Three	$203,205.99	$3,907.81
Sheridan, IL—Southeast Illinois	July, 1996	Two	$82,602.00	$1,588.50
Denver, CO—Northern Colorado	August, 1996	One	$41,813.00	$804.10
Fayetteville, AR—Northwest Arkansas	August, 1996	One	$41,313.00	$794.48
Ramseur, NC—North Carolina	October, 1996	Two	$97,430.95	$1,873.67
Tampa, FL—Central Florida	October, 1996	Two	$70,045.92	$1,347.04
Orlando, Florida	March, 1997	One	$14,598.00	$280.73
Savannah, Georgia	April, 1997	Two	$44,883.00	$863.13
Cape Coral, Florida	April, 1997	Three	$104,995.00	$2,019.13
Mesa, Arizona—Northern Arizona	June, 1997	Three	$42,613.50	$819.49
Westminster, Colorado	July, 1997	One	$102,164.50	$1,964.70
Valparaiso, Florida	August, 1997	One	$64,105.00	$1,232.79

Affiliate Sales

Also included is the Affiliate-owned business experience for the period of January 1 through December 31, 1998. The Affiliate-owned business, which started in 1980, covers approximately 250 Auto Dealerships in the state of Illinois.

The affiliate-owned business is similar to that operated by the franchisees, except that the affiliate business also provides leather furniture repair services to individual consumers as well as to commercial accounts.

Franchisees are not prohibited from providing leather furniture repair services; however, most franchises are not currently in the practice of rendering services to those markets, although we encourage franchisees to expand into those markets.

The gross sales figures appearing in these statements should not be construed as the "profit" which might be experienced by a franchisee with a similar sales volume. An individual franchisee will incur various expenses for continuing services and royalty fees, interest rates, advertising contributions, general insurance, legal and accounting fees, employee benefits, income taxes and other expenditures. Each of these factors, as well as the actual accounting, operational and management procedures employed by a franchisee, may significantly affect profits realized in any given operation. The nature of these variables and the economic discretion exercised by individual franchisees renders a determination of the profit level a franchisee will attain impossible to ascertain.

Substantiation of the data used in preparing the accompanying statement will be made available to Franchisee upon reasonable request.

Affiliate-Owned for the Year Ended December 31, 1998

	Date Started	Total Annual Sales	Average Weekly Sales
TRUCK #1—KG	June, 1986	$73,698.00	$1,417.27
TRUCK #2—KM	November, 1986	$81,375.00	$1,564.90
TRUCK #3—KF	June, 1988	$114,303.00	$2,198.13
TRUCK #4—TS	July, 1988	$104,075.00	$2,001.44
TRUCK #5—GF	June, 1991	$101,744.57	$1,956.63
TRUCK #6—BC	March, 1992	$64,887.50	$1,247.84
TRUCK #7—BV*	May, 1993	$29,652.56	$570.24
TRUCK #8—TC*	October, 1994	$43,202.00	$830.81
TRUCK #9—SB	September, 1995	$119,233.00	$2,292.94
TRUCK #10—JS	July, 1996	$73,724.00	$1,417.77
TRUCK #11—MD	December, 1996	$87,608.00	$1,684.77
TRUCK #12—LS*	May, 1997	$45,375.00	$872.60
TRUCK #13—DS	August, 1997	$63,525.00	$1,221.63

Trucks #7, 8 & 12 are devoted entirely to leather furniture repair.

DR. VINYL & ASSOC.
821 NW Commerce St.
Lee's Summit, MO 64086
Tel: (800) 531-6600 (816) 525-6060
Fax: (816) 525-6333
E-Mail: tbuckley@drvinylcom
Internet Address: www.drvinyl.com
Contact: Mr. Tom Buckley, Jr., President

Description: We offer vinyl, leather and velour fabric repair and coloring, auto windshield repair, dashboard and hard plastic repair, vinyl striping and protective molding to new and used car dealers.

# Franchised Units:	145 Units
# Company-Owned Units:	2 Units
Total # Units:	147 Units
Founded In:	1972
1st Franchised In:	1980

Average Total Investment:	35-40K
Franchise Fee:	19.5K
On-Going Royalty:	7%
Advertising Fee:	1%
Financial Assistance:	Yes(B)
Site Selection Assistance:	N/A
Lease Negotiation Assistance:	N/A
Contract Terms (Init./Renew):	10/10

Initial Training Provided:2 Weeks Corporate Office; 2 Weeks Field Training.

Of the 118 Dr. Vinyl Businesses currently in operation, 85 have been in business for at least 2 years. Based on royalty fee reports, the average gross sales of those 85 Dr. Vinyl Businesses is $119,158. 28 of the 85 franchisees have sales above the average stated.

Except as stated above, DR. VINYL does not furnish or authorize its salespersons to furnish any oral or written information or representations or statements of actual sales, costs, income or profits of a Dr. Vinyl Business. Actual results vary from business to business and DR. VINYL cannot estimate the results of any particular franchisee. You must execute a disclosure acknowledgment statement (Exhibit G) whereby you acknowledge that no earnings claims other than those set forth above have been made to you.

ACTUAL RESULTS VARY FROM BUSINESS TO BUSINESS AND DR. VINYL CANNOT ESTIMATE THE RESULTS OF ANY PARTICULAR FRANCHISEE. FINANCIAL RESULTS MAY DIFFER FROM THE FIGURES PRESENTED ABOVE. YOU SHOULD MAKE YOUR OWN INVESTIGATION TO DETERMINE WHETHER YOUR FRANCHISE DR. VINYL BUSINESS WILL BE PROFITABLE.

KITCHEN SOLVERS
401 Jay St.
La Crosse, WI 54601
Tel: (800) 845-6779 (608) 791-5516
Fax: (608) 784-2917
E-Mail: dave@kitchensolvers.com
Internet Address: www.kitchensolvers.com
Contact: Mr. David Woggon, Dir. of Franchise Operations

Description: Specialize or diversify... It's your option. "10 in 1" business concept offered by the most experienced kitchen remodeling franchise system in the United States. Home-based business with no inventory required. Complete start-up and on-going marketing program, experienced technical support. Call for a FREE introductory video.

# Franchised Units:	106 Units
# Company-Owned Units:	1 Units
Total # Units:	107 Units
Founded In:	1982
1st Franchised In:	1984
Average Total Investment:	24.2-36K
Franchise Fee:	8-14K
On-Going Royalty:	4-6%
Advertising Fee:	0%
Financial Assistance:	Yes(D)
Site Selection Assistance:	Yes
Lease Negotiation Assistance:	No
Contract Terms (Init./Renew):	10/10

Initial Training Provided:6 Days La Crosse, WI (Refacing); 3 Days Houston, TX (Recoloring). Pre-Training Program.

Except as attached as Exhibit 4, KSI does not furnish or authorize its salespersons to furnish any oral or written information concerning the actual or potential sales, costs, income or profits of a "Kitchen Solvers" franchise. Actual results will vary from franchise to franchise and KSI cannot estimate the results of any particular franchise.

Attached as Exhibit 4 to this Offering Circular is an Earnings Claim, which includes, as qualified in Exhibit 4, (i) an unaudited Statement of Average Sales, Average Expenses and Average Gross Profit for kitchens remodeled by 21 franchisees who submitted specific information on kitchens that the franchisees remodeled during the period October 1, 1996 to September 30, 1997 and (ii) an unaudited Statement of Average Sales, Average Expenses and Average Gross Profit for kitchens remodeled by 13 franchisees who submitted specific information on kitchens that the franchisees remodeled during 1998. A franchisee's financial results may differ from the information set forth on Exhibit A. Substantiation of all data illustrated in Exhibit A will be made available to you upon reasonable demand.

Statement of Average Sales, Expenses and Gross Profit for the Period of Time from January 1, 1998 to December 31, 1998

These figures are taken from reports by 13 franchisees who submitted specific information on the kitchens that they remodeled during the period from January 1, 1998, to December 31, 1998. A total of 455 kitchens were included in this Statement.

Average Total Sales Price	$4,162.50
Average Material Expenses	$1,774.00
(does not include installation cost)	
Average Gross Profit	$2,388.50

THESE SALES, EXPENSES, AND GROSS PROFIT ARE AVERAGES FOR 13 FRAN-CHISEES AND SHOULD NOT BE CON-SIDERED AS THE ACTUAL OR PROBABLE SALES, INCOME, GROSS OR NET PROFITS OR EARNINGS THAT WILL BE REALIZED BY ANY FRANCHISEE. THE KITCHEN SOLVERS, INC. HAS NOT AUDITED OR REVIEWED THE FRANCHISEES' FINAN-CIAL RECORDS IN COMPILING THIS INFORMATION, AND THERE ARE NO ASSURANCES THAT GENERALLY ACCEPTED ACCOUNTING PRINCIPLES WERE USED BY THE FRANCHISEES. THE KITCHEN SOLVERS, INC. DOES NOT REP-RESENT THAT ANY FRANCHISEE CAN EXPECT TO ATTAIN SUCH SALES, INCOME, GROSS OR NET PROFITS, OR EARNINGS.

As mentioned above, the averages identified in the Statement are based on specific sales price, material expenses, and gross profit for a total of 455 kitchens remodeled by 13 franchisees. The total sales volume of the 13 franchisees ranged from a low of $35,240.80 (10 kitchens sold) to a high of $349,876.00 (95 kitchens sold). Another 57 franchisees reported total sales by month but not on a per kitchen basis. The average total sales price of the 70 franchisees was $4,211. Of the 70 franchisees who reported information to The Kitchen Solvers, Inc. related to their sales for fiscal year 1998, 23 of the 70 franchisees (33%) attained the average total sales price of $4,211 for kitchens in their areas. It should be noted that several of these franchisees do not remodel countertops as part of their remodeling of kitchens, which would reduce the sales price for a remodeling job.

The 57 franchisees who did not submit informa-tion for each kitchen remodeled did not report sufficient data to The Kitchen Solvers, Inc. related to expenses and gross profit to determine the per-centage of franchisees who attained the averages noted above. The average gross profit as listed here does not include such overhead expenses such as advertising, installation, telephone, insur-ance, office rental, secretarial help (if needed), etc., or the payment of continuing license fees. These expenses will vary a great deal depending on each Franchisee's location and particular situ-ation. Therefore, each prospective franchisee will have to estimate these figures for themselves. Each prospective franchisee can make their own projec-tions as to what sales they plan to make per week or month.

All figures used in determining the average gross profit in this report are on file and a matter of record in The Kitchen Solvers, Inc.'s records. This information may be obtained upon request.

Statement of Average Sales, Expenses and Gross Profit for the Period of Time From October 1, 1996 to September 30, 1997
These figures are taken from reports by 21 franchisees who submitted specific information on the kitchens that they remodeled during the period from October 1, 1996, to September 30, 1997. A total of 154 kitchens were included in this Statement.

Average Total Sales Price	$3,763
Average Material Expenses	$1,754
(does not include installation cost)	
Avenge Gross Profit	$2,009

THESE SALES, EXPENSES, AND GROSS PROFIT ARE AVERAGES FOR 21 FRANCHISEES AND SHOULD NOT BE CONSIDERED AS THE ACTUAL OR PROBABLE SALES, INCOME, GROSS OR NET PROFITS OR EARNINGS THAT WILL BE REALIZED BY ANY FRANCHISEE. THE KITCHEN SOLVERS, INC. HAS NOT AUDITED OR REVIEWED THE FRANCHISEES' FINANCIAL RECORDS IN COMPILING THIS INFORMATION, AND THERE ARE NO ASSURANCES THAT GENERALLY ACCEPTED ACCOUNTING PRINCIPLES WERE USED BY THE FRANCHISEES. THE KITCHEN SOLVERS, INC. DOES NOT REPRESENT THAT ANY FRANCHISEE CAN EXPECT TO ATTAIN SUCH SALES, INCOME, GROSS OR NET PROFITS, OR EARNINGS.

As mentioned above, the averages identified in the Statement are based on specific sales price, material expenses, and gross profit for a total of 154 kitchens remodeled by 21 franchisees. Another 46 franchisees reported total sales by month but not on a per kitchen basis. Of the 67 franchisees who reported information to The Kitchen Solvers, Inc. related to their sales for fiscal year 1996/1997, 27 of the 67 franchisees (40%) attained the average total sales price of $3,763 for kitchens in their areas. The average total sales price of the 67 franchisees was $3,622. It should be noted that several of these franchisees do not remodel countertops as part of their remodeling of kitchens, which would reduce the sales price for a remodeling job.

The 46 franchisees who did not submit information for each kitchen remodeled did not report sufficient data to The Kitchen Solvers, Inc. related to expenses and gross profit to determine the percentage of franchisees who attained the averages noted above. The average gross profit as listed here does not include such overhead expenses such as advertising, installation, telephone, insurance, office rental, secretarial help (if needed), etc., or the payment of continuing license fees. These expenses will vary a great deal depending on each Franchisee's location and particular situation. Therefore, each prospective franchisee will have to estimate these figures for themselves. Each prospective franchisee can make their own projections as to what sales they plan to make per week or month.

All figures used in determining the average gross profit in this report are on file and a matter of record in The Kitchen Solvers, Inc.'s records. This information may be obtained upon request.

KITCHEN TUNE-UP
813 Circle Dr.
Aberdeen, SD 57401-3349

Tel: (800) 333-6385 (605) 225-4049
Fax: (605) 225-1371
E-Mail: kituneup@midco.net
Internet Address: www.kitchentuneup.com
Contact: Mr. Craig Green, Franchise Acquisitions Dir.

Description: America's #1 home improvement franchise. We offer 'Kitchen Solutions For Any

Budget.' Cabinet restoration, cabinet refacing and custom cabinetry along with shelf lining, replacement hardware and cabinet organization systems. Excellent initial and on-going training and support. High residential and commercial potential. Home-based and retail locations available.

# Franchised Units:	321 Units
# Company-Owned Units:	1 Units
Total # Units:	322 Units
Founded In:	1975
1st Franchised In:	1988

Average Total Investment:	28-35K
Franchise Fee:	15K
On-Going Royalty:	4.5-7%
Advertising Fee:	0%
Financial Assistance:	Yes(D)
Site Selection Assistance:	Yes
Lease Negotiation Assistance:	Yes
Contract Terms (Init./Renew):	10/10

Initial Training Provided:2 Weeks Pre-training Home Study, 6-10 Days Corporate Office, 12 Wks. Home Study, On-Going.

CAUTION: THE INFORMATION PROVIDED BELOW REPRESENTS AVERAGE GROSS VOLUMES FOR THE CATEGORIES OF FRANCHISEES NOTED. THIS GROSS VOLUME INFORMATION IS NOT A FORECAST, PROJECTION, OR PREDICTION OF HOW YOUR FRANCHISE WILL PERFORM. THESE GROSS VOLUME FIGURES SHOULD NOT BE RELIED UPON AS THE ACTUAL OR POTENTIAL GROSS VOLUME THAT WILL BE REALIZED BY YOU. IT IS LIKELY THAT YOUR GROSS VOLUME WILL DIFFER FROM THE INFORMATION IN THIS EARNINGS CLAIM. KTU DOES NOT REPRESENT THAT YOU, OR ANY FRANCHISEE, CAN EXPECT TO ATTAIN THESE FIGURES. YOUR DECISION TO BUY A KITCHEN TUNE-UP FRANCHISE MUST BE BASED UPON YOUR INDEPENDENT ANALYSIS OF THE BUSINESS CONCEPT. IF YOU RELY ON THE GROSS VOLUME INFORMATION, YOU MUST ACCEPT THE RISK OF NOT DOING AS WELL.

As of December 31, 2000, KTU had 119 individual franchisees. Each month those franchisees provide KTU with information regarding the amount of business conducted during the prior month. The royalties which are paid to KTU are based upon that business information and KTU relies on that information in its relationship with its franchisees. The following averages are based upon actual gross volume information provided to US by franchisees who were in business for the full calendar year of 1999. As defined in section 1 of the Franchise Agreement, "Gross Volume" means your cumulative total of YOUR sales.

The top 5 franchisees (4% of all franchisees) operated their business full-time and averaged $410,573 in average gross volume per franchisee.

The top 20 franchisees (17% of all franchisees) operated their business full-time and averaged $251,105 in annual gross volume per franchisee.

The top 50 franchisees (42% of all franchisees) averaged $162,776 in annual gross volume per franchisee, with 80% being full-time operators and 20% being part-time.

The 20 franchisees (17% of all franchisees) with the lowest gross volume averaged $38,620 in annual gross volume; 90% of those franchisees were part-time operators. Most of the franchisees in the lowest gross volume group only provide 1 or 2 of the total package of services available to the public from KTU franchisees.

For the KTU System, as a whole, the annual gross volume was earned by the franchisees as follows:

Months	Percent of Systemwide Annual Gross Volume Earned Per Calendar Month
January	6%
February	6.1%
March	8%
April	8.8%
May	9.8%
June	9.6%
July	9%
August	8.3%
September	8.6%
October	8.8%

Months	Percent of Systemwide Annual Gross Volume Earned Per Calendar Month
November	9.2%
December	7.8%
	100.0%

Substantiation of the data used in preparing this earnings claim will be made available to YOU upon reasonable request.

MIRACLE METHOD

4239 N. Nevada, # 110
Colorado Springs, CO 80907
Tel: (800) 444-8827 (719) 594-9196
Fax: (719) 594-9282
E-Mail: cpistor@miraclemethodusa.com
Internet Address: www.miraclemethodusa.com
Contact: Mr. Chuck Pistor, President

Description: Make money in the growing remodeling industry by running your own bath and kitchen refinishing business. Save customers money by refinishing instead of replacing. Bathtubs, tile, showers, counter tops and more. Excellent income potential!

# Franchised Units:	97 Units
# Company-Owned Units:	0 Units
Total # Units:	97 Units
Founded In:	1979
1st Franchised In:	1980
Average Total Investment:	25-50K
Franchise Fee:	16.5K
On-Going Royalty:	5-7.5%
Advertising Fee:	1%
Financial Assistance:	Yes(D)
Site Selection Assistance:	No
Lease Negotiation Assistance:	No
Contract Terms (Init./Renew):	5
Initial Training Provided:	1 Week at Headquarters Location.

Representations Regarding Earnings Capability

Attached hereto as Exhibit I is the Miracle Method Franchise Budget Assumptions. Other than as specifically set forth in Exhibit I, no representations or statements of actual, or average, or projected, or forecasted sales, profits, or earnings are made to you with respect to the franchise. Neither Miracle's sales personnel nor any employee or officer of Miracle is authorized to make any claims or statements as to the earnings, sales, or profits, or prospects or chances of success that you can expect or that present or past franchises have had, other than as set forth in Exhibit I. Miracle recommends that applicants for Miracle Method franchises make their own investigation and determine whether or not the franchises are profitable.

Miracle Method Franchise Budget Assumptions*

Gross Income

Achievable Work per Day per Technician	$300–500

Cost of Goods

Labor Costs as Percent of Gross Income	25–35%
Materials as Percent of Gross Income	7.5–10%
Advertising as Percent of Gross Income	5–10%
Franchise Service Fee as Percent of Gross Income	5–7.5%

Operating Expenses	*Annually*
Rent for Office/Showroom of 1,000–1,500 SF	$6,000–10,000
Truck Payment	$2,000–4,000
Fuel per Truck	$1,000–1,500
Maintenance per Truck	$750–1,250
Salary + Taxes per Assistant	$18,000–20,000
Electricity + Water + Gas	$2,400–4,200
Property Insurance	$400–750
Vehicle Insurance Each	$800–1,500
Liability Insurance	$2,000–4,000
Health Medical Insurance per Person	$3,300–4,800
Office Supplies	$1,200–3,600
Telephone Each	$600–1,500

Operating Expenses	Annually
Postage	$180–1,200
Miscellaneous	$300–2,400
Estimated Total	**$38,930–60,700**

Capital Items	Initial
Franchise Fee	$16,500
Equipment	$4,000
Professional Fees	$500–3,000
Trucks Down Payment Each	$800–3,000
Computer/Printer/Software	$1,800–5,000
Fax Machine	$250–500
Telephone System	$300–2,000
Extra Spray Guns and Equipment Each	$0–2,000
Showroom Display	$500–1,000
State License Fees (If Applicable)	$100–500
Start-up Advertising	$2,000–6,000
Office Fixtures/Equipment	$1,750–2,800
Insurance Down Payment	$0–200
Working Capital	$1,000–3,000
Estimated Total	**$29,500–49,500**

*This schedule has been prepared as a reference only. Actual future operating results will depend on individual franchise conditions including, but not limited to market, economic and geographic conditions. Your results will also vary greatly depending on the number of technicians you hire. These estimates are based on the operating experience as reported by at least 75% of Miracle Method franchisees on average over the last five years. A NEW FRANCHISEES INDIVIDUAL FINANCIAL RESULTS ARE LIKELY TO DIFFER FROM THESE RESULTS. Data used as the basis for these assumptions will be made available upon reasonable request to a registered franchise prospect. A prospective franchise should consult with appropriate financial, business and legal advisors in evaluating the above information. Any actual or projected sales, costs, income, gross or net profits disclosed above should not be considered as the actual or probable sales, costs, income, gross or net profits which will be realized by a prospective franchisee and that as a prospective franchisee, you must accept the risk of not doing as well.

PERMA-GLAZE

1638 S. Research Loop Rd., # 160
Tucson, AZ 85710
Tel: (800) 332-7397 (520) 722-9718
Fax: (520) 296-4393
E-Mail: permaglaze@permaglaze.com
Internet Address: www.permaglaze.com
Contact: Mr. Dale R. Young, President

Description: PERMA GLAZE specializes in multi-surface restoration of bathtubs, sinks, countertops, appliances, porcelain, metal, acrylics, cultured marble and more. PERMA GLAZE licensed representatives provide valued services to hotels/ motels, private residences, apartments, schools, hospitals, contractors, property managers and many others.

# Franchised Units:	177 Units
# Company-Owned Units:	1 Units
Total # Units:	178 Units
Founded In:	1978
1st Franchised In:	1981
Average Total Investment:	22-25K+
Franchise Fee:	19.5K+
On-Going Royalty:	6/5/4%/$200 Min.
Advertising Fee:	$1,800/Yr.
Financial Assistance:	No
Site Selection Assistance:	Yes
Lease Negotiation Assistance:	N/A
Contract Terms (Init./Renew):	10/10
Initial Training Provided:	5 Days Tucson, AZ.

Perma-Glaze Refinishing Business

Set forth below is a Statement of the high and low Range of Costs of Products Used and Charges for a Residential Refinishing Job Involving a Standard Size Bathtub as reported by us and certain of our Perma-Glaze licensees. The Statement describes the typical high and low range of the cost of Perma-Glaze Products and other products used in refinishing a standard size residential bathtub which does not need significant restoration or other repair work and is serviced by a trained and experienced technician (this refinishing job is referred to as an "Average Residential Tub Job"). The Statement also describes the typical high and low range of charges for an Average Residential Tub Job. These charges are subject to various factors, including: (1) the appeal of and demand for this work in the locality of the job site; (2) price and other competition from other tub refinishing businesses in proximity to the job site; (3) labor and fixed overhead costs; (4) federal, state and local taxes; (5) media, marketing and advertising costs; and (6) general economic conditions. The Statement does not disclose any costs or expenses in conducting an Average Residential Tub Job other than the cost of product used in the refinishing process.

We have based our Statement on the actual results of all of our Perma-Glaze Businesses located throughout the United States as reported to us by licensees. We will make available to you substantiation of the information used in preparing this Statement upon reasonable request, although we will maintain the confidentiality of those Businesses' locations.

THE STATEMENT DISCLOSES THE RANGE OF COSTS OF PRODUCTS USED AND CHARGES OF CERTAIN EXISTING PERMA-GLAZE, BUSINESSES FOR AN AVERAGE RESIDENTIAL TUB JOB. THIS STATEMENT SHOULD NOT BE CONSIDERED AS THE ACTUAL OR POTENTIAL REVENUE OR EXPENSES THAT YOU WILL REALIZE. WE DO NOT REPRESENT THAT YOU CAN EXPECT TO ATTAIN ANY OF THE REVENUE OR EXPENSE LEVELS DISCLOSED IN THE STATEMENT. YOUR OWN FINANCIAL RESULTS MAY DIFFER FROM THIS STATEMENT.

OTHER THAN THE STATEMENT, NO REPRESENTATIONS OR STATEMENTS OF ACTUAL, AVERAGE, PROJECTED OR FORECASTED SALES, REVENUE, EARNINGS OR PROFITS ARE MADE TO PROSPECTIVE LICENSEES. NEITHER OUR SALES PERSONNEL NOR ANY EMPLOYEE OR OFFI-CER OF OURS IS AUTHORIZED TO MAKE ANY CLAIMS OR STATEMENTS AS TO THE REVENUE, EARNINGS, SALES, OR PROFITS OR PROSPECTS OR CHANCES OF SUCCESS THAT YOU CAN EXPECT OR THAT PRESENT OR PAST LICENSEES HAVE HAD. WE HAVE SPECIFICALLY INSTRUCTED OUR SALES PERSONNEL, AGENTS, EMPLOYEES AND OFFICERS THAT THEY ARE NOT PERMITTED TO MAKE SUCH CLAIMS OR STATEMENTS AS TO REVENUE, EARNINGS, SALES OR PROFITS OR THE PROSPECTS OR CHANCES OF SUCCESS, NOR ARE THEY AUTHORIZED TO REPRESENT OR ESTIMATE DOLLAR FIGURES AS TO A SPECIFIC PERMA-GLAZE BUSINESS. YOU SHOULD NOT RELY ON UNAUTHORIZED REPRESENTATIONS AS TO REVENUE, EARNINGS, SALES PROFITS, OR PROSPECTS OR CHANCES OF SUCCESS.

Statement of the High and Low Range of Costs of Products Used and Charges for a Residential Refinishing Job Involving a Standard Size Bathtub

Product Costs: $40–60 per Job

Charges: $225–400 per Job

A trained and experienced technician usually can perform 2 Average Residential Tub Jobs in an 8 hour work day, subject to travel times between job sites and the restorative/repair work required before commencing the refinishing aspects of these jobs. However, we do not represent that you can perform this volume of work which will depend, among other things, upon your efforts and your ability to obtain customers.

Thermal-Ation Insulating Business.
We do not furnish or authorize our salespersons to furnish any oral or written information concerning the actual or potential sale, costs, income or profits of Thermal-Ation licensees. Actual results vary from unit to unit, and we cannot estimate the results of any particular franchise.

DEFINITIVE FRANCHISOR DATA BASE
AVAILABLE FOR RENT

SAMPLE FRANCHISOR PROFILE

Name of Franchise:	**AARON'S RENTAL PURCHASE**
Address:	309 East Paces Ferry Rd., N.E.
City/State/Zip/Postal Code:	Atlanta, GA 30305-2377
Country:	U.S.A.
800 Telephone #:	(800) 551-6015
Local Telephone #:	(404) 237-4016
Alternate Telephone #:	
Fax #:	(404) 240-6540
E-Mail:	billwilson@aaronfranchise.com
Internet Address:	www.aaronsfranchise.com
# Franchised Units:	136
# Company-Owned Units:	199
# Total Units:	335
Company Contact:	Mr. Todd Evans
Contact Title/Position:	VP Franchise Development
Contact Salutation:	Mr. Evans
President:	Mr. R. Charles Loudermilk, Sr.
President Title:	Chairman/Chief Executive Officer
President Salutation:	Mr. Loudermilk
Industy Category (of 54):	37/Rental Services
IFA Member:	International Franchise Association
CFA Member:	

Key Features

☙ Number of Active North American Franchisors	~ 2,150
% US	~85%
% Canadian	~15%
☙ Data Fields (See Above)	23
☙ Industry Categories	45
☙ % With Toll-Free Telephone Numbers	67%
☙ % With Fax Numbers	97%
☙ % With Name of Preferred Contact	99%
☙ % With Name of President	97%
☙ % With Number of Total Operating Units	95%
☙ Guaranteed Accuracy - $.50 Rebate/Returned Bad Address	
☙ Converted to Any Popular Data Base or Contact Management Program	
☙ Initial Front-End Cost	$550
☙ Quarterly Up-Dates	$75
☙ Mailing Labels Only - One-Time Use	$350

For More Information, Please Contact
Source Book Publications
1814 Franklin Street, Suite 820, Oakland, California 94612
(800) 841-0873 ❖ (510) 839-5471 ❖ FAX (510) 839-2104

Business: financial services

ACE — AMERICA'S CASH EXPRESS

1231 Greenway Dr., # 800
Irving, TX 75038
Tel: (800) 713-3338 (972) 550-5000
Fax: (972) 582-1406
E-Mail: rpryor@acecashexpress.com
Internet Address: www.acecashexpress.com
Contact: Mr. Richard Pryor, Manager of Franchise Development

Description: Cash in with the leader in retail financial services! ACE is a 30-year-old publicly-traded company operating and franchising over 900+ locations across 29 states. ACE offers customers a number of financial services, including check cashing, bill payments, money orders, wire transfers, short-term loans or cash advances, prepaid telecommunication products and other related services.

# Franchised Units:	120 Units
# Company-Owned Units:	<u>791</u> Units
Total # Units:	911 Units
Founded In:	1968
1st Franchised In:	1996
Average Total Investment:	77.5-186.1K
Franchise Fee:	15/30K
On-Going Royalty:	5%/$850 Min
Advertising Fee:	3%
Financial Assistance:	Yes(I)
Site Selection Assistance:	Yes
Lease Negotiation Assistance:	NA
Contract Terms (Init./Renew):	10/5

Initial Training Provided: 10 Days Corporate Office (excludes travel and lodging expenses).

We do not furnish or authorize our salespersons to furnish any oral or written information concerning the actual, average or projected *sales* of your business or the actual, average or projected *costs* of doing business *except* as hereunder described.

We have instructed all of our employees that they are not permitted to make any claims of sales or costs *except* as hereunder described and, we will not be bound by any allegations of unauthorized representations as to sales or costs except as set forth herein.

The following results are averages of the 515 company-owned stores that have been opened for a period of 24 months or longer as of June 30, 1998 and for a period of 12 months or longer as of June 30, 1997. These results are actual store level performance used in our Annual Reports, and we believe represent a true picture of a mature store.

All Ace Cash Express franchise stores opened for the full calendar year of 1997 had average sales of approximately $338,000. This number was reported by 22 franchise stores with approximately 77% of all reporting Ace Cash Express franchise stores below these results and approximately 23% of the reporting franchise stores surpassing these results. Since the profit of a store is dependent on various factors, we highly recommend that prospective franchisees make their own independent investigation to determine whether or not the franchise may be profitable, and consult with advisors prior to executing the Franchise Agreement.

A new franchisee's individual financial results are likely to differ from the above stated results. The results during the first 12 to 24 months of operation will vary greatly depending on owner involvement, advertising, location, size of market, awareness in market and other factors. We feel you should be prepared to suffer negative cash flow for a minimum of 6 months.

The following are averages of store revenue, and expenses of all company-owned Ace Cash Express stores opened for a period of 24 months or longer as of June 30, 1998 and for a period of 12 months or longer as of June 30, 1997. We have provided a 2 year comparison of these stores for you to evaluate. We will provide you with substantiation of the averages described below upon your reasonable request. The revenue numbers do not include revenues from any Ace Cash Express Kiosk store.

Ace Cash Express Same Store Sales

	Fiscal Year		Average per Store		% of Revenue	
	1997 Actual	1998 Actual	1997	1998	1997	1998
Check Fees[1]	$49,897,265	$51,979,850	$96,888	$100,932	65.1%	63.5%
Loan Fees	5,327,231	8,304,618	10,344	16,125	7.0%	10.1%
Tax Check Fees	7,549,703	7,313,739	14,660	14,201	9.9%	8.9%
Filling Fees[2]	358,756	259,362	697	504	0.5%	0.3%
Money Orders	2,585,969	2,603,512	5,021	5,055	3.4%	3.2%
New Customers[3]	1,866,700	1,837,834	3,625	3,569	2.4%	2.2%
Money Transfer	3,359,510	3,035,190	6,523	5,894	4.4%	3.7%
Other	5,645,720	6,519,284	10,963	12,659	7.4%	8.0%
Total Revenue	76,590,854	81,853,389	148,720	158,939	100.0%	100.0%
Salaries & Benefits	22,105,488	22,632,678	42,923	43,947	28.9%	27.7%
Rent	9,010,586	9,252,038	17,496	17,965	11.8%	11.3%
Other Occupancy	3,360,337	3,280,906	6,525	6,371	4.4%	4.0%
Armored & Security	3,049,323	3,329,412	5,921	6,465	4.0%	4.1%
Returns, Net of Collections	4,670,838	4,719,659	9,070	9,164	6.1%	5.8%
Cash Shorts	1,624,078	1,517,656	3,154	2,947	2.1%	1.9%
Other	5,194,214	5,457,370	10,086	10,597	6.8%	6.7%
Interest	456,668	794,470	887	1,543	0.6%	1.0%
Total Expenses	49,471,532	50,984,189	96,061	98,998	64.6%	62.3%
Center Contribution to Profit	27,119,322	30,869,200	52,659	59,940	35.4%	37.7%
Average Center Count	515	515				

Note 1: Tax Check Fees — cashing of tax refunds.
Note 2: Filing Fees — Electronic tax return filing.
Note 3: New Customers — The Company charges a one time fee for new check cashing customers to cover the costs of initial set up in the Ace customer data base and identification verification.

UNITED CHECK CASHING

325 Chestnut St., # 1005
Philadelphia, PA 19106
Tel: (800) 626-0787 (215) 238-0300
Fax: (215) 238-9056
E-Mail: UnitedCC12@aol.com
Internet Address: www.unitedcheckcashing.com
Contact: Mr. Seth N. Schonberg, Development Director

Description: UNITED CHECK CASHING is the convenience financial center of the new millennium. Our friendly centers offer more than just check cashing. We are the nation's one-stop center for electronic bill payment, money orders, Western Union, faxes, copies, notary, tax preparation and much, much more!

# Franchised Units:	76 Units
# Company-Owned Units:	3 Units
Total # Units:	79 Units
Founded In:	1977
1st Franchised In:	1992
Average Total Investment:	156.8K
Franchise Fee:	21.5K
On-Going Royalty:	.2% Volume
Advertising Fee:	10%/Royal.
Financial Assistance:	Yes(I)
Site Selection Assistance:	Yes
Lease Negotiation Assistance:	Yes
Contract Terms (Init./Renew):	15/15

Initial Training Provided: 1 Week Corporate Headquarters; 1 Week+ in Open Store; 1 Week+ Store Opening.

Exhibit 5 of this offering circular contains earnings information based upon the actual operating history of all System franchisees operating United Check Cashing Centers for the full 12 months of calendar year 1998 and a projection of operating expenses and projected profits for hypothetical United Check Cashing Centers cashing $4,000,000, $7,000,000, $10,000,000, $15,000,000 and $20,000,000 in checks annually.

These projections were based upon various factors as described in Exhibit 5, but were not prepared in accordance with the statement on Standards of Accountant's Services on Prospective Financial Information.

Actual results will vary from franchise to franchise and United cannot estimate the results of any particular franchise. A new franchisee's financial results are likely to differ from the results stated in the earnings claim.

SUBSTANTIATION OF THE DATA USED IN PREPARING THIS EARNINGS CLAIM WILL BE MADE AVAILABLE TO PROSPECTIVE FRANCHISEES ON REASONABLE REQUEST.

Disclosure of Actual and Projected Sales Together with Statement of Bases and Assumptions

Statement of Bases and Assumptions

The income information reflected in the chart below is based upon actual operating history of the 62 United Check Cashing Centers operating for the full 12 months of calendar year 1998. Below is a breakdown of the total face amount of checks cashed by these centers during calendar year 1998. These figures do not reflect the fee actually derived by the respective franchisees for performing check cashing services and do not include revenue derived from providing any other goods or services.

Actual Volumes of Checks Cashed for Franchised Centers in Operation During Full 12 Months of Calendar Year 1998

Checks Cashed (Dollars)	Number of Centers	Percentage of Total
3,000,000	2	3.23%
4,000,000	1	1.61%
5,000,000	5	8.06%
6,000,000	4	6.45%
7,000,000	7	11.29%
8,000,000	8	12.90%
9,000,000	7	11.29%

Checks Cashed (Dollars)	Number of Centers	Percentage of Total
10,000,000	7	11.29%
11,000,000	6	9.68%
12,000,000	5	8.06%
13,000,000	1	1.61%
14,000,000	1	1.61%
15,000,000	2	3.23%
16,000,000	2	3.23%
20,000,000	2	3.23%
22,000,000	2	3.23%
Total	62	100.00%

Estimated Expenses and Return Based on Sales

The chart on the following page reflects a projection of operating expenses and projected profits for a typical United Check Cashing Center cashing $4,000,000, $7,000,000, $10,000,000, $15,000,000, and $20,000,000 in checks annually. These figures are based upon information obtained from System franchisees in response to a survey performed by United and other factors as described in the notes below the cart. Approximately 20% to 30% of System franchisees responded to this survey. Expense figures of franchised centers vary by franchise and are not included here. Net Profit, as reflected in the chart, assume that the franchisee's

check cashing fee equal 1.75% and 2% of the face value of the checks.

The Net Profit figures in the chart do not provide for debt service and assume that the franchisee will not finance any part of the initial investment. The figures in the chart also do not reflect depreciation expense or license and compliance fees which may be imposed by the state and/or municipality in which the Franchised Business is located.

THE SALES, EXPENSES AND PROFIT FIGURES CONTAINED IN THE FOLLOWING CHART ARE ONLY ESTIMATES AND SHOULD NOT BE CONSIDERED AS THE SALES, EXPENSES OR PROFITS THAT WILL BE REALIZED BY ANY PARTICULAR FRANCHISEE. UNITED DOES NOT REPRESENT THAT ANY FRANCHISEE CAN EXPECT TO ATTAIN THESE SALES, EXPENSES OR PROFIT LEVELS. IF YOU RELY ON THESE FIGURES, YOU MUST ACCEPT THE RISK OF NOT DOING AS WELL

SUBSTANTIATION OF THE DATA USED IN PREPARING THIS EARNINGS CLAIM WILL BE MADE AVAILABLE TO PROSPECTIVE FRANCHISEES ON REASONABLE REQUEST.

Estimated Expenses and Return Based on Sales

Volume of Checks Cashed	$4,000,000	$7,000,000	$10,000,000	$15,000,000	$20,000,000
Check Fee Income @ 1.75%[1]	$70,000	$122,500	$175,000	$262,500	$350,000
Other Income[2]	16,800	29,400	42,000	63,000	84,000
Total income	$86,800	$151,900	$217,000	$325,500	$434,000
Expenses					
Rent[3]	$21,600	$21,600	$21,600	$21,600	$21,600
Office Supplies[3]	1,800	2,100	2,400	2,700	3,000
Maintenance and Repairs[3]	1,000	1,000	1,000	1,000	1,000
Phone[4]	2,796	3,396	3,696	3,696	3,696
Utilities[3]	3,840	3,840	3,840	3,840	3,840
Film Expense[3]	1,070	1,070	1,070	1,070	1,070
Delivery[5]	1,196	2,392	2,392	3,588	3,588
Legal and Accounting[6]	2,500	2,500	2,500	2,500	2,500
Advertising[7]	800	1,400	2,000	3,000	4,000
Payroll[8]	N/A	16,640	41,640	48,296	48,296
Payroll Taxes[8]	N/A	1,830	4,580	5,313	5,313

Insurance[9]	2,792	2,792	2,792	2,792	2,792
Bank Service[3]	2,800	4,900	7,000	10,500	14,000
Security[10]	700	700	700	700	700
Royalty @ 0.2%	8,000	14,000	20,000	30,000	40,000
Bad Check Expense @ 0.0005%[11]	2,000	3,500	5,000	7,500	10,000
Total Expenses	$52,894	$83,660	$122,210	$148,095	$165,395
Net Profit @ 1.75%	$33,906	$68,240	$94,790	$177,405	$268,605
Net Profit @ 2%	$43,906	$85,740	$119,790	$214,905	$318,505

Notes to Estimated Expenses and Return Based on Sales

Note 1. The check fee income is given on an average of 1.75%, however, many United Check Cashing Centers obtain rates that are 2% or higher, and a few are lower than 1.75%. Fees for check cashing will vary based on state regulations and market conditions. (See summary of state check cashing regulations attached as Exhibit 10 of this offering circular.)

Note 2. Other Income represents commissions received from the sale of money orders, money transfers, bill payments collection, lottery services, photocopying, fax, notary, and film developing services. It also includes income derived from the sale of I.D. cards, stamps, envelopes, cigarettes, beepers and miscellaneous items and services. The figures in the chart are based on randomly selected survey results of 15 United Check Cashing Center franchisees. United used the actual operating results of these 15 franchised Centers to calculate their "Other Income" as an actual percentage of "Total Income." United then applied the average of these percentages (19.354483%) to the Total Income figures reflected in the chart.

Note 3. The figures in the chart represent average expense figures based upon survey results.

Note 4. The figures in the chart are based on actual operating expenses of United's franchisees and affiliate-owned United Check Cashing Centers maintaining seven telephone lines.

Note 5. Delivery expense is based upon an average cost of $23 per delivery. The number of deliveries you will need will depend upon a variety of factors including the dollar amounts of checks cashed and money orders sold.

Note 6. Legal and Accounting expenses were based upon survey results.

Note 7. Advertising expense is calculated at 10% of a franchisee's annual Royalty Fee, which is consistent with United's standard form of franchise agreement through March 30, 1999. United revised its standard form of franchise agreement on March 31, 1999. Under the revised franchise agreement, United can require you to spend 3% of your Gross Receipts on local advertising, or contribute up to that amount to a group advertising cooperative. See Items 6 and 11 of this offering circular for more information about required advertising expenses and contributions. United also has the right to require you to contribute up to $1,000 per year to a National Advertising fund, which contribution is not reflected in the chart.

Note 8. Payroll and Payroll Expenses assume that the franchisee will act as a full time owner/operator, and does not include a salary for the owner. The payroll figure at the $4,000,000 volume assumes that the franchisee will work full time and will require no other employees. The $7,000,000 volume allows for an additional 40 hours at $8.00 per hour; the $10,000,000 volume includes a manager's salary of $25,000 and an additional 40 hours at $8.00; the $15,000,000 volume allows for a manager and 56 hours at $8.00; and the $20,000,000 volume allows for a manager's salary and 56 hours at $8.00 per hour.

Note 9. Insurance expense includes coverage for property, liability, worker's compensation and fidelity. The figures in the chart are based on the insurance premiums paid by affiliated-owned United Check Cashing Centers.

Note 10. Security expense represents the cost of surveillance monitoring services.

Note 11. Bad Check Expense is based upon actual operating results of affiliate-owned United Check Cashing Centers.

Business: advertising & promotion

SUPER COUPS
180 Bodwell St.
Avon, MA 02322
Tel: (800) 626-2620 (508) 580-4340
Fax: (508) 588-3347
E-Mail: gliset@supercoups.com
Internet Address: www.supercoups.com
Contact: Mr. Glen R. Liset, VP Sales & Marketing

Description: SUPER COUPS is one of the top co-op direct mail companies in America. We specialize in developing an integrated marketing solution for local and regional businesses, featuring co-op coupon mailings, co-op TV and internet advertising. We are known for our personalized training, outstanding field support and state-of-the-art production facilities.

# Franchised Units:	434 Units
# Company-Owned Units:	4 Units
Total # Units:	438 Units
Founded In:	1984
1st Franchised In:	1983
Average Total Investment:	41K
Franchise Fee:	32K
On-Going Royalty:	$148/Mailing
Advertising Fee:	$500/Yr.
Financial Assistance: Yes(I) (D – direct, or I – indirect)	
Site Selection Assistance:	No
Lease Negotiation Assistance:	No
Contract Terms (Init./Renew):	10/10
Initial Training Provided: 1 Week Headquarters, Avon, MA; 1 Week In Field.	

The following information reflects experiences of our Franchisees while Mailhouse was the franchisor. MailCoups continues to operate the Franchise business in substantially the same manner as Mailhouse had done, according to the terms of our franchise agreements.

Mailhouse had 69 franchisees as of January 1, 1998. Of these 69 franchisees, 58 had been in the Franchise system for at least 12 months, and 11 were new franchisees scheduled to begin mailing in 1998. The 58 franchisees in the system for at least 12 months each completed mailings in the last 12 months, and each met his or her mailing requirements for 1997.

Among these 58 franchisees, the number of envelopes mailed ranged from 200,000 to 9,747,500. Mailhouse did not track these franchisees specific sales, income or profits, and neither do we. To prepare this claim, we asked all franchisees' to provide us with limit sales figures for 1997. By the time this claim was prepared in December 1998, 42 out of the 58 franchisees provided us with this information. To avoid distorted results, the chart omits information reported by one franchisee who reported 9,747,500 mailings and Gross Sales of $6,311,399.

The chart sets out information about the number of mailings, Gross Sales and Net Sales and manufacturing costs of the reporting franchisees. The chart organizes the Franchisees roughly into thirds, distinguishing the top, middle and bottom thirds according to Gross Sales. For each group, we have calculated their ranges of Gross Sales and Average Production Costs paid to Mailhouse and charges Mailhouse collected from Franchisees under their

Franchise Agreements: Royalty Fees, Manufacturing Charges, Postage and Tracking Fees.

The franchisees listed represent 70.68% of the 58 franchisees in the system for at least 12 months. "Gross Sales" means the sales a franchisee made before any costs or expenses were deducted. "Net Sales" means the sales a franchisee made after deducting production costs paid to Mailhouse. We make no representation concerning the costs (other than production costs paid to Mailhouse), income or profits of any franchisee. While franchisees carry varying amounts of receivables, receivables are not distinguished for purposes of this sample.

CAUTION: A new Franchisee's individual financial results are likely to differ from the result stated in the earnings claim.

41 Reporting Franchisees (of 58)

	Average Gross Sales in Dollars	Range of Gross Sales in Dollars	Average Production Costs Paid to Mailhouse	Average Net Sales in Dollars	Range of Net Sales in Dollars	Average Number of Envelopes Mailed	Range of Envelopes Mailed
Top 13	$540,459.21	$984,021.00–296,000.00	$329,064.39	$211,394.82	$569,130.00–97,655.00	1,001,635	2,357,500–300,000
Middle 15	$235,177.93	$286,099.00–187,900.00	$153,226.13	$81,951.70	$122,946.11–43,580.00	451,083	1,378,750–260,000
Bottom 13	$119,789.37	$161,137–66,278	$88,442.93	$31,346.43	$69,669.00–4,987.28	251,538	360,000–240,000
Overall	$295,387.82	$984,021–66,278	$188,438.75	$106,949.07	$569,130.00–4,987.28	562,378	2,357,500–240,000

We will substantiate the data used in preparing this earnings claim on reasonable demand by a prospective franchisee. Be advised, however, that this information was not prepared by a statistician or an accountant. The figures here may be based on records and financial statements that have not been compiled under generally accepted accounting principles. The underlying data may or may not be audited.

Some franchisees experienced the sales and mailings described in this claim. There is no assurance that any other franchisee will do as well. If you rely on these figures, you accept the risk that you may not do as well. Any actual or projected sales and mailings should not be considered as the actual or

probable sales that will be realized by any franchisee. We do not represent that any franchisee can expect to attain such sales.

We urge you to consult with appropriate financial, business and legal advisors in connection with using the information in this earnings claim. If you become a Super Coups franchisee, your results are likely to differ from the figures presented in this claim.

We do not authorize our salespersons to furnish any oral or written information concerning the actual or potential sales, costs, income or profits of a franchised business beyond those contained in this earnings claim.

CAUTION: THE SALES AND MAILING FIGURES STATED ABOVE ARE THE RESULTS OF SOME FRANCHISEES AND SHOULD NOT BE CONSIDERED AS THE ACTUAL OR POTENTIAL SALES OR MAILINGS THAT ARE REALIZED BY OTHER FRANCHISEES OR THAT MAY BE REALIZED BY YOU. WE DO NOT REPRESENT THAT YOU CAN EXPECT TO ATTAIN THESE SALES OR MAILINGS.

VAL-PAK DIRECT MARKETING

8605 Largo Lakes Dr.
Largo, FL 33773
Tel: (800) 237-6266 (727) 393-1270
Fax: (727) 392-0049
E-Mail: david_elmer@valpak.com
Internet Address: www.valpak.com
Contact: Mr. David Elmer, Director, Franchise Sales

Description: North America's oldest and largest local co-operative direct mail advertising franchisor, with distribution of over 490 million coupon envelopes annually to over 53 million unduplicated homes and businesses. Subsidiary of Cox Enterprises, Inc. VAL-PAK OF CANADA is the Canadian franchisor.

# Franchised Units:	240 Units
# Company-Owned Units:	<u>6</u> Units
Total # Units:	246 Units
Founded In:	1968
1st Franchised In:	1989
Average Total Investment:	25-85K
Franchise Fee:	7K
On-Going Royalty:	0%
Advertising Fee:	0%
Financial Assistance:Yes(I) (D – direct, or I – indirect)	
Site Selection Assistance:	N/A
Lease Negotiation Assistance:	N/A
Contract Terms (Init./Renew):	10/5

Initial Training Provided:5 Days Home Study with Trainer; 2 Weeks Corporate Headquarters; On-Going, On- and Off-Site

The following is certain information which you may find useful in formulating your own estimates of the potential cash flow of a VAL-PAK franchise. Many of the key items of information which are essential in preparing a meaningful cash flow analysis are not provided because they vary so significantly among geographic markets, and because many of the expense items to be considered are largely within your control (such as office rent, car expenses, etc.). Accordingly, the selected information set forth below is provided to you with the understanding that you will do your own research to develop data with which to perform your analysis. Val-Pak suggests that you contact a number of VAL-PAK franchisees to discuss the missing items of information and to compare their experiences with the information which is provided below. In talking to franchisees about selling prices of coupons, be sure to distinguish between their asking price (also referred to as their "rate card") and their actual selling price for advertising, and to ask what kind of discounts they provide for volume purchases or annual contracts with advertisers.

You should also keep in mind that the performance of franchisees varies dramatically among markets for a variety of reasons, including differences in sales and management abilities, demographics, the business environment in a particular market, the history of a particular franchise and the strength of competing advertisers in a given market. Therefore, you cannot assume that the information provided to you by a VAL-PAK franchisee is necessarily relevant to your market. Of course, if you are buying an existing Val-Pak franchise, you should ask for the seller's historical financial information, although you should be aware that Val-Pak does not review franchisees' financial statements and bears no responsibility for the accuracy of same. Accordingly, you should carefully review any financial information received from a selling franchisee with your professional financial advisors.

You should also research the prices charged by competing advertisers in your prospective market to determine the degree of price competition you will face. Even if a selling franchisee has historically sold VAL-PAK advertising at above average prices in his or her market, it is not safe to assume that you will be able to charge those same prices in the future, especially if major competitors are providing significant price competition.

Finally, keep in mind that the information below does not take into account many of the variables which can affect your cash flow. It is intended merely as a starting place for your analysis. Reviewing this limited amount of information cannot substitute for thorough research on your part and a careful evaluation of this franchise opportunity with professional, financial and legal advisors. Subject to the foregoing, you may wish to consider the following items:

1. For purposes of preparing cash flow projections, you may find it helpful to assume that you will make the minimum required Mailings per year, taking into account that the minimum requirements may be phased in (as described in Item 12). This suggestion does not constitute any assurance that you will meet the minimum performance requirements.

2. The average number of advertising inserts sold by franchisees per mailing (the "piece count") in fiscal year ending December 26, 1998 was 23. 11 pieces per mailing. This figure is somewhat skewed by the fact that certain franchisees with many years of experience have piece counts significantly higher than the average, while franchisees opening new markets are likely to have piece counts below the average. Again, if you are purchasing an established franchise, your seller can provide you with important historical information on piece counts. If you are purchasing a franchise in an inactive market, you will need to contact relatively new VAL-PAK franchisees in similar markets, and make an honest assessment of your own sales ability and that of your planned sales staff. Keep in mind that the average piece count does not represent the minimum number that you should expect to sell. Typically, franchisees who meet or exceed this average generally have a highly motivated and professional sales staff, and have developed client relationships over a number of years.

3. Prices charged by franchisees to advertisers for certain popular products range from $210 to $500 per 10,000 households mailed. Val-Pak does not have access to any average figures for the franchise network as a whole, and any such average could be misleading given the wide disparity of pricing among different markets. Based on the experience of Val-Pak's affiliate, Val-Pak Franchise Operations, Inc., and based on informal discussions with franchisees, Val-Pak believes that this range represents typical pricing of certain popular products, but is aware that many sales occur outside of this range as well. This does not constitute any representation that you can obtain such prices in your market. The figures for your market will depend on a variety of factors, including among others, your product mix, the size and loyalty of the existing customer base, if any, pricing strategies of local competitors, local economic conditions, and your own sales and sales management abilities.

4. Val-Pak believes that a well-managed VAL-PAK franchise should be able to collect at least 40% of all receivables for a given Mailing by the Final Order date for such Mailing (i.e., 10 days before the scheduled Mailing date), and should be able to collect additional increments of 5% by the Mailing date, 30% within 30 days after the Mailing, 15% within 60 days, and 8% within 90 days after the Mailing. (This assumes a maximum bad debt of only 2%, which is discussed in paragraph 5 below.) Val-Pak believes that some franchisees have been successful in achieving these collection goals, but has no way of knowing whether VAL-PAK franchisees as a group achieve these targets. Collection rates will vary from market to market, especially where a selling franchisee has allowed clients to pay slowly in the past, or where local economic conditions make slow payment more prevalent.

5. The figure of 2% for bad debt used in paragraph 4 is a goal rather than an average, but Val-Pak believes that it represents a reasonable goal based on the experience of Val-Pak Franchise Operations, Inc. and on figures communicated to Val-Pak informally by some of its franchisees. Val-Pak has seen some instances where a particular franchisee had a much higher bad debt ratio, and where bad debt has been a significant factor in the failure of a franchise. Val-Pak has no reliable information on what the average bad debt percentage is among Val-Pak franchisees as a whole.

6. The percentage of sales accounted for by you as the franchisee rather than by a sales representative is something that is entirely within your control, and you should make the appropriate assumptions with regard to this figure.

7. To the extent that you use commissioned sales representatives, you are free to pay any amount of commission that you desire. Based on informal discussions with franchisees, Val-Pak believes that a commission rate in the range of 18% is typical among its franchisees. Since this figure is within your control, you should make appropriate adjustments. If you are purchasing an existing VAL-PAK franchise, you should obtain information from the seller as to their commission structure, and you should ask whether there is any additional compensation to sales representatives, such as incentive bonuses.

8. You should include in your analysis all applicable taxes, including those required under federal, state and local law. You should consult with your professional advisors regarding applicable taxes.

9. The fixed costs of production for VAL-PAK Envelopes for a Mailing to 10,000 homes (1 NTA) are about $1,660 (including postage); however, franchisees will receive production credits (national sales credits) if Val-Pak has sold and mailed national advertising inserts into your Territory for the same Mailing. In fiscal year ending December 26, 1998, franchisees received an average of $189 per NTA per Mailing in production credits.

10. The variable costs of production for each advertising insert to be included in VALPAK Envelopes depends on a number of factors, including the print run quantity and the advertising product sold (2-color v. 4-color, size, special graphics, etc.) and the extent to which the inserts are the same in each NTA mailed. For a Mailing of LC2O advertising inserts, one of the most popular products, the variable costs would likely range from $122 to $145 per 10,000, depending on the total print run quantity. For a Mailing of a 4-color premium product, the variable costs would likely range from $150 to $215 depending on the total print run quantity. Your own production costs may differ from those set forth above because of the number of variables which affect pricing. Val-Pak's prices are subject to change at any time, and should be expected to increase over time, especially in view of the volatility in paper costs. The production costs are also based on a certain product mix which may differ significantly from the product mix which your clients desire. If you have questions regarding production costs for specific product mixes, based on the size of your Territory and your assumptions regarding numbers of NTAs mailed and piece counts, you may request further information by way of Supplemental Earnings Claim, as explained below.

11. Your analysis of a VAL-PAK franchise should include estimates of expenses for all applicable items, including office rent, office staff salaries, your own salary, phone/fax charges, postage and courier charges, travel, auto expense, insurance, advertising expenses, Dealer Association fees and the costs of marketing materials. All of these items are based largely on factors within your control, for which you can obtain information through your own research. Since these amounts are to a great degree a matter of personal preference, Val-Pak has included no estimates for these items, and you should make appropriate assumptions. Please see Items 6 and 7 for a description of certain expense

items which you are likely to incur in operating a VAL-PAK franchise. However, you should also be aware that the expense items listed above and those listed in Items 6 and 7, taken together, are by no means exhaustive. There are likely to be additional expenses that Val-Pak has not listed, some of which may be unique to your market or situation.

Val-Pak will substantiate the information above on request.

If you would like to obtain information which is more specific to the Territory which you are considering purchasing, you may request such information from Val-Pak. If Val-Pak is able to provide additional information specific to your Territory, it will do so in the form of a Supplemental Earnings Claim. PLEASE BE ADVISED THAT NO ONE OTHER THAN AN OFFICER OF VAL-PAK IS AUTHORIZED TO PROVIDE A SUPPLEMENTAL EARNINGS CLAIM OR

TO DISCUSS THE INFORMATION CONTAINED ABOVE. ACCORDINGLY, EXCEPT FOR A SUPPLEMENTAL EARNINGS CLAIM PROVIDED TO YOU BY AN OFFICER OF THE CORPORATION, WITH A RECEIPT FOR SAME EXECUTED BY YOU AND RETURNED TO VAL-PAK, YOU SHOULD DISREGARD ANY INFORMATION, ORAL OR WRITTEN, THAT IS PROVIDED TO YOU BY ANY PERSON, WHETHER EMPLOYED BY VAL-PAK OR OTHERWISE, WHICH CONFLICTS WITH OR SUPPLEMENTS THE INFORMATION SET FORTH ABOVE.

THE FIGURES PROVIDED IN THIS ITEM 19 SHOULD NOT BE CONSIDERED AS THE ACTUAL OR PROBABLE RESULTS THAT YOU WILL OR CAN REALIZE. THE EXPERIENCE OF AN INDIVIDUAL FRANCHISEE IS LIKELY TO DIFFER FROM THE INFORMATION SET FORTH ABOVE.

Business: telecommunications/ miscellaneous

THE ALTERNATIVE BOARD TAB®

ALTERNATIVE BOARD, THE (TAB)
225 E. 16th Ave., Penthouse
Denver, CO 80203-1622
Tel: (800) 219-7718 (303) 839-1200
Fax: (800) 420-7055
E-Mail: info@TheAlternativeBoard.com
Internet Address: www.TheAlternativeBoard.com
Contact: Ms. Tamyra A. Wallace, Dir. Facilitator Development

Description: TAB Facilitators develop and facilitate small peer advisory groups of presidents, CEOs, and business owners who meet once a month. Each business owner discusses challenges or opportunities he or she is having in his or her business. Solutions and strategies are provided by the facilitator and other group members. Senior level executive and/or business consulting experience required.

# Franchised Units:	36 Units
# Company-Owned Units:	14 Units
Total # Units:	50 Units
Founded In:	1990
1st Franchised In:	1996
Average Total Investment:	32.4-51.7K
Franchise Fee:	34.9K
On-Going Royalty:	10%
Advertising Fee:	1%
Financial Assistance:No (D – direct, or I – indirect)	
Site Selection Assistance:	N/A
Lease Negotiation Assistance:	N/A
Contract Terms (Init./Renew):	10/10
Initial Training Provided:4 Days Denver, CO; 3 Weeks Franchisee's Territory Field Support Training.	

Except as provided in this Item 19, we do not furnish or authorize our sales persons to furnish any oral or written information concerning the actual or potential sales, costs, income or profits of the Business. The chart listed below is not intended to project any results from any particular franchise. It is meant solely for the purpose of helping you do your own estimate of face-to-face monthly hours which may be spent and TAB Group Membership Dues which may be received, based upon whatever number of TAB Group Members you decide to use as a goal. We recommend that you contact our franchisees and ask their results before doing any personal estimates. Actual results may vary from Business to Business and we cannot estimate the results of any particular franchise.

As of December 31, 1998, approximately 67.8% of TAB Group Members were Four Hour Members and approximately 32.2% were Three Hour Members (See Item 6, footnote 2, for a definition of these Member types).

TAB Members (1)	4-Hour TAB Groups	4-Hour TAB Members (2)	3-Hour TAB Groups	3-Hour TAB Members (2)	Estimated Face To Face Monthly Hours (3)	Estimated Monthly Membership Dues (4)
10	1	7	1	3	15	$4,350
18	1	12	1	6	21	$7,710
28	2	19	1	9	33	$12,060
38	3	26	2	12	48	$16,410
48	3	33	2	15	56	$20,760

THERE IS NO GUARANTEE THAT A FRANCHISEE'S RESULTS WILL BE THE SAME AS WHAT IS SET FORTH IN THE CHART. THE ESTIMATED MONTHLY MEMBERSHIP DUES IN THE ABOVE CHART ARE ONLY TO BE USED FOR YOUR CALCULATIONS BASED UPON WHATEVER ASSUMPTIONS OF MEMBERSHIP YOU MAKE AFTER DOING YOUR OWN DUE DILIGENCE BY CONTACTING CURRENT FRANCHISEES. INFORMATION IN THE CHART SHOULD NOT BE CONSIDERED A PREDICTION BY US OF YOUR EARNING ABILITY.

A Summary of Factual Basis for Data

The chart above states the monthly revenues that may be derived by a franchisee from TAB Group Membership Dues based on a specified number of TAB Group Members (see the first column) paying the currently suggested monthly dues of $295 per month for Three Hour Members and $495 per month for Four Hour Members. The suggested monthly dues which we currently recommend vary with the geographic area. They range from $295 to $350 per month for Three Hour Members, who also receive a one hour quarterly Private Session, and $495 to $550 per month for Four Hour Members, who also receive a one-hour monthly Private Session with their Facilitator in addition to their monthly TAB Group Meeting. We have only included the minimum monthly dues of $295 for Three Hour Members and $495 for Four Hour Members in the chart above, however.

The chart also does not include any revenues franchisees may earn from the currently suggested initiation fees to be collected from new TAB Group Members, or from providing additional services such as consulting or selling business educational products to TAB Group Members and those met through marketing for TAB Group Members. We believe that some franchisees earn more revenue from providing consulting and other income opportunities that evolve from TAB Group Members and from clients met through marketing for TAB Group Members, than they earn from Membership Dues. The differences in revenue from such other opportunities is due to several factors, including the desire to provide such other services and products, the range in rates that franchisees may charge for various kinds of additional consulting services and the range in the amount of consulting services that franchisees want to provide. We do not make any suggestions regarding rates for additional consulting work.

TAB Group Members customarily pay Membership Dues in advance. Data used to compile the above will be made available to you on your reasonable request at TAB's offices.

Footnotes — Significant assumptions on which the information is based.

1. In presenting this data, we do not estimate the length of time it will take for any particular franchisee to sign up Members for TAB Groups. Your ability to sell TAB Group Memberships is a major factor in determining your profitability and is dependent on many factors including; sales ability and efforts, your support staff, competition within your market area, the type and reputation of business consulting that you are offering and other factors.

2. We recommend that TAB Groups consist of no more than 12 Members each, and that no TAB Group begins monthly meetings until the group has a minimum of four Members. Meetings are held once a month for each TAB Group established.

3. Face-to-face estimated hours consist of hours spent in TAB Group Meetings and in Private Sessions with Members.

4. Recommended dues are based on our experience. Existing TAB Group Members have accepted and paid dues in these amounts. You may charge a lesser or greater amount for dues.

MISTER MONEY — USA
238 Walnut St.
Fort Collins, CO 80524
Tel: (800) 827-7296 (970) 493-0574
Fax: (970) 490-2099
E-Mail: tim@mistermoney.com
Internet Address: www.mistermoney.com
Contact: Mr. Don Ettinger, Franchise Sales Director

Description: MISTER MONEY — USA franchises offer pawn loans, payday loans, check cashing, money orders, and other financial services. Franchisees operate full-service retail stores or loan only outlets. MISTER MONEY — USA stores are modern, customer friendly and located in solid blue collar areas.

# Franchised Units:	25 Units
# Company-Owned Units:	14 Units
Total # Units:	39 Units
Founded In:	1976
1st Franchised In:	1996
Average Total Investment:	65-200K
Franchise Fee:	21.5-24.5K
On-Going Royalty:	3-5%
Advertising Fee:	3%
Financial Assistance:Yes(D) (D – direct, or I – indirect)	
Site Selection Assistance:	Yes
Lease Negotiation Assistance:	Yes
Contract Terms (Init./Renew):	5/5
Initial Training Provided:10-14 Days Fort Collins, CO.	

Mister Money intends you to have a sense of the earnings potential in any given market of your choice. In this regard, Mister Money will assist you through an analytical process used in making market evaluations and construing pro forma financial statements useful in making informed decisions. Actual results vary from store to store and Mister Money cannot estimate the results of any particular franchise.

Mister Money has operating experience with regard to 26 franchised stores. Mister Money Financial Services, Inc. owns and operates 12 pawnshops doing business under the trade name Mister Money or The Mister.

In the following table, Mister Money provides financial data showing sales and loans outstanding for each of the stores owned by Mister Money

Financial Services, Inc. and the length of time the stores have been operated by Mister Money or its affiliates. Population data for each town in which Mister Money Financial Services, Inc. has a store is also provided. The basis of the earnings from these stores may not be the same as your store. A franchisee's results are dependent, in part, upon economic conditions, type of community where located, attitude and background of people who live in the marketing area of the franchise, interest rates permitted in the state or municipality where a store is located, ability to judge the fair market value of the pawned goods, amount of pawn loans made, required holding after a forfeiture, and percentage of redemptions versus forfeitures. Your results may vary from those of the Mister Money Financial Services, Inc. owned stores.

Loans Outstanding, Yearly Retail Sales, and Population as of December 31, 1998

Mister Money Financial Services, Inc., Stores	Year Operations Began	Current Loans Outstanding	1998 Sales[1]	U.S. City[2] Census Population
Ft. Collins, CO North	April, 1976	$174,727	$421,123	100,300
Ft. Collins, CO South	July, 1993	$331,527	$775,770	100,300
Colorado Springs, CO	July, 1988	$188,617	$379,190	311,900
Security, CO	November, 1988	$126,997	$169,080	14,000
Loveland, CO	February, 1989	$180,851	$277,610	43,800
Cheyenne, WY	August, 1987	$106,808	$204,474	53,000
Scottsbluff, NE	October, 1990	$73,227	$171,919	14,100
Casper, WY	August, 1991	$197,504	$362,715	47,400
Pueblo, CO North	June, 1992	$111,401	$235,666	101,600

Loan Only Mister Money Financial Services, Inc., Stores	Year Operations Began	Current Loans Outstanding	1998 Sales[1]	U.S. City[2] Census Population
Ft. Dodge, IA	August, 1994	$80,059	$120,801	25,900
Ames, IA	March, 1995	$59,628	N/A	47,400
Mason City, IA	March, 1995	$37,653	$57,855	29,500

1. The sales figures are for goods only. Interest earned on loans is not reflected.

2. Population figures are January 1, 1994, estimated by Market Statistics for places of 25,000 or more and other principal business centers; 1990 census figures or recent estimated by Rand McNally for other places. Source: Commercial Atlas and Marketing Guide, Rand McNally, 126th edition, 1995.

3. Converted from a loan only to full service mid-year.

At your request, Mister Money will prepare and deliver to you an estimate of your possible earnings for a particular location or circumstance from this offering circular. The earnings claim will be in writing and based upon a profile developed by Mister Money Financial Services, Inc. from operations of its stores and from Mister Money — USA, Inc. franchised stores.

A statement substantiating the data used in preparing any earnings claim will be made available to you upon reasonable request.

Child development/ education/products

COMPUTERTOTS/COMPUTER EXPLORERS
10132 Colvin Run Rd.
Great Falls, VA 22066
Tel: (800) 531-5053 (703) 759-1938
Fax: (703) 759-7411
E-Mail: sgould@computertots.com
Internet Address: www.computertots.com
Contact: Ms. Sandy Gould, Franchise Development Director

Description: A worldwide network of computer education services for children. Programs are offered through learning centers and outreach programs at private and public educational facilities. The program was established in 1984 and has grown to be one of the largest programs of it kind in the U.S. today. Programs currently operate in the U.S. and 9 other countries. International franchising has occurred through licensing partnerships; the company is actively seeking international candidates.

# Franchised Units:	207 Units
# Company-Owned Units:	2 Units
Total # Units:	209 Units
Founded In:	1984
1st Franchised In:	1988
Average Total Investment:	38-43.8K
Franchise Fee:	10-29.9K
On-Going Royalty:	8%/$350
Advertising Fee:	1%
Financial Assistance:No (D – direct, or I – indirect)	
Site Selection Assistance:	N/A
Lease Negotiation Assistance:	N/A
Contract Terms (Init./Renew):	10/10
Initial Training Provided:	7 Days Great Falls, VA.

Exhibit F contains historical financial information about our franchisees' annual gross sales. We will provide you with substantiation of the annual gross sales figures in Exhibit F on request.

Except as disclosed in Exhibit F, we do not furnish or authorize our salespersons to furnish any oral or written information on the actual or potential sales, costs, income or profits of a COMPUTERTOTS/COMPUTER EXPLORERS business. Actual results may vary from unit to unit, and we cannot estimate the results of any particular franchised business.

Exhibit F
Average Annual Gross Sales of Franchise Territories (1996–1998)

We had 123 franchise territories reporting gross sales for the full 12 months of 1998. One of those territories did not operate because of the franchisee's health difficulties. This exhibit describes the results achieved by the remaining 122 reporting franchise territories.

Of the 122 territories, 107 (87%) achieved annual gross sales at or above the quotas stated in their franchise agreements.

Of the 122 territories, 44 (36%) achieved annual gross sales at or above the average annual gross sales of $83,552 for all reporting territories in 1998.

The results achieved by franchise territories that did not report gross sales for the full 12 months in any year (such as franchise territories that started operations mid-year), and franchise territories that were transferred and assigned new franchise numbers, are not included in this exhibit.

Gross sales represent the actual revenues collected by franchise territories. While franchise territories carry varying amounts of receivables, receivables are not included in gross sales. Business expenses such as the following must be paid out of gross sales: salaries and benefits; commercial office rent (not required); continuing franchise fees (8%, subject to monthly minimums), and advertising and promotional contributions; equipment; office supplies and expenses; marketing materials and expenses; travel expenses; amortization; depreciation; and taxes.

The gross sales figures stated in this exhibit are substantiated by unaudited reports submitted to us by our franchisees. Relevant portions of those reports will be made available to you on reasonable request.

CAUTION: THE GROSS SALES FIGURES STATED IN THIS EXHIBIT SHOULD NOT BE CONSIDERED AS THE ACTUAL OR POTENTIAL GROSS SALES FIGURES THAT WILL BE REALIZED BY ANY PROSPECTIVE FRANCHISEE. WE DO NOT REPRESENT THAT YOU CAN EXPECT TO ATTAIN ANY OF THE GROSS SALES FIGURES INDICATED.

Average Annual Gross Sales of Franchise Territories (Territories Reporting for Full 12 Months in 1998)

	1998
Average for Whole Reporting System [1]	$83,552
Top Franchise Territory	$290,497
Average for: [2]	
Top 10% of Territories	$232,500
Top 25% of Territories	$172,167
Top 50% of Territories	$127,952
Top 75% of Territories	$101,704

1. 122 of 123 reporting territories are included in the average. One territory reported for the full 120 months in 1998, but did not operate because of the franchisee's health difficulties. That territory is not included in the average.
2. The percentage is of the total number of reporting territories (e.g., 122 reporting territories; the top 10%=10% of 122 or the top 12 reporting territories).

FASTRACKIDS INTERNATIONAL LTD.
6900 E. Belleview Ave.
Englewood, CO 80111
Tel: (888) 576-6888 (303) 224-0200
Fax: (303) 224-0222
E-Mail:
Internet Address: www.fastrackids.com

Contact: Mr. Kevin Krause, Director Franchise Development

Description: FASTRACKIDS ® is a remarkable new, technologically-advanced educational system designed to enrich the knowledge of young children. FASTRACKIDS (R) enrichment education

**"Enrichment Education
for Tomorrow's Leaders"**

# Franchised Units:	50 Units
# Company-Owned Units:	0 Units
Total # Units:	50 Units
Founded In:	1998
1st Franchised In:	1998
Average Total Investment:	8.7-34.4K
Franchise Fee:	5-15K
On-Going Royalty:	1.5%
Advertising Fee:	5%
Financial Assistance:Yes(B) (D – direct, or I – indirect)	
Site Selection Assistance:	Yes
Lease Negotiation Assistance:	No
Contract Terms (Init./Renew):	5/5
Initial Training Provided: 3-4 Days in Denver, CO.	

encourages the development of a child's creativity, leadership, speaking and communication skills in a stimulating, high-participation learning environment.

Attached to this Offering Circular as *Attachment I* are charts which indicate teaching days and revenues generated under various enrollment scenarios ("Enrollment Charts"), one for a FasTracKids Academy and one for a Mini-Academy. The Enrollment Charts indicate teaching schedules and estimated revenues of a FasTracKids Business franchise based on number of classes held and Student enrollment levels. The Enrollment Charts have not been prepared in accordance with the statement on Standards for Accountant's Services on Prospective Financial Information. The information contained in the Enrollment Charts is not intended to express or infer an estimate, projection or forecast of actual teaching obligations, income, sales, profits or earnings to be obtained with any particular franchise. The information presented is limited specifically to an estimate of gross revenues, after certain operating expenses, which could he obtained from conducting classroom courses at a FasTracKids Business utilizing the FasTracKids Educational Package and the FasTracKids Materials. The Enrollment Charts do not estimate or project all expenses you may incur in operating your FasTracKids Business. We do not represent the length of time it will take you to operate your FasTracKids Business in order to realize any gross revenues or whether you will be able to realize any revenues from operating your FasTracKids Business. Your individual gross revenue margins are likely to differ from the results in the Enrollment Charts, and you may not be able to schedule your

actual classes as time efficiently as shown on the Enrollment Charts.

Attachment I sets forth the factual basis for the data in the Enrollment Charts and the significant assumptions used in compiling the data. The information which substantiates the data in the Enrollment Charts will be made available to you on your reasonable request.

Except for the Enrollment Charts, we do not furnish, or make, or authorize our sales personnel to furnish or make, any oral or written information concerning the actual, average, projected, forecasted or potential sales, cost, income or profits of a FasTracKids Business. Actual results will vary from franchise to franchise and we cannot estimate the results of any particular franchise. You should make your own investigation to determine whether or not your FasTracKids Business will be profitable. We are not bound by allegations of any unauthorized representations as to earnings, sales, profits, prospects or chances of success.

Attachment I
Enrollment Charts
YOU SHOULD NOTE THAT THE INFORMATION CONTAINED IN THIS DOCUMENT IS NOT INTENDED TO EXPRESS OR INFER AN ESTIMATE, PROJECTION OR FORECAST OF ACTUAL TEACHING OBLIGATIONS, INCOME, SALES, PROFITS OR

EARNINGS TO BE DERIVED IN CONNECTION WITH ANY PARTICULAR FRANCHISE. THE INFORMATION PRESENTED IS LIMITED TO AN ESTIMATE OF REVENUE POTENTIALLY OBTAINABLE BASED ON CERTAIN ENROLLMENT LEVELS. WE MAKE NO REPRESENTATION AS TO WHETHER YOU WILL EVER BE ABLE TO OBTAIN THE ENROLLMENT LEVELS SET FORTH IN THIS DOCUMENT AND, IF SOLD, THE LENGTH OF TIME IT WILL TAKE YOU TO REACH THOSE LEVELS IN ORDER TO REALIZE ANY REVENUE LEVELS.

CAUTION: YOUR ACTUAL FINANCIAL RESULTS ARE LIKELY TO DIFFER FROM THE FIGURES PRESENTED. WE DO NOT REPRESENT THAT YOU CAN EXPECT TO ATTAIN THE GROSS REVENUE RESULTS OR TEACHING SCHEDULES CONTAINED IN THIS EXHIBIT.

Enrollment Scenarios — FasTracKids[SM] Academy ($1,500 Enrollment Fee)

This chart is designed to show varying teaching day possibilities/revenues at various enrollment levels.

Teaching Days/Enrollments Based on 3 Classes per Day; 16 Students per Class

Hours			Mon.			Tues.			Wed.			Thurs.			Fri.
T			16			16			16			16			16
10:30/12:30			16			16			16			16			16
2:00/4:00			16			16			16			16			16
Student: Cumulative Total			48			96			144			192			240
Monthly Enrollments	16	32	48	64	80	96	112	128	144	160	176	192	208	224	240
Income:															
Monthly Revenue[1]: $125 X # of Enrollments	$2,000	$4,000	$6,000	$8,000	$10,000	$12,000	$14,000	$16,000	$18,000	$20,000	$22,000	$24,000	$26,000	$28,000	$30,000
Franchise Share[2] of Monthly Revenues (62.5%)	$1,250	$2,500	$3,750	$5,000	$6,250	$7,500	$8,750	$10,000	$11,250	$12,500	$13,750	$15,000	$16,250	$17,500	$18,750
Expenses:															
Learning Station Lease[3]	$170	$170	$170	$170	$170	$170	$170	$170	$170	$170	$170	$170	$170	$170	$170
Gross Operating Margin[4,5]	$1,080	$2,330	$3,580	$4,830	$6,080	$7,330	$8,580	$9,830	$11,080	$12,330	$13,580	$14,830	$16,080	$17,330	$18,580

Enrollment Scenarios — FasTracKids[SM] Mini Academy ($1,500 Enrollment Fee)

This chart is designed to show varying teaching day possibilities/revenues at various enrollment levels.

Teaching Days/Enrollments Based on 3 Classes per Day; 8 Students per Class

Hours			Mon.			Tues.			Wed.			Thurs.			Fri.
8:00/10:00			8			8			8			8			8
10:30/12:30			8			8			8			8			8
2:00/4:00			8			8			8			8			8
Student: Cumulative Total			24			48			72			96			120
Monthly Enrollments	8	16	24	32	40	48	56	64	72	80	88	96	104	112	120
Income:															
Monthly Revenue[1]: $125 X # of Enrollments	$1,000	$2,000	$3,000	$4,000	$5,000	$6,000	$7,000	$8,000	$9,000	$10,000	$11,000	$12,000	$13,000	$14,000	$15,000
Franchise Share[2] of Monthly Revenues (62.5%)		$625	$1,250	$1,875	$2,500	$3,125	$3,750	$4,375	$5,000	$5,625	$6,250	$6,875	$7,500	$8,125	$8,750	$9,375

Hours					Mon.			Tues.			Wed.			Thurs.			Fri.
Expenses:																	
Learning Station Lease[3]	$150	$150	$150	$150	$150	$150	$150	$150	$150	$150	$150	$150	$150	$150	$150		
Classroom Facility[4] (10% of Enrollment)	$100	$200	$300	$400	$500	$600	$700	$800	$900	$1,000	$1,100	$1,200	$1,300	$1,400	$1,500		
Gross Operating Margin[5,7]	$375	$900	$1,425	$1,950	$2,475	$3,000	$3,525	$4,050	$4,575	$5,100	$5,625	$6,150	$6,675	$7,200	$7,725		
Teacher: ($20 per Classroom Hr., plus 2 Hrs. per Wk. Preparation)						$1,120	$1,280	$1,440	$1,600	$1,760	$1,920	$2,080	$2,240	$2,400	$2,560		
Gross Operating Margin with Teacher[6]						$1,880	$2,245	$2,610	$2,975	$3,340	$3,705	$4,070	$4,435	$4,800	$5,165		

FasTracKids International, Ltd. Summary of Factual Basis and Significant Assumptions for Statement

This Statement ("Statement") is based on estimate revenues based on different Student enrollment levels less certain expenses. It is not based upon actual experience of franchised FasTracKids Academies or Mini-Academies.

The Statement contains two different enrollment scenarios, one for a FasTracKids Academy franchise and one for a Mini-Academy franchise. A franchisee that operates a FasTracKids Academy typically has an existing business, such as a school, pre-school, daycare center or health and fitness center, and desires to add a FasTracKids Academy as an additional component of its business operation. These franchisees generally already have teaching staff available and an existing facility. The chart for this type of franchise contemplates no additional expenses for a teaching staff. A franchisee that operates a Mini-Academy typically is an individual who desires to operate small classes, sometimes on a part-time basis. A Mini-Academy franchisee normally will need to locate a place to conduct classes, which may be a school, pre-school, daycare center, health and fitness center or other business location. A Mini-Academy franchisee may conduct classes or hire a Facilitating Instructor to conduct the classes. The chart for a Mini-Academy contemplates expenses for rent and a Facilitating Instructor.

The Statement assumes that the enrollment fee is paid monthly. Our current suggested enrollment price for one Student attending the complete 48-week course is $1,500. You may charge a fee which is higher or lower than our suggested minimum enrollment price. The Statement sets forth estimated revenues at our suggested enrollment price.

The Statement does not contemplate all expenses you may incur, such as start-up expenses and certain standard business expenses. We do not require our franchisees to provide us with financial statements. Therefore, we cannot accurately estimate standard operating business expenses.

The Statement does not factor in your initial franchise fee or other start-up expenses you may incur. The initial franchise fee for a FasTracKids Academy franchise is $15,000 and for a Mini-Academy franchise is $5,000. See Item 7 of the Offering Circular for other initial investment expenses.

The recommended Student to teaching staff ratio is 8 to 1. The maximum number of Students who may be in one class in a FasTracKids Academy is 16 without our prior written consent. The maximum number of Students who may be in one class in a Mini-Academy is 8 without our prior written consent. The Statement assumes a maximum class size for each type of franchise and that a franchisee will fill a class to the maximum number of Students before opening another class.

Each class is typically two hours in duration, held once a week. The Statement is based on a maximum potential of three classes per day, five days per week. The Statement contemplates that you will fill three classes in one day to the maximum number of Students allowed for each type of franchise before you enroll any Students in classes to be held on a different day. You may conduct any number of classes on any days you desire. The Statement does not consider weekend classes, although you are not prohibited from conducting classes on the weekend. A FasTracKids Academy franchisee may conduct several classes at the same time. The Statement contemplates only one class being conducted at a time. A Mini-Academy may only conduct one class at a time.

Since FasTracKids Academy franchisees typically operate at a school, pre-school, daycare center, health and fitness center or similar operation and already have teaching facilities, the Statement assume there will be no out-of-pocket expenses for rent. The Statement contemplates rent for a Mini-Academy to be 10% of enrollment fees. Your actual rent may be based on square footage, percentage of enrollment fees or any other basis. See Item 7 of the FasTracKids Franchise Offering Circular for a more detailed discussion of rent expenses.

The Statement contemplates that a franchisee will rent the FasTrack Learning Station™ rather than purchase it, and that a FasTracKids Academy franchisee will acquire the large interactive white board while a Mini-Academy franchisee will acquire a small interactive white board. The Statement contemplates a monthly lease rate of $170 for the FasTrack Learning Station™ with the large interactive white board and $150 for the FasTrack Learning Station™ with the small interactive white board based on a 60 month lease with a $1.00 buyout at the end of the lease term based on interest rates in effect as of the date of this Statement. See Item 7 of the FasTracKids Franchise Offering Circular for a more detailed discussion of the acquisition costs of the FasTrack Learning Station™.

Since we have no franchisees who have operated continuously for a year or more, the Statement does not include results of our franchised FasTracKids Businesses. Further, in presenting this data, we do not estimate the length of time it

will take for any particular franchisee to obtain any specific enrollment levels. Your ability to enroll Students into your FasTracKids Business is a major factor in determining your profitability and is dependent on your sales ability and efforts, your sales and marketing staff, competition within your market and other market factors. YOU ARE CAUTIONED THAT YOU MAY NEVER REALIZE THE ENROLLMENT OF GROSS REVENUE LEVELS PRESENTED IN THIS DATA IF YOU ARE UNABLE TO PROMOTE THE ENROLLMENT OF STUDENTS INTO YOUR FASTRACKIDS BUSINESS.

Notes to Enrollment Charts
THE FOLLOWING NOTES APPLY TO THE ENROLLMENT SCENARIOS FOR A FASTRACKIDS ACADEMY:

1. $1,500 per enrollment paid monthly ($125.00 per month x 12 months).

2. Franchisees approximate share of revenues (after deducting Maintenance and Usage Fees [34%]. Royalties [1½%], Estimated Cost of FasTracKids Materials [1%], Shipping and Handling Fees [½%] and Miscellaneous [½%]).

3. Assumes Franchisee chooses to lease the FasTrack Learning Station™ at $170 per month (smaller board available at $150 per month).

4. Assumes Franchisee staff does all teaching.

5. Assumes Franchisee has existing space, Facilitating Instructor and teaching assistants available without cost; does not contemplate expenses other than the FasTrack Learning Station™.

THE FOLLOWING NOTES APPLY TO THE ENROLLMENT SCENARIOS FOR A FASTRACKIDS MINI-ACADEMY:

1. $1,500 per enrollment paid monthly ($125.00 per month x 12 months).

2. Franchisees approximate share of revenues (after deducting Maintenance and Usage Fees

[34%], Royalties [1½%], Estimated Cost of FasTracKids Materials [1%], Shipping and Handling Fees [½%] and Miscellaneous [½%]).

3. Assumes Franchisee chooses to lease the Fas-Track Learning Station™ at $150 per month.

4. Assumes Franchisee "partners" with a pre-school, church or other organization for 10% of enrollment revenue in exchange for space.

5. Assumes Franchisee does all teaching.

6. Assumes Franchisee hires the Facilitating Instructor to teach classes.

7. Does not consider expenses except for the FasTrack Learning Station™, classroom space (10% or enrollment revenue) and, if applicable, a Facilitating Instructor.

THE STATEMENT IS MERELY AN ESTIMATE AND SHOULD NOT BE CONSIDERED AS THE ACTUAL OR POTENTIAL TEACHING SCHEDULES, SALES, PROFITS OR EARNINGS THAT WILL BE REALIZED BY ANY SPECIFIC FRANCHISEE. WE DO NOT REPRESENT THAT YOU CAN EXPECT TO ATTAIN THESE OR ANY SPECIFIC ENROLLMENT OR GROSS REVENUE MARGINS.

YOUR ABILITY TO ACHIEVE ANY LEVEL OF NET INCOME WILL DEPEND UPON FACTORS NOT WITHIN OUR CONTROL, INCLUDING THE OCCURRENCE OF CERTAIN START UP AND OPERATING EXPENSES AND THE AMOUNT OF THOSE EXPENSES, AND YOUR LEVEL OF EXPERTISE. FURTHER, THE ABOVE FIGURES DO NOT ACCOUNT FOR INTEREST EXPENSE, APPRECIATION OR DEPRECIATION OF ASSETS OR OTHER OVERHEAD, CAPITAL EXPENSES AND CARRYING COSTS WHICH WILL VARY FROM FRANCHISEE TO FRANCHISEE.

A FRANCHISEE'S INDIVIDUAL FINANCIAL RESULTS ARE LIKELY TO DIFFFR FROM THE RESULTS PRESENTED.

If any prospective distributor or franchisee has any questions regarding the figures and assumptions contained in the charts or desires any additional information or documents to verify or supplement the information contained in the charts, please write or call us and substantiating materials pertaining to this data will be made available for inspection at our headquarters and will be provided upon request.

INTERNATIONAL, INC.
an MDC Company

KIDDIE ACADEMY INTERNATIONAL
108 Wheel Rd.
Bel Air, MD 21015
Tel: (800) 5-KIDDIE (410) 515-0788
Fax: (410) 569-2729
E-Mail:
Internet Address: www.kiddieacademy.com

Contact: Ms. Kathy Barry, Franchise Development

Description: We offer comprehensive training and support without additional cost. KIDDIE ACADEMY's step-by-step program assists with staff recruitment, training, accounting support, site selection, marketing, advertising and curriculum. A true turn-key opportunity that provides on-going support so you can focus on running a successful business.

# Franchised Units:	40 Units
# Company-Owned Units:	11 Units
Total # Units:	51 Units
Founded In:	1981

1st Franchised In:	1992	
Average Total Investment:	180-260K	
Franchise Fee:	40K	
On-Going Royalty:	7%	
Advertising Fee:	0%	
Financial Assistance:Yes(I) (D – direct, or I – indirect)		

Site Selection Assistance:	Yes
Lease Negotiation Assistance:	Yes
Contract Terms (Init./Renew):	10/5
Initial Training Provided:2 Weeks Owner Train., Corp. HQ; 1 Wk. Director Train., Corp. HQ; 3-5 Day Staff Training.	

Except for the average gross revenues stated below, Kiddie Academy does not furnish or authorize its salespersons to furnish any oral or written information concerning the actual or potential sales, costs, income or profits of a Kiddie Academy Center. THE FOLLOWING INFORMATION SHOULD NOT BE CONSIDERED AS THE ACTUAL OR POTENTIAL REVENUE OR RESULTS OF ANY PARTICULAR KIDDIE ACADEMY CENTER. WE DO NOT REPRESENT, NOR SHOULD YOU EXPECT, THAT YOU CAN ATTAIN THESE REVENUE LEVELS. ACTUAL RESULTS VARY FROM UNIT TO UNIT AND KIDDIE ACADEMY CANNOT ESTIMATE THE RESULTS OF ANY PARTICULAR FRANCHISE. YOUR ACTUAL FINANCIAL RESULTS ARE LIKELY TO VARY FROM THE FIGURES PRESENTED BELOW.

Gross revenues represent the amount of tuition charged for enrollment at the Kiddie Academy Center. The average gross revenues are before costs and expenses, that vary greatly depending on location and other circumstances. You should consult with a legal, financial or business advisor about these figures.

The information below has been gathered from the financial information reported to us during the 1998 fiscal year by our 40 operating franchisees under their reporting requirements (see Item 9 of this offering circular). Supporting data will be available to prospective franchisees on reasonable request. WE HAVE NOT CONDUCTED AN INDEPENDENT INVESTIGATION TO VERIFY THESE FIGURES.

The charts below divide the Kiddie Academy Centers into two classifications: (1) Mature Centers (centers that have been operational for at least 24 months) and (2) Ramping Centers (centers that have been operational for less than 24 months). The time periods expressed in this chart are not meant to be an indication as to when or if a center will reach maturity. Each center's growth rate will vary by location, programs, and franchisee marketing efforts and management skills. Substantiation of the date used in preparing this earning claim will be made available to the prospective franchisee on reasonable request.

For Fiscal Year Ended September 27, 1998
Mature Centers (open for more than 24 months)

	Student Capacity (Determined by State regulation)			
	Less than 115 children	Between 116 and 150 children	Over 150 children	All Centers
Number of Centers	8	8	6	22
Average Student Capacity	102	133	170	136
Maximum average weekly revenue at full enrollment (Capacity)	$13,659	$17,782	$23,483	$17,838
Actual Average Weekly Revenue during fiscal year 1998	$10,157	$13,648	$18,116	$13,597

	Student Capacity (Determined by State regulation)			
	Less than 115 children	Between 116 and 150 children	Over 150 children	All Centers
Utilization (Actual divided by Maximum)	74.40%	76.70%	77.10%	76.20%
Centers operating above average	5 (62.5%)	3 (37.5%)	4 (66.7%)	12 (54.5%)

Ramping Centers (open for less than 24 months) [Annualized]

	Student Capacity (Determined by State regulation)			
	Less than 115 children	Between 116 and 150 children	Over 150 children	All Centers
Number of Centers	3	9	6	18
Average Student Capacity	104	135	169	141
Maximum average weekly revenue at full enrollment (Capacity)	$12,978	$174,944	$22,816	$18,983
Average Weeks Open	47	33.8	28.3	34.2
Actual Average Weekly Revenue during fiscal year 1998	$5,346	$10,267	$6,292	$8,122
Annualized Utilization (Actual divided by Maximum)	37.00%	57.20%	27.60%	42.80%
Centers operating above average	2 (62.5%)	4 (44.4%)	4 (66.7%)	9 (50.0%)

The utilization data in this chart was annualized using average weekly amounts to be able to compare and combine centers that operated for varying time periods during the fiscal year ended on September 27, 1998.

THE ABOVE DATA WAS PREPARED WITHOUT AN AUDIT. PROSPECTIVE FRANCHISEES SHOULD BE ADVISED THAT NO CERTIFIED PUBLIC ACCOUNT HAS AUDITED THESE FIGURES OR EXPRESSED HIS OR HER OPINION WITH REGARD TO THEIR CONTENT OR FORM.

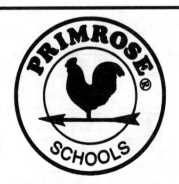

PRIMROSE SCHOOLS
199 S. Erwin St.
Cartersville, GA 30120
Tel: (800) 745-0677 (770) 606-9600
Fax: (770) 606-0020
E-Mail: psfcfranchise@mindspring.com
Internet Address: www.primroseschools.com
Contact: Mr. Ray Orgera, VP Franchise Development

Description: Educational child-care franchise, offering a traditional pre-school curriculum and programs while also providing quality childcare services. Site selection assistance, extensive training, operations manuals, building plans, marketing plans and on-going support.

# Franchised Units:	103 Units
# Company-Owned Units:	1 Units
Total # Units:	104 Units
Founded In:	1982
1st Franchised In:	1989

Average Total Investment:	1.3-2MM
Franchise Fee:	48.5K
On-Going Royalty:	7%
Advertising Fee:	1%
Financial Assistance:Yes(I) (D – direct, or I – indirect)	
Site Selection Assistance:	Yes
Lease Negotiation Assistance:	Yes
Contract Terms (Init./Renew):	11/10

Initial Training Provided: 1 Week Home Office; 1 Week at Existing School; 1 Week at Franchisee's New School.

Summary of Revenue of Company and Franchised Schools during the Period January 1, through December 31, 1998.

This Summary sets forth the median school revenue achieved by 30, 136 capacity franchised Primrose facilities, ("Smaller Facilities"), 16, 176 capacity franchised Primrose facilities, ("Larger Facilities"), 3, 136 capacity franchised facilities which were expanded to 176 capacity facilities during 1998 ("Expanded Facilities"), and the PSFC-owned Primrose facility for the year ended December 31, 1998. The data is based on revenue reported by PSFC and its franchisees. On December 31, 1998 there were 62 total Primrose facilities open and in operation for at least one month of the year. Of those 62, 30 Smaller Facilities and 32 Larger Facilities were open. However, the median revenue reported herein is based solely on the 30 Smaller Facilities, 3 expanded facilities and 16 Larger Facilities that were opened and in operation for at least one full year. All of the Primrose facilities opened and in operation are located in Georgia, Alabama, Tennessee, North Carolina, Colorado and Texas. As of the date of this Summary, no Primrose facility has ceased operation.

The median revenue for the year ending December 31, 1998, was $773,348 for the Smaller Facilities, $986,222 for the Larger Facilities, $907,579 for the Expanded Facilities, and $696,249 for the PSFC-owned Primrose facility. The high revenue produced by a franchised Primrose Smaller Facility was $975,818, and the low revenue for a Smaller Facility was $447,294. The high revenue for a Larger Facility was $1,165,379, and the low revenue for the Larger facility was $491,458. The high revenue for an Expanded Facility was $951,278, and the low revenue for the Expanded Facility was $837,808.

Median Revenues

Franchised Smaller Facilities	$773,348
Franchised Larger Facilities	$986,222
Franchised Expanded Facilities	$907,579
PSFC-Owned Primrose Facilities	$696,249

High and Low Annual Revenue

High, Smaller Facilities	$975,818
High, Larger Facilities	$1,165,379
High, Expanded Facilities	$951,278
Low, Smaller Facilities	$447,294
Low, Larger Facilities	$491,458
Low, Expanded Facilities	$837,808

Range of Annual Revenue Smaller Facility

Average Annual Revenue	Percentage of Franchised Primrose Facilities within Ranges	Aggregate Percentages of Franchised Primrose Facilities Equaling or Exceeding Revenue Ranges
More than $754,000	60%	60%
Between $699,000 and $753,999	14%	74%
Between $556,000 and $698,999	23%	97%
Less than $555,999	3%	100%

131

Range of Annual Revenue Larger Facilities

Average Annual Revenue	Percentage of Franchised Primrose Facilities within Ranges	Aggregate Percentages of Franchised Primrose Facilities Equaling or Exceeding Revenue Ranges
More than $969,000	56%	56%
Between $883,000 and $968,999	13%	69%
Between $806,000 and $882,999	18%	87%
Less than $805,999	13%	100%

Range of Annual Revenue Expanded Facilities

Average Annual Revenue	Percentage of Franchised Primrose Facilities within Ranges	Aggregate Percentages of Franchised Primrose Facilities Equaling or Exceeding Revenue Ranges
More than $754,000	100%	100%
Between $699,000 and $753,999	0%	100%
Between $556,000 and $698,999	0%	100%
Less than $555,999	0%	100%

All **Average Annual Revenue** categories used above in this report are consistent in their ranges from the 1996 and 1997 reports. PSFC has continued to use these ranges to simplify year-to-year comparisons for you. The Expanded Facility category is a new category and we have used the "Smaller Facility" range due to these schools having been smaller facilities for much of this year. Please note that had we used the Larger Facility range chart 100% of the Expanded Facilities would have fallen above the $806,000 revenue level.

All Primrose facilities included in this Summary are located in free standing buildings.

Explanatory Notes to Summary:
1. PSFC is unaware of any material differences between the franchised Primrose facilities whose results are reflected in this Summary and any Primrose facility that may be opened in the future.

2. You are responsible for developing you own business plan for your Primrose facility, including capital budgets, financial statements, projections and other appropriate factors, and

you are encouraged to consult with you own accounting, business and legal advisors in doing so. The business plan should make necessary allowances for economic downturns, periods of inflation and unemployment, and other negative economic influences.

3. This summary should not be considered to be the actual or probable revenues that you will experience. PSFC does not represent that you can expect to obtain the results set forth in this Summary. Actual results vary from franchisee to franchisee and PSFC cannot estimate the results of any particular franchisee. Significant variations in revenues and expenses exist among franchisees for a variety of reasons, such as the length of time the Primrose facility has been open, location, the franchisee's prior business experience, competition, and other factors.

4. You should fully understand that historical revenues may not correspond to future revenues due to a variety of factors. AS WITH ANY BUSINESS, THE INITIAL FINANCIAL PERFORMANCE OF YOUR

PRIMROSE FACILITY IS LIKELY TO BE LESS FAVORABLE THAN THOSE REPRESENTED HEREIN.

5. Except as set forth in this summary, PSFC does not furnish or authorize its personnel to furnish any oral or written information concerning the actual or potential revenues, costs, income or profits of a franchise, and PSFC will not be bound by allegations of any unauthorized representation as to earnings, revenues, expenses, profits, prospects or chances for success.

6. Substitution for the data set forth in this Summary will be made available to you by PSFC upon reasonable request.

Education/Personal Development/Training

BERLITZ INTERNATIONAL
400 Alexander Park Dr.
Princeton, NJ 08540-6306
Tel: (800) 626-6419 (609) 514-3046
Fax: (609) 514-9675
E-Mail: frank.garton@berlitz.com
Internet Address: www.berlitz.com
Contact: Mr. Frank Garton, VP Worldwide
Franchising

Description: Language instruction, publishing and translation services

# Franchised Units:	50 Units
# Company-Owned Units:	350 Units
Total # Units:	400 Units
Founded In:	1900
1st Franchised In:	1996
Average Total Investment:	150-300K
Franchise Fee:	30-50K
On-Going Royalty:	10%
Advertising Fee:	2%
Financial Assistance:No (D – direct, or I – indirect)	
Site Selection Assistance:	Yes
Lease Negotiation Assistance:	Yes
Contract Terms (Init./Renew):	10/10
Initial Training Provided:2 Weeks Home Office; 2 Weeks Division Training, 2 Weeks On-Site	

Statement of Selected Financial Performance Results and Indicators

Set forth below is a summary of selected financial performance results and indicators for the period January 1 through December 31, 1997 for Berlitz-owned and operated Language Centers in the United States. These Language Centers have been divided into three groups based upon the aggregate number of lessons furnished at the Language Centers in 1997. The data presented for each category reflects the mean average result for the group.

Revenues and Costs			
	Language Centers furnishing fewer than 7,001 lessons in 1997	Language Centers furnishing from 7,001 to 12,000 lessons in 1997	Language Centers Furnishing from 12,000 to 20,000 Lessons in 1997
Gross Revenue	$216,096	$433,661	$662,077
Teacher Costs	51,046	107,660	169,609
Variable Costs	34,347	68,035	89,092
Fixed Costs	87,512	131,127	162,735
Royalties	21,581	43,366	66,208
Earnings Before Income Taxes	21,581	83,473	174,433
Number of Language Centers in Group	8	28	14

Performance Indicators			
	Language Centers furnishing fewer than 7,001 lessons in 1997	Language Centers furnishing from 7,001 to 12,000 lessons in 1997	Language Centers furnishing from 12,000 to 20,000 lessons in 1997
Average Revenue per Lesson	$36.09	$36.92	$36.47
Average Cost per Lesson	$10.81	$11.55	$11.39
Teacher Salary Ratio (TSR)	30.0%	31.3%	31.2%
Variable Cost Percentage (excludes TSR)	15.9%	15.7%	13.5%
Fixed Cost Percentage (excludes Rent)	30.5%	22.9%	18.5%
Rent Percentage	10.0%	7.3%	6.1%
Royalties	10.0%	10.0%	10.0%
Breakeven Point Ratio	80.2%	61.1%	48.3%
Earnings Before Income Taxes Percentage	10.0%	19.3%	26.4%
Average Number of Lessons	4,723	9,321	14,892

Notes to Statement

1. The Statement presented above reflects the results of operations of 50 Language Centers owned and operated by Berlitz in the United States throughout the 1997 fiscal year.

2. No franchised Language Centers are included in this Statement. Of the 3 franchised Language Centers operating in the United States as of December 31, 1997, one commenced operations in March 1997 and 2 commenced opera-

tions in September 1997. As a result, these franchised Language Centers do not offer sufficient financial history upon which to base an earnings claim.

3. "Gross Revenue" includes income from tuition, registration fees, tuition forfeitures and reinstatements, sale of merchandise such as books and cassettes, revenue from Berlitz Publishing and Berlitz Jr. products, Cross-Cultural services, commissions from Berlitz Study Abroad and revenue from non-Berlitz products and services.

4. "Teacher Costs" include teachers' salaries and related payroll expenses such as payroll taxes and vacation pay.

5. "Variable Costs" includes expenses such as advertising and promotion, commissions and bonuses payable to center directors, materials and supplies, miscellaneous expenses, and bad debt.

6. "Fixed Costs" include expenses such as depreciation and amortization, administrative salaries and related payroll expenses, rent, postage and supplies, insurance, communications expenses, taxes (other than income tax), premises upkeep, travel, and miscellaneous expenses.

7. Royalties are calculated at 10 percent of gross revenue.

8. Performance Indicators are computed as follows:

    A. *Average Revenue per Lesson:* Tuition revenue divided by total lessons given.
    B. *Average Cost per Lesson:* Teacher costs divided by total lessons given.
    C. *Teacher Salary Ratio (TSR):* Teacher costs as a percentage of tuition revenue.
    D. *Variable Cost Percentage (excludes TSR):* Variable costs, excluding teacher costs, as a percentage of gross revenue.
    E. *Fixed Cost Percentage (excludes Rent):* Fixed costs, excluding rent, as a percentage of gross revenue.
    F. *Rent Percentage:* Rental costs as a percentage of total sales and revenue. Language center space ranges from approximately 1,100-4,300 square feet.
    G. *Breakeven Point Ratio:* Fixed costs (including rent) as a percentage of gross revenue less variable and teacher costs.

9. The average Language Center whose results are included in this Statement has been in operation for ten years or more, and no Language Center whose results are included has been in operation for less than four years.

10. There are no material differences between the operations of the Language Centers whose results are reflected in the Statement and the Language Centers being franchised by Franchisor. Both Berlitz-owned and operated Language Centers and franchised Language Centers will operate under the same System, and with similar operating requirements.

11. You will incur other expenses of doing business which are not reflected in this Statement. These additional expenses are likely to be significant, and will vary widely among franchisees. The additional categories of expenses which will be incurred by franchisees include, but are not necessarily limited to, the following: (i) franchisee's draw; (ii) advertising contributions and expenses; (iii) various taxes, such as federal, state and local income taxes; (iv) voluntary employee benefits, such as health, vacation, and pension plan contributions; (v) accounting and legal fees related to the establishment and operation of the franchise; and (vi) interest or finance charges for any monies borrowed in connection with establishing and operating the Language Center.

12. This Statement was prepared from unaudited internal operating records of Berlitz-owned Language Centers.

13. Substantiation of the data set forth in this Statement will be made available to you upon reasonable request.

14. THE INFORMATION SET FORTH IN THIS STATEMENT REFLECTS THE AGGREGATE RESULTS OF INDIVIDUAL LANGUAGE CENTERS, AND SHOULD NOT BE CONSIDERED AS THE ACTUAL OR PROBABLE RESULTS THAT WILL BE ACHIEVED BY YOU. ACTUAL RESULTS VARY FROM LANGUAGE CENTER TO LANGUAGE CENTER, AND WE CANNOT ESTIMATE THE RESULTS OF ANY INDIVIDUAL LANGUAGE CENTER. WE DO NOT REPRESENT THAT YOU CAN EXPECT TO OBTAIN THE RESULTS SET FORTH IN THIS STATEMENT. A NEW FRANCHISEE'S FINANCIAL RESULTS ARE LIKELY TO BE LOWER.

CRESTCOM INTERNATIONAL, LTD.
6900 E. Belleview Ave.
Englewood, CO 80111
Tel: (888) CRESTCOM (303) 267-8200
Fax: (303) 267-8207
Internet Address: www.crestcom.com
Contact: Mr. Kelly Krause, Dir. Int'l. Marketing

Description: CRESTCOM is rated the #1 management training company of 1999 by Entrepreneur and other magazines. CRESTCOM uses a unique combination of video instruction and live facilitation to teach management, sales and office personnel. Internationally-renowned business/management training personalities appear on CRESTCOM videos. The company is active in 50 countries and CRESTCOM's materials are translated into 20+ languages.

# Franchised Units:	117 Units
# Company-Owned Units:	0 Units
Total # Units:	117 Units
Founded In:	1987
1st Franchised In:	1992
Average Total Investment:	44.4-72K
Franchise Fee:	35-52.5K
On-Going Royalty:	1.5%
Advertising Fee:	N/A
Financial Assistance:	Yes (D – direct, or I – indirect)
Site Selection Assistance:	N/A
Lease Negotiation Assistance:	N/A
Contract Terms (Init./Renew):	7/7/7
Initial Training Provided:	7-10 Days Denver, CO, Phoenix, AZ or Sacramento, CA.

Attached to this Offering Circular as *Attachment I* is our Estimate of Gross Revenue Margins Before Expenses on Sale of Materials ("Estimate of Gross Revenue Margins"). The Estimate of Gross Revenue Margins has not been prepared in accordance with the statement on Standards for Accountant's Services on Prospective Financial Information. The information contained in the Estimate of Gross Revenue Margins is not intended to express or infer an estimate, projection or forecast of income, sales, profits or earnings to be obtained with any particular franchise. The information presented is limited specifically to an estimate of gross revenues, before operating expenses, which could be obtained from the sale of the Materials you are entitled to receive from the certificate you receive when you pay the initial franchise fee or from the sale of ordered Materials from us. The information also shows the average gross revenue results of our U.S. franchisees who were operating continuously throughout the 1998 calendar year. We do not represent the length of time it will take you to sell the Materials in order to realize any gross revenues or whether you will be able to sell the initial Materials. Your individual gross revenue margins are likely to differ from the results in the Estimate of Gross Revenue Margins.

Attachment I sets forth the factual basis for the data in the Estimate of Gross Revenue Margins and the significant assumptions used in compiling the data. The information which substantiates the data in the Estimate of Gross Revenue Margins will be made available to you on your reasonable request. Except for the Estimate of Gross Revenue Margins, we do not furnish, or make, or authorize

137

our sales personnel to furnish or make, any oral or written information concerning the actual, average, projected, forecasted or potential sales, cost, income or profits of a CRESTCOM Business. Actual results vary from franchise to franchise and we cannot estimate the results of any particular franchise. You should make your own investigation to determine whether or not your CRESTCOM Business will be profitable. We are not bound by allegations of any unauthorized representations as to earnings, sales, profits, prospects or chances of success.

Attachment I
Estimate of Gross Revenue Margins before Expenses on Sale of Materials
YOU SHOULD NOTE THAT THE INFORMATION CONTAINED IN THIS DOCUMENT IS NOT INTENDED TO EXPRESS OR INFER AN ESTIMATE, PROJECTION OR FORECAST OF INCOME, SALES, PROFITS OR EARNINGS TO BE DERIVED IN CONNECTION WITH ANY PARTICULAR FRANCHISE. THE INFORMATION PRESENTED IS LIMITED TO AN ESTIMATE OF GROSS REVENUE MARGINS, BEFORE OPERATING EXPENSES, WHICH COULD BE DERIVED FROM THE SALE OF THE MATERIALS. WE MAKE NO REPRESENTATION AS TO WHETHER YOU WILL EVER BE ABLE TO SELL ANY OF THE MATERIALS AND, IF SOLD, THE LENGTH OF TIME IT WILL TAKE YOU TO RESELL THE MATERIALS PURCHASED IN ORDER TO REALIZE ANY GROSS REVENUES.

CAUTION: YOUR ACTUAL FINANCIAL RESULTS ARE LIKELY TO DIFFER FROM THE FIGURES PRESENTED. WE DO NOT REPRESENT THAT YOU CAN EXPECT TO ATTAIN THE GROSS REVENUE MARGINS CONTAINED IN THIS EXHIBIT.

Crestcom International, Ltd. Estimate of Gross Revenue Margins before Expenses

Initial Inventory Margins[2]							
Type of Franchise[1]	Materials	Suggested Minimum Retail Price (per Participant)	Total	Fees: Paid to Us[3]	Shipping (Est. ½%)[3]	Total Fees and Shipping Costs[3]	Gross Margin[4,5]
Executive	BPM Materials (36 Participants)	$3,000	$108,000	$38,340	$540	$38,880	$69,120
Standard	BPM Materials (24 Participants)	$3,000	$72,000	$32,760	$360	$33,120	$38,880

Re-Order Margins per Participants[2]							
Type of Franchise[1]	Materials (per Participant)	Suggested Minimum Retail Price	Distributors Cost as % of Suggested Retail[6]	Fees as % of Suggested Retail[3]	Est. Shipping as % of Suggested Retail[3]	Total % of Suggested Retail	Gross Margin[4,5] (%/$s)
Executive	BPM Materials	$3,000	3.73%	35.50%	0.50%	39.73%	60.27% $1,808
Standard	BPM Materials	$3,000	3.73%	45.50%	0.50%	49.73%	50.27% $1,508

Average Gross Revenue Margins before Expenses on Sale of Materials — 1998[7,8,9]			
Franchisees	Average Sales[10,11]	Estimated Gross Margin %[5,12]	Average Gross Margins[4]
Top 1/3 — U.S. Franchisees	$400,421	60%	$240,253
Middle 1/3 — U.S. Franchisees	$174,836	60%	$104,902
Lower 1/3 — U.S. Franchisees	$87,867	60%	$52,720

THE ACCOMPANYING FOOTNOTES ARE AN INTEGRAL PART OF THESE CHARTS AND SHOULD BE READ IN THEIR ENTIRETY FOR A FULL UNDERSTANDING OF THE INFORMATION CONTAINED IN THESE CHARTS.

Summary of Factual Basis for Data

❧ The initial franchise fee for a U.S. executive franchise is $52,500. The initial franchise fee for a standard U.S. franchise is $35,000.

❧ Upon payment in full of the initial franchise fee, franchisees acquiring an executive franchise receive our Fast Start Kit containing an initial inventory of training and sample materials, along with a certificate to acquire sufficient materials to supply *36 participants (5 groups of four and 8 groups of two) for The BULLET PROOF® Manager ("BPM") training program.* Materials are provided against the certificate as sales are made and distribution and royalty fees are paid. The merchandise credit must be used within 30 months following the completion of your initial training course.

❧ Upon payment in full of the initial franchise fee, franchisees acquiring a standard franchise receive our Fast Start Kit containing the same initial inventory of training and sample materials as our franchisees obtaining executive franchises, along with a certificate to acquire sufficient materials to supply *24 participants (3 groups of four and 6 groups of two) for BPM training.* Materials are provided against the certificate as sales are made and distribution and royalty fees are paid. The merchandise credit must be used within 30 months following the completion of your initial training course.

❧ In 1996, 1997 and 1998, clients attending The BULLET PROOF® Manager training program enrolled, on average, more than three managers per session, although your experience may differ. At three attendees per client, upon the purchase of a franchise an executive franchisee would receive sufficient Materials for approximately twelve clients and a standard franchisee would receive sufficient Materials for approximately eight clients.

❧ Based on the current suggested minimum retail price, *the value of the merchandise credit for an executive franchise is $108,000, and for a standard franchise is $72,000.*

❧ Our current suggested retail price for one participant to The BULLET PROOF® Manager training program is $3,000. You may charge a fee which is higher or lower than our suggested minimum retail price. Many of our U.S. franchisees and affiliates are currently charging $3,300 or more per participant. We have created a promotional video which uses $3,300 per participant to demonstrate gross margin potentials. However, we have used a suggested minimum retail price of $3,000 in these charts so as not to inflate gross margin projections.

❧ The projected gross revenue margins reflected above are based on cost and retail values of our program materials ("Materials") existing as of January 1999. Data has been compiled based on the experience of franchisees and distributors in our system. Our system is comprised of franchisees operating within the United States and franchisees and distributors operating in other countries. Our foreign franchise/distributorship programs operate in a manner similar to our franchise system within the United States as it relates to the information contained in this chart, although retail prices for the Materials distributed internationally frequently differ from the suggested retail price presented in this chart and are often subject to customs and duty expenses as well as higher shipping costs. International prices are also subject to change with exchange rate fluctuations. The results of our foreign franchise/distributorship programs are not included in this data.

❧ In presenting this data, we do not estimate the length of time it will take for any particular franchisee or distributor to sell either the initial inventory of Materials or ongoing reorders of Materials in order to realize any of the gross

139

revenue margins presented. Your ability to sell the Materials is a major factor in determining your profitability and is dependent upon your sales ability and efforts, your sales and marketing staff, competition within your market and other market factors. YOU ARE CAUTIONED THAT YOU MAY NEVER REALIZE THE GROSS REVENUE MARGINS PRESENTED IN THIS DATA IF YOU ARE UNABLE TO RESELL ALL OR A PORTION OF THE MATERIALS PURCHASED BY YOU.

FOOTNOTES — Significant Assumptions Upon Which the Information is Based

1. The investment for an executive franchise is $52,500 and the investment for a standard franchise is $35,000. The investment referred to is the initial franchise fee paid to us only and not other investment costs. You should refer to Item 7 of the Offering Circular for a discussion of other initial investment considerations.

2. Upon the purchase of a franchise, an executive franchise is furnished with training and sample items and sufficient Materials to supply 36 of The BULLET PROOF® Manager participants. A standard franchisee receives the same training and sample items and sufficient Materials to supply 24 of The BULLET PROOF® Manager participants. The suggested minimum retail price is $3,000 per participant. However, you may charge a fee which is higher or lower than our suggested minimum retail price. We do not represent that sales of the Materials will occur within any particular time frame, if at all. The costs charged by us and the suggested minimum retail price of the Materials are based on the costs and prices in effect as of the date of this Offering Circular and are subject to change. You are not required to charge your clients the suggested minimum retail price for the Materials. Other market conditions, such as competition, market recognition, quality of training conducted by you and location may affect your actual retail pricing. The gross margins set forth in each chart relate only to The BULLET PROOF® Manager training. We may offer other programs with greater or lesser margins.

3. The aggregate fees paid to us for the initial inventory of Materials is 35½% of the retail price of the Materials for franchisees acquiring our executive franchise and 45½% for franchisees acquiring our standard franchisee. This is comprised of (a) Distribution Fee of 34% for executive franchisees and 44% for standard franchisees and, (b) Royalty Fee of 1½%. In addition, we estimate shipping costs at ½% of the retail price of the Materials. This may be higher if the initial inventory is shipped in several shipments or subsequent shipments are for small quantities of materials. The fees due us are paid as proceeds from The BULLET PROOF® Manager training program are received by you. We recommend that you require the Materials be paid for by a client on a cash basis or on a basis of 25% down, with the balance payable in 30, 60 and 90 days. The charts assume all funds are collected during the calendar quarter of the sale. Many franchisees provide additional Materials for cash purchasers as a bonus for early payment. You are not required to give bonus Materials and the costs of any bonus Materials are not reflected in the charts.

4. The gross margins are not adjusted for start up and operating expenses you may incur. Operating expenses vary substantially and are based on particular factors relevant to each franchisee. You may incur operating expenses for a video player, automobile, telephone, fax, car phone, answering machine, seminar related expenses, marketing and advertising expenses, telemarketing expenses including the salaries, commissions and other expenses to employ one or more telemarketers to solicit business for you, as well as other isolated and/or recurring expenses. You may operate from an office location although most of our franchisees operate out of their homes.

5. The majority of revenues generated by our franchisees currently result from the enrollment of participants in The BULLET

PROOF® Manager program and only gross margins from the enrollments in this program are shown. We offer other training programs to our franchisees and distributors and you are permitted to sell Materials or enroll attendees in courses other than The BULLET PROOF® Manager training program. The margins on those programs may be less than the margins for The BULLET PROOF® Manager training program.

6. The "Distributors Costs" relate to the costs of Materials only. They do not include the initial investment in the franchise, start-up costs, overhead, seminar costs, marketing costs, salaries or commissions, the franchisee's (and its authorized representatives') time or effort, bonus merchandise, or any other expenses associated with the franchise. It also assumes that videos which are loaned by the franchisee to its clients come from the franchisee's own inventory. The actual cost of the Materials for participants in The BULLET PROOF® Manager training program or other CRESTCOM programs varies. Depending on the number of participants a client enrolls, the mix of materials the client receives is different. Based on our Franchisees' reorder costs, the average expense for required Materials for one participant in The BULLET PROOF® Manager training program is currently $112 or 3.73% of the current suggested retail price of $3,000.

7. The Average Gross Revenue Margins chart was compiled based on actual sales of The BULLET PROOF® Manager training program and other sales by our existing franchisees during our fiscal year ending December 31, 1998. More than 90% of all sales revenues were derived from The BULLET PROOF® Manager training program.

8. Only active U.S. franchisees, who are franchisees operating on a full-time basis for the entire fiscal year in the United States of America, and their sales are shown. In 1998, we had 18 active U.S. franchisees. Franchises who did not operate for the entire fiscal year are not shown. Some franchisees first operate their Businesses on a part-time basis and later operate on a full-time basis. Other franchisees did not operate on a full-time basis due to personal or family illnesses or other personal or business reasons. No attempt is made to estimate potential profits, income or earnings. We cannot accurately determine expenses because some of our franchisees have other business interests in addition to their CRESTCOM Business.

9. Only franchisees actively operating executive franchise programs are shown. Although we have offered our standard franchise programs since 1995, we have not awarded any standard franchises. Therefore, no results for a standard franchise are shown.

10. The total of sales is based on sales reports provided by the franchisees to us. We have not audited these sales reports and cannot guarantee their accuracy. We do not require our franchisees to provide us with financial statements. Many of our franchisees provide other services to their clients in addition to the management, sales and personnel development training programs we offer, including other training related services. We do not require that the franchisees provide us with financial information relating to these other services. The chart does not include sales by our international franchisees or distributors.

11. There is a large variation in the range of sales generated by our franchisees. Of the 18 franchisees reported in the chart, total sales varied from a low of less than $45,000 to a high of more than $675,000. These amounts do not include sales of salespersons of a franchisee, except for two family-operated franchises that have individual family members as salespersons. We consolidated the sales results of all of the family members for those two franchises. Also, some franchisees who did not operate on a full-time basis for the entire fiscal year generated less total sales than the low amount noted in this Footnote although some generated total sales in excess of that amount. Of the franchisees shown in this chart, 40% met or exceeded the total average sales volume

141

levels. Generally speaking, those franchisees with more experience in utilizing our training and sales techniques are the higher producers.

12. For purposes of this chart, we have estimated a gross margin percentage of 60%. In determining this percentage, we deducted the distribution fee (34%) and royalty fee (1.5%) paid to us, and our estimate of distribution costs (3.73%) and shipping costs (0.5%) as shown in the preceding chart. We then rounded to the nearest whole percentage number.

THESE CHARTS OF GROSS REVENUE MARGINS ARE MERELY ESTIMATES AND SHOULD NOT BE CONSIDERED AS THE ACTUAL OR POTENTIAL SALES, PROFITS OR EARNINGS THAT WILL BE REALIZED BY ANY SPECIFIC FRANCHISEE. WE DO NOT REPRESENT THAT YOU CAN EXPECT TO ATTAIN THESE OR ANY SPECIFIC GROSS REVENUE MARGINS.

YOUR ABILITY TO ACHIEVE ANY LEVEL OF NET INCOME WILL DEPEND UPON FACTORS NOT WITHIN OUR CONTROL, INCLUDING THE OCCURRENCE OF CERTAIN START UP AND OPERATING EXPENSES AND THE AMOUNT OF THOSE EXPENSES, AND YOUR LEVEL OF EXPERTISE. FURTHER, THE ABOVE FIGURES DO NOT ACCOUNT FOR INTEREST EXPENSE, APPRECIATION OR DEPRECIATION OF ASSETS, RENT, OR OTHER OVERHEAD, CAPITAL EXPENSES AND CARRYING COSTS WHICH WILL VARY FROM FRANCHISEE TO FRANCHISEE.

A FRANCHISEE'S INDIVIDUAL FINANCIAL RESULTS ARE LIKELY TO DIFFER FROM THE RESULTS PRESENTED.

If any prospective distributor or franchisee has any questions regarding the figures and assumptions contained in the charts or desires any additional information or documents to verify or supplement the information contained in the charts, please write or call us and substantiating materials pertaining to this data will be made available for inspection at our headquarters and will be provided upon request.

HUNTINGTON LEARNING CENTER

496 Kinderkamack Rd.
Oradell, NJ 07649
Tel: (800) 653-8400 (201) 261-8400
Fax: (201) 261-3233
E-Mail: hlcorp@aol.com
Internet Address: www.huntingtonlearning.com
Contact: Mr. Richard C. Pittius, VP Franchise

Description: Offers services to 5-19 year-olds, and occasionally to adults, in reading, spelling, phonics, language development study skills and mathematics, as well as programs to prepare for standardized entrance exams. Instruction is offered in a tutorial setting and is predominately remedial in nature, although some enrichment is offered.

# Franchised Units:	151 Units
# Company-Owned Units:	54 Units
Total # Units:	205 Units
Founded In:	1977
1st Franchised In:	1985
Average Total Investment:	136.8-188.6K
Franchise Fee:	34K
On-Going Royalty:	8%/$1.2K minimum
Advertising Fee:	2%/$300 Min
Financial Assistance:Yes(D) (D – direct, or I – indirect)	
Site Selection Assistance:	Yes
Lease Negotiation Assistance:	Yes
Contract Terms (Init./Renew):	10/10
Initial Training Provided:2 1/2 Weeks at Oradell, NJ.	

THIS ITEM 19 IS NOT A REPRESENTATION, PROMISE, OR FORECAST; NOR IS IT AN ESTIMATE OF THE SALES, EXPENSES, PROFITS, OR EARNINGS THAT MAY OR

CAN BE ACHIEVED BY YOU OR ANY PROSPECTIVE FRANCHISEE. YOUR RESULTS ARE LIKELY TO DIFFER FROM THE RESULTS STATED IN THIS ITEM 19. HUNTINGTON DOES NOT REPRESENT THAT YOU CAN EXPECT TO ATTAIN ANY SPECIFIED SALES OR INCUR ANY SPECIFIED EXPENSES.

Huntington Learning Centers differ from each other in a multitude of important ways, including their market area and geographic location and the number of children and population contained thereabout and the economic and financial circumstances of this population. Huntington Learning Centers also differ from each other in their physical, marketing, employee, and manager's characteristics and in many other factors that may or may not exist or be similar to the factors that exist in any other location or geographic area or market area that may be considered by you or any prospective franchisee. Actual sales, expenses, profits, and earnings vary from one Huntington Learning Center to another by significant amounts, and Huntington cannot and does not estimate or forecast the sales, expenses, profits, or earnings that may be achieved by you. Huntington does not authorize its officers or sales personnel to furnish you with any oral or written information about actual or potential sales, expenses, profits, or earnings of Huntington Learning Centers, other than the specific information contained in this Item 19. Revenue at your Franchised Center business is determined by many factors, including factors exogenous to the business and factors such as the way you operate your business, the number

of inquiries, conversion of these inquiries to enrolled students, program duration, and receipts. You should consult with financial, business, and legal advisors about this Item 19 and the Franchise Agreement. This Item 19 contains no information about future, projected, or forecasted sales; or about actual, average, projected, or forecasted expenses, profits, or earnings. The data used to compile this Item 19 will be made available to any prospective franchisee upon reasonable written request.

Gross revenues ("sales") in this Item 19 were reported to Huntington by its franchised Huntington Learning Centers in operation for an entire calendar year, and for concurrent equal periods of time. Huntington has not audited nor in any other manner substantiated the truthfulness, accuracy, or completeness of any information supplied by its franchisees. If a Huntington Learning Center was transferred from one franchisee to another, its results under the different franchisees are included as the results of one Huntington Learning Center. Sales by Huntington Learning Centers owned or operated by Huntington or its affiliates as of the end of a calendar year are not included in this Item 19. If a Huntington Learning Center was transferred from (to) Huntington or a Huntington affiliate to (from) a franchisee, its results are reported as of (to) the transfer date.

The following table presents the number of franchised Huntington Learning Centers open during each year, their average annual sales, and the number and percent that achieve annual sales greater than each year's average.

Sales of Franchised Huntington Learning Centers				
Year	Number in operation for the entire year	Average annual sales of centers in operation for the entire year	Number and percent in operation for the entire year that achieved annual sales greater than that year's average	
			Number	Percent
1991	68	$156,311	31	46%
1992	69	$186,160	32	46%
1993	72	$210,661	34	47%
1994	75	$233,833	31	41%
1995	85	$243,493	38	45%
1996	91	$285,472	42	46%
1997	110	$319,943	49	44%

SYLVAN LEARNING CENTERS

1000 Lancaster St.
Baltimore, MD 21202
Tel: (800) 284-8214 (410) 843-8000
Fax: (410) 843-8717
E-Mail: irene.vavas@educate.com
Internet Address: www.educate.com
Contact: Ms. Flo Schell, VP Franchise System Dev.

Description: SYLVAN is the leading provider of educational services to families, schools and industry. It provides computer-based testing services internationally for academic admissions, professional licensure and certification programs.

SYLVAN services kindergarten through adult-levels from more than 800 SYLVAN LEARNING CENTERS worldwide.

# Franchised Units:	720 Units
# Company-Owned Units:	80 Units
Total # Units:	800 Units
Founded In:	1979
1st Franchised In:	1980
Average Total Investment:	92-165K
Franchise Fee:	38-46K
On-Going Royalty:	8-9%
Advertising Fee:	1.5%
Financial Assistance:Yes(B) (D – direct, or I – indirect)	
Site Selection Assistance:	Yes
Lease Negotiation Assistance:	No
Contract Terms (Init./Renew):	10/10
Initial Training Provided:6 Days Baltimore, MD; 5 Days in Various Other Locations.	

As of December 31, 1998, SYLVAN had 595 licensed Centers subject to revenue reporting requirements. Of these, there were 549 franchised Centers operating continuously in the U.S. throughout the 12 calendar months of 1998. Of those 549 Centers, the following "Revenue Ranking Report" or "Report" provides the 1998 annual gross revenues of 546 Centers (three Centers that did not report fully their 1998 revenues are omitted from the Report). The Report does not include any Center that operated for only a part of 1998 because it either closed during that year, or opened after January of that year. The revenues shown on the Report are the revenues upon which licensees' monthly royalty fees were calculated.

SYLVAN offered substantially the same services to all of the licensed Centers included in the Revenue Ranking Report and substantially all the Centers offered the same instructional services in reading, math, study skills and algebra. Many factors or variables affect the gross revenues of Centers. Among these are:

- the licensee's knowledge of its local market
- the amount and effectiveness of advertising
- the telemarketing skills of Center personnel in dealing with inquiries from prospective clients
- the presence in the market of other learning centers and tutors

- the demographics of the market served by the Center
- the location and appearance of the Center
- the licensee's standing in the community and relationships with local school and business leaders

Your licensed Center will likely be affected by one or more of these factors, some to a greater extent than others.

Prior to May 5, 1995, SYLVAN sold "A," "B," and "C" type territories, with respective demographic ranges of:

20,000 to 30,000 school age children for an "A" territory
10,000 to 20,000 school age children for a "B" territory
5,000 to 10,000 school age children for a "C" territory

Since May 5, 1995, SYLVAN has offered only A and B type territories, with respective demographic ranges of:

18,000 to 30,000 school age children for an "A" territory

8,000 to 18,000 school age children for a "B" territory

Since SYLVAN no longer sells "C" type territories, and because "C" type territories are routinely "upgraded" to "B" territories whenever they are sold, the licenses renewed, or upon the request of the licensee in the following Report, we have included 32 "C" type territories sold before May 5, 1995 in the "B" territory list of Centers. These "C" territories should have demographic profiles that are within the current "B" territory range. You should keep in mind the demographic ranges we reference above and the demographics of the particular area that you may be considering when evaluating the following Report. You should also keep in mind that the demographic range for any given Center may vary from the norms for "A" and "B" type territories. Reasons for this include different demographic criteria in existence at the time the territory was first sold and population increases or decreases occurring since the time of sales. Consequently, some "B" Centers operate in territories that meet the current "A" territory demographic profile.

In some cases, licensees open and operate more than one Center in their Territory. We include these additional, or "satellite," Centers in the Report as independent Centers and categorize them as "A" or "B" Centers corresponding to the "A" or "B" Territory in which they are located. In the Report that follows, there are 79 of these "A" satellite centers, and 9 "B" satellite Centers.

We do not require our licensees to report fixed and variable expenses, and accordingly, we cannot estimate the average "break-even" sales volume of the reporting Centers. We expect that our licensees' fixed and variable expenses vary widely from Center to Center. As a result, even if your gross revenues fall within the reported range of

revenues experienced by our licensees, there is no guarantee that your Center will be profitable. The data received from reporting Centers was accumulated using a uniform method that included direct reports to SYLVAN by the licensees. SYLVAN has not independently verified the figures given by the licensed Centers. SYLVAN does not require its licensees to utilize a uniform accounting method and therefore cannot confirm whether their revenue figures were compiled in accordance with generally accepted accounting principles.

THE ACTUAL GROSS SALES FIGURES THAT FOLLOW IN THE REPORT ARE OF LICENSEE OPERATED CENTERS AND SHOULD NOT BE CONSIDERED AS THE ACTUAL OR PROBABLE GROSS SALES THAT WILL BE REALIZED BY ANY LICENSEE. SYLVAN DOES NOT REPRESENT THAT YOU CAN EXPECT TO ATTAIN THESE LEVELS OF GROSS SALES OR THAT IF YOU DO, YOUR CENTER WILL BE PROFITABLE.

We will provide you with substantiation of the data used in preparing this Revenue Ranking Report upon your reasonable request, however, this does not require us to disclose the identity of any specific licensee or require us to release data without the consent of any specific licensee.

1998 Revenue Ranking Report
U.S. Sylvan Learning Centers Open
Continuously for all Twelve Months of
Calendar Year 1998
THIS REPORT HAS BEEN PREPARED WITHOUT AN AUDIT. PROSPECTIVE LICENSEES SHOULD BE ADVISED THAT NO CERTIFIED PUBLIC ACCOUNTANT HAS AUDITED THESE FIGURES OR EXPRESSED AN OPINION WITH REGARD TO THEIR CONTENT OR FORM.

	"A" Territory Centers				
	1998 Calendar Year Revenues				
Ranking in Order of Revenues	1998 Sum of Revenues Reported	Ranking in Order of Revenues	1998 Sum of Revenues Reported	Ranking in Order of Revenues	1998 Sum of Revenues Reported
1	1,048,801	36	585,777	71	494,468
2	929,919	37	583,633	72	493,705
3	890,035	38	581,651	73	490,878
4	878,099	39	580,704	74	489,256
5	841,910	40	578,618	75	488,368
6	838,992	41	576,518	76	485,268
7	827,435	42	560,504	77	483,681
8	798,990	43	557,717	78	482,834
9	788,473	44	554,071	79	482,649
10	784,689	45	553,310	80	481,393
11	779,557	46	550,008	81	479,690
12	756,549	47	549,208	82	479,516
13	753,219	48	548,466	83	475,308
14	734,372	49	533,820	84	474,184
15	722,901	50	531,476	85	469,698
16	703,800	51	529,327	86	467,886
17	703,134	52	528,537	87	466,895
18	699,307	53	524,405	88	465,978
19	697,011	54	523,928	89	465,357
20	683,728	55	519,090	90	465,351
21	677,269	56	510,792	91	461,696
22	668,312	57	510,076	92	459,579
23	660,309	58	508,821	93	456,978
24	651,886	59	507,809	94	455,125
25	644,157	60	507,715	95	454,658
26	643,088	61	506,480	96	454,227
27	642,452	62	506,085	97	453,795
28	639,499	63	505,076	98	450,386
29	612,085	64	504,590	99	450,116
30	610,837	65	503,902	100	449,175
31	597,990	66	502,719	101	448,768
32	593,117	67	502,583	102	447,115
33	590,635	68	498,096	103	446,579
34	590,113	69	495,703	104	441,913
35	587,014	70	494,850	105	440,072

"A" Territory Centers 1998 Calendar Year Revenues					
Ranking in Order of Revenues	1998 Sum of Revenues Reported	Ranking in Order of Revenues	1998 Sum of Revenues Reported	Ranking in Order of Revenues	1998 Sum of Revenues Reported
106	437,230	141	391,975	176	350,848
107	435,913	142	389,762	177	349,041
108	434,019	143	388,063	178	348,087
109	433,665	144	386,692	179	347,181
110	431,813	145	385,871	180	346,972
111	431,418	146	377,523	181	346,944
112	430,397	147	376,606	182	346,611
113	429,119	148	376,298	183	345,496
114	425,643	149	375,887	184	344,793
115	424,554	150	374,676	185	343,656
116	424,229	151	373,068	186	343,274
117	424,189	152	372,689	187	339,916
118	423,969	153	372,452	188	338,917
119	423,429	154	370,815	189	338,629
120	420,788	155	370,554	190	338,512
121	419,033	156	366,748	191	338,448
122	417,258	157	365,849	192	338,294
123	415,479	158	365,673	193	337,504
124	414,304	159	365,529	194	336,573
125	414,225	160	364,953	195	334,302
126	413,812	161	364,508	196	333,544
127	412,926	162	363,960	197	332,001
128	411,831	163	363,596	198	331,553
129	407,700	164	362,507	199	330,362
130	405,321	165	360,198	200	329,174
131	403,849	166	359,024	201	328,848
132	403,451	167	358,751	202	327,987
133	402,382	168	358,310	203	326,343
134	400,597	169	357,968	204	326,302
135	399,746	170	357,269	205	324,861
136	399,032	171	354,620	206	324,336
137	396,504	172	354,466	207	322,582
138	395,039	173	353,985	208	321,858
139	394,351	174	353,759	209	321,210
140	392,380	175	352,559	210	321,012

"A" Territory Centers 1998 Calendar Year Revenues					
Ranking in Order of Revenues	1998 Sum of Revenues Reported	Ranking in Order of Revenues	1998 Sum of Revenues Reported	Ranking in Order of Revenues	1998 Sum of Revenues Reported
211	316,838	246	288,996	281	260,193
212	316,462	247	288,984	282	259,480
213	315,768	248	288,927	283	258,914
214	314,260	249	287,478	284	258,636
215	313,697	250	287,256	285	258,179
216	313,385	251	285,450	286	257,588
217	312,754	252	284,805	287	252,173
218	312,398	253	283,610	288	252,000
219	311,966	254	283,104	289	251,408
220	311,543	255	282,875	290	250,951
221	310,495	256	282,169	291	250,021
222	310,004	257	281,799	292	248,211
223	309,927	258	280,153	293	246,512
224	309,887	259	280,056	294	245,109
225	308,416	260	279,866	295	242,983
226	307,597	261	279,376	296	242,961
227	306,938	262	278,870	297	242,503
228	304,642	263	277,213	298	242,412
229	304,362	264	275,701	299	240,993
230	303,876	265	275,679	300	240,305
231	303,293	266	274,648	301	239,796
232	302,825	267	274,141	302	239,161
233	300,634	268	274,134	303	238,940
234	299,237	269	274,120	304	238,789
235	294,984	270	273,572	305	238,660
236	294,502	271	272,471	306	237,186
237	294,439	272	270,037	307	237,148
238	293,385	273	267,500	308	236,906
239	293,368	274	266,971	309	235,930
240	292,152	275	266,968	310	235,559
241	292,053	276	263,230	311	235,170
242	291,154	277	263,177	312	235,081
243	291,018	278	261,041	313	234,544
244	290,353	279	260,469	314	234,018
245	289,926	280	260,211	315	233,861

| | "A" Territory Centers | | | | |
| | 1998 Calendar Year Revenues | | | | |
Ranking in Order of Revenues	1998 Sum of Revenues Reported	Ranking in Order of Revenues	1998 Sum of Revenues Reported	Ranking in Order of Revenues	1998 Sum of Revenues Reported
316	233,802	351	187,259	386	122,886
317	233,710	352	185,753	387	118,414
318	233,342	353	185,696	388	114,565
319	232,444	354	182,286	389	113,580
320	232,372	355	181,924	390	107,603
321	231,903	356	181,909	391	105,519
322	230,038	357	181,871	392	104,796
323	229,552	358	181,488	393	103,013
324	228,295	359	180,735	394	100,195
325	227,608	360	180,700	395	93,512
326	227,494	361	177,987	396	93,111
327	226,964	362	176,833	397	77,782
328	224,723	363	174,843	398	74,268
329	223,764	364	167,821	399	63,699
330	223,250	365	166,458		
331	221,158	366	166,201		
332	218,837	367	164,888		
333	216,744	368	163,825		
334	216,510	369	163,099		
335	215,599	370	162,194		
336	214,843	371	157,995		
337	214,699	372	156,231		
338	213,776	373	153,390		
339	212,244	374	148,288		
340	210,581	375	144,761		
341	205,833	376	141,975		
342	201,591	377	141,067		
343	201,445	378	139,742		
344	201,011	379	137,411		
345	200,504	380	134,398		
346	200,176	381	132,508		
347	195,584	382	132,451		
348	194,867	383	131,796	Total Revenue	$142,891,829
349	193,936	384	127,775	Average	$358,125
350	191,572	385	127,659	Median	$329,174

"B" Territory Centers 1998 Calendar Year Revenues					
Ranking in Order of Revenues	1998 Sum of Revenues Reported	Ranking in Order of Revenues	1998 Sum of Revenues Reported	Ranking in Order of Revenues	1998 Sum of Revenues Reported
1	930,099	36	310,120	71	230,999
2	876,672	37	307,369	72	230,676
3	865,659	38	299,311	73	230,166
4	572,253	39	292,276	74	228,991
5	543,143	40	291,131	75	227,900
6	460,786	41	289,399	76	225,100
7	456,774	42	289,282	77	224,614
8	446,393	43	288,113	78	222,215
9	436,219	44	282,671	79	220,738
10	404,726	45	281,571	80	219,347
11	401,982	46	277,112	81	219,085
12	396,967	47	276,745	82	216,788
13	390,577	48	276,391	83	214,827
14	385,802	49	274,014	84	214,428
15	380,799	50	270,489	85	212,605
16	378,731	51	267,447	86	212,540
17	371,686	52	266,835	87	205,198
18	366,707	53	266,728	88	205,182
19	364,184	54	264,701	89	203,565
20	360,313	55	263,648	90	203,432
21	358,234	56	262,905	91	201,818
22	348,880	57	260,674	92	201,194
23	345,981	58	259,887	93	197,784
24	343,625	59	253,854	94	196,570
25	343,095	60	252,608	95	195,762
26	337,188	61	251,232	96	194,487
27	337,131	62	249,233	97	192,728
28	333,496	63	245,748	98	188,979
29	329,213	64	243,913	99	182,021
30	324,376	65	242,955	100	178,284
31	319,395	66	240,270	101	177,213
32	317,877	67	237,079	102	175,370
33	317,824	68	236,990	103	174,971
34	317,089	69	235,526	104	172,337
35	316,437	70	231,577	105	168,717

\"B\" Territory Centers 1998 Calendar Year Revenues					
Ranking in Order of Revenues	1998 Sum of Revenues Reported	Ranking in Order of Revenues	1998 Sum of Revenues Reported	Ranking in Order of Revenues	1998 Sum of Revenues Reported
106	167,820	141	91,490		
107	167,010	142	86,268		
108	165,913	143	82,147		
109	164,497	144	81,841		
110	163,124	145	71,876		
111	161,989	146	69,364		
112	158,726	147	65,376		
113	158,680				
114	158,433				
115	157,597				
116	157,349				
117	156,316				
118	156,131				
119	155,446				
120	154,404				
121	142,659				
122	140,409				
123	137,806				
124	136,568				
125	125,432				
126	124,863				
127	124,536				
128	121,893				
129	119,724				
130	116,354				
131	115,615				
132	114,032				
133	113,981				
134	111,694				
135	109,090				
136	106,016				
137	100,108				
138	98,891			Total Revenue	$36,585,768
139	94,364			Average	$248,883
140	93,186			Median	$228,991

Employment & personnel

Dynamic People

Skilled People With People Skills

DYNAMIC PEOPLE
3535 Piedmont Rd., NE
Atlanta, GA 30305
Tel: (800) 933-9976 (404) 240-3000

Fax: (404) 240-3084
Contact: Ms. Mary Jane Good, Regional Vice President

# Franchised Units:	10 Units
# Company-Owned Units:	1 Unit
Total # Units:	11 Units

NOTE: THIS INFORMATION RELATES ONLY TO THE TEMPORARY HELP BUSINESS. WE HAVE NO EARNINGS CLAIMS INFORMATION FOR THE PERMANENT PLACEMENT BUSINESS.

DYNAMIC does not represent to potential franchisees what projected sales, earnings or profits should be because these vary widely from franchise to franchise. It may be helpful, however, for you to know the following average Bill Rate, Gross Margin Percentage and Weekly Hour numbers for our franchises for the DYNAMIC fiscal year ended October 29, 1995, October 27, 1996 and November 2, 1997. The data below comes from the payroll and billing information which DYNAMIC processes on a weekly basis. It is not audited. The data is from franchises which were in operation as of October 29, 1995, October 27, 1996, and November 2, 1997, respectively, and which had been in business at least one year as of those respective dates. As of October 29, 1995, 7 franchises at locations throughout the United States met this criteria and all are included in the following statistics relating to that date. As of October 27, 1996, 7 franchises (including one which was franchised then re-acquired by DYNAMIC during the fiscal year) at locations throughout the United States met this criteria and all are included in the following statistics relating to that date. As of November 2, 1997, 6 franchises at locations throughout the United States met this criteria and all are included in the following statistics relating to that date.

Bill Rate. Bill Rate is the amount per hour billed to the DYNAMIC client using temporary services.

Average Bill Rate for 12 months ending October 29, 1995, was $11.68.
(Five of seven offices exceeded this Average)

Average Bill Rate for 12 months ending October 27, 1996, was $12.15.
(Four of seven offices exceeded this Average)

Average Bill Rate for 12 months ending November 2, 1997, was $14.51.
(Two of six offices exceeded this Average)

A number of factors influence the Bill Rate in a particular market, such as prevailing wages, unemployment levels, skill level of the temporary employees, and competition.

Gross Margin Percentage. Gross Margin Percentage is Gross Margin stated as a percentage of net billings. That is, the net billings during applicable accounting periods less all payroll and other direct labor costs, divided by net billings, and multiplied by 100%.

$$\text{GM\%} = \frac{\text{Net Billings - (Payroll \& other Direct Labor Costs)}}{\text{Net Billings}} \times 100\%$$

Average GM% for 12 months ending October 29, 1995 was 26.37%.
(Four of seven offices exceeded this Average)

Average GM% for 12 months ending October 27, 1996 was 25.21%.
(Three of seven offices exceeded this Average)

Average GM% for 12 months ending November 2, 1997 was 23.70%.
(Two of six offices exceeded this Average)

Gross Margin Percentage varies from franchise to franchise based on skill mix, unemployment levels, the local economy, competition and other factors.

Weekly Hours. Weekly hours are the total number of hours of temporary help billed per week by a franchise.

Average Weekly Hours for 12 months ending October 29, 1995 was 2,090.
(Three of seven offices exceeded this Average)

Average Weekly Hours for 12 months ending October 26, 1996 was 1,997.
(Three of seven offices exceeded this Average)

Average Weekly Hours for 12 months ending November 2, 1997 was 2,293.61.
(Two of six offices exceeded this Average)

The number of Average Weekly Hours varies greatly between different franchises and with time within the same franchise. It is influenced by factors such as sales and marketing effort, local economy, availability of workers, competition, projects, time of the year and quality of service being provided.

We provide substantiation of the data used in preparing this earnings claim to prospective franchisees upon reasonable request.

OTHER THAN THE DIRECT LABOR COSTS INHERENT IN THE GROSS MARGIN PERCENTAGE NUMBERS, WE PRESENT NO INFORMATION CONCERNING EXPENSES.

YOU SHOULD DRAW NO INFERENCE AS TO EXPENSES OR NET PROFITS OF EXISTING OR FUTURE FRANCHISED BUSINESSES FROM THE DATA.

THE NUMBERS PRESENTED HERE ARE AVERAGES OF SPECIFIC FRANCHISES AND YOU SHOULD NOT CONSIDER THEM AS THE ACTUAL OR POTENTIAL BILL RATE, GROSS MARGIN PERCENTAGE, AND WEEKLY HOUR NUMBERS THAT YOU OR ANY OTHER FRANCHISE WILL REALIZE. WE DO NOT REPRESENT THAT YOU OR ANY OTHER FRANCHISEE CAN EXPECT TO ATTAIN THESE BILL RATE, GROSS MARGIN PERCENTAGE, AND WEEKLY HOUR NUMBERS OR ANY OTHER SALES, PROFITS OR EARNINGS.

We developed the following table to assist you in identifying some of the significant variables you should consider in purchasing a DYNAMIC franchise. The table is set up so you can use it in your conversations with existing franchisees. WE MAKE NO REPRESENTATION THAT THIS TABLE INCLUDES ALL OF THE SIGNIFICANT VARIABLES WHICH MAY APPLY TO YOUR PROPOSED OFFICE OR WHICH MAY EFFECT YOUR PROPOSED MARKET AND WE MAKE NO REPRESENTATION AS TO WHAT YOUR EXPENSES WILL BE. WE PROVIDE THIS TABLE WITH THE UNDERSTANDING THAT YOU MAY USE IT AS A STARTING POINT FOR YOUR ANALYSIS, BUT THAT YOU MUST DETERMINE HOW APPLICABLE THIS MODEL IS TO YOUR SPECIFIC CIRCUMSTANCE.

Expense Items	Franchisee: Market:	Franchisee: Market:	Franchisee: Market:	Franchisee: Market:	Franchisee: Market:
Rent					
Associates Payroll					
Utilities					
Repairs & Maintenance					
Telephone					
Postage					
Courier					
Office Supplies					
Forms & Brochures					
Promotional Materials					
Professional Fees					
Taxes & Licenses					
Dues & Subscriptions					
Equipment					
Miscellaneous Expenses					
Furniture					
Total Operations					
Newspaper Advertising					
Business & Sales Promo.					
Other Advertising					
Total Advertising					
Total Expenses					

HOME INSTEAD SENIOR CARE

604 N. 109th Court
Omaha, NE 68154
Tel: (888) 484-5759 (402) 498-4466
Fax: (402) 498-5757
E-Mail: homeinsted@aol.com
Internet Address: www.homeinstead.com
Contact: Mr. Jeff Huber, Franchise Development Manager

Description: HOME INSTEAD SENIOR CARE is America's largest, most successful, non-medical companionship and home care franchise. Entrepreneur and other leading business publications have ranked us one of the top opportunities in all of franchising. The elderly market we serve is the fastest growing segment of the population. Services such as companionship, light housework, errands and meal preparation assist the elderly in remaining in their homes rather than being institutionalized.

# Franchised Units:	159 Units
# Company-Owned Units:	1 Units
Total # Units:	160 Units
Founded In:	1994
1st Franchised In:	1995
Average Total Investment:	21-27.7K
Franchise Fee:	15.5K
On-Going Royalty:	5%
Advertising Fee:	0%
Financial Assistance: No (D – direct, or I – indirect)	
Site Selection Assistance:	Yes
Lease Negotiation Assistance:	No
Contract Terms (Init./Renew):	10/10
Initial Training Provided: 1 Week Corporate Headquarters; 2 Days Visit Franchise Office	

Exhibit X is a statement of the gross sales for the HOME INSTEAD SERNIOR CARE BUSINESS operated by the Franchisor in Omaha, Nebraska. Franchisor commenced operation of its HOME INSTEAD SENIOR CARE BUSINESS in Omaha, Nebraska on June 1, 1994. In November, 1995, Franchisor transferred a portion of its customer accounts to a new franchisee and in September, 1996 transferred a portion of its customers accounts to another new franchisee. Except as set forth in Exhibit X, HOME INSTEAD, does not furnish or authorize sale persons to furnish any oral or written information, representations or statements of actual sales, costs, income or profits of a HOME INSTEAD SENIOR CARE franchised business.

ACTUAL RESULTS VARY FROM FRANCHISEE TO FRANCHISEE AND HOME INSTEAD CANNOT ESTIMATE THE RESULTS OF ANY PARTICULAR FRANCHISEE. A NEW FRANCHISEE'S FINANCIAL RESULTS MAY DIFFER FROM THE FIGURES PRESENTED. YOU SHOULD MAKE YOUR OWN INVESTIGATION AND DETERMINE WHETHER YOUR FRANCHISED HOME INSTEAD SENIOR CARE BUSINESS WILL BE PROFITABLE. HOME INSTEAD DOES NOT GUARANTEE THAT A FRANCHISEE WILL HAVE INCOME.

Exhibit X
STATEMENT OF THE ANNUAL GROSS SALES FOR THE SINGLE HOME INSTEAD SENIOR CARE BUSINESS OPERATED BY FRANCHISOR IN THE OMAHA, NEBRASKA TERRITORY.

As of December 31, 1998, there are 150 HOME INSTEAD SENIOR CARE franchised businesses in operation. All of the franchised businesses are comparable to the franchise being offered.

Set forth below is the actual annual gross sales of the HOME INSTEAD SENIOR CARE BUSINESS operated by the Franchisor in Omaha, Nebraska, commencing with the first day of operation on June 1, 1994.

ACTUAL GROSS SALES OF THE HOME INSTEAD SENIOR CARE BUSINESS OPER-

ATED BY FRANCHISOR IN OMAHA, NEBRASKA, COMMENCING ON

THE FIRST DAY OF OPERATION ON JUNE 1,1994

Year of Operation by Franchisor	Annual Gross Sales
First Seven Months of Operation, Commencing June 1, 1994–December 31, 1994	$67,891.00
Second Year of Operation — 1995 January 1, 1995–December 31, 1995	$353,300.00
Third Year of Operation — 1996 January 1,1996–December 31, 1996	$428,121.00
Fourth Year of Operation — 1997 January 1, 1997–December 31,1997	$431,382.00
Fifth Year of Operation — 1998 January 1,1998–December 31, 1998	$553,625.00

The information presented is based upon the actual gross sales of the company-owned HOME INSTEAD SENIOR CARE BUSINESS operated by the Franchisor in Omaha, Nebraska, since June 1, 1994.

SUBSTANTIATION OF THE DATA IN THIS EARNINGS CLAIM WILL BE MADE AVAILABLE TO YOU ON REASONABLE REQUEST.

A NEW FRANCHISEE'S INDIVIDUAL RESULTS ARE LIKELY TO DIFFER

FROM THE RESULTS STATED IN THE GROSS SALES ABOVE. THESE SALES SHOULD NOT BE CONSIDERED AS THE ACTUAL OR POTENTIAL SALES, PROFITS OR EARNINGS THAT WILL BE REALIZED BY ANY OTHER FRANCHISEE. THE FRANCHISOR DOES NOT REPRESENT THAT ANY FRANCHISEE CAN EXPECT TO ATTAIN THESE SALES.

MRI® Management Recruiters·

MANAGEMENT RECRUITERS/SALES CONSULTANTS
200 Public Sq., 31st Fl.
Cleveland, OH 44114-2301
Tel: (800) 875-4000 (216) 696-1122
Fax: (216) 696-6612
E-Mail: webmaster@brilliantpeople.com
Internet Address: www.brilliantpeople.com
Contact: Mr. Robert A. Angell, VP Franchise Marketing

Description: Complete range of recruitment and human resource services, including: permanent executive, mid-management, professional, marketing, sales management and sales placement; temporary professional and sales staffing; video-conferencing; permanent and temporary office support personnel; with coverage on all continents. Franchises available ourside of North America through our wholly-owned subsidiary, the Humana Group International.

# Franchised Units:	791 Units
# Company-Owned Units:	39 Units
Total # Units:	830 Units
Founded In:	1957
1st Franchised In:	1965
Average Total Investment:	110-145K
Franchise Fee:	72.5K

On-Going Royalty:	7%	Lease Negotiation Assistance:	Yes
Advertising Fee:	0.5%	Contract Terms (Init./Renew):	5-20/10
Financial Assistance:Yes(I) (D – direct, or I – indirect)		Initial Training Provided:3 Weeks Headquarters, Cleveland, OH; 10 Days Franchisee's Location.	
Site Selection Assistance:	Yes		

We prepare an Operating Ratio Study each year (the "Study"). In addition to providing it to our franchised and company offices, we are providing it to you as part of this Earnings Claim. The most recent Study is for 1998. The Study is based on the actual operating results of 467 offices that were in operation for the entire year. We base it on the data reported to us by the offices.

The Study is divided by size of offices, measured by the average number of recruiters, or "filled desks" that the office had during the year, as reported by the office. If the owner is working actively as a recruiter, as we expect you to do, the owner is included in the number. The three office size categories are 2 to 4 desks, 5 to 7 desks, and 8 and above. There were 137 one-desk offices, which are not included in the Study. Nine offices did not report their operating results in time for preparation of the Study. There were 446 franchised and 21 company-owned offices included. There were 285 offices (all franchised) in the 2-4 desk category of the Study, 92 (86 franchised and 6 company-owned) in the 5-7 desk category, and 90 (75 franchised and 15 company-owned) in the 8 and up category. For purposes of the Study, an office that combines both Management Recruiters and Sales Consultants operations is treated as a single office.

The offices are located in 48 states, Puerto Rico, and Mexico. We attach no relevance to the geographical locations of the offices in the Study, since each office may do business anywhere in the country.

Substantiation of the data used in preparing the Study will be made available to you on reasonable request.

A NEW FRANCHISEE'S INDIVIDUAL FINANCIAL RESULTS ARE LIKELY TO DIFFER FROM THE RESULTS STATED IN THE EARNINGS CLAIM.

The Study follows on the next five pages, followed by additional information.

March 22, 1999

To:	All Management Recruiters Offices
	All Sales Consultants Offices
	All CompuSearch Offices
From:	William E. Aglinsky
Subject:	1998 Operating Ratio Study

The primary factor that determines the success of your office is volume of placements. However, effective control over expenses can significantly increase an office's profitability at any given level of sales volume. To provide you with a guideline for use in analyzing and controlling your expenses, we have compiled the annual Operating Ratio Study from Income Reports submitted by Management Recruiters, Sales Consultants and CompuSearch offices.

We have again combined the operating results of Management Recruiters offices with the operating results of Sales Consultants and CompuSearch offices. Prior year studies indicate that expenses generally do not vary significantly among offices of similar size and profitability. Combining the MR's with the SC's and CS's creates a larger population and makes it statistically possible to have larger size categories.

During 1998 many offices participated in the new businesses introduced in late 1993 (DayStar, Inter-Exec, Conferview and Sales Staffers). The receipts from these services are not subject to the royalty obligation and are shown as a separate line item identified as "net cash in-other receipts". Because the expenses related to generating income for these businesses may not be easily separated from other costs of operation they are included with the total costs.

During 1998 many offices employed research assistants and project coordinators in order to increase production and to reduce overall personnel costs. A new line item was created in 1995 to separately report compensation related to research assistants and project coordinators. However, some offices may not have reported this compensation expense separately and may have combined it with account executive compensation. Approximately 53% of the offices in this study reported this expense separately from account executive compensation.

The 1998 Operating Ratio Study results are expressed on an annual basis. All dollar amounts are rounded to the nearest hundred dollars.

The study is based on Income Reports for the twelve-month period of January 1998 through December 1998. All MR, SC and CS offices, which were open the entire 1998 calendar year and averaged two or more filled desks, are included in this study, except for nine offices, which failed to submit their data as of the date required. Offices opened subsequent to January 1, 1998 are not included in the study because their operating results are not representative of the results of more tenured offices. This year, we have again grouped the offices into three desk size categories:

2-4, 5-7, and 8 or more desks. The categorization is based on the average number of filled desks during 1998. We are distributing the studies for all three size categories to all offices.

The report format of the Operating Ratio Study conforms very closely to the Form 10 Income Report, which is our source document. In each category, each line item represents the dollar average of the reported results of all offices in the category, which are then also expressed as percentages of the average net cash-in for the category.

As with previous Operating Ratio Studies, we have used "Quartile Analysis" in the presentations of the operating ratio results. The HIGH QUARTILE column reflects the average operating results of offices whose net profit ranks in the upper 25% of offices in their size category. The MIDDLE RANGE column reflects the average operating results of offices whose net profit ranks in the middle 50% of offices in their size category.

I hope that this study will provide you with some meaningful information to use while evaluating your own operating results and managing your business for increased profitability. Please feel free to call if you have any questions or comments.

Offices with 2 to 4 Desks

There were 285 2–4 desk franchised offices which were open the entire year and which were included in the Study. Here are the percentages of these offices that achieved or surpassed the results shown:

	High Quartile		Mid Range	
	$	%	$	%
Income				
Net Cash In — Permanent	719,000		340,300	
Net Cash In — Other Receipts	4,100		3,100	
Net Cash In	723,100	100.00%	343,400	100.00%
	Note a		Note c	
Operating Expenses				
Account Executive Compensation	146,500	20.26%	74,200	21.61%
Research Assistant & Project Coordinator	19,400	2.68%	10,200	2.97%

	High Quartile		Mid Range	
	$	%	$	%
Office Payroll	31,300	4.33%	19,600	5.71%
Hospitalization & Insurance	14,000	1.94%	10,100	2.94%
Payroll & Other Taxes	23,700	3.28%	16,100	4.69%
Advertising	5,500	0.76%	3,200	0.93%
Dues & Subscriptions	1,800	0.25%	1,900	0.55%
Equipment lease, depreciation, etc.	15,000	2.07%	13,000	3.79%
Office Supplies & Expenses	10,400	1.44%	9,800	2.85%
Professional Services	6,700	0.93%	4,500	1.31%
Rent & Utilities	18,100	2.50%	15,200	4.43%
Telephone	20,800	2.88%	15,600	4.54%
Travel & Entertainment	14,600	2.02%	9,600	2.80%
Miscellaneous & Repairs	7,000	0.97%	5,400	1.57%
Total Expenses	334,800	46.30%	208,400	60.69%
Net profit before royalties and owner/manager compensation	388,300	53.70%	135,000	39.31%
	Note b		Note d	
Note a: 10.5%. Note b: 8.8%. Note c: 49.5%. Note d: 47.8%.				

Offices with 5 to 7 Desks

There were 86 5-7 desk franchised offices, which were, open the entire year and which were included in the Study. Here are the percentages of these offices that achieved or surpassed the results shown:

	High Quartile		Mid Range	
	$	%	$	%
Income				
Net Cash In — Permanent	1,300,200		799,500	
Net Cash In — Other Receipts	2,400		5,700	
Net Cash In	1,302,600	100.00%	805,200	100.00%
	Note a		Note c	
Operating Expenses				
Account Executive Compensation	385,500	29.59%	284,600	35.35%
Research Assistant & Project Coordinator	64,700	4.97%	34,300	4.26%
Office Payroll	44,100	3.39%	38,300	4.76%
Hospitalization & Insurance	28,000	2.15%	20,700	2.57%

	High Quartile		Mid Range	
	$	%	$	%
Payroll & Other Taxes	45,200	3.47%	32,800	4.07%
Advertising	14,700	1.13%	6,700	0.83%
Dues & Subscriptions	3,900	0.30%	3,200	0.40%
Equipment Lease, Depreciation,etc.	15,500	1.19%	16,800	2.09%
Office Supplies & Expenses	25,000	1.92%	20,200	2.51%
Professional Services	13,300	1.02%	10,400	1.29%
Rent & Utilities	36,100	2.77%	26,500	3.29%
Telephone	38,000	2.92%	27,400	3.40%
Travel & Entertainment	34,000	2.61%	17,400	2.16%
Miscellaneous & Repairs	14,800	1.14%	10,100	1.25%
Total Expenses	762,800	58.56%	549,400	68.23%
Net profit before royalties and owner/manager compensation	539,800	41.44%	255,800	31.77%
	Note b		Note d	
Note a: 12.8%. Note b: 9.3%. Note c: 48.8%. Note d: 50.0%.				

Offices with 8 or more Desks

There were 75 8+ desk franchised offices which were open the entire year and which were included in the Study. Here are the percentages of these offices that achieved or surpassed the results shown:

	High Quartile		Mid Range	
	$	%	$	%
Income				
Net Cash In — Permanent	3,658,000		1,732,300	
Net Cash In — Other Receipts	23,200		15,100	
Net Cash In	3,681,200	100.00%	1,747,400	100.00%
	Note a		Note c	
Operating Expenses				
Account Executive Compensation	1,508,900	40.99%	703,700	40.27%
Research Assistant & Project Coordinator	195,300	5.31%	77,100	4.41%
Office Payroll	94,000	2.55%	86,300	4.94%
Hospitalization & Insurance	69,700	1.89%	44,800	2.56%
Payroll & Other Taxes	127,500	3.46%	74,700	4.27%
Advertising	41,000	1.11%	18,100	1.04%

	High Quartile		Mid Range	
	$	%	$	%
Dues & Subscriptions	8,400	0.23%	5,500	0.31%
Equipment Lease, Depreciation,etc.	47,500	1.29%	33,100	1.89%
Office Supplies & Expenses	43,800	1.19%	32,200	1.84%
Professional Services	27,900	0.76%	16,500	0.94%
Rent & Utilities	81,800	2.22%	55,900	3.20%
Telephone	76,200	2.07%	50,700	2.90%
Travel & Entertainment	85,300	2.32%	32,100	1.84%
Miscellaneous & Repairs	11,900	0.32%	11,800	0.68%
Total Expenses	2,419,200	65.72%	1,242,500	71.11%
Net profit before royalties and owner/manager compensation	1,262,000	34.28%	504,900	28.89%
	Note b		Note d	
Note a: 4.0%. Note b: 2.7%. Note C: 45.3%. Note d: 48.0%.				

As stated in the Study, the number of placements made will be the primary determining factor in your success. This in turn will be affected by your effort and ability and the effort and ability of persons you hire as account executives. We stress the importance of your personal production on your desk. It is a major part of a smaller office's cash receipts and profitability. This is particularly important in the early years of your operation and will continue to be important for the majority of our offices. While changes in the economy can affect our business, offices that respond flexibly to changing demands can remain profitable even during downturns in the economy.

Variations in expenses do affect profitability. The study shows that the major categories of expense are account executive compensation, office payroll, rent, and telephone. The advice of our regional management staff and the guidance provided by the Study can help you prudently control your expenses.

NORRELL SERVICES
3535 Piedmont Rd. NE
Atlanta, GA 30305
Tel: (800) 765-6342 (404) 240-3687
Fax: (404) 240-3014
E-Mail: cebz65a@prodigy.com
Internet Address: www.norrell.com
Contact: Mr. Les Wharton, VP Legal Affairs

Description: NORRELL SERVICES is a national provider of both short- and long-term staffing services. We offer traditional temporary help, project and managed staffing services to businesses, including clerical and light-industrial applications. Our competitive differences include no up-front fees, turn-key training and on-going support of our franchisees.

# Franchised Units:	114 Units
# Company-Owned Units:	161 Units
Total # Units:	275 Units
Founded In:	1961
1st Franchised In:	1966
Average Total Investment:	75.7-176.4K

Franchise Fee:	0	Lease Negotiation Assistance:	No
On-Going Royalty:	Varies	Contract Terms (Init./Renew):	10/15
Advertising Fee:	0%	Initial Training Provided:130-135 Hrs.	
Financial Assistance:Yes(I) (D – direct, or I – indirect)		Classroom Atlanta; 40+ Wks Pre-Open. In-Field; 80-120 Hrs. Pre/Post-Opening.	
Site Selection Assistance:	Yes		

NORRELL does not represent to potential franchisees what projected sales, earnings or profits should be because these vary widely from franchise to franchise. It may be helpful, however, for you to know the following average Bill Rate, Gross Margin Percentage and Weekly Hour numbers for the top one-third, middle one-third and lower one-third of the franchises in total Gross Margin for the NORRELL fiscal years ended October 29, 1995, October 27, 1996, and November 2, 1997. We also show you what the franchises in these groups paid to us in fees and royalties from the fee and royalty chart as a percentage of revenue. This data comes from the payroll and billing information NORRELL processed on a weekly basis. It is not audited. The data comes from franchises which were operating as of October 29, 1995, October 27, 1996, and November 2, 1997, respec-

tively, and which had been in business at least one year as of those respective dates. As of October 29, 1995, 94 franchises (including 3 offices which were company-owned and franchised during the year) at locations throughout the United States met this criteria and all are included in the statistics. As of October 27, 1996, 105 franchises (including 1 office which was franchised and reacquired by NORRELL during the year) at locations throughout the United States met this criteria and all are included in the statistics. As of November 2, 1997, 117 franchises (including 2 offices which were company-owned and franchised during the year and 7 offices which were franchised and reacquired by NORRELL at the end of the fiscal year) at locations throughout the United States met this criteria and all are included in the statistics.

Bill Rate. Bill Rate is the amount per hour billed to the NORRELL client using temporary services.

Average Bill Rates for 12 months ending October 29, 1995:

Top 1/3	(31 out of 94)	$10.87/Hr.
Middle 1/3	(32 out of 94)	$10.26/Hr.
Lower 1/3	(31 out of 94)	$9.44/Hr.

29 of 94 offices had Bill Rates less than $9.44/Hr.

Average Bill Rates for 12 months ending October 27, 1996:

Top 1/3	(35 out of 105)	$11.19/Hr.
Middle 1/3	(35 out of 105)	$10.51/Hr.
Lower 1/3	(35 out of 105)	$10.00/Hr.

37 of 105 offices had Bill Rates less than $10.00/Hr.

Average Bill Rates for 12 months ending November 2, 1997:

Top 1/3	(39 out of 117)	$11.22/Hr.
Middle 1/3	(39 out of 117)	$10.84/Hr.
Lower 1/3	(39 out of 117)	$10.81/Hr.

50 of 117 offices had Bill Rates less than $10.81/Hr.

A number of factors influence the Bill Rate in a particular market such as prevailing wages, unemployment levels, skill level of the temporary employees, and competition.

Gross Margin Percentage. Gross Margin Percentage is Gross Margin stated as a percentage of net billings. That is, the net billings during applicable accounting periods less all payroll and other direct labor cost, divided by net billings, then multiplied by 100%.

GM% = <u>Net Billings - (Payroll & other Direct Labor Costs)</u> x 100%
Net Billings

Average GM% for 12 months ending October 29, 1995:

Top 1/3	(31 out of 94)	23.00%
Middle 1/3	(32 out of 94)	22.91%
Lower 1/3	(31 out of 94)	21.29%

31 of 94 offices had GM% less than 2 1.29%.

Average GM% for 12 months ending October 27, 1996:

Top 1/3	(35 out of 105)	22.11%
Middle 1/3	(35 out of 105)	23.39%
Lower 1/3	(35 out of 105)	21.38%

40 of 105 offices had GM% less than 21.38%.

Average GM% for 12 months ending November 2, 1997:

Top 1/3	(39 out of 117)	21.33%
Middle 1/3	(39 out of 117)	21.52%
Lower 1/3	(39 out of 117)	21.39%

41 of 117 offices had GM% less than 21.33%.

Gross Margin Percentage varies from franchise to franchise based on skill mix, unemployment levels, the local economy, competition, etc.

Weekly Hours. Weekly hours are the total number of hours of temporary help a franchisee billed per week.

Average Weekly Hours for 12 months ending October 29, 1995:

Top 1/3	(31 out of 94)	7,700 hrs/wk.
Middle 1/3	(32 out of 94)	3,848 hrs/wk.
Lower 1/3	(31 out of 94)	2,147 hrs/wk.

19 of 94 offices had less than 2,147 hrs/wk.

Average Weekly Hours for 12 months ending October 27, 1996:

Top 1/3	(35 out of 105)	7,529 hrs/wk.
Middle 1/3	(35 out of 105)	3,512 hrs/wk.
Lower 1/3	(35 out of 105)	2,037 hrs/wk.

15 of 105 offices had less than 2,037 hrs/wk.

Average Weekly Hours for 12 months ending November 2, 1997:

Top 1/3	(39 out of 117)	7,735.72 hrs/wk.
Middle 1/3	(39 out of 117)	3,191.63 hrs/wk.
Lower 1/3	(39 out of 117)	1,899.55 hrs/wk.

22 of 117 offices had less than 1,899.55 hrs/wk.

The number of Average Weekly Hours varies greatly between different franchises and with time within the same franchise. Factors such as sales and marketing effort, local economy, availability of workers, competition, projects, time of the year, and quality of service being provided influence weekly hours.

Fee and Royalty as a Percentage of Net Billing. Since our fee and royalty varies based on volume of Gross Margin dollars (see Item 6), it also varies as a percentage of net billings. But some historical averages of the fee and royalty stated as a percentage of net billings may help you in comparing our offering to others.

Fee and royalty as a percentage of net billings for 12 months ending October 29, 1995:

Top 1/3	(31 out of 94)	10.05%
Middle 1/3	(32 out of 94)	11.18%
Lower 1/3	(31 out of 94)	10.73%

Fee and royalty as a percentage of net billings for 12 months ending October 27, 1996:

Top 1/3	(35 out of 105)	9.82%
Middle 1/3	(35 out of 105)	11.21%
Lower 1/3	(35 out of 105)	10.74%

Fee and royalty as a percentage of net billings for 12 months ending November 2, 1997:

Top 1/3	(32 out of 96)	9.49%
Middle 1/3	(32 out of 96)	10.04%
Lower 1/3	(32 out of 96)	10.55%

A prospective franchisee should note in using the data that two franchisees whose franchises began operation before 1978, John Keenan Company and Sivad Services Corporation, pay NORRELL a fee and royalty less than the standard amount of Gross Margin (Sivad Services Corporation owned all of the 7 franchised offices noted earlier which NORRELL reacquired). The remainder of our franchisees are on our current fee and royalty rate described in Item 6. You should note, when reviewing the figures for the 12 months ending October 29, 1995, that the fee and royalty as a percentage of net billings for the Middle 1/3 and Lower 1/3 are slightly affected by a royalty waiver program in effect for new offices during the first 12 months of operation. One office in each of these categories participated in the program for the 12 months ending October 29, 1995. You should note, when reviewing the figures for the 12 months ending October 27, 1996, that the fee and royalty as a percentage of net billings for the Top 1/3, Middle 1/3 and Lower 1/3 are slightly affected by a royalty waiver program in effect for new offices during the first 12 months of operation. One office in the Top 1/3 category, one office in the Middle 1/3 category, and eight offices in the Bottom 1/3 category participated in the program for the 12 months ending October 27, 1996. You should note, when reviewing the figures for the 12 months ending November 2, 1997, that the fee and royalty as a percentage of net billings for the Middle 1/3 and Lower 1/3 are slightly affected by a royalty waiver program in effect for new offices opened by existing franchisees during the first 12 months of operation. Three offices in the Middle 1/3 category, and four offices in the Bottom 1/3 category participated in the program for the 12 months ending November 2, 1997.

We provide substantiation of the data used in preparing this earnings claim to prospective franchisees upon reasonable request.

OTHER THAN THE DIRECT LABOR COSTS INHERENT IN THE GROSS MARGIN PERCENTAGE NUMBERS, WE PRESENT NO INFORMATION CONCERNING EXPENSES. YOU SHOULD DRAW NO INFERENCE AS TO EXPENSES OR NET PROFITS OF EXISTING OR FUTURE FRANCHISED BUSINESSES FROM THE DATA.

THE NUMBERS PRESENTED HERE ARE AVERAGES OF SPECIFIC FRANCHISES AND YOU SHOULD NOT CONSIDER THEM AS THE ACTUAL OR POTENTIAL BILL RATE, GROSS MARGIN PERCENTAGE, AND WEEKLY HOUR NUMBERS THAT YOU OR ANY OTHER FRANCHISE WILL REALIZE. WE DO NOT REPRESENT THAT YOU OR ANY OTHER FRANCHISEE CAN EXPECT TO ATTAIN THESE BILL RATE, GROSS MARGIN PERCENTAGE, AND WEEKLY HOUR NUMBERS OR ANY OTHER SALES, PROFITS OR EARNINGS.

ALSO, A NEW FRANCHISEE'S FINANCIAL RESULTS WILL MOST LIKELY DIFFER SIGNIFICANTLY FROM THOSE PRESENTED HERE, AS THE FRANCHISES INCLUDED IN THESE NUMBERS HAD ALL BEEN IN OPERATION MORE THAN ONE YEAR.

We developed the following table to assist you in identifying some of the significant variables you should consider in purchasing a NORRELL franchise. The table is set up so you can use it in your conversations with existing franchisees. WE MAKE NO REPRESENTATION THAT THIS TABLE INCLUDES ALL OF THE SIGNIFICANT VARIABLES WHICH MAY APPLY TO YOUR PROPOSED OFFICE OR WHICH MAY AFFECT YOUR PROPOSED MARKET AND WE MAKE NO REPRESENTATION AS TO WHAT YOUR EXPENSES WILL BE. WE PROVIDE THIS TABLE WITH THE UNDERSTANDING THAT YOU MAY USE IT AS A STARTING POINT FOR YOUR ANALYSIS, BUT THAT YOU MUST DETERMINE HOW APPLICABLE THIS MODEL IS TO YOUR SPECIFIC CIRCUMSTANCE.

Expense Items	Franchisee: Market:	Franchisee: Market:	Franchisee: Market:	Franchisee: Market:	Franchisee: Market:
Rent					
Associates Payroll					
Utilities					
Repairs & Maintenance					
Telephone					
Postage					
Courier					
Office Supplies					
Forms & Brochures					
Promotional Materials					
Professional Fees					
Taxes & Licenses					

Expense Items	Franchisee: Market:	Franchisee: Market:	Franchisee: Market:	Franchisee: Market:	Franchisee: Market:
Dues & Subscriptions					
Equipment					
Miscellaneous Expenses					
Furniture					
Total Operations					
Newspaper Advertising					
Business & Sales Promo.					
Other Advertising					
Total Advertising					
Total Expenses					

Food: donuts/ cookies/bagels

BREADSMITH
418 E. Silver Spring Dr.
Whitefish Bay, WI 53217
Tel: (414) 962-1965
Fax: (414) 962-5888
E-Mail: marcc@breadsmith.com
Internet Address: www.breadsmith.com
Contact: Mr. Marc L. Cayle, Director of
Development

Description: Award-winning, European, hearth-bread bakery, featuring fresh-from-scratch crusty breads, gourmet jams and coffee. Open kitchen concept reveals an eight-ton, stone hearth oven imported from France used to bake the hand-crafted loaves each morning. BREADSMITH has been ranked by Bon Appetit, Best of Philadelphia, Madison, WI, Orange Co., CA, Detroit, MI, Minneapolis, MN, Milwaukee, WI and Cleveland, OH as the best bread store in America.

# Franchised Units:	50 Units
# Company-Owned Units:	3 Units
Total # Units:	53 Units
Founded In:	1993
1st Franchised In:	1994
Average Total Investment:	210.5-386K
Franchise Fee:	25K
On-Going Royalty:	7%
Advertising Fee:	0%
Financial Assistance:Yes(I) (D – direct, or I – indirect)	
Site Selection Assistance:	Yes
Lease Negotiation Assistance:	Yes
Contract Terms (Init./Renew):	15/15
Initial Training Provided:2 Weeks Corporate Store; 10 Days Franchisee Store.	

Statement of Actual Earnings

The following represents examples of sales, expenses and net income achieved by three of our stores in 1998. These statements are intended to show examples of a low, medium, and high performing store. The sales numbers are actual numbers taken from three specific stores. The expense numbers are also actual numbers, except that we increased the expenses in certain indicated places where we believe the actual numbers may not be indicative of what a typical franchisee would incur, and we deleted expenses for interest, depreciation, amortization, income taxes, manager's salary, and owner's draw. All of these changes are explained in the footnotes to the statements.

	Low Sales Example[1]	Medium Sales Example[2]	High Sales Example[3]
Sales	**$162,181.40**	**$404,474.50**	**$642,834.51**
Cost of Goods Sold	41,034.37	76,631.76	130,089.31
Royalty[4]	11,352.70	28,313.22	44,998.42
Margin	109,794.33	299,529.52	467,746.78
Labor[5]	39,473.65	142,369.40	178,446.32
Marketing	10,285.32	10,338.91	12,856.69[6]
General and Administrative[7]	43,878.20	65,607.28	79,070.76
Total Expense	$93,637.17	$218,315.59	$270,373.77
Net Income before interest, depreciation, amortization, income taxes and manager's salary or owner's draw	$16,157.16	$81,213.93	$197,373.01

During 1998, we had 40 full service stores in operation for the entire year, including 2 stores that we own, and 1 store that we owned for part of the year. Of those stores, all 40, or 100%, had sales that equaled or exceeded the low sales example, 17 stores, or 42.5%, had sales that equaled or exceeded the medium sales example, and 4 stores, or 10%, had sales that equaled or exceeded the high sales example. Because we had to prepare this information in February, 1999, at that time, we only had operating costs from 10 of these stores. All 10 stores, or 100%, had net income before interest, income taxes, depreciation, amortization, manager's salary or owner's draw (collectively, Net Income) that equaled or exceeded the Net Income shown for the low sales example, 5 stores, or 50%, had Net Income that equaled or exceeded the amount shown in the medium sales example, and 1 store, or 10%, had Net Income that equaled or exceeded the amount shown in the high sales example. Based upon operating costs we have seen from prior years, we believe the operating costs of these stores are representative of operating costs throughout our system.

The following chart shows the sales ranges for the 40 full service BreadsmithTM bakery stores that were operating through all of 1998.

	Under $200,000	$200,000–299,000	$300,000–399,999	$400,000–499,999	$500,000–599,999	$600,000–699,999	$700,000 and up
Percentage of Stores In Range	12.5%	22.5%	22.5%	17.5%	10.0%	10.0%	5.0%
Number of Stores In Range	5	9	9	7	4	4	2

All of the information contained in this Item 19 was taken from unaudited financial reports provided to us by our individual franchise owners. We are not aware of any reason this information is not accurate, but we have not checked the information for accuracy. We recommend a particular accounting method or system to you. This system is consistent with generally accepted accounting principles. To the best of our knowledge, each of the stores that reported to us used this accounting method or system. Most of the stores in our system offer the same products as those you will offer in your stores. However, there are stores that, with our consent, have added additional products.

If you want substantiation of any of the data or information we used in preparing the numbers in this Item 19, we will make it available to you upon reasonable request.

THESE STATEMENTS OF SALES, INCOME, GROSS OR NET PROFITS ARE BASED ON HISTORICAL RESULTS AND SHOULD NOT BE CONSTRUED AS THE ACTUAL OR PROBABLE SALES, INCOME, GROSS OR NET PROFITS THAT WILL BE REALIZED BY ANY FRANCHISEE. WE DO NOT REPRESENT THAT ANY FRANCHISEE

CAN EXPECT TO ATTAIN SUCH SALES, INCOME, GROSS OR NET PROFITS.

1   This is a franchise store that opened in January 1996. The store has 1500 sq. ft. and is located in a small community strip center in a suburban shopping district. There are approximately 60,000 people residing within three miles of this site and approximately 130,000 residing within five miles of the site.

2   This is a 1,000 sq. ft. store that we own. We opened the store in June 1993. It is located in an inline street front in a semi-urban shopping district. Our store is surrounded by boutique shops and has a lot of pedestrian traffic. The population within three miles of this store is close to 170,000 and the population within five miles is about 390,000.

3   This is a franchise store. It has almost 1,600 sq. ft., and it opened in June 1997. It is located on a major roadway in a small community strip center. The surrounding area is a shopping district and there is a large mall two blocks away. The population within three miles of the site is about 46,000, and the population within five miles is about 95,000.

4   We adjusted the royalties to 7% of sales, the royalty you would pay if you own only one Breadsmith™ store.

5   Labor includes wages, payroll taxes, health benefits, recruiting and uniforms. However, when calculating labor, we subtracted any amount paid to the manager, in the case of our company-owned store, and to the owner-manager, in the case of the franchise stores. These examples, therefore, all assume that you are the manager and that your salary is paid from any net income at the end of the year.

6   The marketing for this store was actually less than listed. We believe all stores should spend at least 2% of their sales on marketing, and that is the number we put into this statement.

7   These amounts include all other expenses, including but not limited to office supplies, postage, professional fees, entertainment, kitchen supplies, trash removal, rent, building and equipment maintenance, insurance, linen, utilities, and permits. However, we have eliminated interest expense, income taxes, depreciation and amortization.

GREAT HARVEST BREAD CO.
28 S. Montana St., Dillon, MT 59725-2434
Tel: (800) 442-0424 (406) 683-6842
Fax: (406) 683-5537
E-Mail: inquiry@greatharvest.com
Internet Address: www.greatharvest.com
Contact: Ms. Lisa Wagner, Director of Franchise Growth

# Franchised Units:	140 Units
# Company-Owned Units:	1 Units
Total # Units:	141 Units
Founded In:	1976
1st Franchised In:	1978
Average Total Investment:	89-234K
Franchise Fee:	24K
On-Going Royalty:	7/6/5%
Advertising Fee:	0%
Financial Assistance: Yes (D – direct, or I – indirect)	
Site Selection Assistance:	Yes
Lease Negotiation Assistance:	Yes
Contract Terms (Init./Renew):	10
Initial Training Provided: 2 Weeks Host Bakeries; 1 Week at Headquarters; 3 Trainers for Opening.	

Description: Neighborhood bread bakery, specializing in whole wheat breads from scratch.

Chart 1 in Exhibit J is the actual monthly and yearly Gross Sales of 131 Great Harvest franchised bread companies and 40 Satellites that operated during the period from December 1997 through November 1998. (While we have disclosed the 40 Satellites separately in Chart 2, Chart 1's Gross

Sales numbers include Satellite Gross Sales.) Some of the bread companies in the chart, or their Satellites, did not operate for the entire 12 month period (as noted). However, the bar graph following Charts 1 and 2 includes only 115 franchised bread companies that were open for the full 12 month period.

Notes to Monthly Gross Sales:
1. We obtained these sales figures from monthly reports received from the franchised bread companies, and we have not independently audited them. Certain bread companies had not reported all monthly sales figures to us for the 12 month period presented. The monthly sales amounts presented in bold, italicized type represent our estimates for these unreported months, based on each bread company's specific historical sales performance, relative to the other bread companies in our system for each unreported month.

2. The 8 regions presented in Charts 1 and 2 encompass bread companies in the following states:

Region	States Included
Central	Illinois, Kansas, Minnesota, Missouri, Nebraska, North Dakota, South Dakota, Wisconsin
Central East	Indiana, Kentucky, Michigan, Ohio
Northeast	Connecticut, Maryland, Massachusetts, New Jersey, New York, Pennsylvania, Virginia
Northwest	Alaska, Idaho, Oregon, Washington
Rocky Mountain	Colorado, Montana, Utah
South Central	Alabama, Texas, Tennessee
Southeast	Florida, North Carolina
Southwest	Arizona, California, New Mexico, Nevada

3. The franchised bread companies are substantially similar to the franchises we offer in all states. All bread companies are owner-managed and receive substantially the same services.

4. The Gross Sales reports we have listed should not be used as a measure of profitability. Your bread company's actual performance will be affected by the specific conditions in your bread company's market. These conditions include location, amount of time in business, sales mix of products, lease terms, financing costs, taxes, labor costs, supply costs, local economic and regulatory conditions, franchisee's management skills, and competition. The numbers we have presented in the first 2 charts are "gross" numbers and do not reflect the expenses of the bread companies presented.

From December 1997 through November 1998, the average reported total Gross Sales of the franchised bread companies that were open for the full 12 month period (including any associated Satellite sales) were $475,258. Of the bread companies open for the full 12 month period, 45.3% exceeded this average.

The third set of information in Exhibit J (beginning with the page marked "3rd Set") sets forth the average operating results of 4 different groups of franchised bread companies (including any related Satellites) — (1) 31 reporting bread companies open 72 months or more as of December 31, 1997; (2) 19 reporting bread companies open 48 to 71 months as of December 31, 1997; (3) 29 reporting bread companies open 24 to 47 months as of December 31, 1997; and (4) 19 reporting bread companies open 12 to 23 months as of December 31, 1997. We based this presentation on financial information that franchisees reported to us. We have not audited this information or otherwise verified its accuracy. The reporting franchisees reported their numbers for their most recent 12 months of operations ended the last month of their 1997 fiscal years. (Some franchisees have elected a fiscal year other than a calendar year.) The amounts presented on these four pages do not include the results of 9 of our franchisees in operation during the entire 1997 year, as these franchisees failed to report their 1997 financial results to us. Had these non-reporting franchisees' results been included with those of the 98 reporting franchisees, the amounts would differ, perhaps significantly, from those reported. We have not adjusted the numbers to conform the accounting practices that each bread company uses. Differences in depreciation methods, cash or accrual methods of accounting, and the like affect the comparability of the information presented.

THE INFORMATION IN THIS ITEM IS TO HELP OUR FRANCHISE CANDIDATES AND THEIR PROFESSIONAL ADVISORS EVALU-ATE OUR FRANCHISE OPPORTUNITY. WE DO NOT REPRESENT THAT ANY NEW FRANCHISEE CAN EXPECT TO ATTAIN THESE RESULTS. A NEW FRANCHISEE'S INDIVIDUAL FINANCIAL RESULTS ARE LIKELY TO DIFFER FROM THESE RESULTS BECAUSE ALL OF THE FACTORS NOTED ABOVE AFFECT FRANCHISEES DIFFERENTLY.

THE RECORDS UPON WHICH THESE FIGURES ARE BASED ARE AVAILABLE FOR YOUR INSPECTION UPON REASONABLE REQUEST.

SAINT LOUIS BREAD COMPANY, INC.
7930 Big Bend Blvd.
Webster Groves, MO 63119
Tel: (800) 301-5566 (314) 918-7779
Fax: (314) 918-7773
E-Mail: slbfrandev@aol.com
Internet Address: www.panerabread.com
Contact: Mr. P.J. Evans, VP Franchise Development

Description: Founded in Saint Louis in 1987, SAINT LOUIS BREAD has expanded into new markets over the past few years, with strong consumer acceptance for its unique concept. Each SAINT LOUIS BREAD bakery-cafe features a comfortable neighborhood setting where residents can relax and enjoy a wide range of fresh-baked sourdough breads, along with other fresh-baked goods, bagels and hearty made-to-order sandwiches, salads and soups.

# Franchised Units:	37 Units
# Company-Owned Units:	<u>67</u> Units
Total # Units:	104 Units
Founded In:	1987
1st Franchised In:	1993
Average Total Investment:	550-650K
Franchise Fee:	35K
On-Going Royalty:	5%
Advertising Fee:	Up to 5%
Financial Assistance:No (D – direct, or I – indirect)	
Site Selection Assistance:	Yes
Lease Negotiation Assistance:	No
Contract Terms (Init./Renew):	20/Agrmt.
Initial Training Provided: 10 Weeks St. Louis, MO.	

Statement of Average Gross Sales of Panera Bread Bakery-Cafés for the 52-Week Period Ending December 26, 1998.

Average Gross Sales

Company-owned Bakery-Cafés	$1,237,422
Franchisee-owned Bakery-Cafés	$1,281,497
Company and Franchisee-owned Bakery-Cafés	$1,248,158

THESE RESULTS ARE AVERAGES OF SPECIFIC PANERA BREAD BAKERY-CAFÉS AND SHOULD NOT BE CONSIDERED AS THE ACTUAL OR PROBABLE RESULTS THAT WILL BE REALIZED BY YOU. WE DO NOT REPRESENT THAT YOU CAN EXPECT TO ATTAIN THESE FINANCIAL RESULTS. YOUR OWN FINANCIAL RESULTS ARE LIKELY TO DIFFER FROM THESE RESULTS. IF YOU ARE PURCHASING THE ASSETS OF EXISTING COMPANY-OWNED BAKERY-CAFÉS, YOU SHOULD NOT RELY ON THE STATEMENT OF AVERAGE GROSS SALES, BUT SHOULD INSTEAD REVIEW

THE ACTUAL FINANCIAL RESULTS OF THE BAKERY-CAFÉ(S) BEING PURCHASED. SIMILARLY, PROSPECTIVE FRANCHISEES OF NONTRADITIONAL LOCATIONS SHOULD NOT RELY ON THE FOREGOING STATEMENT OF AVERAGE GROSS SALES, SINCE IT IS NOT RELEVANT TO THOSE TYPES OF LOCATIONS. WE MAKE NO CLAIM REGARDING THE ACTUAL OR POTENTIAL SALES OR PROFITS OP NON-TRADITIONAL LOCATIONS.

Information Regarding Statement of Average Gross Sales.

The Statement of Average Gross Sales consists of the mean averages of the reported annual gross sales of 59 Company-owned Bakery-Cafés and 19 Franchisee-owned Bakery-Cafés open during the entire 52-week reporting period ending December 26, 1998. Some of the Company-owned Bakery-Cafés included in the Statement are smaller than the current prototype and/or are open for shorter hours during the day than the current prototype. The Average Gross Sales of Company-owned bakery-cafés would have been higher if those bakery-cafés had been excluded. The gross sales of the Rendezvous Café at the Galleria in Richmond Heights, Missouri have been included in the Average Gross Sales set forth above and the range of sales stated below. Substantiation of the information used in preparing the Statement of Average

Gross Sales will be made available to you upon reasonable request. However, we will not disclose the identity or sales data of any particular Panera Bread Bakery-Café without the consent of that owner, except to any applicable state registration authorities or except in connection with the sale of a particular existing Panera Bread Bakery-Café that we own.

Of the 78 Panera Bread Bakery-Cafés (which includes the Rendezvous Café) used for calculating the Average Gross Sales for the 52-week reporting period ending December 26, 1998, (i) the 59 Company-owned Panera Bread Bakery-Cafés had gross sales ranging between $290,297 and $2,124,614, of which 26 (44%) attained or surpassed $1,237,422 in gross sales (the average gross sales of Company-owned Panera Bread Bakery-Cafés), and (ii) the 19 Franchisee-owned Panera Bread Bakery-Cafés had gross sales ranging between $870,428 and $1,971,900 of which 8 (42%) attained or surpassed $1,281,497 in gross sales (the average gross sales of franchisee-owned Panera Bread Bakery-Cafés).

The gross sales of Franchisee-owned Bakery-Cafés were derived from unaudited financial reports submitted by Franchisees for the purpose of computing royalties. The gross sales of Company-owned Bakery-Cafés were compiled by Panera on the basis of generally accepted accounting principles, consistently applied.

Statement of Average Net Profit and EBITDA of Company-Owned Bakery-Cafés for the 52-Week Period Ending December 26, 1998.

	Average Amount	% of Average Gross Revenues	No .Attaining or Surpassing % of Avg. Gross Rev.	% Attaining or Surpassing % of Avg. Gross Rev.
Gross Revenues[1]	$1,275,365	100	N/A	N/A
Discounts[2]	537,943	3	26	44
Gross Sales[3]	1,237,422	97	33	56
Cost of Sales[4]	438,331	34.4	27	46
Gross Profit	799,091	62.6	26	44
Labor[5]	334,003	26.2	29	49
Operating Expenses[6]	82,591	6.5	32	54
Advertising Expenses	16,171	1.3	41	69

	Average Amount	% of Average Gross Revenues	No .Attaining or Surpassing % of Avg. Gross Rev.	% Attaining or Surpassing % of Avg. Gross Rev.
Fixed Expenses[7]	69,097	5.4	31	53
Occupancy Expenses[8]	88,562	6.9	34	58
Net Profit	208,668	16.4	26	44
Depreciation	57,216	4.5	33	56
EBITDA[9]	265,884	20.9	26	44

THESE RESULTS ARE AVERAGES OF COMPANY OWNED PANERA BREAD BAKERY-CAFES AND SHOULD NOT BE CONSIDERED AS THE ACTUAL OR PROBABLE RESULTS THAT WILL BE REALIZED BY YOU. WE DO NOT REPRESENT THAT YOU CAN EXPECT TO ACHIEVE THESE FINANCIAL RESULTS. YOUR OWN FINANCIAL RESULTS ARE LIKELY TO DIFFER FROM THESE RESULTS. IF YOU ARE PURCHASING THE ASSETS OF EXISTING COMPANY-OWNED BAKERY-CAFÉS, YOU SHOULD NOT RELY ON THE AVERAGE GROSS REVENUES AND AVERAGE PROFIT AND LOSS INFORMATION SET FORTH ABOVE, BUT SHOULD INSTEAD REVIEW THE ACTUAL FINANCIAL RESULTS OF THE BAKERY-CAFÉ(S) BEING PURCHASED. SIMILARLY, PROSPECTIVE FRANCHISEES OF NON-TRADITIONAL LOCATIONS SHOULD NOT RELY ON THE FOREGOING STATEMENT OF AVERAGE GROSS REVENUES AND AVERAGE PROFIT AND LOSS, SINCE SUCH STATEMENT IS NOT RELEVANT TO THOSE TYPES OF LOCATIONS. WE MAKE NO CLAIM REGARDING THE ACTUAL OR POTENTIAL REVENUES OR PROFITS OF NON-TRADITIONAL LOCATIONS.

Information Regarding Statement of Average Gross Revenues and Average Profit and Loss Statement of Company-Owned Bakery-Cafés. The Statement of Average Gross Revenues and Average Profit and Loss Statement of Company-Owned Bakery-Cafés consists of the mean averages of 59 Company-owned Bakery-Cafés open during the entire 52-week period ending December 26, 1998. Some of the Company-owned Bakery-Cafés included in the Statement are smaller than the current prototype and/or are open for shorter hours during the day than the current prototype. The Average Gross Sales of Company-owned bakery-cafés would have been higher if those bakery-cafés had been excluded. The gross revenues of the Rendezvous Café at the Galleria in Richmond Heights, Missouri have been included in the Statement of Average Gross Revenues and Average Profit and Loss set forth above. Substantiation of the information used in preparing the Statement of Average Gross Revenues and Average Profit and Loss will be made available to you upon reasonable request. However, we will not disclose the identity, revenue or other items of income or expense of any particular Company-owned Panera Bread Bakery-Café, except to any applicable state registration authorities or except in connection with the sale of a particular existing Panera Bread Bakery-Café that we own. The Statement of Average Gross Revenues and Average Profit and Loss for Company-owned Bakery-Cafés was prepared on the basis of generally accepted accounting principles, consistently applied. The footnotes listed below are an integral part of the Statement of Average Gross Revenues and Average Profit and Loss and should be read in conjunction therewith. The Statement of Average Profit and EBITDA does not include amortization of initial franchise fees or royalties, which a franchisee would have to pay to us, or bank financing charges, which can vary greatly.

Sales volumes of Panera Bread Bakery-Cafés vary considerably due to a variety of factors, such as: local popularity of Panera Bread Bakery-Cafés; hours of operation; size of the Bakery-Café; competition from other restaurants, especially fast food businesses in proximity to the Bakery-Café; traffic flow, accessibility and visibility of the Bakery-Café; the economic conditions in the locality of the Bakery-Café; and the business abilities and efforts of Franchisees.

Except for the above Statements, and except as otherwise expressly stated in this Item 19, no representations or statements of actual, average, projected or forecasted sales, expenses, profits or earnings of Panera Bread Bakery-Cafés are made to prospective Franchisees. None of our officers or employees are authorized to make any claims or statements as to the earnings, expenses, sales or profits or prospects or chances of success that you can expect or that have been experienced by us or by present or past Panera Bread Bakery-Cafés. We have specifically instructed our officers and employees that they are not permitted to make claims or statements as to the earnings, expenses, sales or profits or the prospects or chances of success, nor are they authorized to represent or estimate dollar figures as to any particular Panera Bread Bakery-Café or any particular site for a Panera Bread Bakery-café.

---

[1] Gross Revenues is comprised of Gross Sales (see footnote 3 below) and the dollar amount of coupons and other promotional discounts, but does not include sales or service taxes.

[2] Discounts consist of the dollar amount of coupons and other promotional discounts.

[3] Gross Sales has the same meaning as set forth in the Franchise Agreement, i.e., the aggregate gross amount of all sales of food, beverages and other products sold and services rendered in connection with the Panera Bread Bakery/Café, including monies derived from sales at or away from the Panera Bread Bakery-Café, whether for cash or credit, but excluding (1) all federal, state or municipal sales or service taxes collected from customers and paid to the appropriate taxing authorities; and (2) all customer refunds and adjustments and promotional discounts made by the Panera Bread Bakery-Café.

[4] Cost of Sales includes the cost of food, paper and other products. The cost of frozen dough products included in the Cost of Sales set forth above was 27% of the average retail price charged by Company-owned Panera Bread Bakery-Café's for finished products made from the dough product during the first fiscal quarter and 22.1% of the Retail Price thereafter. Currently, such frozen dough products are supplied to you by Bunge through a Distributor at a cost of 22.1% of the Retail Price. See Item 8.

[5] Labor includes wages paid to management (but does not include any wages or overhead above the store management level) and employees of the Bakery-Café, including shift supervisors, bakers and associates, management bonuses, payroll taxes, the cost of group insurance, workers compensation, vacation and other employee benefits.

[6] Operating Expenses includes bank charges, the cost of utilities, repairs and maintenance, smallwares and hardwares, cleaning supplies, office supplies, telephone, trash removal, uniforms, point-of-sale maintenance, flowers, pest control, music, parking and employee advertising, and other miscellaneous operating expenses.

[7] Fixed Expenses includes taxes, depreciation, the cost of insurance, leased equipment and licenses, and other miscellaneous fixed expenses.

[8] Occupancy Expenses includes base rent, percentage rent, common area maintenance, real estate taxes, promotional and other miscellaneous lease expenses.

[9] EBITDA means earnings before income taxes, depreciation and amortization.

HAPPY & HEALTHY PRODUCTS
1600 S. Dixie Hwy., # 200
Boca Raton, FL 33432
Tel: (800) 764-6114 (561) 367-0739
Fax: (561) 368-5267
E-Mail: generalmanager@fruitfull.com
Internet Address: www.fruitfull.com
Contact: Ms. Rosemary Harris, General Manager

Description: A wholesale distributorship for the sale of frozen fruit bars, FRUITFULL, through dedicated freezers placed in retail locations or in retailer's own freezers. Super Grand, Grand and

Standard wholesale franchisees will receive the services of an independent marketing consultant who will provide on-site training in identifying and negotiating agreements to place freezers. Training includes stocking, collection and route service procedures dealing with frozen storage supplies.

# Franchised Units:	113 Units
# Company-Owned Units:	0 Units
Total # Units:	113 Units
Founded In:	1991
1st Franchised In:	1993
Average Total Investment:	23-54K
Franchise Fee:	17-24K
On-Going Royalty:	0%
Advertising Fee:	0%
Financial Assistance: Yes(I) (D – direct, or I – indirect)	
Site Selection Assistance:	N/A
Lease Negotiation Assistance:	N/A
Contract Terms (Init./Renew):	10/5
Initial Training Provided: 1 or 2 Weeks in Franchise MSA.	

As of the date of this Offering Circular, the Company charges Retail Franchisees 42¢ per juice based fruit bar and 44¢ per cream based fruit bar. Super Grand Wholesale, Grand Wholesale and Standard Wholesale Franchisees pay 41.5¢ per juice based fruit bar and 43.5¢ per cream based fruit bar. Master Distributors currently pay 38¢ per juice based fruit bar and 40¢ per cream based fruit bar.

Franchisees are entitled to a 2% discount for prepaid orders. If a Franchisee prepays, Retail Franchisees will pay .4116¢ per juice based fruit bar and .4312¢ per cream based fruit bar. Super Grand Wholesale, Grand Wholesale and Standard Wholesale Franchisees will pay .4067¢ per juice based fruit bar and .4263¢ per cream based fruit bar.

The recommended wholesale price for both juice and cream based bars is 70¢ each. If selling the juice and cream based FRUITFULL® bars at the recommended wholesale price of 70¢ each, Super Grand, Grand and Standard Wholesale Franchisees will make a gross profit of 28.5¢ per juice based bar and 26.5¢ per cream based bar. Master Distributors will make a gross profit of 32¢ per juice based bar and 30¢ per cream based bar.

If a franchisee takes advantage of H&H's prepay discount and sells the juice and cream based FRUITFULL® bars at the recommended wholesale price of 70¢ each, Super Grand, Grand and Standard Wholesale Franchisees will make a gross profit of 29¢ per juice based bar and 27¢ per cream based bar. Master Distributors will make a gross profit of 32.5¢ per juice based bar and 30.5¢ per cream based bar.

Additionally, all H & H Franchisees may sell H & H Products, including FRUITFULL®, from a freezer cart at special events such as street fairs, festivals and sporting events. The recommended retail price for FRUITFULL® at these events is $2.00–$2.50 for both juice and cream based fruit bars.

If selling the bars at retail events at the recommended retail price of $2.00–$2.50 each, a Retail Only Franchisee will make a gross profit of $1.58–$2.08 per juice based bar and $1.56–$2.06 per cream based bar depending on the retail price.

If selling the bars at retail events at the recommended retail price of $2.00–$2.50 each, a Super Grand, Grand and Standard Wholesale Franchisee will make a gross profit of $1.59–$2.09 per juice based bar and $1.57–$2.07 per cream based bar depending on the retail price.

If selling the bars at retail events at the recommended retail price of $2.00–$2.50 each, Master Distributors will make a gross profit of $1.62–$2.12 per juice based bar and $1.60–$2.10 per cream based bar depending on the retail price.

The recommended wholesale and retail prices listed above are based on information the Company has obtained from its current Franchisees. The product costs are based upon the prices that H & H currently charges its Franchisees. Various market, geographic, competition and economic factors may require you to charge prices other than the recommended prices listed above and, therefore, **the gross profits that you derive may differ from those listed above.** The Company suggests that Franchisees use the recommended wholesale and retail prices. However, the Company does not mandate or require Franchisees to use such prices and Franchisees are free to sell products at whatever price they choose. There may be different wholesale and retail prices from one H & H Franchised business to another H & H Franchised business.

The gross profits listed above do not take into account costs other than the costs that you will pay for the various products. There will be other costs and expenses incurred in operating your Franchised Business. See Item 7 of this Offering Circular for your estimated initial investment.

Other than the information stated above, the Company does not furnish or authorize its salespersons to furnish any other information, either oral or written, concerning the actual or potential sales, costs, income or profits of a H & H Franchised Business. Actual results vary from H & H Franchised Business to H & H Franchised Business and the Company can not estimate or guarantee the results of any particular franchise.

We have specifically instructed sales persons, agents, employees and officers that except what is listed above, that they are not permitted to make claims or statements as to earnings, sales or profits or prospects or chances of success, nor are they authorized to represent or estimate dollar figures as to any particular H & H Franchised Business. You should not rely on unauthorized representations as to earnings, sales, profits or prospects or chance of success.

Substantiation of the data used in preparing the information set forth above will be made available upon reasonable request.

KOHR BROS. FROZEN CUSTARD
2115 Berkmar Dr.
Charlottesville, VA 22901
Tel: (888) 527-9783 (804) 975-1500
Fax: (804) 975-1505
E-Mail: dennis.poletti@kohrbros.com
Internet Address: www.kohrbros.com
Contact: Mr. Dennis G. Poletti, Exec. Director

Description: KOHR BROS. is the original frozen custard since 1919. Our stores, which are bright and easily maintained, offer a simple and unique frozen dessert concept.

# Franchised Units:	30 Units
# Company-Owned Units:	11 Units
Total # Units:	41 Units
Founded In:	1919
1st Franchised In:	1994
Average Total Investment:	145.9-277.5K
Franchise Fee:	27.5K
On-Going Royalty:	5%
Advertising Fee:	0.5%
Financial Assistance:Yes(I) (D – direct, or I – indirect)	
Site Selection Assistance:	Yes
Lease Negotiation Assistance:	Yes
Contract Terms (Init./Renew):	5/3/5
Initial Training Provided:6 Days in Corporate Offices; 3 Says at Franchisee Unit.	

Representations Regarding Earnings Capability

Attached to this Offering Circular as Exhibit E is a summary of the annual average earnings of stores owned and operated by Parent, for a 12 year period ending in 1998 and a summary of franchise store operating results for a period of five (5) years. THE SALES, PROFITS OR EXPENSES REPORTED FOR PARENT-OWNED STORES SHOULD NOT BE CONSIDERED AS THE ACTUAL OR POTENTIAL SALES, PROFITS OR EARNINGS THAT WILL BE REALIZED BY ANY FRANCHISE. COMPANY DOES NOT REPRESENT THAT ANY FRANCHISEE CAN EXPECT TO ATTAIN ANY PARTICULAR SALES, INCOME, GROSS OR NET PROFITS.

Except for the attached, Company does not furnish or authorize its salespersons to furnish any oral or written information concerning the actual or potential sales, costs, income or profits of a KOHR BROS.® store. Actual results vary from unit to unit, and Company cannot estimate results of any particular franchise.

Exhibit E to the Offering Circular
Kohr Bros. Franchise Systems, Inc. (Company)

KOHR BROTHERS, INC.'s (Company's Parent) 12 Year Summary
of Earnings Company's Parent Store Profitability 1998 Update

Year	No. of Stores	Gross Revenue	Average Store Revenue	Average Increase In Sales	Net Store Profit	Average Store Profit	Average Increase In Profit	Profit as a % of Sales
1987	7	$1,141,872	$163,125		$296,951	$42,422		26.01%
1988	7	$1,121,222	$160,175	-1.81%	$231,144	$33,021	-22.16%	20.62%
1989	7	$1,302,217	$162,777	1.62%	$352,036	$50,291	52.30%	27.03%
1990	8	$1,566,988	$195,874	22.29%	$523,721	$65,465	30.17%	33.42%
1991	8	$1,805,825	$225,728	15.24%	$679,433	$84,929	29.73%	37.62%

Year	No. of Stores	Gross Revenue	Average Store Revenue	Average Increase In Sales	Net Store Profit	Average Store Profit	Average Increase In Profit	Profit as a % of Sales
1992	9	$1,972,468	$219,163	-2.91%	$632,242	$70,249	-17.29%	32.05%
1993	9	$2,179,120	$242,124	10.48%	$756,813	$84,090	19.70%	34.73%
1994	9	$2,261,855	$251,317	3.80%	$853,983	$94,887	12.84%	37.76%
1995	9	$2,453,164	$272,574	8.46%	$923,024	$102,558	8.08%	37.63%
1996	8	$2,509,980	$313,748	15.11%	$1,004,440	$125,555	22.42%	40.02%
1997	8	$2,675,650	$334,456	6.60%	$1,110,749	$138,844	10.58%	41.51%
1998	10*	$3,353,561	$335,356	0.27%	$1,430,533	$143,053	3.03%	42.66%
Averages:			$239,701	7.19%		$86,280	13.58%	34.25%
*Pad site which operated less than a full year (less than 3 months) not included.								
								Company's Parent
12 Year Average Annual Company's Parent Store Profit:								34.25%

Basis of Compilation of Company's Parent Data

The information set out above represents a summary of the annual total and average earnings of KOHR BROS. stores operated by Company's Parent, Kohr Brothers, Inc., for the 12 year period beginning in 1987 and ending in 1998. All financial statements for the 12 year period were audited by an independent accounting firm.

These figures represent only the performance of stores that were in operation during an entire "season." "Season" means the period beginning approximately on Palm Sunday weekend and ending approximately on Halloween weekend of each year, for an average of approximately 200 days in length. However, stores are only open an average of approximately 153 days within that 200 day period as stores are open on weekends only, early and late in the season at most summer resort locations. The stores owned and operated by Kohr Brothers, Inc. included in the statement have offered substantially the same products and services to the public as the Franchised Store will offer. Essentially the same services are available to franchised businesses as have been available to the stores owned and operated by Kohr Brothers, Inc.

The average annual store profits appearing in this earnings claim summary should not be construed as the "profit" which might be experienced by a franchisee with similar store revenue. An individual franchisee is likely to experience expense variation, as detailed in this entire section.

The information contained herein was compiled from the audited financial statements of Kohr Brothers, Inc. from 1987 through 1998. The information reflects store profits only and does not include certain items of corporate income or expense which related to the overall administration, supervision and management of the existing stores or the capital costs of developing new locations. The stores included in the summary use a uniform accounting system. The enclosed information has not been prepared on a basis consistent with generally accepted accounting principles. Specific assumptions used in the presentation of the statements are indicated below.

Company's Parent Store Profit does not take into account:

1. *Expense Variations.* a) At well established locations, advertising expenditures have traditionally averaged 0.05% of Gross Sales as brand equity is well-established. However, beginning in 1997, Company's Parent stores contributed 0.5% of revenue to the Franchise System's Advertising and Development Fund; b)The franchise agreement calls for 1% local and 0.5% Fund advertising, but the franchisee may find it necessary to spend more than this

amount. Store management may also vary a great deal. The profits shown are net of competitive store managers' compensation; c) The Cost of goods sold should be higher for the franchisee because the company-owned operations account for Kohr Brothers proprietary products at cost. Company's Parent-owned stores do not pay any sales royalties. The Franchise Agreement calls for You to make weekly sales royalty payments of 5% of Gross Sales; and d) Other expense variations are also likely as labor and rent costs are different for each location.

2. *General and Administrative Expenses.* No attempt has been made to allocate the administrative overhead of the Company's Parent which includes legal, accounting, insurance, office expenses, etc.

3. *Capital Expenditures.* No attempt has been made to allocate the capital expenditures of Company's Parent. Capital expenditures include repayment of principal, capitalized expenditures, income taxes, dividends, etc.

The stores upon which these results are based are seasonal businesses operating approximately 200 days per year and are located primarily in resort areas. A store operating annually may achieve different results. Although Company is unable to estimate the performance of a business in a non-resort type setting, the results which follow include net store profits from year round franchised mall and pad site locations. Many of Kohr Bros., Inc.'s (Company's Parent) highest volume stores have been established and in continuous operation for 70 to 80 years (i.e., seasons). Conversely, Your store may have to develop its own brand equity in a new location if customers are not familiar with Kohr Bros.® trademark products.

You must pay to Company a Continuing Services and Royalty Fee in an amount equal to 5% of the Gross Receipts of the Franchised Store, as described in Item 6 of this Offering Circular. The Company's Parent stores included in the Twelve Year Summary of Earnings did not pay a Continuing Services and Royalty Fee. Thus, the Average Annual Store Profit must be adjusted to provide for a deduction of a Continuing Services and Royalty Fee of 5% of the Gross Receipts.

The average annual store profit figure does not take into account any cost of capital employed. Capital costs include the franchise fee, expenses incurred during training and designing the store and the cost of leasehold improvements, signage and equipment as well as the down payment on leases, insurance and working capital.

Substantiation of the data used in preparing the accompanying statements will be made available to You upon reasonable request.

During each of the 1 year periods from 1987 through 1998, certain stores exceeded the average while others failed to meet the average as follows:

Kohr Brothers, Inc. 12 Year Store Performance Analysis

Year	Number of Stores	Average Store Sales	Number of Stores with Sales Below Average	Number of Stores with Sales Above Average
1987	7	$163,125	3	4
1988	7	$160,175	3	4
1989	7	$162,777	3	4
1990	8	$195,874	4	4
1991	8	$225,728	3	5
1992	9	$219,163	4	5
1993	9	$242,124	5	4
1994	9	$251,317	5	4
1995	9	$272,574	4	5

Year	Number of Stores	Average Store Sales	Number of Stores with Sales Below Average	Number of Stores with Sales Above Average
1996	8	$313,748	3	5
1997	8	$334,456	4	4
1998	10	$335,356	4	6
12 Year Average:	8	$239,701	4	5 Company's Parent

Days Stores Open — 1998				
	11	128		
	12	145		
	13	195		
	14	144		
	21	139	61	364 Days
	23	139	62	363 Days
	24	107		
	31	198		
	41	178		
9 Resort Store Avg.:		153 Days		
1 Year-round Store:				
Days Stores Open — 1998				
	61	364 Days		

During each year of the 12 year period, the average break even point was as follows:

Year	Lowest Annual Sales*	Highest Annual Sales
1987	$47,305	$230,577
1988	$54,691	$245,011
1989	$73,147	$273,136
1990	$76,454	$294,528
1991	$87,957	$356,223
1992	$103,534	$344,975
1993	$101,831	$391,098
1994	$93,173	$398,741
1995	$89,542	$432,202
1996	$112,795	$444,821
1997	$113,830	$475,654
1998	$128,399	$538,356
12 Yr. Avg.:	$90,222	$368,777

*Includes an 8´ x 10´ two (2) machine kiosk.

Year	Average Store Sales	Average Store Profit	Average Sales Break Even Pt.
1987	$163,125	$42,422	$120,703
1988	$160,175	$33,021	$127,154
1989	$162,777	$50,291	$112,486
1990	$195,874	$65,465	$130,409
1991	$225,728	$84,929	$140,799
1992	$219,163	$70,249	$148,914
1993	$242,124	$84,090	$158,034
1994	$251,317	$94,887	$156,430
1995	$272,574	$102,558	$170,016
1996	$313,748	$125,555	$188,193
1997	$334,456	$138,844	$195,612
1998	$335,356	$143,053	$192,303
12 Yr. Avg.:	$239,701	$86,280	$153,421

SUCH ACTUAL SALES, INCOME, GROSS OR NET PROFITS INCLUDED ABOVE ARE OF

Year	Average Store Sales	Average Store Profit	Average Sales Break Even Pt.
1992	$219,163	$70,249	$148,914
1993	$242,124	$84,090	$158,034
1994	$251,317	$94,887	$156,430
1995	$272,574	$102,558	$170,016
1996	$313,748	$125,555	$188,193
1997	$334,456	$138,844	$195,612
1998	$335,356	$143,053	$192,303
12 Yr. Avg.:	$239,701	$86,280	$153,421

SPECIFIC STORES OWNED BY COMPANY'S PARENT AND SHOULD NOT BE CONSIDERED AS THE ACTUAL OR PROBABLE SALES, INCOME, GROSS OR NET PROFITS THAT WILL BE REALIZED BY ANY FRANCHISEE. COMPANY DOES NOT REPRESENT THAT ANY FRANCHISEE CAN EXPECT TO ATTAIN THESE SALES, INCOME, GROSS OR NET PROFITS. COMPANY PROVIDES SUCH DATA FOR INFORMATIONAL PURPOSES ONLY.

Company:

Company is Kohr Bros. Franchise Systems, Inc., which was incorporated in Delaware on July 16, 1993 for the purpose of developing and implementing a program for the franchising of KOHR BROS.® franchises. Company has limited experience in franchising a business offering and selling frozen custard and related food products and beverages. All of the businesses included in the 12 Year Summary of Earnings are owned and/or operated by Company's Parent, KOHR BROTHERS, INC. Because Company has limited experi-

ence in offering franchises for sale, it must rely upon the experience of its current franchises to suggest that a franchise can or will reach or exceed the average earnings and profitability figures described below. **There is no assurance You will do as well. If You rely upon these figures, You must accept the risk of not doing as well.**

There is no assurance that any return on a particular investment can be expected whatsoever as there are substantial risk factors associated with the retail food businesses. **The greatest risk may be if You agree to pay too much rent relative to the business that a particular location can generate.** Also, there are the risks of adverse weather conditions during peak sales periods and the risk that leases may not be renewed at affordable rates, that foot traffic at a given location may go down over time, along with many other risks which cannot be insured against. The prior performance of stores operated by Company's Parent, Kohr Brothers, Inc., and by other franchises, upon which the above figures are based, cannot be used to accurately project future returns.

ANY PROSPECTIVE FRANCHISEE MUST CONSIDER THAT A SUBSTANTIAL PORTION OF, OR EVEN ALL OF HIS OR HER INVESTED CAPITAL MAY BE ENTIRELY LOST. THESE FIGURES ARE NOT TO BE RELIED UPON AS TO HOW ANY FRANCHISE STORE WILL PERFORM. NEITHER KOHR BROTHERS, INC. NOR KOHR BROS. FRANCHISE SYSTEMS, INC. PROVIDES ANY FRANCHISEE WITH ANY GUARANTEE OF ANY RETURN WHATSOEVER FROM AN INVESTMENT IN A KOHR BROS.® FRANCHISE.

KOHR BROS. FRANCHISE SYSTEMS 5 Year Summary of Earnings Franchise Store Profitability 1998 Update

Year	No. of Stores	Gross Revenue	Average Store Revenue	Average Increase In Sales	Net Store Profit	Average Store Profit	Average Increase In Profit	Profit as a % of Sales
1994*	1	$242,180	$242,180		$79,392	$79,392		32.78%
1995*	2	$556,372	$278,186	14.87%	$172,502	$86,251	8.64%	31.00%
1996*	4	$1,290,800	$322,700	16.00%	$438,050	$109,513	26.97%	33.94%
1997	5	$1,713,470	$342,694	6.20%	$584,158	$116,832	6.68%	34.09%

Year	No. of Stores	Gross Revenue	Average Store Revenue	Average Increase In Sales	Net Store Profit	Average Store Profit	Average Increase In Profit	Profit as a % of Sales
1998**	13	$3,528,766	$271,444	-20.79%	$1,029,593	$79,199	-32.21%	29.18%
Averages:			$291,441	4.07%		$94,237	2.52%	32.20%

*Calendar year reporting except one store listed each year open only 7–8 months.

**Financial results for stores operated full year/season — 3 additional stores did not report (last four quarters reported — 10/1/97–9/30/98)

								Franchise
				5 Year Average Annual Franchise Store Profit:				32.20%

Year	Number of Stores	Average Store Sales	Number of Stores with Sales Below Average	Number of Stores with Sales Above Average
1994	1	$242,180	0	0
1995	2	$278,186	1	1
1996	4	$322,700	2	2
1997	5	$342,694	3	2
1998	13	$271,444	5	8
5 Year Average:	5	$291,441	3	3 Franchise

Year	Lowest Annual Sales	Highest Annual Sales
1994	$242,180	$242,180
1995	$224,505	$328,581
1996	$292,720	$404,049
1997	$200,182	$447,063
1998	$123,578	$443,125
5 Year Average:	$216,633	$373,000 Franchise

**KOHR BROS. FRANCHISE SYSTEMS 5 Year Summary
of Earnings Franchise Store Profitability 1998 Update (Continued)**

Year	Average Store Sales	Average Store Profit	Average Sales Break Even Point
1994	$242,180	$79,392	$162,788
1995	$278,186	$86,251	$191,935
1996	$322,700	$109,513	$213,187
1997	$342,694	$116,832	$225,862
1998	$271,444	$79,199	$192,245
5 Year Average:	$291,441	$94,237	$197,203 Franchise

A NEW FRANCHISEE'S INDIVIDUAL FINANCIAL RESULTS ARE MORE THAN LIKELY TO DIFFER SUBSTANTIALLY FROM THE RESULTS STATED ABOVE.

Basic Cost of Franchise Store/Site Development: (Does not include the Franchise Fee or the very variable costs of Travel & Board for Franchisee Training, Initial Inventory and Grand Opening Expenses)								
Type of Stores	Stores	Type of Location	Avg. Sq. Ft.	Atty., Architect & Other	Leasehold Improvements	Equip. & Smallwares	Fixtures & Signage	Totals
Single Concept	12	Mall	581	$9,426	$96,197	$82,288	$17,092	$205,003
Dual Concept	6	Mall	493	$7,408	$95,971	$76,375	$16,165	$195,918
Single Concept Pad Site	1	Pad Site	545	$9,349	$180,859	$69,670	$15,100	$274,662
Dual Concept Pad Site	None	Pad Site	N/A	N/A	N/A	N/A	N/A	N/A
(Only 19 of 27 reported to date)								

KOHR BROS. FRANCHISE SYSTEMS 1998 Historical Earnings & Hypothetical Return on Investment Based upon Average Franchise Store Profitability
Hypothetical Return for Kohr Bros. Franchise (with and without the use of Leverage)

		Non-Leveraged Scenario		Leveraged Scenario			Alternative Investment	Alternative Investment
Cash Flow		Hypothetical Cash Flow **232,503** Invested. Cash Flow Reinvested at 5.00%	Hypothetical Store Cash Flow Reinvested. Cash on Cash ROI	Debt Service for 157,503 (Debt) at 10%	Hypothetical Cash Flow **75,000** Invested. Cash Flow Reinvested at 5.00%	Hypothetical Store Cash Flow Reinvested. Cash on Cash ROI	**232,503** Invested in CD at 5%	**75,000** Invested in CD at 5%
Year 1	65,935	65,935	28%	40,158	25,777	34%	244,128	78,750
Year 2	65,935	135,166	30%	40,158	52,843	36%	256,335	82,688
Year 3	65,935	207,859	31%	40,158	81,262	38%	269,151	86,822
Year 4	65,935	284,187	33%	40,158	111,103	40%	282,609	91,163
Year 5	65,935	364,331	34%	40,158	142,435	42%	296,739	95,721
Year 6	65,935	448,483	36%		215,491	97%	311,576	100,507
Year 7	65,935	536,842	38%		292,201	102%	327,155	105,533
Year 8	65,935	629,619	40%		372,746	107%	343,513	110,809
Year 9	65,935	727,034	42%		457,318	113%	360,688	116,350
Year 10	65,935	829,321	44%		546,118	118%	378,723	122,167
Total Cash Flow (10 Years)		829,321			546,118		378,723	122,167
Hypothetical Average Annual Return		35.67%			72.82%		16.29%	16.29%

Assumptions

Assumed Development Cost & Franchise Fee	232,503
Average Annual Net Operating Revenues	271,444
Average Annual Total Operating Expenses	191,937
Average Annual Net Store Profit	79,507
Assumed Annual G&A Factor ONE STORE	5.00%

The above chart illustrates the potential benefits of leverage when compared with an all cash investment in a franchise. For comparison purposes only, the historical average of all franchise operations for the last quarter of 1997 and the first three quarters of 1998 are used — those franchises which reported data. **There is absolutely no assurance whatsoever that Your results from operating a Kohr Bros. Franchise will be as profitable or even profitable at all.** Therefore, the above numbers should not be relied upon as an indication of how Your franchise might perform and are provided strictly for illustration and informational purposes only.

RITA'S ITALIAN ICE
1525 Ford Rd.
Bensalem, PA 19020
Tel: (800) 677-RITA (215) 633-9899
Fax: (215) 633-9922
E-Mail:
Internet Address: www.ritasice.com
Contact: Ms. Sandee Devine, Franchise Licensing
Manager

Description: Retail outlets selling Italian ices.

# Franchised Units:	207 Units
# Company-Owned Units:	<u>3</u> Units
Total # Units:	210 Units
Founded In:	1984
1st Franchised In:	1989
Average Total Investment:	133-242K
Franchise Fee:	25K
On-Going Royalty:	6.5%
Advertising Fee:	2.5%
Financial Assistance:Yes(I) (D – direct, or I – indirect)	
Site Selection Assistance:	Yes
Lease Negotiation Assistance:	Yes
Contract Terms (Init./Renew):	10/10
Initial Training Provided:6 Days Corporate Office; 2-4 Days On-Site.	

Included in this Item 19 are Rita's estimates of (1) actual 1998 average sales of Proprietary Products at franchised Shops ("Average Sales"), described in I, below, and (2) actual 1998 average food costs for ingredients for the Proprietary Products at franchised Shops ("Food Costs"), described in II, below.

I. 1998 Average Sales of Proprietary Products at Franchised Shops

The following chart represents our estimates of the Average Sales of franchised shops for water ice, gelati, custard and Misto shakes in 1998:

	Shops Open More Than 1 Full Season	Shops Open More Than 3 Full Seasons	Shops Open More Than 5 Full Seasons
Average Sales	$177,481	$185,188	$198,149
Median Sales	$183,313	$182,266	$182,266
Number of Shops in Category	153	68	22
Number of Shops Above Average Sales/% of Total	73/48%	31/46%	9/41%
Number of Shops Below Average Sales/% of Total	80/52%	37/54%	13/59%

Although Rita's obtained reports from Franchisees as to Gross Sales at franchised Shops for a portion of the 1998 season, in order to prepare the Average Sales figure for the entire selling season in this Item 19 it was necessary for Rita's to estimate Average Sales from franchised Shops. Rita's describes below how Rita's estimated the Average Sales contained in this Item 19.

The Average Sales estimate described in this Item 19 represents only the sales by Franchisees of Proprietary products containing the proprietary Rita's Mixes. These Proprietary Products were water ice, gelati, custard and Misto shakes. Not included in the Average Sales calculations described in this Item 19 are any other products sold by Franchisees, such as pretzels and promotional items.

A Shop is considered open for more than 1 full season when it has been open for an entire selling season for which Rita's requires operation plus some portion of the prior season. A Shop is considered open for more than 3 full seasons when it has been open for 3 entire selling seasons for which Rita's requires operation plus some portion of the prior selling season. A Shop is considered open for more than 5 full selling seasons when it has been open for 5 entire selling seasons for which Rita's requires operation plus some portion of the prior selling season. An entire season for which Rita's requires operation is typically from March 20 (the first day of Spring) through September 15.

Florida franchised Shops may have been open for as many as ten to twelve months. Where a Shop was open for a period longer than the selling season, all sales for such Shop were included in Rita's determination of Average Sales. Figures from the 28 franchised Shops opened after March 1, 1998 have not been included in the Average Sales calculation, as franchised Shops that have been open for less than twelve months are less likely to achieve Average Sales in that first twelve month period (e.g., because the Franchisee must spend disproportionate amounts of time and money developing the market by creating greater customer awareness and controlling wastage and food costs).

As noted in Item 6 of this Offering Circular, each Franchisee must pay to Rita's a Royalty Fee in the amount of 6½% of the projected sales to be made by a Franchisee based on a Franchisee's purchase of Rita's proprietary Rita's Mixes. In calculating the Royalty Fee, Rita's estimates the projected sales that can be expected to be made from a Franchisees purchase of Rita's Mixes, based on the amount of Rita's Mixes required for use in Rita's recipes for each product.

In calculating the Average Sales, Rita's estimated Franchisees' Average Sales based on the amount of Rita's Mixes purchased, Franchisees' prices, and the percentage of each type of Proprietary Product sold by Franchisees relative to all Proprietary Products sold (the "Product Percentages"). The historical data from which Rita's calculated the Product

Percentages was provided to Rita's by approximately 62% of Rita's Franchisees who submitted cash register tapes for one randomly selected day each month during the 1998 selling season. Rita's knows the prices charged by each Franchisee because each Franchisee must notify Rita's of its prices so that Rita's may calculate the Royalty Fee to be paid by such Franchisee. Rita's calculated the percentage of sales by Franchisees represented by each Proprietary Product and the average selling price for each Proprietary Product during the 1998 season to determine the expected revenue from a given amount of Rita's Mixes.

The Product Percentages for the 1998 season, as determined from Franchisees' franchised Shop register tapes (described in I, above) was as follows:

Proprietary Product by Size	Percentage of All Proprietary Products Required for Sale
Small Water Ice	11.63%
Medium Water Ice	17.40%
Large Water Ice	11.16%
Quart Water Ice	8.76%
Medium Gelati	20.03%
Large Gelati	11.26%
Small Custard	4.32%
Medium Custard	3.76%
Large Custard	1.16%
Large Misto Shake	7.87%
Super Misto Shake	2.65%
Total	**100%**

The Product Percentages vary based upon a Franchisee's location.

In calculating the Royalty Fee and Average Sales, Rita's also assumed that some "wastage" would occur. Rita's defines "wastage" as the Rita's Mix that will not be used in Proprietary Products that are sold (e.g., product that will be thrown away or given away in connection with promotions).

The Royalty Fee calculation for the 1998 season provided for 7% wastage; accordingly, when Rita's estimated projected sales on which a Franchisee owed Rita's a Royalty Fee, Rita's reduced its projections of sales expected to be made from a given amount of Rita's Mixes by 7%.

Four groups (3 pairs and 1 group of 3) of franchised Shops purchased Rita's Mixes together due to common ownership. In those cases, individual store usage could not be determined. Some Shops may have been open longer than other Shops under the same ownership. In order to approximate sales at each Shop under common ownership, Rita's used the Franchisee's reports of Gross Sales at each such Shop (which reports were collected for approximately one-half the 1998 selling season) to allocate sales between Shops. The estimated sales for each Shop were included in our calculation of Average Sales.

Sales figures for franchised Shops owned and operated by Rita's affiliates are included in the calculations of Average Sales. The Rita's System has its highest concentration of Shops in the Delaware Valley (including portions of Delaware, Pennsylvania and New Jersey). Of the 69 Shops located outside the Delaware Valley which were included in the determination of Average Sales, the average sales for such Shops was approximately 9% lower than the Average Sales for Shops open for more than 1 full season; 8.5% lower than the Average Sales for Shops open for more than 3 full seasons; and 7% lower than Average Sales for Shops open for more than 5 full seasons. If you operate a franchised Shop in areas other than the Delaware Valley, you must accept the possibility that you may achieve Gross Sales figures lower than the Average Sales.

II. 1998 Food Costs for Proprietary Products at Franchised Shops

Rita's estimates that Rita's Franchisees' Food Costs represent 13.45% of Franchisees' revenue from sales of the Proprietary Products. Rita's has calculated the estimated Food Costs of 13.45% based on (1) portions for ingredients required in Rita's proprietary recipes, (2) 1998 prices for such ingredients, (3) the System-wide average selling price in 1998 for each Proprietary Product sold, and (4) a weighted average of Proprietary Products sold as determined by Franchisee reports of Product Percentages in 1998 (as defined in I, above). Rita's

calculation of Food Costs assumes that proper recipes are followed, Franchisees adhere to proper serving sizes for Proprietary Products, and Franchisees maintain product wastage levels of 7%.

Rita's does not obtain reports from Franchisees as to Food Costs at franchised Shops. Accordingly, to prepare the Food Costs figures in this Item 19 it was necessary for Rita's to estimate the Food Costs figures from franchised Shops. Rita's does not know what percentage of Franchisees incurred actual Food Costs higher or lower than the estimated Food Costs of 13.45%. Rita's describes below how it estimated the Food Costs contained in this Item 19.

The calculation of Food Costs contained in this Item 19 represents Food Costs only for the products that Rita's requires each Franchisee to sell (i.e., small, medium, large and quart water ice; medium and large gelati; small, medium and large custard; and large and super Misto shakes). As described in I, above, approximately 62% of Rita's Franchisees operating in 1998 for at least one full season provided Rita's with their cash register tapes for one randomly selected day each month of the selling season. Rita's used this sampling of register tapes to estimate the Food Costs in the 1998 season. Rita's can estimate the total cost of the ingredients for each Proprietary Product because the recipes for each Proprietary Product are prescribed by Rita's, Franchisees were required in 1998 to purchase the Rita's Mixes from Rita's, and Franchisees may also purchase the remaining ingredients from Rita's. Rita's has used the prices it charged in 1998 to Franchisees for ingredients. Rita's has determined the average selling price (not including sales tax) for each Proprietary Product during the 1998 season based on the prices submitted by Franchisees. In order to approximate the food costs resulting from wastage, in calculating Food Costs for this Item 19, Rita's reduced the average selling price for each Proprietary Product by 7%. To determine the total pre-tax sales represented by the register tapes, as adjusted to reflect wastage, Rita's multiplied the adjusted average selling price by the number of units of each Proprietary Product sold (as reflected on the register tapes). Rita's also estimated the total cost of ingredients necessary to produce the total sales represented by the register tapes by multiplying the total number of each Proprietary Product sold by the estimated total costs for the ingredients for each item. Rita's determined estimated total costs for all sales represented by the register tapes by adding the estimated total costs for each Proprietary Product. Rita's determined Food Costs by dividing the estimated total costs by the pre-tax adjusted sales. From this calculation, Rita's determined Food Costs to be 13.45% of Franchisees' sales of all Proprietary Products.

As described in Item 6, above, each Franchisee must pay to Rita's a Royalty Fee based upon the amount of Rita's Mixes purchased by the Franchisee. This Royalty Fee has not been included in the calculations to determine Food Costs in this Item 19. As a Franchisee, payment of the Royalty Fee would be an additional cost.

The calculations in this Item 19 used in determining Food Costs are made under the assumption that Franchisees adhere to Rita's proprietary recipes and serving sizes. Although Rita's has provided each Franchisee with training and support to assist each Franchisee in adhering to these recipes and serving sizes, Rita's Franchisees have indicated to Rita's that an indeterminate number of Franchisees may serve portions to customers larger than those Rita's specifies.

Food Costs vary depending on store location, menu, Product Percentages, seasonal variances in raw material prices, and Franchisees' ability to effectively control costs. The average new Franchisee generally finds the first year of operation of each franchised Shop to be the most challenging. During the first year of operation a new Franchisee typically experiences higher wastage levels due to sampling, couponing and other promotional programs designed to build brand and product acceptance and due to higher amounts of "throw-aways" resulting from inexperience in planning. Historical costs do not correspond to future costs because of factors such as inflation, changes in menu and market driven changes in raw material costs.

* * *

Rita's does not furnish, or authorize its sales persons to furnish, any oral or written information concerning the actual, or average, or projected, or forecasted, or potential sales, costs, earnings or profits of a franchise other than as set forth in this Item.

Rita's Franchisees provided Rita's with actual gross sales for a portion of the 1998 season, but we have not relied on these reports in this Item 19. Actual sales and food costs vary from franchise to franchise, and Rita's cannot estimate the sales or food costs for a particular franchise. Rita's recommends that you make your own independent investigation to determine whether or not the franchise may be profitable, and consult with an attorney and other advisors prior to executing the Development Agreement or the Franchise Agreement.

THE ESTIMATED SALES AND COSTS CONTAINED IN THIS ITEM 19 ARE ESTIMATES OF THE AVERAGE SALES AND FOOD COSTS OF EXISTING FRANCHISES DESCRIBED AND SHOULD NOT BE CONSIDERED AS THE ACTUAL OR PROBABLE AVERAGE SALES OR FOOD COSTS THAT WILL BE REALIZED OR INCURRED BY ANY PROSPECTIVE FRANCHISEE. THE FRANCHISOR DOES NOT REPRESENT THAT ANY FRANCHISEE CAN EXPECT TO ATTAIN SUCH SALES OR TO INCUR SUCH FOOD COSTS. NONE OF THIS INFORMATION IS INTENDED AS A REPRESENTATION OF WHAT AVERAGE SALES YOU CAN EXPECT TO ACHIEVE OR FOOD COSTS YOU CAN EXPECT TO INCUR AT ANY PARTICULAR LOCATION.

SOME FRANCHISED SHOPS HAVE ACHIEVED THESE RESULTS AND INCURRED THESE COSTS. THERE IS NO ASSURANCE THAT YOU WILL DO AS WELL. IF YOU RELY UPON RITA'S FIGURES, YOU MUST ACCEPT THE RISK OF NOT DOING AS WELL.

RITA'S WILL MAKE AVAILABLE TO YOU FOR INSPECTION AND REVIEW THE DATA UTILIZED IN FORMULATING THE INFORMATION CONTAINED IN THIS ITEM 19 UPON REASONABLE REQUEST FROM YOU.

Food: quick-service/ takeout

BOJANGLES' FAMOUS CHICKEN 'N BISCUITS
P. O. Box 240239
Charlotte, NC 28224
Tel: (800) 366-9921 (704) 527-2675
Fax: (704) 523-6676
E-Mail: msandefer@bojangles.com
Internet Address: www.bojangles.com
Contact: Mr. Mike Sandefer, Director Franchise Development

Description: BOJANGLES OPERATES DURING ALL 3 DAY-PARTS. Breakfast items are available all day long. Our menu in unique, and flavorful, with chicken prepared either spicy or traditional Southern-style. Restaurants operate in traditional locations and non-traditional locations in convenience stores.

# Franchised Units:	110 Units
# Company-Owned Units:	<u>160</u> Units
Total # Units:	270 Units
Founded In:	1977
1st Franchised In:	1979
Average Total Investment:	200K-1.2MM
Franchise Fee:	12 or 20K
On-Going Royalty:	4%
Advertising Fee:	1%
Financial Assistance:No (D – direct, or I – indirect)	
Site Selection Assistance:	Yes
Lease Negotiation Assistance:	No
Contract Terms (Init./Renew):	20/10
Initial Training Provided:6 Weeks	
Training Units (Sevveral Locations); 1 Week Bo-U Corporate Office.	

This earnings claim contains information about our Full Size Restaurants and Express Restaurants. Sales and expenses shown for restaurants owned by our affiliate, Bojangles' Restaurants, Inc., are based on our 1998 fiscal year which was December 29, 1997, to January 3, 1999. "Company-owned" restaurants or "Bojangles'-owned" restaurants refers to restaurants owned by our affiliate, Bojangles' Restaurants, Inc. Annual sales shown for franchised restaurants may be based on our fiscal year or the calendar year depending on how a particular franchisee has reported sales.

1. **Full Size Restaurants:**
Set forth below is information concerning the gross sales of franchised and Bojangles'-owned

full size restaurants which were in operation continuously throughout the period January 1 through December 31, 1998 and which were operating as of the date of this offering circular, as well as two line-item expenses incurred by Bojangles'-owned full size restaurants.

2. **Express Restaurants:**

Set forth below is information concerning the average monthly gross sales of all operating, franchised and Bojangles'-owned Express Restaurants from their opening (but excluding their first month's operations) through December 31, 1998.

I. Full Size Restaurants
Table A: Annual Gross Sales Range of Restaurants by State

State	Over $1,600,000		$1,400,000–1,599,999		$1,200,000–1,399,999		$1,000,000–1,199,999		$800,000–999,999		$600,000–799,999		Less than $600,000		Total Number of Restaurants	
	Franchised	Company Owned	Franchised	Company Owned	Franchised	Company Owned	Franchised	Company Owned	Franchised	Company Owned	Franchised	Company Owned	Franchised	Company Owned	Franchised	Company Owned
North Carolina	24	2	7	3	7	14	4	20	2	26	3	16	0	2	47	83
South Carolina	0	1	0	0	0	3	1	6	1	9	0	12	0	4	2	35
Georgia	0	0	0	0	1	0	1	1	3	1	2	2	0	0	7	4
Virginia	0	0	1	0	0	0	0	0	2	0	0	0	3	0	6	0
Pennsylvania	0	0	0	0	0	0	0	0	1	0	0	0	1	0	2	0
Kentucky	0	0	0	0	0	0	0	0	1	0	2	0	1	0	4	0
Tennessee	0	0	0	0	0	0	0	0	3	0	3	0	0	0	6	0
Total	24	3	8	3	8	17	6	27	13	36	10	30	5	6	74	122

Table B: Summary of Gross Sales Ranges of Full Size Restaurants by Percentage

Gross Sales	Percentage of Franchise Restaurants	Percentage of Bojangles'-Owned Restaurants	Percentage of All Restaurants
Over $1,600,000	32.4%	2.5%	13.8%
$1,400,000–1,599,999	10.8%	2.5%	5.6%
$1,200,000–1,399,999	10.8%	13.9%	12.8%
$1,000,000–1,199,999	8.1%	22.1%	16.8%
$800,000–999,999	17.6%	29.5%	25.0%
$600,000–799,999	13.5%	24.6%	20.4%
Under $600,000	6.8%	4.9%	5.6%

Table C: Average Gross Sales of Full Size Restaurants

	Arithmetic	Median
Franchise	$1,312,312	$1,332,663
Company	$965,084	$938,213

Table E: Selected Expenses of Bojangles'-Owned Full Size Restaurants

Expense Category	Average Cost
Food and Paper	33.8%
Labor	31.9%

Table D: Gross Sales Range of Full Size Restaurants

	High	Low
Franchise	$2,550,098	$153,866
Company	$1,895,759	$510,627

189

II. Express Restaurants
Average Monthly Sales of Express Restaurants

Bojangles'-Owned

State	Opened	Seating	Average Monthly Gross Sales
1. Georgia[11]	May 1995	20	$49,773
2. Georgia[11]	June 1995	30	$33,116
3. South Carolina	September 1995	18	$43,825
4. South Carolina	October 1996	20	$33,907
5. South Carolina	January 1996	26	$59,677
6. South Carolina	July 1998	44	$65,186
7. North Carolina	December 1995	100	$28,309
8. North Carolina	May 1997	38	$52,525
9. North Carolina	July 1997	70	$48,511

Franchise

State	Opened	Seating	Average Monthly Gross Sales
1. North Carolina	November 1994	96	$92,181
2. North Carolina	January 1998	54	$92,515
3. North Carolina	September 1998	48	$60,147
4. North Carolina	November 1998	62	$69,433
5. South Carolina	August 1996	45	$63,378
6. South Carolina	August 1996	50	$36,120
7. South Carolina	November 1996	30	$41,068
8. South Carolina	June 1997	58	$47,201
9. South Carolina	August 1997	24	$38,356
10. South Carolina	September 1997	22	$25,003
11. South Carolina	November 1997	12	$33,007
12. South Carolina	April 1998	32	$17,961
13. South Carolina	June 1998	28	$21,072
14. Virginia	June 1996	80	$85,088
15. Virginia	March 1998	42	$42,547
16. Virginia	October 1998	38	$28,364
17. West Virginia	May 1996	80	$32,851
18 . West Virginia	September 1996	50	$22,976
19. Georgia	July 1998	52	$69,138

Footnotes:

1. The gross sales information set forth in this Item 19 refers only to full size free-standing restaurants which are 2,800 to 4,800 square feet. As of the end of the 1998 fiscal year, we also operated 5 and franchised 4 "Mini-Bo" restaurants which are smaller size freestanding restaurants 1,800 to 2,400 square feet; operated 1 and franchised 2 "Drive-thru" restaurants without interior seating; operated 9 and fran-

chised 20 "Express" units operated in connection with other brands and businesses such as malls or convenience stores and which are between 700 and 2,400 square feet.

2. Sixteen franchisees own an aggregate of the 74 franchised full size restaurants whose results are included in tables A–D.

3. The results of the following full size restaurants are excluded from this earnings claim:

   a. Nineteen Bojangles'-owned and six franchised restaurants which were open less than a full year as of December 31, 1998.

   b. Fifteen franchised restaurants that were closed in 1998 or are otherwise not operating as of the date of this Offering Circular.

   c. Eighteen restaurants which were acquired by Bojangles from franchisees in 1998. Six of the 18 are located in North Carolina and 12 are located in South Carolina. Two of the 18 have been closed.

4. No operating Express restaurants have been excluded from this earnings claim.

5. We have permitted some franchisees of full size restaurants to reduce the number of menu items offered by their restaurants.

6. We relied on the royalty reports submitted by franchised restaurants and the internal reports prepared by company personnel for Bojangles'-owned restaurants, when preparing this earnings claim. Although these results are unaudited, we have no reason to question the accuracy of the reports submitted to us.

7. The information concerning expenses of all company restaurants that appears in Table E reflects the 1998 results of the 156 Bojangles'-owned restaurants whose results are reflected in Tables A–D. Labor costs include crew employee wages and benefits, management wages and benefits including unit directors and general managers (who manage 2 to 3 units each) but exclude wages and benefits of area managers (multi-unit supervisors). Benefits required by state and federal law, worker's compensation, payroll taxes including FICA and FUTA expenses, payroll charges, group insurance costs and company paid vacations are also included in labor costs. Food costs include costs of all food and food components, and paper sold and condiments given at retail level, but excludes costs of supplies and uniforms. You will incur other costs in addition to the two selected expense categories described in Table E.

8. The information contained in this earnings claim refers to specific franchise and Bojangles'-owned restaurants, and should not be considered as the actual or potential sales or costs that will be achieved by your restaurant. Actual results vary from restaurant to restaurant and we cannot estimate the results of any specific restaurant. A new franchisee's results are likely to differ from those of established restaurants. We recommend that you make your own independent investigation to determine whether or not a franchise may be profitable, and consult with an attorney or other advisors before signing any franchise agreement.

9. We will provide substantiation for the information contained in this earnings claim upon reasonable request.

10. The results of the first month of operations of Express Restaurants have been excluded when calculating their monthly gross sales.

11. These restaurants do not have drive-thru windows.

12. This restaurant is a hybrid Full Size and Express Restaurant. It is attached to a convenience store, but its size is more similar to a Full Size Restaurant. Its results are reflected in the Table for Express Restaurants.

13. These Express units share seating with other food service operations in the same building,

191

but only sales from the Bojangles' operations are included.

14. Except for the information contained in this offering circular, we do not furnish or authorize our salespersons to furnish any oral or written information concerning the actual, average, projected or forecasted sales, costs, income or profits of a Bojangles-owned or franchised full size restaurant, "Mini-Bo," "Drive-thru," or "Express" restaurant.

BUFFALO WILD WINGS

600 S. Highway 169, 1919 Interchange Tower
Minneapolis, MN 55426
Tel: (800) 499-9586 (612) 593-9943
Fax: (612) 593-9787
E-Mail: bill@bw3.com
Internet Address: www.bw3.com
Contact: Mr. Bill McClintock, VP Franchise Development

Description: BUFFALO WILD WINGS has a sports-themed environment, complete with large-screen TV's, interactive games and memorabilia, with an inexpensive a la carte menu, concentrating buffalo wings, great sandwiches and 12 proprietary sauces.

# Franchised Units:	80 Units
# Company-Owned Units:	<u>26</u> Units
Total # Units:	106 Units
Founded In:	1982
1st Franchised In:	1991
Average Total Investment:	522-850K
Franchise Fee:	25-30K
On-Going Royalty:	5%
Advertising Fee:	3%
Financial Assistance:No (D – direct, or I – indirect)	
Site Selection Assistance:	Yes
Lease Negotiation Assistance:	Yes
Contract Terms (Init./Renew):	10/5/5
Initial Training Provided:	3 Weeks Training.

During the fiscal year ended December 27, 1998, all of the System Restaurants which had been in operation at least 18 months (66 out of 86) had average gross sales of $1,247,768. This figure represents the actual average gross sales of 57 Franchised Restaurants and 9 Restaurants owned by Parent and its subsidiaries and affiliates. Out of the 66 Restaurants, the lowest gross sale figure was $708,803 and the highest gross sale figure was $2,739,659. Of the 66 Restaurants, 30 (45%) have gross sales in excess of the average. Of the 66 Restaurants, 55 (83%) have gross sales over $1,000,000. All Restaurants considered offer substantially the same products and services as will be offered from Franchised Restaurants.

We have made no material assumptions in producing the gross sales figures described above. Substantiation of the actual gross sales amounts set forth in this section of the Offering Circular will be made available to you upon reasonable request.

WE DO NOT REPRESENT THAT YOU CAN EXPECT TO ATTAIN THESE SALES. THERE IS NO ASSURANCE THAT YOU WILL DO AS WELL. IF YOU RELY ON THESE FIGURES, YOU MUST ACCEPT THE RISK OF NOT DOING AS WELL. YOUR FINANCIAL RESULTS ARE LIKELY TO DIFFER FROM THE RESULTS SHOWN.

WE HAVE BASED THE CLAIMS UPON OUR RECORDS AND CONSOLIDATED FINANCIAL STATEMENTS AND HAVE COMPILED THE CLAIMS TO THE EXTENT POSSIBLE IN A MANNER CONSISTENT WITH GENERALLY ACCEPTED ACCOUNTING PRINCIPLES.

Gross sales do not represent actual or potential income of a Franchised Restaurant and you should not rely on them in calculating prospective profitability. The profitability of individual restaurants depends on a number of factors which may vary due to individual characteristics of the franchised business. Factors affecting net profits may include but are not limited to costs of labor and rental, compliance and supplies. In addition, net profitability will be affected by required contributions for advertising and promotions as well as continuing fees paid to us.

Substantiation of the actual sales data will be made available to you upon reasonable request.

BETTER BREAD. BETTER SUBS.™

COUSINS SUBS
N83 W13400 Leon Rd.
Menomonee Falls, WI 53051
Tel: (800) 238-9736 (262) 253-7700
Fax: (262) 253-7705
E-Mail: dkilby@cousinssubs.com
Internet Address: www.cousinssubs.com
Contact: Mr. David K. Kilby, Executive Vice President

Description: COUSINS SUBS celebrates over 27 years as an exceptionally high-volume, fast service concept in up-scale, in-line, free-standing and non-traditional locations. # 1 sub sandwich chain for five years running (Income Opportunities Magazine). Midwest, Southwest and South development available for single, multiple and area developers.

# Franchised Units:	110 Units
# Company-Owned Units:	<u>35</u> Units
Total # Units:	145 Units
Founded In:	1972
1st Franchised In:	1985
Average Total Investment:	165-253K
Franchise Fee:	15K
On-Going Royalty:	4-6%
Advertising Fee:	2%
Financial Assistance:Yes(I) (D – direct, or I – indirect)	
Site Selection Assistance:	Yes
Lease Negotiation Assistance:	Yes
Contract Terms (Init./Renew):	10/10

Initial Training Provided:1 Wk Corp. HQ;4 Wks Training Store;10 Days Franchisee's New Store;3 Field Visits/mo 1st yr

The following Gross Receipts of Cousins Subs Shops are for the calendar year ending December 31, 1998.

Cousins does not furnish or authorize its salespersons to furnish any oral or written information concerning the actual or potential sales, costs, income or profits of a Cousins Subs Shop. Actual results vary from unit to unit, and Cousins cannot estimate the results of any particular franchise.

Exhibit H
Statement of Gross Receipts

Ranges of Gross Receipts of Franchised Shops for the calendar year 1998 which have been open for more than 1 year but less than 2 years as of December 31, 1998

Range of Receipts	No. of Shops	% of Total
$50,000–99,999	1	5.00%
$100,000–149,999	0	—
$150,000–199,999	5	25.00%
$200,000–249,999	5	25.00%
$250,000–299,999	1	5.00%
$300,000–349,999	4	20.00%
$350,000–399,999	0	—
$400,000–449,999	2	10.00%
$450,000–499,999	1	5.00%
$500,000–549,999	1	5.00%
$550,000–599,999	0	—
$600,000–649,999	0	—
Total	20	100.00%

All of these Shops are Highly Efficient Concept Shops. 5 of these are located in Arizona. The remainder are located in Midwestern markets.

Ranges of Gross Receipts of Franchised Shops for the calendar year 1998 which have been open for more than 2 years as of December 31, 1998

Range of Receipts	No. of Shops	% of Total
$100,000–149,999	1	1.53%
$150,000–199,999	3	4.62%
$200,000–249,999	5	7.69%
$250,000–299,999	11	16.92%
$300,000–349,999	9	13.85%
$350,000–399,999	13	20.00%
$400,000–449,999	3	4.62%
$450,000–499,999	2	3.08%
$500,000–549,999	6	9.23%
$550,000–599,999	2	3.08%
$600,000–649,999	3	4.62%
$650,000–699,999	2	3.08%
$700,000–749,999	3	462%
$750,000–799,999	0	—
$800,000–849,999	0	—
$850,000–899,999	0	—
$900,000–949,999	1	1.53%
$950,000–999,999	0	—
$1,000,000–1,049,999	1	1.53%
Total	65	100.00%

24 of these Shops are Original Concept Shops. The remainder are Highly Efficient Concept Shops. 13 of these are located in Arizona, the rest are located in Midwestern markets. Of the Highly Efficient Concept Shops, 1 Shop gross receipts ranged from $100,000 to $149,999; 3 ranged from $150,000 to $199,999; 5 ranged from $200,000 to $249,999; 11 from $250,000 to $299,999; 1 ranged from $300,000 to $349,999; 7 ranged from $350,000 to $399,999; 2 ranged from $400,000 to $449,999; 2 ranged from $450,000 to $499,999; 3 ranged from $500,000 to $549,999; 1 from

$600,000 to $649,000; 1 from $700,000 to $749,999.

These numbers include shops in convenience stores and other alternative venues. Gross receipts for such shops ranged from $100,000 to $349,000.

Ranges of Gross Receipts of affiliated owned for shops for calendar year 1998 open for more than 1 year as of December 31, 1998

Range of Receipts	No. of Shops	% of Total
$250,000–299,999	0	—
$300,000–349,999	0	—
$350,000–399,999	1	2.78%
$400,000–449,999	1	2.78%
$450,000–499,999	3	8.33%
$500,000–549,999	2	5.56%
$550,000–599,999	1	2.78%
$600,000–649,999	3	8.33%
$650,000–699,999	1	2.78%
$700,000–749,999	9	25.00%
$750,000–799,999	3	8.33%
$800,000–849,999	2	5.56%
$850,000–899,999	2	5.56%
$900,000–949,999	2	5.56%
$950,000–999,999	3	8.33%
$1,000,000–1,049,999	3	8.32%
Total	36	100.00%

2 shops are Highly Efficient Concept with Gross Receipts from $400,000 to $449,999 & $800,000 to $849,999. All the others are Original Concept Shops.

The gross receipt figures set forth in this Statement have not been audited by Cousins. The figures used in this Statement are gross receipt figures. Net income will vary from Shop to Shop depending upon such factors as rental or real estate costs, costs of goods sold, labor costs and other costs relating to the operation of the Shop.

Cousins or its affiliates offered substantially the same services to all of the Shops described in this Statement. These Shops offered substantially the same products and services to the public.

All of the Shops report gross receipts information to Cousins based upon a uniform reporting system. Cousins believes that this Statement is consistent with generally accepted accounting principles, to the extent applicable.

CULVERS FRANCHISING SYSTEM
107 Berkley Blvd., # A
Baraboo, WI 53913
Tel: (608) 356-5938
Fax: (608) 356-9017
E-Mail: katee@baraboo.com
Internet Address: www.culvers.com
Contact: Mr. Tom Wakefield, Franchise Sales

Description: The menu at CULVERS FROZEN CUSTARD is a bit of a flashback to the simple, honest taste of the 1950's hamburger stand. We have converted our ideas about quality and freshness into a new kind of restaurant where the tastes of butterburgers and frozen custard keep customers coming back. By serving good food at a good value, we've managed to become the largest frozen custard establishment in the United States.

# Franchised Units:	84 Units
# Company-Owned Units:	3 Units
Total # Units:	87 Units
Founded In:	1984
1st Franchised In:	1987
Average Total Investment:	800K-1.8MM
Franchise Fee:	42.5K
On-Going Royalty:	4%
Advertising Fee:	2%
Financial Assistance:No (D – direct, or I – indirect)	
Site Selection Assistance:	Yes
Lease Negotiation Assistance:	Yes
Contract Terms (Init./Renew):	15/15
Initial Training Provided:16 Weeks in Central, WI.	

The "Schedule of Restaurant Financial Data" discloses the total and average sales and selected costs of the three corporate-owned restaurants operated by Culver Franchising System, Inc. for the entire fiscal year ending December 31, 1998.

These corporate-owned Restaurants are located in Sauk City, Spring Green, and Prairie du Chien, Wisconsin. The buildings housing the Restaurants are single-purpose, one story and free-standing, seating 88 to 98 guests at one time, which is comparable to the restaurants expected to be operated pursuant to the Franchise Agreement.

Substantially the same services were offered to the corporate-owned Restaurants as are provided to the Franchise Owners; however, we do not provide certain services to Franchise Owners as financing, accounting, legal, personnel, construction, management, financial and food and labor cost systems.

The corporate-owned Restaurants offered substantially the same products and services to the general public as the Restaurants to be operated pursuant to the Franchise Agreement.

The following Schedule was prepared on a basis consistent with generally accepted accounting principles and the same accounting system was used for each corporate-owned Restaurant. The figures used in the Schedule are based on an annual performance.

195

Schedule of Corporate-Owned Restaurant Data			
	3 Restaurant Total	Average	% of Sales
Sales	$3,139,000	$1,046,000	100
Food & Paper Costs	$1,111,000	$370,000	35.4
Labor Costs*	$1,165,000	$388,000	37.1
Other Controllable Expenses**	$271,000	$90,000	8.6
Income before Royalties, Interest, Depreciation, Occupancy Costs and Taxes	$600,000	$200,000	19.1

*Labor Costs include manager salaries, crew wages, payroll taxes, bonuses, and other benefits.
**Other Controllable Expenses are those expenses over which on-site management has the ability to control, in part or in whole, and includes such items as supplies, chemicals, uniforms, telephone, utilities, insurance (general liability and property), cash overages or shortages, local marketing, legal, accounting, and repairs.

SUCH SALES, INCOME, GROSS OR NET PROFITS ARE OF SPECIFIC RESTAURANTS OWNED AND OPERATED BY CFSI AND SHOULD NOT BE CONSIDERED AS THE ACTUAL OR PROBABLE SALES, INCOME, GROSS OR NET PROFITS THAT WILL BE REALIZED BY ANY FRANCHISE OWNER. CFSI DOES NOT REPRESENT THAT ANY FRANCHISE OWNER CAN EXPECT TO ATTAIN SUCH SALES, INCOME, GROSS OR NET PROFITS. YOUR RESULTS WILL VARY AND SUCH VARIANCES MAY BE MATERIAL AND ADVERSE.

Substantiation of the data used in preparing the Schedule will be made available upon reasonable demand. THE INFORMATION PRESENTED ABOVE HAS NOT BEEN AUDITED.

The average statements shown in the Schedule DO NOT include the following items of expense which have to be calculated and included separately for every franchised restaurant:

&- Royalty Fees consistent with current contractual requirements under the Franchise Agreement.
&- Depreciation of property and equipment.
&- Rent, interest or other financing cost for land, buildings, equipment, and inventory.
&- Initial franchise fee and organization costs.
&- Any management fees.
&- Income taxes and property taxes.

These excluded items affect the net income and/or cash flow of any restaurant and must be carefully considered and evaluated by any prospective licensee. The actual performance of any restaurant will depend on a number of factors specific to the property including, but not limited to. the above factors.

The Restaurants and restaurants to be operated pursuant to the Franchise Agreement have the following similarities:

&- Each Restaurant operates under the name "Culver's Frozen Custard." Each Restaurant generally offers the same selection of menu items and are opened from 10 a.m. to 10 p.m. every day.

Sales and operating results of the Restaurants and the restaurants to be operated pursuant to the Franchise Agreement are effected by the following:

&- Economic and weather conditions of various geographic areas.
&- Competition from a variety of other restaurants, including fast food business. Some restaurants have greater competition than others.
&- Different acquisition, development, construction and property costs.
&- Local property tax rates.
&- State laws concerning employee costs
&- Different traffic counts, accessibility and visibility. The location of each restaurant may

have a significant impact on sales and operating income.

❧ Different benefits from advertising. Some Restaurants do not receive the benefits of television advertising. Some Restaurants are not grouped in such a way that local television or other media advertising can be efficiently obtained.

❧ Although each Restaurant has seating and parking, the amount of seating and parking varies among the Restaurants.

❧ All Restaurants have been in business for different periods of time and therefore have experienced varying periods of time to become established in their respective markets.

❧ Each Restaurant may set its own prices for menu items.

❧ Each Restaurant may experience varying food costs due to geographic area and economies of scale due to the grouping of Restaurants in any single geographic area.

❧ The quality and effectiveness of management of each Restaurant varies.

The following information is based on 53 franchised Restaurants and does not include the 16 franchised restaurants that opened during 1998 or one franchised restaurant that closed for part of the year.

	Number of Restaurants		
Range of Gross Sales	Company-Owned	Franchise	Total
$1,500,001–1,900,000	0	11	11
$1,200,001–1,500,000	1	19	20
$900,001–1,200,000	1	18	19
$500,000–900,000	1	5	6
Totals	3	53	56
Average Sales	$1,046,381	$1,272,220	$1,260,122

FIGARO'S ITALIAN KITCHEN
1500 Liberty St., S. E., # 160
Salem, OR 97302
Tel: (888) FIGAROS (503) 371-9318
Fax: (503) 363-5364
E-Mail: figaros@cyberhighway.net
Internet Address: www.figaros.com
Contact: Mr. Max Bennett, Franchise Sales Director

Description: A store offering a limited menu of we-bake or you-bake pizza, lasagna, calzones and other food and beverage products which are prepared for take-out baking and consumption.

# Franchised Units:	80 Units
# Company-Owned Units:	0 Units
Total # Units:	80 Units
Founded In:	1981
1st Franchised In:	1986
Average Total Investment:	154.5-181.5K
Franchise Fee:	18.5K
On-Going Royalty:	5%
Advertising Fee:	2%
Financial Assistance:Yes (D – direct, or I – indirect)	
Site Selection Assistance:	Yes
Lease Negotiation Assistance:	Yes
Contract Terms (Init./Renew):	5/5/5/5
Initial Training Provided:12 Days Salem Training Stores.	

Except for Exhibit H to the Offering Circular "1997 Sales Averages" and "Financial Statement Cost Averages," Company does not furnish or authorize its salespersons to furnish any oral or written information concerning the actual or potential sales, costs, income or profits of a FIGA-

RO'S store. Actual results vary from unit to unit and FIGARO'S ITALIAN PIZZA, INC. cannot estimate results of any particular franchise. Exhibit H does not apply to Satellite, Co-Branding or Supermarket franchises.

However, under law we may give a prospective franchisee who is seeking to buy a specific operating unit actual operating results of that unit, together with the last known address of each owner of the unit during the prior three years.

Figaro's Italian Pizza, Inc. Exhibit H to the Offering Circular

Existing Store Growth Monthly Averages and Selected Cost Account Averages

The information included in this Earnings Claim represents amounts reported to Company by its franchisees, subject to the assumptions outlined below. While we believe these figures to be reliable, we did not audit these reports or the franchisees, and therefore cannot guarantee their accuracy.

SUCH ACTUAL SALES, AVERAGE SALES, AND COSTS ARE OF SPECIFIC FRANCHISED STORES AND SHOULD NOT BE CONSIDERED AS THE ACTUAL OR POTENTIAL SALES, AVERAGE SALES OR PERCENTAGE INCREASES THAT WILL BE REALIZED BY ANY FRANCHISEE. FRANCHISOR DOES NOT REPRESENT THAT ANY FRANCHISEE (CAN EXPECT TO ATTAIN THESE SALES FIGURES OR OVERALL PERCENTAGE INCREASES.

THE ACTUAL SALES, AVERAGE SALES AND COSTS SHOULD NOT BE CONSTRUED AS THE "PROFIT" WHICH MIGHT BE EXPERIENCED BY A FRANCHISEE WITH A SIMILAR SALES VOLUME, WHICH IS IMPOSSIBLE TO PREDICT. SEE RISK FACTORS IN PAGE ii AND ITEM 1 OF THE OFFERING CIRCULAR.

THESE FIGURES DO NOT APPLY TO SUPERMARKET, CO-BRANDING, OR SATELLITE FRANCHISES.

The cost figures are for selected items only, and do not make allowances for many other expenses which may arise in the operation of your FIGARO'S Franchised Store, but which may not be listed here. These figures may vary substantially from store to store and franchise to franchise.

The franchised stores included have offered substantially the same products and services to the public as will be offered from your franchised store. The franchised stores included in the statement do not use a uniform accounting system.

Substantiation of the data used in preparing the accompanying Earnings Claim will be made available to a prospective franchisee upon reasonable request.

Figaro's Existing Store Growth (Comparing Only Stores That Have Been Opened a Minimum of 13 Months)

	1997 Monthly Gross Sales Avg.	1996 Monthly Gross Sales Avg.
January	$28,759	$24,706
February	26,804	24,694
March	28,954	28,182
April	28,796	25,761
May	29,352	27,692
June	27,025	25,182
July	25,437	24,718
August	27,265	26,155
September	25,939	26,067
October	28,887	28,198
November	27,255	28,384
December	30,130	30,264
Yearly Totals:	$334,603	$320,003

NOTE: THE TERM "GROSS SALES" SHALL MEAN AND INCLUDE THE TOTAL OF ALL SALES, LESS DISCOUNTS OF FOOD PRODUCTS, BEVERAGES, AND OTHER MERCHANDISE AND PRODUCTS TO CUSTOMERS OF FIGARO'S, WHETHER OR NOT SOLD AT OR FROM THE FRANCHISED STORE LESS ANY

SALES TAX, USE TAX, OR SERVICE TAXES COLLECTED AND/OR PAID TO THE APPROPRIATE TAXING AUTHORITY, AND LESS CUSTOMER REFUNDS.

Selected Financial Statement Cost Accounts Non-Weighted Averages For 1997

	Low	High	Average	No. of Stores
Food %	24.2	31.2	26.3	49
Paper %	3.9	5.2	4.3	48
Beverage %	0.9	2.2	1.4	49
Management %	3.2	9.7	6.5	39
Crew Labor %	8.6	18.2	13.5	45
Lease (Monthly $)	709.0	2,406.0	1,468.0	48
Discounts %	3.7	13.8	8.6	44
Supplies (Yearly $)	250.0	5,096.0	1,561.0	37
Repair & Maint. (Yearly $)	319.0	7,420.0	2713	44
Uniforms (Yearly $)	134.0	1,354.0	522.0	37
Utilities (Yearly $)	4,040.0	10,746.0	6,107.0	47

NOTE: 82 FIGARO'S STORES WERE OPERATING AT CLOSE OF 1997 (DECEMBER 31, 1997). 14 STORES WERE WINCO SUPERMARKETS (FINANCIAL STATEMENTS ARE NOT REQUIRED NOR PROVIDED FROM THIS GROUP). THE REMAINING 68 STORES ARE REQUIRED TO PROVIDE FINANCIAL STATEMENTS.

OF THESE 68 STORES: FOUR STATEMENTS WERE NOT APPLICABLE FOR THIS CALCULATION DUE TO IMPROPER GROUPING OF EXPENSES; ONE STORE OPENED IN LATE DECEMBER OF 1997; NINE FINANCIAL STATEMENTS WERE NOT OBTAINABLE; AND THE REMAINING 54 STATEMENTS WERE UTILIZED FOR THE ABOVE CALCULATIONS.

EACH OF THE ABOVE ACCOUNTS DOES NOT REFLECT AN AVERAGE FOR THE ENTIRE GROUP OF 54 STORES. A FEW STORES WERE MISSING FROM EACH FOR ONE OF THE FOLLOWING REASONS: SOME ACCOUNTS WERE NOT INDIVIDUALLY IDENTIFIED FOR CALCULATION ON FRANCHISEE FINANCIAL STATEMENTS; SOME ACCOUNTS WERE MISSING; AND SOME ACCOUNTS WERE COMBINED WITH OTHER ACCOUNTS MAKING IT IMPOSSIBLE TO IDENTIFY THE ENTRY.

FRULLATI CAFÉ & BAKERY
15150 Preston Rd., # 300
Dallas, TX 75248
Tel: (800) 289-8291 (972) 401-9730

Fax: (972) 401-9731
E-Mail: comments@frullati.com
Internet Address: www.frulatti.com
Contact: Ms. Nicole Rayborn, Franchise Director

Description: FRULLATI CAFÉ & BAKERY, the fresh franchise alternative in fast food. Featuring something fresh for every taste, FRULLATI's lite fare menu includes: fruit smoothies, frozen yogurt, deli sandwiches, healthy snacks, fresh baked bread, cookies and gourmet coffee. If the taste of success by owning one or a chain of FRULLATI CAFÉs sounds appetizing, here's the opportunity for you.

We have FRULLATI CAGE & BAKERY franchise opportunities coming to your neighborhood.

# Franchised Units:	60 Units
# Company-Owned Units:	<u>40</u> Units
Total # Units:	100 Units
Founded In:	1985
1st Franchised In:	1994
Average Total Investment:	150-275K
Franchise Fee:	20K

On-Going Royalty:	6%
Advertising Fee:	1%
Financial Assistance:Yes(I) (D – direct, or I – indirect)	
Site Selection Assistance:	Yes
Lease Negotiation Assistance:	Yes
Contract Terms (Init./Renew):	10/10
Initial Training Provided:	3 Weeks Dallas, TX.

Except as provided below, we do not furnish or authorize our salespersons to furnish any oral or written information concerning the actual or potential sales, costs, income or profits of a Cafe. Actual results vary from Cafe to Cafe and we cannot estimate the results of any particular franchisee.

Analysis of Gross Sales of Affiliate-Owned Cafes and Franchised Cafes for Period Ending December 27, 1998

1. *Introduction.* The financial information contained in this Item 19 is provided to assist you in conducting your own financial analysis of the Cafe franchise opportunity we described in this Offering Circular and for the purpose of planning your budget and estimating your need for operating capital. This Item 19 contains information concerning the Gross Sales of certain affiliate-owned and franchised Cafes that have been open and operating for the entire fiscal year ending December 27, 1998, and certain information concerning the operating costs of particular affiliate-owned Cafes for the fiscal year ending December 27, 1998 (the "Analysis"). This Analysis does not contain any information concerning the operating costs of any franchised Cafes, nor does it contain any information concerning any of the other operational expenses you may incur for financing, interest, depreciation, amortization, taxes and other costs associated with the operation of the Cafe, based on your particular circumstances.

As of December 27, 1998, we had a total of 85 Affiliate-owned and franchised Cafes. The ranges of the Gross Sales have been provided reflecting the Gross Sales of 51 Cafes that were open and in operation during the entire 13, 4 week periods (the "Statement Period"), ending December 27, 1998. These 51 Cafes consist of 12 Cafes operated by our affiliates in the geographic markets where our affiliates expect to concentrate their expansion: and 39 Cafes operated by Franchisees. Our affiliates also operated 13 Cafes in geographic markets that they do not expect to expand; these Cafes are not included in this analysis. Twenty of our affiliate-owned and franchised Cafes were not in continuous operation during the entire Statement Period and financial information from those Cafes were not included in this analysis. One other Frullati Cafe owned by Our affiliate that was open and in continuous operation during this Statement Period is located in a secured access facility in Dallas, Texas for bank data processing and is not open to the public. No information from this Cafe was included in this analysis. The Gross Sales figures provided above were compiled by Us from the financial statements of affiliate-owned Cafes and the royalty reports We received from franchisees.

In addition to the Gross Sales ranges, certain operating costs, expressed as a percentage of Gross Sales, have been provided based on the experience of the 12 Cafes owned and operated by our affiliates in the geographic markets in which they expect to expand, as described below.

The Gross Sales and expense percentages provided should be carefully evaluated by you solely in the context of the specific operations and geographic markets of the Cafes included in the Analysis. The affiliate-owned Cafes included in this analysis have conducted operations with the Dallas/Fort Worth Area. To the extent your general trade area comprises a market area which is geographically different from the markets of the existing Cafes (see Item 20), it is likely that the operational results of your Cafe will vary materially from the results of the existing Cafes. Variables which differ from region to region and which are likely to materially affect Cafe Gross Sales and expenses include, but are not limited to, general population of market, general economic conditions in market, recognition and patronage of the Marks and your Cafe products and services, availability and costs of supplies (see Note 3 below of Cost Analysis below), shipping/delivery costs, costs of labor, property costs, financing costs (including interest), and local and state taxes. The operations of the Cafes described in this Analysis are substantially similar to the franchise offered under this Offering Circular.

The information relating to Gross Sales provided by our Franchisees and used by us in determining the Gross Sales ranges and percentages described in the chart below has not been audited by an independent certified public accountant and such information has not necessarily been prepared on a basis consistent with generally accepted accounting principles. Our affiliate-owned Cafes are audited on a consolidated basis. The Gross Sales and expense figures presented were compiled from the information we received from our affiliates and Franchisees. We have not verified the information provided by our Franchisees, and we do not have the data and have not compared whether the expense data submitted by each individual franchised Cafe for each separately provided expense item appropriately reflects the types of expenses which would be incurred by the Cafe you will operate. Further, we do not represent that the information we received from our franchisees was prepared according to generally accepted accounting principles. Substantiation of financial information contained in this Item 19 is available on reasonable request.

THE FINANCIAL INFORMATION IN THIS ANALYSIS CONCERNING SALES, INCOME, GROSS OR NET PROFITS, OR EARNINGS ARE BASED ON THE RESULTS OF EXISTING AFFILIATE-OWNED AND FRANCHISED CAFES, BUT ARE THE RESULTS OF ANY PARTICULAR CAFE, AND SHOULD NOT BE CONSIDERED TO BE THE ACTUAL OR PROBABLE SALES, INCOME, GROSS OR NET PROFITS, OR EARNINGS THAT MAY BE REALIZED BY ANY FRANCHISEE. WE DO NOT REPRESENT THAT YOU CAN EXPECT TO ATTAIN THE SALES, INCOME, GROSS OR NET PROFITS, OR EARNINGS OF THOSE CAFES. YOUR RESULTS ARE LIKELY TO DIFFER FROM THE RESULTS OF OTHER CAFES, AND FROM THE RESULTS OBTAINED FROM THIS ANALYSIS. WE DO NOT MAKE ANY REPRESENTATIONS THAT YOU MAY OR WILL DERIVE INCOME FROM THE CAFE WHICH EXCEEDS THE INITIAL PAYMENT FOR OR INVESTMENT IN THE CAFE.

YOU ARE URGED TO CONSULT WITH APPROPRIATE FINANCIAL, BUSINESS AND LEGAL ADVISORS IN CONNECTION WITH THE INFORMATION LISTED IN THIS ANALYSIS.

2. *Frullati Cafe Gross Sales Information.* The following table sets forth ranges of Gross Sales with respect to the continuous operations of 51 Cafes during the one-year period ending December 27, 1998, as more particularly described above.

The ranges of Gross Sales have been prepared from financial reports submitted by our affiliates and franchisees, as described above.

Average Gross Sales of Affiliate-Owned and Franchised Cafes for Fiscal Year Ending December 27, 1998
The average Gross Sales of the 12 affiliate-owned Cafes for fiscal year 1998 was $484,519. The aver-

age Gross Sales for the 39 franchised Cafes for fiscal year 1998 was $339,226. We calculated these arithmetic mean averages by totaling the Gross Sales of all of the affiliate-owned Cafes used in this Analysis and dividing by 12, and totaling the sales of all of the franchised Cafes used in this Analysis and dividing by 39. We then divided the affiliate-owned and franchised Cafes into 3 ranges based on the volume of Gross Sales experienced by the Cafes. We then also calculated the arithmetic mean average of Gross Sales volume experienced by the affiliate-owned and franchised Cafes used in this Analysis (Low, Medium and High volume Cafes). Listed in the chart below is the number and percentage of affiliate-owned and franchised Cafes falling within each category, the arithmetic mean average Gross Sales volume for affiliate-owned and franchised Cafes falling within the range, and the number and percentage of franchised Cafes achieving the average Gross Sales volume within the range.

Gross Revenue Range	(Low) $145,000–300,000	(Medium) $300,001–400,000	(High) $400,001–Greater
Number of Affiliate-owned Cafes Reported Within Range	2	2	8
Percentage of Affiliate-owned Cafes Included Within Range	16.67%	16.67%	66.66%
Average Affiliate-owned Cafe Gross Sales Within Range	$278,714	$337,129	$572,819
Number of Franchised Cafes Reported Within Range	13	17	9
Percentage of Franchised Cafes Included Within Range	33.33%	43.59%	23.08%
Average Franchised Cafe Gross Sales Within Range	$244,395	$336,111	$482,085
Number and Percentage of Franchised Cafes Achieving Average Within Range	8 or 62%	8 or 47%	3 or 33%

3. *Affiliate Operated Frullati Cafe Operating Cost Analysis (1).* In this Analysis, we have expressed certain expense items as a percentage of Gross Sales. The expense percentages are based on expenses (expressed as percentages of Gross Sales) or the 12 affiliate-owned Cafes open and operating during fiscal year 1998 as more particularly described above. Each percentage given on this Analysis reflects the mean average of the applicable expense item provided by the Cafes (i.e.. the aggregate sum of the expenses of all Cafes described above divided by the number of those Cafes). No percentage given on this Analysis is the actual expense percentage experienced by any one affiliate-owned Cafe and the actual expense percentages for the Cafes on any particular expense item may vary significantly. Further, no franchised Cafe data was considered in this cost Analysis, so since we do not have sufficient data on the operating expenses of franchisees, we do not know and cannot represent the number or percentage of franchised Cafes that obtained these expense percentages. Of the 12 affiliate-owned Cafes on which this information is based, 6 (or 50.00%) achieved the percentage level of operating income described below and 4 (or 33.33%) achieved the percentage level of the net income before occupancy costs, interest, depreciation and income taxes (NIBOIDT) described below.

	Estimated Expense (Percent of Gross Sales)	Comments
Gross Sales (2)	100%	Varies depending on the Cafe; Mean Average Gross Sales $440,458.
Cost of Goods Sold (3)	28%	Varies depending on Cafe; Mean Average 31% of Gross Sales.
Gross Profit	72%	(Gross Sales less Cost of Sales)
Labor (4)	22%	Varies typically based on Gross Sales of Cafe
Operating Income	50%	(Gross Profit less Labor)
Other Costs:		
Repairs & Maintenance and General & Administrative (5)	6%	Repairs & Maintenance and General & Administrative on a per store basis
Insurance (6)	1%	Insurance varies from $1,500 to $2,500, but generally less than 1%
Advertising (7)		Franchise Agreement requires 1%, but Malls may require approx. 2%, which is included in Occupancy costs
Utilities (7)		Typically we budget $500 per month for electricity which is also generally included in Occupancy costs
Net income before occupancy costs, interest, depreciation & income taxes (NIBOIDT) (7)	43%	Operating Income less Total Other Costs
Royalty Fee (8)	6%	
Marketing Fees	0.25%	

Notes to Cost Analysis

1. THIS ANALYSIS DESCRIBES CERTAIN AVERAGE COSTS AND EXPENSES INCURRED BY CERTAIN AFFILI-ATE-OWNED CAFES DURING FISCAL YEAR ENDING DECEMBER 27, 1998 EXPRESSED AS A PERCENTAGE OF GROSS SALES. THIS ANALYSIS DOES NOT INCLUDE SOME SUBSTANTIAL INITIAL ONE TIME EXPENSES SUCH AS THE FRANCHISE FEE AND EXPENSES FOR LEASEHOLD IMPROVEMENTS, AND FURNITURE AND EQUIPMENT (IF PURCHASED RATHER THAN LEASED) (SEE ITEMS 5, 6 AND 7 OF THE OFFER-ING CIRCULAR).

YOU SHOULD NOTE THAT IF YOU HAVE SELECTED AND OBTAINED OUR APPROVAL OF THE SITE FOR THE CAFE AT THE TIME OF SIGNING THE FRANCHISE AGREEMENT, THE CAFE WILL BE TYPICALLY OPEN AND IN OPERATION APPROXIMATELY 3 TO 6 MONTHS FOLLOWING THE DATE YOU SIGN THE FRANCHISE AGREEMENT (SEE ITEM 11 OF THE OFFERING CIRCULAR) AND IT IS NOT ANTIC-IPATED THAT YOU WILL RECEIVE SALES BEFORE THAT TIME. CERTAIN OPERATIONAL EXPENSES SUCH AS EXPENSES FOR INITIAL INVENTORY, LABOR, PRE-OPENING ADVERTISING,

GENERAL ADMINISTRATIVE, PROPERTY TAXES AND RENT (IF ANY), INSURANCE, AND DEBT SERVICE, WILL BE INCURRED BY YOU BEFORE THE OPENING OF THE CAFE AND YOU SHOULD CONSIDER THESE OPERATIONAL EXPENSES (AS WELL AS THE INITIAL ONE TIME EXPENSES DESCRIBED ABOVE) IN PLANNING YOUR BUDGET AND ESTIMATING YOUR NEED FOR OPERATING CAPITAL. YOU SHOULD ALSO NOTE THAT IF YOU HAVE NOT SELECTED (AND OBTAINED OUR APPROVAL OF) A SITE AT THE TIME YOU SIGN THE FRANCHISE AGREEMENT, THE CAFE TYPICALLY WILL BE OPEN AND OPERATING NO SOONER THAN APPROXIMATELY 6 MONTHS FOLLOWING THE DATE YOU SIGN THE FRANCHISE AGREEMENT, UNLESS YOU ACQUIRE AN EXISTING CAFE DEVELOPED BY ONE OF OUR AFFILIATES.

YOU SHOULD ALSO NOTE THAT WHEN YOU OPEN THE CAFE AND COMMENCE OPERATIONS, THERE IS LIKELY TO BE A ONE (1) TO THREE (3) MONTH "STABILIZATION" PERIOD DURING WHICH THE EXPENSES INCURRED BY YOU FOR COST OF SALES (SEE NOTE 3 BELOW) AND LABOR (SEE NOTE 4 BELOW) MAY BE HIGHER THAN THE EXPENSES INCURRED BY YOU SUBSEQUENT TO THAT PERIOD. THE INCREASED AMOUNT OF THOSE EXPENSES DURING THE "STABILIZATION" PERIOD IS LIKELY TO RESULT FROM OVER-STAFFING AND EXCESS FOOD PREPARATION BY YOU ARISING FROM YOUR LACK OF SALES TREND EXPERIENCE IN YOUR MARKET AREA.

WE MAKE NO REPRESENTATIONS OR WARRANTIES THAT YOU WILL EXPERIENCE SIMILAR EXPENSE OR INCOME PERCENTAGES.

2. Gross Sales includes the total selling price of all services and products and all income of every other kind and nature related to the Cafe (including, income related to catering and delivery activities, and any sales or orders of food products or food preparation services provided from or related to the Cafe), whether for cash or credit and regardless of collection in the case of credit. Gross Sales expressly excludes the following: (a) Receipts from the operation of any public telephone installed in the Cafe, or products from vending machines located at the Cafe, except for any amount representing your share of the revenues; (b) Sums representing sales taxes collected directly from customers, based on present or future laws of federal, state or local governments, collected by you in the operation of the Cafe, and any other tax, excise or duty which is levied or assessed against you by any federal, state, municipal or local authority, based on sales of specific merchandise sold at or from the Cafe, provided that the taxes are actually transmitted to the appropriate taxing authority; (c) Returns to shippers or manufacturers; and (d) Proceeds from isolated sales of trade fixtures not constituting any part of your products and services offered for resale at the Cafe nor having any material effect on the ongoing operation of the Cafe required under the Franchise Agreement.

3. Costs of sales represents the consumable food, beverage and paper products used in serving food and beverages to customers, as well as food waste. Under the terms of the Franchise Agreement, you must purchase these products solely from Approved Suppliers (see Item 8). For the existing Cafes, we have arranged for certain volume purchasing discounts through certain Approved Suppliers, and those purchasing discounts are reflected in the expense percentage figures supplied by the Cafes. The volume purchasing discounts are available at the sole discretion of the Approved Suppliers and we cannot guarantee that the volume purchasing discounts will be available to any Cafe. In addition, if you are located outside the state of Texas, we are unable to estimate whether any of the existing volume discount purchasing

arrangements will be available to you or the amount of any additional shipping costs you may incur in purchasing from Approved Suppliers. The prices of products purchased outside of the volume discounts from Approved Suppliers are likely to be higher than prices paid by existing Cafes.

As stated above in Note 1, the costs of sales is likely to be higher during the 1 to 3 month "stabilization" period following the opening of the Cafe. Any expense percentage figure provided for costs of sales does not reflect this increased amount of costs of sales because of the length of time of operations of the reporting Cafes as described above.

4. Under the Franchise Agreement, you must engage sufficient personnel to operate the Cafe, including a manager if you do not elect to personally manage the Cafe (see Item 15). Although you may work in your Cafe, some of the Cafes will hire a manager and an assistant manager to operate the Cafe. The typical Cafe employs a total of 6 to 10 full-time and part-time individuals to operate each Cafe. Generally, 3 to 7 employees (including a manager or assistant manager) operate the Cafe during each work shift and there are generally 2 work shifts per day. The number of employees necessary to operate the Cafe during each shift will vary depending on the time of day (e.g., dinner or lunch shifts) and from unit to unit (e.g., traffic count for the location). In estimating labor expenses, you should include the compensation for personnel, payroll taxes, vacation benefits, the paid portion of group health benefits, and expenses related to workers compensation claims. Salaries, wages and related payroll costs may vary substantially depending on the geographic location of your Cafe, the supply of and demand on the local labor pool, state and federally mandated minimum wage laws and the level of benefits (i.e., medical insurance, vacation and bonuses) provided by you. Under the Franchise Agreement, you must maintain worker's compensation insurance on all your employees in amounts provided by applicable law (or at your election, any legally appropriate

alternative providing reasonable compensation for injured workers) (see Item 8).

As stated above, your expenses for labor are likely to be higher during the 1 to 3 month "stabilization" period following the opening of the Cafe. In addition, any expense percentage figure provided does not reflect any overhead or salary paid to any area managers or home office personnel. Franchisees who operate multiple units may need these additional personnel.

5. In estimating the costs of repairs and maintenance, you should include estimated non-capitalized repairs and maintenance expenses including, but not limited to, heating/cooling unit, plumbing, and equipment. Repairs and maintenance costs will vary depending on the age and condition of the building and labor costs in the geographic area. General and administrative expenses should include your estimated expenses for accounting and book-keeping services, legal and other professional services, bank charges, late charges and penalties, contract labor, donations, dues and subscriptions, laundry and linen services, licenses and fees, office supplies, pest control, postage/freight, returned checks, telephone, trash pickup, travel-auto, uniforms, small equipment purchases and rental, and other miscellaneous expenses. General and administrative expenses vary significantly among the Cafes and any percentage for this expense item provided in the Analysis reflects the mean average of the range of reported expenses.

6. Under the Franchise Agreement, you must maintain Comprehensive General Liability Insurance, including broad form contractual liability, broad form property damage, personal injury, advertising injury, completed operations, products liability and fire damage coverage, in the amount of $1,000,000 combined single limit; "All Risks" coverage for the full cost of replacement of the Cafe premises and all other property in which we may have an interest with no coinsurance clause; crime insurance for employee dishonesty in the amount of $10,000 combined single limit; business interruption

insurance in a sufficient amount to cover profit margins, maintenance of competent and desirable personnel and fixed expenses for a period of at least 90 days; and automobile liability coverage, including coverage of owned, non-owned and hired vehicles, with coverage in amounts not less than $1,000,000 combined single limit (see Item 8). Costs of insurance may vary depending on the insurer, the location of your Cafe, and other factors. Any expense percentage figure provided does not include the Cafes' expenses for worker's compensation insurance (see Note 4 above) and does not include expenses for automobile insurance. As noted in Item 7, insurance costs are estimated to range from $1,500 to $2,500 in annual premiums.

7. Estimates for rent should be calculated based on obtaining 400 to 600 square feet of space in a food court, or 800 to 1,500 square feet of in-line space, in a regional mall. The figures in Item 7 assume that you will purchase all equipment. Costs for rent in a regional shopping mall and equipment rent vary significantly based on the geographic location of the Cafe. You should contact rental agents, landlords and equipment leasing companies in the area in which the Cafe will be located to estimate the amount of these expenses. As of the date of this Offering Circular, the average occupancy costs for all Company-owned and franchised Cafes was $[36,722] per year, or $[3,227] per month. The lowest occupancy cost for any Cafe we had last year was $[6,580] and the highest was $[67,500]. If you have already identified a site for your Cafe, you should consider your actual cost for this expense item.

Under the Franchise Agreement, you must spend 1% of the Gross Sales of your Cafe on local advertising. In addition, although we currently do not require you to do so, we have the right to require you to pay a continuing weekly advertising fee contribution to us of 1% (which may be increased up to 3½%) of your Gross Sales for the Fund as well as contribute to an advertising Cooperative. We may increase the amount of the Fund contribution

as described in Item 6. We may also require you to pay for Yellow Pages or other business listing advertising. The Franchise Agreement does not otherwise require you to participate in advertising and promotional activities on an individual basis; however, you may elect to do so in your sole discretion. Also, your landlord may require you to contribute toward a common mall advertising program, which may exceed the 1% we require. Typically, these contributions are included in occupancy costs. We will allow you to credit your landlord contributions toward meeting our local advertising requirements. The costs of any individual advertising and promotional activities conducted by you will depend on the amount and type of advertising and the particular market.

In estimating the costs of utilities, you should include monthly expenses for gas, electricity, water, sewer, and any other utility charges applicable to your Cafe. Utility expenses may vary significantly depending on geographic area. Any expense percentage amount given does not include charges for initial installation. Generally, we budget $500 a month for electricity, but this and other utility costs are included within occupancy costs for mall Cafes.

If you finance the leasehold improvements for the Cafe or any equipment to be used in connection with the Cafe, you should estimate both the interest expense and the principal portion of debt service for inclusion in conducting your own analysis. The amount of your taxable income will vary according to capital expenditures, depreciation and amortization and the amount of your Principal Portion of Debt Service (which is added to your Net Operating Cash Flow for purposes of calculating taxable income). You are urged to consult with tax advisors in estimating your taxable income and corresponding income tax.

8. Under the Franchise Agreement, you must pay a weekly royalty fee of 6% of Gross Sales. The affiliate-owned Cafes used in this Analysis do not.

JIMMY JOHN'S GOURMET SANDWICH SHOPS
600 Tollgate Rd.
Elgin, IL 60123
Tel: (800) 546-6904 (847) 888-7206
Fax: (847) 888-7070
E-Mail:
Internet Address: www.jimmyjohns.com
Contact: Ms. Linda Kelley, Franchise President

Description: World's greatest gourmet sandwich shop. All the sandwiches are made on fresh-baked french bread or 7-grain honey wheat bread. We only use the highest-quality meats available with garden fresh veggies that are brought in and sliced each morning.

# Franchised Units:	51 Units
# Company-Owned Units:	9 Units
Total # Units:	60 Units
Founded In:	1983
1st Franchised In:	1993
Average Total Investment:	Up to 203.4K
Franchise Fee:	12.5-25K
On-Going Royalty:	6%
Advertising Fee:	4.5%
Financial Assistance:No (D – direct, or I – indirect)	
Site Selection Assistance:	Yes
Lease Negotiation Assistance:	No
Contract Terms (Init./Renew):	10/5/5
Initial Training Provided:3 Weeks in Champaign, IL.	

Included as Exhibit G to the Offering Circular is a statement of actual sales of the affiliate-owned JIMMY JOHN'S restaurants. Except for this statement, Company does not furnish or authorize its salesperson to furnish any oral or written information concerning the actual or potential sales, costs, income or profits of a JIMMY JOHN'S restaurant. Actual results vary from unit to unit and JIMMY JOHN'S FRANCHISE, INC. cannot estimate results of any particular franchise.

Jimmy John's Franchise, Inc. Statement of Actual Sales from July 1, 1997 through June 30, 1998

Exhibit G to the Offering Circular
The information included herein represents the sales experience, subject to the assumptions outlined below, of affiliate-owned businesses for the period of July 1, 1997 through June 30, 1998. These figures reflect the average sales, food costs and labor costs per store for seven (7) affiliate-owned stores, all of which were managed by Jimmy John's Enterprises, Inc. formerly known as Jimmy John's, Inc. of Urbana that were in operation for a twelve (12) month period. The restaurants are located in Illinois, Indiana and Michigan.

SUCH ACTUAL SALES, INCOME, GROSS OR NET PROFITS ARE OF SPECIFIC AFFILIATE-OWNED AND OPERATED BUSINESSES AND SHOULD NOT BE CONSIDERED AS THE ACTUAL OR POTENTIAL SALES, INCOME, GROSS OR NET PROFITS THAT WILL BE REALIZED BY ANY FRANCHISEE. FRANCHISOR DOES NOT REPRESENT THAT ANY FRANCHISEE CAN EXPECT TO ATTAIN THESE SALES, INCOME, GROSS OR NET PROFITS.

The annual average results of an average restaurant based on the seven (7) affiliate-owned restaurants is as follows:

Gross Sales	$568,372.81	100.00%
Food	153,650.53	27.03%
Labor	156,332.28	27.51%
Net Income from Operations	$172,875.11	30.42%

Gross Sales
Of the seven (7) restaurants operating for the twelve (12) month period from July 1, 1997 through June 30, 1998, Gross Sales per restaurant

averaged FIVE HUNDRED SIXTY-EIGHT THOUSAND THREE HUNDRED SEVENTY-TWO AND 81/100 Dollars ($568,372.81). For the twelve (12) month period, three (3) of Jimmy John's Gourmet Sandwich Shops restaurants exceeded the average and four (4) of the stores had sales below the average. The highest grossing store had sales of EIGHT HUNDRED THIRTY-SIX THOUSAND ONE HUNDRED THIRTY-TWO and 20/100 Dollars ($836,132.20), and the lowest grossing store had sales of THREE HUNDRED TWENTY-FIVE THOUSAND SIX HUNDRED FORTY-SEVEN and 93/100 Dollars ($325,647.93).

Net Income from Operations
Net income from operations includes gross sales, less food costs and all expenses incurred by the restaurant including labor. Net income from operations of the seven (7) restaurants averages ONE HUNDRED SEVENTY-TWO THOUSAND EIGHT HUNDRED SEVENTY-FIVE AND 11/100 Dollars ($172,875.11). Three (3) restaurants exceeded the average net income from operations while four (4) restaurants had net income below the average. The highest net income was THREE HUNDRED ONE THOUSAND THREE HUNDRED FORTY-FOUR and 46/100 Dollars ($301,344.46) and the lowest was THIRTY-NINE THOUSAND SIX HUNDRED THIRTY-SEVEN and 67/100 Dollars ($39,637.67).

Operating Expenses
1. *Food Cost.* The food cost includes all food items as well as paper costs such as cups, napkins, etc.

Food costs for all seven (7) restaurants averaged ONE HUNDRED FIFTY-THREE THOUSAND SIX HUNDRED FIFTY and 53/100 Dollars ($153,650.53). Three (3) restaurants exceeded the average and four (4) had food costs below the average. The lowest food cost was NINETY-ONE THOUSAND FOURTEEN and 63/100 Dollars ($91,014.63) and the highest was TWO HUNDRED TWENTY-THREE THOUSAND FOUR HUNDRED FORTY-SIX and 69/100 Dollars ($223,446.69). On average, food costs

equaled twenty-seven and three-one hundredths percent (27.03%) of Gross Sales.

2. *Labor.* The cost of labor covers all hourly and salaried employees including a manager's salary. The expense for management personnel may vary depending on the extent of Franchisee's involvement in the day-to-day operation of the Franchised Restaurant.

The average cost of labor, including a manager's salary, was ONE HUNDRED FIFTY-SIX THOUSAND THREE HUNDRED THIRTY-TWO and 28/100 Dollars ($156,332.28). Three (3) restaurants exceeded the average and four (4) were below the average. The highest labor cost was TWO HUNDRED FOURTEEN THOUSAND FIVE HUNDRED SEVENTY-EIGHT and 39/100 Dollars ($214,578.39) and the lowest was ONE HUNDRED FOURTEEN THOUSAND FORTY-SIX and 77/100 Dollars ($114,046.77). On average, labor (including a manager's salary) equaled twenty-seven and fifty-one one-hundredths percent (27.51%) of Gross Sales.

Other Considerations
Because most of these businesses are located near college campuses, the business is somewhat seasonal. Sales typically drop off in June, July, August and December when colleges are not in session.

Basis of Compilation
The affiliate-owned and operated restaurants included in the statement have offered the same products and services to the public as will be offered by the Franchised Restaurant. Essentially the same services are available to franchised restaurants as have been available to the affiliate-owned and operated restaurants.

The businesses included in the statement use a uniform accounting system. The statement has been prepared on a basis consistent with generally accepted accounting principles. Specific assumptions used in the presentation of the statement are indicated above.

The actual sales figures appearing in these statements should not be construed as the "profit" which might be experienced by a franchisee with a similar sales volume. The nature of these variables and the economic discretion exercised by individual franchisees renders a determination of the profit level a franchisee will attain is impossible to ascertain.

Substantiation of the data used in preparing the accompanying statement will be made available to a prospective franchisee upon reasonable request.

MANCHU WOK
816 S. Military Trail, Unit # 6
Deerfield Beach, FL 33442
Tel: (800) 423-4009 (954) 481-9555
Fax: (954) 481-9670
E-Mail: alechudson@manchuwok.com
Internet Address: www.manchuwok.com/index2.html
Contact: Mr. Alec Hudson, Franchise Sales Manager

Description: MANCHU WOK is one of the largest Chinese quick service franchises in North America. MANCHU WOK operates in over 225 food court locations in large regional malls. MANCHU WOK franchisees are enjoying profitable growth; many owning multiple locations.

# Franchised Units:	140 Units
# Company-Owned Units:	<u>47</u> Units
Total # Units:	187 Units
Founded In:	1980
1st Franchised In:	1980
Average Total Investment:	260-306K
Franchise Fee:	20K
On-Going Royalty:	7%
Advertising Fee:	1%
Financial Assistance:Yes(I) (D – direct, or I – indirect)	
Site Selection Assistance:	Yes
Lease Negotiation Assistance:	Yes
Contract Terms (Init./Renew):	5/5
Initial Training Provided:3-4 Weeks at Corporate Site.	

For the fiscal year ended, April 30, 1998, there were 89 Company-owned and operated MANCHU WOK® Outlets and 66 franchised MANCHU WOK® Outlets in operation in the United States for the full fiscal year. Of this total, approximately 93% had annual sales volumes in excess of $200,000; approximately 71% had annual sales volume in excess of $300,000; approximately 54% had annual sales volume in excess of $400,000; approximately 27% had annual sales volume in excess of $500,000; and approximately 18% had annual sales volumes in excess of $600,000.

The restaurant operations statements included in this Item show annual sales volumes of $350,000, $450,000 and $650,000. These restaurant operations statements have been modified from the actual results of Company-owned and operated MANCHU WOK® Outlets to provide information more relevant to a prospective franchisee. Specific assumptions used in the presentation of these income statements are indicated following the restaurant operations statements.

THESE SALES, PROFITS OR EARNINGS ARE AVERAGES OF SPECIFIC MANCHU WOK® OUTLETS AND SHOULD NOT BE CONSIDERED AS THE ACTUAL OR POTENTIAL SALES, PROFITS OR EARNINGS THAT WILL BE REALIZED BY A POTENTIAL FRANCHISEE. THE FRANCHISOR DOES NOT REPRESENT, WARRANT OR OTHERWISE GUARANTEE THAT ANY FRANCHISEE CAN EXPECT TO ATTAIN THESE SALES, PROFITS OR EARNINGS. A NEW FRANCHISEE'S INDIVIDUAL FRANCHISE RESULTS ARE LIKELY TO DIFFER FROM THE RESULTS STATED IN THE RESTAURANT OPERATIONS STATEMENTS SHOWN BELOW. SUBSTANTIATION OF THE DATA

USED IN PREPARING THIS EARNINGS CLAIM WILL BE MADE AVAILABLE TO YOU UPON REASONABLE REQUEST.

The information presented in the pro forma Restaurant Operations Statements shown below is based on the averages of 39 Company-owned and operated MANCHU WOK® Outlets that have been operating for at least one year, which are similar to comparable independent franchised MANCHU WOK® Outlets. The data used was received from Outlets using a uniform accounting system and the respective pro forma Restaurant Operations Statements were prepared on a basis consistent with generally accepted accounting principles. The Company-owned and operated MANCHU WOK® Outlets do not receive any services which are not generally available to independent franchisees.

However, the Outlet profit figures appearing below should not be construed as the "profit" which might be experienced by a franchisee with a similar sales volume. An individual franchisee is likely to experience variations, including, but not limited to, depreciation and amortization, occupancy costs, restaurant wages and benefits, legal and accounting fees and other discretionary expenses. Company-owned MANCHU WOK® Outlets are not required to pay the initial franchise fee paid by independent franchisees, and are not required to make monthly royalty payments which are made by independent franchisees. In addition, a franchisee may incur various amounts of interest expense depending on how the investment is financed.

Each of these items, as well as the actual accounting and operational methods employed by a franchisee, may significantly impact profits realized in any particular operation. The nature of these variables and the economic discretion exercised by individual franchisees renders a determination of the number of franchisees attaining a given profit level impracticable to ascertain. Computation of all actual, average, projected or forecasted sales, profit or earnings, and a list of addresses of current Company-owned MANCHU WOK® Outlets will be made available to you upon your written request.

Of our sixty-six (66) franchisees that were open for the full fiscal year ended April 30, 1998, sixty-one (61) of such franchisees (92%) had sales in excess of $200,000; forty-six (46) of such franchisees (70%) had sales in excess of $300,000; and thirty-five (35) of such franchisees (53%) had sales in excess of $400,000; seventeen (17) of such franchises (26%) had sales in excess of $500,000; and twelve (12) of such franchisees (18%) had sales in excess of $600,000.

Manchu Wok® — United States Pro Forma Restaurant Operations Statement

Sales	$350,000		$450,000		$650,000+	
Cost of Sales						
Food & Beverage	99,639	30.90%	126,711	28.20%	172,010	26.50%
Paper	12,250	3.50%	15,750	3.50%	22,750	3.50%
Total Cost of Sales	111,889	34.40%	142,461	31.70%	194,760	30.00%
Labor and Benefits Mngt. Wages & Benefits	73,226	23.70%	89,540	19.90%	116,157	7.90%
Advertising	3,500	1.00%	4,500	1.00%	6,500	1.00%
Royalties	24,500	7.00%	31,500	7.00%	45,500	7.00%
Other Direct Expenses	28,521	7.80%	30,246	6.70%	34,340	5.30%
Profit Before Committed Cost	108,364	26.10%	151,753	33.70%	252,743	38.80%
Rent and Occupancy Costs	60,719	18.10%	72,531	16.10%	104,985	16.10%

Sales	$350,000		$450,000		$650,000+	
Taxes, Licenses, Insurance (excludes depn.)	3,583	1.50%	4,951	1.10%	7,030	1.10%
Restaurant Profit	44,062	12.60%	61,239	13.60%	146,596	22.60%

1. All figures based on an average of actual results achieved for the period May 1, 1997, to April 30, 1998, by 39 Company-owned MANCHU WOK® Outlets located in the United States.

2. Labor costs exclude Manager's salary and benefits.

3. Other direct expenses include expenses such as mall promotions, telephone, utilities, maintenance and repairs, smallwares, office supplies, laundry and miscellaneous expenses.

4. Rent and occupancy costs will vary depending upon lease terms and location.

5. Figures exclude depreciation and finance charges.

6. Financial results vary based on individual operator's performance.

MCDONALD'S
One McDonald's Plaza, Kroc Dr.
Oak Brook, IL 60523
Tel: (630) 623-6196
Fax: (630) 623-5645
E-Mail:
Internet Address: www.mcdonalds.com
Contact: Franchise Department,

# Franchised Units:	19607 Units
# Company-Owned Units:	5729 Units
Total # Units:	25336 Units
Founded In:	1955
1st Franchised In:	1956
Average Total Investment:	433.8-1,361K
Franchise Fee:	45K
On-Going Royalty:	12.5%
Advertising Fee:	4%
Financial Assistance:No (D – direct, or I – indirect)	
Site Selection Assistance:	N/A
Lease Negotiation Assistance:	N/A
Contract Terms (Init./Renew):	20/20
Initial Training Provided:	NR

Description: Quick-service restaurant.

In 1998, of the approximately 10,400 domestic traditional McDonald's restaurants open at least one year as of December 31, 1998, approximately 72% had annual sales volumes in excess of $1,300,000; approximately 53% had annual sales volumes in excess or $1,500,000; and approximately 35% had annual sales volumes in excess of $1,700,000.
In 1998, the average annual sales volume of domestic traditional McDonald's restaurants open at least one year was $1,580,000. The highest and lowest annual sales volume in 1998 for these domestic McDonald's restaurants was $6,830,000 and $185,000, respectively.

The pro forma statements included show annual sales volumes of $1,300,000, $1,500,000, and $1,700,000. These pro forma statements have been derived from company-operated and independent franchisee traditional restaurant statements to provide information more relevant to a prospective franchisee. Specific assumptions used in the presentation of these pro forma statements are indicated above and below each statement.

The pro forma statements are based upon a total of 8,578 domestic traditional restaurants open at least one year, of which 1,414 were company-operated restaurants and 7,164 were independent

211

franchises. Both company-operated and independent franchises are similar with respect to their operations and operating results and are subject to the same monthly franchise fee structure and receive similar services from McDonalds. A NEW FRANCHISEE'S INDIVIDUAL FINANCIAL RESULTS MAY DIFFER FROM THE RESULTS STATED IN THE PRO FORMA STATEMENTS FOR THE REASONS STATED ON THE FOLLOWING PAGE. Computations of all actual, average, projected or forecasted sales, profit or earnings, range of years in operation, and list of addresses of current company-operated restaurants will be made available to prospective franchisees upon reasonable request.

THESE SALES, PROFITS OR EARNINGS ARE AVERAGES OF SPECIFIC FRANCHISES AND SHOULD NOT BE CONSIDERED AS THE ACTUAL OR POTENTIAL SALES, PROFITS OR EARNINGS THAT WILL BE REALIZED BY ANY OTHER FRANCHISEE. MCDONALD'S DOES NOT REPRESENT THAT YOU CAN EXPECT TO ATTAIN THESE SALES, PROFITS OR EARNINGS.

As previously stated, the information reported in these profit and loss statements reflect the operating results for restaurants open the entire year and are similar for both Company-operated and independent franchises. However, the net operating income figures appearing below should not be construed as the "profit" which might be experienced by a franchisee with a similar sales volume. An individual franchisee is likely to experience expense variations, including but not limited to, depreciation and amortization, interest rate, franchise fees (including rent paid to McDonald's), general insurance, legal and accounting fees, store management benefits (life and health insurance, etc.); salaries and benefits of non-restaurant personnel; income taxes; cost of an automobile used in the business, if any; and other discretionary expenditures.

Additionally accounting, operational and management methods employed by a franchisee, different geographic areas of the country and menu price variations, may significantly affect profits realized in any given operation. The nature of these variables makes it difficult to determine the number of franchisees that will attain a given profit level.

01 Net Sales	$1,300,000	100.00%	$1,500,000	100.00%	$1,700,000	100.00%
04 Total Cost of Sales	405,021	31.16%	464,296	30.95%	523,572	30.80%
05 Gross Profit	894,979	68.84%	1,035,704	69.05%	1,176,428	69.20%
25 Total Controllable Expenses	526,217	40.48%	589,939	39.33%	653,661	38.45%
26 Profit After Controllables	368,762	28.37%	445,765	29.72%	522,767	30.75%
35 Total Other Expenses	284,027	21.85%	315,152	21.01%	346,276	20.37%
36 Net Operating Income	84,735	6.52%	130,613	8.71%	176,491	10.38%

Note: The table above reflects operating results based upon existing stores.

Total Other Expenses — For all sales volumes, includes rent paid to McDonald's equal to 9.8% of Sales, Depreciation, Amortization and Interest of $63,528, and Service Fees of 4.0% of gross sales. Other Miscellaneous Operating Expenses are $41,099, $44,624 and $48,148 for the $1.3 million, $1.5 million and $1.7 million stores, respectively.

Depreciation, Amortization and Interest included in Total Other Expenses will vary based upon the purchase price and required

reinvestment of the specific restaurant acquired.

Total Controllable Expenses — Includes franchisee's salary as manager.

THESE SALES, PROFITS OR EARNINGS ARE AVERAGES OF SPECIFIC FRANCHISES AND SHOULD NOT BE CONSIDERED AS THE ACTUAL OR POTENTIAL SALES, PROFITS OR EARNINGS THAT WILL BE REALIZED BY ANY OTHER FRANCHISE. MCDONALD'S DOES NOT REPRESENT THAT ANY FRANCHISEE CAN EXPECT TO ATTAIN THESE SALES, PROFITS OR EARNINGS.

PIZZA OUTLET
2101 Greentree Rd., # A-202
Pittsburgh, PA 15220
Tel: (888) 816-2116 (412) 279-9100
Fax: (412) 279-9781
E-Mail: jbullian@pizzaoutlet.com
Internet Address: www.pizzaoutlet.com
Contact: Mr. Joseph M. Bullian, Director Franchise Marketing

Description: PIZZA OUTLET provides delivery and carry-out service of pizza, subs, wings, breadsticks and drinks. Streamlined operations and a compact menu provide for low start-up costs and ease of operation. On-going support at every level is provided, including a marketing effort with a national focus.

# Franchised Units:	70 Units
# Company-Owned Units:	<u>33</u> Units
Total # Units:	103 Units
Founded In:	1988
1st Franchised In:	1994
Average Total Investment:	95-185K
Franchise Fee:	15K
On-Going Royalty:	4%
Advertising Fee:	1%
Financial Assistance:No (D – direct, or I – indirect)	
Site Selection Assistance:	Yes
Lease Negotiation Assistance:	No
Contract Terms (Init./Renew):	10/5
Initial Training Provided:4 Weeks	
Corporate Office; 1 Week On Site of Franchise During Opening.	

Representations Regarding Earnings Capability

We have attached our Representations Regarding Earnings Capability as Exhibit "A" to this Offering Circular.

We will make available substantiation of the data used in preparing the earnings claim to prospective franchisees upon reasonable request.

Please note that we have not prepared the earnings claim attachment of future performance in accordance with the Statement on Standards for Accountant's Services on Prospective Financial Information.

WE PROVIDE THIS DATA FOR INFORMATIONAL PURPOSES ONLY. THIS DATA DOES NOT CONSTITUTE A REPRESENTATION AS TO WHAT YOU MAY EARN. EARNINGS CAN CHANGE DRAMATICALLY WITH A VARIETY OF FACTORS, INCLUDING LOCATION AND MANAGEMENT EXPERIENCE. YOU SHOULD NOT RELY ON THESE FIGURES IN DETERMINING YOUR LIKELIHOOD OF SUCCESS.

Exhibit A
Pizza Outlet, L.P. Representation of Earnings Claim

CAUTION: SOME OUTLETS HAVE ACHIEVED THE SALES AND EARNINGS DESCRIBED BELOW. THERE IS NO ASSURANCE YOU'LL DO AS WELL. IF YOU RELY UPON OUR FIGURES, YOU MUST ACCEPT THE RISK OF NOT DOING AS WELL.

Of the 103 total stores open as of December 27, 1998, 33 were company-owned stores. Of these 33 stores, 23 were open for the entire fiscal years ending December 27, 1998 and December 31, 1997.

The average gross sales for these 23 company-owned stores was $485,863.
The gross sales of these 23 stores ranged from $290,342 to $781,237.

The following information is based on income statements from 20 representative stores, or 87% of the 23 company-owned stores open for the entire 1997 and 1998 fiscal years.

The stores with the highest and lowest sales volumes and 1 additional store not in the Pittsburgh Market were not used.

NO FRANCHISED STORES WERE USED IN THE PREPARATION OF THIS CLAIM. ALL STORES USED IN THIS CLAIM ARE IN THE PITTSBURGH MARKET.

The 3 groups of stores averaged to provide representative sample stores from the 23 company-owned stores open for the entire 1997 and 1998 fiscal years follow:

Above Average Store: $554,987 average gross sales from 6 stores with gross sales ranging from $539,617 to $587,363.

Average Store: $495,453 average gross sales from 8 stores with gross sales ranging from $470,621 to $534,828.

Below Average Store: $429,551 average gross sales from 6 stores with gross sales ranging from $379,912 to $466,354.

THE FOREGOING IS PROVIDED FOR INFORMATIONAL PURPOSES ONLY. SUCH DOES NOT CONSTITUTE A REPRESENTATION AS TO WHAT YOU MAY EARN. EARNINGS ARE BASED UPON A VARIETY OF FACTORS, INCLUDING LOCATION AND MANAGEMENT EXPERIENCE. YOU SHOULD NOT RELY ON THESE FIGURES IN DETERMINING YOUR LIKELIHOOD OF SUCCESS.

Income Statements — FY 1998

	Above Average Store		Average Store		Below Average Store	
	$	%	$	%	$	%
Gross Sales (1)	$554,986.92	100.00%	$495,452.61	100.00%	$429,550.91	100.00%
Cost of Sales:						
Purchases (2)	$180,305.74	32.49%	$163,571.01	33.01%	$138,820.54	32.32%
Wages (3)	$143,755.91	25.90%	$129,760.07	26.19%	$116,697.84	27.17%
Total Cost of Sales	$324,061.65	58.39%	$293,331.09	59.20%	$255,518.38	59.49%
Gross Profit	$230,925.27	41.61%	$202,121.52	40.80%	$174,032.53	40.51%
Expenses:						
Payroll Related (4)	$20,057.01	3.61%	$17,671.09	3.57%	$15,595.79	3.63%
Rent	$14,877.38	2.68%	$11,384.31	2.30%	$16,961.81	3.95%
Utilities	$12,413.01	2.24%	$12,902.60	2.60%	$14,133.81	3.29%
General Operating (5)	$18,638.46	3.36%	$18,664.03	3.77%	$18,952.68	4.41%
Store Repair and Maintenance	$5,203.04	0.94%	$5,420.69	1.09%	$5,512.37	1.28%
Advertising (6)	$33,299.22	6.00%	$29,727.16	6.00%	$25,773.05	6.00%
Royalty Fee (7)	$22,199.48	4.00%	$19,818.10	4.00%	$17,182.04	4.00%
Delivery Expense	$22,665.85	4.08%	$19,358.54	3.91%	$15,129.37	3.52%
Total Expenses (8)	$149,353.43	26.91%	$134,946.52	27.24%	$129,240.92	30.09%
Operating Profit (9)	$81,571.84	14.70%	$67,175.00	13.56%	$44,791.61	10.43%
Projected "Cash On Cash" Returns						
Initial Investment (10)	$135,000.00		$135,000.00		$135,000.00	

	Above Average Store		Average Store		Below Average Store	
	$	%	$	%	$	%
Return on 100% Invested Equity		60%		50%		33%
Return on 50% Invested Equity (11)		94%		73%		40%
Return on 25% Invested Equity (11)		162%		119%		53%

ABOVE FIGURES ARE BASED ONLY ON COMPANY-OWNED STORES OPEN PRIOR TO DECEMBER 31, 1996 IN THE PITTSBURGH MARKET.

Notes

1. Gross Sales: Does not include discounts or sales tax.

2. Purchases: Average actual cost of food, beverages and paper products used by the stores in each store category.

3. Wages: Average of the actual management and hourly labor cost incurred by the stores in each category. It does not include bonuses or officers' salaries.

4. Payroll Related: Includes health insurance according to PO policy for 1998. Includes workers compensation insurance costs for the stores in each category (these costs will vary with the state in which a franchised store operates as well as other factors). Does not include bonuses of any kind.

5. General Operating: Includes store office expenses, legal and professional costs, permits, uniforms and liability insurance.

6. Advertising: The 6% expenditure is the minimum obligation under the franchise agreement

7. Royalty Fee: The 4% fee adds the franchisee's obligation under the agreement.

8. Does not include corporate main office overhead expenses charged to stores.

9. Operating Profit: Earnings before interest, taxes, depreciation and amortization.

10. Initial Investment: This is the average projected cost from the range of costs detailed in Item 7 of the current offering circular.

11. Return on Equity Investment lower than 100% was calculated as follows:
    Debt Service:
    $67,500 @ 12% amortized over 5 years is
        $1,502 per month x 12 = $18,024
    $101,250 @ 12% amortized over 5 years is
        $2,252 per month x 12 = $27,024
    Cash Flow: Operating Profit — Debt Service

    Return on Invested Equity: Cash Flow/ Invested Equity

POPEYES CHICKEN & BISCUITS
5555 Glenridge Connector NE, # 300
Atlanta, GA 30342
Tel: (800) 848-8248 (404) 459-4450
Fax: (404) 459-4533
E-Mail:

Internet Address: www.afc-online.com
Contact: Director of Franchising,

Description: POPEYES CHICKEN & BISCUITS, the world's second-largest chicken chain, is owned by AFC Enterprises, Inc., one of the world's largest restaurant parent companies and the winner of the 1997 MUFSO Operator of the Year and Golden Chain awards. POPEYES is famous for its New

Orleans-style chicken, buttermilk biscuits and signature side items. The brand name has a presence in 40 states and 23 countries worldwide. 1997 system sales were $847 million. POPEYES' Internet Web site is www.popeyes.com.

# Franchised Units:	1013 Units
# Company-Owned Units:	119 Units
Total # Units:	1132 Units
Founded In:	1972
1st Franchised In:	1976

Average Total Investment:	209.8-320.6K
Franchise Fee:	15K
On-Going Royalty:	5%
Advertising Fee:	3%
Financial Assistance:Yes(I) (D – direct, or I – indirect)	
Site Selection Assistance:	Yes
Lease Negotiation Assistance:	Yes
Contract Terms (Init./Renew):	20/10
Initial Training Provided:	4 Weeks Atlanta, GA.

The following four (4) Tables present information about the annual sales, during the period December 28, 1997 through December 27, 1998, of Popeye's Chicken & Biscuits restaurants that were open throughout the entire period.

Table 1: Free-Standing Restaurants
A. Amount and Distribution of Annual Sales

Annual Sales Level (2)	Consolidated	# Units	Company	# Units	Franchise	# Units
$1,300+	11.1%	81	8.3%	8	11.5%	73
$1,200–1,299	4.0%	29	4.2%	4	3.9%	25
$1,100–1,199	4.8%	35	4.2%	4	4.9%	31
$1,000–1,099	94%	69	14.6%	14	8.6%	55
$900–999	10.9%	80	13.5%	13	10.5%	67
$800–899	12.7%	93	10.4%	10	13.0%	83
$700–799	14.5%	106	24.0%	23	13.0%	83
$600–699	13.0%	95	12.5%	12	13.0%	83
$500–599	11.1%	81	7.3%	7	11.6%	74
$400–499	6.1%	45	1.0%	1	6.9%	44
$300–399	2.2%	16	0.0%	–	2.5%	16
< $300	0.4%	3	0.0%	–	0.5%	3
Total	100.0%	733	100.0%	96	100.0%	637
Number of Units		733		96		637

B. Arithmetic Average

Consolidated	Company	Franchise
$871,722	$901,948	$867,167

C. Sales Range

	Company	Franchise	Consolidated
High	$1,918,947	$2,764,227	$2,764,227
Low	$483,083	$205,952	$205,952

Additional footnotes follow Table 4 and form an integral part of this Table.

Table 2: In-Line Restaurants
A. Amount and Distribution of Annual Sales

Annual Sales Level (2)	Consolidated	#Units	Company	#Units	Franchise	#Units
$1,300+	6.0%	7	0.0%	–	6.6%	7
$1,200–1,299	2.6%	3	9.1%	1	1.9%	2
$1,100–1,199	8.5%	10	9.1%	1	8.5%	9
$1,000–1,099	4.3%	5	0.0%	–	4.7%	5
$900–999	6.0%	7	18.2%	2	4.7%	5
$800–899	5.1%	6	0.0%	–	5.7%	6
$700–799	7.7%	9	0.0%	–	8.5%	9
$600–699	18.8%	22	27.3%	3	17.9%	19
$500–599	12.8%	15	27.3%	3	11.3%	12
$400–499	15.4%	18	9.1%	1	16.0%	17
$300–399	9.4%	11	0.0%	–	10.4%	11
< $300	3.4%	4	0.0%	–	38%	4
Total	100.0%	117	100.0%	11	100.0%	106
Number of Units		117		11		106

B. Arithmetic Average

Consolidated	Company	Franchise
$733,509	$752,640	$731,524

C. Sales Range

	Company	Franchise	Consolidated
High	$1,236,563	$1,893,202	$1,893,202
Low	$441,302	$253,025	$253,025

Footnotes follow Table 4 and form an integral part of this Table.

Table 3: Mall/Food-Court Restaurants
A. Amount and Distribution of Annual Sales

Annual Sales Level (2)	Consolidated	# Units	Company	# Units	Franchise	# Units
$1,300+	7.7%	2	0.0%		7.7%	2
$1,200–1,299	0.0%	–	0.0%		0.0%	–
$1,100–1,199	3.8%	1	0.0%		3.8%	1
$1,000–1,099	7.7%	2	0.0%		7.7%	2
$900–999	3.8%	1	0.0%		3.8%	1
$800–899	15.4%	4	0.0%		15.4%	4
$700–799	11.5%	3	0.0%		11.5%	3
$600–699	15.4%	4	0.0%		15.4%	4
$500–599	3.8%	1	0.0%		3.8%	1
$400–499	15.4%	4	0.0%		15.4%	4
$300–399	15.4%	4	0.0%		15.4%	4
< $300	0.0%	–	–		0.0%	–

Annual Sales Level (2)	Consolidated	# Units	Company	# Units	Franchise	# Units
Total	100.0%	26	0.0%	–	100.0%	26
Number of Units		26		–		26

B. Arithmetic Average

Consolidated	Company	Franchise
$757,003	$52	$757,003

C. Sales Range

	Company	Franchise	Consolidated
High	$797,776	$2,204,310	$2,204,310
Low	$797,776	$379,080	$379,080

Includes one airport food court restaurant with 1998 annual sales of $2,204,310. Footnotes follow Table 4 and form an integral part of this Table.

Table 4: Supermarket Restaurants
A. Amount and Distribution of Annual Sales

Annual Sales Level (2)	Consolidated	# Units	Company	# Units	Franchise	# Units
$1,300+	0.0%	–	0.0%	–	0.0%	–
$1,200–1,299	0.0%	–	0.0%	–	0.0%	–
$1,100–1,199	0.0%	–	0.0%	–	0.0%	–
$1,000–1,099	0.0%	–	0.0%	–	0.0%	–
$900–999	0.0%	–	0.0%	–	0.0%	–
$800–899	0.0%	–	0.0%	–	0.0%	–
$700–799	0.0%	–	0.0%	–	0.0%	–
$600–699	12.5%	1	14.3%	1	0.0%	–
$500–599	37.5%	3	28.6%	2	100.0%	1
$400–499	25.0%	2	28.6%	2	0.0%	–
$300–399	12.5%	1	14.3%	1	0.0%	–
< $300	12.5%	1	14.3%	1	0.0%	–
Total	100.0%	8	100.0%	7	100.0%	1
Number of Units		8		7		1

B. Arithmetic Average

Consolidated	Company	Franchise
$480,978	$471,431	$547,810

C. Sales Range

	Company	Franchise	Consolidated
High	$671,986	$547,810	$671,986
Low	$281,886	$547,810	$281,886

The following footnotes form an integral part of this Table.

Notes:

1. The restaurants whose results are reflected in the foregoing Tables were in operation continuously throughout the period December 28, 1997 through December 27, 1998. Results of restaurants which either opened or closed during this period are not included.

2. For purposes of this Item 19, restaurant concepts are defined as follows:

   Free-Standing Restaurants: Any type of restaurant other than the other restaurant categories defined below.

   In-line Restaurants: Restaurants located in traditional "strip style" retail shopping centers.

   Mall/Food Court Restaurants: Restaurants located within the confines of shopping malls and other food court locations, such as free-standing food court buildings, airports, and amusement parks.

   Supermarket Locations: Restaurants located within the premises of supermarket locations which typically have the following features: large retail space (over 15,000 square feet of supermarket space); a wide range of grocery product offerings; and/or large parking areas (over 20 spaces).

3. As shown in the foregoing Tables, sales volumes vary considerably due to a variety of factors, such as demographics of the restaurant trade area; competition from other restaurants in the trade area, especially other quick service restaurants; traffic flow; accessibility and visibility; economic conditions in the restaurant trade area; advertising and promotional activities; and the business abilities and efforts of the management of the restaurant.

4. The results shown for franchise restaurants have been taken from royalty reports submitted by franchisees. We have not audited these royalty reports but have no information to believe that they are unreliable. The results shown for company-owned restaurants are taken from reports prepared by company personnel at each restaurant, and are unaudited.

5. These sales figures are for specific franchise and company restaurants and should not be considered as the actual or potential sales that will be achieved by any other franchise restaurant. We do not represent that any franchisee can expect to attain these sales results. Actual results vary from restaurant to restaurant and we cannot estimate the results of any specific restaurant. A new franchisee's results are likely to be lower than the results shown above. We recommend that you make your own independent investigation to determine whether or not the franchise may be profitable, and consult with an attorney or other advisors before signing any franchise agreement.

6. Upon reasonable request, substantiation for the information appearing in these Tables will be made available to you.

7. Except for the information set forth in this Item 19, we do not furnish or authorize our salespersons to furnish any oral or written information concerning the actual, average, projected, or forecasted sales, costs, income, or profits (the "earnings capability") of a restaurant. We specifically instruct our sales personnel, agents, and employees that they are not permitted to make any claims or statements concerning a specific franchisee's earnings capability or chances for success, and we will not be bound by allegations of any unauthorized representations as to earnings capability or chances for success.

TACO JOHN'S INTERNATIONAL
808 W. 20th St.
Cheyenne, WY 82001

Tel: (800) 877-7886 (307) 635-0101
Fax: (307) 638-0603
E-Mail:
Internet Address: www.tacojohns.com
Contact: Ms. Roberta A. Coates, Vice President/ General Counsel

Description: Mexican fast-food restaurant franchisor.

# Franchised Units:	443 Units
# Company-Owned Units:	17 Units
Total # Units:	460 Units
Founded In:	1969
1st Franchised In:	1985
Average Total Investment:	100-550K
Franchise Fee:	10-19.5K

On-Going Royalty:	4%
Advertising Fee:	3.5%
Financial Assistance:	No (D – direct, or I – indirect)
Site Selection Assistance:	Yes
Lease Negotiation Assistance:	No
Contract Terms (Init./Renew):	20/10/10
Initial Training Provided:	NR

We have attached to this Offering Circular as Exhibit F a Statement of Per Restaurant Average Gross Sales and Ranges of Gross Sales for Taco John's Restaurants for the year ending 1998. The statement should be read along with all of the related information about its factual basis and the material assumptions underlying it.

We will provide you with substantiation of the data used to prepare this earnings claim if you request substantiation.

Your individual financial results are likely to differ from the results shown in this claim. This claim is not a representation or guarantee that you will or may achieve any level of sales included in the claim. We do not make any representation or guarantee of future sales or profits.

Exhibit F
Statement of Per Restaurant Average Sales
Set out below is a Statement of Per Restaurant Average Sales for Taco John's Restaurants for the year ending December 31, 1998. Included in the table are 373 Taco John's Restaurants, which were in operation throughout 1998. The Notes that follow the Statement explain the data included in the Statement and you should review them carefully.

1998 Per Restaurant Average Sales
(See Note 4)

("PSA"): $448,900
(See Note 1)

Media Efficient Markets
(See Note 2)

# of Stores and %			PSA
41	(11%)	Located in cities over 20,000 population	$636,700
57	(15%)	Located in towns under 20,000 population	$457,300
7	(2%)	Mall locations (Note 3)	$455,600
105	(28%)	Average for Media Efficient Markets	$527,200

Non-Media Efficient Markets

126	(34%)	Located in cities over 20,000 population	$440,200
117	(31%)	Located in town under 20,000 population	$410,900
25	(7%)	Mall locations (Note 3)	$341,300
268	(72%)	Average for Non-Media Efficient Markets	$418,200

373	(100%)	Total

Notes to Statement of Per Restaurant Average Sales

1. The foregoing is a statement of the average sales of the 373 Taco John's Restaurants in operation throughout 1998. The Taco John's Restaurants included in this statement sell substantially the same products and services as the franchised Taco John's Restaurants offered pursuant to this Offering Circular. The sales information for the franchised stores included in the Statement is information as reported by the franchisees and has not been audited or otherwise verified. The foregoing statement is only a statement of sales of Taco John's Restaurants and is not a statement of profits or earnings.

2. By "media efficient" we mean that the amount of money spent for advertising media within a

specific market would buy 7,000 Target Rating Points of advertising on an annual basis.

3. Mall locations are a separate category because they are located in a self-contained trade area. Mall sales volume is not related to residential demographics, but rather to the size of the mall, the number of employees in the mall, and pedestrian traffic counts in the food court.

4. Sales is the total receipts of all sales of the restaurant, but does not include sales tax or equivalent taxes.

Statement of Per Mexpress Average Sales

1998 Per Mexpress Average Sales: $99,400
(See Notes 1, 2 and 3)

Notes to Statement of Per Mexpress Average Sales

1. The foregoing is a statement of the average sales of the 39 Taco John's Mexpress in operation throughout 1998. The Taco John's Mexpresses included in this statement sell substantially the same products and services as the franchised Taco John's Mexpress Restaurants offered pursuant to the Offering Circular. The sales information for the franchised stores included in the statement is information as reported by franchisees and has not been audited or otherwise verified.

2. The foregoing is a statement of sales of Taco Johns Mexpresses and is not a statement of profits or earnings.

3. Sales is the total receipts of all sales of the Mexpress, but does not include sales tax or equivalent taxes.

WETZEL'S PRETZELS
65 N. Raymond Ave., # 310
Pasadena, CA 91103
Tel: (626) 432-6900

Fax: (626) 432-6904
E-Mail: wetzelsgw@aol.com
Internet Address: www.wetzels.com
Contact: Mr. Anthony Parete, Executive VP

Bakery Sales — Calendar Year 1998 (Stores open the entire calendar year)

Store	Amount
1	617,953
2	533,230
3	518,330
4	461,884
5	401,852
6	365,540
7	361,538
8	356,496
9	352,706
10	346,299
11	321,039
12	312,021
13	308,005
14	293,456
15	282,903

Store	Amount
16	263,805
17	256,359
18	252,873
19	247,419
20	245,805
21	245,133
22	234,682
23	226,724
24	219,139
25	203,616
26	197,056
27	169,541
Total 27 Stores	8,595,404
Average Store Volume	318,348

Notes to Items in Table:

1. Chart Includes all bakeries that were open for the entire 12 months ended December

31, 1998. Of the 27 bakeries open for the 12-month period, 14 were in California, 3 in Puerto Rico, 2 in Nebraska, 2 in New Jersey, 1 in Florida, 1 in Texas, 1 in Georgia, 1 in Mississippi, 1 in Kansas, and 1 in Oregon. Two of the stores included above were company-owned the entire year and 25 stores were franchised. The franchises are substantially similar to the franchises being offered in this and other states.

2. The figures for franchised bakeries were provided to Wetzel's Pretzels by franchised store owners. In most cases Wetzel's Pretzels was able to verify these figures through polling the stores' cash registers. In all cases these sales figures have been used as the basis for collection of royalties.

3. Three of the bakeries included in the above table are at street locations. Wetzel's Pretzels believes that mall locations are far more suitable for its bakeries than street locations and is unlikely to approve a street location in the future. Certain expenses associated with mall locations will be higher on average than similar expenses at street locations. However, Wetzel's Pretzels believes that higher sales volumes at mall locations will more than offset these increased expenses in most cases.

4. The data presented above was collected at a time when the U.S. and state economy was generally expansive. Your bakery's sales and expenses are likely to be affected by national, state, and local economic conditions, including rate of inflation, level of employment, and degree of consumer confidence.

5. The figures above reflect the owners' gross revenue before subtraction of any of the expenses they incur in operating their bakeries. The profitability of your WETZEL'S® PRETZELS bakery will depend not only on the level of gross revenue you achieve but also upon your ability to minimize costs. Expenses may vary on the basis, among other things, of the cost of labor and the availability of desirable mall locations in your geographic area. You should conduct an independent investigation of the expenses you will incur in operating your WETZEL'S® PRETZELS bakery.

6. Each of the bakeries used in compiling the figures above had been in operation for at least 12 months. You should expect results that are materially less favorable during your bakery's first 12 months of operation.

7. Wetzel's Pretzels will show you substantiation of the data used in preparing the table above in response to your reasonable request.

8. You should regard the information shown above only as an indication of historical performance and not as a prediction of future performance. Actual results are likely to vary from one bakery to another. The results of your franchised bakery may differ substantially from those shown above.

WINGSTOP
1212 Northwest Hwy.
Garland, TX 75041
Tel: (972) 686-6500
Fax: (972) 686-6502
E-Mail: jimdeering@worldnet.att.net
Internet Address: www.wingstop.com

Contact: Mr. James P. Deering, Director of Franchising

Description: The Arlington Morning News wrote: ' With the somewhat rough-and-ready air of an early century barnstormers' aircraft hanger, WINGSTOP treads the line between neighborhood hang and a casual, laid-back dinner-snack spot. The place's signature chicken wings, however, are righteously assertive, distinctive and anything but bland . . ' WINGSTOP is fun! WINGSTOP is focused! WINGSTOP is growing fast!

# Franchised Units:	16 Units	Advertising Fee:	2%
# Company-Owned Units:	1 Units	Financial Assistance:Yes(I) (D – direct,	
Total # Units:	17 Units	or I – indirect)	
Founded In:	1994	Site Selection Assistance:	Yes
1st Franchised In:	1997	Lease Negotiation Assistance:	Yes
Average Total Investment:	167.1-211.1K	Contract Terms (Init./Renew):	10/10
Franchise Fee:	20K	Initial Training Provided:2 Weeks Corporate Store;	
On-Going Royalty:	5%	1 Week Franchise Store.	

As of May 22, 1999, seven of the 11 Stores in the Wingstop chain had been operating for at least six months. They included our Flagship Store and six franchised Stores. Following is information about the average weekly sales of those seven Stores. We will provide substantiation of the data we used in calculating the averages upon receipt of a written request from you.

For the first 20 weeks of 1999, the average weekly sales of the seven Stores that had been operating for at least six months as of May 22, 1999 were $9,045. Two of the seven Stores, including our Flagship Store, achieved weekly sales averages more than 5.5% above the average; three of the seven Stores achieved weekly sales averages within 5.5% of the average; and two of the seven Stores achieved weekly sales averages more than 5.5% below the average.

Two of the other four Stores had been operating for more than two months, but less than six months, as of May 22, 1999. These two Stores were averaging weekly sales of $6,850 as of May 22, 1999. The other two Stores had been open for less than two months as of May 22, 1999 and neither had held its Grand Opening. In our judgment, neither Store had been open long enough as of that date to establish a sales pattern.

YOUR STORE'S WEEKLY GROSS SALES MAY DIFFER FROM THOSE OF STORES CURRENTLY IN OUR SYSTEM. In determining how relevant their sales data may be to your situation, we caution you to keep the following points in mind. We also urge you to discuss and analyze this information with your own business, financial and legal advisers.

❧ We collected all of the sales data by electronically polling each Stores electronic cash register. The information is unaudited, and we have relied on franchisee assurances that the information we received from them is accurate and reliable.

❧ The information covers only the first 20 operating weeks of 1999, which extended from January 3rd through May 22nd. Sales averages for this period may not be indicative of the weekly sales average that any of the seven Stores will achieve for all of 1999 or any other full year.

❧ Our Flagship Store is the only Store that has been operating for more than 15 months. It has not experienced significant seasonal variations in sales during its 5-year history.

❧ All seven Stores are located in Texas, which enjoys moderate winter weather. None of the seven Stores missed a single day of operation during 1999 on account of weather conditions.

❧ All seven Stores are located at least four miles driving distance apart; none of them experiences competition from any other Wingstop Store.

❧ All seven Stores are located in major metropolitan markets in which competition from other quick service food restaurants is substantial, but in which large consumer populations reside.

❧ The information relates only to sales; you can draw no inferences with respect to any Store's profitability.

Except for the information presented above, we do not use or furnish statements of actual, average, projected or forecasted sales, costs, profits or earnings in marketing our franchises. We will not guarantee, nor do we represent, that you will or can expect to attain any specific amount or range of sales, profits or earnings from the operation of your Store. Actual results may vary from unit to unit, and we cannot estimate the results of any franchisee.

Except for the information presented above, we do not authorize any of our officers, employees or sales representatives to make any claims, statements or representations regarding the sales, costs, profits or earnings, or the prospects or chances of success, that you can expect to achieve or that any other franchisee has achieved. We specifically instruct our representatives not to make such claims, statements or representations, and you are cautioned not to rely on any claims, statements or representations any person makes in disregard of these instructions. We accept no responsibility for, and will not be bound by, any unauthorized claims, statements or representations regarding your potential sales, costs, profits, earnings, prospects or chances of success.

ZERO'S SUBS
2106 Pacific Ave.
Virginia Beach, VA 23451
Tel: (800) 588-0782 (757) 425-8306
Fax: (757) 422-9157
E-Mail: zeros@norfolk.infi.net
Internet Address: www.zeros.com
Contact: Mr. Charles J. McCotter, Executive Vice President

Description: Specializes in hot, oven-baked submarine sandwiches made-to-order with quality ingredients. We also serve pizzas, salads, soups, kids meals, meal deals and desserts. All priced for today's budget. Catering and party subs complement any special event. The uniqueness of ZERO'S SUBS will bring customers back.

# Franchised Units:	45 Units
# Company-Owned Units:	6 Units
Total # Units:	51 Units
Founded In:	1969
1st Franchised In:	1990
Average Total Investment:	120-170K
Franchise Fee:	15K
On-Going Royalty:	6%
Advertising Fee:	2%
Financial Assistance:	Yes(I) (D – direct, or I – indirect)
Site Selection Assistance:	Yes
Lease Negotiation Assistance:	Yes
Contract Terms (Init./Renew):	15/15
Initial Training Provided:	3-6 Weeks in Virginia Beach, VA.

We do not make any representations or statements of actual, or average, or projected, or forecasted sales, profits, or earnings to franchisees with respect to franchises, except for the statement of actual income and expenses with respect to Zero's restaurants which appear under this item.

We do not furnish or authorize our salespersons to furnish any oral or written information concerning the actual, average, projected, forecasted, or potential sales, costs, income, or profits of a franchise other than as set forth in this Item.

We specifically instruct our sales personnel, agents, employees, and officers that they are not permitted to make any claims or statements as to the earnings, sales, or profits, or prospects or chances of success, nor do we authorize them to represent or estimate dollar figures as to any franchisee's operation. We will not be bound by any unauthorized representations as to earnings, sales, profits, or prospects or chances for success.

You should disregard any unauthorized information, whether oral or written, concerning the actual, average, projected, forecasts, or potential sales, costs, income or profits, or the prospects or chances of success, or representations or estimated dollar figures as to a franchisee's operation.

Actual results vary from franchise to franchise, and we cannot estimate the results of a particular franchise. We recommend that you make your own independent investigation to determine whether or not the franchise may be profitable, and consult with an attorney and other advisors prior to executing the Development Agreement or Franchise Agreement.

The summary statement set forth is a statement of actual average annual income and expenses as of December 31, 1998, for the five (5) Zero's Subs restaurants operated by Zero's affiliated, X.S., Inc. which have been in operation at least six (6) months.

As of December 31, 1998, Zero's affiliate X.S., Inc. operated six (6) restaurants. Five (5) of which have been included in the summary statement below. (The sixth restaurant has been excluded due to a contract of sale). Two (2) of these are free standing locations; one (1) a conversion of a fast food operation; and two (2) are inline strip center locations, information for which is included in this earnings claim. Restaurants utilize a building of approximately 1,200–3,200 square feet. These restaurants provide seating for approximately 30–60 customers. Each of the restaurants is similar equipped.

We based the results of operations described in this Item upon the unaudited profit and loss statements prepared by Zero's affiliate, X.S., Inc. in accordance with generally accepted accounting practices for the period January 1, 1998 through December 31, 1998 with respect to the five (5) restaurants operated as of December 31, 1998, which had been in operation for at least six (6) full calendar months as of that date.

The summary statement of average actual annual income, food costs and labor reflects only operating expenses and does not include capital expenses, other controllable expenses, or fixed expenses including any land, building or equipment rent, debt service, depreciation, advertising, administra-

tive expenses such as accounting or legal expenses, taxes, licenses or insurance, and does not include royalties payable by a franchisee.

The five (5) restaurants operated by Zero's affiliate, X.S., Inc. are located in the state of Virginia. Restaurants located in other geographic area may experience different results. A variety of factors influence the results of operations, including location, demographics, local economic conditions and weather.

SUCH ACTUAL SALES, INCOME, GROSS OR NET PROFITS ARE OF ZERO'S AFFILIATE, X.S., INC. OWNED UNITS AND SHOULD NOT BE CONSIDERED AS THE ACTUAL OR PROBABLE SALES, INCOME, GROSS OR NET PROFITS THAT WILL BE REALIZED BY ANY FRANCHISEE. WE DO NOT REPRESENT THAT YOU CAN EXPECT TO ATTAIN SUCH SALES, INCOME, GROSS OR NET PROFITS.

SOME ZERO'S RESTAURANTS OWNED BY ZERO'S AFFILIATE, X.S., INC. HAVE SOLD THIS AMOUNT. THERE IS NO ASSURANCE THAT YOU WILL DO AS WELL. IF YOU RELY UPON OUR FIGURES, YOU MUST ACCEPT THE RISK OF NOT DOING AS WELL.

The following table sets out the average annual net sales, food cost and labor related expenses. Based upon actual annual sales for the period January 1, 1998 through December 31, 1998 for the five (5) locations operated by X.S., Inc. which have been in operation for at least six (6) months as of such date.

Annual

	Amount	Percentage of Average Monthly Sales
Average Annual Sales (Note 1)	$412,267	100%
Food Cost (Note 2)	$108,720	26.38%
Labor Related Expenses (Note 3)	$109,617	26.59%

225

The following restaurants were included in the summary statements:

Location	Date of Opening
Virginia Beach, Virginia (Oceanfront)	March 21, 1967
Norfolk, Virginia (Hampton Blvd.)	August 1, 1968
Virginia Beach, Virginia (Hilltop)	November 1, 1978
Virginia Beach, Virginia (Lynnhaven)	March 1, 1986
Norfolk, Virginia (Wards Corner)	May 20, 1994

Note 1: Net sales reflect total average sales exclusive of sales tax collected and paid to state and local governmental authorities. These net sales are an average of the annual sales for each of the five (5) restaurants included in the sample. Annual sales volume will also vary depending upon other factors including location, demographics, general economic conditions, weather conditions, menu mix, competition and other seasonal factors as well as the efforts of the individual restaurant management team.

Note 2: Food costs are an average of the actual total costs for the five (5) Zero's restaurants included in the summary statement. Food costs have been adjusted by three (3%) percent based on free food given by coupon accounted for as advertising expense.

Note 3: Labor related expenses include the annual salary paid by X.S., Inc. to a Manager, one assistant manager and one shift supervisor for each restaurant. Included in labor related expenses are amounts paid or accrued by X.S., Inc. for employee payroll taxes, insurance and worker's compensation. X.S., Inc. provides insurance at one hundred (100%) for it's manager in each restaurant

Worker's compensation expense is based upon X.S., Inc.'s experience rating. The experience rating for a franchisee may be different than X.S., Inc.'s experience rating.

Local market conditions and state and federal minimum wage requirements may affect wages and labor related expenses.

UPON YOUR WRITTEN REQUEST WE WILL MAKE AVAILABLE TO YOU FOR INSPECTION AND REVIEW ALL DATA UTILIZED IN FORMULATING THE ACTUAL AVERAGE SALES, PROFITS OR EARNINGS CONTAINED IN THIS STATEMENT DATA UTILIZED IN DRAFTING THIS STATEMENT WAS PREPARED BASED UPON A UNIFORM ACCOUNTING SYSTEM AND GENERALLY ACCEPTED ACCOUNTING PRACTICES, AND THE INFORMATION PROVIDED HEREIN WAS PREPARED BASED UPON THIS DATA.

Food: restaurant/ family-style

BIG BOY RESTAURANT & BAKERY
4199 Marcy Dr.
Warren, MI 48091
Tel: (800) 837-3003 (810) 755-8114
Fax: (810) 757-4737
E-Mail:
Internet Address:
Contact: Mr. Ronald E. Johnston, Executive Vice President

Description: Full-service family restaurant with over 60 years of success. BIG BOY'S comprehensive menu features a daily breakfast and fruit buffet, soup, salad and fruit bar, in-store bakery and award-winning desserts, in addition to traditional favorites. Industry leader in managed profitability.

# Franchised Units:	429 Units
# Company-Owned Units:	<u>74</u> Units
Total # Units:	503 Units
Founded In:	1936
1st Franchised In:	1952
Average Total Investment:	600K-1.8MM
Franchise Fee:	40K
On-Going Royalty:	4%
Advertising Fee:	3%
Financial Assistance:No (D – direct, or I – indirect)	
Site Selection Assistance:	Yes
Lease Negotiation Assistance:	Yes
Contract Terms (Init./Renew):	20

Initial Training Provided:6-8 Weeks In-Unit; 1-2 Weeks at Corporate Headquarters.

In this Item, Elias makes certain disclosures concerning sales and expenses for Big Boy Restaurants. In doing so, only actual and average sales (and costs of operations as a percentage of sales) of existing, free-standing, company-operated restaurants in Michigan are disclosed ("Designated Company Restaurants.") In referring to these sales and expenses, you must understand that the results of the Designated Company Restaurants may differ from a franchised restaurant for several reasons, including: varying building occupancy rates (rent); differences in market penetration and its affect on advertising budgets and market presence; and differences in wage rates and taxes, depending on the state or city in which the restaurant is located and differences in food costs (food costs may be higher for those restaurants that cannot be serviced by Elias' Commissary or which are outside of Elias' approved distributors' service area.) General economic conditions beyond Elias' control and its franchisees' control are also important: inflationary pressures, unemployment, energy shortfalls and related or similar conditions, depending on their existence and degree, may adversely affect the market for a franchisee's business with a corresponding adverse affect on earnings.

In 1998, of the Designated Company Restaurants, approximately 88% had annual sales volumes in excess of $1,000,000, approximately 53% had annual sales volumes in excess of $1,200,000; approximately 35% had annual sales volumes in excess of $1,500,000; and approximately 12% had annual sales volumes in excess of $1,800,000. In 1998 the average annual sales volume of Designated Company Restaurants was $1,383,436. The highest and lowest annual sales volume in 1998 for these Designated Company Restaurants was $2,310,880 and $931,620, respectively.

In 1998, the average break-even cash flow point for Designated Company Restaurants, insofar as sales and expenses are concerned, was approximately $1,000,000. This break-even point may vary based on many factors such as menu price, food and labor costs, reinvestment, special location, a franchisee's operational and management methods, legal and accounting fees, insurance expenses, depreciation expenses, interest expense and miscellaneous non-controllables.

The Designated Company Restaurants proforma statements set forth below were calculated using actual sales through Period 13 of 1998 (from December 29, 1997 through December 27, 1998), for restaurants with annual sales volumes of $1,000,000, $1,200,000, $1,500,000 and $1,800,000. (The actual sales ranges used for these four models were, respectively, $931,629–1,001,820; $1,102,626–1,148,813; $1,373,516–1,574,156; and $1,807,871–2,310,880.) Specific assumptions used in these proforma statements include franchise fees of 3% and advertising fees of 2% in the calculation of G & A Expenses. Cash flow is calculated before depreciation and financing expense, and after a 5% occupancy rate assumption which is included in the Operating Expenses assumption.

	$1,000,000 Model	
	Dollars	%
Sales	$1,000,000	100.00%
Cost of Sales	$302,000	30.20%
Hourly	$223,700	22.37%
Management	$55,000	5.50%
Facilities	$35,300	3.53%
Other Expenses	$334,800	33.48%
Cash Flow	$49,200	4.92%

	$1,200,000 Model	
	Dollars	%
Sales	$1,200,000	100.00%
Cost of Sales	$367,200	30.60%
Hourly	$277,560	23.13%
Management	$45,240	3.77%
Facilities	$37,680	3.14%
Other Expenses	$396,600	33.05%
Cash Flow	$75,720	6.31%

	$1,500,000 Model	
	Dollars	%
Sales	$15,000,000	100.00%
Cost of Sales	$450,900	30.36%
Hourly	$333,600	22.24%
Management	$60,600	4.04%
Facilities	$44,250	2.95%
Other Expenses	$470,100	31.34%
Cash Flow	$140,550	9.37%

	$1,800,000 Model	
	Dollars	%
Sales	$1,800,000	100.00%
Cost of Sales	$536,400	29.80%
Hourly	$382,140	21.23%
Management	$55,980	3.11%
Facilities	$43,200	2.40%
Other Expenses	$546,660	30.37%
Cash Flow	$235,620	13.09%

The proforma statements are based upon approximately 17 Designated Company Restaurants open at least one year which are similar to comparable franchises operating in Michigan. The data used was received from restaurants using a uniform accounting system, whose operating statements were prepared on a basis consistent with generally accepted accounting principles. Both Elias operated and independent franchises are similar with respect to their operations and operating results and are subject to the same franchise fee rate and receive similar services from Elias. A NEW FRANCHISEE'S INDIVIDUAL FINANCIAL RESULTS ARE LIKELY TO DIFFER FROM THE RESULTS STATED IN THE PROFORMA STATEMENT. Designated Company Restaurants are not required to pay the initial franchise fee paid by independent franchisees.

Substantiation of the data used in preparing the earnings claim will be made available to the prospective franchisee on reasonable request.

THESE SALES, CASH FLOW, PROFITS OR EARNINGS ARE AVERAGES OF SPECIFIC DESIGNATED COMPANY RESTAURANTS AND SHOULD NOT BE CONSIDERED AS THE ACTUAL OR POTENTIAL SALES, PROFITS OR EARNINGS THAT WILL BE REALIZED BY ANY OTHER FRANCHISEE. THE FRANCHISOR DOES NOT REPRESENT THAT ANY FRANCHISEE CAN EXPECT TO ATTAIN THESE SALES, PROFITS OR EARNINGS.

Boston Pizza

BOSTON PIZZA
5500 Parkwood Way, # 200
Richmond, BC V6V 2M4 CANADA
Tel: (800) 887-7757 (604) 270-1108
Fax: (604) 270-4168
E-Mail:
Internet Address:
Contact: Mr. Rick Villalpando, Director of Franchising

Description: BOSTON PIZZA is Canada's most successful casual dining pizza and pasta franchise operation, with over 100 locations and system-wide sales in excess of $175 million.

# Franchised Units:	118 Units
# Company-Owned Units:	1 Units
Total # Units:	119 Units
Founded In:	1963
1st Franchised In:	1968
Average Total Investment:	800-950K
Franchise Fee:	45K
On-Going Royalty:	7%
Advertising Fee:	3%
Financial Assistance:Yes(I) (D – direct, or I – indirect)	
Site Selection Assistance:	Yes
Lease Negotiation Assistance:	Yes
Contract Terms (Init./Renew):	10/10
Initial Training Provided:8 Weeks Richmond, BC, Corporate Training Centre.	

The following chart represents a pro forma statement of (estimated) income for a 5,500 square foot restaurant and lounge with 208 seats. (The pro forma statement assumes a full liquor license has been granted, i.e. beer, wine and mixed drinks). BPR has no significant operating experience of its own, therefore, this pro forma statement is based upon the experience of, and the results of the operations of franchisees of BPI, BPR's affiliate, in Canada. These figures were compiled based on the actual financial statements and rate of sales analysis for food costs, for the year ended December 31, 1997, of 11 generally representative Canadian Boston Pizza franchisees. These franchisees make up approximately 10% of all BPI's Canadian Franchisees. To prepare the $1,600,000 Cdn. pro forma, these 11 franchisees were grouped together. Of the 11 franchisees, 4 achieved annual sales in excess of $2,000,000 Cdn. and they make up the $2,000,000 Cdn. pro forma. For each category, franchisees' expense results were averaged for each expense item to derive the final pro forma expense figure. Consequently, on an expense by expense basis, there is not one franchisee that has achieved each of the expense figures in the pro forma. Annual sales for all of BPI's Canadian franchisees for the year ended December 31, 1997 range from $650,000 to $3,075,000 Cdn. Detailed financial statements for BPI's other Canadian franchisees were not available.

Boston Pizza Full Service Restaurant with Lounge 5,500 Square Feet
(Figures Shown in Canadian Dollars)

Annual Sales[1]	$1,600,000	100.0%	$2,000,000	100.0%
Food Sales	1,249,600	78.1%	1,600,000	80.0%
Cost of Sales	312,400	25.0%	400,00	25.0%
Gross Profit	937,200	58.6%	1,200,000	60.0%
Liquor Sales	350,400	21.9%	400,000	20.0%
Cost of Sales	115,632	33.0%	128,000	32.0%
Gross Profit	234,768	14.7%	272,000	13.6%
Annual Gross Profit	$1,171,968	73.3%	$1,472,000	73.6%
Expenses				
Accounting & Legal[2]	10,880	0.7%	14,000	0.7%
Advertising & Promotion[3]	113,600	7.1%	132,000	6.6%
Bank Charges[4]	12,000	0.7%	12,000	0.6%
Delivery[5]	9,600	0.6%	12,000	0.6%
Franchise Fee[6]	89,040	5.6%	113,400	5.7%
Laundry & Cleaning[7]	24,000	1.5%	28,000	1.4%
Leased Equipment[8]	8,000	0.5%	24,000	1.2%
Insurance[9]	4,800	0.3%	6,000	0.3%
Office & Sundry[10]	36,800	2.3%	46,000	2.3%
Rent & Common Area Costs[11]	123,200	7.7%	176,000	8.8%
Repairs & Maintenance[12]	24,000	1.5%	30,000	1.5%
Supplies[13]	32,000	2.0%	40,000	2.0%
Telephone & Utilities[14]	32,000	2.0%	38,000	1.9%
Wages & Benefits[15]	417,600	26.1%	452,000	22.6%
Annual Expenses	937,520	58.6%	1,123,400	56.2%
Operating Income	234,448	14.7%	348,600	17.4%
Miscellaneous Income	16,000	1.0%	20,000	1.0%
Profit Available before Debt Services, Taxes and Depreciation	$250,448	15.7%	$368,600	18.4%

Readers are cautioned that the notes that follow on the next page are an integral part to these projections.

Notes Boston Pizza Restaurants Projections:

1. For the twelve months ended December 31, 1997 the average sales for the 94 stores that operated continuously throughout the year was $1,600,000 per store.

   During this year, 21.3% of the above mentioned stores exceeded sales of $2,000,000 per store.

2. Accounting & Legal represents the cost of an external accountant's preparation of unaudited

monthly and annual financial statements, as well as miscellaneous legal expenses.

3. Advertising and promotion represents all national advertising costs required under BPI's franchise agreement, as well as the cost of local advertising conducted by the individual franchisee.

4. Bank charges include credit card and bank fees.

5. Delivery represents the costs for a delivery driver, including insurance, gas and repair and maintenance of the delivery vehicle.

6. Franchisee fee is based on a royalty rate of 7% of food sales, plus miscellaneous income.

7. Laundry and cleaning represents the cost of hiring outside suppliers to clean uniforms, and to clean the restaurant.

8. Leased equipment includes the annual costs associated with leasing the kitchen and other equipment for use in the restaurant.

9. Insurance represents the annual cost of maintaining liability, property and casualty insurance policies for the restaurant.

10. Office and sundry includes the ongoing cost of purchasing office supplies and sundry items for the restaurant.

11. Rent and common area costs include base rent expenses, plus charges for the maintenance of common areas that may be imposed under the lease. Free-standing locations will not incur the expense of common area maintenance

12. Repairs and maintenance represent the costs associated with the ongoing repairs to the interior of the restaurant and to all of the restaurant equipment, as may be required by BPI's franchise agreement or by necessity to operate the restaurant. This item does not include the cost of renovation that may be required every 7 years by BPI under the franchise agreement.

13. Supplies include the ongoing costs of purchasing paper supplies (including, napkins and tablecloths), small wares and any other supplies necessary to operate the restaurant that were not previously included in the "office and sundry" expense category.

14. Telephone and utilities include the costs of maintaining the phone system, which on average consists of 4 lines, as well as the annual costs for electricity, gas and other utilities.

15. Wages and benefits represent the wages and benefits paid to restaurant employees, which typically range from 30 to 45 individuals, as well as the restaurant's general manager. It does not include any payments to the franchisee (except as general manager, if applicable).

The projections are only estimates of how we think a Boston Pizza Restaurant will perform in Canada. The conversion of these figures into U.S. dollars will not accurately portray the projected performance of a Boston's The Gourmet Pizza Restaurant in the United States. Factors such as differing market and economic conditions, labour rates and fluctuating exchange rates must be taken into consideration. Thus, actual results of your Boston's The Gourmet Pizza Restaurant are likely to differ, perhaps substantially, from the estimates in these pro forma statements. There is no assurance that your Boston's The Gourmet Pizza Restaurant will perform as well. If you rely on our figures, you must accept the risk of not doing as well.

This statement has been prepared by BPR without review by an independent accountant. Actual earnings from the operation of a franchised business are inherently subject to uncertainty and variations depending upon changing events and economic conditions. There can be no guaranty that these statements accurately predict the earnings of any franchisee. Substantiation of the data used in preparing this statement will be made available upon reasonable request.

Other than as noted in this Item 19, BPR does not furnish or authorize its salespersons to furnish any oral or written information concerning the actual or potential sales, costs, income or profits of a Boston's the Gourmet Pizza restaurant. Actual results vary from unit to unit and BPR cannot estimate the results of a particular Franchised Business.

CHARLEY'S STEAKERY
6610 Busch Blvd., # 100
Columbus, OH 43229
Tel: (800) 437-8325 (614) 847-8100
Fax: (614) 847-8110
E-Mail: franchising@charleyssteakery.com
Internet Address: www.charleyssteakery.com
Contact: Mr. Richard A. Page, Vice President Development

Description: CHARLEY'S STEAKERY is a progressive quick-service restaurant with over 100 locations across the United States and Canada. The heart of CHARLEY'S menu consists of freshly-grilled Steak and Chicken Subs, fresh-cut fries and freshly squeezed lemonade. CHARLEY'S open kitchen environment and freshly-prepared products are unique in the fast-food industry.

# Franchised Units:	92 Units
# Company-Owned Units:	<u>10</u> Units
Total # Units:	102 Units
Founded In:	1986
1st Franchised In:	1991
Average Total Investment:	124.5-294.5K
Franchise Fee:	19.5K
On-Going Royalty:	5% or $200/mon
Advertising Fee:	.25%
Financial Assistance:	Yes(I) (D – direct, or I – indirect)
Site Selection Assistance:	Yes
Lease Negotiation Assistance:	Yes
Contract Terms (Init./Renew):	10/10
Initial Training Provided:	3 Weeks at Columbus, OH.

We provide as part of this Offering Circular, information regarding the earnings capability of our franchisees. This information is attached hereto as Exhibit G.

While this information is provided to assist in the analysis of a Charley's Steakery Grilled Subs & Salads® Franchise, YOU ARE ADVISED THAT EACH NEW FRANCHISEE'S INDIVIDUAL FINANCIAL RESULTS CAN BE DIFFERENT FROM THE RESULTS STATED IN EXHIBIT G. THE INFORMATION SUPPLIED IN EXHIBIT G1 IS BASED UPON AVERAGES OF SIX (6) OF OUR AFFILIATE'S RESTAURANTS (CHARLEY'S STEAKERY, INC.) WHICH ARE OPERATED IN COLUMBUS (3), LANCASTER (1), CLEVELAND (1), OHIO, ATLANTA, GEORGIA (1) AND WHICH OPERATE AS AFFILIATES OF US. THE INFORMATION SUPPLIED IN EXHIBIT G2 IS BASED UPON AVERAGES OF TWO (2) OF OUR AFFILIATE'S RESTAURANTS (CHARLEY'S STEAKERY, INC.) WHICH ARE OPERATED IN LANCASTER, OHIO AND CLEVELAND, OHIO. CHARLEY M. SHIN, OUR CEO, OWNS 100% OF CHARLEY'S STEAKERY, INC.

We do not have any "company-owned" Restaurants, however we do have an affiliated company, Charley's Steakery, Inc. One of the six Restaurants met or exceeded the average in Exhibit G1 and one of the two Restaurants met or exceeded the average in Exhibit G2.

The following sales information relates solely to historical sales information regarding existing affiliated Restaurants (as noted above). No inference as to expenses, cost of goods, or profits under existing or future outlets should be drawn from the following sales information.

Upon your request, we will make available to you the substantiating data used in preparing the averages of earnings capability presented in Exhibit G.

Information Regarding Earning Capability of Gosh Enterprises, Inc.'s Franchisees
THE RESTAURANT BUSINESS IS HIGHLY COMPETITIVE AND IS AFFECTED BY, AMONG OTHER THINGS, CHANGES IN A GEOGRAPHIC AREA, CHANGES IN EATING HABITS AND PREFERENCES, LOCAL, REGIONAL AND NATIONAL ECONOMIC CONDITIONS, POPULATION TRENDS AND TRAFFIC PATTERNS. THE PRINCIPAL BASES OF COMPETITION IN THE INDUSTRY ARE THE QUALITY AND PRICE OF THE FOOD PRODUCTS SERVED, RESTAURANT LOCATION, QUALITY AND SPEED OF SERVICE, ADVERTISING, NAME IDENTIFICATION AND ATTRACTIVENESS OF FACILITIES. IN ADDITION, THE ACQUISITION OF SITES IS HIGHLY COMPETITIVE WITH OTHER RESTAURANT CHAINS AND RETAIL BUSINESSES FOR SUITABLE SITES FOR THE DEVELOPMENT OF NEW RESTAURANTS.

The following figures are based on six of Franchisor's affiliate Charley's Steakery, Inc.'s Restaurants, three of which are located in Columbus, Ohio, one of which is located in Lancaster, Ohio, one of which is located in Cleveland, Ohio, and one of which is located in Atlanta, Georgia[1]. These Restaurants are operated by an affiliate of Franchisor and the figures below are the average figures of these six (6) Restaurants from September 30, 1996 through September 28, 1997, and should not be considered as the actual or potential sales, cost of goods, operating expenses, or profit that will be realized by any other franchise. The Franchisor does not claim that any Franchisee can expect to attain these sales or profits.

Sales	(100%)	$588,553[1]
Cost of Sales	(54.6%)	$321,375
Gross Profit	(45.4%)	$267,178
Operating Expenses	(25.9%)	$152,338
Operating Income[2]	(19.5%)[3]	$114,840

These affiliated Restaurants' numbers reflect a 5% royalty fee and actual advertising expense. It should be noted that the affiliate which owns these Restaurants is the originator of the business concept, and as such presumably has above-average knowledge and expertise with regard to the franchise business. Additionally, because of its ownership of multiple locations and its status as an incorporated affiliate of the Franchisor, the affiliate may be able to take advantage of greater economies of scale that may not be available to the individual franchisee.

THE RESTAURANT INDUSTRY IS INTENSELY COMPETITIVE BASED ON PRICE, SERVICE, THE TYPE AND QUALITY OF FOOD OFFERED, LOCATION AND OTHER FACTORS. THE FRANCHISOR HAS MANY WELL ESTABLISHED COMPETITORS WITH SUBSTANTIALLY GREATER FINANCIAL RESOURCES AND A LONGER HISTORY OF OPERATIONS THAN THE FRANCHISOR, INCLUDING COMPETITORS ALREADY ESTABLISHED IN REGIONS INTO WHICH A FRANCHISEE MAY BE CONSIDERING A RESTAURANT.

UPON REASONABLE REQUEST, FRANCHISOR WILL MAKE AVAILABLE TO THE REQUESTING FRANCHISEE, THE SUBSTANTIATING DATA USED IN PREPARING THE ABOVE FIGURES. A NEW FRANCHISEE'S INDIVIDUAL FINANCIAL RESULTS ARE LIKELY TO DIFFER FROM THE RESULT STATED IN THE EARNINGS CLAIM.

Information Regarding Earning Capability of Gosh Enterprises, Inc.'s Franchisees
THE RESTAURANT BUSINESS IS HIGHLY COMPETITIVE AND IS AFFECTED BY, AMONG OTHER THINGS, CHANGES IN A GEOGRAPHIC AREA, CHANGES IN EATING HABITS AND PREFERENCES, LOCAL, REGIONAL AND NATIONAL ECONOMIC CONDITIONS, POPULATION TRENDS AND TRAFFIC PATTERNS. THE PRINCIPAL BASES OF COMPETITION IN THE INDUSTRY ARE THE QUALITY AND PRICE OF THE FOOD PRODUCTS SERVED,

RESTAURANT LOCATION, QUALITY AND SPEED OF SERVICE, ADVERTISING, NAME IDENTIFICATION AND ATTRACTIVENESS OF FACILITIES. IN ADDITION, THE ACQUISITION OF SITES IS HIGHLY COMPETITIVE WITH OTHER RESTAURANT CHAINS AND RETAIL BUSINESSES FOR SUITABLE SITES FOR THE DEVELOPMENT OF NEW RESTAURANTS.

The following figures are based on two of Franchisor's affiliate Charley's Steakery, Inc.'s Restaurants, located in regional malls, one of which is located in Lancaster, Ohio, one of which is located in Cleveland, Ohio. These Restaurants are operated by an affiliate of franchisor and the figures below are the average figures of these two (2) Restaurants from September 30, 1996 through September 28, 1997, and should not be considered as the actual or potential sales, cost of goods, operating expenses, or profit that will be realized by any other franchise in a regional mall food court location. The Franchisor does not claim that any Franchisee can expect to attain these sales or profits.

Sales	(100%)	$471,320
Cost of Sales	(54.2%)	$255,666
Gross Profit	(45.8%)	$215,654
Operating Expenses	(23.1%)	$108,651
Operating Income[2]	(22.7%)[3]	$107,003

These affiliated Restaurants are required to pay all royalty and advertising fees at rates identical to those paid by all other franchisees. It should be noted that the affiliate which owns these Restaurants is the originator of the business concept, and as such presumably has above-average knowledge and expertise with regard to the franchise business. Additionally, because of its ownership of multiple locations and its status as an incorporated affiliate of the Franchisor, the affiliate may be able to take advantage of greater economies of scale that may not be available to the individual franchisee.

THE RESTAURANT INDUSTRY IS INTENSELY COMPETITIVE BASED ON PRICE, SERVICE, THE TYPE AND QUALITY OF FOOD OFFERED, LOCATION AND OTHER FACTORS. THE FRANCHISOR HAS MANY WELL ESTABLISHED COMPETITORS WITH SUBSTANTIALLY GREATER FINANCIAL RESOURCES AND A LONGER HISTORY OF OPERATIONS THAN THE FRANCHISOR, INCLUDING COMPETITORS ALREADY ESTABLISHED IN REGIONS INTO WHICH A FRANCHISEE MAY BE CONSIDERING A RESTAURANT.

UPON REASONABLE REQUEST FRANCHISOR WILL MAKE AVAILABLE TO THE REQUESTING FRANCHISEE, THE SUBSTANTIATING DATA USED IN PREPARING THE ABOVE FIGURES.

---

[1]   These locations consist of University, Convention Center, Airport, malls and a downtown location.

[2]   One unit (17%) exceeded this average sales number.

[3]   This figure represents profit before depreciation, amortization, interest income and expense, and income taxes.

[4]   The percentage figures represent the percentage of the item compared to sales.

[2]   This figure represent profits before depreciation, amortization, interest income and expense, and income taxes.

[3]   The percentage figures represent the percentage of the item compared to sales.

CHEDDAR'S CASUAL CAFÉ
616 Six Flags Dr., # 116
Arlington, TX 76011
Tel: (817) 640-4344
Fax: (817) 633-4452

Contact: Mr. Larry D. Zimmerman, Director
Franchise Development

Description: Full-service restaurant. Terrific price/value, with traditional menu, in pleasing ambiance.

# Franchised Units:	16 Units
# Company-Owned Units:	14 Units
Total # Units:	30 Units
Founded In:	1978
1st Franchised In:	1984
Average Total Investment:	1.5-1.9MM+
Franchise Fee:	30K
On-Going Royalty:	3%

Advertising Fee:	0%
Financial Assistance: No (D – direct, or I – indirect)	
Site Selection Assistance:	Yes
Lease Negotiation Assistance:	Yes
Contract Terms (Init./Renew):	20/20
Initial Training Provided: 12 Weeks Arlington, TX.	

Statement of Average Sales and Expenses

The following statement of Averages Unit Sales and Expenses sets forth the average sales and expenses of OUR-operated restaurants for OUR fiscal years ending ("FYE"), December 31, 1996, December 31, 1997, and December 31, 1998. The total number of CHEDDAR'S-operated restaurants included in the calculation of average results for each fiscal year are shown in the table below.

During the Fiscal Year ending 1998, six (6) of twelve (12) of OUR company-operated restaurants (opened the entire year) achieved annual sales at or above the Company average annual sales of $2,750,280 during the full calendar year 1998.

During the Fiscal Year ending 1998, six (6) of fifteen (15) Franchisee-operated restaurants achieved annual sales at or above the reported Franchisee annual sales average of $2,486,640. The one additional Franchise-operated restaurant opened in 1998, and, although it achieved weekly sales volumes above the Franchisee-operated restaurant volumes during 1998, it did not operate for a full year and did not experience sufficient sales history to project average annual volumes.

Cheddar's, Inc. Historical Performance Review

	FYE 12/31/96	FYE 12/31/97	FYE 12/31/98
Company Units open at year end	12	12	12
No. of unit weeks	621	624	624
Sales per Unit week	$48,003	$50,903	$52,890
Franchised Units open at year end	12	14	15
No. of Franchised Unit weeks	560	674	694
Franchise Unit sales per Unit week	$46,763	$47,565	$47,820
System wide sales	$55,996,867	$63,812,693	$66,169,933
Total Units open at year end	24	26	27
System wide Unit weeks	1,181	1,298	1,318
System wide sales per Unit weeks	$47,415	$49,170	$50,221

All of OUR company-operated restaurants offer substantially the same products and services to the public that Franchised Units are expected to offer.

Certain charges which YOU will be required to pay to US and other differences in the expenses which YOU may incur if YOU desire to obtain a franchise (including, but not limited to, a development fee, initial franchise fee, and ongoing royalty expenditures) are noted in the "Bases and Assumptions" for the data contained in this analysis. Such charges are not included in the calculation of average results set forth below. The sales made and expenses incurred by YOU in connection with operation of a Franchised Unit are likely to be different from the sales and expenses of OUR company-operated restaurants and will be directly affected by many factors such as competition in the market, the quality of YOUR management and service at the Franchised Unit, YOUR contractual relationships with lessors and vendors, the extent to which YOU finance the operation of the Franchised Unit, YOUR legal, accounting and other professional fees and certain benefits and economies of scale which WE may have derived as a result of operating multiple restaurants on a consolidated basis. Accordingly, this analysis is provided as reference information only for YOU in connection with other information and is not intended by US to be used as a statement or forecast of sales, costs or profits that may be achieved by any Franchised Unit.

YOU are urged to consult with appropriate financial, business, tax, accounting and legal advisors in connection with the information set forth in this analysis.

THIS ANALYSIS IS NOT BASED UPON THE ACTUAL EXPERIENCE OF FRANCHISED UNITS. THE AVERAGE SALES, COSTS, INCOME OR PROFITS REFLECTED IN THE ANALYSIS ARE OF CHEDDAR'S-OPERATED RESTAURANTS FOR THE PERIOD INDICATED AND SHOULD NOT BE CONSIDERED AS THE ACTUAL OR POTENTIAL SALES, COSTS, INCOME, OR PROFITS THAT WILL BE REALIZED BY YOU. WE DO NOT REPRESENT THAT YOU CAN EXPECT TO ATTAIN SUCH SALES, COSTS, INCOME, OR PROFITS OR ANY PARTICULAR LEVEL OF SALES, COSTS, INCOME OR PROFITS. IN ADDITION, WE DO NOT REPRESENT THAT YOU WILL DERIVE INCOME THAT EXCEEDS THE INITIAL PAYMENT FOR OR INVESTMENT IN OUR FRANCHISE. YOUR SUCCESS LARGELY DEPENDS UPON YOUR ABILITY, AND YOUR INDIVIDUAL FINANCIAL RESULTS ARE LIKELY TO DIFFER FROM THE INFORMATION DESCRIBED HEREIN. SUBSTANTIATION OF THE DATA USED IN PREPARING THIS ANALYSIS WILL BE MADE AVAILABLE UPON REASONABLE REQUEST.

THIS ANALYSIS DOES NOT INCLUDE ANY ESTIMATES OF THE FEDERAL INCOME TAX THAT WOULD BE PAYABLE ON THE NET INCOME FROM A RESTAURANT OR STATE OR LOCAL NET INCOME OR GROSS PROFITS TAXES THAT MAY BE APPLICABLE TO THE PARTICULAR JURISDICTION IN WHICH A RESTAURANT MAY BE LOCATED. EACH FRANCHISEE IS STRONGLY URGED TO CONSULT WITH ITS TAX ADVISER REGARDING THE IMPACT THAT FEDERAL, STATE AND LOCAL TAXES WILL HAVE ON THE AMOUNTS SHOWN IN THIS ANALYSIS.

Statement of Average Sales and Expenses of Cheddar's-Operated Cheddar's Casual Cafe Restaurants (a) (In Thousands of Dollars)

	Fifty-Two Weeks ended		Fifty-Two Weeks ended		Fifty-Two Weeks ended	
	12/31/96	%	12/31/97	%	12/31/98	%
Avg. Food Sales	$2,237.5	89.6	$2,374.1	89.4	2,455.3	89.3
Avg. Liquor Sales	258.7	10.4	272.8	10.6	295.0	10.7
Total Avg. Sales	$2,496.2	100.0	$2646.9	100.0	2750.3	100.0
Total Avg. Sales/Week (c)	48.0	100.0	50.9	100.0	52.9	100.0
Gross Profit (e)	1,765.0	70.7	1,872.4	70.2	1,934.6	70.3
Operating Expenses						
Labor Cost (f)	705.6	28.3	734.3	27.7	793.4	28.8
Marketing (g)	2.1	0.1	1.4	0.1	1.8	0.1
Rep. & Main. (h)	116.4	4.7	124.4	4.9	121.6	4.4
R.E. Taxes (i)	24.8	1.0	24.8	1.0	28.7	1.0
Cont. Op. Exp. (j)	318.1	12.7	304.4	11.5	302.9	11.0
Total Operating Expenses	1,167.0	46.8	1189.3	44.9	1,248.4	45.0
Total Operating Cash Flow	$598.3	24.0	$668.6	25.3	$663.1	24.1

Bases and Assumptions

(a) OUR Company-operated restaurants utilize a uniform accounting system and the data pertaining to such restaurants was prepared by OUR in-house accountants on a basis consistent with generally accepted accounting principles during the covered periods. The information contained in the foregoing statement has not been audited. Substantiation of the data used in preparing the statement will be made available upon reasonable request.

(b) Sales includes the total of all food sales and all beverage sales, including liquor, wine and beer sales. The Franchise Agreement requires that YOU pay a royalty fee of 3.0% of the sale price to the extent includable in the "Gross Sales" as defined in the Franchise Agreement of such items.

(c) Represents the total of OUR company-operated sales for each respective year-end divided by the total number of weeks the CHEDDAR'S-operated units were open for business in each respective year.

(d) Cost of sales includes the total of all food costs, costs of bar mixes and all liquor, wine and beer costs. WE have purchased many items utilized in the operation of the company operated restaurants pursuant to certain arrangements negotiated with suppliers and distributors which may have permitted CHEDDAR'S to purchase and have delivered such items at a volume discount. To the extent such arrangements are changed, are not available to YOU or are discontinued, the freight, shipping and handling costs and the mark-up imposed on such items may vary.

(e) Gross Profit is calculated by subtracting the total Cost of Sales from the Total Sales.

(f) Labor Cost includes employee and manager training expenses, employee salaries, wages and benefits and management salaries, expenses and benefits. The costs of providing group medical and dental insurance for employees will vary depending on many factors, including

but not limited to, the extent and amount of coverage provided and the loss experience of the group. YOU, with a smaller total employee base may encounter higher relative costs than US in providing comparable health benefits. Other benefits which YOU elect to provide to YOUR employees, such as the amount of vacation time and vacation pay provided to employees, are factors which will affect total labor and operating costs.

(g) YOU are not required to contribute to any advertising fund administered by US. YOU are not required to expend any minimum amount for local advertising.

(h) Repairs and maintenance expenses include repairs and maintenance on both building and equipment, plus third party contracted recurring maintenance and recurring janitorial services.

(i) Taxes refers to real estate taxes and assessments levied against the property upon which the restaurant is located. Income taxes are not included as a component of Restaurant Operating Cash Flow. Sales and use taxes are included in other costs when applicable. Sales and use taxes which are collected by US on behalf of the taxing authority are excluded from both sales and expenses. The amount of rate of taxation for all such taxes varies from jurisdiction to jurisdiction. YOU should consult with YOUR tax advisors regarding the impact such taxes will have on this analysis.

(j) Controllable Operating Expenses are those expenses over which on-site management has the ability to control, in part or in whole, and includes such items as supplies, laundry and linen, licenses, Legal Fees, uniforms, telephone, utilities, insurance (general liability, property and Workers' Compensation), security costs, credit card charges, cash overages and shortages, transportation, shipping and handling charges for food and beverage products and other items.

(k) Total Operating Cash Flow is calculated by deducting all direct Operating Expenses from Gross Profit, and is before any depreciation, interest and income taxes are deducted. You should consult with YOUR tax attorney and advisors regarding tax consequences and depreciation of assets.

The Total Operating Cash Flow does not reflect any allocation of expenses incurred by US for various corporate administrative and overhead expenses allocated on a System-wide basis such as regional, divisional and corporate management expenses, and other non-operating expenses.

DAMON'S INTERNATIONAL
4645 Executive Dr.
Columbus, OH 43220
Tel: (614) 442-7900
Fax: (614) 538-2517
E-Mail: kclark@damons.com
Internet Address: www.damons.com
Contact: Mr. Ed Williams, VP of Development

Description: DAMON'S... A dining event in a casual dining restaurant, dedicated to exceeding your expectations in all areas of operation. The 128-unit chain is famous for its award-winning BBQ ribs, prime rib and onion loaf. DAMON'S features 10' screens and is a state-of-the-art electronic sports/entertainment facility.

# Franchised Units:	129 Units
# Company-Owned Units:	21 Units
Total # Units:	150 Units
Founded In:	1979
1st Franchised In:	1982
Average Total Investment:	940K-2.7MM
Franchise Fee:	50K
On-Going Royalty:	4%
Advertising Fee:	5%
Financial Assistance: Yes(I) (D – direct, or I – indirect)	
Site Selection Assistance:	Yes
Lease Negotiation Assistance:	Yes
Contract Terms (Init./Renew):	10/3-5

Initial Training Provided: 8 Weeks In-Restaurant Training; 1 Week Training at Home Office.

Damon's International provides information regarding the earnings capability of Damon's International's franchisees. This information is in Exhibit C of this Offering Circular.

While this information is provided to assist in the analysis of a Damon's® franchise, YOU ARE ADVISED THAT EACH NEW FRANCHISEE'S INDIVIDUAL FINANCIAL RESULTS ARE LIKELY TO BE DIFFERENT FROM THE RESULTS STATED IN EXHIBIT C. THE INFORMATION SUPPLIED IS BASED UPON AVERAGES OF DAMON'S INTERNATION-ALS FRANCHISES.

Upon your request, Damon's International will make available to you the substantiating data used in preparing the averages of earnings capability presented in Exhibit C.

Exhibit C
Information Regarding Earnings Capability of Damon's International Franchise Corp.'s Franchisees
THE RESTAURANT BUSINESS IS HIGHLY COMPETITIVE AND IS AFFECTED BY, AMONG OTHER THINGS, CHANGES IN A GEOGRAPHIC AREA, CHANGES IN EATING HABITS AND PREFERENCES, LOCAL, REGIONAL AND NATIONAL ECONOMIC CONDITIONS, POPULATION TRENDS AND TRAFFIC PATTERNS. THE PRINCIPAL BASES OF COMPETITION IN THE INDUSTRY ARE THE QUALITY AND PRICE OF THE FOOD PRODUCTS SERVED, RESTAURANT LOCATION, QUALITY AND SPEED OF SERVICE, ADVERTISING, NAME IDENTIFICATION AND ATTRACTIVENESS OF FACILITIES ARE ALSO VERY IMPOR-TANT. IN ADDITION, THE ACQUISITION

OF SITES IS HIGHLY COMPETITIVE WITH OTHER RESTAURANT CHAINS AND RETAIL BUSINESS FOR SUITABLE SITES FOR THE DEVELOPMENT OF NEW RESTAURANTS.

Averages for Franchisor's Franchisee Owned and Operated Restaurants
THE AVERAGE ANNUAL AND WEEKLY SALES OF 108 FRANCHISED RESTAURANTS OPERATED CONTINUOUSLY DURING THE ONE YEAR PERIOD BEGINNING JUNE 30, 1997 AND ENDING JUNE 30, 1998 (INCLUDING 16 RESTAURANTS OPERATED BY FRANCHISOR'S AFFILIATE, DAMON'S RESTAURANT, INC.), IS:

Annual Average: $2,055,131.71

Weekly Average: $39,521.63

DAMON'S INTERNATIONALS FRANCHISEES OPERATE DAMON' S® RESTAURANTS IN A VARIETY OF FORMATS. THE FOLLOWING AVERAGE ANNUAL SALES ARE A FURTHER BREAKDOWN OF THE 108 FRANCHISED RESTAURANTS BY FORMAT TYPE DURING THE SAME ACCOUNTING PERIOD NOTED ABOVE:

Free Standing Buildings Originally Constructed According to Our Specifications (based on 28 units): $2,454,836.17 [1]

All Free Standing Buildings Including Those Converted to Accommodate Damon's® Restaurants (based on 60 units — including the 28 units above): $2,271,240.82 [2]

In-Line Retail Space (Strip-Centers) (based on 29 units): $1,958,784.39 [3]

Hotel Locations (based on 19 units): $1,519,738.33 [4]

TO FURTHER ASSIST YOU IN ANALYZING THE EARNINGS AND OPERATING COSTS INVOLVED WITH A DAMON'S® RESTAURANT THE FOLLOWING INFORMATION WAS TAKEN FROM THE OPERATION OF OUR AFFILIATE'S (DAMON'S RESTAURANT, INC'S) 16 FRANCHISE LOCATIONS DURING THE PERIOD OF JUNE 30, 1997 THROUGH JUNE 30, 1998. ALTHOUGH OUR AFFILIATE OPERATES UNDER FRANCHISE AGREEMENTS AT EACH LOCATION, YOU SHOULD CONSIDER THESE FIGURES TO BE TAKEN FROM COMPANY-OPERATED LOCATIONS SINCE OUR AFFILIATE IS SO CLOSELY ALIGNED WITH DAMON'S INTERNATIONAL:

Category	Free-Standing	In-Line	Hotel	Overall
No. of Units	7	7	2	16
Sales	100%	100%	100%	100%
Cost of Sales	32–35%	31–34%	32–33%	31–35%
Gross Margin	65–68%	66–69%	67–68%	65–69%
Labor Expense	25–32%	28–31%	26–36%	25–36%
Contribution to Profit	35–42%	36–41%	32–40%	32–42%
Operating Expenses	21–26%	21–28%	24–26%	21–28%
Income*	14–25%	13–22%	9–20%	9–25%

*These averages represent income before depreciation, amortization, occupancy costs, royalties, interest income and expense, corporate, general and administrative expense, management fees, and income taxes.

Definition of Certain Accounting Terms Used in the above Table:

Sales means the food and beverage sales of the restaurant.

Cost of Sales means the cost of the food and beverages sold.

Labor Expense means salaries and hourly wages, worker's compensation, FICA, state and federal unemployment taxes.

Operating Expenses means the cost incurred to operate the restaurant: Payroll Expenses (which include wages, salaries, vacation, payroll taxes and worker's compensation), Controllable Expenses (which include, but are not limited to, advertising, china, glassware, silver, cleaning, supplies, dining room supplies, discounts, linens, office supplies, kitchen supplies, paper goods, repairs, uniforms, gas, electric, water and sewage, trash, telephone and service contacts), and other Miscellaneous Operating Expenses (such as accounting, credit card charges, health insurance, subscriptions and travel).

ALL OF THE INFORMATION PRESENTED IN THIS EXHIBIT ARE AVERAGES OF FRANCHISES OPEN DURING THE PERIODS SPECIFIED, AND SHOULD NOT BE CONSIDERED AS THE ACTUAL OR POTENTIAL SALES.

THESE SALES, PROFITS, INCOME OR EARNINGS ARE AVERAGES OF SPECIFIC FRANCHISE(S) AND SHOULD NOT BE CONSIDERED AS THE ACTUAL OR POTENTIAL SALES, PROFITS OR EARNINGS THAT WILL BE REALIZED BY ANY OTHER FRANCHISE. WE DO NOT CLAIM THAT ANY FRANCHISEE CAN EXPECT TO ATTAIN THESE SALES, PROFITS OR EARNINGS.

THE RESTAURANT INDUSTRY IS INTENSELY COMPETITIVE BASED ON PRICE, SERVICE, THE TYPE AND QUALITY OF FOOD OFFERED, LOCATION AND OTHER FACTORS. THE COMPANY HAS MANY WELL ESTABLISHED COMPETITORS WITH SUBSTANTIALLY GREATER FINANCIAL RESOURCES AND A LONGER HISTORY OF OPERATIONS THAN OURS, INCLUDING COMPETITORS ALREADY ESTABLISHED IN REGIONS IN WHICH A FRANCHISEE MAY BE CONSIDERING A RESTAURANT.

UPON YOUR REQUEST, WE WILL MAKE AVAILABLE TO YOU THE SUBSTANTIATING DATA USED IN PREPARING THE ABOVE AVERAGES.

[1] A breakdown of the units shows that 1 unit averaged over $4 million in sales, 3 units averaged between $3 million and $4 million in sales, 6 units averaged between $2.5 million and $3 million in sales, 11 units averaged between $2 million and $2.5 million in sales, and 7 units average between $1.6 million and $2 million in sales.

[2] A breakdown of the units shows that 1 unit averaged over $4 million in sales, 6 units average between $3 million and $4 million in sales, 10 units averaged between $2.5 million and $3 million in sales, 22 units avenged between $2 million and $2.5 million in sales, 14 units averaged between $1.6 million and $2 million in sales, and 7 units averaged between $1.1 million and $1.6 million in sales.

[3] A breakdown of the units shows that 5 units averaged over $2.5 million in sales, 9 units averaged between $2 million and $2.5 million in sales, 9 units avenged between $1.6 million and $2 million in sales, and 6 units averaged between $1.1 million and $1.6 million in sales.

[4] A breakdown of the units shows that 4 units averaged between $2 million and $2.3 million in sales, 4 units average between $1.5 million and $2 million in sales, and 11 units average between $1 million and $1.5 million in sales.

GOLDEN CORRAL FAMILY STEAKHOUSE
5151 Glenwood Ave., # 300
Raleigh, NC 27626-0502
Tel: (800) 284-5673 (919) 881-4647
Fax: (919) 881-5252
E-Mail:
Internet Address: www.goldencorralrest.com
Contact: Mr. Peter Charland, VP Franchise
Development

Description: We offer nearly 25 years of proven success in the family steakhouse market segment. The metromarket concept features in-store bakery, dessert bar and our Golden Choice Buffet, in addition to our up-dated core menu. The layout of our metro market restaurant, as well as our expanded food offering, enables each customer to define his own experience each time he visits a GOLDEN CORRAL.

# Franchised Units:	297 Units
# Company-Owned Units:	<u>152</u> Units
Total # Units:	449 Units
Founded In:	1973
1st Franchised In:	1986
Average Total Investment:	1.2-3.3MM
Franchise Fee:	40K
On-Going Royalty:	4%
Advertising Fee:	2%
Financial Assistance:No (D – direct, or I – indirect)	
Site Selection Assistance:	Yes
Lease Negotiation Assistance:	No
Contract Terms (Init./Renew):	15/5
Initial Training Provided:12 Weeks Headquarters and Field.	

We do not make any representations or statements of actual, or average, or projected, or forecasted sales, profits, or earnings to franchisees except for the information which appears in this Item. We specifically instruct our sales personnel, agents, employees, and officers that they are not permitted to make any claims or statements as to the earnings, sales, or profits, or prospects or chances of success, nor do we authorize them to represent or estimate dollar figures as to any franchisee's operation. Any representations as to earnings, sales, profits, or prospects or chances for success, except as set forth in this Item, are unauthorized.

You should disregard any unauthorized information, whether oral or written, concerning the actual, average, projected, forecasted, or potential sales, costs, income or profits, or the prospects or chances of success, or representations or estimated dollar figures as to a franchisee's operation. You should immediately notify Golden Corral of any such unauthorized information or representation by contacting either Mr. Larry I. Tate, Vice President of Franchising, or Mr. Robert B. Heyward, Vice President and Secretary, in writing at P.O. Box 29502, Raleigh, North Carolina 27626.

Actual results vary from franchise to franchise, and we cannot estimate the results of a particular franchise. A new franchisee's results are likely to differ from the results shown in this Item. We recommend that you make your own independent investigation to determine whether or not the franchise may be profitable, and consult with an attorney and other advisors prior to executing the Area Development Agreement or Franchise Agreement.

At your written request, we will make available to you for inspection and review all data utilized in compiling the results presented in this Item.

A. Statement of Average Monthly Sales, Selected Expenses and Operating Income for GCC Operated Restaurants
The summary statements set forth in this Section A are statements of the average monthly net sales, operating costs and expenses, and net operating income based upon actual sales for the period January 1, 1998 through December 30, 1998, by building design, for the 116 GCC operated Restaurants utilizing the Metro Market, GC-11M or GC-11S building designs, and which had been in operation at least 6 months as of December 31,

1998. On December 31, 1998, there were a total of 125 Restaurants using one of these 3 Restaurant designs, but 9 of these 125 Restaurants had not been in operation for at least 6 months and, therefore, their results are not included in the summary statements.

Summary Statements Average Monthly Results

Category	Metro		GC-11M		GC-11S	
	Amount	% of Sales	Amount	% of Sales	Amount	% of Sales
Net Sales (Note 5)	$237,453	100.00%	$205,003	100.00%	$143,601	100.00%
Operating Costs and Expenses:						
Food Cost	92,157	38.81%	80,742	39.39%	56,935	39.65%
Labor Related Expenses (Note 6)	61,164	25.76%	54,254	26.46%	39,232	27.32%
Controllable Expenses (Note 7)	27,287	11.49%	23,119	11.28%	17,092	11.90%
Total Operating Costs & Expenses (Note 8)	180,608	76.06%	158,115	77.13%	113,259	78.87%
Net Operating Income (Notes 9, 10)	$56,845	23.94%	$46,888	22.87%	$30,342	21.13%

Included in the above chart are 3 GC-11M Restaurants that utilize a specialized equipment package and floor plan (hereinafter referred to as "Strata Restaurants"). These 3 Strata Restaurants have been in operation for at least 6 months but less than one year, and their average monthly sales and net operating income are as follows:

Location	Average Monthly Sales	Average Monthly Net Operating Income
Durham, NC	$332,345	$84,233
Fayetteville, NC	$243,296	$61,203
Albany, GA	$260,070	$49,822

The accompanying Notes form an integral part of this summary statement

Notes to Summary Statement of Average Monthly Results of GCC Operated Restaurants:

Note 1: The number of Restaurants utilizing the Metro Market, GC-11M, or GC-11S building designs operated by GCC as of December 31, 1998 and in operation for at least 6 months as of December 31, 1998 by building design type, is as follows:

Building Type	Operated at December 31, 1998	Open At Least 6 Months
Metro (aka GC-10)	57	57
GC-11M	37	30
GC-11S	31	29

Note 2: The summary statements reflect only operating expenses, and do not include capital expenses or fixed expenses such as (but not limited to) any land, building and/or equipment rent, debt service, depreciation, advertising, administrative expenses such as accounting or legal expenses, taxes, licenses or insurance. These expenses also do not include (i) a 4% royalty on Gross Sales which is payable by a franchisee; (ii) the cost of any additional supervisory personnel; or (iii) any expenses for transportation, room and board for attending training refresher courses.

Note 3: The 57 Metro Restaurants are located in the states of Colorado (1); Florida (3); Georgia (1); Missouri (1); New Mexico (3); North Carolina (10); Oklahoma (5); and Texas (33). The 30 GC-11M Restaurants are located in the states of Alabama (1); Colorado (2); Florida (6); Georgia (1); Kansas (1); Kentucky (1); New Mexico (1); North Carolina (8);

South Carolina (1); and Texas (8). The 29 GC-11S Restaurants are located in the states of Colorado (1); Florida (3); Kansas (1); Kentucky (1); Missouri (2); New Mexico (3); North Carolina (4); Oklahoma (5); and Texas (9).

Note 4: The summary statements are based on the unaudited profit and loss statements prepared by GCC in accordance with generally accepted accounting principles for the period January 1, 1998 through December 30, 1998.

Note 5: Net sales reflect the total average monthly sales for the Restaurants included in the sample, and do not include sales taxes. Variations among Restaurants may be caused by a variety of factors, such as location, demographics, general economic conditions, weather conditions, menu mix, competition and other seasonal factors as well as the efforts of the individual Restaurant management team. The range of variation is as follows:

Net Sales	Metro	GC-11M	GC-11S
Average From Summary Statements	$237,453	$205,003	$143,601
Range of Sales: Highest	$367,853	$332,345	$212,360
Lowest	$106,144	$125,261	$85,254
Number of Units Above Average	27 (47%)	16 (53%)	13 (45%)
Number of Units Below Average	30 (53%)	14 (47%)	16 (55%)

Note 6: Labor related expenses include: (i) the salary and bonuses paid by GCC to management for each Restaurant; (ii) the average expense for employees' wages, including pre-opening training wages for all other Restaurant employees; and (iii) amounts paid or accrued by GCC for employee payroll taxes, group insurance and workers' compensation.

The management team generally receives a monthly salary and a monthly bonus based upon the operating cash flow of their Restaurant. In 1998, these amounts were:

	Management Level	Total Monthly Avg. Salary & Bonus
Metro	1 General Manager 2 Associate Managers	$12,350
GC-11M	1 General Manager 1 Associate Manager	$8,738
GC-11S	1 General Manager	$4,887

As of January 1, 1999, (i) it is a requirement that all GC-11S Restaurants must have a General Manager and an Associate Manager instead of only a General Manager as shown above; and (ii) any GC-11M Restaurant with annualized sales of more than $2,700,000 must have 3 managers instead of the 2 managers as reflected in the chart.

GCC provides group insurance for Restaurant employees, and pays approximately 80% of this expense for the management team and their dependents in each Restaurant. Group insurance for other employees is at the employee's expense. This group insurance coverage is not available to franchisees. You may establish your own insurance program if desired.

Workers' compensation expense is based upon GCC's experience rating. Workers compensation expense varies at each location, based upon state rates and GCC's experience. The experience rating for a franchisee may be different than GCC's experience rating.

Local market conditions and state and federal minimum wage requirements may affect wages and labor related expense.

Note 7: Controllable expenses include utilities purchased prior to opening and included as an expense item not otherwise in equipment, maintenance expense, and sanitation supplies.

Utilities expenses vary significantly with sales volume but remain relatively stable as a percentage of sales. Utilities expenses also may be dependent upon factors such as local utility rates and weather conditions.

Maintenance expenses reflect maintenance at newly constructed facilities with new equipment. Maintenance expenses may be affected by the age and condition of the building and/or equipment, quality of construction, environmental impact and other factors.

Note 8: The range of variation of total operating costs and expenses is as follows:

Operating Costs and Expenses	Metro	GC-11M	GC-11S
Average from Summary Statements	$180,608	$158,115	$113,259
Range: Highest	$261,097	$248,112	$157,921
Lowest	$87,816	$100,283	$74,020
Number of Units Above Average	27 (47%)	16 (53%)	16 (55%)
Number of Units Below Average	30 (53%)	14 (47%)	13 (45%)

Note 9: The range of variation of net operating income is as follows:

Net Operating Income	Metro	GC-11M	GC-11S
Average from Summary Statements	$56,845	$46,888	$30,342
Range: Highest	$106,756	$84,233	$54,439
Lowest	$722	$9,381	$7,231
Number of Units Above Average	32 (56%)	18 (60%)	15 (52%)
Number of Units Below Average	25 (44%)	12 (40%)	14 (48%)

Note 10: Net operating income excludes those expenses described in Note 2. The amount of some of your fixed expenses, such as rent or debt service related to land, building and/or equipment, will depend, in part, on your total initial investment. See Item 7 for an estimate of your initial investment.

B. Statement of Average Sales of Franchised Restaurants
The following table provides sales information for the period January 1, 1998 through December 30, 1998, by building design, about the 134 franchised Restaurants utilizing the Metro Market, GC-11M, or GC-11S building designs which had been in operation at least 6 months as of December 31, 1998. On December 31, 1998, we had 9 other franchised Restaurants which utilized one of these 3 Restaurants designs that had not been in operation for at least 6 months as of December 31, 1998, and, accordingly, their results are not included in this table.

	Metro	GC-11M	GC-11S
Number operating at December 31, 1998	71	47	25
Number operating at least 6 months	69	44	21
Average monthly sales	$254,495	$207,017	$158,772
Range of sales: Highest	$385,639	$356,446	$219,318
Lowest	$116,739	$116,543	$99,994
Number Above Average	34 (49%)	22 (50%)	11 (52%)
Number Below Average	35 (51%)	22 (50%)	10 (48%)

We have not audited those franchisee-prepared results which have been reported to us by our franchisees, but have no reasonable basis to question their reliability. These Restaurants are located in Alabama, Arizona, Arkansas, California, Colorado, Delaware, Florida, Georgia, Indiana, Kansas, Kentucky, Louisiana, Maryland, Michigan, Missouri, Mississippi, Montana, Nebraska, New Mexico, New York, North Carolina, Ohio, Oklahoma, Pennsylvania, South Carolina, South Dakota, Tennessee, Texas, Utah, Virginia, Washington, and West Virginia.

This table does not include the results of those franchised Restaurants described in Item 1 who do not utilize a Metro Market, GC-11M, or GC-11S Restaurant design. There are 152 such Restaurants and they utilize older and smaller Restaurant design configurations, none of which are currently being built.

THE RESULTS WHICH APPEAR IN THIS ITEM SHOULD NOT BE CONSIDERED AS THE ACTUAL OR PROBABLE SALES, INCOME, GROSS OR NET PROFITS THAT WILL BE REALIZED BY ANY FRANCHISEE. WE DO NOT REPRESENT THAT YOU CAN EXPECT TO ATTAIN SUCH SALES, INCOME, GROSS OR NET PROFITS. THERE IS NO ASSURANCE THAT YOU WILL DO AS WELL. IF YOU RELY UPON OUR FIGURES, YOU MUST ACCEPT THE RISK OF NOT DOING AS WELL.

HUDDLE HOUSE® RESTAURANTS

HUDDLE HOUSE RESTAURANT
2969 E. Ponce de Leon Ave.
Decatur, GA 30030
Tel: (800) 478-9089 (404) 377-5700
Fax: (404) 377-0497
E-Mail: jbardill@msn.com
Internet Address: www.huddlehouse.com
Contact: Mr. John Bardill, Director Franchise Development

Description: HUDDLE HOUSE restaurants are 24-hour, diner-style restaurants which offer a wide variety of tasty menu items for all day parts. Our 35 years of experience has allowed us to develop a 1-stop opportunity for our franchise owners. We will show you the way, from initial site selection and construction and training, marketing and on-going operations support. We also maintain competitively-priced food and equipment divisions for the benefit of our franchised system.

# Franchised Units:	306 Units
# Company-Owned Units:	24 Units
Total # Units:	330 Units
Founded In:	1964
1st Franchised In:	1966
Average Total Investment:	40-750K
Franchise Fee:	20K
On-Going Royalty:	4%
Advertising Fee:	0.5%
Financial Assistance:N/A (D – direct, or I – indirect)	
Site Selection Assistance:	Yes
Lease Negotiation Assistance:	Yes
Contract Terms (Init./Renew):	15/5x3
Initial Training Provided:5 Weeks Metro Atlanta, GA; 7-10 Days On-Site Pre-Opening and Opening.	

HHI does not furnish or authorize its sales personnel to furnish any oral or written information concerning the potential or projected sales, costs, income or profits of a HUDDLE HOUSE® restaurant.

Below are certain UNAUDITED historical sales and selected cost figures. Substantiation of the data used in preparing these sales and cost amounts are available upon your reasonable request.

THE FIGURES BELOW ARE AVERAGES AND SHOULD NOT BE CONSIDERED AS THE ACTUAL OR POTENTIAL SALES OR COSTS THAT YOU WILL REALIZE. HHI DOES NOT REPRESENT OR INFER THAT YOU CAN EXPECT TO ATTAIN THE SAME OR SIMILAR SALES OR COSTS.

THE SELECTED COSTS ARE NOT THE ONLY COSTS INVOLVED IN THE OPERATION OF A FRANCHISE. YOU SHOULD

SEEK THE COUNSEL OF A QUALIFIED FINANCIAL CONSULTANT TO HELP YOU DETERMINE ALL COSTS INVOLVED.

YOUR FINANCIAL RESULTS ARE LIKELY TO DIFFER, POSSIBLY MATERIALLY, FROM THOSE SHOWN BELOW.

Interim Sales — New Franchised Units (sales from May 3, 1998 – January 30, 1999 for fiscal year ending May 1, 1999)

Average of reported daily sales = $1,515
Highest daily sales avg. reported = $2,963
Lowest daily sales average reported = $698

7 of 19 (36.8%) units reported average daily sales above the new unit average.

NOTE: These figures are based on unaudited daily sales reported to HHI by its franchisees during the 39 week period ending 1/30/99 for 19 new franchises which opened for business during such period. The total number of days reported for the 19 franchisees was 1,966. The average number of days reported was 103. The highest number of days reported was 272. The lowest number of days reported was 0 which relates to a unit that opened January 14, 1999.

Interim Food Cost (costs from May 3, 1998 – January 30, 1999 for fiscal year ending May 1, 1999)

Average of reported food cost percentages = 31.45%
Highest percentage food cost reported = 46.52%
Lowest percentage food cost reported = 24.29%

4 out of 12 (33.3%) units reported food cost percentages at or below the average.

Interim Supply Cost (costs from May 3, 1998 – January 30, 1999 for fiscal year ending May 1, 1999)

Avg. of reported supply cost % = 1.15%

Highest % supply cost reported 4.28%
Lowest % supply cost reported = 0.00%
(4 units reported $0 supply cost)

6 out of 12 (50.0%) units reported supply cost percentages at or below the average.

Interim Labor Cost (costs from May 3, 1998 – January 30, 1999 for fiscal year ending May 1, 1999)

Avg. of reported labor cost % = 35.41%
Highest percentage labor cost % = 56.03%
Lowest percentage labor cost % = 22.68%

7 out of 12 (58.3%) units reported labor cost percentages at or below the average.

Interim Utility Cost (costs from May 3, 1998 – January 30, 1999 for fiscal year ending May 1, 1999)

Avg. of reported utility cost % = 4.42%
Highest % utility cost reported = 14.59%
Lowest % utility cost reported = 0.39%

8 out of 12 (66.7%) units reported percentage utility cost percentages at or below the average.

Interim Maintenance Cost (costs from May 3, 1998 – January 30, 1999 for fiscal year ending May 1, 1999)

Average of reported maintenance cost percentages = 1.14%
Highest percentage maintenance cost reported 8.53%
Lowest percentage maintenance cost reported = 0% (one unit reported $0 maintenance cost)

7 out of 12 (58.3%) units reported maintenance cost percentages at or below the average.

NOTE: The selected costs presented above are based on unaudited profit and loss statements as reported to HHI by its franchisees. The costs represent each franchisee's most recent 9 month period (or the greatest portion reported) which ended within HHI's fiscal year 5/3/98 – 5/1/99. The number of reporting periods was 39 out of a possible 68, which represents 57.35% of possible reporting periods. The average number of reporting periods reported per franchisee was 3.25. The lowest number of periods from reporting franchisees was 1 period; the highest number of periods reported for any franchise was 6 periods. The number of units operating at least one month under a franchise agreement during this period was 15. Reporting was received from 12 (80.0%) units.

Sales — New Franchised Units

Average of reported daily sales = $1,257
Highest daily sales avg. reported = $2,050
Lowest daily sales average reported = $768

10 of 20 (50.0%) units reported average daily sales above the new unit average.

NOTE: These figures are based on unaudited daily sales reported to HHI by its franchisees during HHI's 52-week period within the fiscal year ending 5/2/98 for 20 new franchises which opened for business during such year. The total number of days reported for the 20 franchisees was 4,714. The average number of days reported was 236. The highest number of days reported was 354. The lowest number of days reported was 5.

Sales — All Franchised Units

Annual Average of all reported daily sales = $1,187
Highest daily sales avg. reported = $2,475
Lowest daily sales average reported = $567

134 of 299 (44.82%) units reported average daily sales at or above the average.

NOTE: These sales are based on unaudited daily sales reported to HHI by its franchisees during HHI's 52-week period within the fiscal year ended 5/2/98 for 299 franchised units operating during this period. The total number of days reported was 102,906. The average number of days reported was 344. The highest number of days reported was 364. The lowest number of days reported was 5.

Food Cost

Avg. of reported food cost % = 29.42%
Highest % food cost reported = 44.19%
Lowest % food cost reported = 21.03%

113 out of 208 (54.33%) units reported food cost percentages at or below the average.

Supply Cost

Avg. of reported supply cost % = 2.08%
Highest % supply cost reported = 5.70%
Lowest % supply cost reported = 0.19%
(27 units reported $0 supply cost)

102 out of 208 (49.04%) units reported supply cost percentages at or below the average.

Avg. of reported labor cost % = 25.20%
Highest % labor cost reported = 55.19%
Lowest % labor cost reported = 12.70%

108 out of 208 (51.93%) units reported labor cost percentages at or below the avg.

Labor Cost

Average of labor cost % = 25.20%
Highest % labor cost reported = 55.19%
Lowest % labor cost reported = 12.70%

108 out of 208 (51.93%) units reported labor cost percentages at or below the avg.

Utility Cost

Avg. of reported utility cost % = 5.85%
Highest % utility cost reported = 10.27%
Lowest % utility cost reported = 2.82%

101 out of 208 (48.56%) units reported percentage utility cost percentages at or below the average.

Maintenance Cost

Average of reported maintenance cost percentages = 2.25%
Highest percentage maintenance cost reported = 14.71%
Lowest percentage maintenance cost reported = 0.08%
(two units reported $0 maintenance cost)

127 out of 208 (61.06%) units reported maintenance cost percentages at or below the average.

NOTE: The selected costs presented above are based on unaudited profit and loss statements as reported to HHI by its franchisees. The costs represent each franchisee's most recent 12 month period (or the greatest portion reported) which ended within HHI's fiscal year 5/4/97 – 5/2/98. The number of reporting periods was 1,960 out of a possible 3,393, which represents 57.77% of possible reporting periods. The average number of reporting periods reported per franchisee was 9.43. The lowest number of periods from reporting franchisees was 3 periods; the highest number of periods reported for any franchise was 12 periods. The number of units operating at least one month under a franchise agreement during this period was 296. Reporting was received from 208 (70.27%) units.

Sales — Specific HHI Company-Owned Units

Average daily sales reported for all company operated units = $935
Highest daily sales avg. reported = $1,575
Lowest daily sales average reported = $ 593

14 out of 37 units (37.84%) meet or surpass above average.

The figures shown above are for 37 units that were operated by HHI for all or part of the 52-week period May 4, 1997 – May 2, 1998. The averages are based on 10,058 total reported days of sales. The average number of days reported for these units was 272. The highest number of days reported was 364. The lowest number of days reported was 2.

22 of the above units were specific HHI operated units for the complete 52-week period:

Average daily sales reported for 52-week units = $915
Highest daily sales avg. reported = $1,575
Lowest daily sales average reported = $ 594

9 out of 22 units (40.91%) meet or surpass above average.

PEPE'S MEXICAN RESTAURANT
1325 W. 15th St.
Chicago, IL 60608
Tel: (312) 733-2500

Fax: (312) 733-2564
E-Mail:
Internet Address:
Contact: Mr. Edwin A. Ptak, Corporate Counsel

Description: A full-service Mexican restaurant, serving a complete line of Mexican food, with liquor, beer and wine. Complete training and help in remodeling, site selection, equipment purchasing and running the restaurant provided.

# Franchised Units:	56 Units
# Company-Owned Units:	1 Units
Total # Units:	57 Units
Founded In:	1967
1st Franchised In:	1968
Average Total Investment:	75-300K

Franchise Fee:	15K
On-Going Royalty:	4%
Advertising Fee:	3%
Financial Assistance:No (D – direct, or I – indirect)	
Site Selection Assistance:	Yes
Lease Negotiation Assistance:	Yes
Contract Terms (Init./Renew):	20
Initial Training Provided: 4 Weeks Headquarters.	

As of December 31, 1998, Pepe's Incorporated had 55 Franchise units and 1 company unit operating in the states of Illinois and Indiana. Listed below is a schedule of the actual Reported Net Sales amounts for these units divided into 4 sales ranges. The term Reports Net Sales is defined as gross sales less sales tax. Pepe's is Franchising two types of restaurants. The first type is our Pepe's Mexican Restaurant and it has a full liquor license, waiter or waitress services and serves a full menu of Mexican food. The second type of restaurant is a Pepe's Mexican Express concept which has limited seating, no liquor, counter service and a limited menu. The sales for the Express units are typically lower than the full menu Pepe's Mexican Restaurant. I have not included those units which did not report sales for the full year or were not in operation for the entire year.

Substantiation of the data used to prepare this statement will be available to a prospective Franchisee upon demand.

The sales figures utilized are based on the sales figures reported by the Franchisees to Pepe's. While Franchisor has audited several restaurants during last year, it can't independently verify the sales figures of every unit.

THESE SALES, PROFITS OR EARNINGS ARE AVERAGES OF SPECIFIC FRANCHISES AND SHOULD NOT BE CONSIDERED AS THE ACTUAL OR POTENTIAL SALES, PROFITS OR EARNINGS THAT WILL BE REALIZED BY ANY OTHER FRANCHISEE. THE FRANCHISOR DOES NOT REPRESENT THAT ANY FRANCHISEE CAN EXPECT TO ATTAIN THESE SALES, PROFITS OR EARNINGS.

Range of Sales	Number of Restaurants	Percentage
$200,000.00–300,000.00	14	35%
$300,000.00–400,000.00	15	38%
$400,000.00–500,000.00	6	15%
Over $500,000.00	5	12%
	40	100%

PERKINS RESTAURANT & BAKERY
6075 Poplar Ave., # 800
Memphis, TN 38119-4709
Tel: (800) 877-7375 (901) 766-6400
Fax: (901) 766-6482
E-Mail: franchise@perkinsrestaurants.com
Internet Address: www.perkinsrestaurants.com

Contact: Mr. Robert J. Winters, VP Franchise Development

Description: Full-service family-style restaurant, offering breakfast, lunch and dinner, along with proprietary bakery items at moderate prices.

# Franchised Units:	332 Units
# Company-Owned Units:	<u>140</u> Units
Total # Units:	472 Units
Founded In:	1958
1st Franchised In:	1958

Average Total Investment:	1.0-1.7MM
Franchise Fee:	40K
On-Going Royalty:	4%
Advertising Fee:	3%
Financial Assistance:No (D – direct, or I – indirect)	
Site Selection Assistance:	Yes
Lease Negotiation Assistance:	Yes
Contract Terms (Init./Renew):	20/10-20
Initial Training Provided:8-12 Weeks	
Management Training at Various Locations.	

Average Sales and Selected Costs of Restaurants Owned and Operated by the Licensor

The Schedule of Restaurant Financial Data (the "Schedule") discloses the average sales and selected costs of 133 Perkins restaurants owned and operated by Perkins (which comprise all restaurants owned and operated by Perkins with the exception of seven restaurants opened and three restaurants closed during 1998) for the entire fiscal year ending December 31, 1998 (referred to as the "Restaurants").

The following table groups the Restaurants into ranges of annual sales volume disclosing the number of Restaurants within each range and further disclosing the average sales volume of each range.

	Average Annual Sales Volume	Sales Volume Range of Restaurants Included	Number of Restaurants in Range
Average Restaurant No. 1	$1,232,382	$ 800,000–1,539,000	43
Average Restaurant No. 2	$1,783,673	$1,540,000–2,049,000	45
Average Restaurant No. 3	$2,396,148	$2,050,000–3,167,000	45

The Restaurants are distributed throughout the north central and midwestern United States with the greatest concentrations in Minnesota, Wisconsin, Missouri, Nebraska, Iowa, and Florida. They are located predominantly in metropolitan areas on or near major traffic thoroughfares. The buildings housing the Restaurants are predominantly single-purpose, one story and free-standing, seating from 90 to 250 guests at one time, which are comparable to the restaurants expected to be operated pursuant to the License Agreement.

The location of the Restaurants used to compile the information disclosed in the Schedule are categorized by state, as follows:

Average Restaurant No. 1 (43 locations): Florida — 5, Illinois — 4, Iowa — 5, Kansas — 2, Michigan — 2, Minnesota — 11, Missouri — 6, Nebraska — 2, Oklahoma — 3, Wisconsin —3.

Average Restaurant No. 2 (45 locations): Florida — 4, Iowa — 6, Michigan — 2, Minnesota — 15, Missouri — 2, Nebraska — 3, Kansas — 2, North Dakota — 2, Wisconsin — 4, Pennsylvania — 3, Illinois — 2.

Average Restaurant No 3 (45 locations): Florida — 10, Illinois — 2, Iowa — 5, Michigan — 1, Minnesota — 12, Missouri

— 2, Wisconsin — 7, Pennsylvania — 4, North Dakota — 1, Tennessee — 1.

Substantially the same services were offered by Perkins to the Restaurants as are provided to the licensees; however, Perkins does not provide certain services to licensees which are normally provided by the owner such as financing, accounting (unless the licensee has elected to enter the Accounting Services Agreement), legal, personnel, construction (unless the licensee has elected to use Perkins' Construction Management Program), management, financial and food and labor cost systems.

The Restaurants offered substantially the same products and services to the public as the restaurants to be operated pursuant to the License Agreement.

The following Schedule was prepared on a basis consistent with generally accepted accounting principles and the same accounting system was used for each Restaurant. The figures used in the Schedule are based on an annual performance.

SUCH SALES, INCOME, GROSS OR NET PROFITS ARE OF SPECIFIC RESTAURANTS OWNED AND OPERATED BY PERKINS AND SHOULD NOT BE CONSIDERED AS THE ACTUAL OR PROBABLE SALES, INCOME, GROSS OR NET PROFITS THAT WILL BE REALIZED BY ANY LICENSEE. PERKINS DOES NOT REPRESENT THAT ANY LICENSEE CAN EXPECT TO ATTAIN SUCH SALES, INCOME, GROSS OR NET PROFITS. YOUR RESULTS WILL VARY AND SUCH VARIANCES MAY BE MATERIAL AND ADVERSE.

Substantiation of the data used in preparing the Schedule will be made available upon reasonable request.

THE INFORMATION PRESENTED BELOW HAS NOT BEEN AUDITED.

Perkins Family Restaurants, L.P. Schedule of Restaurant Financial Data (Dollars in Thousands)

	Average Restaurant No. 1		Average Restaurant No. 2		Average Restaurant No. 3	
	Amount	% of Annual Sales	Amount	% of Annual Sales	Amount	% of Annual Sales
Net Food Sales	$ 1,232	100.0%	$ 1,783	100.0%	$ 2,396	100.0%
Food Cost	325	26.4%	464	26.0%	619	25.8%
Gross Profit	907	73.6%	1,319	74.0%	1,777	74.2%
Labor:						
Mgmt	80	6.5%	105	5.9%	130	5.4%
Hourly	303	24.6%	430	24.1%	548	22.9%
Total	383	31.1%	535	30.0%	678	28.3%
Benefits:						
Payroll tax	43	3.5%	60	3.4%	77	3.2%
Vacation/sick	10	0.8%	14	0.8%	20	0.8%
Work comp/other	13	1.1%	17	0.9%	22	0.9%
Total	66	5.4%	91	5.1%	119	5.0%
DOE						
Supplies	34	2.8%	47	2.6%	64	2.7%
Menus/guest cks/ Placemats/toys	3	0.2%	5	0.3%	5	0.2%

	Average Restaurant No. 1		Average Restaurant No. 2		Average Restaurant No. 3	
	Amount	% of Annual Sales	Amount	% of Annual Sales	Amount	% of Annual Sales
Uniforms/laundry	6	0.5%	7	0.4%	8	0.3%
Smallwares/Other	1	0.1%	2	0.1%	3	0.1%
Total	44	3.6%	61	3.4%	80	3.3%
R&M	19	1.5%	26	1.4%	29	1.2%
Outside Services	20	1.6%	20	1.1%	27	1.1%
Utilities	58	4.7%	65	3.6%	80	3.3%
LSM	21	1.7%	29	1.6%	33	1.4%
Administrative						
Travel	0	0.0%	1	0.1%	0	0.0%
Classified advertising	1	0.1%	1	0.1%	1	0.0%
Office supplies	2	0.2%	3	0.2%	3	0.1%
Legal/bank fees/bad debt	9	0.7%	12	0.7%	15	0.6%
Miscellaneous	3	0.2%	3	0.2%	3	0.1%
Total	15	1.2%	20	1.1%	22	0.9%
Total Operating Expense	626	50.8%	847	47.4%	1,068	44.6%
Total Controllable Income	281	22.8%	472	26.5%	709	29.6%
Non-Controllable Expense						
Advertising	38	3.1%	55	3.1%	73	3.0%
Property insurance	8	0.6%	10	0.6%	12	0.5%
Property taxes	18	1.5%	23	1.3%	22	0.9%
Employee insurance	22	1.8%	27	1.5%	33	1.4%
Other	7	0.6%	12	0.7%	16	0.7%
Total	93	7.5%	127	7.1%	156	6.5%
Cash flow from Operations	188	15.3%	345	19.4%	553	23.1%
Rent	92	7.5%	91	5.1%	109	4.5%
Net Cash flow from Operations	$96	7.8%	$254	14.3%	$444	18.5%

The average statements shown in the Schedule DO NOT include the following items of expense which have to be calculated and included separately for every restaurant:

a. Royalty Fees consistent with current contractual requirements under the License Agreement (see Exhibit B).

b. Depreciation of property and equipment.

c. Interest or other financing costs for land, buildings, equipment and inventory.

d. Initial license fee and organization costs (see Item 5).

e. Any accounting, legal or management fees.

f. Income taxes, property taxes, and insurance costs.

These excluded items affect the net income and/or cash flow of any restaurant and must be carefully considered and evaluated by any prospective licensee. The actual performance of any restaurant will depend on a number of factors specific to the property including, but not limited to, the above factors.

The Restaurants and restaurants to be operated pursuant to the License Agreement have the following similarities:

a. Each Restaurant operates under the name "Perkins," "Perkins 'Cake & Steak," "Perkins Restaurant" or "Perkins Family Restaurant."

b. Each Restaurant generally offers the same selection of menu items and the majority are open 24 hours a day.

Sales and operating results of the Restaurants and the restaurants to be operated pursuant to the License Agreement are affected by the following:

a. Economic and weather conditions of various geographic areas.

b. Competition from a variety of other restaurants, including fast food businesses. Some restaurants have greater competition than others.

c. Different acquisition, development construction and property costs.

d. Local property tax rates.

e. State laws affecting employee costs.

f. Different traffic counts, accessibility and visibility. The location of each restaurant may have a significant impact on sales and operating income.

g. Different benefits from advertising. Some Restaurants do not receive the benefits of tele-

vision advertising. Some Restaurants are not grouped in such a way that local television or other media advertising can be efficiently obtained.

h. Although each Restaurant has seating and parking, the amount of seating and parking varies among the Restaurants.i. All Restaurants have been in business for different periods of time and therefore have experienced varying periods of time to become established in their respective markets.

j. Each licensee may set its own prices for menu items.

k. Each Restaurant may experience varying food costs due to geographic area and economies of scale due to the grouping of Restaurants in any single geographic area.

l. The quality and effectiveness of management of each Restaurant varies.

The following information is based on 321 licensed restaurants and does not include 35 licensed restaurants that opened and 16 that closed during 1998.

a. To Perkins' knowledge, the approximate percentage of total sales for licensed restaurants that were in operation during the entire year ending December 31, 1998 that actually fell within the sales ranges shown in the Schedule were 55.1% for the sales range of Average Restaurant No. 1; 26.5% for the sales range of Average Restaurant No. 2; and 13.1% for the sales range of Average Restaurant No. 3.

b. Perkins does not have any knowledge of the percentage of licensed restaurants which during the same year actually attained or surpassed the levels of income before royalties, advertising, occupancy costs and taxes as set forth in the Schedule.

c. Within a range of annual sales volumes from $800,000 to $3,167,000 for Restaurants owned and operated by Perkins, to Perkins' knowledge approximately 94.7% of reporting licensed restaurants that were in operation during the

253

entire year actually fell within such range of sales. Annual sales volumes of reporting licensed restaurants for the year ending December 31, 1998 ranged from $345,300 to $3,441,500.

Substantiation of the data used in preparing the above statement will be made available upon

request. Because Perkins does not require that licensed restaurants follow a particular accounting system, Perkins cannot certify that the licensed restaurants follow generally accepted accounting principles. Perkins will not disclose the identity of any specific licensee whose data has been used to compile any information in this item except to the agency(ies) with which this filing is made.

PIZZERIA UNO CHICAGO BAR & GRILL

100 Charles Park Rd.
Boston, MA 02132-4985
Tel: (800) 449-8667 (617) 323-9200
Fax: (617) 218-5376
E-Mail: randy.clifton@pizzeriauno.com
Internet Address: www.pizzeriauno.com
Contact: Mr. Randy M. Clifton, VP Worldwide Franchising

Description: A casual theme restaurant with a brand name signature product - UNO's Original Chicago Deep Dish Pizza. A full, varied menu with broad appeal and a flair for fun and comfortable decor in a facility that attracts guests of all ages.

# Franchised Units:	71 Units
# Company-Owned Units:	<u>99</u> Units
Total # Units:	170 Units
Founded In:	1943
1st Franchised In:	1979
Average Total Investment:	900K-1.7MM
Franchise Fee:	35K
On-Going Royalty:	5%
Advertising Fee:	1%
Financial Assistance: Yes(I) (D – direct, or I – indirect)	
Site Selection Assistance:	Yes
Lease Negotiation Assistance:	Yes
Contract Terms (Init./Renew):	15/10
Initial Training Provided: 8 Weeks in a Training Restaurant; 2 Weeks On-Site Staff Training.	

Except as described below, no representations or statements of actual, average, projected, or forecasted sales, profits, or earnings are made to franchisees or developers. We do not furnish or authorize our salespersons to furnish any oral or written information concerning the actual, average, projected, forecasted, or potential sales, costs, income or profits of your business.

We specifically instruct our sales personnel, agents, employees and officers that they are not permitted to make such claims or statements as to the earnings, sales or profits, or prospects or chances of success, nor are they authorized to represent or estimate dollar figures as to a franchisee's or developer's operation. We will not be bound by allegations of any unauthorized representations as to earnings, sales, profits, or prospects or chances for success.

Actual results vary from franchise to franchise, and we cannot estimate the results of a particular franchise. We recommend that prospective franchisees and developers make their own independent investigation to determine whether or not the franchise may be profitable, and consult with an attorney and other advisors prior to executing the Franchise Agreement or the Development Agreement.

Analysis of Average Sales and Expenses for Franchisor-Operated Full-Service Uno Restaurants

Bases and Assumptions
The sales information which follows was aggregated from affiliate-owned and franchised restaurants open for the entire fiscal year ended September 27, 1998. The expense information which follows was aggregated from affiliate-owned

restaurants only, since expense data is not available for franchised restaurants. The Table included in the analysis contains the number and percentage of affiliate-owned Uno restaurants which, during the period September 29, 1997 to September 27, 1998, reported annual gross sales within the following ranges: under $1,500,000; $1,501,000 to $1,800,000; $1,801,000 to $2,100,000; and over $2,100,000. This analysis was constructed using the arithmetic mean (average) annual sales and expenses of all 90 restaurants that were open and operated by us during the entire aforementioned period. However, certain charges which you will be required to pay to us under the Franchise Agreement (see Items 5 and 6) and other differences in the expenses of a franchised Uno restaurant are included in the table, as noted below.

The affiliate-owned restaurants used in this analysis are substantially similar to the franchised Uno restaurants. However, the amount of sales and expenses incurred will vary from restaurant to restaurant. In particular, the sales and expenses of your Restaurant will be directly affected by factors which include the Restaurant's geographic location; competition in the market; presence of other Uno restaurants; the quality of both management and service at the Restaurant; contractual relationships with lessors and vendors; the extent to which you finance the operation of a restaurant; your legal, accounting and other professional fees; federal, state and local income taxes, gross profits taxes or other taxes; cost of any automobile used in the business; other discretionary expenditures;

accounting methods used and certain benefits and economies of scale which we may derive as a result of operating Uno restaurants on a consolidated basis. A NEW FRANCHISEE'S INDIVIDUAL FINANCIAL RESULTS ARE LIKELY TO DIFFER FROM THE RESULTS DESCRIBED BELOW.

As of the 1998 fiscal year end, the average time in operation of the affiliate-owned restaurants included in this analysis is 7.6 years. The restaurants included in this analysis are located in the following states:

	Number of Restaurants
Colorado	3
Connecticut	6
Florida	5
Illinois	6
Maine	1
Maryland	4
Massachusetts	24
Missouri	1
New Hampshire	3
New Jersey	1
New York	18
Ohio	1
Pennsylvania	3
Rhode Island	1
Vermont	1
Virginia	10
Washington, D.C.	2
Total	90

Statement of Average Sales (in thousands) for all Full-Service Restaurants for the Fiscal Year ended September 27, 1998

	(1)	(2)	(3)	(4)
1. Annual Sales Range	Under $1,500	$1,501–1,800	$1,801–2,100	Over $2,100
2. Number of restaurants within the range/% of total affiliate-owned restaurants within the range	28/31.1	19/21.1	17/18.9	26/28.9
3. Number of franchised restaurants within the range/% of total franchised restaurants within the range	24/41.4	15/25.9	7/12.1	12/20.7

Uno Restaurant Corporation Statement of Average Sales and Expenses of Affiliate-Owned Full Service Pizzeria Uno Restaurants for the Fiscal Year Ended September 27, 1998

Profit & Loss Period 12 Ended September 27, 1998 Consolidated Earnings Claim Disclosure Pro Forma Per Store Estimates

($s In Thousands) (Gross Sales Level)	Under $1,500		$1,501–1,800		$1,801–2,100		Over $2,100	
Sales								
1. Net Sales	1,331.6	100.0%	1,661.6	100.0%	1,933.9	100.0%	2,512.2	100.0%
2. Total Cost of Sales (Food and Beverage Costs)	364.2	27.4%	441.0	26.5%	512.0	26.5%	637.6	25.4%
Labor								
3. Direct Labor	281.3	21.1%	333.8	20.1%	372.7	19.3%	453.1	18.0%
4. Management Salary	115.8	8.7%	121.1	7.3%	138.3	7.2%	155.1	6.2%
5. Payroll Taxes & Benefits	71.0	5.3%	78.0	4.7%	89.7	4.6%	110.6	4.4%

($s In Thousands) (Gross Sales Level)	Under $1,500		$1,501–1,800		$1,801–2,100		Over $2,100	
Total Labor	468.1	35.2%	532.9	32.1%	600.7	31.1%	718.8	28.6%
Gross Profit	499.2	37.5%	687.8	41.4%	821.1	42.5%	1,155.8	46.0%
Controllables								
6. Paper Goods	16.7	1.3%	21.3	1.3%	24.3	1.3%	31.1	1.2%
7. Smallwares	10.9	0.8%	12.5	0.8%	15.0	0.8%	19.4	0.8%
8. Other Controllables	31.8	2.4%	34.2	2.1%	38.7	2.0%	43.4	1.7%
Total Controllables	59.4	4.5%	68.0	4.1%	78.0	4.0%	93.9	3.7%
Income after Controllables	439.9	33.0%	619.8	37.3%	743.1	38.4%	1,061.9	42.3%
Other Expenses								
9. Advertising & Business Co-op	39.9	3.0%	49.8	3.0%	58.0	3.0%	75.4	3.0%
10. Royalties	66.6	5.0%	83.1	5.0%	96.7	5.0%	125.6	5.0%
11. Legal & Accounting	5.0	0.4%	5.0	0.3%	5.0	0.3%	5.0	0.2%
12. Repairs & Maintenance	42.3	3.2%	46.1	2.8%	48.4	2.5%	55.8	2.2%
13. Utilities	65.7	4.9%	60.9	3.7%	68.7	36%	73.5	2.9%
14. Other Noncontrollables	20.1	1.5%	22.8	1.4%	26.7	1.4%	31.3	1.2%
15. Occ. Costs Excl. Rent & Taxes	19.7	1.5%	20.8	1.2%	25.0	1.3%	32.3	1.3%
Total Other Expenses	259.3	19.5%	288.5	17.4%	328.6	17.0%	398.9	15.9%
Earnings before Rent, Depr. & Interest	180.6	13.6%	331.3	19.9%	414.5	21.4%	663.0	26.4%

Each of the 90 affiliate-owned Uno restaurants utilized a uniform accounting system and the data pertaining to such restaurants was prepared on a basis consistent with generally accepted accounting principles during the covered period. The information contained in this analysis has generally not been audited. The following notes should assist in interpretation of the foregoing table of results.

1. *Net Sales* (line 1). The net sales are based on the average volume of the restaurants that fall into each revenue range.

2. *Total Cost of Sales* (line 2). You will have the opportunity to take advantage of volume discounts on particular items negotiated by us; however, availability of such volume discounts is generally limited to geographic areas in which our affiliates currently operate Uno restaurants. The cost of items such as produce, which are often purchased locally, may vary according to the location of the Restaurant. Additionally, freight and shipping costs and the amount of mark-up imposed by suppliers will also vary.

3. *Direct Labor* (line 3). Labor for a Restaurant generally necessitates a range of 40–80 employees, including both full-time and part-time workers.

4. *Management Salary* (line 4). This category assumes one designated general manager, 1 manager and 1 assistant manager and includes an amount for bonuses.

5. *Payroll Taxes and Benefits* (line 5). This category includes amounts for worker's compensation, group insurance expenses, payroll taxes and vacation pay. The amounts stated reflect administrative costs incurred by Uno restaurants and exclude all other general and administrative costs incurred for payroll matters which are handled by our corporate or regional office. The costs of labor and related payroll expenses may vary substantially depending on the geographic location of the Restaurant.

6. *Other Controllables* (line 8). Other controllable expenses include the following costs: janitorial service; office supplies; entertainment; laundry; telephone; cash shortages; and miscellaneous.

7. *Advertising and Business Coop* (line 9). These expenses represent the advertising and business coop contributions you are required to pay to us as described in Item 6. Specifically, you are required to pay a monthly fee of up to 1% of Gross Revenues, for business coop services. This fee includes your share of costs that are incurred by us for the benefit of the System. Article 7 of the Franchise Agreement further details and explains this expense. You are also required to expend a minimum of 2% of Gross Revenues on local marketing as described in Item 6. We have not accounted for the impact of a System wide Media Fund Fee of up to 1% of Gross Revenues, because the fee has never yet been actually implemented.

8. *Royalties* (line 10). You will be required to pay a continuing royalty fee of 5% of Gross Revenues as described in Item 6.

9. *Other Noncontrollables* (line 14). This category of expenses includes amounts for bank processing charges, dues, licenses, subscriptions, menus, guest checks and recruitment.

10. *Occupancy Costs excluding Rent and Taxes* (line 15). This category includes insurance, security, trash services and extermination. We may have derived a benefit in the form of lower premiums for insurance based on the number of Uno restaurants owned by our affiliates and our loss control programs. You should inquire about the cost of insurance, which may vary substantially depending on the geographic location of the Restaurant.

11. *Other Information.* We are also presenting in the following paragraphs a Comparison of certain financial information received from our franchisees along with the average financial results of the 90 affiliate-owned Uno restaurants. However, while we suggest that our franchisees utilize a uniform accounting system in reporting, which is consistent with generally accepted accounting principles, it should be expressly noted that we cannot attest to (i) the accuracy of the information received from our franchisees or (ii) whether such information was actually prepared in accordance with generally accepted accounting principles.

The numbers and percents indicated in the first table in lines (2) and (3) relate to the 90 affiliate-owned restaurants and 58 franchised restaurants open during all of fiscal year 1998 (September 29, 1997 to September 27, 1998). In addition, the average annual sales volume for all affiliate-owned restaurants as described above was $1,856,092. This sales volume was attained or surpassed by 40 (or 44.4%) of the affiliate-owned restaurants and 19 (or 32.8%) of the franchised restaurants.

The highest annual sales volume of an affiliate-owned restaurant was $3,345,810. The lowest annual sales volume of an affiliate-owned restaurant was $885,362. The highest annual sales volume of a franchised restaurant was $3,550,437. The lowest annual sales volume of a franchised restaurant was $651,999.

Substantiation of the data used in preparing the earnings claim described above will be made available to you on reasonable request.

SANDELLA'S CAFÉ

9 Brookside Place
West Redding, CT 06896
Tel: (888) 544-9984 (203) 544-9984
Fax: (203) 544-7749
E-Mail: bmajor@sandellas.com
Internet Address: www.sandellas.com
Contact: Mr. Bruce J. Major, Chief Development Officer

Description: Positioned in the explosive wrap market, SANDELLA'S is carving a market niche in fresh, distinctive food at affordable prices. The

SANDELLA'S concept combines the convenience and value of quick-service concepts with the quality, freshness and variety associated with up-scale, casual full-service dining.

# Franchised Units:	10 Units
# Company-Owned Units:	3 Units
Total # Units:	13 Units
Founded In:	1994
1st Franchised In:	1998
Average Total Investment:	145-245K
Franchise Fee:	20K
On-Going Royalty:	6%
Advertising Fee:	3 + 1%
Financial Assistance:Yes(I) (D – direct, or I – indirect)	
Site Selection Assistance:	Yes
Lease Negotiation Assistance:	Yes
Contract Terms (Init./Renew):	10/10
Initial Training Provided:6 Days Georgetown, CT; 10 Days in Store.	

THE PURPOSE OF THE FOLLOWING SITE SELECTION PRO FORMA WORKSHEET IS TO HELP YOU TO EVALUATE POTENTIAL SITES. IT IS MERELY AN OUTLINE TO ASSIST YOU IN THE SITE SELECTION PROCESS.

YOU MUST COMPLETE THIS WORKSHEET USING YOUR OWN RESOURCES, RESEARCH AND ADVISORS. UNDER NO CIRCUMSTANCE WILL SANDELLA'S OR ANY OF ITS OFFICERS, DIRECTORS, MANAGERS OR EMPLOYEES ASSIST YOU IN COMPLETING THIS WORKSHEET OR, FOLLOWING ITS COMPLETION, COMMENT IN

ANY WAY ON ITS PREPARATION, COMPLETENESS, ACCURACY OR THE CONCLUSIONS OR INFERENCES YOU ESTABLISH.

THE WORKSHEET IS NOT BASED ON ANY FRANCHISED OPERATIONS OR SPECIFIC COMPANY-OWNED CAFÉS.

THE PERCENTAGES SHOWN ON THE FOLLOWING PRO FORMA WORKSHEET HAVE NOT BEEN AUDITED OR REVIEWED BY ANY OUTSIDE ACCOUNTING FIRM. PROSPECTIVE FRANCHISEES AND OTHERS REVIEWING THESE PERCENTAGES SHOULD BE ADVISED THAT

NO CERTIFIED PUBLIC ACCOUNTANT HAS AUDITED THE PERCENTAGES PRESENTED ON THE PRO FORMA WORKSHEET, AND THAT SANDELLA'S DOES NOT PRESENT THIS INFORMATION IN ACCORDANCE WITH THE STATEMENT ON STANDARDS FOR ACCOUNTANTS' SERVICES ON PROSPECTIVE FINANCIAL INFORMATION (OR ITS SUCCESSOR) ISSUED BY THE AMERICAN INSTITUTE OF CERTIFIED PUBLIC ACCOUNTANTS.

Sandella's will make available to you upon reasonable request the methodology, data, and assumptions it used in arriving at the Site Selection Pro Forma Worksheet, and will otherwise substantiate it. However, understand that Sandella's is under no obligation to disclose to you specific information for any particular Café.

Site Selection Pro Forma Worksheet for Self-Evaluation Purposes	Targeted Percentage of Sales	Estimated Amount (in Dollars)
Sales Revenues from sale of food and beverages. This is a number you must estimate yourself, based on visits to your proposed site, talking with other businesses in the area and help from your professional advisors.	100%	
Cost of Goods Sold Subject to product mix and your ability to effectively manage inventory, waste, theft and purchases.	32–35%	
Labor Does not include salary for you or your Manager. You should talk with other businesses in the area to help determine market wage rates and availability. This cost is subject to the number of hours you work, your ability to manage other people and the wages you pay them. Sandella's recommends that you try to manage your labor costs to achieve this percentage range.	15–20%	
Rent Sandella's recommends that you not pay more than this percentage of your estimated sales for rent.	10–12%	
Operating Expenses Subject to local rates for utilities, trash collection, sanitation, insurance, music, legal services, accounting services, etc., and your ability to control these costs. Sandella's recommends that you not pay more than this percentage of your estimated sales for operating expenses.	7–10%	
Continuing Royalty You pay this percentage to Sandella's — see Item 6.	6%	
Local Advertising Required minimum percentage paid to third parties — see Item 6.	3%	
System Marketing Contribution You pay this percentage to Sandella's — see Item 6.	1%	
Total Costs	74–87%	
Operating Margin	13–26%	

The purpose of the above worksheet is to help you evaluate a potential site. You should look at other businesses in the area to help determine the demand for Sandella's products, competition, rental rates, costs of labor, operating expenses, and other factors that will affect how your business performs. The above chart does not include the debt service costs that you must pay if you finance any portion of your initial investment.

THE PERCENTAGES FOR YOUR CAFÉ WILL BE MATERIALLY DIFFERENT FROM THOSE SHOWN ON THE ABOVE PRO FORMA IF YOUR SALES ESTIMATE PROVES TO BE INACCURATE.

IF YOU RELY ON SANDELLA'S FIGURES IN THE ABOVE PRO FORMA WORKSHEET, YOU MUST ACCEPT THE RISK THAT YOUR CAFÉ MAY NOT DO AS WELL. SANDELLA'S DOES NOT MAKE ANY REPRESENTATION THAT YOUR CAFÉ WILL BE PROFITABLE OR THAT YOU WILL BE ABLE TO ACHIEVE THESE PERCENTAGES.

SANDELLA'S CAN IN NO WAY WARRANT, REPRESENT, PROMISE, PREDICT OR GUARANTEE THAT YOU CAN OR WILL ATTAIN ANY OF THE FINANCIAL RESULTS SET FORTH IN THE SITE SELECTION PRO FORMA WORKSHEET. ACTUAL RESULTS WILL VARY FROM CAFÉ TO CAFÉ AND SANDELLA'S CANNOT ESTIMATE THE RESULTS OF ANY PARTICULAR FRANCHISE.

THE ACTUAL SALES AND EARNINGS OF YOUR BUSINESS WILL BE AFFECTED BY MANY FACTORS, INCLUDING YOUR OWN EXPERIENCE, ABILITY, EFFORTS, AND CONTROL OF YOUR CAFÉ, AS WELL AS FACTORS OVER WHICH YOU DO NOT HAVE CONTROL, SUCH AS LOCAL CONDITIONS, COMPETITION, BUSINESS CYCLES AND THE PERFORMANCE OF THE NATIONAL AND GLOBAL ECONOMY.

Food: Specialty

It's a matter of taste

the coffee beanery, ltd. ®

COFFEE BEANERY, THE
3429 Pierson Place Rd.
Flushing, MI 48433
Tel: (800) 728-2326 (810) 728-2326
Fax: (810) 733-6847
E-Mail: franchiseinfo@CoffeeBeanery.com
Internet Address: www.CoffeeBeanery.com
Contact: Mr. Kevin Shaw, VP Franchise
Development

Description: THE COFFEE BEANERY, LTD. offers a variety of investment levels with storefront cafes being the main growth vehicle in the future. The cornerstone and foundation of the business is the exceptional quality of its own hand-roasted coffee. Our customers enjoy the best coffee and assorted products available from a network of over 180 opened franchised and corporate locations. Our operations department and training are superb.

# Franchised Units:	159 Units
# Company-Owned Units:	27 Units
Total # Units:	186 Units
Founded In:	1976
1st Franchised In:	1985
Average Total Investment:	140-250K
Franchise Fee:	5-25K
On-Going Royalty:	6%
Advertising Fee:	2%
Financial Assistance:Yes(I) (D – direct, or I – indirect)	
Site Selection Assistance:	Yes
Lease Negotiation Assistance:	Yes
Contract Terms (Init./Renew):	5,10,15+
Initial Training Provided:3.5 Days Corporate Office, Flushing, MI; 21 Days Flint or Birmingham, MI Corp. Store.	

We furnish and authorize our salespersons to furnish written information concerning the actual sales of our corporately-operated THE COFFEE BEANERY, LTD. Stores, to the extent shown in the attached financial statements and Exhibit C-1. We also furnish and authorize all salespersons to furnish the information concerning the gross sales of Franchisee-operated Stores shown on Exhibit C.

CAUTION — THE GROSS SALES FIGURES CONTAINED IN EXHIBITS C AND C-1 SHOULD NOT BE CONSIDERED THE ACTUAL, POTENTIAL OR PROBABLE GROSS

SALES THAT WILL BE REALIZED BY ANY FRANCHISEES. THE FRANCHISOR DOES NOT PROVIDE ANY GUARANTEE OR ASSURANCE THAT ANY FRANCHISEE MAY ATTAIN SUCH GROSS SALES, OR ANY INCOME OR PROFIT WHICH COULD BE DERIVED FROM SUCH GROSS SALES. YOUR RESULTS ARE LIKELY TO DIFFER FROM THE RESULTS STATED IN THE EARNINGS CLAIM. IF ANYONE RELIES ON THESE FIGURES, THEY MUST ACCEPT THE RISK OF NOT DOING AS WELL.

SUBSTANTIATION OF THE DATA USED IN PREPARING THE EARNINGS CLAIMS WILL BE MADE AVAILABLE TO PROSPEC-TIVE FRANCHISEES ON REASONABLE REQUEST.

Exhibit C
Actual Gross Sales Information on All Franchised Stores
The Franchisor furnishes and authorizes its representatives to furnish the following information concerning the actual gross sales of all Franchise operated Stores that have been operational for at least one (1) full year as of June 30, 1998. These figures are for the preceding twelve (12) months prior to that date. The figures are divided by concept, and the Stores used in this table are given in alphabetical order by names of the malls or sites in which they are located, but not in the order the actual gross sales figures are listed.

Store Gross Sales	Number of Full Years in Operation as of June 30, 1998
Mall Stores	
881,677	8
732,162	20
649,324	12
638,095	8
634,471	5
627,124	5
585,362	7
561,878	9
559,212	6

Store Gross Sales	Number of Full Years in Operation as of June 30, 1998
Mall Stores	
531,562	17
531,042	10
512,896	7
509,422	4
485,377	12
483,023	7
466,190	6
466,078	9
460,460	6
451,856	5
449,384	5
444,902	4
423,858	7
421,792	8
421,490	5
420,766	5
418,928	5
417,339	5
414,388	5
412,273	9
412,217	7
404,196	4
401,502	4
393,910	6
393,906	8
391,249	10
388,518	7
382,522	7
377,452	4
374,966	1
370,391	4
370,148	2
369,077	6
366,147	7
360,271	9
355,034	7
354,044	5
353,697	7

Store Gross Sales	Number of Full Years in Operation as of June 30, 1998
Mall Stores	
353,212	10
352,493	8
349,751	6
347,763	4
344,934	8
343,328	8
336,069	9
335,559	5
335,182	10
334,399	3
334,292	6
331,470	7
329,592	6
329,013	4
321,669	3
321,518	4
321,188	1
321,518	4
315,647	5
314,555	4
309,788	8
303,329	4
299,421	4
299,161	7
290,483	7
287,846	3
282,494	3
279,728	5
278,710	10
276,020	7
270,530	4
269,993	10
263,370	5
259,527	7
256,851	7
256,155	7
250,603	10
244,012	4

Store Gross Sales	Number of Full Years in Operation as of June 30, 1998
Mall Stores	
243,411	5
234,933	6
233,058	5
224,726	3
221,617	5
219,594	9
205,634	5
189,162	3
180,910	5
180,630	10
107,026	9
Average $371,624	7

Store Gross Sales	Number of Full Years in Operation as of June 30, 1998
Carts and Kiosks	
393,980	2
297,870	3
251,034	5
228,731	6
198,842	3
183,473	2
163,707	5
160,773	3
148,071	2
144,923	1
141,318	3
115,703	4
85,119	4
84,930	4
74,107	2
Average $178,172	3

Store Gross Sales	Number of Full Years in Operation as of June 30, 1998
Streetfront Cafes; Mixed Use and Airports	
604,195	3
560,545	15
389,720	7
384,287	2
369,522	3
352,827	8
337,768	2
288,482	5
277,538	1
254,660	3
242,432	5
204,114	2
88,619	1
Average $334,971	5

Locations of Mall Stores used in this Table are (in alphabetical order):

Acadiana (LA); Aurora Mall (CO); Beach Place (FL); Beaver Valley (PA); Belden Village (OH); Berkshire Mall (PA); Boulevard Mall (NY); Briarwood; Brunswick Square (NJ); Charleston Place (SC); Charlottesville (VA); Cherry Hill (NJ); Christiana Mall (DE); Coliseum Mall (VA); Colonie Center (NY); Columbiana Centre (SC); Columbus City Center (OH); Concord Mall (DE); Coolsprings Galleria (TN); Crabtree Valley (NC); Crossgates Mall (NY); Cumberland Mall (GA); Dayton Mall (OH); Del Amo (CA); Dover Mall (DE); Echelon (NJ); Enfield Square (CT); Fayette Mall (KY); Florence Mall (KY); Forest Fair (OH); Granite Run Mall (PA); Hamilton Mall (NJ); Hulen Mall (TX); Jefferson Valley Mall (NY); King of Prussia (PA); Lakeforest Mall (MD); Lakeside Mall; Lakeline Mall (TX); Laurel Center Mall (MD); Laurel Park Place; Lincolnwood (IL); Mall at Green Hills (TN); Media City Center (CA); Meriden Mall; Monmouth Mall (NJ); Montgomery Mall (PA); Moorestown Mall (NJ); Nanuet

(NY); Newport Center (NJ); Northeast Mall (TX); Northland Mall (OH); Oakland Mall; Oxford Valley Mall (PA); Oxmoor Center (KY); Panama City (FL); Paradise Valley (AZ); Paramus Park (NJ); Park Plaza (AR); Patrick Henry (VA); Peachtree Mall (GA); Pembroke Lakes Mall (FL); Pentagon (VA); Post Oak Mall (OK); Quail Springs Mall (OK); Quaker Bridge Mall (NJ); Regency Square (VA); River Oaks (IL); Rockaway Townsquare (NJ); Roosevelt Field Mall (NY); Salisbury Centre (MD); Santa Rosa (FL); Southland Mall; Southpark (VA); Spotsylvania Mall (VA); St. Charles Towne Center (MD); Summit Place Mall; Sunrise Mall (NY); Superstition Springs (AZ); The Mall at Steamtown (PA); The Parks at Arlington Mall (TX); The Meadows (NV); Turtle Creek (MS); Twelve Oaks Mall; Tysons Corner (VA); Valley View Mall (TX); Virginia Center Commons (VA); Vista Ridge (TX); West County (MO); Westfartns Mall (CT); Westland Center; Westshore Mall; Wheaton Plaza (MD); White Flint Mall (MD); White Plains (NY); Woodbridge (NJ); and Woodland Mall. [Except as indicated otherwise, these stores are all located in Michigan. See Exhibits "A" and "B".]

Locations of Carts and Kiosks used in this Table are (in alphabetical order):

Acadiana (LA); Ballston Commons (VA); Blue Ridge Mall (MO); Briarwood Mall; Columbiana Mall (SC); Cortana Mall (LA); Lakeside Mall; Laurel Park Place; South Square Mall (NC); St. Matthews (KY); The Parks at Arlington Mall (TX); Townsquare Mall (KY); Viewmont Mall (PA); Westfarms Mall (CT); and Woodland Mall. [Except as indicated otherwise, these stores are all located in Michigan. See Exhibits "A" and "B"]

Locations of Streetfront Cafes and Mixed Use Stores used in this Table are (in alphabetical order):

Broadway at the Beach; Denver International Airport (CC)); El Premier Centre (FL); Georgetown (WDC); Loehmann's Fashion Island (FL); Main Street—Greenville (SC); Main Street—Royal Oak; Marketplace at Pelican Bay (FL); Renaissance Center; Tower City Centre

(OH); Tower Place (OH); Town Center Plaza (KS); and Walnut Street (PA). [Except as indicated otherwise, these stores are all located in Michigan. See Exhibits "A" and "B".]

Exhibit C-1 Actual Gross Sales Information on All Corporate Stores

The Franchisor furnishes and authorizes its representatives to furnish the following information concerning the actual gross sales of all Corporately operated Stores that have been operational for at least one (1) full year as of June 30, 1998. These figures are for the preceding twelve (12) months prior to that date. The figures are divided by concept, and the Stores used in this table are given in alphabetical order by names of the malls or sites in which they are located, but not in the order the actual gross sales figures are listed.

Store Gross Sales	Number of Full Year in Operation as of June 30, 1998
Mall Stores	
480,352	16
479,636	8
426,546	6
345,170	11
342,499	4
332,545	8
324,039	6
309,220	4
304,120	10
297,562	4
293,489	5
289,562	8
241,708	6
222,797	13
Average $335,785	8

Carts and Kiosks	
212,742	4
159,838	5
149,145	6
Average $173,908	5

Store Gross Sales	Number of Full Year in Operation as of June 30, 1998
Streetfront Cafes; Mixed Use and Airports	
1,071,549	5
791,452	6
715,211	6
377,017	8
360,871	3
356,801	1
324,556	4
99,744	1
Average $512,150	4

Locations of Mall Stores used in this Table are (in alphabetical order):

Bellevue Mall (TN); Birchwood Mall; Eastland Mall; Fashion Square; Galleria at Southbay (CA); Genesee Valley; Mall of America (MN); Manhattan Mall (NY); Midway Mall (OH); Natick Mall (MA); Oakdale Mall (NY); The Shops at Liberty Place (PA); Sandusky (OH); and Willow Grove Park (PA). [Except as indicated otherwise, these stores are all located in Michigan. See Exhibits "A" and "B".]

Locations of Carts and Kiosks used in this Table are (in alphabetical order):

Fisher Building; Manhattan Mall (NY); Kroger—Sterling Heights; Kroger—West Bloomfield; Kroger—Ann Arbor; and Wayne State. [Except as indicated otherwise, these stores are all located in Michigan. See Exhibits "A" and "B".]

Locations of Streetfront Cafes and Mixed Use Stores used in this Table are (in alphabetical order):

Brickell Avenue (FL); 569 Lexington Avenue (NY); LaGuardia Airport (NY); Main Street — Rochester; Pittsburgh International Airport (PA); Sunny Isles Beach (FL); and Woodward Avenue — Birmingham. [Except as indicated otherwise, these stores are all located in Michigan. See Exhibits "A" and "B".]

CLASSIC SUBS

QUIZNO'S CLASSIC SUBS
1099 18th St. # 2850
Denver, CO 80202-9275
Tel: (800) 335-4782 (303) 291-0999
Fax: (303) 291-0909
E-Mail:
Internet Address: www.quiznos.com
Contact: Ms. Patricia Meyer, Director Franchise
Sales

Description: QUIZNO'S CLASSIC SUBS is an up-scale, Italian-theme sub sandwich restaurant that features 'the best sandwich you will ever eat.' QUIZNO'S subs are oven-baked and made with our special recipe bread, QUIZNO'S special dressing and the highest-quality meats and cheeses. With 600 units open across the U. S., Canada and Puerto

Rico, our success will continue as we double the number of units open in the coming year. Franchisees are supported at both the corporate level and by one of our 100 area owners.

# Franchised Units:	584 Units
# Company-Owned Units:	28 Units
Total # Units:	612 Units
Founded In:	1981
1st Franchised In:	1984
Average Total Investment:	129-199K
Franchise Fee:	20K
On-Going Royalty:	6%
Advertising Fee:	1%
Financial Assistance:Yes(I) (D – direct, or I – indirect)	
Site Selection Assistance:	Yes
Lease Negotiation Assistance:	Yes
Contract Terms (Init./Renew):	15
Initial Training Provided:11 Days Regional Market; 11 Days Corporate Office Denver, CO.	

We have compiled the following information regarding average per Restaurant sales during fiscal years 1996 and 1997 at all QUIZNO'S Restaurants operating as of December 31, 1996 and December 31, 1997, respectively:

As of December 31, 1996, there were a total of 156 QUIZNO'S Restaurants, 9 of which were owned by us or our affiliates. All of these Restaurants were operational. Of the 156 Restaurants, 89 had been open for business all of 1996, under the same ownership. The following data has been compiled from the information reported by these 89 Restaurants for the period from January 1,1996 through December 31, 1996. We have not undertaken an independent investigation to verify the amounts reported.

The average gross sales for the period for all 89 Restaurants was $300,580. Of the 89 Restaurants which were open for all of 1996, 47% met or exceeded the average gross sales figure set forth above.

As of December 31, 1997, there were a total of 275 QUIZNO'S Restaurants, 17 of which were

owned by us or our affiliates. All of these Restaurants were operational. Of the 275 Restaurants, 108 had been open for business all of 1997, under the same ownership. The following data has been compiled from the information reported by these 108 Restaurants for the period from January 1, 1997, through December 31, 1997. We have not undertaken an independent investigation to verify the amounts reported.

The average gross sales for the period for all 108 Restaurants was $316,259. Of the 108 Restaurants which were open for all of 1997, 42% met or exceeded the average gross sales figure set forth above.

The products and services offered by each Restaurant, although essentially the same, may vary to some degree based on the individual Franchisee's direction. The sales volume attainable by each Restaurant depends on many factors including, but not limited to, geographic differences, competition within the immediate market area, the quality and service provided to customers by the Restaurant, as well as their own marketing and sales efforts.

YOUR ACTUAL FINANCIAL RESULTS ARE LIKELY TO DIFFER FROM THE FIGURES PRESENTED.

THE SALES FIGURES ABOVE ARE AVERAGES OF HISTORICAL DATA OF SPECIFIC FRANCHISES. THEY SHOULD NOT BE CONSIDERED AS POTENTIAL SALES THAT MAY BE REALIZED BY YOU. WE DO NOT REPRESENT THAT YOU CAN EXPECT TO ACHIEVE THESE SALES LEVELS. ACTUAL RESULTS VARY FROM RESTAURANT TO RESTAURANT AND WE CANNOT ESTIMATE THE RESULTS OF ANY PARTICULAR FRANCHISE.

SUBSTANTIATION OF THE ABOVE AVERAGES IS AVAILABLE TO YOU AT OUR OFFICES IF YOU REQUEST PROVIDED IT DOES NOT REQUIRE THE DISCLOSURE OF THE IDENTITY OF ANY RESTAURANT OWNER

OTHER THAN THE ABOVE INFORMATION, WE DO NOT FURNISH OR AUTHORIZE OUR SALESPERSONS TO FURNISH ANY ORAL OR WRITTEN INFORMATION CONCERNING THE ACTUAL OR POTENTIAL SALES, INCOME OR PROFITS OF A QUIZNO'S RESTAURANT.

Schlotzsky's Deli

SCHLOTZSKY'S DELI
203 Colorado St.
Austin, TX 78701
Tel: (800) 846-2867 (512) 236-3600
Fax: (512) 236-3650
E-Mail:
Internet Address: www.schlotzskys.com
Contact: Ms. Joyce Cates,

Description: SCHLOTZSKY'S DELI is a franchised restaurant, serving a menu of sandwiches, pizza and salads on SCHLOTZSKY'S baked-fresh-daily sourdough bread. Restaurants are designed to provide fresh, clean environments with an in-store bakery.

# Franchised Units:	760 Units
# Company-Owned Units:	23 Units
Total # Units:	783 Units
Founded In:	1971
1st Franchised In:	1977
Average Total Investment:	1.3-2.3MM
Franchise Fee:	30K
On-Going Royalty:	6%
Advertising Fee:	1%
Financial Assistance:Yes (D – direct, or I – indirect)	
Site Selection Assistance:	Yes
Lease Negotiation Assistance:	Yes
Contract Terms (Init./Renew):	20/10
Initial Training Provided: 3 Weeks in Austin, TX.	

Our Earnings Claim includes a chart of system-wide sales from 1994 to 1998 sales summary charts showing sales by Restaurant type, and two reports of actual sales of certain Restaurants. The first report covers Restaurants that were open and reporting sales for the full year ending December 1998. The second report covers Restaurants reporting sales for less than the full year ending December 1998 (see Exhibit G).

YOUR INDIVIDUAL FINANCIAL RESULTS ARE LIKELY TO DIFFER FROM THE SALES RESULTS SHOWN IN THIS EARNINGS CLAIM.

SUCH ACTUAL SALES ARE SALES OF SPECIFIC FRANCHISED AND COMPANY-OWNED UNITS AND SHOULD NOT BE CONSIDERED AS THE ACTUAL OR PROBABLE SALES THAT WILL BE REALIZED BY ANY FRANCHISEE. WE DO NOT REPRESENT THAT ANY FRANCHISEE CAN EXPECT TO ATTAIN SUCH SALES.

CAUTION — SOME OUTLETS HAVE SOLD THIS AMOUNT. THERE IS NO ASSURANCE YOU'LL DO AS WELL. IF YOU RELY UPON OUR FIGURES, YOU MUST ACCEPT THE RISK OF NOT DOING AS WELL

Exhibit G

This Earnings Claim includes a chart showing information about systemwide sales, including information about Restaurants operated in the United States and in other countries (the "Sales Chart"), two charts showing information about sales by Restaurant type (the "Sales Summary Charts") and two sales reports (the "Full Sales Period Report" and the "Short Sales Period Report") of actual sales reported during 1998 for Restaurants in the United States, as described below.

Systemwide Sales

The Sales Chart covers systemwide sales and average weekly sales for each year from 1994 to 1998 and provides information about the number of Restaurants open at year end at each of such years. The information provided includes data for the Restaurants operated throughout our system, which includes Restaurants in the United States, the District of Columbia and several foreign countries. In reviewing this information it is important to note that, because Restaurants operated in foreign countries may have limited menus, may offer some different products and may not report sales in the same manner as Restaurants in the United States, data from sales at such Restaurants will not be comparable on a Restaurant-by-Restaurant basis with sales at U.S. Restaurants. In addition, data in the Sales Chart includes information for Restaurants which were not open, or not reporting sales, for the full period covered and includes some estimated sales data. The data includes information for Restaurants that were open for a full year as well as Restaurants that closed or opened during the year, and, as a result, were open for only a portion of that period. The average weekly sales numbers indicate weighted average numbers, which means that the data is adjusted or "weighted" based on the number of weeks the store was actually open during the period. However, the weighted average number will necessarily differ from the average that would be obtained if actual sales data were available for each Restaurant in the chart for the full year of each of the years covered by the chart. While we believe that information about weighted average weekly sales provides some relevant information for you to consider when viewed

in context as described in this report, it should not be relied on as any statement or representation by us that you will achieve such sales levels and should only be viewed in connection with all other relevant data, including the two sales reports described below, which report sales by Restaurant for certain Restaurants in the United States. Those reports include information about the location, opening date and type of each Restaurant — factors which we believe are relevant to Restaurant sales.

Sales Summary Charts

The lowest, highest and weighted average sales reported by the Restaurants in the Full Sales Period Report and the Short Sales Period Report (the "Sales Reports") described below, for each of the Restaurant types (P27, P32, PP and Other) described in Note 6 of this Earnings Claim are included in two charts. The first chart is the chart of *Earnings Claim Information by Restaurant Type for Restaurants Open and Reporting Sales for the Full Year Ending December 1998* and the second chart is the chart of *Earnings Claim Information by Restaurant Type for Restaurants Reporting Sales for Less Than the Full Year Ending December 1998*. This information was compiled from the sales reported in the two Sales Reports to assist you in your review of this information and should be viewed only in conjunction with all of the information in this Earnings Claim. Certain of the Restaurants in the Sales Summary Charts show sales for Restaurants that were open for as short a period as one week and/or closed within the reporting period. As described in Note 7 of this Earnings Claim, sales reported during a short period of time, especially at a time when a Restaurant has recently opened or shortly before the Restaurant is closed should be viewed with caution because the sales of such Restaurants for the long term operation of the Restaurant may be significantly different as compared with the sales in the short period reported. See Note 7.

Sales Reports

The first report of Restaurant sales (the "Full Sales Period Report") covers reported sales for 1998 for Restaurants open and reporting sales for a full year ending December 1998. A sales distribution chart for such Restaurants are included. The sales distribution chart for the Full Sales Period Report describe sales distributions by percentage for the Restaurants that actually attained or surpassed the sales levels indicated in the charts during the periods covered. A chart showing the geographical distribution of the Restaurants reporting is also included.

The second report of Restaurant sales (the "Short Sales Period Report") covers reported sales for Restaurants which were open and reported sales for at least one week during 1998, but were not open and reporting sales for a full year ending December 1998. The Short Sales Period Report includes Restaurants that opened in a prior year and reopened in 1998 after remodeling or relocation, Restaurants that closed at some time during 1998 and Restaurants that for any other reason reported sales in 1998 for less than the full twelve month period ending December 1998. A sales distribution chart for such Restaurants is included. The sales distribution chart for the Short Sales Period Report describes sales distribution by percentage for the Restaurants that actually attained or surpassed the sales levels indicated in the chart during the periods such Restaurants were reporting sales for the periods covered. A chart showing the geographical distribution of the Restaurants reporting is also included.

Sales figures from Restaurants not reporting results for the full period that they were open are not included in the Full Sales Period Report described above. Such Restaurants are more likely to have had lower sales, on average, than the Restaurants included in the two Sales Reports.

1. The attached sales information was taken from the sales reports provided to us from both franchised and Company-operated Restaurants and compiled by us as a part of our business records. Such reports are derived from gross revenues.

2. Substantially the same services were offered by us to all Restaurants. All Restaurants offered substantially the same products or services, with the exception of (i) certain Restaurants which offered a more limited menu, either because of lease or similar restrictions or because they were developed before the current menu was required; (ii) the Restaurant located at 218 South Lamar, Austin, TX, which is a company-owned Restaurant that is substantially larger than typical franchised Restaurants and has an expanded offering of products including products not generally available to be offered by franchisees ("Additional Products"); and (iii) the Restaurant located at 106 E. Sixth Street, Austin, TX, which is a company-owned Restaurant that is larger than typical franchised Restaurants and also offers some Additional Products. The sales noted in the sales reports for the Restaurants at 218 South Lamar and 106 E. Sixth Street have been adjusted, however, to exclude sales attributable to Additional Products.

3. As of December 31, 1998, there were 730 Restaurants licensed to operate in the United States, some of which were temporarily closed for remodeling, relocation or other reasons, or not yet opened for business on that date. 701 Restaurants (franchised and company-operated) were open and doing business in the United States on December 31, 1998.

4. The data for franchised Restaurants used in compiling this Earnings Claim was based on reports made to us by Franchisees. At the current time we do not require that Restaurants follow a particular system or method of accounting. We have no knowledge or information as to whether the accounting systems or methods used by Franchisees are consistent with generally accepted accounting principles or whether the accounting systems or methods actually utilized have been consistently applied. Therefore, it is reasonable to assume that this claim was not prepared on a basis consistent with generally accepted accounting principles.

5. There are no accounting adjustments necessary to reconcile Restaurant-by-Restaurant data, but in reviewing the data it is important to note the factors, described in Note 6 below, which may cause material differences in sales performance and the special information regarding the Short Sales Period Report, included in Note 7 below.

6. FACTORS WHICH MAY CAUSE MATERIAL DIFFERENCES IN THE SALES PERFORMANCE OF RESTAURANTS ARE:
    a. Management, attitude, expertise, and time spent;
    b. Restaurant type and size;
    c. Location, access, and visibility of Restaurant;
    d. Advertising and promotional activities;
    e. Cost of advertising (larger markets = higher cost);
    f. Local economic conditions, unemployment, etc.; and
    g. Area demographic factors
        i. Income level;
        ii. Population density; and
        iii. Age of Restaurant.

We have developed and made available for use by franchisees a series of prototype Restaurant designs and specifications for freestanding Restaurants, and certain of such designs and specifications may be adapted for use in other Restaurants. During 1995 and 1996 a limited number of freestanding Restaurants using an early version of one of the prototype designs were constructed. A significant number of freestanding Restaurants that opened during 1997 and 1998 were constructed using a prototype design. The information about the Restaurants on the following sales reports includes a designation of Restaurant type as P27, P32, PP or Other. Those designations indicate restaurant types described as follows:

Prototype 2700 ("P27") — A Restaurant which is a freestanding building of approximately 2700 square feet originally constructed and equipped to be a Schlotzsky's® Deli restaurant using prototype plans developed for P27 Restaurants by Schlotzsky's, Inc.

Prototype 3200 ("P32") — A Restaurant which is a freestanding building of approximately 3200 square feet originally constructed and equipped to be a Schlotzsky's® Deli restaurant using prototype plans developed for P32 Restaurants by Schlotzsky's, Inc.

Pre-Prototype ("PP") — A Restaurant which is a freestanding building of varying size, from approximately 2100 to 3100 square feet, originally constructed and equipped to be a Schlotzsky's® Deli restaurant using certain design elements, or a previous version of the design elements, which are now incorporated into the prototype plans developed by Schlotzsky's, Inc for its P27 and P32 restaurants (the "Prototype Restaurants").

Other — A Restaurant of varying size which was not constructed and equipped using prototype plans developed by Schlotzsky's, Inc. These Restaurants may be situated in strip shopping centers in an "in-line" (tenants on both sides) or "end-cap" (end of the building) space or they may be in non-traditional locations (such as airports) or in a free standing building which was converted/remodeled from a business that was not originally a Schlotzsky's® Deli restaurant.

The prototype plans for the P27 and P32 restaurants (the "Prototype Restaurants") evolved over a period beginning in 1995 through approximately October 1996, in the case of the P27 restaurants, and December 1996, in the case of the P32 restaurants, when the architectural plans for the Prototype Restaurants were substantially standardized. The restaurants designated Pre-Prototype range from restaurants which may have only a few design elements similar to the Prototype Restaurants to restaurants which are very similar to the Prototype Restaurants. The architectural plans and specifications for the Prototype Restaurants may continue to be refined and modified infrequently in the future. The plans for equipping Prototype Restaurants may change more frequently as we add, modify and upgrade requirements for equipment

It is important to note that while the Prototype Restaurants were built using the applicable prototype plans, there are some minor variations among them. The square footage is *approximately* 2,700 or 3,200 square feet and the specific buildings may have some differences as constructed due to local conditions or restrictions, lot size or configuration or other special conditions or circumstances applicable to the individual restaurants. Most Prototype and Pre-Prototype Restaurants have a drive-thru while the Restaurants in the "Other" category may or may not have a drive-thru.

We have provided this information about store type to assist you in your analysis and review. We believe that the fact that a freestanding Restaurant is constructed using a prototype design is a significant factor which may cause a material difference in sales performance. However, store type is only one of many factors that must be considered in assessing the potential success of a restaurant and should be viewed only in conjunction with all other available information. There can be no assurance that Restaurants constructed using prototype designs and specifications will have sales significantly different from sales at other Restaurants and you should expect that your sales results will differ even if you build a Restaurant which would be included in one of the types listed above. By providing information about store type we are not representing that your sales will be the same as or similar to the sales of any particular restaurant of the same type or to the average sales of restaurants of that type.

7. SPECIAL FACTORS APPLICABLE TO SHORT SALES PERIOD REPORT: In addition to the other factors noted above, it is important to note that sales reported in the Short Sales Period Report were, in most cases, for periods of less than a full year, including sales reported for a period as short as one week. Our experience indicates that sales reported during the first few months of a Restaurant's opening may be much less indicative of Restaurant sales than sales reported for

longer periods. Also, the shorter the period of sales reported, the less reliable, generally, the reported sales will be in forecasting sales for the long term operations of the Restaurant. In addition, because many of the Restaurants included in the Short Sales Period Report opened after January 1, 1998, they include a significantly higher concentration of Restaurants using prototype designs as compared with the Restaurants included in the Full Sales Period Report. As noted above, Restaurant type, including whether a Restaurant is freestanding or is constructed using a prototype design, may be a significant factor which may cause a material difference in the sales performance of a Restaurant as compared with Restaurants of a different type.

Data substantiating the information contained in this Earnings Claim will be made available upon reasonable request.

YOUR INDIVIDUAL FINANCIAL RESULTS ARE LIKELY TO DIFFER FROM THE SALES RESULTS SHOWN IN THIS EARNINGS CLAIM.

SUCH ACTUAL SALES ARE SALES OF SPECIFIC FRANCHISED AND COMPANY-OWNED UNITS AND SHOULD NOT BE CONSIDERED AS THE ACTUAL OR PROBABLE SALES THAT WILL BE REALIZED BY ANY FRANCHISEE. WE DO NOT REPRESENT THAT ANY FRANCHISEE CAN EXPECT TO ATTAIN SUCH SALES.

CAUTION: SOME OUTLETS HAVE SOLD THIS AMOUNT. THERE IS NO ASSURANCE YOU'LL DO AS WELL. IF YOU RELY UPON OUR FIGURES, YOU MUST ACCEPT THE RISK OF NOT DOING AS WELL.

Systemwide Sales and Average Weekly Sales (1994–1998)
Schlotzsky's® Deli Restaurants System Wide Information * 1994–1998

	1994	1995	1996	1997	1998
Weighted Average Weekly Sales (systemwide)	$6,276	$7,086	$7,867	$8,753	$9,671
Restaurants Open At Year End**	353	463	573	673	750
Systemwide Sales	$98 Million	$143 Million	$202 Million	$270 Million	$349 Million

*Includes information for U.S. and international Restaurants
**Includes Restaurants that were temporarily closed for remodeling, relocation or other reasons, or not yet opened for business on December 31, 1998.

Sales Summary Chart
Earnings Claim Information by Restaurant Type for Restaurants Open and Reporting Sales for the Full Year Ending December 1998

	Prototype 2700	Prototype 3200	Pre-Prototype	Other
Weighted Average Weekly Sales of Group (1)	$12,182	$17,215	$13,072	$8,807
Lowest Average Weekly Sales (2)	$6,431	$9,332	$6,752	$1,817
Highest Average Weekly Sales (3)	$17,263	$25,072	$26,815	$56,845*

*This restaurant is a Company-owned restaurant that is substantially larger than the typical franchised restaurant. It has an expanded offering of products. The amounts shown in this report were adjusted to exclude sales attributable to additional products.

Earnings Claim Information by Restaurant Type for Restaurants Reporting Sales for Less Than the Full Year Ending December 1998

	Prototype 2700	Prototype 3200	Pre-Prototype	Other
Weighted Average Weekly Sales of Group (1)	$16,731	$18,520	$7,054	$8,995
Lowest Average Weekly Sales (2)(4)	$9,749	$8,991	$7,054	$993
Highest Average Weekly Sales (3)	$26,437	$35,527	$7,054	$26,617

Notes:

1. The Weighted Average Weekly Sales is the weighted average weekly sales of the group of Restaurants in the applicable Restaurant type category.

2. The Lowest Average Weekly Sales is the lowest of the average weekly sales reported for that Restaurant type of all the Restaurants reporting sales in that Restaurant type category.

3. The Highest Average Weekly Sales is the highest of the average weekly sales reported for that Restaurant type of all the Restaurants reporting sales in that Restaurant type category.

4. The Restaurants in this lowest category include Restaurants that were open for as short a period as one week and/or closed within the reporting period. As described in Note 7 of this Earnings Claim, sales reported during a short period of time, especially at a time when a Restaurant has recently opened or shortly before the Restaurant is closed should be viewed with caution because the sales of such Restaurants for the long term operation of the Restaurant may be significantly different as compared with the sales in the short period reported. See Note 7.

Note: The UFOC provides the address, 1998 Sales and Average Weekly Sales for each of the operating units used in the Summary Charts. Because of space limitations, this detail is not included.

STEAK-OUT CHAR-BROILED DELIVERY

1967 Lakeside Pkwy., # 420
Tucker, GA 30084
Tel: (770) 493-6110
Fax: (770) 493-6093
E-Mail: jmccord@steakout.com
Internet Address: www.steakout.com
Contact: Mr. Joseph M. McCord, Vice President

Description: STEAK-OUT franchising specializes in home and office deliveries of charbroiled steaks, chicken and burgers - other menu items include salads and desserts. The only full meal delivery service expanding nationwide. Customers absolutely love our combination of quality food and delivery service. America's finest delivery.

# Franchised Units:	74 Units
# Company-Owned Units:	3 Units
Total # Units:	77 Units
Founded In:	1986
1st Franchised In:	1987
Average Total Investment:	199.7-291K
Franchise Fee:	24.5K
On-Going Royalty:	5%
Advertising Fee:	2%
Financial Assistance:Yes(I) (D – direct, or I – indirect)	
Site Selection Assistance:	Yes
Lease Negotiation Assistance:	Yes
Contract Terms (Init./Renew):	10/10
Initial Training Provided:4-5 Weeks Training Center at Atlanta, GA.	

We make no earnings claims. The historical information listed below is supplied by our franchisees. This information was reported to us by Franchisees for Steak-Out Units that were open for the entire fifty-three (53) week period from December 29, 1997 to January 3, 1999.

As used in the following chart: "Net Sales" are defined as gross sales less sales tax; "Food, Labor and Coupon Cost" includes the cost of food sold, packaging, salary and hourly unit labor (exclusive of payroll taxes, workers' compensation, insurance and meat cutters labor) and expenses associated with coupon offers; and the "percentage" relates to net sales.

All Steak-Out Units offer substantially the same products and services to the public. None of the franchised Steak-Out Units have customarily received services not generally available to other franchises and substantially the same services will be offered to you.

We do not provide you with projections or with forecasts of probable sales, profits or earnings you may achieve, and we do not assure you that you will attain results at the same levels as those in existing franchises.

YOU ARE URGED TO CONSULT WITH APPROPRIATE FINANCIAL, BUSINESS AND

LEGAL ADVISORS IN CONNECTION WITH THE HISTORICAL INFORMATION. SUBSTANTIATION OF THE DATA USED IN PREPARING THIS ITEM 19 WILL BE MADE AVAILABLE TO YOU ON REASONABLE REQUEST.

Category	Total Units	Highest Unit	Lowest Unit
Average Weekly Net Sales	$14,853.00	$40,848.00	$7,494.00
Average Weekly Carry-Out %	19.89%	39.58%	5.33%
Average Weekly Daytime %	39.18%	68.93%	22.69%
Average Weekly Food and Labor Cost %	Food 33.63% Labor 25.72%	Food 37.56% Labor 31.65%	Food 28.94% Labor 21.01%

*The highest unit/lowest unit columns in each category do not represent one unit, but the highest and lowest Unit for each category from the Units open the entire year.

The average time in operation of the Steak-Out Units included in the foregoing information is approximately 5.5 years. We emphasize that, while the above information represents actual sales and costs figures for the period noted as reported to us, the results are, to a large extent, determined by the quality of the management of the units. Among the determinant factors are the energy and dedication of the franchisees, and the quality of the franchisees' food and service. For you to assume that you will achieve similar results, you must realize that similar dedication to managing the Unit is required.

Hairstyling salons

COST CUTTERS®
FAMILY HAIR CARE

We're your style:

COST CUTTERS FAMILY HAIR CARE
7201 Metro Blvd.
Minneapolis, MN 55439
Tel: (800) 858-2266 (612) 947-7328
Fax: (612) 947-7301
E-Mail: jcook@regiscorp.com
Internet Address: www.costcutters.com
Contact: Ms. Jen Cook, Franchise Development Coord.

Description: COST CUTTERS FAMILY HAIR CARE is a value-priced, family hair salon chain with over 850 locations in 45 states. COST CUTTERS offers its customers high-quality hair care services and products in an attractive atmosphere and at affordable prices.

# Franchised Units:	774 Units
# Company-Owned Units:	31 Units
Total # Units:	805 Units
Founded In:	1968
1st Franchised In:	1982
Average Total Investment:	67.7K-123.8K
Franchise Fee:	19.5/12.5K
On-Going Royalty:	6%/4%-Yr. 1
Advertising Fee:	5%
Financial Assistance:	Yes(I)
Site Selection Assistance:	Yes
Lease Negotiation Assistance:	Yes
Contract Terms (Init./Renew):	15/15
Initial Training Provided:	1 Week at National HQ; 1 Week On-Site; Several On-Site Visits Prior to Opening.

COST CUTTERS provides prospective franchisees with information regarding the average sales of franchised Cost Cutters Businesses.

COST CUTTERS COMPILES THESE AVERAGE SALES FIGURES FROM GROSS REVENUES SUPPLIED BY COMPANY-OWNED SALONS AND SPECIFIC FRANCHISEES AND YOU SHOULD NOT CONSIDER THESE FIGURES AS THE ACTUAL OR POTENTIAL SALES YOU WILL REALIZE. COST CUTTERS DOES NOT REPRESENT THAT YOU CAN EXPECT TO ATTAIN THESE SALES. YOUR FINANCIAL RESULTS ARE LIKELY TO DIFFER FROM THE AVERAGE SALES FIGURES PRESENTED BELOW.

COST CUTTERS DOES NOT PROVIDE PROJECTIONS OR FORECASTS OF SALES, PROFITS OR EARNINGS. SUBSTANTIATION OF THE AVERAGE SALES OF COMPANY-OWNED AND FRANCHISED COST CUTTERS BUSINESSES WILL BE PROVIDED TO YOU UPON REASONABLE REQUEST. COST CUTTERS requires its franchisees to adopt, install and maintain designated bookkeeping, accounting, auditing and record keeping systems. The particular accounting methods required by COST CUTTERS are in accordance with generally accepted accounting principles and, to the best of COST CUTTERS' knowledge, these accounting principles are substantially adhered to by COST CUTTERS' franchisees. Neither COST CUTTERS nor COST CUTTERS' independent certified public accountant has independently audited or verified the sales reports.

All Cost Cutters Businesses offer substantially the same products and services to the public. None of the franchised Cost Cutters Businesses have received services that are not generally available to other franchisees, and substantially the same services will be offered to new franchisees.

The following chart shows the average annual sales for company-owned and franchised Cost Cutters Businesses, by region, for COST CUTTERS' 1998 fiscal year. The average sales figures are derived from sales reports from those company-owned and franchised Cost Cutters Businesses that were in operation for that full period and that provided COST CUTTERS with weekly statements of Gross Revenues for all weeks during that period.

THE FOLLOWING INFORMATION RELATES SOLELY TO HISTORICAL SALES INFORMATION PROVIDED BY COST CUTTERS AND FRANCHISEES FOR EXISTING COMPANY-OWNED AND FRANCHISED COST CUTTERS BUSINESSES. YOU SHOULD NOT DRAW ANY INFERENCE AS TO EXPENSES, COST OF GOODS, OR PROFITS OF EXISTING OR FUTURE FRANCHISED COST CUTTERS BUSINESSES FROM THE FOLLOWING AVERAGE SALES FIGURES.

Average Sales of Cost Cutters Businesses*

Region	Average Annual Sales Per Business	Percentage of Businesses Exceeding Average	Number of Businesses Used in Calculating Average
Black	$214,344	37%	78
Blue	$195,231	36%	42
Gold	$271,909	38%	91
Gray	$224,213	46%	92
Green	$253,574	36%	103
Purple	$225,638	41%	71
Red	$243,545	38%	76
National Average	$237,142		553

Key to Regions

Black	Minnesota, Montana, North Dakota, South Dakota
Blue	California, Idaho, Nevada, Oregon, Washington
Gold	Michigan, Wisconsin
Gray	Alabama, Florida, Georgia, Kentucky, Louisiana, Mississippi, North Carolina, South Carolina, Tennessee, Virginia, West Virginia
Green	Arizona, Arkansas, Colorado, New Mexico, Oklahoma, Texas, Utah, Wyoming
Purple	Connecticut, Delaware, Maine, Maryland, Massachusetts, New Hampshire, New Jersey, New York, Ohio, Pennsylvania, Rhode Island, Vermont
Red	Illinois, Indiana, Iowa, Kansas, Missouri, Nebraska

*240 operational Cost Cutters Businesses have been excluded in computing these average sales figures because they were not open for the full period or had not reported sales for the full year.

In addition to the average sales information stated above, COST CUTTERS provides prospective franchisees with the following information regarding the average income and expenses of franchised Cost Cutters Businesses. Except for the total sales figure set forth on the following chart which reflects the national average as stated above, the following information is a consolidated year-to-date average for 336 Cost Cutters Businesses that have been open for more than 12 consecutive months and whose cost and expense percentages reported to COST CUTTERS have been reviewed by COST CUTTERS' internal audit department. Of the 793 Cost Cutters Businesses that were operational as of September 24, 1998, 96 had not been open for more than 12 consecutive months. The cost and expense percentages were provided by franchisees and, although they have been reviewed by COST CUTTERS' internal audit department, these percentages have not been audited by COST CUTTERS or by any independent certified public accountant or other third party.

In addition, Franchisees whose methods of recording sales and expenses were not in accordance with the policies and procedures recommended by COST CUTTERS have not been included in the following averages. In certain cases, information for periods less than 12 months has been annualized.

COST CUTTERS COMPILES THE FOLLOWING CONSOLIDATED AVERAGE INCOME AND EXPENSE FIGURES FROM INFORMATION COST CUTTERS' FRANCHISEES PROVIDE TO COST CUTTERS. YOU SHOULD NOT CONSIDER THESE FIGURES AS THE ACTUAL OR POTENTIAL INCOME OR EXPENSES THAT YOU WILL REALIZE. COST CUTTERS DOES NOT REPRESENT THAT YOU CAN EXPECT TO ATTAIN THE INDICATED INCOME OR EXPENSES. YOUR INDIVIDUAL FINANCIAL RESULTS ARE LIKELY TO DIFFER FROM THE RESULTS PRESENTED BELOW. COST CUTTERS WILL PROVIDE TO YOU SUBSTANTIATION OF THE INFORMATION PRESENTED BELOW UPON REASONABLE REQUEST.

Account Description		Year-To-Date Percentage
Total Sales	$237,142	
Weekly Sales	$4,355	100.00%
Cost of Sales		
Total Labor		44.96%
Total Supplies		10.62%
Continuing Fees		4.10%
Total Cost of Sales		59.67%
Gross Profit		40.33%
Operating Expenses		
Total Advertising		4.18%
Total Insurance		1.41%
Total Rent		9.69%
Total Maintenance		1.22%
Total Operating Expenses		21.05%
Net Cash Flow From Operations		19.27%

YOU SHOULD NOT CONSIDER THE FOLLOWING INVESTMENT COST ASSUMPTIONS AND CASH FLOW RETURN ON INVESTMENT INFORMATION AS THE ACTUAL INVESTMENT COSTS OR THE ACTUAL CASH FLOW RETURN ON INVESTMENT THAT YOU WILL REALIZE. COST CUTTERS DOES NOT REPRESENT THAT YOU CAN EXPECT TO EXPEND THE INDICATED AMOUNTS ON YOUR INVESTMENT OR ATTAIN THE INDICATED CASH FLOW RETURN ON INVESTMENT. YOUR INDIVIDUAL COSTS AND FINANCIAL RESULTS ARE LIKELY TO DIFFER FROM THE COSTS AND RESULTS PRESENTED BELOW.

Investment Cost Assumptions

	1st Salon	2nd Salon
Initial Franchise Fee	$19,500	$12,500
Grand Opening Advertising	5,000	5,000
Signage	4,000	4,000
Furniture, Fixtures and Equipment	18,000	18,000

	1st Salon	2nd Salon
Leasehold Improvement	21,000	21,000
Prepaid Rent and Security Deposit	2,100	2,100
Initial Inventory	5,000	5,000
Computer Hardware & Software	4,000	4,000
Working Capital	6,000	6,000
Total	$84,600	$77,600
Cash Flow Return on Investment	54.02%	58.89%

Except as stated in writing in COST CUTTERS' Uniform Franchise Offering Circular, COST CUTTERS does not furnish or authorize its salespersons to furnish any oral or written information concerning the actual or potential sales, costs, income or profits of a Cost Cutters Business. Actual results of Cost Cutters franchises vary from unit to unit, and COST CUTTERS cannot estimate the potential results of any particular franchise.

GREAT CLIPS

3800 W. 80th St., # 400
Minneapolis, MN 55431-4419
Tel: (800) 947-1143
Fax: (612) 844-3443
E-Mail: maryjo.keefe@greatclips.com
Internet Address: www.greatclipsfranchise.com
Contact: Franchise Development,

Description: High-volume haircutting salon, specializing in haircuts for the entire family. Unique, attractive decor, with quality, comprehensive advertising programs. Strong, hands-on support to franchisees, excellent training programs. We offer real value to our customers. Tremendous growth opportunities.

# Franchised Units:	1304 Units
# Company-Owned Units:	18 Units
Total # Units:	1322 Units
Founded In:	1982
1st Franchised In:	1983
Average Total Investment:	87.2-161.5K
Franchise Fee:	17.5K
On-Going Royalty:	6%
Advertising Fee:	5%
Financial Assistance:	Yes(I)
Site Selection Assistance:	Yes
Lease Negotiation Assistance:	Yes
Contract Terms (Init./Renew):	10/5/5

Initial Training Provided:5 Days Minneapolis, MN; 2.5 Weeks Local Market.

Great Clips provides prospective franchisees with information regarding the average sales, expenses and cash flows of certain franchised GREAT CLIPS units. Great Clips will substantiate the information set forth in this Item 19, upon reasonable request, provided, however, that such substantiation shall not disclose the sales, expenses or cash flows of any specific franchised unit without the written authorization of the franchisee, except as required by any applicable state or federal registration authorities.

OTHER THAN AS SPECIFICALLY DISCLOSED IN THIS ITEM 19, GREAT CLIPS DOES NOT MAKE ACTUAL, AVERAGE, PROJECTED OR FORECASTED SALES, EXPENSES, PROFITS, CASH FLOW OR EARNINGS INFORMATION AVAILABLE TO PROSPECTIVE FRANCHISEES. THERE IS NO GUARANTY THAT ANY NEW FRANCHISEE WILL ATTAIN THE AVERAGE SALES, EXPENSES, PROFITS, CASH FLOW OR EARNINGS LEVELS ATTAINED BY ANY EXISTING FRANCHISEES.

GREAT CLIPS HAS COMPILED THESE AVERAGE SALES, EXPENSES, PROFITS, CASH FLOW OR EARNINGS FIGURES FROM INFORMATION SUPPLIED BY GREAT CLIPS FRANCHISEES AND THEY SHOULD NOT BE CONSIDERED AS THE ACTUAL OR POTENTIAL SALES,

EXPENSES, PROFITS, CASH FLOW, OR EARNINGS THAT WILL BE REALIZED BY ANY OTHER FRANCHISEE. GREAT CLIPS DOES NOT REPRESENT THAT ANY FRANCHISEE CAN EXPECT TO ATTAIN THESE SALES, EXPENSES, PROFITS, CASH FLOW OR EARNINGS. A NEW FRANCHISEE'S INDIVIDUAL FINANCIAL RESULTS ARE LIKELY TO DIFFER FROM THE AVERAGE FIGURES PRESENTED BELOW.

The average sales, expenses and cash flows of the GREAT CLIPS units were obtained from operating statements submitted to Great Clips by its franchisees. Most franchisees use a cash versus accrual system for producing their financial statements which may produce slight differences between the actual date of occurrence of expenses and the date such expenses are reported on the franchisee's financial statements. Neither Great Clips nor its independent certified public accountants have independently audited or verified these franchisee statements. The information received in these statements, to the best of Great Clips' knowledge, is accurate and complete.

All GREAT CLIPS units offer substantially the same services and products to the public. The actual sales, expenses and cash flow results of any franchised GREAT CLIPS unit may vary substantially from these averages. Sales, expenses and cash flow results depend upon many independently variable factors including, but by no means limited to, the location and visibility of the unit, local traffic patterns, the demographic composition and trends of the market area served by the unit, the competitive environment, public awareness of and goodwill associated with the name "GREAT CLIPS," the region and market area in which the unit is located, the length of time the unit has been in operation, the quality of the management and service at the unit, the individual skills of the franchisee and other factors. This information is therefore limited in its usefulness and should only be utilized as a reference for you to use in conducting your own independent analysis of the business.

THE FOLLOWING TABLE CONTAINS INFORMATION RELATING SOLELY TO HISTORICAL SALES, EXPENSE AND CASH FLOW DATA COMPILED FROM EXISTING FRANCHISED GREAT CLIPS UNITS. THE TABLE IS QUALIFIED IN ITS ENTIRETY BY ALL THE INFORMATION, NOTES, CAUTIONARY STATEMENTS AND QUALIFICATIONS CONTAINED IN THIS ITEM 19.

Average Operating Cash Flow of Certain Great Clips Units

General Description and Methodology
The following statement (hereinafter referred to as the "Average Operating Cash Flow Statement") consists of the average sales, expenses and operating cash flow of certain GREAT CLIPS units. The statement is based on a sample of 405 units that were open two years or longer as of January 1, 1998, and operating as of the date of this offering circular.

The total potential sample of units opened for two years or longer, as of January 1, 1998, consisted of 586 shops. The sample was reduced by eliminating any unit for which Great Clips had insufficient data to be reasonably assured of having accurate and complete expense information (181 units).

The 181 units eliminated due to insufficient data were not distributed evenly over the entire database, based on total sales. Of the missing shops, 56 had total sales at or above the median for the total sample and 125 had total sales below the median for the total sample. If all 181 of these shops had been included in the sample, it would have reduced the median total sales in the sample by 5.92% and the net operating cash flow by a somewhat larger percent.

Average sales used in this table were the actual reported sales of each unit during 1998. The expense data used in the preparation of this table was taken from actual unit operating statements, provided by the franchisee, for each unit in the sample. The time frame or accounting period of these operating statements was the most current available to Great Clips, but, in most cases, did not match the exact time frame from which sales figures were drawn.

279

The methodology used was to calculate each unit's reported expenses as a percentage of total sales, then to apply this expense percentage to the total sales for 1998 to compute the operating cash flow figure. Great Clips feels that this is the method that produces the fairest representation of the current operating averages for these sample units.

The 405 units included in this sample are located in the following states/provinces:

1. Arizona (40)
2. California (9)
3. Colorado (41)
4. Florida (15)
5. Georgia (41)
6. Idaho (3)
7. Illinois (19)
8. Indiana (35)
9. Iowa (12)
10. Kansas (6)
11. Maryland (1)
12. Minnesota (65)
13. Missouri (42)
14. Nebraska (10)
15. North Carolina (11)
16. Ohio (4)
17. Oregon (5)
18. Utah (6)
19. Washington (15)
20. Wisconsin (20)
21. Washington DC (1)
22. British Columbia (4)

The average annualized total sales for this group of 405 units is $274,313. A total of 172 units, or 42.47%, exceed this average. The average total of all expenses for this group of 405 units is $231,117. A total of 240 units, or 59.26%, have total expenses lower than the average figure of

$231,117. The average operating cash flow for this group of 405 units is $43,196. A total of 179 units, or 44.20%, had total average operating cash flow in excess of the average of $43,196.

THE FOLLOWING AVERAGE OPERATING CASH FLOW INFORMATION SHOULD NOT BE CONSTRUED AS ACTUAL OR PROBABLE RESULTS THAT WILL BE REALIZED BY A FRANCHISEE. IT IS BASED ON OPERATING RESULTS OF UNITS IN OPERATION SINCE AT LEAST JANUARY 1, 1996.

Average Operating Cash Flow Statement

Revenues[1]		
Service Sales	$252,834	92. 17%
Product Sales	21,479	7.83%
Total Revenues	$274,313	100.0%
Expenses		
Labor[2]	$135,689	49.47%
Occupancy[3]	23,032	8.40%
Products[4]	14,331	5.22%
Royalties[5]	16,517	6.02%
Advertising[6]	15,520	5.66%
Other[7]	26,028	9.49%
Total Expenses	$231,117	84.25%
Operating Cash Flow[8]	$43,196	15.75%

Averages Based on Sales Range

Salons				Expense as a Percent of Sales					
Sales Range ($000)	Number	%	Average Sales in Range	Labor	Occupancy	All Other	Total	Cash Flow (%)	Cash Flow ($)
<$150	16	4.0%	$134,115	57.6%	13.1%	31.5%	102.2%	-2.2%	($2,953)
$150–199	74	18.3%	$173,797	54.0%	11.9%	28.1%	94.1%	5.9%	$10,270
$200–249	101	24.9%	$227,607	50.6%	10.1%	27.5%	88.2%	11.8%	$26,907
$250–299	84	20.7%	$275,040	48.6%	8.5%	26.5%	83.6%	16.4%	$45,196
$300–349	59	14.6%	$322,974	48.6%	7.2%	26.2%	82.0%	18.0%	$58,127
$350–399	34	8.4%	$370,445	47.5%	6.4%	24.8%	78.7%	21.3%	$79,029
$400–449	13	3.2%	$418,615	47.9%	5.8%	23.9%	77.6%	22.4%	$93,576
$450+	24	5.9%	$537,739	47.0%	5.7%	24.5%	77.3%	22.7%	$122,267
All Salons in Sample	405	100.0%	$274,313	49.5%	8.4%	26.4%	84.3%	15.8%	$43,196

Notes:

1. *Revenues.* Average sales based on actual operating results as reported by franchisees to Great Clips.

2. *Labor.* Includes all employee related expenses including: wages, salary, bonus, commission, payroll taxes, insurance benefits, other benefits, and workman's compensation expenses.

excludes, if identifiable, any labor expense related to general manager or franchisee.

3. *Occupancy.* Includes all rent, common area maintenance, real estate taxes plus percentage rent paid, if any. Also includes any other lease related charges such as maintenance, security, trash removal, merchant association dues or charges or shopping center promotional expenses.

4. *Products.* Includes the cost of all product purchased for resale or for back bar customer service usage plus all freight or delivery costs associated with this product.

5. *Royalties.* All units in the system pay identical continuing franchise fees of 6%. The model is not exactly 6% due to the fact that the franchisees predominately use a cash rather than accrual basis for accounting purposes.

6. *Advertising.* All units in the system pay identical amounts of 5% of gross sales into the North American Advertising Fund. In addition, virtually all franchisees participate in other discretionary advertising on a local or regional basis.

7. *Other.* This category includes all other cash expense items and categories not included elsewhere. These would include: travel and entertainment, supplies, dues and subscriptions, telephone, utilities, non-real estate repairs and maintenance, insurance, postage, freight, bad debts, taxes and fees, cash over/short, recruitment expense, laundry, meals, equipment purchase, credit card charges, accounting and legal, employee theft/losses, deposits, bank charges, uniforms, licenses, contributions, meeting expenses, janitorial, bad checks, printing, inventory differences, computer charges and convention expenses.

8. *Operating Cash Flow.* This figure does not include any provision for income taxes or for non-cash expenses such as depreciation or amortization. It also does not include any reserve for future capital expenditures.

Newly opened units tend to have average sales and cash flow significantly below the average for the units included in the earnings claim sample above. This is especially true of new units opened by new franchisees in markets that have few existing units. Certain markets have substantially higher real estate costs than others and any prospective franchisee is urged to verify this along with all other expense factors in relation to local market conditions. Markets with many units and correspondingly larger cooperative advertising budgets tend to have units with higher revenues and cash flows than markets with few existing units.

You are responsible for developing your own business plan for your proposed GREAT CLIPS unit, including capital budgets, pro forma financial statements, sales and expense projections and other elements appropriate to the particular circumstances of the proposed unit. In developing the business plan, you are cautioned to make necessary allowance for changes in financial results that may occur due to any of the factors listed above, for any and all ranges of general economic conditions that may exist now or in the future, or for any other circumstances that may impact the operation and performance of the business.

No representations or statements of actual, average or projected sales profits or earnings are made to applicants for GREAT CLIPS franchises except as stated in this Item 19. Neither Great Clips' sales personnel nor any employee or officer of Great Clips is authorized to make any claims or statements as to the earnings, sales, expenses, cash flows, or profits or prospects or chances of success that any franchisee can expect or that present or past franchisees have had, other than as stated in this Item 19. Great Clips specifically instructs its sales personnel, agents, employees and officers that they are not permitted to make any such claims or statements, nor are they authorized to represent or estimate dollar figures as to existing or future GREAT CLIPS shop operations, other than as stated in this Item 19. Great Clips recommends that applicants for GREAT CLIPS franchises make their own investigation and determine whether or not existing shops are profitable and whether their shop is likely to be profitable.

Great Clips will not be bound by allegations of any unauthorized representations as to earnings, sales, profits or prospects or chances of success.

SPORT CLIPS
PMB 266, P. O. Box 3000
Georgetown, TX 78627-3000
Tel: (800) 872-4247 (512) 869-1201
Fax: (512) 869-0366
E-Mail: bjboecker@aol.com
Internet Address: www.sportclips.com
Contact: Ms. Beth Boecker, Market Development Coord.

Description: Sports-themed haircutting salons, appealing primarily to men and boys. Unique design, proprietary haircutting system and complete support at the unit level. Retail sale of Paul Mitchell hair care products, sports apparel and memorabilia.

# Franchised Units:	28 Units
# Company-Owned Units:	4 Units
Total # Units:	32 Units
Founded In:	1995
1st Franchised In:	1995
Average Total Investment:	100-150K
Franchise Fee:	15K
On-Going Royalty:	6%
Advertising Fee:	$250/Wk.
Financial Assistance:	No
Site Selection Assistance:	Yes
Lease Negotiation Assistance:	Yes
Contract Terms (Init./Renew):	5/5

Initial Training Provided:3 Days in Georgetown, TX for Franchisee; 2 Wks. in Austin, TX for Manager; 2 Wks. Locally.

Last year was the first time that Sport Clips made available any information concerning the actual or potential sales, costs, income or profits of the Franchised Business, since the operating history of Sport Clips stores was relatively short. The *sales and expense information* presented last year reflected the average for the three company-owned stores in operation in Austin for the entire calendar year of 1997, although only one had been open more than twelve months prior to January 1, 1997. This data is re-stated below.

During 1999, only two company-owned stores were owned by Sport Clips, Inc. for the entire year due to acquisitions, sales and swaps. The data presented below is for the four stores that were owned by Sport Clips, Inc. at the end of 1999. The two Austin stores were in the data presented last year, and were owned for the entire year. One Houston store was purchased from a corporate officer franchisee in March, 1999, and the other was acquired in a swap with an Austin franchisee in August, 1999. The sales and expenses for the two Houston stores have been annualized based on performance since they were acquired in March and in August, 1999.

The following data include all direct costs of operating the stores, but do not include provisions for royalties, overhead and/or administrative costs, accounting and legal fees, financing or equipment leasing costs. These numbers are unaudited but are believed by Management to be substantially accurate in all material respects. (ACTUAL RESULTS VARY FROM UNIT TO UNIT, AND SPORT CLIPS CANNOT ESTIMATE THE RESULTS OF ANY PARTICULAR FRANCHISE.)

	Average for 1997	Austin #1	Austin #2	Houston #1	Houston #2	Average for Four Stores, 1998
Sales	$270,707	$348,018	$327,090	$299,158	$258,162	$308,107 100%
Variable Costs (1)	$28,817	$20,019	$17,734	$21,589	$17,881	$19,317 6%
Payroll (2)	$141,523	$198,154	$182,178	$149,973	$135,612	$166,468 54%
Occupancy (3)	$34,115	$34,214	$34,213	$60,918	$45,558	$43,726 14%
Advertising (4)	$15,797	$14,598	$15,492	$13,971	$13,143	$14,301 5%
Miscellaneous (5)	$1,134	$2,638	$2,416	$2,125	$2,767	$2,486 <1%
Operating Profit Profit as % of Sales	$49,322 18%	$78,395 23%	$75,057 23%	$50,582 17%	$43,201 17%	$61,809 20%

Notes:

1. Variable Costs include operating supplies, cost of goods sold, bank service charges, credit card discounts, and classified ads to recruit stylist.

2. Payroll includes direct payroll, payroll taxes and fringe benefits. Austin stores have a higher base pay for stylists than most other markets due to a very tight labor market.

3. Occupancy includes rent, pass-through expenses from the landlord, utilities, phone charges, repairs and maintenance. Houston store #1 is in a very upscale center and has unusually high rent. Houston store #2 has a training center and is larger than most Sport Clips stores, therefore has higher rent.

4. Advertising includes the weekly payments to the Ad Fund plus other advertising and marketing expenses for the store.

5. Miscellaneous expense includes magazine subscriptions, store insurance and overages and/or shortages from the cash drawer.

6. During 1998, the base haircut price in Austin was $10.95; this was increased to $11.95, a 9.1% increase, in January, 1999. The base price in Houston was $10.95 until August, 1998,

when it was raised to $11.95. In Houston store #1 above, the lowest priced service was increased to $13 in August, 1998, which includes the Sport Clips haircut and a complimentary shampoo service.

THIS FINANCIAL INFORMATION HAS BEEN PREPARED BY SPORT CLIPS WITHOUT REVIEW BY AN INDEPENDENT ACCOUNTANT. ACTUAL EARNINGS FROM THE OPERATION OF A FRANCHISED BUSINESS ARE INHERENTLY SUBJECT TO UNCERTAINTY AND VARIATIONS DEPENDING UPON CHANGING EVENTS AND ECONOMIC CONDITIONS. THERE CAN BE NO GUARANTEE THAT THESE STATEMENTS PREDICT THE EARNINGS OF ANY FRANCHISEE. ANYONE WHO USES THE ABOVE INFORMATION TO PREPARE HIS OWN PRO FORMA STATEMENT MUST ACCEPT THE RISK THAT HIS OWN SPORT CLIPS STORE MAY PERFORM SUBSTANTIALLY WORSE THAN THOSE INCLUDED IN THE AVERAGES ABOVE.

SUBSTANTIATION OF THE DATA USED IN PREPARING THESE STATEMENTS WILL BE MADE AVAILABLE UPON REASONABLE REQUEST.

FIT AMERICA
401 Fairway Dr., # 200
Deerfield Beach, FL 33441
Tel: (800) 221-1186 (954) 570-3211
Fax: (954) 570-8608
E-Mail: fitstores@aol.com
Internet Address: www.fitamerica.com
Contact: Mr. Jack Farland, Dir. Franchise Development

Description: Retail store operation offering the finest all-natural herbal products, comprehensive education and training, and unparalleled, free customer service, as well as motivation to help people lose weight.

# Franchised Units:	72 Units
# Company-Owned Units:	0 Units
Total # Units:	72 Units
Founded In:	1992
1st Franchised In:	1996
Average Total Investment:	25-45K
Franchise Fee:	8.4K
On-Going Royalty:	$400/Mo.
Advertising Fee:	$165/Mo.
Financial Assistance:	No
Site Selection Assistance:	Yes
Lease Negotiation Assistance:	Yes
Contract Terms (Init./Renew):	2/2

Initial Training Provided:3 Days Corporate Headquarters; 1 Week at Already Existing Site; 2 Weeks Franchisee's Store.

Representations Regarding Earnings Capability

We do not furnish or authorize our salespersons to furnish any oral or written information concerning the actual or potential sales, costs, income or profits of a Fit Americastore aside from what is disclosed in this Offering Circular, except that we may supplement what is disclosed in this Offering Circular from time to time. Exhibit R summarizes the monthly sales made by franchisees in 1997 and 1998. These are based upon purchases of product from us, and do not represent either the actual income experienced by a franchisee or the franchisee's profitability. Actual income and profitability results vary from store to store based on a number of factors including pricing, the amounts spent on advertising, salaries, rent and other items. We do not estimate the profitability of any particular franchise.

In 1998, the average monthly sales per store for all franchise stores open in 1998 was $43,330.02, with the range being $76,337.99 at the high end for a store group comprised of eight stores and $11,567.38 at the low end for a single store franchise. The average for franchises owning and operating one store in the same period was $42,462.95, with the range being $73,559.22 on the high end and $11,567.38 on the low end. The 1998 analysis includes new stores that were open for only a fraction of the year.

The comparable figures for 1997 show an average of $35,232.48 per store for all franchise stores, the range being $80,107.08 for a five store group and $13,570.92 for a single store franchise. For single store franchises, the average is $27,118.58 with the high store being $39,072.22 and the low store being $13,570.92. The 1997 analysis includes new stores that are open for only a fraction of the year.

Comparison of the 1997 and 1998 results shows an increase in average monthly sales of 56.58% for single store franchises and 22.98% increase in average monthly sales per store when all stores are included.

A new franchisee's individual financial results are likely to differ from the results shown in Exhibit R. We will permit you to examine the materials that substantiate the figures above

Caution: These figures are only estimates of what we think you may earn. There is no assurance you'll do as well. If you rely upon our figures, you must accept the risk of not doing as well.

Exhibit R

Fit America Monthly Sales Volume by Store Owner Group

Notes

1. The monthly sales volumes in this Exhibit R are based upon our records of what each franchisee purchased from us during the calendar years 1997 and 1998. Since the sales of product take place after the purchase date from us, it is possible that purchases made at the end of 1997 were actually sold in 1998, and purchases made at the end of 1998 were sold in 1999.

2. The monthly sales figures are based upon the franchisee's purchase price and the suggested retail price of each product. Since a franchisee may sell a product for a price other than the suggested retail price, a franchisee's actual experience may differ from our estimates.

3. The monthly sales figures do not include sales tax or other adjustments such as returns.

4. Exhibit R includes all franchisees in 1997 and 1998.

5. You are permitted to examine the information that was used to produce Exhibit R.

Caution: The figures in Exhibit R are only estimates. There is no assurance that you'll do as well. If you rely upon our figures, you must accept the risk of not doing as well.

Owner Designated Code	Area(s)	1998		1997	
		Average Monthly Sales per Store	Number Stores Owned	Average Monthly Sales per Store	Number Stores Owned
—	Pittsburgh, Long Is.	$76,337.99	8	$71,416.97	5
—	North Jersey	$70,451.80	7	$80,107.08	5
—	New York City	$76,326.32	5	$45,276.19	5
—	Houston, Texas	$43,152.90	4	$39,493.78	4
—	North Jersey	$48,383.79	3	$43,592.51	2
—	South Florida	$35,555.03	3	$41,202.43	2
—	South Florida	$18,057.95	3	—	0
—	Philadelphia Area	$43,743.07	2	$32,264.74	1
—	Tampa Area	$19,088.00	2	$20,097.43	1

Owner Designated Code	Area(s)	1998		1997	
		Average Monthly Sales per Store	Number Stores Owned	Average Monthly Sales per Store	Number Stores Owned
—	North Jersey	$73,559.22	1	$40,423.15	1
—	North Jersey	$65,693.61	1	$19,165.35	2
—	New York City	$55,683.71	1	$49,991.26	2
—	North Jersey	$49,998.65	1	$39,072.22	1
—	Long Island	$50,583.51	1	$17,106.27	1
—	North Jersey	$41,205.32	1	$22,518.47	1
—	New York City	$44,323.20	1	$29,811.76	1
—	New York City	$42,419.62	1	$35,427.64	1
—	North Jersey	$32,542.85	1	$26,693.58	1
—	Pennsylvania	$28,730.75	1	$21,318.21	1
—	Central Florida	$13,247.57	1	$16,099.65	2
—	South Florida	$12,608.24	3	—	0
—	North Jersey	$11,567.38	1	$13,570.92	1
	Mean per Month	$43,330.02		$35,232.48	
	Median per Month	$44,033.13		$33,846.19	
	Std. Dev.	$20,797.81		$17,658.43	
	Standard Range — Low	$22,532.21		$17,574.05	
	Standard Range — High	$64,127.83		$52,890.91	
			%		%
	Number & Percent Stores Below Standard Range	5	23%	3	15%
	Number & Percent Stores Above Standard Range	5	23%	2	10%

MEDICAP PHARMACY
4700 Westown Pkwy, # 300
West Des Moines, IA 50266-6730
Tel: (800) 445-2244 (515) 224-8400
Fax: (515) 224-8415
E-Mail:
Internet Address: www.medicapRX.com
Contact: Mr. Calvin C. James, VP Franchise Development

Description: MEDICAP PHARMACY - convenient, low-cost, professional pharmacies. The stores operate in an average of 1,500 square feet. We average 90% RX and the remaining 10% over-the-counter products, including MEDICAP-brand private label. We specialize in starting new stores and converting existing full-line drug stores and independent pharmacies to the MEDICAP concept. We teach independent pharmacists how to survive in today's marketplace.

# Franchised Units:	172 Units
# Company-Owned Units:	15 Units
Total # Units:	187 Units

Founded In:	1971	Financial Assistance:	Yes(I)
1ˢᵗ Franchised In:	1974	Site Selection Assistance:	Yes
Average Total Investment:	20-300.5K	Lease Negotiation Assistance:	Yes
Franchise Fee:	8.5-15K	Contract Terms (Init./Renew):	20/20
On-Going Royalty:	2/4%	Initial Training Provided: 5 Days Headquarters; 3	
Advertising Fee:	1%	Days On-Site; 3 Days Computer.	

Average Pharmacy Revenues

The following data represents average revenues and number of prescriptions filled in Medicap Pharmacy® stores for the 12 month periods ended June 30, 1998, and June 30, 1999. These averages are based on averages for all pharmacies that operated as Medicap Pharmacy® stores for at least one full year before the start of each year indicated below. (For example, all stores included in the averages for the period ended June 30, 1999, began operating as a Medicap Pharmacy® store on or before July 1, 1997.)

	12 Months Ended June 30, 1999	12 Months Ended June 30, 1998
Average Retail Revenues	$1,400,113	$1,198,163
Average Prescriptions Filled	39,895	37,300

As of June 30, 1999, there were 148 pharmacies operating under the Medicap Pharmacy® name. Of these pharmacies, 120 operated for the entire period from July 1, 1997 through June 30, 1999, and were used in preparing the 1999 averages. 38% of these pharmacies had revenues higher than the average for the 12 months ended June 30, 1999, and 38% filled more prescriptions than the average for the 12 months ended June 30, 1999. 111 of these franchises were owned by independent franchisees and 9 were owned by us or our affiliates. 41% of the independent franchisees' pharmacies had revenues higher than the average for the 12 months ended June 30, 1999, and 41% filled more prescriptions than the average for the 12 months ended June 30, 1999.

As of June 30, 1998, there were 145 pharmacies operating under the Medicap Pharmacy® name. Of these pharmacies, 116 operated for the entire period from July 1, 1996 through June 30, 1998, and were used in preparing the 1998 averages. 36% of these pharmacies had revenues higher than the average for the 12 months ended June 30, 1998, and 35% filled more prescriptions than the average for the 12 months ended June 30, 1998. 109 of these franchises were owned by independent franchisees and 7 were owned by affiliates of ours. 38% of the independent franchisees' pharmacies had revenues higher than the average for the 12 months ended June 30, 1998, and 40% filled more prescriptions than the average for the 12 months ended June 30, 1998.

We also tracked the same store percentage increases from 1997 to 1998. Average revenues of stores open during the entire 12 months ended June 30, 1997, increased by 16% in the 12 months ended June 30, 1999. 111 of these franchises were owned by independent franchisees, and 40% of those franchisees had revenue increases that exceeded the average. The average number of prescriptions filled by these stores increased by 12.7% during this same period. 111 of these franchises were owned by independent franchisees, and 35.1% of these franchisees had increases in the number of prescriptions filled that exceeded the average.

Average Adjusted Net Income

The average adjusted net income for Medicap Pharmacy® stores in calendar year 1998 was $122,008. This represented a $15,953 increase, or 15%, over the same store's average for 1997. This information is taken from all pharmacies operating as Medicap Pharmacy® stores for all of 1997 and all of 1998. This included 92 pharmacies. Of these pharmacies, 47% exceeded the average adjusted net income for 1998, and 47% exceeded the average adjusted net income for 1997.

The average adjusted net income for Medicap Pharmacy® stores in calendar year 1997 was

$106,055. This represented a $3,916 increase, or 3.7%, over the same store's average for 1996. This information is taken from all pharmacies operating as Medicap Pharmacy® stores for all of 1996 and all of 1997. This included 105 pharmacies. Of these pharmacies, 47% exceeded the average adjusted net income for 1997, and 44% exceeded the average adjusted net income for 1996.

We prepared this average adjusted net income information from reports of net income sent to us by our franchisees. We added back deductions taken for interest, income taxes, depreciation, amortization, and salary paid to the pharmacy manager (or owner/manager). We then averaged the net results for all pharmacies.

Additional Information
THESE STATEMENTS OF AVERAGE REVENUES, AVERAGE NET INCOME, AND AVERAGE PRESCRIPTIONS FILLED ARE BASED ON HISTORICAL RESULTS AND SHOULD NOT BE CONSTRUED AS THE ACTUAL OR PROBABLE REVENUES, NET INCOME, GROSS OR NET PROFITS, OR NUMBER OF PRESCRIPTIONS FILLED, THAT WILL BE REALIZED BY ANY FRANCHISEE. MEDICAP DOES NOT REPRESENT THAT ANY FRANCHISEE CAN EXPECT TO ATTAIN THESE AVERAGE REVENUES, INCREASES, NET INCOME OR NUMBER OF PRESCRIPTIONS FILLED.

THESE FIGURES WERE PREPARED WITHOUT AN AUDIT. PROSPECTIVE FRANCHISEES OR SELLERS OF FRANCHISES SHOULD BE ADVISED THAT NO CERTIFIED PUBLIC ACCOUNTANT HAS AUDITED THESE FIGURES OR EXPRESSED HIS/HER OPINION WITH REGARD TO THE CONTENT OR FORM.

The information used in this section was taken from information provided to us by our franchisees. We have no reason to doubt the accuracy of the information, but we have not verified it, and the information has not been audited. We do recommend our franchisees use a particular accounting method or system, and we believe the vast majority of our franchisees use this system and that these numbers were computed using that system. The system uses generally accepted accounting principles.

We anticipate you will provide similar goods and services as the pharmacies we used in compiling information for this Item 19. We will provide substantially similar training and services to you as we provided to the owners of these pharmacies.

If you want substantiation of any of the data or information we used in preparing the numbers in this Item 19, we will make it available to you upon reasonable request.

PEARLE VISION CENTER
1925 Enterprise Pkwy.
Twinsburg, OH 44087
Tel: (800) 282-3931 (330) 486-3000
Fax: (330) 486-3425
E-Mail: g.helwig@mciworldcom.net
Internet Address: www.pearlevision.com
Contact: Mr. Greg Hilwig, Dir. Franchise Stores

Description: PEARLE VISION, the largest optical franchisor, offers the ability for qualified individuals to benefit from PEARLE's strong name recognition and operating systems developed over the past 36 years. We have been franchising for 16 years.

# Franchised Units:	323 Units
# Company-Owned Units:	368 Units
Total # Units:	691 Units
Founded In:	1961
1st Franchised In:	1980
Average Total Investment:	135-2.5MM
Franchise Fee:	30K
On-Going Royalty:	7%
Advertising Fee:	9%
Financial Assistance:	Yes(B)
Site Selection Assistance:	NR
Lease Negotiation Assistance:	No
Contract Terms (Init./Renew):	10/10
Initial Training Provided:	Varies Dramatically With Skill Assessment of Franchisee.

The following is unaudited sales information for franchised Pearle Vision stores operational for the 12 month period ending December 31, 1997, and reporting 12 full calendar months of sales information for that period. A description of the material assumptions and sources from which the data was derived is set forth in the footnotes below.

Sales Data for Stores Operating for the Full Calendar Year 1997

Average Annual Sales	$ 694,603
Median Sales	$ 567,200
Minimum Sales	$ 171,400
Maximum Sales	$ 2,792,700
Total Number of Stores	263
Number of Stores Meeting or Exceeding the Average	92

1. The results shown in Table I are based on unaudited sales reports submitted to Us by Franchisees for the period from January 1, 1997 to December 31, 1997. While We routinely audit franchisee sales reports, We have not investigated and are unable to independently verify the accuracy of this information.

2. As of December 31, 1997, there were 329 Pearle Vision surfacing or finishing stores operated by Franchisees, 322 of which were operational during all or a portion of the period from January 1, 1997 to December 31, 1997. Of these 322 stores, 263 stores had been in operation for and reported a full 12 calendar months of sales for the reporting period. The remaining 58 franchised stores were either not operational for a full 12 calendar months as of December 31, 1997 or had failed to report sales for one or more months during the reporting period and are therefore not included in this statement.

3. This statement includes sales information from: 1) 119 surfacing stores which have the capacity to grind lenses to prescription specifications and cut stock lenses to fit frames to create finished products on site, usually within one hour; 2) 143 finishing stores which have the capacity to cut stock lenses to fit frames to create finished products, but must rely on third party laboratories to fulfill orders which require lenses to be ground to fill unique or unusual prescriptions; and 3) 1 Limited Public Access Dispensary which is located within another medical facility, such as a hospital or clinic and has the capacity only to dispense finished products which are manufactured at an off-site facility.

4. The stores included in this statement range in age from 1 to approximately 17 years and are located in 38 states. The stores are found within a large range of commercial areas including single store markets, suburban communities and urban population centers.

5. The surfacing stores included in this statement average approximately 3,000 to 3,200 square feet and are located primarily in regional and super regional shopping centers. The finishing stores included in this statement average approximately 1,500 to 2,200 square feet and are located primarily in regional shopping centers. Both types of stores are located in strip centers, stand alone stores and enclosed malls.

6. Factors which could affect sales at a particular store include temporary interruption in availability or unavailability of an on site professional to perform eye exams; temporary construction of surrounding facilities which may impair visibility of or access to the store; state licensing requirements or prohibitions which may require changes in certain critical operational aspects of the store, square footage of the store; demographics of the population within the store's trading area; the number of consumers utilizing managed vision care programs within the store's trading area; and the number of other Pearle Vision stores located in or near your market.

7. We offered substantially the same products, services, training and support to all of the stores included in this statement and the stores offered substantially the same products and services to the public.

8. Substantiation of the data used in preparing this statement will be made available upon reasonable request.Except for the information in this Item 19, we do not authorize our salespersons to furnish any oral or written information concerning the actual or potential sales, costs, income or profits of a Pearle Vision store.

THIS SALES DATA IS OF SPECIFIC FRANCHISEE OWNED UNITS AND SHOULD NOT BE CONSIDERED AS THE ACTUAL OR PROBABLE SALES THAT YOU WILL REALIZE. WE DO NOT REPRESENT THAT ANY FRANCHISEE CAN EXPECT TO ATTAIN THE SAME OR SIMILAR ACTUAL OR AVERAGE LEVEL OF SALES. ACTUAL RESULTS MAY VARY FROM STORE TO STORE AND WE CANNOT ESTIMATE THE RESULTS OF ANY PARTICULAR FRANCHISE. WE ENCOURAGE YOU TO REVIEW THIS MATERIAL WITH YOUR ATTORNEY OR ACCOUNTANT.

Laundry & dry cleaning

EAGLE CLEANERS
1750 University Dr., # 111
Coral Springs, FL 33071
Tel: (800) 275-9751 (954) 346-9501
Fax: (954) 346-9505
E-Mail:
Internet Address:
Contact: Mr. Gerard J. Teeven, President

Description: Franchisor of state-of-the-art dry-cleaning stores, offering turn-key plants and drop stores, complete training, site evaluation and a marketing strategy that separates us from the rest of the dry cleaning industry.

# Franchised Units:	92 Units
# Company-Owned Units:	0 Units
Total # Units:	92 Units
Founded In:	1991
1st Franchised In:	1993
Average Total Investment:	200-250K
Franchise Fee:	15K
On-Going Royalty:	5%/$195
Advertising Fee:	3%
Financial Assistance:	Yes(I)
Site Selection Assistance:	Yes
Lease Negotiation Assistance:	Yes
Contract Terms (Init./Renew):	10/10

Initial Training Provided:3 Weeks Coral Springs, FL; 1 Week Opening; 90-120 Post-Opening.

Other than the information presented in Exhibit I, Eagle Cleaners does not furnish or authorize its salespersons to furnish any oral or written information concerning the actual or potential sales, costs, income or profits of your Eagle Cleaners Franchise. Actual results vary from Franchise to Franchise, and Eagle Cleaners cannot estimate the results of any particular franchise. You should not rely on unauthorized representations as to earnings, sales, profits or prospects or chances of success.

Exhibit I

Plant Store, Multi-Unit Development and Drop Store Program Statement of Actual Gross Revenues of Certain Eagle Cleaners Stores
EAGLE CLEANERS COMPILED THE GROSS REVENUE FIGURES IN THE TABLE FROM INFORMATION SUPPLIED BY ITS FRANCHISEES AND SHOULD NOT BE CONSIDERED AS THE ACTUAL OR POTENTIAL GROSS REVENUES THAT WILL BE REALIZED BY ANY OTHER FRANCHISEE. EAGLE CLEANERS DOES NOT REPRESENT

THAT ANY FRANCHISEE CAN EXPECT TO ATTAIN THESE GROSS REVENUES. A NEW FRANCHISEE'S INDIVIDUAL FINANCIAL RESULTS ARE LIKELY TO DIFFER FROM THE GROSS REVENUE FIGURES PRESENTED BELOW.

EAGLE CLEANERS OBTAINED THE GROSS REVENUE FIGURES FROM THE INFORMATION SUBMITTED BY ITS FRANCHISEES FROM THE REQUIRED PERIODIC GROSS REVENUE REPORTS. NEITHER EAGLE CLEANERS NOR AN INDEPENDENT CERTIFIED PUBLIC ACCOUNTANT HAS INDEPENDENTLY AUDITED OR VERIFIED THE GROSS REVENUE REPORTS.

ALL EAGLE CLEANERS STORES OFFER SUBSTANTIALLY THE SAME SERVICES TO THE PUBLIC. NONE OF THE FRANCHISED EAGLE CLEANERS STORES RECEIVED ANY SERVICES NOT GENERALLY AVAILABLE TO OTHER FRANCHISEES AND SUBSTANTIALLY THE SAME SERVICES WILL BE OFFERED TO NEW FRANCHISEES.

EAGLE CLEANERS DOES NOT PROVIDE PROSPECTIVE FRANCHISEES WITH PROJECTIONS OR FORECASTS OF GROSS REVENUES, PROFITS OR EARNINGS. ACTUAL RESULTS MAY VARY BY REGION, MARKET POTENTIAL, THE FRANCHISEE'S MANAGERIAL SKILL, COMPETITION AND OTHER FACTORS BEYOND EAGLE CLEANER'S CONTROL. THERE IS NO GUARANTEE THAT ANY NEW FRANCHISEE WILL ATTAIN THE GROSS REVENUE LEVELS ATTAINED BY THE EXISTING FRANCHISEES. SUBSTANTIATION OF THE GROSS REVENUES OF FRANCHISED EAGLE CLEANERS STORE WILL BE PROVIDED TO PROSPECTIVE FRANCHISEES UPON REASONABLE REQUEST.

THE FOLLOWING CHART CONTAINS INFORMATION RELATING SOLELY TO HISTORICAL GROSS REVENUE INFORMATION REGARDING EXISTING FRANCHISED EAGLE CLEANERS STORES. NO INFERENCE AS TO EXPENSES, COSTS OF GOODS OR PROFITS RELATING TO EXISTING OR FUTURE FRANCHISED EAGLE CLEANERS STORES SHOULD BE DRAWN FROM THEM.

The following chart shows the average Gross Revenues, the percent of Stores exceeding the average, and the high Gross Revenue volume and low Gross Revenue volume for franchised Eagle Cleaners Stores based on the number of years in operation. The Gross Revenue figures are for the 12-month period from January 1 through December 31, 1997 only. Eagle Cleaners derived the Gross Revenue figures from periodic Gross Revenue reports it received from those franchised Eagle Cleaners Stores that were open for the entire period stated. In all instances, the Stores had completed a full year of operation before inclusion in the table. Gross Revenues of any Eagle Cleaners Stores within your territory are likely to differ substantially during the first year of operation. The term "Gross Revenues" is defined in the Franchise Agreement and is the basis for payment of royalties.

Number of Years Franchised Store Completed in Business as of 12/31/97	Number of Franchised Stores Eligible[1] to Report for Period	Number of Eligible[1] Franchised Stores Reporting for Period[2]	Total Gross Revenues of Reporting Stores	Average Volume of Reporting Stores During Reporting Period	% of Reporting Stores Meeting or Exceeding Average Volume	Highest Volume During Reporting Period	Lowest Volume During Reporting Period
Completed 1 Year	11	11	$2,384,592	$238,459	40%	$418,202	$115,000
Completed 2 Years	10	7	2,614,773	326,847	38%	623,837	203,885
Completed 3 Years	14	10	2,110,031	211,003	50%	377,615	82,982

Number of Years Franchised Store Completed in Business as of 12/31/97	Number of Franchised Stores Eligible[1] to Report for Period	Number of Eligible[1] Franchised Stores Reporting for Period[2]	Total Gross Revenues of Reporting Stores	Average Volume of Reporting Stores During Reporting Period	% of Reporting Stores Meeting or Exceeding Average Volume	Highest Volume During Reporting Period	Lowest Volume During Reporting Period
Completed 4 Years	6	6	1,499,200	241,533	67%	385,001	78,538

1. Only Stores that were open for the entire period (and were in operation at least 1 year) are eligible to be included in this table.

2. While all Stores are required to report Gross Revenues, Eagle Cleaners has not yet received all reports from some of the Stores.

CAUTION: THERE IS NO ASSURANCE THE EAGLE CLEANERS FRANCHISEES IN YOUR AREA WILL DO AS WELL AS THESE UNITS. IF YOU RELY UPON THESE FIGURES, YOU MUST ACCEPT THE RISK OF NOT DOING AS WELL.

Lawn & garden

NATURALAWN OF AMERICA
1 E. Church St.
Frederick, MD 21701
Tel: (800) 989-5444 (301) 694-5440
Fax: (301) 846-0320
E-Mail: natlawn@erols.com
Internet Address: www.nl-amer.com
Contact: Mr. Randy Loeb, VP Franchise Development

Description: NATURALAWN of America is the only nationwide lawn care franchise offering an environmentally friendly lawn care service incorporating natural, organic-based fertilizers and biological controls. Our franchise owners provide residential and commercial customers with fertilization, weed control, insect control, disease control and lawn diagnosis services using safer and healthier products, eliminating the need for harsh chemicals and pesticides.

# Franchised Units:	46 Units
# Company-Owned Units:	2 Units
Total # Units:	48 Units
Founded In:	1987
1st Franchised In:	1989
Average Total Investment:	50-125K
Franchise Fee:	29.5K
On-Going Royalty:	7-9%
Advertising Fee:	0%
Financial Assistance:	Yes(B)
Site Selection Assistance:	N/A
Lease Negotiation Assistance:	Yes
Contract Terms (Init./Renew):	5/10

Initial Training Provided: 1 Week + 3 Days + 3 Days Corporate Headquarters; 2 Days Regionally 3-4 Times Per Year.

Except for the Analysis of Average Gross Sales for NaturaLawn of America Businesses described in Exhibit C, NaturaLawn of America, Inc. does not furnish or authorize its salespersons to furnish any oral or written information concerning the actual or potential sales, costs, income or profits of a NaturaLawn or America business. Actual results vary from unit to unit and we cannot estimate the results of any particular franchise. Substantiation of the data used in preparing the analysis contained in Exhibit C will be made available on reasonable request

Exhibit C
Analysis of Average Gross Sales for NaturaLawn of America Businesses
Except as provided in this Exhibit C, we do not furnish or authorize our salespersons to furnish any oral or written information concerning the actual or potential sales, costs, income or profits

of a franchised Franchised Business. Actual results vary from Franchised Business to Franchised Business and we cannot estimate the results of any particular franchisee.

Listed below is an analysis of average Gross Sales experienced by NaturaLawn of America service businesses that (i) were owned and operated by franchisees and our affiliates described in Item 1, and (ii) that were open and in operation continuously throughout the 12 month period ended December 31, 1998. As of December 31, 1998 we had 36 lawn care businesses owned and operated by franchisees and 3 owned and operated by our affiliates. The operations of the Franchised Businesses described in this analysis are substantially similar to the Franchise offered under this offering circular.

Gross Sales Analysis

Of the 36 Franchised Businesses, 30 were open and operating in accordance with the System for the entire 12-month period ending December 31, 1998. As of December 31, 1998, 6 of the 36 Franchised Businesses were either not open for the full year, or were not operating full-time in accordance with the System. We compiled the figures provided below based on the weekly remittance reports filed by those Franchised Businesses with the payment of service fees due to us during that period (see Item 6), and the deposit information we received from the franchisees. We also included the Gross Sales information from the 3 lawn care businesses operated by our affiliates that were also open and operating for the entire 12-month period ("Company-Operated Businesses"). The information provided by franchisees that we used in preparing the numerical values included in this analysis has not been audited by an independent certified public accountant, Further, we have not independently verified the Gross Sales data provided by the franchisees, and cannot attest whether it was prepared on a basis consistent with generally accepted accounting principles.

The 30 Franchised Businesses were open and in operation for varying periods of time: (i) 10 of those Franchised Businesses were in operation for 2 years or less; (ii) 5 Franchised Businesses were in operation from 3 to 5 years; and (iii) 15 Franchised Businesses were in operation for more than 5 years. The 3 Company-Operated Businesses used in this analysis were open and in operation for more than 5 years. The lengths of operation are approximations based on the date the respective franchise agreements were signed and the date company-operated businesses began operations. The 33 NaturaLawn of America Businesses used in this analysis were dispersed primarily throughout the Eastern and Mid-Atlantic States. See Item 20 for a description of the location of our Franchised and Company-owned businesses by State.

The following is an analysis of the average Gross Sales reported by those 33 businesses, We totaled the Gross Sales for each of the 30 reporting Franchised Businesses and the 3 company-operated lawn care businesses for the 12-month period ending December 31, 1998. We then calculated the arithmetic mean average Gross Sales for all of the 33 businesses by adding the total Gross Sales for all of the 30 reporting Franchised Businesses and the 3 Company-operated lawn care businesses and then dividing by 33. The average Gross Sales were $388,165 for the 33 NaturaLawn of America businesses. The highest volume Franchised Business had Gross Sales of $1,761,082 and the lowest volume Franchised Business used in this analysis had Gross Sales of $75,538 For the 12-month period ending December 31, 1998. The highest volume company-owned lawn care business had Gross Sales of $1,068,326, and the lowest volume company-owned lawn care business had Gross Sales of $274,618.

We further divided the data into categories based on whether the business had been open less than 2 years to show the results of start-up operations and those businesses that had been operating 5 years or more to show the results of more mature operations. We calculated the arithmetic mean average Gross Sales results for both Company-operated and Franchised Businesses for each of those categories in the same manner described above (totaled the Gross Sales for all businesses within the category, and divided by the number of businesses). The following is the results of that analysis:

System Wide Numbers (All Businesses; 3 Company-operated + 30 Franchised)
Total Sales Volume = $12,809,470
Average Sales Volume = $388,165 (33 Businesses)

10 NaturaLawn of America Businesses (or 30.4%) met or exceeded the average shown.

Franchised Numbers (30 Franchised Businesses)
Total Sales Volume = $11,097,355
Average Sales Volume = $369,911

8 Franchised Businesses (or 26.7%) met or exceeded the average shown.

Company-Operated Numbers (3 Company-operated Businesses)
Total Sales Volume = $1,712,115
Average Sales Volume = $570,705

1 Company-operated Business (or 33.3%) met or exceeded the average shown.

Five or More Years Numbers (All Businesses — 3 Company-operated + 13 Franchised)
Total Sales Volume = $10,112,549
Average Sales Volume = $561,808

5 (1 Company-operated Business and 4 Franchised Businesses) (or 27.8%) met or exceeded the average shown.

Five or More Years Numbers (15 Franchised Businesses)
Total Sales Volume = $8,400,434
Average Sales Volume = $560,029

4 Franchised Businesses (or 13.4%) met or exceeded the average shown.

Five or More Years Numbers (3 Company-Operated Businesses)
Total Sales Volume = $1,712,115
Average Sales volume = $570,705
1 Company-operated Business (or 33.3%) met or exceeded the average shown

1997 1 Year Start Up Numbers (5 Franchised Businesses)
Total Sales Volume = $677,540
Average Sales Volume = $135,508

3 Franchised Businesses (or 60%) met or exceeded the average shown.

You should carefully evaluate the information provided solely in the context of the specific operations and geographic markets where you will operate your Franchised Business. The Franchised Businesses used in this analysis were geographically dispersed as stated in Item 20. To the extent your proposed trade area comprises a market area that is geographically different from the markets of the Franchised Businesses included in this analysis, it is likely that the operational results of your Franchised Business will vary materially from the results of these Franchised Businesses. Variables which differ from region to region and which are likely to materially affect the Gross Sales, costs and expenses of your Franchised Business may include, among others, general population of the market, general economic conditions in the market, recognition and patronage of the Marks, the products and services offered from your Franchised Business, competition and price of competitive products and services in the market, and your ability to generate repeat customers and create customer loyalty. You should consider carefully the difference between the geographic area in which you plan to locate your Franchised Business and those Franchised Businesses from which the information in this Item 19 was gathered.

The financial information provided in this analysis is Gross Sales information, and the analysis does not contain any information concerning operating costs. Operating costs will vary substantially from Franchised Business to Franchised Business. You must consider the operating costs for your proposed geographic area and your circumstances. We recommend you review this analysis with your business advisors. Interest expense, interest income, depreciation, amortization and other income or expenses will also vary substantially from Franchised Business to Franchised Business depending on the amount and kind of financing you obtain to establish the franchised Business. You should consult with your tax advisor regarding depreciation and amortization schedules and the period over which the assets of the Franchised Business nay be amortized or depreciated, as well as the effect, if any, of recent or proposed tax legislation.

YOU ARE URGED TO CONSULT WITH APPROPRIATE FINANCIAL, BUSINESS AND LEGAL ADVISORS AND TO CONDUCT YOUR OWN ANALYSIS WITH THE INFORMATION CONTAINED IN THIS ITEM 19. THE GROSS SALES DESCRIBED IN THE ANALYSIS ARE OF CERTAIN FRANCHISED AND COMPANY-OWNED NATURALAWN OF AMERICA BUSINESSES AND SHOULD NOT BE CONSIDERED AS THE ACTUAL OR POTENTIAL SALES, COSTS, INCOME OR PROFITS THAT YOU WILL REALIZE. WE DO NOT REPRESENT THAT ANY FRANCHISEE CAN EXPECT TO ATTAIN THE GROSS SALES LEVELS DESCRIBED IN THIS OFFERING. IN ADDITION, WE DO NOT REPRESENT THAT ANY FRANCHISEE WILL DERIVE INCOME THAT EXCEEDS THE INITIAL PAYMENT FOR OR INVESTMENT IN THE FRANCHISED BUSINESS. YOUR SUCCESS LARGELY WILL DEPEND ON YOUR ABILITY, AND THE INDIVIDUAL FINANCIAL RESULTS OF ANY FRANCHISED BUSINESS ARE LIKELY TO DIFFER FROM THE INFORMATION DESCRIBED IN THIS ITEM 19 EXHIBIT. SUBSTANTIATION OF THE DATA USED IN PREPARING THIS ANALYSIS WILL BE MADE AVAILABLE ON REASONABLE REQUEST.

SPRING-GREEN.

SPRING-GREEN LAWN CARE
11909 Spaulding School Dr.
Plainfield, IL 60544
Tel: (800) 435-4051 (815) 436-8777
Fax: (815) 436-9056

Internet Address: www.spring-green.com
Contact: Ms. Nancy Babyar, Franchise Development Rep.

# Franchised Units:	92 Units
# Company-Owned Units:	15 Units
Total # Units:	107 Units

Statement of Average Gross Profit Margin of Certain Spring-Green Franchisees During 1997

Revenue	100%
Material Costs	12.3%
Direct Labor Costs	15.75%
Total Cost of Sales	28.05%
Gross Profit	71.95%

A NEW FRANCHISEE'S GROSS PROFIT MARGIN IS LIKELY TO DIFFER FROM THE 1997 AVERAGE GROSS PROFIT MARGIN STATED ABOVE, AND WE DO NOT REPRESENT THAT ANY FRANCHISEE CAN EXPECT TO ATTAIN THE 1997 AVERAGE GROSS PROFIT MARGIN. THE FOREGOING STATEMENT OF AVERAGE GROSS PROFIT MARGIN DOES NOT ACCOUNT FOR CERTAIN COSTS AND EXPENSES A FRANCHISEE MAY INCUR ON A REGULAR BASIS INCLUDING, WITHOUT LIMITATION, ROYALTY AND SERVICE FEES, ADVERTISING FEES AND EXPENDITURES, LEASE PAYMENTS, EQUIPMENT PAYMENTS, DEBT SERVICE, INSURANCE, MANAGEMENT AND ADMINISTRATIVE EXPENSES AND OTHER MISCELLANEOUS EXPENSES.

The Statement of Average Gross Profit Margin of Certain Spring-Green Franchisees During 1997 (the "Gross Profit Margin Statement" or "Statement") comprises the average gross profit margin of certain Spring-Green franchisees operating during the 1997 lawn care season. The Statement was compiled from financial statements submitted by 30 of the 68 Spring-Green Franchisees who were operational for the entire 1997 lawn care season. These 30 franchisees operated 49 of the 105 franchised territories which were operational during the entire year. Data concerning the remaining 38 franchisees were not included in the Statement due to insufficient information from these franchisees. It is unknown to us whether the inclusion of such data, if available, would have a material effect on the gross profit margin shown.

The cost of materials as a percentage of revenues actually incurred in fiscal 1997 by the 30 franchisees upon which the Gross Profit Margin Statement is based ranges from 6.99% to 28.61%. We attribute this variance primarily to factors such as variances in the cost of materials purchased by franchisees, variances in pricing of lawn and tree care applications to customers and variances in the franchisees' efficiency in lawn and tree care applications. Additionally, we believe that inconsistent accounting treatment by some franchisees in the booking of inventory purchases may have contributed to the wide variation of the percentages. Nevertheless, we believe that the average percentage shown in the Statement is reasonably accurate. Twelve or 40% of the 30 franchisees upon which the statement is based experienced a materials cost percentage which was either equal to or lower than the average materials cost percentage contained in the statement.

The cost of direct labor as a percentage of revenues actually incurred in fiscal 1997 by the 30 franchisees upon which the Gross Profit Margin Statement is based ranges from 0% to 26.8%. Direct labor costs includes only compensation (excluding payroll taxes, medical insurance and other fringe benefits) for employees who perform lawn and tree care services and excludes compensation of the franchisee and other administrative and office personnel. We attribute the variance in the percentage of direct labor cost primarily to the extent to which the franchisee employed others to perform application services, with franchisees who performed all application services themselves incurring no direct labor costs. Direct labor costs tended to be lower than average for full time owner-operators with small operations, who performed most of the application services themselves, and tended to be higher than the average for franchisees with large operations, where almost all of the application services were performed by employees. The variance is also due to the different levels of compensation paid to employees who performed application services. Finally, we believe

that some franchisees may have mischaracterized compensation of employees who performed, at least in part, some administrative functions as direct labor expense in their reports to us causing the high end of the direct labor range to become exaggerated. Twelve or 40% of the 30 franchisees upon which the Average Gross Margin Statement is based experienced a direct labor cost percentage that was either equal to or lower than the average labor cost percentage contained in the statement.

Gross profits as a percentage of revenues actually incurred by the 30 franchisees upon which the Statement is based ranged from 56.99% to 89.71%. Seventeen or 56.67% of the 30 franchisees, upon which the Statement is based, met or exceeded the average gross profit percentage contained in the Statement.

Substantiation of the data used to prepare the Gross Profit Margin Statement will be made available to prospective Franchisees upon reasonable request.

We do not disclose actual or average revenues of Businesses due to the significant variations experienced by franchisees. Since most customers use the same lawn care services from year to year, the customer base of a Business tends to be cumulative, especially in the early years of operation. Accordingly, the revenues of the business will tend to be cumulative with the number of years that the business has been in operation. Revenues of Businesses also vary as a result of the number of franchised territories that a franchisee operates. Finally, revenues for a franchisee's first year of operation will vary significantly depending upon when, during that year, the franchisee commences operation. Franchisees who begin operations before the spring season of the year may generate significantly higher revenues for that year than franchisees who begin later in the year.

Prospective Franchisees are encouraged to obtain further financial and operating information from existing Spring-Green franchisees and other industry sources.

Weed Man

WEED MAN
2399 Royal Windsor Dr.
Mississauga, ON L5J 1K9 CANADA
Tel: (905) 823-8550
Fax: (905) 823-4594
E-Mail: weedman@netcom.ca
Internet Address: www.weed-man.com
Contact: Mr. Michael J. Kernaghan, Vice President

Description: Professional lawn care services.

Franchised Units: 130 Units

# Company-Owned Units:	2 Units
Total # Units:	132 Units
Founded In:	1970
1st Franchised In:	1976
Average Total Investment:	75K
Franchise Fee:	20-34K
On-Going Royalty:	$7.9K/Vehcl.
Advertising Fee:	20% Royalty
Financial Assistance:	No
Site Selection Assistance:	Yes
Lease Negotiation Assistance:	No
Contract Terms (Init./Renew):	10/10
Initial Training Provided:	1 Week Mississauga, ON.

Except for the "STATEMENT OF CERTAIN GROSS MARGIN OF CERTAIN WEEDMAN FRANCHISEES DURING 1996," that follows, we do not furnish or authorize our salespersons to furnish any oral or written information concerning the actual or potential sales, costs, income or profits of a Weed Man Business. Actual results vary from unit to unit and we cannot estimate the results of any particular franchise.

Statement of Average Gross Margin of Certain Weed Man Franchisees During 1996

Revenue	100%
Direct Expenses	
Material Costs	10.8%
Direct Labor Costs	17.1%
Trucks & Equipment Costs	7.4%
Depreciation	0.4%
Total Direct Expenses	35.7%
Gross Margin	**64.3%**

YOUR GROSS MARGIN IS LIKELY TO DIFFER FROM THE 1996 AVERAGE GROSS MARGIN STATED ABOVE, AND WE DO NOT REPRESENT THAT YOU CAN EXPECT TO ATTAIN THE 1996 AVERAGE GROSS MARGIN. THE FOREGOING STATEMENT OF AVERAGE GROSS MARGIN DOES NOT ACCOUNT FOR CERTAIN COSTS AND EXPENSES YOU MAY INCUR ON A REGULAR BASIS INCLUDING, WITHOUT LIMITATION, ROYALTY AND SERVICE FEES, ADVERTISING FEES AND EXPENDITURES, DEBT SERVICE, INSURANCE, MANAGEMENT, SELLING AND ADMINISTRATIVE EXPENSES AND OTHER MISCELLANEOUS EXPENSES.

The Statement of Average Gross Margin of Certain Weed Man Franchisees During 1996 (the "Gross Margin Statement" or "Statement") comprises the average gross Margin of certain Weed Man franchisees operating in the United States and Canada during the 1996 lawn care season. The Statement was compiled from financial statements submitted by 5 of the 130 Weed Man franchisees who were operational for the entire 1996 lawn care season. The performance of all franchise owners in the Weed Man System in Canada or the United States. The franchise operations on which the Statement is based were selected because they provided 1996 performance to Weed Man. You should note that of these five franchisees one is located in the United States and four are in Canada; their results may be affected substantially by the location of their business.

The cost of materials as a percentage of revenues actually incurred in fiscal 1996 by the 5 franchisees upon which the Gross Margin Statement is based ranges from 9.6% to 13.0%. We attribute this variance primarily to factors such as variances in the cost of materials purchased by franchisees, variances in pricing of lawn applications to customers and variances in the franchisees' efficiency in lawn care applications. Three (3) or 60.0% of the 5 franchisees upon which the Statement is based experienced a materials cost percentage which was either equal to or lower than the average materials cost percentage contained in the Statement.

The cost of direct labor as a percentage of revenues actually incurred in fiscal 1996 by the 5 franchisees upon which the Gross Margin Statement is based ranges from 13.1% to 21.1%. Direct labor costs includes compensation (including payroll taxes, and other fringe benefits) for employees who perform lawn care services and excludes compensation of the franchisee and other administrative and marketing personnel. We attribute the variance in the percentage of direct labor cost primarily to the extent to which the franchisee employed others to perform application services, with franchisees who performed all application services themselves incurring no direct labor costs. Direct labor costs tended to be lower than average for full time owner-operators with small operations, who performed most of the application services themselves, and tended to be higher than the average for franchisees with large operations, where almost all of the application services were performed by employees. The variance is also due to the different levels of compensation paid to employees who performed application services. Two (2) or 40.0% of the 5 franchisees upon which the Average Gross Margin Statement is based experienced a direct labor cost percentage that was either equal to or lower than the average labor cost percentage contained in the Statement.

Truck & Equipment costs as a percentage of revenues actually incurred in fiscal 1996 by the 5 franchisees upon which the Gross Margin Statement is based ranges from 5.2% to 16.2%. We attribute the variation to a number of reasons. Depending on the age of the business, some trucks are owned and others are leased. Normally, in the early years, this percentage is higher when the trucks are not owned. In the more mature franchises, the expenses reflect the higher maintenance costs associated with theses vehicles. Three (3) or 60.0% of the 5 franchisees upon which the Average Gross Margin Statement is based experienced a truck & equipment cost percentage that was either equal

to or lower than the average truck & labor cost percentage contained in the Statement.

The depreciation costs as a percentage of revenues actually incurred in fiscal 1996 by the 5 franchisees upon which the Gross Margin Statement is based ranges from 0.2% to 0.8%. The variation is a reflection of the various lives of the franchisees equipment. Four (4) or 80.0% of the 5 franchisees upon which the Average Gross Margin Statement is based experienced a depreciation cost percentage that was either equal to or lower than the average depreciation cost percentage contained in the Statement.

Gross margin as a percentage of revenues actually incurred by the 5 franchisees upon which the Statement is based ranged from 54.0% to 69.6%. Four (4) or 80.0% of the 5 franchisees, upon which the Statement is based, met or exceeded the average gross margin percentage contained in the Statement.

Substantiation of the data used to prepare the Gross Margin Statement will be made available to prospective Franchisees upon reasonable request.

We do not disclose actual or average revenues of Businesses due to the significant variations experienced by franchisees. Since most customers use the same lawn care services from year to year, the customer base of a Business tends to be cumulative, especially in the early years of operation. Accordingly, the revenues of the business will tend to be cumulative with the number of years that the business has been in operation. Revenues of Businesses also vary as a result of the number of franchised territories that a franchisee operates. Revenues for a franchisee's first year of operation will vary significantly depending upon when, during that year, the franchisee commences operation. Franchisees who begin operations before the Spring season of the year may generate significantly higher revenues for that year than franchisees who begin later in the year.

Prospective Franchisees are encouraged to obtain further financial and operating information from existing Weed Man franchisees and other industry sources.

DEFINITIVE FRANCHISOR DATA BASE AVAILABLE FOR RENT

SAMPLE FRANCHISOR PROFILE

Name of Franchise:	**AARON'S RENTAL PURCHASE**
Address:	309 East Paces Ferry Rd., N.E.
City/State/Zip/Postal Code:	Atlanta, GA 30305-2377
Country:	U.S.A.
800 Telephone #:	(800) 551-6015
Local Telephone #:	(404) 237-4016
Alternate Telephone #:	
Fax #:	(404) 240-6540
E-Mail:	billwilson@aaronfranchise.com
Internet Address:	www.aaronsfranchise.com
# Franchised Units:	136
# Company-Owned Units:	199
# Total Units:	335
Company Contact:	Mr. Todd Evans
Contact Title/Position:	VP Franchise Development
Contact Salutation:	Mr. Evans
President:	Mr. R. Charles Loudermilk, Sr.
President Title:	Chairman/Chief Executive Officer
President Salutation:	Mr. Loudermilk
Industy Category (of 54):	37/Rental Services
IFA Member:	International Franchise Association
CFA Member:	

Key Features

❧ Number of Active North American Franchisors	~ 2,150
% US	~85%
% Canadian	~15%
❧ Data Fields (See Above)	23
❧ Industry Categories	45
❧ % With Toll-Free Telephone Numbers	67%
❧ % With Fax Numbers	97%
❧ % With Name of Preferred Contact	99%
❧ % With Name of President	97%
❧ % With Number of Total Operating Units	95%
❧ Guaranteed Accuracy - $.50 Rebate/Returned Bad Address	
❧ Converted to Any Popular Data Base or Contact Management Program	
❧ Initial Front-End Cost	$550
❧ Quarterly Up-Dates	$75
❧ Mailing Labels Only - One-Time Use	$350

For More Information, Please Contact
Source Book Publications
1814 Franklin Street, Suite 820, Oakland, California 94612
(800) 841-0873 ❖ (510) 839-5471 ❖ FAX (510) 839-2104

worldfranchising.com
the definitive source of up-to-date franchising information.

Visit our Newest Website

www.worldfranchising.com

The Web's most comprehensive and up-to-date site on franchising. Unique features include:

Extensive, Searchable Franchisor Database that includes over 1,000 North American Franchisors. Profiles include all of the data in *Bond's Franchise Guide*, as well as a **direct link** to the franchisor's home page. The Franchisor Database is searchable by:

> Alphabet.
> Industry Category (Over 45 Distinct Categories).
> Average Total Investment.
> Average Franchise Fee.
> Total Number of Operating Units.

Franchise Attorneys.

Franchise Consultants and Service Providers.

International Franchising Section.

Recommended Reading, including on-line ordering capabilities.

Franchise Trade Shows, Expos and Seminars.

Franchise Associations.

All data updated throughout the year to ensure accurate and current information.

Lodging

▲Bass
Hotels & Resorts℠

BASS HOTELS & RESORTS
3 Ravinia Dr., # 2900
Atlanta, GA 30346
Tel: (770) 604-2166
Fax: (770) 604-2107
E-Mail: hifranchise@basshotels.com
Internet Address: www.basshotels.com
Contact: Mr. Brown Kessler, VP Franchise Sales

Description: BASS HOTELS & RESORTS, the hotel business of Bass PLC of the United Kingdom, operates or franchises more than 2,700 hotels and 450,000 guest rooms in more than 90 countries and territories. Franchisor of Holiday Inn, Holiday Inn Express, Crowne Plaza, STAYBRIDGE SUITES and INTER-CONTINENTAL HOTELS.

# Franchised Units:	2465 Units
# Company-Owned Units:	266 Units
Total # Units:	2731 Units
Founded In:	1952
1st Franchised In:	1952
Average Total Investment:	40-150K/Room
Franchise Fee:	500/Rm,40Kmin
On-Going Royalty:	5%
Advertising Fee:	2.5-3%
Financial Assistance:	
Site Selection Assistance:	No
Lease Negotiation Assistance:	Yes
Contract Terms (Init./Renew):	10

Initial Training Provided: Varying fees required. Programs supported by franchisor.

This section contains information regarding the average performance figures for franchised hotels only, for nine of the ten US hotel brands described below in the Holiday Inn system. The statement sets forth the Average Room Rate, the Average Occupancy Rate, and the Average Revenue Per Available Room for the fiscal year October, 1997 through September, 1998. Each of these terms is explained below. All information presented in these system averages is based principally on information received from independent franchise owners, and has not been audited or otherwise verified by us.

Immediately following the statement is additional information that you should carefully consider in order to understand this performance information in the appropriate context.

During fiscal year 1998, average performance figures for Holiday Inn hotels were as follows:

1. **Average Room Rate:** $71.93
   A total of 541 hotels or 28.0% of all hotels in the study period achieved or surpassed this Average Room Rate.

2. **Average Occupancy Rate:** 65.4%
   A total of 942 hotels or 48.8% of all hotels in the study period achieved or surpassed this Average Occupancy Rate.

3. **Average Revenue Per Available Room ("RPAR"):** $47.07
   A total of 630 hotels or 32.6% of all hotels in the study period achieved or surpassed this Average RPAR.

These averages are based on performance information for all 1,930 franchised Holiday Inn hotels in operation in the US for revenues reported and estimated during fiscal year 1998. System Averages were used for any period for which a hotel did not report. The data includes 993 Holiday Inn hotels; 39 Holiday Inn Hotel & Suites; 62 Holiday Inn Select hotels; 20 Holiday Inn SunSpree Resort hotels; 48 Crowne Plaza hotels; 3 Crowne Plaza Resort hotels; 1 Crowne Plaza Suites hotel; 665 Holiday Inn Express hotels; and 99 Holiday Inn Express Hotel & Suites operating during this period.

In compiling the data, we used the following calculations:

The "Average Room Rate was calculated by dividing the total amount of room rental revenues reported by franchisees by the total number of guest rooms rented at the franchised hotels during the study period.

The "Average Occupancy Rate" was calculated by dividing the number of guest room nights reported rented by the total number of rooms available for rent.

The "RPAR" was calculated by multiplying the Average Room Rate for each hotel by its Average Occupancy Rate.

The information presented represents system wide averages for franchised hotels; it excludes results for hotels owned or operated by HHFI and its affiliates. Individual financial results for each Holiday Inn, Holiday Inn Hotel & Suites, Holiday Inn Select, Holiday Inn SunSpree Resort, Crowne Plaza, Crowne Plaza Resort, Crowne Plaza Suites, Holiday Inn Express, Holiday Inn Express Hotel & Suites, Staybridge Suites or other Holiday Inn brand hotel are likely to differ substantially from these figures.

A number of factors will directly affect the financial results of your Hotel. These include the general market for hotel services purchased by the traveling public, the economic strength of the particular market in which the Hotel is located, the length of time the Hotel has been affiliated with Holiday Inn hotels, and the efficiency with which you operate the Hotel.

Substantiation of the data used in preparing the information in this section is available to you on reasonable request.

MICROTEL INNS
13 Corporate Square, # 250
Atlanta, GA 30329
Tel: (888) 771-7171 (404) 321-4045
Fax: (404) 231-4482
E-Mail:
Internet Address: www.microtelinn.com
Contact: Mr. Steve Romaniello, EVP Franchising

# Franchised Units:	49 Units
# Company-Owned Units:	<u>2</u> Units
Total # Units:	51 Units

This section contains information regarding the average performance figures for franchised Microtel Hotels. The statements below include the Average Room Rate, the Average Occupancy Rate, and the Revenue Per Available Room for the 12-month period January 1998 through December 1998. Each of these terms is described below. The Microtel Hotels described in this section are Microtel Hotels that were operated by franchisees who executed franchise agreements both with MISF and with Hudson (which were assigned to USFS pursuant to the Joint Venture Agreement.) All information presented in these system averages we base principally on information received from independent franchise owners, and we have not audited or otherwise verified the information.

The averages and figures below are based on performance information for 12 consecutive months for the 21 Microtel Hotels which have been in operation for at least 24 months before December 31, 1998. None of the Microtel Hotels in the sample were Microtel Suites. As of December 31, 1998, there were 97 other Microtel Hotels that were not in operation for the full 24 month period. Due to the traditional stabilization period for room rates and occupancy, the 97 newest properties have been omitted from the averages.

Immediately following the statement is additional information that you should carefully consider in order to understand this performance information in the appropriate context.

During the period January 1998 through December 1998, the average performance of the Microtel hotels in the sampling (open at least 24 months) was as follows:

1. **Average Room Rate: $40.43**

A total of 15 Microtel Hotels, or 56% of the 27 sampled Microtel Hotels in the study period, achieved or surpassed this Average Room Rate, and 12 were below this rate. The lowest Average Room Rate of the sample Hotels was $35.49, and the highest was $48.56.

2. **Average Occupancy Rate: 69%**

A total of 15 Microtel Hotels, or 56% of the 27 sampled Microtel Hotels in the study period, achieved or surpassed this Average Occupancy Rate, and 12 were below this rate. The lowest Average Occupancy Rate of the sample Hotels was 49.5% and the highest was 87.9%.

3. **Revenue Per Available Room ("RevPar"): $27.95**

A total of 14 Microtel Hotels, or 52% of the 27 sampled Microtel Hotels in the study period, achieved or surpassed this RevPar, and 13 were below this amount. The lowest RevPar of the sample Hotels was $19.00, and the highest was $37/21.

In compiling the data, we used the following calculations:

The "Average Room Rate" was calculated by dividing the total amount of room rental revenues reported by franchisees by the total number of reported guest rooms rented at the hotels during the study period.

The "Average Occupancy Rate" was calculated by dividing the number of guest room nights reported rented by the total number of rooms available for rent during the period.

The "Revenue Per Available Room" was calculated by multiplying the Average Room Rate for each Microtel Hotel by its Average Occupancy Rate.

The information presented represents system wide averages for franchised hotels; it excludes results for hotels noted above that are not in the sample. Individual financial results for each Microtel Inn, Microtel Inn & Suites, or Microtel Suites are likely to differ substantially from these figures. The figures above are averages of historical data of specific franchises. They should not be considered as potential sales that may be realized by you. We do not represent that you can expect to achieve these sales levels.

A number of factors will directly affect the financial results of your Hotel. These include the general market for hotel services purchased by the traveling public, the economic strength of the particular market in which the Hotel is located, the length of time the Hotel has been affiliated with Microtel Hotels, and the efficiency with which you operate the Hotel.

Substantiation of the data used in preparing the information in this section is available to you on reasonable request.

EXCEPT AS STATED ABOVE, WE DO NOT FURNISH OR AUTHORIZE OUR SALES-PERSONS TO FURNISH ANY ORAL OR WRITTEN INFORMATION CONCERNING ACTUAL, PROJECTED OR POTENTIAL COSTS, EXPENSES OR PROFITS OF A PRO-POSED HOTEL.

MOTEL 6
14651 Dallas Pkwy., # 500
Dallas, TX 75240
Tel: (888) 842-2942 (972) 702-6951
Fax: (972) 386-4107
E-Mail: arcioto@airmail.net
Internet Address: www.motel6.com
Contact: Mr. Dean Savas, Vice President Franchise

Description: Quality product, proven operational results, easy to operate. Many open motels available. Well-established brand. Part of Accor organization, largest owner/operator of economy lodging in the U.S.

# Franchised Units:	134 Units
# Company-Owned Units:	<u>722</u> Units
Total # Units:	856 Units
Founded In:	1962
1st Franchised In:	1996
Average Total Investment:	1-3MM
Franchise Fee:	25K
On-Going Royalty:	4%
Advertising Fee:	3.5%
Financial Assistance:	No
Site Selection Assistance:	No
Lease Negotiation Assistance:	No
Contract Terms (Init./Renew):	10-15/10

Initial Training Provided: 1.5 Weeks Dallas, TX for Owners and Managers.

Statement of Average Revenues and Expenses for Motel 6 Properties Owned or Leased by Us During the Period January 1, 1997 – December 31, 1997[1]

Number of Properties: 691[2]
Average Property Size: 113 Rooms
Average Daily Rate: $35.46[3]
Average Occupancy: 65.1%[4]

Revenues

	Mean Average[5]	Percentage of Mean Average Revenues[6]	Median Average[7]
Room Rental Revenues	$956,085	98.9%	$857,646
Other Revenues	$10,674	1.1%	$9,240
Total Revenues	**$966,759**	100.0%	**$866,886**
Operating Expenses			
Salaries and Wages[9]	$177,099	18.3%	$167,592
Employee Benefits[10]	$38,361	4.0%	$29,392

	Mean Average[5]	Percentage of Mean Average Revenues[6]	Median Average[7]
Supplies[11]	$36,203	3.7%	$33,703
Repairs and Maintenance[12]	$32,862	3.4%	$29,905
Utilities[13]	$82,182	8.5%	$75,765
Billboards/Local Marketing[14]	$11,313	1.2%	$10,075
Security Services[15]	$9,091	0.9%	$752
Travel and Other[16]	$23,296	2.4%	$20,794
Total Operating Expenses	$410,407	42.4%	$367,978
Controllable Profit	$556,352	57.6%	$498,908
Overhead & Company Expense[17]	$76,523	7.9%	$68,518
Income from Operations Before Fixed Expenses[18]	$479,829	49.7%	$430,390

THE INFORMATION SET FORTH ABOVE WAS COMPILED FROM DATA FROM COMPANY-OWNED OR LEASED MOTELS AND SHOULD NOT BE CONSIDERED AS THE AVERAGE OR PROBABLE SALES, EXPENSES OR INCOME THAT SHOULD OR WOULD BE REALIZED BY YOU. WE DO NOT REPRESENT THAT YOU CAN EXPECT TO ATTAIN SIMILAR RESULTS. A NEW FRANCHISEE'S RESULTS ARE LIKELY TO DIFFER FROM THE RESULTS SET FORTH IN THIS STATEMENT PRIMARILY BECAUSE "STARTUP" MOTELS TRADITIONALLY EXPERIENCE LOWER REVENUES AND HIGHER COSTS THAN THOSE WHICH HAVE BEEN OPERATING FOR SOME TIME.

OTHER THAN AS SET FORTH IN THIS ITEM 19, WE DO NOT FURNISH, OR AUTHORIZE OUR SALESPERSONS TO FURNISH, ORAL OR WRITTEN INFORMATION CONCERNING ACTUAL OR POTENTIAL SALES, COSTS, INCOME OR PROFITS OF A MOTEL 6 UNIT. ACTUAL RESULTS VARY FROM PROPERTY TO PROPERTY AND WE CANNOT ESTIMATE THE RESULTS OF ANY PARTICULAR FRANCHISE.

1. No franchised operations are included in the information contained in this Item.

2. This Statement reflects the results of 691 Motels owned or leased by us and open throughout the entire period January 1 – December 31, 1997. In addition to these Motels, during 1997 we (i) managed (but did not own or lease) 3 Motels; (ii) owned or leased 49 Motels which were not open throughout the entire year; and (iii) owned or leased 8 motels which did not operate under the Motel 6 name or System.

3. This is the mean average of the rate paid by guests for lodging in all the properties described in note 2 above, for the calendar year 1997. Rate and occupancy are the traditional measures of motel revenue generation, and vary from property to property based on such factors as stay demand in the immediate market, the number and type of competitive properties, the quality and physical condition of the property, service levels, location, visibility and accessibility, brand affiliation (or lack thereof), marketing efforts and effectiveness, prevailing rates in the market, facility reputa-

tion, convenience to destinations or generators of motel stays and other factors.

4. This is the mean average of all room stays in the properties described in note 2 above, and has been calculated by dividing the number of room stays by the number of available room-nights in those same properties.

5. This is the mean average which has been calculated by aggregating the total revenues or expenses for a given category and thereafter dividing it by the number of properties contributing to such revenues or expenses.

6. This percentage reflects the relationship between a specific expense or revenue shown in the "mean average" column and the total revenues of the average property.

7. The "median average" is the point at which half the properties reported higher results, and half the properties reported lower results.

8. "Other revenues" includes revenue primarily from vending sales and guest laundry. Motel 6 guests are required to pay in advance (checkout is not necessary). Under the Motel 6 System, guests do not pay for local telephone calls and are not permitted to incur "room charges" for long-distance telephone calls and other services. Thus, non-room sales are limited to those which can utilize a point-of-sale payment procedure, as with coin-operated or "card-swipe" machinery; as a result, "other revenue" sources are less significant for Motel 6 properties than in the lodging industry generally.

9. We hire and train professional managers, who are paid a wage somewhat below industry averages but are generally furnished personal lodging in a "manager's apartment" built into the motel facility. You are not required to construct or furnish a manager's apartment; if you hire a manager to operate your property, but do not provide an apartment, you may pay a higher wage expense, but would save construction and furnishing costs which, in turn, may

reduce your financing expenses. In addition to management personnel, a Motel 6 Motel will require desk clerks to staff the front desk 24 hours per day. Variable salary costs, depending upon number of rooms occupied, include those for laundry workers, housekeepers, security services and maintenance workers, as necessary.

10. The bulk of this expense consists of payroll taxes and workers' compensation expenses. This entry also includes the cost of our employee benefits package which includes a pension plan, a 401(k) plan and company-subsidized medical coverage. You are not required to offer similar benefits to your employees or any specific level or type of employee benefits. Accordingly, the level and cost of such benefits will be determined by you, and by the requirements of applicable laws.

11. The largest single expense in this category is for linen and bedding, but this category also includes expendable supplies furnished to guests for their use, cleaning supplies, paper goods and items of a similar nature. Expenditures for such items generally vary with occupancy more than any other factor. We are able, by reason of our size and purchasing power, to secure advantageous pricing on most supplies, but you may not be able to purchase supplies at similar prices.

12. This expense includes repairs and maintenance both within guest rooms and in common areas of the property. The extent of needed repairs or maintenance will vary with the quality and durability of construction, furnishings and other materials in the property; occupancy levels; types of guests; unusual climatic conditions; weather and other factors.

13. This expense includes gas, water, electricity, telephone, trash disposal and expenses of a similar nature. The properties reflected in this Statement are predominantly exterior-door motel designs in which heated or cooled air is lost to the atmosphere whenever an entry door is opened; we believe that an interior-

corridor design may experience greater operating efficiencies. Utility charges vary with local suppliers and utility companies, as well as occupancy and climate.

14. This expense consists primarily of the cost of highway billboards announcing the proximity of a Motel 6 property, directions for finding it, and the price of a single-occupancy room. Our guest surveys indicate that highway billboards are an important tool in attracting guests. The outdoor advertising industry is geographically diverse, as are the laws and regulations which apply to billboard advertising. Costs vary widely among locations, and you should check the availability and costs in the vicinity of your intended location.

15. This expense consists primarily of third-party security services hired to patrol the Motel grounds and vicinity for the protection of guests, staff and parked automobiles. The necessity or desirability of such services varies from location to location based on such factors as the surrounding neighborhood, guest and visitor demographics, adequate lot lighting and mechanical security devices, whether the location has a history of problems and crime trends in the market area. Such services are usually provided by local companies or agencies, and you should be able to secure cost estimates locally. As indicated by the disparity between the mean and median averages for this item, the necessity for security services is very location specific.

16. This expense includes such items as travel, relocation, training, recruitment, meals, attendance at meetings and miscellaneous smaller categories (losses, legal expense, dues and subscriptions, financial and collection charges and credit card commissions). You will experience some or all such costs, but expenses vary widely among properties. You are obligated to pay any applicable salaries, travel, lodging and meal costs of your employees while undergoing our training program.

17. This expense includes costs experienced by us for marketing, reservations, administrative and company expenses, field and training expenses, a corporate overhead allocation and some minor management-fee expenses. You are unlikely to experience these costs in the same proportions, and may not experience some such costs at all. However, you will experience expenses not incurred by us in our operations or reflected in this Statement, such as marketing contributions, reservations fees and franchise fees (as described in Item 6 of this Offering Circular), which, in combination with other "overhead" expenses for accounting, administration and management, will likely exceed our "Overhead and Company Expenses" entry shown.

18. From Income from Operations Before Fixed Expenses, you must deduct such capital expenses as interest on mortgages and/or other loans, lease payments, the cost of periodic motel refurbishment, etc. The level of financing-related costs you may experience will be a function of your individual equity and financing structure and, thus, no meaningful estimate can be given here. Periodic refurbishment costs will vary with the quality of original materials used in the construction and furnishing of your Motel, the degree of usage it experiences and factors such as climate and maintenance practices. The Franchise Agreement requires you to replace, refurbish or maintain capital items to ensure continued acceptable quality of the guest experience and conformity with our minimum specifications. You also must deduct fixed expenses such as property taxes, licenses, insurance, etc. These fixed expenses like capital expenses, vary widely by location and individual circumstances.

19. Substantiating material for this Statement is available for inspection by you upon request.

Statement of Average Revenues and Expenses for Motel 6 Properties with 70 Rooms or Less Owned or Leased by Us during the Period January 1, 1997 – December 31, 1997[1]

Number Of Properties: 40[2]
Average Property Size: 60 Rooms
Average Daily Rate: $38.39[3]
Average Occupancy: 74.1%[4]

Revenues

	Mean Average[5]	Percentage of Mean Average Revenues[6]	Median Average[7]
Room Rental Revenues	$626,809	99.1%	$605,199
Other Revenues[8]	5,792	0.9%	5,259
Total Revenues	$632,601	100.0%	$610,458
Operating Expenses			
Salaries and Wages[9]	$129,073	20.4%	$129,165
Employee Benefits[10]	36,102	5.7%	30,338
Supplies[11]	24,078	3.8%	24,105
Repairs and Maintenance[12]	18,876	3.0%	17,372
Utilities[13]	50,705	8.0%	47,291
Billboards/Local Marketing[14]	5,540	0.9%	1,844
Security Services[15]	3,627	0.6%	0
Travel and Other[16]	15,538	2.5%	15,421
Total Operating Expenses	$283,539	44.8%	$265,536
Controllable Profit	$349,062	55.2%	$344,922
Overhead & Company Expense[17]	$50,110	7.9%	$48,099
Income from Operations Before Fixed Expenses[18]	$298,952	47.36%	$296,823

THE INFORMATION SET FORTH ABOVE WAS COMPILED FROM DATA FROM COMPANY-OWNED OR LEASED MOTELS AND SHOULD NOT BE CONSIDERED AS THE AVERAGE OR PROBABLE SALES, EXPENSES OR INCOME THAT SHOULD OR WOULD BE REALIZED BY YOU. WE DO NOT REPRESENT THAT YOU CAN EXPECT TO ATTAIN SIMILAR RESULTS. A NEW FRANCHISEE'S RESULTS ARE LIKELY TO DIFFER FROM THE RESULTS SET FORTH IN THIS STATEMENT PRIMARILY BECAUSE "STARTUP" MOTELS TRADITIONALLY EXPERIENCE LOWER REVENUES AND HIGHER COSTS THAN THOSE WHICH HAVE BEEN OPERATING FOR SOME TIME.

OTHER THAN AS SET FORTH IN THIS ITEM 19, WE DO NOT FURNISH, OR AUTHORIZE OUR SALESPERSONS TO FURNISH, ORAL OR WRITTEN INFORMATION CONCERNING ACTUAL OR POTENTIAL SALES, COSTS, INCOME OR PROFITS OF A MOTEL 6 UNIT. ACTUAL RESULTS VARY FROM PROPERTY TO PROPERTY AND WE

CANNOT ESTIMATE THE RESULTS OF ANY PARTICULAR FRANCHISE.

1. No franchised operations are included in the information contained in this Item.

2. This Statement reflects the results of 40 Motels owned or leased by us and open throughout the entire period January 1 – December 31, 1997 which have a room count of equal to or less than 70 rooms per property.

3. This is the mean average of the rate paid by guests for lodging in all the properties described in note 2 above, for the calendar year 1997. Rate and occupancy are the traditional measures of motel revenue generation, and vary from property to property based on such factors as stay demand in the immediate market, the number and type of competitive properties, the quality and physical condition of the property, service levels, location, visibility and accessibility, brand affiliation (or lack thereof), marketing efforts and effectiveness, prevailing rates in the market, facility reputation, convenience to destinations or generators of motel stays and other factors.

4. This is the mean average of all room stays in the properties described in note 2 above, and has been calculated by dividing the number of room stays by the number of available room-nights in those same properties.

5. This is the mean average which has been calculated by aggregating the total revenues or expenses for a given category and thereafter dividing it by the number of properties contributing to such revenues or expenses.

6. This percentage reflects the relationship between a specific expense or revenue shown in the "mean average" column and the total revenues of the average property.

7. The "median average" is the point at which half the properties reported higher results, and half the properties reported lower results.

8. "Other revenues" includes revenue primarily from vending sales and guest laundry. Motel 6 guests are required to pay in advance (check-out is not necessary). Under the Motel 6 System, guests do nor pay for local telephone calls and are not permitted to incur "room charges" for long-distance telephone calls and other services. Thus, non-room sales are limited to those which can utilize a point-of-sale payment procedure, as with coin-operated or "card-swipe" machinery; as a result, "other revenue" sources are less significant for Motel 6 properties than in the lodging industry generally.

9. We hire and train professional managers, who are paid a wage somewhat below industry averages but are generally furnished personal lodging in a "manager's apartment" built into the motel facility. You are not required to construct or furnish a manager's apartment; if you hire a manager to operate your property, but do not provide an apartment, you may pay a higher wage expense, but would save construction and furnishing costs which, in turn, may reduce your financing expenses. In addition to management personnel, a Motel 6 Motel will require desk clerks to staff the front desk 24 hours per day, as well as a head housekeeper. Variable salary costs, depending upon number of rooms and occupancy, include those for laundry workers, housekeepers, security services and maintenance workers, as necessary.

10. The bulk of this expense consists of payroll taxes and workers' compensation expenses. This entry also includes the cost of our employee benefits package which includes a pension plan, a 401(k) plan and company-subsidized medical coverage. You are not required to offer similar benefits to your employees or any specific level or type of employee benefits. Accordingly, the level and cost of such benefits will be determined by you, and by the requirements of applicable laws.

11. The largest single expense in this category is for linen and bedding, but this category also includes expendable supplies furnished to

guests for their use, cleaning supplies, paper goods and items of a similar nature. Expenditures for such items generally vary with occupancy more than any other factor. We are able, by reason of our size and purchasing power, to secure advantageous pricing on most supplies, but you may not be able to purchase supplies at similar prices.

12. This expense includes repairs and maintenance both within guest rooms and in common areas of the property. The extent of needed repairs or maintenance will vary with the quality and durability of construction, furnishings and other materials in the property; occupancy levels; types of guests; unusual climatic conditions; weather and other factors.

13. This expense includes gas, water, electricity, telephone, trash disposal and expenses of a similar nature. The properties reflected in this Statement are predominantly exterior-door motel designs in which heated or cooled air is lost to the atmosphere whenever an entry door is opened; we believe that an interior-corridor design may experience greater operating efficiencies. Utility charges vary with local suppliers and utility companies, as well as occupancy and climate.

14. This expense consists primarily of the cost of highway billboards announcing the proximity of a Motel 6 property, directions for finding it, and the price of a single-occupancy room. Our guest surveys indicate that highway billboards are an important tool in attracting guests. The outdoor advertising industry is geographically diverse, as are the laws and regulations which apply to billboard advertising. Costs vary widely among locations, and you should check the availability and costs in the vicinity of your intended location.

15. This expense consists primarily of third-party security services hired to patrol the motel grounds and vicinity for the protection of guests, staff and parked automobiles. The necessity or desirability of such services varies from location to location based on such factors

as the surrounding neighborhood, guest and visitor demographics, adequate lot lighting and mechanical security devices, whether the location has a history of problems and crime trends in the market area. Such services are usually provided by local companies or agencies, and you should be able to secure cost estimates locally. As indicated by the disparity between the mean and median averages for this item, the necessity for security services is very location specific.

16. This expense includes such items as travel, relocation, training, recruitment, meals, attendance at meetings and miscellaneous smaller categories (losses, legal expense, dues and subscriptions, financial and collection charges and credit card commissions). You will experience some or all such costs, but expenses vary widely among properties. You are obligated to pay any applicable salaries, travel, lodging and meal costs of your employees while undergoing our training program.

17. This expense includes costs experienced by us for marketing, reservations, administrative and company expenses, field and training expenses, a corporate overhead allocation and some minor management-fee expenses. You are unlikely to experience these costs in the same proportions, and may not experience some such costs at all. However, you will experience expenses not incurred by us in our operations or reflected in this Statement, such as marketing contributions, reservations fees and franchise fees (as described in Item 6 of this Offering Circular), which, in combination with other "overhead" expenses for accounting, administration and management, will likely exceed our "Overhead and Company Expenses" entry shown.

18. From Income from Operations Before Fixed Expenses, you must deduct such capital expenses as interest on mortgages and/or other loans, lease payments, the cost of periodic Motel refurbishment, etc. The level of financing-related costs you may experience will be a function of your individual equity and

financing structure and, thus, no meaningful estimate can be given here. Periodic refurbishment costs will vary with the quality of original materials used in the construction and furnishing of your Motel, the degree of usage it experiences and factors such as climate and maintenance practices. The Franchise Agreement requires you to replace, refurbish or maintain capital items to ensure continued

acceptable quality of the guest experience and conformity with our minimum specifications. You also must deduct fixed expenses such as property taxes, licenses, insurance, etc. These fixed expenses like capital expenses, vary widely by location and individual circumstances.

19. Substantiating material for this Statement is available for inspection by you upon request.

RED ROOF INNS
14651 Dallas Pkwy., # 500
Dallas, TX 75240
Tel: (888) 842-2942 (972) 702-5963
Fax: (972) 702-3610
E-Mail: arcinfo@airmail.net
Internet Address: www.redroofinns.com
Contact: Mr. Dean Savas, VP Franchise

Description: RED ROOF is a strong, proven brand, delivering excellent results. Now a part of Accor, the world's leading owner/operator in economy lodging. Through franchising, this brand offers many opportunities to interested entrepreneurs in open markets throughout the U.S.

# Franchised Units:	70 Units
# Company-Owned Units:	<u>258</u> Units
Total # Units:	328 Units
Founded In:	1972
1st Franchised In:	1996
Average Total Investment:	2.6-5.0MM
Franchise Fee:	30K
On-Going Royalty:	4.5%
Advertising Fee:	4%
Financial Assistance:	
Site Selection Assistance:	N/A
Lease Negotiation Assistance:	N/A
Contract Terms (Init./Renew):	20/10
Initial Training Provided:	1.5 Weeks for Owners and Managers in Dallas, TX.

Average Occupancy Rate, Average Daily Room Rate, Average RevPAR and Gross Operating Profit Margin

At the end of 1997, there were 254 company-owned open and operating Red Roof Inns. The Inn data presented in this Item 19 is based on 223 Inns open at the beginning of the fiscal year following four successive quarters as an open and operating fully renovated or constructed property (the "Comparable Inns"). Red Roof Inns, Inc. believes that the other 31 Inns acquired or developed (the "Newly Acquired inns") which do not meet the definition of a Comparable Inn have not been operated by us for a sufficient period to provide meaningful period-to-period comparisons, as we have closed a significant number of rooms at the Newly Acquired Inns for conversion and,

therefore, the Average Daily Room Rates and the Average Occupancy Rate for these Newly Acquired Inns are not comparable to those of a Comparable Inn. Newly Acquired Inns historically begin with a lower Average Occupancy Rate and Average Daily Room Rate and improve over time following completion of specified renovations and refurbishments (if a conversion Inn) and as these Newly Acquired Inns implement our operating standards and become integrated into our central reservation system. With regard to the Comparable Inns, based on a 52 week comparison, the Average Occupancy Rate was 71.0% and the Average Daily Room Rate was $47.49. The Average Occupancy Rate ranged from a high of 87.4% to a low of 42.4%. 118 of the Comparable Inns achieved or exceeded 71.0% in occupancy (105 below). The Average

Daily Room Rate ranged from a high of $75.32 to a low of $35.35. 84 of the Comparable Inns (37.7%) were above the Average Daily Room Rate of $47.49. The "Average Occupancy Rate" is the weighted average occupancy rate reported for all 223 Comparable Inns, which is calculated as a percentage of the number of rooms occupied to the total number of rooms available during 1997. The "Average Daily Room Rate" is the weighted average daily room rate before allowances reported for all 223 Comparable Inns, which is calculated by dividing the total amount of room revenues by the total number of rooms occupied during 1997. The average RevPAR during 1997 was $33.72 and the gross operating profit margin for 1997 was 60.0% The "average RevPAR" is calculated by multiplying average occupancy by the Average Daily Room Rate. The "gross operating profit margin" is revenues less operating expenses but before fixed expenses, royalty, marketing and reservation fees.

For the 13 weeks ended April 4, 1998, there were open and operating 258 company-owned and 7 franchised Red Roof Inns. The Inn data presented in this Item 19 is based on 243 Inns open (the "Comparable Inns"). Red Roof Inns, Inc. believes that the other 15 Inns acquired or developed (the "Newly Acquired Inns") which do not meet the definition of a Comparable Inn have not been operated by us for a sufficient period to provide meaningful period-to-period comparisons, as we have closed a significant number of rooms at the Newly Acquired Inns for conversion and, therefore, the Average Daily Room Rates and the Average Occupancy Rate for these Newly Acquired Inns are not comparable to those of a Comparable Inn. Newly Acquired Inns historically begin with a lower Average Occupancy Rate and Average Daily Room Rate and improve over time following completion of specified renovations and refurbishments (if a conversion Inn) and as these Newly Acquired Inns implement our operating standards and become integrated into our central reservation system. However, since 250 company plus 7 franchised inns ("All Inns") are used in the data provided by Smith Travel Research and referenced in our advertisements directed at prospective franchisees from time to time, All Inns data for the 13 weeks period ended April 4, 1998 is also included.

With regard to the **Comparable Inns**:

Based on the 13 weeks ended April 4, 1998, the Average Occupancy Rate was 72.2% and the Average Daily Room Rate was $43.31, as compared to the 13 weeks ended April 5, 1997 when the Average Occupancy Rate was 63.8% and Average Daily Room Rate was $45.52. The average RevPAR during the 13 weeks ended April 4, 1998 was $31.27 as compared to the 13 weeks ended April 5, 1997 when the average RevPAR was $29.04.

With regard to **All Inns**:

Based on the 13 weeks ended April 4, 1998, (as reported to Smith Travel Research) all company and franchised Inns' Average Occupancy Rate was 71.0% and the Average Daily Room Rate was $44.18, as compared to the 13 weeks ended April 5, 1997 when the Average Occupancy Rate was 63.8% and Average Daily Room Rate was $46.02. The average RevPAR for all 265 Inns during the 13 weeks ended April 4, 1998 was $31.37 as compared to the average RevPAR for all 249 Inns during to the 13 weeks ended April 5, 1997 when the average RevPAR was $29.36.

The above figures represent averages, and we do not claim that you can expect to attain the same Average Occupancy Rate, Average Daily Room Rate, average RevPAR and gross operating profit margin with your Inn. The Average Occupancy Rate, Average Daily Room Rate, average RevPAR and gross operating profit margins will vary from Inn to Inn and will depend upon many variables and factors, including size, location and relative locations of competitors, seasonality, competition, general economic conditions, the length of time your Inn has been open or affiliated with us, and the efficiency with which you operate your Inn.

YOU SHOULD UNDERSTAND THAT YOUR RESULTS ARE LIKELY TO DIFFER SUBSTANTIALLY FROM THE AVERAGE DAILY ROOM RATE, AVERAGE OCCUPANCY RATE, AVERAGE REVPAR AND GROSS OPERATING PROFIT MARGIN INDICATED ABOVE, AND NO ASSURANCES CAN BE GIVEN THAT ANY PAR-

TICULAR RESULTS CAN BE ACHIEVED BY YOU.

We will provide you with substantiation of the data used in preparing this Item 19 upon your request.

We are under no obligation to disclose specific information for a particular Inn in the System.

SUPER 8 MOTELS

1 Sylvan Way
Parsippany, NJ 07054
Tel: (800) 889-8847 (973) 496-5250
Fax: (973) 496-5351
E-Mail:
Internet Address: www.super8.com
Contact: Mr. Michael O'Hara, Sr. VP Franchise Sales

# Franchised Units:	1715 Units
# Company-Owned Units:	0 Units
Total # Units:	1715 Units

Average Occupancy Rate and Average Daily Room Rate

THE AVERAGE OCCUPANCY RATE AND AVERAGE DAILY ROOM RATE OF A FACILITY NEW TO THE CHAIN ARE LIKELY TO DIFFER FROM THE RESULTS STATED BELOW. WE DO NOT REPRESENT THAT YOU WILL ACHIEVE THESE RESULTS AT YOUR FACILITY. NO INFERENCE AS TO EXPENSES, COSTS OF SERVICES, OR PROFITS RELATING TO EXISTING OR FUTURE FACILITIES SHOULD BE DRAWN FROM THE FOLLOWING INFORMATION.

For the period from January 1, 1998 through December 31, 1998, there were 1,597 Chain Facilities which were operating all 12 months. These Chain Facilities achieved an average occupancy rate of 60.83%. with 855 of them (53.54%) meeting or exceeding this average. The average daily room rate for the 1,597 Chain Facilities during the period was $43.99, with 677 (42.39%) meeting or exceeding this average.

This information was obtained from the monthly revenue reports of Chain Facilities and is believed to be reliable. For any months in which Chain Facilities did not submit revenue reports, we estimated their occupancy and average daily rates based upon their performance during the same month of the prior year, or if not available, based upon the performance of similar Facilities during the same month of the prior year. Occupancy and room rates vary from Chain Facility to Chain Facility and depend on many factors, including competition, general economic conditions, the length and intensity of the hotel trading seasons, management decisions to raise or lower rates to induce changes in occupancy or revenue, geographic location, climate, weather conditions, and cost factors. You set your own room rates.

Reservation Activity of the Central Reservation System

THE FOLLOWING RESERVATION INFORMATION PROVIDES CHAIN-WIDE TOTALS AND AVERAGES. THE CONTRIBUTION THAT THE CENTRAL RESERVATION SYSTEM WILL MAKE TO A NEW FACILITY'S REVENUES, RATES OR OCCUPANCY IS LIKELY TO VARY FROM THE AVERAGES PRESENTED BELOW.

From January 1, 1998 through December 31, 1998, 6,932,031 telephone calls were received by the Central Reservation System. From such calls, reservations for 3,476,848 room nights were booked. This number is net of cancellations received by the Central Reservation System, but includes cancellations and "no shows" at the Facility level that were not reported to the Central Reservation System. Estimated Gross Room Sales generated from such reservations were $173,621,152, representing in excess of 17.17% of Gross Room Revenues accrued by all open and operating Chain Facilities during the period. The estimated average daily room rate for these room nights booked through the Central Reservation System was $49.94.

From January 1, 1998 through December 31, 1998, reservations for 20,058 room nights were booked through the Internet. This number is net of cancellations communicated through the Internet, but includes cancellations and no-shows at the Facility level. Estimated Gross Room Revenues from these reservations were $1,060,260, at an average daily rate of $52.86.

Substantiation of the data used in calculating the average rates and reservation figures presented in this Item will be made available to you after reasonable request. We will not disclose the performance data of a specific Chain Facility and its identity without the franchisee's consent.

Operating Revenue and Expenses

We requested information from all Chain Facility franchisees on the rate, occupancy, revenue and cost structure of their Chain Facilities in 1998 and generally excluded information from Chain Facilities operating less than 12 full months. Information on 465 Chain Facilities is presented in the

following table. The responses are grouped by the number of guest rooms, and data is presented on the basis of per occupied room, percent of gross sales, and per available room. The information is believed to be reliable, but has not been independently verified or audited. Substantiation of the data will be made available to you after reasonable request.

THE SURVEY INCLUDES THE RESULTS OF 465 CHAIN FACILITIES, REPRESENTING 29% OF THE 1,597 CHAIN FACILITIES OPERATING FOR ALL 12 MONTHS OF 1998. THE RESULTS OF THE SURVEY ARE AVERAGES THAT COULD VARY MATERIALLY FROM THE RESULTS OF A SPECIFIC UNIT. YOUR FACILITY'S RESULTS AND PERFORMANCE ARE LIKELY TO DIFFER MATERIALLY FROM THE SURVEY RESULTS, INCLUDING FROM THE RESULTS OF THE CATEGORY IN WHICH YOUR FACILITY FALLS. NUMEROUS FACTORS THAT MAY OR MAY NOT HAVE AFFECTED THE SURVEY RESULTS COULD AFFECT THE RESULTS OR PERFORMANCE OF YOUR FACILITY, INCLUDING, FOR EXAMPLE, INFLATION SINCE 1998, LOCAL ECONOMIC AND LODGING MARKET CONDITIONS, LABOR COSTS, UTILITY COSTS, MANAGERIAL EXPERTISE, COMPETITION, PROXIMITY TO ATTRACTIONS AND DEMAND GENERATORS, WEATHER CONDITIONS AND OTHER FACTORS.

Super 8 Motels, Inc. Survey by Property Size 1998 Grand Total

	25 to 45			46 to 55			56 to 61		
	Per Occupied Room	Percent of Room Sales	Per Available Room	Per Occupied Room	Percent of Room Sales	Per Available Room	Per Occupied Room	Percent of Room Sales	Per Available Room
Number of Motels Reporting	58			81			91		
Average Room/Motels	39.90			49.83			59.51		
Occupancy %	64.51%			57.96%			63.44%		
Average Daily Rate	$44.53	100.00%	$28.72	$44.02	100.00%	$25.51	$42.93	100.00%	$27.24
Telephone Revenue	$0.55	1.23%	$0.35	$0.56	1.27%	$0.32	$0.53	1.24%	$0.34
Net Vending/Lobby Revenue	$0.24	0.54%	$0.15	$0.13	0.30%	$0.08	$0.15	0.35%	$0.10
Other Revenue	$0.28	0.62%	$0.18	$0.17	0.38%	$0.10	$0.20	0.46%	$0.12
Total Operating Revenue	$45.59	102.39%	$29.41	$44.87	101.94%	$26.01	$43.82	102.06%	$27.80
Motel Operating Expenses									
Management Wages	$2.19	4.92%	$1.41	$2.03	4.61%	$1.18	$2.01	4.67%	$1.27
Front Desk Wages	$4.94	11.09%	$3.19	$4.34	9.85%	$2.51	$4.35	10.13%	$2.76

	25 to 45			46 to 55			56 to 61		
	Per Occupied Room	Percent of Room Sales	Per Available Room	Per Occupied Room	Percent of Room Sales	Per Available Room	Per Occupied Room	Percent of Room Sales	Per Available Room
Housekeeping Wages	$3.21	7.20%	$2.07	$3.25	7.38%	$1.88	$3.25	7.57%	$2.06
Other Wages	$0.81	1.81%	$0.52	$0.91	2.06%	$0.53	$0.96	2.24%	$0.61
Unclassified Wages	$0.01	0.02%	$0.01	$0.02	0.05%	$0.01	$0.11	0.27%	$0.07
Payroll Taxes/Benefits	$1.41	3.17%	$0.91	$1.31	2.99%	$0.76	$1.37	3.20%	$0.87
Total Payroll Costs	$12.57	28.22%	$8.11	$11.86	26.94%	$6.87	$12.05	28.07%	$7.65
Property Taxes	$1.76	3.95%	$1.13	$1.73	3.92%	$1.00	$1.75	4.07%	$1.11
Cleaning Supplies	$0.23	0.52%	$0.15	$0.17	0.38%	$0.10	$0.15	0.36%	$0.10
Laundry/Linen Supplies	$0.55	1.24%	$0.36	$0.63	1.44%	$0.37	$0.57	1.33%	$0.36
Guest Room Supplies	$0.40	0.90%	$0.26	$0.41	0.93%	$0.24	$0.38	0.88%	$0.24
Other Supplies	$0.51	1.15%	$0.33	$0.40	0.91%	$0.23	$0.42	0.97%	$0.26
Super 8 Ad Fund Contribution	$0.66	1.49%	$0.43	$0.72	1.64%	$0.42	$0.72	1.68%	$0.46
Other Adv/Promo	$0.74	1.66%	$0.48	$0.56	1.26%	$0.32	$0.66	1.54%	$0.42
Continental Breakfast	$0.49	1.10%	$0.32	$0.58	1.31%	$0.33	$0.55	1.27%	$0.35
Utilities	$2.63	5.91%	$1.70	$2.38	5.41%	$1.38	$2.43	5.65%	$1.54
Telephone	$0.70	1.57%	$0.45	$0.67	1.52%	$0.39	$0.57	1.32%	$0.36
Insurance	$0.54	1.22%	$0.35	$0.50	1.14%	$0.29	$0.52	1.20%	$0.33
Repairs and Maintenance	$1.64	3.69%	$1.06	$1.67	3.80%	$0.97	$2.00	4.66%	$1.27
Cable and Satellite TV	$0.50	1.13%	$0.32	$0.49	1.12%	$0.29	$0.49	1.14%	$0.31
Credit Card Expense	$0.67	1.51%	$0.43	$0.67	1.53%	$0.39	$0.59	1.38%	$0.38
Travel and Entertainment	$0.20	0.44%	$0.13	$0.16	0.35%	$0.09	$0.19	0.44%	$0.12
Super 8 Royalty	$2.09	4.70%	$1.35	$1.97	4.48%	$1.14	$1.90	4.43%	$1.21
Management Fees	$1.52	3.41%	$0.98	$1.53	3.49%	$0.89	$1.42	3.31%	$0.90
Legal and Accounting Fees	$0.39	0.87%	$0.25	$0.38	0.86%	$0.22	$0.29	0.68%	$0.19
Other Operating Expenses	$0.57	1.28%	$0.37	$0.51	1.16%	$0.30	$0.71	1.67%	$0.45
Total Operating Expenses	$29.37	65.96%	$18.95	$27.99	63.58%	$16.22	$28.36	66.05%	$17.99
Income Before Debt Service and Depreciation	$16.22	36.43%	$10.47	$16.89	38.36%	$9.79	$15.46	36.01%	$9.81

WE DO NOT FURNISH OR AUTHORIZE OUR SALESPERSONS TO FURNISH ANY ORAL OR WRITTEN INFORMATION CONCERNING ACTUAL, PROJECTED OR POTENTIAL COSTS, EXPENSES OR PROFITS OF A PROPOSED FACILITY.

	62 to 66			67 to 85			86 Rooms or More			All Reporting Models		
	Per Occupied Room	Percent of Room Sales	Per Available Room	Per Occupied Room	Percent of Room Sales	Per Available Room	Per Occupied Room	Percent of Room Sales	Per Available Room	Per Occupied Room	Percent of Room Sales	Per Available Room
Number of Motels Reporting	88			66			81			465		
Average Room/Motels	62.18			76.20			107.64			66.63		
Occupancy %	65.02%			62.83%			63.71%			62.99%		
Average Daily Rate	$41.61	100.00%	$27.05	$46.82	100.00%	$29.42	$45.30	100.00%	$28.86	$44.24	100.00%	$27.87
Telephone Revenue	$0.54	1.31%	$0.35	$0.58	1.25%	$0.37	$0.55	1.22%	$0.35	$0.55	1.25%	$0.35
Net Vending/Lobby Revenue	$0.14	0.33%	$0.09	$0.25	0.53%	$0.16	$0.18	0.40%	$0.12	$0.18	0.40%	$0.11
Other Revenue	$0.15	0.37%	$0.10	$0.18	0.39%	$0.12	$0.30	0.66%	$0.19	$0.22	0.49%	$0.14
Total Operating Revenue	$42.44	102.00%	$27.59	$47.84	102.17%	$30.06	$46.33	102.28%	$29.52	$45.19	102.14%	$28.46
Motel Operating Expenses												
Management Wages	$1.80	4.32%	$1.17	$1.68	3.58%	$1.05	$1.59	3.50%	$1.01	$1.82	4.10%	$1.14
Front Desk Wages	$3.75	9.02%	$2.44	$3.73	7.97%	$2.34	$2.98	6.57%	$1.90	$3.80	8.59%	$2.39
Housekeeping Wages	$3.11	7.48%	$2.02	$3.38	7.23%	$2.13	$3.60	7.96%	$2.30	$3.34	7.56%	$2.11
Other Wages	$1.05	2.53%	$0.68	$1.15	2.46%	$0.72	$1.31	2.90%	$0.84	$1.09	2.46%	$0.69
Unclassified Wages	$0.00	0.00%	$0.00	$0.00	0.01%	$0.00	$0.07	0.16%	$0.05	$0.04	0.10%	$0.03
Payroll Taxes/Benefits	$1.27	3.05%	$0.83	$1.64	3.51%	$1.03	$1.42	3.14%	$0.91	$1.41	3.18%	$0.89
Total Payroll Costs	$10.99	26.40%	$7.14	$11.59	24.76%	$7.28	$10.98	24.23%	$6.99	$11.50	25.99%	$7.24
Property Taxes	$1.59	3.83%	$1.04	$2.29	4.89%	$1.44	$2.05	4.54%	$1.31	$1.89	4.27%	$1.19

	62 to 66			67 to 85			86 Rooms or More			All Reporting Models		
	Per Occupied Room	Percent of Room Sales	Per Available Room	Per Occupied Room	Percent of Room Sales	Per Available Room	Per Occupied Room	Percent of Room Sales	Per Available Room	Per Occupied Room	Percent of Room Sales	Per Available Room
Cleaning Supplies	$0.13	0.31%	$0.08	$0.17	0.37%	$0.11	$0.15	0.33%	$0.10	$0.16	0.36%	$0.10
Laundry/Linen Supplies	$0.65	1.56%	$0.42	$0.57	1.22%	$0.36	$0.50	1.10%	$0.32	$0.57	1.29%	$0.36
Guest Room Supplies	$0.35	0.85%	$0.23	$0.36	0.77%	$0.23	$0.41	0.91%	$0.26	$0.39	0.87%	$0.24
Other Supplies	$0.36	0.85%	$0.23	$0.39	0.84%	$0.25	$0.33	0.72%	$0.21	$0.38	0.86%	$0.24
Super 8 Ad Fund Contribution	$0.69	1.66%	$0.45	$0.63	1.35%	$0.40	$0.49	1.07%	$0.31	$0.63	1.43%	$0.40
Other Adv/Promo	$0.75	1.80%	$0.49	$0.70	1.48%	$0.44	$0.67	1.47%	$0.42	$0.68	1.53%	$0.43
Continental Breakfast	$0.45	1.09%	$0.30	$0.61	1.29%	$0.38	$0.64	1.42%	$0.41	$0.57	1.28%	$0.36
Utilities	$2.27	5.45%	$1.47	$2.50	5.33%	$1.57	$2.26	4.98%	$1.44	$2.37	5.36%	$1.49
Telephone	$0.55	1.32%	$0.36	$0.59	1.26%	$0.37	$0.53	1.18%	$0.34	$0.58	1.32%	$0.37
Insurance	$0.44	1.05%	$0.28	$0.50	1.07%	$0.32	$0.52	1.15%	$0.33	$0.50	1.13%	$0.32
Repairs and Maintenance	$2.09	5.02%	$1.36	$2.52	5.38%	$1.58	$1.85	4.08%	$1.18	$1.99	4.49%	$1.25
Cable and Satellite TV	$0.47	1.13%	$0.31	$0.48	1.03%	$0.30	$0.47	1.04%	$0.30	$0.48	1.09%	$0.30
Credit Card Expense	$0.56	1.36%	$0.37	$0.70	1.49%	$0.44	$0.68	1.51%	$0.43	$0.65	1.46%	$0.41
Travel and Entertainment	$0.17	0.42%	$0.11	$0.22	0.47%	$0.14	$0.17	0.37%	$0.11	$0.18	0.41%	$0.11
Super 8 Royalty	$1.74	4.19%	$1.13	$2.07	4.42%	$1.30	$1.97	4.35%	$1.26	$1.94	4.39%	$1.22
Management Fees	$1.55	3.72%	$1.01	$1.86	3.98%	$1.17	$1.43	3.15%	$0.91	$1.54	3.48%	$0.97
Legal and Accounting Fees	$0.32	0.78%	$0.21	$0.39	0.84%	$0.25	$0.33	0.72%	$0.21	$0.34	0.78%	$0.22
Other Operating Expenses	$0.77	1.85%	$0.50	$1.71	3.65%	$1.07	$1.91	4.22%	$1.22	$1.18	2.67%	$0.74
Total Operating Expenses	$26.90	64.65%	$17.49	$30.85	65.89%	$19.38	$28.34	62.56%	$18.05	$28.52	64.46%	$17.96
Income Before Debt Service and Depreciation	$15.54	37.36%	$10.11	$16.99	36.28%	$10.67	$17.99	39.72%	$11.46	$16.67	37.69%	$10.50

WE DO NOT FURNISH OR AUTHORIZE OUR SALESPERSONS TO FURNISH ANY ORAL OR WRITTEN INFORMATION CONCERNING ACTUAL, PROJECTED OR POTENTIAL COSTS, EXPENSES OR PROFITS OF A PROPOSED FACILITY.

Maid service & home cleaning

COTTAGECARE
6323 W. 110th St.
Overland Park, KS 66211
Tel: (800) 469-6303 (913) 469-8778
Fax: (913) 469-0822
E-Mail: bnagel@cottagecare.com
Internet Address: www.cottagecare.com
Contact: Mr. Brian W. Nagel, Franchise Licensing

Description: Big business approach to housecleaning. We do the marketing and sign up new customers for you! You retain customers and manage the business, not clean houses. "Jumbo"

exclusive territories are 4 times larger than industry standards, leading to 'Jumbo' sales.

# Franchised Units:	53 Units
# Company-Owned Units:	1 Units
Total # Units:	54 Units
Founded In:	1988
1st Franchised In:	1989
Average Total Investment:	35-70K
Franchise Fee:	7.5-19.5K
On-Going Royalty:	5.5%
Advertising Fee:	As needed
Financial Assistance:	Yes(l)
Site Selection Assistance:	Yes
Lease Negotiation Assistance:	Yes
Contract Terms (Init./Renew):	10/10
Initial Training Provided:	2 Weeks Kansas City Headquarters.

Exhibit G
Statement of Actual Gross Sales
CAUTION: THESE SALES, EXPENSES AND BEFORE TAX PROFITS OF FRANCHISEE SHOULD NOT BE CONSIDERED AS THE ACTUAL OR POTENTIAL SALES, EXPENSES OR BEFORE TAX PROFITS THAT WILL BE REALIZED BY ANY FRANCHISEE. CCI DOES NOT REPRESENT THAT ANY FRANCHISEE CAN EXPECT TO OBTAIN THESE SALES, EXPENSES AND BEFORE TAX PROFITS. FURTHERMORE, THESE AVERAGE SALES, EXPENSES AND BEFORE TAX PROFITS WILL HAVE TO BE ADJUSTED FOR THE EXPENSES AND REVENUES THAT ARE UNIQUE TO EACH FRANCHISEE.

As of December 31, 1998, there is 1 COTTAGECARE Business in operation owned by CCI. All of the businesses are comparable to the franchises being offered.

Set forth below are the actual gross sales figures for the twelve month period ending December 31, 1998 for the franchisees operating CottageCare businesses, that utilize the accounting services and procedures recommended by CCI or who have provided CCI with year-end financial reports.

Actual results vary from franchisee to franchisee and depend on a variety of internal and external factors, some of which neither CCI nor you can estimate, including competition, taxes, differences in management skills and experience levels, the availability of financing, general economic climate, demographic of your territory and the social eco-

nomic profile of the population in your territory. We cannot estimate the result of a particular franchise.

WE RECOMMEND THAT YOU MAKE YOUR OWN INDEPENDENT INVESTIGATION TO DETERMINE WHETHER OR NOT THE FRANCHISE MAY BE PROFITABLE, AND CONSULT WITH ANY ATTORNEY OR OTHER ADVISORS BEFORE EXECUTING ANY AGREEMENT.

Franchised Business in Operation over Four Years			
Location	Gross Sales Last 12 Months	Cost of Sales (Percentage)**	Gross Profit
Charlotte, NC	$557,611	67.1	$183,454
Prairie Village, KS	$456,964	61.6	$175,474
KC/KC (MO)	$336,681	63.9	$121,542
Plano, TX	$328,896	57.7	$139,123
Tulsa, OK	$307,822	69.8	$ 92,962
Shawnee, KS	$304,443	66.5	$101,988
St. Louis, MO	$282,384	64.4	$100,529
Seattle, WA	$263,555	65.5	$90,926
Akron, OH	$254,452	72.1	$70,992
Plymouth, MN	$166,691	65.5	$57,508
North Dallas, TX	$151,846	63.2	$55,879
Lilburn, GA	$148,622	64.4	$52,909
Mid-Cities, TX	$145,422	69.7	$44,063
Tempe, AZ	$139,946	65.9	$47,722
Bloomington, MN	$123,852	64.1	$44,463

Franchised Business in Operation Three to Four Years			
Location	Gross Sales Last 12 Months	Cost of Sales (Percentage)**	Gross Profit
Denver North, CO	$403,246	75.8	$97,586
Oklahoma City, OK	$374,567	72.6	$102,631
Raleigh, NC	$288,616	77.6	$64,650
Salt Lake City, UT	$184,952	63.5	$67,507
San Antonio, TX	$164,179	75.9	$39,567
Orlando, FL	$159,310	83.9	$25,649
Richmond, VA	$123,650	67.9	$39,692
Columbus, OH	$116,038	61.8	$44,327

Franchised Business in Operation Two to Three Years			
Location	Gross Sales Last 12 Months	Cost of Sales (Percentage)**	Gross Profit
Edina, MN	$343,361	63.1	$126,700
Calgary, Canada	$322,606	72.0	$90,330
Portland North, OR	$308,516	69.9	$92,863
Portland South, OR	$264,648	71.5	$75,425
Columbus East, OH	$194,126	69.2	$59,791
South Bend, IN	$177,398	70.3	$52,687
Peoria, IL	$134,905	66.1	$45,733
Pittsburgh South, PA	$112,444	65.1*	$39,243
Wichita, KS	$100,727	N/A	N/A
Pittsburgh North, PA	$90,780	64.9*	$31,864

Franchised Business in Operation Less Than Two Years				
Location	Number of Weeks in Operation	Gross Sales	Cost of Sales (Percentage)**	Gross Profit
Colorado Springs, CO	95	$254,415	76.9	$58,770
Little Rock, AR	95	$236,618	61.6	$90,861
Calgary West, Canada	82	$201,101	68.4	$63,548
Milwaukee, WI	62	$196,249	75.7	$47,689
Sarasota, FL	64	$129,329	82.2	$23,021
Austin, TX	68	$123,545	66.6	$41,264
Philadelphia, PA	77	$88,432	71.3	$25,380

Franchised Business in Operation Less Than One Year				
Location	Number of Weeks in Operation	Gross Sales	Cost of Sales (Percentage)**	Gross Profit
Calgary, N/C	33	$50,598	66.3	$17,052
Marietta, GA	24	$28,137	68.1	$8,976
Kansas City/North, MO	17	$27,850	66.9	$9,218
Scottsdale, AZ	15	$18,614	74.1	$4,821
Toronto/Oakville	17	$14,572	N/A	N/A
Las Vegas, NV	13	$12,265	N/A	N/A
Toronto/North	14	$9,493	56.5	$4,129
St. Louis/Manchester	3	$5,588	31.8	$3,811

*Estimated based on incomplete information provided.
**Taken from financial statements provided to CCI.
N/A Information not provided.

Expenses of a CottageCare Business

Variable Expenses

You incur certain variable expenses in the operation of a COTTAGECARE Business. The variable expenses include:

Direct labor
Royalty and service fees
Advertising
Supplies and services

The royalty fees are set forth in the Franchise Agreement.

Fixed Expenses

A COTTAGECARE Business incurs certain fixed expenses. The following explanations assist in compiling a full profile of expenses:

1. Occupancy Expenses. Included in this item are rent, real estate taxes, insurance, repair and maintenance and building licenses expenses. Depending on the area and location of the proposed COTTAGECARE Business, these expenses vary.

2. Utilities. Included in this item are telephone, electricity and heating expenses.

3. Professional Fees. Included in this item are expenses for accounting and legal fees.

4. Crew and Local Advertising. Included in this item are expenses for all local advertising and public relations you elect to do for crew employees.

5. Debt Requirement. Included in this item are expenses for loan principal repayment and applicable interest charges. This expense category varies depending upon loan amount, amortization schedule and interest rates.

6. Owner's Salary. Included in this item are expenses for the owner's salary. This expense varies depending upon the sales volume of the COTTAGECARE Business.

7. Central Telephone System and Software Support.

This information is based upon the operating results of franchisees which have been made available to CCI.

Hourly wages can vary significantly depending on local and regional employment conditions and the availability of labor.

Substantiating material pertaining to this claim is available for inspection at Franchisor's headquarters and will be provided upon reasonable request

YOUR INDIVIDUAL FINANCIAL RESULTS ARE LIKELY TO DIFFER FROM THE RESULTS STATED. THERE IS NO ASSURANCE YOU WILL DO AS WELL.

CAUTION: A FRANCHISEE'S FINANCIAL RESULTS ARE LIKELY TO DIFFER FROM FIGURES PRESENTED. FRANCHISEES MAY GENERATE LOWER REVENUE AND HIGHER EXPENSES THAN SHOWN ABOVE. IT IS STRONGLY RECOMMENDED THAT YOU CONSULT WITH AN INDEPENDENT ADVISOR, SUCH AS AN ACCOUNTANT OR LAWYER TO ADVISE FRANCHISEE REGARDING POTENTIAL REVENUE, EXPENSES, PROFIT AND LOSSES.

THESE SALES, PROFITS OR EARNINGS ARE AVERAGES OF SPECIFIC FRANCHISEES AND COMPANY OPERATED COTTAGECARE BUSINESSES AND SHOULD NOT BE CONSIDERED AS THE ACTUAL OR POTENTIAL SALES, PROFITS OR EARNINGS THAT WILL BE REALIZED BY ANY OTHER FRANCHISEE. THE FRANCHISOR DOES NOT REPRESENT THAT ANY FRANCHISEE CAN EXPECT TO ATTAIN THESE SALES, PROFITS OR EARNINGS.

HOME CLEANING CENTERS OF AMERICA

P. O. Box 11427
Overland Park, KS 66207-1427
Tel: (800) 767-1118 (913) 327-5227
Fax: (913) 327-5272
E-Mail: mcalhoon@aol.com
Internet Address: www.homecleaninginc.com
Contact: Mr. Mike Calhoon, President

Description: Very large franchise zones. Quality Quality Quality. Owners do not clean houses. Every corporate policy is made by the franchise owners. Each and every owner is hand picked - having money is not enough. Corporate 'Mission Statement' is to have the largest grossing, highest-quality offices in the industry.

# Franchised Units:	25 Units
# Company-Owned Units:	0 Units
Total # Units:	25 Units
Founded In:	1981
1st Franchised In:	1984
Average Total Investment:	30-50K
Franchise Fee:	9.5K
On-Going Royalty:	4.5-5%
Advertising Fee:	0%
Financial Assistance:	No
Site Selection Assistance:	Yes
Lease Negotiation Assistance:	Yes
Contract Terms (Init./Renew):	10/10
Initial Training Provided:	5 Days Denver, CO or 5 days at St. Louis, MO.

March 1, 1999

Caution: These figures are only estimates of what we think you may earn. There is no assurance you'll do as well. If you rely upon our figures, you must accept the risk of not doing as well.

Monthly Expenses and Profit Estimates

Percentage of units:	4%	30%	35%	31% (1)
Gross Sales:	$5,000	$10,000	$20,000	$30,000
Labor:	$2,250	$4,500	$9,000	$13,500
Expenses:	$3,800	$4,800	$7,600	$10,200
Profit:	($1,050)	$700	$3,400	$6,300
Percent reaching net:	100%	86%	88%	75% (2)

1. These percentages reflect the percent of all units achieving the gross sales figures in each column.

2. These percentages reflect the percentage of the units achieving the gross sales figure in each column which also achieve the profit level set out, or better.

3. This forecast is based on 1998 performances by all franchises. The range of monthly sales has been from $5,000 to $66,000.

4. Labor figures include gross wages paid to employees. All employees at franchises which have been in business for over one year are typically paid on a commission basis and are considered full-time employees. Some new franchises choose to pay employees on an hourly basis through a start-up phase.

5. The expense projections include insurance, payroll taxes, supplies, driving costs, advertising, royalties and all related office expenses.

6. The profit estimates are before depreciation and taxes.

The Franchisor requires new Franchisees to pay the Franchisor ($2,000) at the time of training to fund an advertising program that will be implemented exclusively in the new Franchisee's zone during the first weeks of operation.

The Franchisee is required to pay (4.5–5%) of gross sales to the Franchisor each month as an on-going royalty.

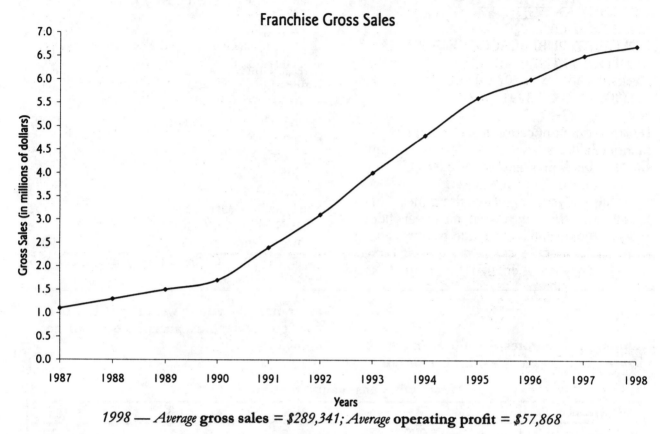

Franchise Gross Sales

*1998 — Average **gross sales** = $289,341; Average **operating profit** = $57,868*

The following schedule represents gross sales volumes and gross profits for Home Cleaning franchise stores for 1998.

THESE SALES AND GROSS PROFITS ARE AVERAGES OF SPECIFIC FRANCHISES AND SHOULD NOT BE CONSIDERED THE ACTUAL OR PROBABLE SALES AND GROSS PROFITS THAT WILL BE REALIZED BY ANY OTHER FRANCHISEE. THE FRANCHISOR DOES NOT REPRESENT THAT ANY FRANCHISEE CAN EXPECT TO ATTAIN SUCH SALES OR GROSS PROFITS.

Schedule of Gross Sales and Gross Profits as of December 31, 1998

Annual Sales	Number of Stores Reporting	Percentage of Stores Reporting
Under $100,000	1	4%
$100,000–200,000	6	26%
$200,001–300,000	9	39%
$300,001–400,000	3	13%
Over $400,000	4	18%
All Stores Reporting	23	100%
Average Gross Sales: $289,341 — Thirty-five percent (35%) achieved this average.		
Average Gross Profit: 40% — Forty percent (40%) achieved this figure in the year ended on December 31, 1998.		

THIS SCHEDULE OF GROSS SALES AND GROSS PROFITS HAS BEEN PREPARED WITHOUT AN AUDIT. PROSPECTIVE FRANCHISEES SHOULD BE ADVISED THAT NO CERTIFIED PUBLIC ACCOUNTANT HAS AUDITED THESE FIGURES OR EXPRESSED HIS OPINION WITH REGARD TO THEIR CONTENT OR FORM.

Information Supporting the Earnings Claim Statement

1. The figures presented on the preceding pages under the heading of Monthly Expenses and Profit Estimates, are based on the performance of all of the Franchisor's franchised outlets, each of which has obtained similar levels of profitability after the first few months of operation. Such outlets are listed on Exhibit A to the Offering Circular.

2. The Franchisor opened a company owned outlet in July, 1981, which it sold in January, 1985. The first franchised outlet was opened to the public on April 27, 1984.

3. The numbers set forth on the Earnings Claim Statement are based on monthly reports received by the Franchisor from all of the franchisees. Copies of these reports are available to the prospective franchisees for inspection at the offices of the Franchisor.

MAID BRIGADE SERVICES
Four Concourse Pkwy., # 200
Atlanta, GA 30328
Tel: (800) 722-6243 (770) 551-9630
Fax: (770) 391-9092
E-Mail: chay@maidbrigade.com
Internet Address: www.maidbrigade.com
Contact: Ms. Cathy Hay, VP Franchise Development

Description: MAID BRIGADE offers the largest territory size with an all-inclusive franchise fee (i.e. territory, equipment and supplies, software, etc.). Lifelong franchise support, plus carefully-designed systems provide the opportunity to develop a large house cleaning business. Franchisee profitability is at the heart of everything we do. Master franchises available outside the USA.

# Franchised Units:	253 Units
# Company-Owned Units:	3 Units
Total # Units:	256 Units
Founded In:	1979
1st Franchised In:	1984
Average Total Investment:	50-60K
Franchise Fee:	16.9K
On-Going Royalty:	7-3%
Advertising Fee:	2%
Financial Assistance:	Yes(I)
Site Selection Assistance:	Yes
Lease Negotiation Assistance:	Yes
Contract Terms (Init./Renew):	10/10

Initial Training Provided:5 Days Atlanta, GA; 8 Days On-Site Week of Opening. Training Videos/Manuals.

We have attached to this Offering Circular as Exhibit H selected gross revenue information regarding the historical revenue performance of our franchisees. Upon reasonable request, we will supply you with data that substantiates this sales information. Other than the information contained in Exhibit H, we do not furnish or authorize our salespersons to give any oral or written information concerning the actual, average, projected or forecasted sales, costs, profits, income or earnings of a particular Franchise. Actual results vary from Franchise to Franchise and from Franchised Business to Franchised Business and we cannot estimate the results of any particular Franchise.

THESE FIGURES SHOW ACTUAL GROSS REVENUES FOR ALL FRANCHISEES AS OF DECEMBER 19, 1998; HOWEVER, THEY SHOULD NOT BE CONSIDERED AS THE ACTUAL OR POTENTIAL GROSS REVE-

NUES THAT WILL BE REALIZED BY ANY NEW FRANCHISEE. WE DO NOT REPRESENT THAT ANY FRANCHISEE CAN EXPECT TO ATTAIN THESE LEVELS OF GROSS REVENUES. WE ENCOURAGE YOU TO REVIEW THIS MATERIAL WITH YOUR ATTORNEY OR ACCOUNTANT. FOR PURPOSES OF THE ACCOMPANYING TABLES, WE HAVE USED THE DEFINITION OF GROSS REVENUE SET FORTH IN THE CURRENT VERSION OF OUR FRANCHISE AGREEMENT — ACTUAL GROSS CHARGES FOR ALL PRODUCTS AND SERVICES PURCHASED BY, OR PROVIDED TO, THE FRANCHISEE'S CLIENTS WHETHER FOR CASH OR CREDIT IN, UPON, FROM, THROUGH OR BY MEANS IN CONNECTION WITH THE FRANCHISED BUSINESS EXCLUDING THE PRICE OF GOODS EXCHANGED FOR GOODS, THE SALE OF WHICH HAS ALREADY BEEN INCLUDED IN GROSS REVENUE AND TAXES COLLECTED.

Franchisees in the Maid Brigade Franchise System as of December 19, 1998 Shown by Region of the Country.

PLEASE READ THE IMPORTANT INFORMATION THAT FOLLOWS THESE FIGURES.

Northeast Region (Connecticut, New Jersey, New York And Pennsylvania)

No. of Weeks Franchisee has been in Operation[†]	Total Gross Revenue Since Opening	Average Weekly Gross Revenue	Weekly Gross Revenue Reported for Week Ended 12/19/98
8 (1)	6,889	861	1,355
500 (3)	1,704,045	3,408	5,739
62 (1)	70,877	1,143	1,063
36 (1)	59,513	1,653	2,390
395 (1)	3,092,901	7,830	16,427
210 (1)	463,990	2,209	1,559
132 (3)	1,205,327	9,131	25,345
26 (1)	28,097	1,081	2,011
297 (1)	782,301	2,634	2,371
* 532 (1)	933,938	1,756	3,792
220 (2)	531,749	2,417	4,792
109 (1)	213,772	1,961	4,207
Averages 2,519	9,086,510	3,607	6,336

Mid-Atlantic Region (Delaware, Maryland and Virginia)

No. of Weeks Franchisee has been in Operation[†]	Total Gross Revenue Since Opening	Average Weekly Gross Revenue	Weekly Gross Revenue Reported for Week Ended 12/19/98
332 (3)	1,277,164	3,847	9,336
* 407 (3)	1,430,447	3,515	4,650
* 442 (4)	2,671,062	6,043	0
183 (3)	332,078	1,815	3,447
501 (12)	13,099,338	26,146	84,470
592 (2)	3,417,502	5,773	6,658

No. of Weeks Franchisee has been in Operation[†]	Total Gross Revenue Since Opening	Average Weekly Gross Revenue	Weekly Gross Revenue Reported for Week Ended 12/19/98
526 (1)	4,289,620	8,155	6,908
538 (3)	3,861,754	7,178	10,662
519 (1)	896,096	1,727	661
585 (2)	8,235,288	14,077	23,742
501 (1)	1,686,342	3,366	7,055
* 595 (3)	2,564,419	4,310	6,094
* 572 (6)	2,767,551	4,838	5,166
382 (2)	2,906,170	7,608	15,567
362 (1)	1,662,501	4,593	5,067
* 542 (1)	2,268,057	4,185	3,484
387 (4)	1,403,779	3,627	7,595
Averages 7,966	54,769,177	6,840	11,797

Southeast Region (Alabama, Florida, Georgia, North Carolina, South Carolina and Tennessee)

No. of Weeks Franchisee has been in Operation[†]	Total Gross Revenue Since Opening	Average Weekly Gross Revenue	Weekly Gross Revenue Reported for Week Ended 12/19/98
517 (1)	995,041	1,925	3,522
464 (4)	2,694,788	5,808	9,964
708 (7)	3,347,659	4,728	2,737
13 (1)	12,508	962	1,687
253 (1)	557,172	2,202	2,810
439 (3)	3,766,269	8,579	10,275
166 (1)	493,840	2,975	6,217
131 (1)	229,191	1,750	2,620
390 (6)	2,650,310	6,796	7,282
610 (4)	2,640,712	4,329	10,004
111 (1)	101,464	914	1,676
216 (4)	761,762	3,527	5,945
191 (3)	624,075	3,267	5,244
45 (1)	41,659	926	1,006
Averages 4,254	18,920,704	4,230	5,070

Southwest Region (Nevada, New Mexico and Texas)

No. of Weeks Franchisee has been in Operation[†]	Total Gross Revenue Since Opening	Average Weekly Gross Revenue	Weekly Gross Revenue Reported for Week Ended 12/19/98
307 (2)	1,155,761	3,765	4,989
9 (1)	8,433	937	2,009
474 (2)	1,715,487	3,619	6,900
426 (1)	1,887,964	4,432	8,620
111 (1)	184,355	1,661	4,943
283 (3)	1,796,777	6,349	11,482
312 (2)	2,145,175	6,876	18,527
17 (1)	21,187	1,246	2,315
Averages 1,922	8,893,952	4,627	8,210

Midwest Region (Illinois, Michigan, Missouri and Ohio)

No. of Weeks Franchisee has been in Operation[†]	Total Gross Revenue Since Opening	Average Weekly Gross Revenue	Weekly Gross Revenue Reported for Week Ended 12/19/98
158 (1)	223,208	1,413	1,822
66 (1)	108,841	1,649	2,327
445 (2)	1,555,820	3,496	5,502
415 (1)	1,922,980	4,634	11,229
220 (1)	348,607	1,585	2,635
75 (1)	154,507	2,060	3,499
Averages 1,379	4,313,963	3,128	4,502

West Region (California, Hawaii, Montana, Oregon and Washington)

No. of Weeks Franchisee has been in Operation[†]	Total Gross Revenue Since Opening	Average Weekly Gross Revenue	Weekly Gross Revenue Reported for Week Ended 12/19/98
14 (1)	6,770	484	1,041
461 (2)	1,975,249	4,285	6,303
283 (3)	2,051,064	7,248	9,554
266 (1)	877,347	3,298	4,510
* 305 (2)	3,201,279	10,496	9,822
111 (1)	136,567	1,230	2,101
447 (5)	6,370,064	14,251	36,183
141 (1)	171,375	1,215	2,123
587 (3)	3,177,177	5,413	7,103
268 (1)	835,690	3,118	5,045
22 (1)	46,576	2,117	3,576

No. of Weeks Franchisee has been in Operation[†]	Total Gross Revenue Since Opening	Average Weekly Gross Revenue	Weekly Gross Revenue Reported for Week Ended 12/19/98
111 (1)	122,841	1,107	1,477
254 (3)	1,451,737	5,716	8,348
* 338 (1)	705,822	2,088	3,791
24 (1)	47,659	1,986	3,257
Averages 3,594	21,122,788	5,877	7,687

† See note 2
* See note 3

1. These charts include only franchisees that were part of our franchise system as of December 19, 1998. Franchisees who were terminated (mutually or unilaterally) or abandoned the system prior to December 19, 1998 are not included. If a Franchise has had multiple owners due to a transfer or sale and the Franchise continued uninterrupted, the Franchise is represented only once in the charts and its cumulative Gross Revenues are shown. *Gross Revenue is shown on a weekly basis not an annual basis.* The chart contains no information regarding Company-owned Franchises because we did not have any such Franchises during our 1998 fiscal year.

2. The figure in parentheses to the right of each entry represents the number of territories associated with that particular Franchise. The total number of territories may vary from the total listed in Item 20 of the Offering Circular because of changes that may have occurred between December 19, 1998 (the date of this document) and December 31, 1998 (our fiscal year end).

3. Gross Revenue information was obtained from our internal records based on franchisees reporting their Gross Revenues when they made royalty payments to us. We had all records for calendar year 1992 to the present and 2/3 of records for all periods before 1992. For the records we did not have, which we estimate to be less than 5% of all records necessary to compile these charts, we received the necessary information from our franchisees or, if the franchisee lacked the necessary data, we extrapolated the figures by using historical information based upon the records we had for 1992-1995. The franchisees marked by "*" are the only franchisees for whom such extrapolation was necessary. We used the following weekly Gross Revenue estimates for extrapolation purposes: $1,538 average weekly Gross Revenue in a franchisee's first full year, $2,885 average weekly Gross Revenue in the second full year and $4,327 average weekly Gross Revenue in the third full year. These averages were obtained from the Gross Revenue data we received from all franchisees for the period between 1992–1995. We believe using data based on all franchisees more accurately reflects the data that was missing than estimating average weekly Gross Revenues for the periods missing based on the average weekly Gross Revenue data for the affected franchisees in 1992-1995 which might have yielded an artificially high average weekly Gross Revenue because in the latter case the data used would have related to a period when the affected franchisees were more experienced and would likely have had higher Gross Revenues. All records we have are available for your review at our corporate headquarters. Gross Revenue information used to compile this chart has not been audited.

4. All states where franchisees are located are represented in the chart. States not represented indicate that there are no franchisees currently located in those states.

5. Franchisees who had multiple territories within multiple regions were listed in the region where their primary location is located.

6. Please be aware that some franchisees added operating territories during the term of their Franchise Agreement. This chart does not show the increase in Gross Revenues that may have occurred as a result of enlarging the franchisee's operating territory.

7. Factors that may affect a franchisee's weekly average Gross Revenues and which may explain why some franchisees have a higher average weekly Gross Revenue than others include: the number of Qualified Households within the franchisee's operating territory; whether the operating territory is in a rural versus an urban setting; prices charged by the franchisee for products and services; the number of maid teams used by the franchisee; the amount of advertising and promotional expenditures undertaken by the franchisee; and the franchisee's business skill. We draw no particular conclusions from a franchisee's weekly Gross Revenue for the week ended December 19, 1998 being greater or less than the franchisee's average weekly Gross Revenue for the period that the franchisee has been in operation. It may be a function of seasonal variations, customer preferences, economic conditions, competition, franchisee efforts and business acumen, and other factors.

8. Of the 12 Franchises in the Northeast region in operation as of December 19, 1998, 2 Franchises or 17% exceeded the average weekly Gross Revenue for the region of $3,607.

9. Of the 17 Franchises in the Mid-Atlantic region in operation as of December 19, 1998, 5 Franchises or 29% exceeded the average weekly Gross Revenue for the region of $6,840.

10. Of the 14 Franchises in the Southeast region in operation as of December 19, 1998, 5 Franchises or 36% exceeded the average weekly Gross Revenue for the region of $4,230.

11. Of the 8 Franchises in the Southwest region in operation as of December 19, 1998, 2 Franchises or 25% exceeded the average weekly Gross Revenue for the region of $4,627.

12. Of the 6 Franchises in the Midwest region in operation as of December 19, 1998, 2 Franchises or 33% exceeded the average weekly Gross Revenue for the region of $3,128.

13. Of the 15 Franchises in the West region in operation as of December 19, 1998, 3 Franchises or 20% exceeded the average weekly Gross Revenue for the region of $5,877.

Caution Important Information
The Gross Revenue results reported above are based upon the performance of all franchisees existing as of December 19, 1998. There is no assurance that you will do as well as any of these franchisees. If you rely upon these figures, you must accept the risk of not doing as well. We make no representation regarding the net earnings of any Franchise or that the information shown is indicative of the success of any Franchise. These charts specifically do not include a Franchise's operating expenses, general and administrative expenses or other factors that may affect profitability.

Sales, expenses and income will vary from Franchised Business to Franchised Business and market to market, and we do not represent that Gross Revenues for the franchisees shown above for the periods indicated will accurately predict the future results for those franchisees or for any potential franchisee. Factors which may affect Gross Revenue, and which you should consider carefully in evaluating this information and in making any decision to purchase a Franchise, include: income and demographic characteristics of a particular market area; competition; expense variables in a particular market (e.g. rent, advertising expense, insurance and labor cost); your business skills, your motivation and effort in operating the Franchise; your financial wherewithal and financial capabilities; your ability to borrow money which may be necessary to operate the Franchise and the terms of debt obligations; conditions generally prevailing in the local and national economy; the number of employees you hire; the size of your operating territory; and your general business acumen.

UPON REASONABLE REQUEST, WE WILL SUPPLY YOU WITH DATA TO SUBSTANTIATE THE ABOVE FIGURES.

MAIDS, THE
4820 Dodge St.
Omaha, NE 68132-4820
Tel: (800) 843-6243 (402) 558-5555
Fax: (402) 558-4112
E-Mail: jbasden@navix.net
Internet Address: www.maids.com
Contact: Mr. Michael P. Fagen, Executive Vice President

Description: AMERICA'S MAID SERVICE - THE MAIDS is the premier residential cleaning franchise. Our cleaning system is the most thorough in the industry and sets us ahead of all competition. We offer low investment, comprehensive training and on-going support that set the industry standard. Call THE MAIDS today and discover why we are AMERICA'S MAID SERVICE.

# Franchised Units:	378 Units
# Company-Owned Units:	50 Units
Total # Units:	428 Units
Founded In:	1979
1st Franchised In:	1980
Average Total Investment:	56-245K
Franchise Fee:	17.5K
On-Going Royalty:	3.3-7%
Advertising Fee:	1%
Financial Assistance:	Yes(I)
Site Selection Assistance:	Yes
Lease Negotiation Assistance:	No
Contract Terms (Init./Renew):	20/20

Initial Training Provided: 8 Days Each in Both Managerial and Technical Training at Headquarters; 90 Days On-Site.

Selected Sales and Income Information of MegaMarket Franchises

The information presented in the next two tables represents the results of operations of the 17 MegaMarket franchises operating as of September 30, 1998 and that submitted the required reports to TMI. A MegaMarket franchise is one that has been in operation for more than two calendar years as of December 31, 1997 and has achieved annual gross sales of at least $500,000.

Sales Results

1. The average monthly gross sales volume in a period of January 1, 1998 through June 30, 1998 for 17 MegaMarket franchises operating as of September 30, 1998 was $72,843, with a low of $47,964 and a high of $105,663.

2. The average monthly gross sales volume increase for these MegaMarket franchises for the period of January 1, 1998 through June 30, 1998 over the same period ending June 30, 1997 was $9,475.

The following table shows the gross sales results for these MegaMarket franchises for the period January 1, 1998 through June 30, 1998:

**THE MAIDS® MegaMarket
Franchises Average Monthly Gross Sales**

Unit #	Region	Gross Sales	+Inc./-Dec.
1	Northeast	75,952	+7,932
2	Northeast	59,789	+18,122
3	Northeast	76,378	+88
4	Northeast	105,663	+6,338
5	Northeast	87,726	+10,020
6	Northeast	77,153	+4,021
7	Northeast	75,251	+9,932
8	Southeast	60,290	+8,623
9	Southeast	84,095	+9,522
10	Midwest	101,501	+19,549
11	Midwest	47,964	+8,579
12	Southwest	57,212	+13,160
13	Southwest	69,705	+19,911

Unit #	Region	Gross Sales	+Inc./-Dec.
14	West	67,941	+1,513
15	West	65,960	+2,370
16	West	48,190	+5,875
17	Canada	77,555	+15,529

Gross Profit Results

1. The average monthly gross profit (as a percentage of gross sales) during the period of January 1, 1998 through June 30, 1998 achieved by these 17 MegaMarket franchises was 26.6%, with a low of 19.0% and a high of 34.4%. The average gross profit figures were computed before income taxes, depreciation, amortization, interest, professional fees, management expense and administrative overhead. 8 of these 17 MegaMarket franchises exceeded the average.

2. Interest expense will vary depending upon the amount and terms of financing utilized by the Franchise Owner. We recommend financing not more than 60% of the initial investment.

3. Depreciation and amortization costs vary depending upon the Initial Fee for the franchise and the cost of capital assets. The Initial Fee for franchises purchased from TMI are $17,500 for the first territory and $14,500 for additional territories, plus the cost of equipment, cars, supplies and other items. Franchise rights and other business assets purchased from an existing Franchise Owners are likely to be considerably different.

4. Management expenses vary depending on the degree of active involvement by the Franchise Owner in the business. The functions of Operations Manager and Sales Manger are often performed by the Franchise Owner, but are sometimes performed by employees.

The following table represents the average results of operations achieved during the period of Janu-

Regular Revenue	$68,150	93.6%
Project Revenue	4,693	6.4%
Revenue Total	**72,843**	**100.0%**
Service Fee	3,950	5.4%
National Ad Fund Fee	817	1.1%
Local Advertising	3,215	4.4%
Direct Labor	27,636	37.9%
Indirect Labor	1,135	1.6%
Outside Services	128	0.2%
Employee Benefits	1,580	2.2%
Uniforms	165	0.2%
Supplies	1,459	2.0%
Rent/Utilities	1,940	2.7%
Auto	3,421	4.7%
Payroll Taxes	3,478	4.8%
Customer Damages	263	0.4%
Telephone	826	1.1%
Insurance WC&PD	2,625	3.6%
Employee Recruiting	333	0.5%
Equip. Rent/Repair	406	0.6%

Miscellaneous	65	0.1%
Operational Expense	53,442	73.4%
Gross Profit	19,401	26.6%

ary 1, 1998 through June 30, 1998 by these 17 MegaMarket franchises:

YOU SHOULD NOT CONSIDER THE FORE-GOING REVENUE, EXPENSE AND GROSS PROFIT FIGURES AS THE ACTUAL REV-

ENUE, EXPENSE AND GROSS PROFIT RESULTS THAT YOU WILL REALIZE. TMI DOES NOT REPRESENT THAT YOU CAN EXPECT TO ATTAIN THE INDICATED RESULTS. YOUR ACTUAL REVENUES, EXPENSES AND GROSS PROFIT RESULTS

MOLLY MAID
A Household Name Since 1979

MOLLY MAID
1340 Eisenhower Pl.
Ann Arbor, MI 48108
Tel: (800) 665-5962 (734) 975-1000
Fax: (734) 975-9000
E-Mail: mak@mollymaid.com
Internet Address: www.mollymaid.com
Contact: Mr. Marc A. Kiekenapp, Director Franchise Development

Description: MOLLY MAID is # I in the industry in residential cleaning and home care service. Ranked in INC 500, Entrepreneur's Top 100, Platinum 200, Entrepreneur 509 and Business Start-Ups

As Top 200 Hottest Franchises. MOLLY MAID's technology won The Windows Worldwide Open in 1995 sponsored by Bill Gates.

# Franchised Units:	526 Units
# Company-Owned Units:	0 Units
Total # Units:	526 Units
Founded In:	1979
Ist Franchised In:	1979
Average Total Investment:	50-60K
Franchise Fee:	16.9K
On-Going Royalty:	3-6%
Advertising Fee:	0-2%
Financial Assistance:	No
Site Selection Assistance:	N/A
Lease Negotiation Assistance:	No
Contract Terms (Init./Renew):	10

Initial Training Provided: 5 Days in Home Office, 6 Months in Right Start Program; 2 Days at Franchise Location.

We have included below certain sales and financial information for MOLLY MAID franchises in operation during 1998. Except for the information contained in this Item, we do not furnish or authorize our salespersons to furnish any oral or written information concerning the actual or potential sales, costs, income, or profits of a franchise. Actual results vary from franchise to franchise, and we cannot and do not estimate the results which any particular franchise may expect to achieve.

As of December 31, 1998, there were 258 MOLLY MAID franchised businesses in operation in the United States owned by 202 franchise owners. Of this, 148 franchised businesses were in operation for at least two full calendar years.

Listed below in Chart 1 is Gross Sales information (not including sales tax) for 1997 and 1998 for each franchised business in operation for at least two calendar years. The information is tabulated and sorted by the total number of years in operation for each franchised business. The Gross Sales information for each franchised business reflects that reported to us by their franchise owners. Also included is the percentage of increase/decrease each franchised business achieved when comparing 1998 Gross Sales to 1997 Gross Sales and a total for each column of information presented by grouping.

Listed below in Chart 2 is the 1998 Gross Sales information for 30 franchised businesses that opened during 1997 and completed their first full calendar year of operation in 1998.

THE RESULTS DESCRIBED IN CHARTS 1 AND 2 ARE THE SALES OF ALL FRANCHISED BUSINESSES OPEN FOR AT LEAST ONE FULL YEAR IN 1998 AND SHOULD NOT BE CONSIDERED AS THE ACTUAL OR PROBABLE SALES YOU WILL REALIZE. YOUR INDIVIDUAL RESULTS ARE LIKELY TO DIFFER FROM THE RESULTS DESCRIBED HERE.

Chart 1: Gross Sales, and Percentage of Increase/Decrease, for 1997 and 1998 as Reported by 148 Franchised Businesses in Operation for Two or More Years as of December 31, 1998.

Calendar Years in Business as of 12/31/98	1997	1998	% Increase/Decrease
2–3 Years	$334,292	$556,935	67%
	$176,027	$357,075	103%
	$148,370	$350,932	137%
	$306,357	$312,662	2%
	$113,830	$268,003	135%
	$161,214	$243,360	51%
	$153,099	$243,143	59%
	$121,255	$213,591	76%
	$204,622	$208,500	2%
	$145,483	$197,698	36%
	$74,983	$196,429	162%
	$106,916	$193,652	81%
	$126,676	$181,617	43%
	$108,159	$157,587	46%
	$78,189	$147,905	89%
	$78,443	$135,778	73%
	$92,336	$113,164	23%
	$86,010	$112,549	31%
Total	$2,616,260	$4,190,579	60%

3–4 Years	$428,223	$572,203	34%
	$287,208	$481,501	68%
	$267,500	$413,149	54%
	$304,149	$407,128	34%
	$288,935	$401,288	39%
	$263,486	$400,395	52%
	$264,479	$370,266	40%
	$214,529	$360,592	68%
	$230,401	$359,836	56%
	$286,839	$344,203	20%

Calendar Years in Business as of 12/31/98	1997	1998	% Increase/Decrease
	$264,301	$339,150	28%
	$221,433	$326,382	47%
	$228,429	$313,120	37%
	$188,015	$278,549	48%
	$213,662	$257,847	21%
	$181,630	$247,290	36%
	$207,131	$247,263	19%
	$167,657	$245,000	46%
	$209,662	$243,189	16%
	$198,877	$236,524	19%
	$194,567	$226,422	16%
	$167,606	$217,728	30%
	$196,575	$205,260	4%
	$166,853	$197,497	18%
	$163,214	$196,428	20%
	$130,263	$158,037	21%
	$172,172	$155,633	-10%
	$121,325	$152,836	26%
	$79,375	$138,457	74%
	$91,967	$135,597	47%
	$92,268	$121,063	31%
	$93,037	$107,522	16%
	$57,507	$93,011	62%
	$82,459	$84,380	2%
	$56,473	$77,457	37%
	$36,551	$31,408	-14%
Total	$ 6,818,753	$ 9,143,608	34%

	1997	1998	% Increase/Decrease
4–5 Years	$621,787	$708,504	14%
	$458,682	$671,599	46%
	$539,966	$592,588	10%
	$466,569	$545,795	17%
	$419,695	$540,913	29%
	$371,746	$499,726	34%
	$365,242	$470,245	29%
	$351,414	$469,147	34%
	$297,471	$452,746	52%
	$299,705	$410,506	37%
	$385,532	$403,849	5%

Calendar Years in Business as of 12/31/98	1997	1998	% Increase/Decrease
	$308,389	$360,490	17%
	$300,000	$350,797	17%
	$288,172	$350,417	22%
	$278,851	$343,557	23%
	$270,704	$339,701	25%
	$306,761	$326,668	6%
	$126,901	$305,068	140%
	$193,355	$293,142	52%
	$194,303	$277,945	43%
	$280,871	$266,492	-5%
	$177,496	$255,248	44%
	$246,241	$243,937	-1%
	$183,770	$242,625	32%
	$190,306	$237,761	25%
	$246,094	$234,507	-5%
	$192,776	$227,532	18%
	$255,155	$220,459	-14%
	$173,252	$191,946	11%
	$148,782	$182,972	23%
	$101,935	$166,745	64%
	$112,951	$124,174	10%
	$97,249	$106,500	10%
	$128,482	$96,193	-25%
Total	$9,380,604	$11,510,491	23%

Calendar Years in Business as of 12/31/98	1997	1998	% Increase/Decrease
5–6 Years	$1,357,787	$1,473,949	9%
	$998,505	$1,267,499	27%
	$718,866	$952,649	33%
	$636,524	$689,132	8%
	$631,904	$888,568	41%
	$511,765	$614,495	20%
	$409,437	$483,390	18%
	$376,912	$492,823	31%
	$353,652	$383,638	8%
	$265,827	$295,564	11%
	$187,293	$226,023	21%
	$178,078	$231,771	30%

Calendar Years in Business as of 12/31/98	1997	1998	% Increase/Decrease
	$148,611	$158,892	7%
	$142,473	$111,377	-22%
	$97,537	$78,235	-20%
	$76,951	$73,226	-5%
Total	**$7,092,122**	**$8,421,230**	**19%**

	1997	1998	%
6 Years +	$982,929	$1,473,529	50%
	$1,055,714	$1,218,721	15%
	$943,184	$997,857	6%
	$840,100	$899,874	7%
	$610,276	$823,011	35%
	$717,247	$816,650	14%
	$826,111	$808,019	-2%
	$765,786	$740,648	-3%
	$555,376	$701,540	26%
	$583,657	$679,220	16%
	$558,335	$663,209	19%
	$512,526	$657,868	28%
	$511,179	$619,173	21%
	$447,088	$605,127	35%
	$617,135	$576,845	-7%
	$478,361	$565,747	18%
	$460,171	$546,959	19%
	$486,204	$528,664	9%
	$516,611	$519,060	0%
	$483,587	$510,996	6%
	$447,199	$486,714	9%
	$455,666	$478,123	5%
	$451,275	$476,355	6%
	$321,010	$462,995	44%
	$411,346	$461,921	12%
	$378,393	$437,678	16%
	$437,526	$426,455	-3%
	$363,766	$419,796	15%
	$394,592	$398,251	1%
	$387,283	$384,457	-1%
	$353,771	$367,223	4%
	$201,744	$309,191	53%
	$293,488	$299,147	2%

Calendar Years in Business as of 12/31/98	1997	1998	% Increase/Decrease
	$293,488	$299,147	2%
	$195,993	$288,662	47%
	$254,849	$286,011	12%
	$338,978	$281,467	-17%
	$222,827	$255,378	15%
	$175,721	$197,298	12%
	$182,855	$194,800	7%
	$168,362	$158,651	-6%
	$173,877	$156,831	-10%
	$145,552	$155,503	7%
	$150,068	$151,760	1%
	$145,116	$142,105	-2%
Total	$20,002,831	$22,629,489	13%

Chart 2: 1998 Gross Sales as Reported by 30 Franchised Businesses That Opened in 1997 and Completed Their First Calendar Year of Operation in 1998.

1998 Gross Sales for 30 Franchised Businesses during Their First Year of Operation In Descending Order Left to Right Column	
$483,582	$204,757
$411,557	$187,497
$386,809	$187,029
$368,217	$184,845
$308,272	$180,267
$305,460	$167,395
$283,664	$131,184
$278,703	$124,371
$238,741	$123,257
$232,936	$120,499
$232,370	$110,510
$231,418	$99,107
$218,271	$81,797
$214,609	$43,147
$205,947	$30,372

Maintenance/cleaning/ sanitation

AEROWEST & WESTAIR SANITATION SERVICES
3882 Del Amo Blvd., # 602
Torrance, CA 90503
Tel: (310) 793-4242
Fax: (310) 793-4250
E-Mail: westsaninc@aol.com
Internet Address: www.members.aol.com/ westsaninc
Contact: Mr. Chris Ratay, Franchise Manager

Description: WEST provides unique odor counteractant dispensers and fluids at cost to franchisees for their service work in the 'high end' market, including hospitals, offices, government and municipal buildings, etc. Administrative support is performed by WEST on behalf of the franchisee, including billings and collections (gross franchise income is advanced at time of billing), allowing franchisees to concentrate on sales and service.

# Franchised Units:	46 Units
# Company-Owned Units:	<u>29</u> Units
Total # Units:	75 Units
Founded In:	1983
1st Franchised In:	1983
Average Total Investment:	3-40K
Franchise Fee:	2K
On-Going Royalty:	35%
Advertising Fee:	0%
Financial Assistance:	Yes(D)
Site Selection Assistance:	N/A
Lease Negotiation Assistance:	N/A
Contract Terms (Init./Renew):	5/1
Initial Training Provided: 1-2 Weeks Local, Near Franchisee's Home.	

As Item 5 describes, West may assign to you existing customers in your area when you sign the franchise agreement. If so, then at the time you sign the franchise agreement, West will document to you the dollar amount of the annualized gross sanitation business of these customers. The figures West gives you will be the actual billings of the specific customers that West assigns to you. The initial development fee described in Item 5 will be based on these actual figures.

You will not be provided with statements of income for any customers other than those that West is assigning to you. West will make no esti-

339

mates or projections of income or earnings. The only statement which West will provide you contains the actual customer billings for the franchise you are purchasing. Therefore, those figures are directly relevant only to that particular franchise.

The example of $23,000 in annualized gross billings in Item 7 is only an example. West does not intend this example as a representation of the actual, average or projected billings of any franchise. West may assign you no customers, or customers with lower or higher annualized billings.

As of November 30, 1998, West had 43 operational franchises (see Item 20 for addresses and telephone numbers of franchisees operational as of the date of this offering circular). Of the 43 franchises in operation on that date, 50% began operations with less than $23,000 in gross billings from customers assigned by West, while 28% began operations with more than $23,000 in gross billings from customers assigned by West. 19% began operations with more than $50,000 in gross billings from customers assigned by West.

In the year ended November 30, 1998, 26% of the franchises in operation exceeded $50,000 in gross billings for that year. The franchise with the highest gross billings of all the franchises in operation during the year ended November 30, 1998 had $125,614 in gross billings, while the franchise with the lowest gross billings during the same period

had $334 in gross billings. The average for all franchises during the same period was $47,480, with the median being $40,418.

"Gross billings" means all customer charges, including charges for labor and materials, which West bills for franchisees, after deducting sales tax receipts. West offers the same services and products to all AEROWEST/WESTAIR franchises, and all AEROWEST/WESTAIR franchises offer substantially the same services and products to the public. All the franchises use the same method of billings-related accounting since West performs all billings-related accounting for them.

West will make substantiation of the data it used in preparing the earnings claim available to prospective franchisees on reasonable request.

THE ABOVE ACTUAL SALES, INCOME OR GROSS OR NET PROFITS ARE OF THE SPECIFIC FRANCHISES IN QUESTION AND SHOULD NOT BE CONSIDERED AS THE ACTUAL OR PROBABLE SALES, INCOME OR GROSS OR NET PROFITS THAT ANY FRANCHISEE WILL REALIZE. WEST DOES NOT REPRESENT THAT ANY FRANCHISEE CAN EXPECT TO ATTAIN THESE SALES, INCOME OR GROSS OR NET PROFITS. A NEW FRANCHISEE'S RESULTS ARE LIKELY TO DIFFER FROM THE RESULTS STATED IN THE EARNINGS CLAIM.

::::: CleanNet USA
Commercial Cleaning Services

CLEANNET USA
9861 Broken Land Pkwy., # 208
Columbia, MD 21046
Tel: (800) 735-8838 (410) 720-6444
Fax: (410) 720-5307
E-Mail:
Internet Address: www.cleannetusa.com
Contact: Mr. Dennis M. Urner, Executive Vice President

Description: Full-service, turn-key commercial office cleaning franchise, offering guaranteed customer accounts, training equipment, supplies, local office support, quality control backup, billing/invoicing and guaranteed payment for services provided. Company also sells master licenses for markets with metropolitan populations of 500,000 and up.

# Franchised Units:	1718 Units
# Company-Owned Units:	7 Units
Total # Units:	1725 Units
Founded In:	1987
1st Franchised In:	1988
Average Total Investment:	2.9-35.7K
Franchise Fee:	2-255K
On-Going Royalty:	3%

Advertising Fee:	0%
Financial Assistance:	Yes(D)
Site Selection Assistance:	Yes
Lease Negotiation Assistance:	Yes

Contract Terms (Init./Renew):	20/20
Initial Training Provided:8 Days -	
2 Weeks Company Offices; 4 Days - 3 Weeks Job	
Site or Master Offices.	

CleanNet does not furnish or authorize its salespersons to furnish any oral or written information concerning the actual or potential sales, costs, income or profits of the Franchised Business. Actual results vary from unit to unit and CleanNet cannot estimate the results of any particular franchise. CleanNet has specifically instructed sales personnel, agents, employees and officers that they are not permitted to make claims or statements as to earnings, sales, profits, or prospects or chances of success, nor are they authorized to represent or estimate dollar figures for those items as to any particular CleanNet franchise. You should not rely on any unauthorized representations.

Initial Volume Fulfillment in Maryland: January – December 1998

The following table demonstrates CleanNet's performance of its obligation to provide Maryland franchisees with initial commercial cleaning business from January through December of 1998, for Maryland Franchisees. For purposes of this table only, Maryland Franchisees are defined as ones who purchased a franchise during the period and are either Maryland residents, or operate their Franchise in the State of Maryland, or both. Franchisees are listed by the packages they selected. Also listed is the amount of time in days that CleanNet had to offer cleaning business under each particular package. For certain franchisees, this time had not yet expired at year end 1998.

CleanNet provides its franchisees with specified amounts of initial business within a specified period of time. In order to inform franchisees of the amount of initial business to be offered under a particular franchise package and for purposes of convenience and consistency with business practices in the janitorial franchise industry, CleanNet describes these packages in terms of monthly Gross Billings to be offered under variously priced packages.

The total revenue, and the total Gross Billing for any specific month, realized by you may not be directly related to CleanNet's performance of its obligation to offer initial business. The amount of revenue is affected by many factors such as (1) the initial business may be offered in stages during the initial offering period; (2) you may not accept all of the accounts offered; or (3) customers may cancel the contract or request a change of franchisees due to poor performance by you. Whether a franchisee maintains the initial business provided by CleanNet depends upon many variables including, the franchisee's ability, timeliness, and dedication. Revenues will be reduced by business expenses associated with servicing customers.

From January 1, 1998 to December 31, 1998, CleanNet granted 50 Franchised Businesses in the State of Maryland. The chart on the following page indicates the initial volume fulfillment related to these franchisees, broken down into package categories.

Initial Volume Fulfillment
Maryland January – December 1998

CleanNet Commercial Cleaning Account Packages (note 1)	P-6 P-6XE	P-8	P-10	P-12	P-14	P-18	P-24	P-30	P-36	P-48	
Amount of Initial Monthly Gross Billing (note 2)	500	667	833	1,000	1,167	1,500	2,000	2,500	3,000	4,000	Totals
Days to Fulfill Package (note 3)	120	120	120	120	120	120	120	120	120	150	
Packages Sold (note 4)	14	6	1	9	3	4	9	1	2	1	50
Packages on Hold (note 5)											

CleanNet Commercial Cleaning Account Packages (note 1)	P-6 P-6XE	P-8	P-10	P-12	P-14	P-18	P-24	P-30	P-36	P-48	
Time to Provide Not Expired (note 9)	5	3	1	4		2	1		1		17
Packages Timely Filled (note 6)	5	1		1	1		1	1			10
Additional Information:											
Packages Adjusted (note 7)											
Full Refunds (note 8)											
Franchisees with Replaceable Volume (note 10)											
Franchisees with Irreplaceable Volume (note 11)											
Franchisees Accepting CleanNet's Performance (note 12)	4	2		4	2	2	7		1	1	23

Notes

1. *CleanNet Commercial Cleaning Account Packages.* The packages listed represent the CleanNet Commercial Cleaning Account Packages sold in Maryland in 1998. More packages were available (see Item 5) but only those packages actually purchased by a Maryland franchisee in 1998 are listed.

2. *Amount of Initial Monthly Gross Billings.* This figure represents the initial monthly Gross Billings CleanNet is to provide under each particular package.

3. *Days to Fulfill Package.* This entry is the number of days CleanNet has to provide the applicable amount of Gross Billings under each particular package.

4. *Packages Sold.* This entry lists the number of each package sold in Maryland in 1998.

5. *Packages on Hold.* Packages are placed on hold when a franchisee requests, in writing, an indefinite hold on CleanNet's provision of accounts (e.g. franchisee requested CleanNet not provide contracts due to family illness).

6. *Packages Timely Filled.* CleanNet completely filled these packages within the specified time.

7. *Packages Adjusted.* CleanNet and the franchisee made a mutually acceptable adjustment to the package (e.g. CleanNet provided a partial refund or provided additional volume).

8. *Full Refunds.* These franchises received a full refund of their initial franchise fee from CleanNet.

9. *Time to Provide Not Expired.* The time for CleanNet to provide initial business under the particular package had not expired at year end.

10. *Franchisees with Replaceable Volume.* These franchisees lost business through no fault of their own during the first 180 days of the account and were thus entitled to replacement business.

11. *Franchisees with Irreplaceable Volume.* These franchisees lost some or all of their initial business as a result of their default (e.g. faulty work, lack of trustworthiness, and failure to service the customer).

12. *Franchisees Accepting CleanNet's Performance.* These franchisees accepted CleanNet's performance, that is, no adjustment was requested.

Initial Monthly Gross Billings in Maryland: January – December 1998

The basis for CleanNet's claim that it will provide monthly Gross Billings is Section I.B.1. of the Franchise Agreement.

In the chart below, CleanNet has calculated the average gross monthly volume of Maryland franchisees who purchased a Franchised Business in 1998. Therefore, the chart includes those whose packages were due to be completely filled by CleanNet in calendar year 1998, as well as franchisees whose packages' time limits for CleanNet to provide initial business expired after December 31, 1998. A total of 50 franchisees joined CleanNet in Maryland in 1998.

The average gross monthly volume was calculated as follows. First, all franchisees were categorized by package size. The franchisees' monthly statements for all months in 1998 were used to determine their gross revenue for 1998 (including monthly cleaning service fees and any special services revenues). The avenge monthly gross volume was calculated for each franchisee by taking his total gross revenue for 1998 and dividing that number by the number of months the franchisee provided services. Finally, for each package category, all of the franchisees average gross monthly volumes were totaled and divided by the number of franchisees

in the category, providing an average monthly gross revenue amount for each package. In addition, a calculation of the average number of months worked by franchisees in each category was made by totaling the number of months worked by all of the franchisees in each category and dividing by the number of franchisees in each category.

YOU SHOULD NOT CONSIDER THE INFORMATION CONCERNING INITIAL BUSINESS TO BE THE ACTUAL OR POTENTIAL SALES, COSTS, INCOME OR PROFITS THAT YOU WILL REALIZE. YOUR SUCCESS WILL DEPEND LARGELY UPON YOUR OWN ABILITY AS WELL AS OTHER FACTORS.

Initial Monthly Gross Billings
Maryland January – December 1998

Monthly Package Size	Number of Franchises	Actual Average Gross Monthly Volume	Average No. of Months Services Performed
500	14	882	5
667	6	801	7
833	1	0	0
1,000	9	762	7
1,167	3	736	6
1,500	4	204	7
2,000	9	1,310	5
2,500	1	4,965	6
3,000	2	1,359	1
4,000	1	2,767	1

Individual Franchisee Average Gross Monthly Billings
Maryland (January – December 1998)

Franchisee No.	Package	Actual Average Gross Monthly Volume (Note 1) (Note 2)	Remarks
807	P-6 ($500)	$276	
796	P-6 ($500)	$368	
803	P-6 ($500)	$1,999	see note 4
810	P-6 ($500)	$0	see note 3
823	P-6 ($500)	$0	see note 3
824	P-6 ($500)	$0	see note 3
826	P-6 ($500)	$0	see note 3
827	P-6 ($500)	$0	see note 3

Franchisee No.	Package	Actual Average Gross Monthly Volume (Note 1) (Note 2)	Remarks
787	P-6 ($500)	$665	see note 4
813	P-6 ($500)	$524	see note 4
795	P-6 ($500)	$764	see note 4
812	P-6 ($500)	$262	
822	P-6 ($500)	$44	
794	P-6 ($500)	$3,061	see note 4
783	P-8 ($667)	$451	
792	P-8 ($667)	$0	see note 3
804	P-8 ($667)	$0	see note 3
806	P-8 ($667)	$884	
820	P-8 ($667)	$0	see note 3
788	P-8 ($667)	$1,070	see note 4
828	P-10 ($833)	$0	see note 3
785	P-12 ($1,000)	$51	
786	P-12 ($1,000)	$615	
811	P-12 ($1,000)	$923	
814	P-12 ($1,000)	$627	
825	P-12 ($1,000)	$0	see note 3
829	P-12 ($1,000)	$0	see note 3
830	P-12 ($1,000)	$0	see note 3
832	P-12 ($1,000)	$0	see note 3
784	P-12 ($1,000)	$1,594	see note 4
791	P-14 ($1,167)	$869	
793	P-14 ($1,167)	$1,160	
818	P-14 ($1,167)	$178	
789	P-18 ($1,500)	$487	
802	P-18 ($1,500)	$125	
808	P-18 ($1,500)	$0	see note 3
821	P-18 ($1,500)	$0	see note 3
782	P-24 ($2,000)	$1,070	
817	P-24 ($2,000)	$0	see note 3
797	P-24 ($2,000)	$1,170	
799	P-24 ($2,000)	$1,607	
800	P-24 ($2,000)	$476	
809	P-24 ($2,000)	$901	
816	P-24 ($2,000)	$325	
819	P-24 ($2,000)	$1,482	
801	P-24 ($2,000)	$3,452	see note 4
798	P-30 ($2,500)	$4,965	see note 4
815	P-36 ($3,000)	$1,359	

Franchisee No.	Package	Actual Average Gross Monthly Volume (Note 1) (Note 2)	Remarks
831	P-36 ($3,000)	$0	see note 3
790	P-36 ($4,000)	$2,767	

Note 1: These amounts are the actual monthly average amounts paid to the individual franchisees during the reporting period (January 1, 1998 to December 31, 1998). These amounts may be more or less than the Gross Monthly Billing (Package Amount) due to the following factors: (a) additional business provided at no cost to the franchisee (Note 5, Below); (b) additional business provided to the franchisee at additional cost (Note 4, Below); (c) franchisees whose packages have been fulfilled by the amount of the agreed upon Gross Monthly Billing, but who have subsequently lost business due to franchisee default, and which is not replaceable by CleanNet; (d) franchisees who have not yet started business due to circumstances explained in Note 3, below.

Note 2: These amounts may include amounts for special or one-time, non-recurring services performed by the individual franchisee. Since Clean-Net's obligation is to fulfill the package with contracts that have an ongoing basis, rather than single-billing, one-time, non-recurring services, there is not a material amount included. CleanNet estimates that the range of special, one-time, or non-recurring business runs from 1–2% of the franchisees normal gross monthly billing. However, in no case, does the performance of special, one-time, or non-recurring business serve to reduce the obligation of CleanNet to provide the agreed amount of Gross Monthly Billings on a recurring basis, and therefore this amount is not counted in the agreed amount for Gross Monthly Billing fulfillment purposes.

Note 3: The Average Gross Monthly Billing of those individual franchisees showing "0" activity denotes that, during the reporting period (January 1, 1998-December 31, 1998), the individual franchisee either (a) had purchased a package, but had not yet begun training and thus had received no contracts, or (b) had purchased a package and had completed training, but the time period during which the accounts are assigned had not yet elapsed, and had received no contracts.

Note 4: The amounts of these individuals' Gross Monthly Billing exceeded the initial package amount due to the fact that an additional fee was paid for the additional business (upgrade), in accordance with the Franchise Fee Schedule, during the reporting period (January 1, 1998 – December 31, 1998). During the reporting period (January 1, 1998 – December 31, 1998), the following franchisees upgraded: Franchisee Number 787 upgraded on July 1, 1998 from a P-6 ($500) to a P-18 ($1,500) package; Franchisee Number 795 did not upgrade (subsequently upgraded in February 1999); Franchisee Number 794 upgraded from a P-6 ($500) to a P-10 ($833) on June 1, 1998; from a P-10 ($833) to a P-18 ($1,500) on June 22, 1998; from a P-l8 ($1,500) to a P-48 ($4,000) on October 1, 1998; and subsequently upgraded from a P-48 ($4,000) to P-72 ($6,000); Franchisee Number 784 upgraded from a P-12 ($1,000) to P-48 ($4,000) on February 18, 1998; Franchisee Number 801 upgraded from a P-24 ($2,000) to a P-36 ($3,000) on June 23, 1998, and from a P-36 ($3,000) to a P-54 ($4,500) on December 10, 1998; Franchisee Number 798 upgraded from a P-30 ($2,500) to a P-48 ($4,000) on May 27, 1998; and from a P-48 ($4,000) to P-90 ($7,500) on October 19, 1998; Franchisee Number 788 did not upgrade (subsequently upgraded from a P-8 ($667) to a P-42 ($3,500) in February 1999; and from a P-42 ($3,500) to a P-60 ($5,000) in May 1999.); Franchisee Number 813 did not upgrade (subsequently upgraded in January 1999 from P-18 ($1,500) to P-30 ($2,500). Franchisee Number 803 did not upgrade (Franchisee was subsequently notified in 1999 of a required upgrade from P-6 ($500) to P-14 ($1,167) level). The amount of the fee due on such additional business is determined by the package level of the Initial Franchise Fee Price Schedule, Item 5, Initial Franchise Fee, and Item 6, Other Fees, and as explained in the Franchise Agreement, Section IV, Fees. All franchisees are required to pay for additional business as it is obtained. The amount of the fee is due immediately upon such determination by CleanNet, and may be paid in frill, or financed by CleanNet in accordance with the terms of the agreement.

This information should not be relied upon by you when considering the purchase of a CleanNet Franchised Business. CleanNet does not represent or warrant that your Franchised Business will perform in accordance with the information provided above. Your individual experience may vary.

The average gross monthly volume reported above is affected by a number of variables, such as: the month in which each franchisee began servicing the customers; whether the franchisor fulfilled its total obligation to provide initial business and the month in which such obligation was completed; whether the franchisee lost customers due to poor service or other default; whether the franchisee lost a customer through no fault of its own, if the customer was obligated to be replaced, and when it was replaced; whether the franchisee purchased or located additional business; whether the franchisee requested that the provision of accounts be delayed; and whether the franchisee performed and received revenue for special services, whether the franchisee rejected any customers, and whether the franchisee upgraded or downgraded the package.

Other factors that affect the amount of revenue you realize include the quality of management and service, the rate of cleaning production you achieve; the extent to which you finance the acquisition and/or operation of the franchise, your

legal, accounting and other professional fees; federal state and local income, gross profits or other taxes; discretionary expenditures; and accounting methods used.

Additional substantiation of the data used in preparing this analysis will be made available upon reasonable request.

YOU ARE CAUTIONED THAT THE MONTHLY REVENUE AVERAGES SET FORTH ABOVE ARE ONLY AVERAGES AS TO THE PARTICULAR MARYLAND FRANCHISEES WHO FIT THE CRITERIA INDICATED (NOT ALL MARYLAND FRANCHISEES CONDUCTING BUSINESS IN 1998 ARE INCLUDED) AND THE DATA ONLY COVERS ONE YEAR OR A PORTION OF ONE YEAR (DEPENDING ON THE FRANCHISEE). THE RESULTS WHICH WOULD BE OBTAINED FOR PRIOR YEARS AND IN FUTURE YEARS MAY VARY SUBSTANTIALLY FROM THE RESULTS SHOWN ABOVE. THERE IS NO ASSURANCE THAT THE FINANCIAL RESULTS WHICH YOU ACHIEVE WILL BE SIMILAR TO THE AVERAGES SHOWN. ACCORDINGLY, YOU SHOULD NOT RELY ON THESE CALCULATIONS AS BEING A PROJECTION, OR FORECAST, OF THE RESULTS WHICH YOU MAY OBTAIN.

COIT

Experience You Can Trust.

COIT SERVICES
897 Hinckley Rd., Burlingame, CA 94010
Tel: (800) 243-8797 (650) 697-5471
Fax: (650) 697-6117
E-Mail: craig@coit.com
Internet Address: www.coit.com
Contact: Mr. Craig Ratkovich, Dir. Franchise Sales

Description: Granting large, exclusive territories, COIT SERVICES provides a proven opportunity in the carpet, upholstery, drapery, area rug and air-duct cleaning business. COIT franchisees enjoy use of a universal 800# (1-800-FORCOIT), along with successful marketing and management programs that have been proven in place for 50 years.

# Franchised Units:	57 Units
# Company-Owned Units:	12 Units
Total # Units:	69 Units
Founded In:	1950
1st Franchised In:	1963
Average Total Investment:	100K
Franchise Fee:	25K
On-Going Royalty:	2-6%
Advertising Fee:	0%
Financial Assistance:	Yes(D)
Site Selection Assistance:	Yes
Lease Negotiation Assistance:	Yes
Contract Terms (Init./Renew):	10/10
Initial Training Provided:	7 Days Corporate Headquarters; 1-2 Weeks in Field.

The 1998 results of 55 franchise locations were included in the earnings information presented below. Nationwide their annual gross sales average was $944,743. Fifteen franchises achieved or exceeded this result. Forty-two franchises achieved sales of at least $125,000 and 47 achieved at least $75,000 in gross sales.

	Number	H.H.	1998	Average
Under 100,000 Households				
Location 1	1	88,200	122,445	
Location 2	1	88,700	141,052	
Location 3	1	59,900	20,488	
Location 4	1	49,300	264,050	
Location 5	1	72,280	4,722	
Location 6	1	64,800	92,732	
Location 7	1	79,900	162,601	
Location 8*	1	54,400		
Sub-Total	8		808,090	101,011
	Number	H.H.	1998	Average
100-200,000 Households				
Location 1	1	127,400	450,286	
Location 2	1	188,300	99,404	
Location 3	1	168,600	800,000	
Location 4	1	152,200	223,413	
Location 5	1	141,000	32,656	
Location 6	1	156,600	220,655	
Location 7	1	115,385	258,376	
Location 8**				
Sub-Total	7		2,084,790	297,827
	Number	H.H.	1998	Average
200-300,000 Households				
Location 1	1	260,300	1,090,773	
Location 2	1	253,000	47,157	
Location 3	1	277,100	72,443	
Location 4	1	233,500	2,316,111	
Location 5	1	253,600	287,669	
Location 6	1	217,500	1,756,870	
Location 7	1	293,500	638,154	
Sub-Total	7		6,209,177	887,025
	Number	H.H.	1998	Average
300-500,000 Households				
Location 1	1	375,100	230,000	
Location 2	1	384,000	192,842	

	Number	H.H.	1998	Average
Location 3	1	509,500	153,348	
Location 4	1	389,300	198,482	
Location 5	1	385,200	165,567	
Location 6	1	417,700	593,589	
Location 7	1	301,800	348,440	
Location 8	1	301,000	67,438	
Location 9	1	320,800	517,098	
Location 10	1	466,100	1,028,969	
Location 11	1	429,900	80,197	
Location 12	1	313,100	684,118	
Location 13	1	300,400	49,941	
Sub-Total	13		4,312,027	331,541
	Number	H.H.	1998	Average
500-750,000 Households				
Location 1	1	717,000	2,660,665	
Location 2	1	582,100	136,998	
Location 3	3	649,300	164,814	
Location 4	1	550,400	2,694,155	
Location 5	1	743,300	513,021	
Location 6	1	551,600	447,537	
Location 7	1	518,500	54,781	
Location 8	1	576,923	3,324,535	
Sub-Total	10		9,996,506	999,651
	Number	H.H.	1998	Average
750-1,000,000 Households				
Location 1	1	931,400	3,301,161	
Location 2	1	863,000	2,648,208	
Location 3	1	864,000	3,272,945	
Location 4	1	960,000	3,295,185	
Location 5	1	890,200	937,379	
Location 6	1	885,700	2,787,296	
Sub-Total	6		16,242,174	2,707,029
	Number	H.H.	1998	Average
1,000,000+ Households				
Location 1	1	N/A	700,000	
Location 2	1	1,202,400	4,857,538	
Location 3	1	1,704,900	3,265,539	
Location 4	1	1,093,700	3,487,009	

	Number	H.H.	1998	Average
Sub-Total	4		12,310,086	3,077,522
Total Operations***	55		51,960,852	944,743
Operations exceeding avg.	15		38,441,879	
Operations exceeding $75k	47			
Operations exceeding $125k	42			
* COIT repurchased in May 1998				
** Closed operations in June 1998				
*** Does not include figures from Thailand				

These figures were obtained from the gross sales reported for 1998 by 55 of the 56 franchises that were operating at the end of the 1998 fiscal year. COIT excluded from these figures the sales information on the Thailand franchisee, information on franchises where sales were not reported in a manner permitting their inclusion (e.g., where multiple franchise owner did not segregate sales per territory) and sales of franchises which had not been in operation for the full year. These figures were compiled from franchisee gross sales reports in accordance with generally accepted accounting principles. The franchisee reports were not audited or independently verified by COIT. Substantiation of the data used in preparing this earnings report will be available to prospective franchisees upon reasonable request.

THE FOREGOING DATA IS NOT NECESSARILY INDICATIVE OF THE SALES LEVELS THAT MAY BE ACHIEVED BY A FRANCHISEE IN ANY MARKET AREA. YOUR RESULTS ARE LIKELY TO DIFFER FROM THE RESULTS REPORTED ABOVE.

While these figures may be useful helping you understand the franchise opportunity offered, factors such as average income levels in the Territory, local advertising costs, number and financial resources of competitors, number of commercial establishment in the Territory, climate and your efforts and business acumen will affect sales. You should bear in mind that these figures are of gross sales only, not profit. They do not account for expenses like royalties, salaries, equipment costs and other operating expenses, which may vary.

JANI-KING INTERNATIONAL
16885 Dallas Pkwy.
Addison, TX 75001
Tel: (800) 552-5264 (972) 991-0900
Fax: (972) 503-0866
E-Mail: info@janiking.com
Internet Address: www.janiking.com
Contact: Mr. Jerry L. Crawford, President

Description: JANI-KING INTERNATIONAL is the world's largest commercial cleaning franchisor, with locations in 11 countries and nearly 100 regions in the U. S. and abroad. Our franchise opportunity includes initial customer contracts, training, continuous local support, administrative and accounting assistance, an equipment leasing program and national advertising. If you are searching for a flexible business opportunity, look no further.

# Franchised Units:	7269 Units
# Company-Owned Units:	35 Units
Total # Units:	7294 Units
Founded In:	1969

1st Franchised In:	1974	Site Selection Assistance:		N/A
Average Total Investment:	2.9-40K	Lease Negotiation Assistance:		N/A
Franchise Fee:	8-33K	Contract Terms (Init./Renew):		20/20
On-Going Royalty:	10%	Initial Training Provided:2 Weeks Local		
Advertising Fee:	0%	Regional Office.		
Financial Assistance:	Yes(D)			

We do not furnish or authorize our salespersons or any employees to furnish any oral or written information concerning the actual or potential sales, costs, income or profits of a JANI-KING franchise. Actual results vary from unit to unit, and we cannot estimate the results of any particular franchise. We have specifically instructed sales personnel, agents, employees and officers that they are not permitted to make claims or statements as to earnings, sales, profits, or prospects or chances of success, nor are they authorized to represent or estimate dollar figures for those items as to any particular JANI-KING franchise. You should not rely on any unauthorized representations.

Analysis of Actual Initial Business Offering Experience

This analysis sets forth information about our performance of the obligation to provide Initial Business for certain Jani-King franchises. The analysis and underlying data is based on information provided by JANI-KING INTERNATIONAL, INC., through its direct and indirect subsidiaries, including any Regional Franchisees of an affiliated subsidiary, for the specified franchises operating within all JANI-KING regions in the United States. The Territory for each franchise is identified more specifically in each franchise agreement.

Under the terms of the Franchise Agreement, we agree to secure and offer you the opportunity to service signed commercial cleaning and/or maintenance contracts that in total would provide a minimum in gross monthly billings in an amount defined as the "INITIAL BUSINESS." These contracts will be secured and offered within the number of days identified in the Franchise Summary of the Franchise Agreement as the "INITIAL OFFERING PERIOD," such time period beginning on the date all required equipment and supplies listed in the "Supply and Equipment Package" and "Additional Electric Equipment" have been obtained and the Acknowledgment of Com-

pletion of Training is signed, or a later date as discussed later in this item. See the schedules and information set forth in Item 11 — Post Opening Obligations.

The analysis is based on data as of December 31, 1998, reported for 11 franchisees located in Maryland that either purchased their franchise between January 1, 1998 and December 31, 1998, or for which time period the Initial Business was to be offered began in 1997, but carried over into 1998. In the calendar year ending December 31, 1997 we sold 9 franchises in Maryland. The time period in which we were required to offer Initial Business to 3 of these franchisees did not expire until after January 1, 1998, and all of those have been included in this analysis. The 6 other franchises sold in 1997 were included in last year's analysis. In the calendar year ending December 31, 1998, we sold 18 franchises in Maryland. The time period in which we were required to provide Initial Business expired for 8 of those franchisees before December 31, 1998. The time period to provide the Initial Business carried over into 1999 for the other 10 franchisees; and therefore, they are not included in this analysis, either because the time period was not scheduled to expire or because the time period was suspended. In the calendar year ending December 31, 1998, we sold a total of 39 franchises. The time period in which we were required to provide Initial Business expired for 24 of those franchisees before December 31, 1998. The percentage of franchises sold in Maryland that are reported in this analysis (11) to the total number of applicable franchises who purchased in 1997 but whose initial offering period did not expire until after January 1, 1998, and who purchased in 1998 and the initial offering period expired before December 31, 1998 (11) is 100%.

The franchises reported in this analysis are listed by ranges of Initial Business obligated to be offered in order to provide a more meaningful presentation of the relevant information about the offering of accounts for Initial Business by JANI-KING. The time period in which the Initial Business is contractually required to be offered is the Initial Offering Period stated in the Franchise Agreement, while the average time period within which the Initial Business was offered represents the actual number of days within which JANI-KING had secured and offered cleaning contracts with gross monthly billings that equal or exceed the total obligation required under each Franchise Agreement for the specified range.

You should particularly note the following: THE INFORMATION CONCERNING FRANCHISEE INITIAL BUSINESS SHOULD NOT BE CONSIDERED AS THE ACTUAL OR POTENTIAL SALES, COSTS, INCOME OR PROFITS THAT YOU WILL REALIZE. YOUR SUCCESS WILL DEPEND LARGELY UPON YOUR OWN ABILITY, AND THE INDIVIDUAL FINANCIAL RESULTS ACHIEVED BY YOU MAY DIFFER FROM THE FRANCHISEE INFORMATION STATED IN THIS OFFERING CIRCULAR. THEREFORE WE DO NOT REPRESENT THAT ALL FRANCHISEES CAN EXPECT TO ACHIEVE THESE GROSS BILLINGS, OR ANY PARTICULAR LEVEL OF SALES, COSTS, INCOME OR PROFITS, OR ANY INCOME THAT EXCEEDS THE INITIAL PAYMENT FOR, OR INVESTMENT IN, THE FRANCHISED BUSINESS. SUBSTANTIATION OF THE DATA USED IN PREPARING THIS ANALYSIS WILL BE MADE AVAILABLE UPON REASONABLE REQUEST.

THE TOTAL REVENUE, AND THE TOTAL GROSS BILLING FOR ANY SPECIFIC MONTH, REALIZED BY YOU MAY NOT BE DIRECTLY RELATED TO OUR PERFORMANCE OF OUR OBLIGATION TO OFFER THE INITIAL BUSINESS REQUIRED BY THE FRANCHISE AGREEMENT. THE AMOUNT OF REVENUE IS AFFECTED BY MANY FACTORS, SUCH AS (1) THE INITIAL BUSINESS MAY BE OFFERED IN STAGES DURING THE INITIAL OFFERING PERIOD; (2) YOU MAY NOT ACCEPT ALL OF THE ACCOUNTS OFFERED; (3) ACCOUNTS MAY CANCEL THE CONTRACT OR REQUEST A CHANGE OF FRANCHISEES DUE TO POOR PERFORMANCE BY YOU; OR (4) THE ACCOUNT MAY GO OUT OF BUSINESS BEFORE THE END OF THE CONTRACT PERIOD.

Other factors that affect the amount of revenue you realize include the quality of management and service, the rate of cleaning production you achieve; the extent to which you finance the acquisition and/or operation of the franchise, your legal, accounting and other professional fees; federal state and local income, gross profits or other taxes; discretionary expenditures; and accounting methods used.

Information Concerning Franchisee Initial Business for Jani-King Maryland Franchisees — 1997–1998

	500	1,000	2,000	Total
Monthly Initial Business Package Purchased ($)	500	1,000	2,000	Total
Time Period (days) in which Initial Business contractually required to be offered[1]	120	120	120	N/A
Monthly Initial Business Package Purchased ($)	500	1,000	2,000	Total
Average time period (days) in which Initial Business was actually offered[1]	22	22	23	N/A
Number of franchisees purchasing within range	4	4	3	11
Percentage[2] of franchisees in which initial business was offered[1] within required period	100	100	100	100
Number of franchises with initial business offered[1] within required period	4	4	3	11

1. Offered means the accounts totally fulfilling the Initial Business were offered to the franchisee. Initial Business Packages not shown indicates that no plans were sold in those ranges for which the Initial Offering Period expired in 1998.

2. Percentage calculated as number of franchises whose Initial Offering Period had expired in 1998 and whose total Initial Business was offered within required time period, divided by the total number of franchises sold during the period whose Initial Offering Period had expired in 1998.

Percentage[3] of Franchisees for all U.S. Regions in Which Initial Business Was Offered[1] within Required Period

Region	%	Region	%
Atlanta	100	Louisville	75
Austin	100	Madison	N/A
Baltimore	100	Memphis	100
Baton Rouge	100	Miami	96
Birmingham	100	Milwaukee	100
Boston	100	Minneapolis	100
Buffalo	100	Mississippi Gulf Coast	100
Charleston	100	Mobile	N/A
Charlotte	95	Nashville	100
Chicago	100	New Jersey	88
Cincinnati	100	New Orleans	100
Cleveland	100	New York	91
Colton	100	Oakland	100
Columbia	100	Oklahoma City	100
Columbus	100	Orlando	100
Dallas	100	Philadelphia	86
Dayton	100	Orlando	100
Denver	100	Pittsburgh	100
Detroit	98	Portland	100
Ft. Worth	100	Raleigh/Durham	100
Greensboro	100	Richmond	100
Greenville/Spartanburg	N/A	St. Louis	100
Hampton Roads	100	Sacramento	100
Hartford	100	Salt Lake City	100
Hawaii	94	San Antonio	100
Houston	100	San Diego	100
Indianapolis	100	San Francisco	93
Jackson	100	Seattle	N/A
Jacksonville	100	Tampa Bay	100
Kansas City	100	Tucson	100
Knoxville	100	Tulsa	100

Region	%	Region	%
Las Vegas	100	Washington D.C.	100
Los Angeles	71		

1. Offered means the accounts totally fulfilling the Initial Business were offered to the franchisee

2. Figures for Washington D.C. included in this chart include franchises sold in District of Columbia, Maryland and Virginia.

3. Percentage calculated as number of franchisees whose Initial Business was offered within required period, divided by the total number of franchises sold during the period and whose Initial Offering Period has expired plus number which has not expired but was offered.

Average Gross Monthly Revenues of Franchisees

The basis for our claim about Initial Contract Business dollar volume is Paragraph 6.1.1 of the Franchise Agreement.

In the chart below, we have calculated the average gross monthly volume of Maryland franchisees sold from the Washington, D.C. regional office who had purchased a franchise and to whom our contractual obligation to offer Initial Contract Business was scheduled to be satisfied in calendar year 1998, which included the 3 franchisees who purchased in 1997 and carried over into 1998 and the 8 franchises sold in 1998 whose Initial Offering Period had expired by December 31, 1998. The chart does not include franchisees with whom our obligation to offer Initial Contract Business expired prior to January 1, 1998, or after December 31, 1998.

To calculate the average monthly volume experienced by these franchisees, we identified from franchise statements the gross revenue, i.e., the gross amount of the monthly cleaning service revenue and special services revenue credited to the franchisee. The franchise statements used were those reflecting 1998 gross revenue beginning with the first month in 1998, respectively, that the franchisee had any monthly revenue and continuing through December 31, 1998. An average gross monthly volume was calculated for each franchisee by dividing each franchisee's 1998 gross revenue by the number of months in their respective reporting period (mean average gross monthly revenue). Then, where there was more than one franchisee in a franchise package category, the average gross monthly revenue and number of months in the reporting period were averaged for all franchisees in each category.

The average gross monthly volume reported below can be affected by a number of variables such as: in which month each franchisee began servicing its customer(s); whether the franchisor fulfilled its total obligation to provide Initial Contract Business and the month in which such obligation was completed; whether the franchisee lost a customer(s) through no fault of its own, and, if there was an obligation for us to replace the customer(s), when it was replaced; whether the franchisee purchased or located additional business; whether the franchisee requested the provision of accounts be postponed; and whether the franchisee performed and received revenue for special services.

Notes:

Initial Contract Monthly Business Package Purchased	Number of Franchisees Purchasing This Package[1]	Average Gross Monthly Volume[2] ($)	Low/High Range of Average Gross Monthly Volumes[3] ($)	Average Months Within Reporting Period[4]
Plan A ($500)	4	1,808	1,498 to 2,166	10
Plan B ($1,000)	4	4,884	2,711 to 6,641	9
Plan C ($2,000)	3	3,214	873 to 4,407	7

1. Franchises purchased whose Initial Contract Monthly Business Offering deadline occurred in 1998.

2. Does not include any sales or other taxes.

3. Indicates the amount of average monthly business of the franchisees (i) with the lowest average gross monthly volume and (ii) with the highest average gross monthly volume.

4. Indicates the mean average of the months of 1998 in which these franchisees accrued gross monthly revenues.

All franchisees listed in the charts above paid Finder's Fees to obtain additional business in excess of

Initial Contract Monthly Business Package Purchased	Number of Franchisees Purchasing This Package	Average Total Revenue for 1998 ($)	Low/High Range of Total Revenue for 1998 ($)	Average Finder's Fees paid in 1998 ($)	Low/High Range of Finder's Fees paid in 1998 ($)
Plan A ($500)	4	17,970	14,984 to 23,304	3,224	1,862 to 5,497
Plan B ($1,000)	4	44,358	13,555 to 66,406	4,898	1,419 to 7,988
Plan C ($2,000)	3	22,175	5,238 to 39,253	3,214	2,123 to 2,648

the amount we are to provide under the particular Plan purchased. The amount of the Finder's Fees paid by those franchisees varied substantially and was calculated in accordance with the methods described in Item 6. As described in Item 6, a franchisee obtaining additional business will pay a Finder's Fee in the form of a down payment and monthly payments over a specified period of time based on a percentage of the amount of the account, the type of account, and the time period for performance. For example, if a franchisee were to receive a $1,000 per month Singe Tenant Account, a franchisee would pay 60% of that monthly amount as a down payment and 20% of the monthly amount for a period of 13 months. If a franchisee were to receive a $1,000 per month Multi-Tenant Account, a franchisee would pay 30% of that monthly amount as a down payment and 5% of that amount for a period of 72 months. There are 6 different types of accounts and payment structures for Finder's Fees described in Item 6 of this Offering Circular which you should review in analyzing this information.

The amounts shown in the chart above are the Low/High Range of the Total Amount of Finder's Fees Paid by franchisees listed in the chart for each Plan for the calendar year ending December 31, 1998. The arithmetic mean Average Finder's Fees paid was calculated by taking the Total Finder's paid by Plan by those franchisees listed in the chart and dividing by the total number of those fran-

chisees. The Low/High Range of Total Revenue figures are the range of total revenues those franchisees received during the calendar year ending December 31, 1998. The arithmetic mean Average Total Revenue figure was calculated by taking the Total Revenues received by Plan by those franchisees listed in the chart and dividing by the total number of those franchisees.

The franchisees included in the above charts were servicing accounts for periods ranging from 1 to 12 months. Because the franchisees have operated their businesses for various lengths of time, have obtained their business required to be offered under the Plan at varying times, and obtained different types of additional business, which required payments of differing amounts at different time periods, there is little or no relationship between the amount of Finder's Fees paid in the chart and the reported Total Revenue and Monthly Volume achieved. We do not represent, and no conclusion can be drawn, that you will receive a particular amount of Revenues or Monthly Volume if you pay a particular amount of Finder's Fees. The information concerning the level of Monthly Volume achieved and Finder's Fees is included in this Offering Circular at the request of the Maryland Division of Securities.

Of the franchisees included in the analysis above, we had 3 franchisees in Plan A who had some business terminate within the first year of the cleaning contract; we had 1 franchisee in Plan B who declined business offered to the franchisee and 3 franchisees who had some business terminate within the first year of the cleaning contract; and we had 2 franchisees in Plan C who declined business offered to the franchisee and 2 franchisees who had some business terminate within the first year of the cleaning contract.

Substantiation of the data used in preparing these statistics will be made available upon request.

YOU ARE CAUTIONED THAT THE MONTHLY REVENUE AVERAGES SET FORTH ABOVE ARE ONLY AVERAGES AS TO THE PARTICULAR MARYLAND FRAN-CHISEES WHO FIT THE CRITERIA INDICATED (NOT ALL MARYLAND FRAN-CHISEES CONDUCTING BUSINESS IN 1998 ARE INCLUDED) AND THE DATE ONLY COVERS ONE YEAR OR A PORTION OF ONE YEAR (DEPENDING ON THE FRAN-CHISEE). THE RESULTS WHICH WOULD BE OBTAINED FOR PRIOR YEARS AND IN FUTURE YEARS MAY VARY SUBSTAN-TIALLY FROM THE RESULTS SHOWN ABOVE. THERE IS NO ASSURANCE THAT THE FINANCIAL RESULTS WHICH YOU ACHIEVE WILL BE SIMILAR TO THE AVERAGES SHOWN. ACCORDINGLY, YOU SHOULD NOT RELY ON THESE CALCULATIONS AS BEING A PROJECTION, OR FORECAST, OF THE RESULTS WHICH YOU MAY OBTAIN.

WE DO NOT FURNISH OR AUTHORIZE OUR SALESPERSONS TO FURNISH ANY OTHER ORAL OR WRITTEN INFORMA-TION CONCERNING THE ACTUAL OR POTENTIAL SALES, COSTS, INCOME OR PROFITS OF A FRANCHISE. ACTUAL RESULTS MAY VARY FROM FRANCHISEE TO FRANCHISEE AND WE DO NOT AND CANNOT GUARANTEE, PROJECT, FORECAST, OR ESTIMATE THE RESULTS OF ANY PARTICULAR FRANCHISEE EXCEPT FOR INFORMATION SPECIFI-CALLY SET FORTH IN THIS OFFERING CIRCULAR.

O . P . E . N .
CLEANING
SYSTEMS

O. P. E. N. CLEANING SYSTEMS
2777 E. Camelback Rd., # 350
Phoenix, AZ 85016
Tel: (800) 777-6736 (602) 224-0440
Fax: (602) 468-3788
E-Mail: info@opencs.com
Internet Address: www.opencs.com
Contact: Mr. Rich Stark, Dir. Franchising & Marketing

Description: O.P.E.N. has been granting commercial cleaning franchises since 1983. Our program is centered around on-going training and support in addition to guaranteed initial customers. All franchises include a customer base, equipment and advanced business training. We also offer Master Franchises on an exclusive basis for certain metropolitan areas.

# Franchised Units:	387 Units
# Company-Owned Units:	3 Units
Total # Units:	390 Units
Founded In:	1983
1st Franchised In:	1983
Average Total Investment:	7-90K
Franchise Fee:	6-45K
On-Going Royalty:	10%
Advertising Fee:	N/A
Financial Assistance:	Yes(D)
Site Selection Assistance:	No

Lease Negotiation Assistance:	Yes
Contract Terms (Init./Renew):	10/10

Initial Training Provided:2 Wks. Regional Office (Janitorial); 4 Wks. Regional Off. & 3 Wks. Master's Off. (Master).

Depending on the package you select, O.P.E.N. is obligated to offer you a specified initial account volume ranging from $500 to $25,000 per month. See the chart in Item 5. See Item 11 for the time periods within which O.P.E.N. must offer accounts. If O.P.E.N. does not offer you the required accounts within the fulfillment period set by your Franchise Agreement, you are entitle to a credit or refund of a portion of your initial fran-

chise fee if you request it. The credit will reduce the amount you owe O.P.E.N. under any promissory note, or you will receive a cash refund. See Item 5. O.P.E.N. America did not grant any janitorial franchises during 1998 and therefore had no performance obligation that year. The obligations of O.P.E.N.'s wholly owned subsidiaries to offer accounts or to make refunds during 1998 is show on the following chart.

1998 Fulfillment of Initial Account Volume Obligations
(Consolidated Numbers for O.P.E.N.'s Three Former Subsidaries)

		Monthly Initial Account Volume Purchased						Total Franchises Sold	
		$.5K	$1K	$1.5K–3K	$4K–7K	$8K–12K	$13K–$25K	#	%
Fulfillment period (days): (Note 1)		120	120	120	150 to 240	270 to 390	420 to 780		
Requirement met within fulfillment period	Number of franchisees offered required initial account volume within fulfillment period	23	5	12	1	1	0	42	78
Requirement excused or not met within fulfillment period	Number of franchisees who accepted delayed performance	0	1	3	0	0	0	4	7
	Number of franchisees to whom offers ceased because of their unacceptable performance	0	0	1	0	0	0	1	2
	Number of franchisees given credit or refunds	0	0	0	0	0	0	0	0
	Number of franchisees in fulfillment period or status indeterminable	2	2	2	1	0	0	7	13
	Subtotals (4 rows above)	2	3	6	1	0	0	12	22
Total Number of Franchises Sold:		25	8	18	2	1	0	54	100

Note 1: O.P.E.N. has 120 days to offer the first $3,000 of initial account volume, and an additional 30 days to offer each additional $1,000 of initial account volume.

During 1998, O.P.E.N.'s three wholly owned subsidiaries received a total of $468,150 in initial franchise fees, and gave credits or refunds totaling $9,584 when they were unable to offer the full initial account volumes to which franchisees were entitled within the fulfillment periods.

The historical performance of O.P.E.N.'s subsidiaries in Arizona, California and Washington may not be relevant to O.P.E.N.'s expansion into new states. O.P.E.N. does not claim that its future performance in supplying accounts will be as good as the 1998 performance shown above. O.P.E.N.'s performance may be affected by factors that it does not control, including economic conditions, the presence of competing janitorial service companies in the geographic area where you are based, the continued willingness of O.P.E.N.'s service contract marketing personnel to remain in O.P.E.N.'s employment and other matters.

Substantiation of the data used in preparing the earnings claim set out above will be made available to you upon reasonable request.

"professional polish"
A Total Franchise System

PROFESSIONAL POLISH
5450 East Loop, 820 South
Fort Worth, TX 76119
Tel: (800) 255-0488 (817) 572-7353
Fax: (817) 561-6193
E-Mail: info@professionalpolish.com
Internet Address:
Contact: Mr. Carren Cavanaugh, President

Description: Janitorial, lawn and building repair. Alto distributor.

# Franchised Units:	30 Units
# Company-Owned Units:	2 Units
Total # Units:	32 Units
Founded In:	1981
1st Franchised In:	1986
Average Total Investment:	14.5K
Franchise Fee:	5K
On-Going Royalty:	15%
Advertising Fee:	0%
Financial Assistance:	Yes(D)
Site Selection Assistance:	Yes
Lease Negotiation Assistance:	Yes
Contract Terms (Init./Renew):	25/25
Initial Training Provided:	10 Days Fort Worth, TX; 30 Days Franchise City.

Actual, Average, Projected or Forecasted Franchisee Sales, Profits, or Earnings:
Franchisees can earn a good income and grow in their Professional Polish franchise. Income earned depends upon the efforts put forth by the franchisee in his/her ability to schedule and complete quality work, and upon how fast and large the Franchisee wants to become.

Local Franchises: The following is what a Franchisee can expect to earn in GROSS PROFITS at specific Gross Sales levels. Professional Polish only publishes these Revenues and Profits and a guide for the potential Franchisee. The actual net profits earned by each Franchisee may vary substantially due to his or her expense structure.

Local Gross Profit:

Gross Revenue	Franchise Fee	Gross Profit
$20,000	$3,000	$17,000
30,000	4,500	25,500
40,000	6,000	34,000

Gross Revenue	Franchise Fee	Gross Profit
40,000	6,000	34,000
50,000	7,500	42,500
60,000	9,000	51,000

These revenues and gross profits demonstrate the ability to earn a good income. The gross revenues depend entirely on how hard the Franchisee is willing to work to expand his/her business, PPI cannot estimate what the Franchisee could earn in net income because PPI's does not have the right to determine the Franchisees' operating cost.

Master Franchise: Due to number of locations, it is not practical to include a list of the locations and potential revenue and profits in this publication. The potential Master Franchisee will be supplied estimates of revenues and gross profits under a separate cover. The potential revenue and earnings of a Master Franchise are determined by location and population.

Property & Casualty Restoration & Reconstruction
Marketing and Consulting

PUROFIRST INTERNATIONAL
5350 NW 35th Ave.
Fort Lauderdale, FL 33309
Tel: (800) 247-9047 (954) 777-2431
Fax: (800) 995-8527
E-Mail: rory@purofirst.com
Internet Address: www.purofirst.com
Contact: Mr. Rory O'Dwyer, Vice President

Description: We have building contractors doing specialty, high-profit, casualty restoration and reconstruction projects. Franchisees work both directly with insurance companies and for the owners. Franchisees work for most national insurance companies. Fast start-up means quicker profits.

# Franchised Units:	98 Units
# Company-Owned Units:	0 Units
Total # Units:	98 Units
Founded In:	1985
1st Franchised In:	1991
Average Total Investment:	63.3-100.5K
Franchise Fee:	30K
On-Going Royalty:	7-2%
Advertising Fee:	0%
Financial Assistance:	Yes(D)
Site Selection Assistance:	No
Lease Negotiation Assistance:	No
Contract Terms (Init./Renew):	10/10
Initial Training Provided:	10 Days Fort Lauderdale, FL; 5 Days Franchise Location.

The information contained in this report represents the information that was reported to us by our franchises. We did not audit or otherwise verify this information. We believe this information to be substantially accurate. The reports that we used to compile this information are available to you for your inspection.

1998 Reported Gross Sales for Purofirst Franchises in Operation for No Less Than Twelve (12) Months

This report for 1998 represents a total of 654 reported months with total gross sales of $34,126,621.66. The average monthly gross sales are $45,869.12. Of the 62 franchises listed, 23 or 36% exceeded this average.

Office Location	Operation Start	Actual Months Reported	Reported Gross Sales
Rockville, Maryland	Jan-95	12	$3,149,170.73
Sevierville, Tennessee	Nov-94	12	$2,287,955.63
Louisville, Kentucky	Sep-94	12	$1,455,825.04
Redding, California	Jan-96	12	$1,309,238.09
Harrisburg, Pennsylvania	Aug-95	12	$1,271,126.96
Hainesport, New Jersey	Apr-94	12	$1,239,295.76
Orlando, Florida	Jun-92	12	$1,182,585.15
Tucson, Arizona	Jul-91	12	$1,108,950.31
Menlo Park, California	Apr-94	12	$1,001,610.97
Ledgewood, New Jersey	Dec-95	12	$895,338.47

Office Location	Operation Start	Actual Months Reported	Reported Gross Sales
Nashville, Tennessee	Dec-95	12	$871,696.51
Santa Rosa, California	Feb-94	12	$776,554.49
Mentone, Indiana	Feb-97	12	$766,200.65
Apple Valley, California	Oct-93	12	$748,633.09
Westerville, Ohio	Oct-96	12	$741,013.30
Sarasota, Florida	Sep-91	12	$736,310.43
Seattle, Washington	Apr-96	12	$717,790.56
Canal Fulton, Ohio	Apr-95	12	$714,482.77
Edgewater, Maryland	Aug-95	12	$666,454.79
Van Nuys, California	Feb-94	12	$657,605.65
Lexington, Kentucky	Sep-96	12	$649,704.17
Needham, Massachusetts	Aug-95	12	$625,676.82
Oakland, California	Jan-93	12	$597,565.01
N. Chatham, New York	Jan-98	12	$549,642.48
San Rafael, California	Apr-92	12	$533,264.11
San Ramon, California	Jun-93	12	$491,672.12
Anaheim, California	Jun-93	12	$484,681.64
Gillette, New Jersey	Oct-95	12	$451,070.50
Newark, Ohio	Apr-95	12	$448,775.40
Santa Clarita, California	Aug-93	12	$447,160.59
Jamesville, New York	Nov-93	12	$387,313.89
Norwell, Massachusetts	Aug-95	12	$378,305.13
Long Beach, N. Carolina	Feb-96	12	$374,777.86
Pittsfield, Massachusetts	Oct-94	12	$363,404.82
Ocean, New Jersey	Nov-95	9	$324,040.17
Gansevort, New York	Aug-95	12	$323,434.96
Baltimore, Maryland	Dec-95	12	$290,348.74
Clute, Texas	Aug-95	12	$285,721.02
Pittsburgh, Pennsylvania	Aug-95	12	$287,477.90
Mt. Pleasant, Pennsylvania	Mar-94	12	$277,177.30
Neshanic Station, New Jersey	Nov-95	12	$270,502.68
Bloomsburg, Pennsylvania	Jan-94	12	$264,180.70
Mt. Pleasant, Michigan	May-97	12	$249,474.97
St. Louis, Missouri	Jun-95	11	$246,240.35
Otego, New York	Jul-97	12	$224,420.94
Strasburg, Pennsylvania	Nov-97	11	$212,503.73
Reading, Pennsylvania	May-97	12	$196,931.60
Santa Cruz, California	Feb-96	12	$194,698.53
Salem, New Hampshire	Oct-93	12	$181,528.25

Office Location	Operation	Actual Months	Reported Gross
	Start	Reported	Sales
Coatesville, Pennsylvania	Jan-93	12	$182,443.58
Bartlesville, Oklahoma	Jul-96	7	$147,539.70
Cassadaga, New York	Dec-97	12	$132,206.95
Hope Mills, N. Carolina	Apr-94	9	$130,940.66
Munising, Michigan	Sep-95	12	$122,135.83
Ontario, California	Mar-94	12	$110,829.65
Tonawanda, New York	Oct-97	12	$109,739.44
Glens Falls, New York	Oct-95	12	$105,894.18
Davis, California	Mar-94	12	$80,454.72
Grand Rapids, Michigan	Jul-97	6	$28,356.71
Monrovia, California	Apr-96	12	$26,521.92
Lombard, Illinois	Jul-92	8	$10,537.65
Mt. Kisco, New York	Dec-96	12	$29,484.94
Ipswich, Massachusetts	Jul-93	12	$0.00

1997 Reported Gross Sales for Purofirst Franchises in Operation for No LessThan Twelve (12) Months

This report for 1997 represents a total of 888 reported months with total gross sales of $33,977,394.00. The average monthly gross sales are $38,263.00. Of the 77 franchises listed, 26 or 34% exceeded this average.

Office Location	Operation	Actual Months	Reported Gross
	Start	Reported	Sales
Rockville, Maryland	Jan-95	12	$2,777,491.00
Sevierville, Tennessee	Nov-94	12	$1,580,651.00
Santa Rosa, California	Feb-94	12	$1,456,302.00
Tucson, Arizona	July-91	12	$1,304,077.00
Louisville, Kentucky	Sept-94	12	$1,141,757.00
Harrisburg, Pennsylvania	Aug -95	12	$924,474.00
Hainesport, New Jersey	Apr-94	12	$924,153.00
N. Chatham, New York	Dec-93	12	$843,706.00
Needham, Massachusetts	Aug-95	12	$810,693.00
Ledgewood, New Jersey	Dec-95	12	$798,312.00
Edgewater, Maryland	Aug-95	12	$726,536.00
Sewickly, Pennsylvania	Aug-95	12	$697,498.00
Van Nuys, California	Feb-94	12	$680,042.00
San Rafael, California	Apr-92	12	$607,961.00
Redmond, Washington	Jul-96	12	$598,385.00
Menlo Park, California	Apr-94	12	$591,526.00
Orlando, Florida	Jun-92	12	$590,674.00
Sarasota, Florida	Sep-91	12	$558,828.00
Williamsburg, Virginia	May-96	12	$553,475.00
San Ramon, California	Jun-93	12	$553,217.00

Office Location	Operation Start	Actual Months Reported	Reported Gross Sales
Elkridge, Maryland	Mar-96	12	$540,864.00
Ocean, New Jersey	Nov-95	12	$508,821.00
Anaheim, California	Jun-93	12	$470,655.00
Santa Clarita, California	Aug-93	12	$464,060.00
Apple Valley, California	Oct-93	12	$442,525.00
Nashville, Tennessee	Dec-95	12	$439,230.00
Dallas, Texas	Jun-94	12	$431,424.00
Pittsfield, Massachusetts	Oct-94	12	$429,394.00
Redding, California	Jan-96	12	$427,363.00
Oakland, California	Jan-93	12	$426,155.00
Westerville, Ohio	Oct-96	12	$420,508.00
Lombard, Illinois	Jul-92	12	$415,028.00
Baltimore, Maryland	Dec-95	12	$413,909.00
Chicago, Illinois	Jan-96	9	$412,704.00
Long Beach, N. Carolina	Feb-96	12	$408,703.00
Warminster, Pennsylvania	Aug-95	9	$378,760.00
Campbell, California	Mar-93	12	$375,465.00
Bloomsburg, Pennsylvania	Jan-94	12	$371,387.00
San Marcos, California	Dec-92	12	$357,474.00
Lewiston, New York	Oct-93	12	$354,899.00
Mt. Pleasant, Pennsylvania	Mar-94	12	$349,924.00
Seattle, Washington	Apr-96	11	$347,424.00
Clute, Texas	Aug-95	12	$333,475.00
Gillette, New Jersey	Oct-95	12	$319,160.00
Hope Mills, N. Carolina	Apr-94	12	$302,522.00
Newark, Ohio	Apr-95	12	$297,749.00
Raleigh, N. Carolina	Jan-96	12	$292,327.00
Canal Fulton, Ohio	Apr-95	12	$290,144.00
Gansevort, New York	Aug-95	12	$265,699.00
St. Louis, Missouri	Jun-95	12	$258,504.00
Camarillo, California	Oct-92	12	$243,145.00
Jamesville, New York	Nov-93	12	$242,713.00
Bartlesville, Oklahoma	Jul-96	12	$241,823.00
Davis, California	Mar-94	10	$233,406.00
Neshanic Station, New Jersey	Nov-95	12	$224,947.00
Salem, New Hampshire	Oct-93	12	$213,124.00
Ontario, California	Mar-94	12	$210,255.00
Fruitland Park, Florida	Jan-95	12	$187,780.00
Skyland, North Carolina	Oct-94	12	$179,856.00

Office Location	Operation Start	Actual Months Reported	Reported Gross Sales
Fresno, California	Oct-95	7	$167,196.00
Coatesville, Pennsylvania	Jan-93	12	$164,477.00
Ithaca, New York	Oct-94	12	$164,065.00
Munising, Michigan	Sep-95	12	$155,544.00
Lexington, Kentucky	Sep-96	12	$152,830.00
Baton Rouge, Louisiana	Aug-95	12	$150,444.00
Norwell, Massachusetts	Aug-95	9	$139,155.00
Glens Falls, New York	Oct-95	11	$122,675.00
South Lyon, Michigan	Nov-96	5	$113,509.00
Monrovia, California	Apr-96	11	$86,369.00
Santa Cruz, California	Feb-96	12	$81,768.00
Long Beach, California	Oct-92	12	$47,448.00
Burgettstown, Pennsylvania	Jan-96	12	$38,054.00
Long Beach, California	Oct-93	12	$36,307.00
Boxborough, Massachusetts	Dec-92	8	$35,995.00
Greenville, Ohio	Sep-96	12	$33,067.00
N. Hollywood, California	Apr-93	6	$32,961.00
Ipswich, Massachusetts	Jul-93	12	$12,467.00
Total			$33,977,394.00

Other than the information set forth above we do not make any representations or statements of past projected, or forecasted sales, profits, or earnings to franchisees with respect to our franchises. We do not furnish or authorize our salespersons to furnish to you any oral or written information concerning projected, forecasted, or potential sales, costs, income, or profits of a franchise.

We specifically instruct our sales personnel, agents, employees, and officers that they are not permitted to make such claims or statements as to the earnings, sales or profits, or prospects or chances of success, nor are they authorized to represent or estimate dollar figures as to a franchisee's operation. We will not be bound by allegations of any unauthorized representations as to earnings, sales, profits, or prospects or chances of success.

Actual results vary from franchise to franchise, and we cannot estimate the results of a particular franchise. We recommend that prospective franchisees make their own independent investigation to determine whether or not the franchise may be profitable, and consult an attorney and other advisors before executing the Franchise Agreement.

These reports do not include franchises that were not in business for a full twelve (12) months in 1997 and 1998. The franchises not included are franchises that were new franchises, transferred, or terminated in 1997 and 1998. These reports do not include information on two (2) franchises that are not obligated to and do not report gross sales.

Your individual financial results are likely to differ from the results reported here.

SPARKLE WASH
26851 Richmond Rd.
Bedford Heights, OH 44146
Tel: (800) 321-0770 (216) 464-4212

Fax: (216) 464-8869
E-Mail: pfunku@en.com
Internet Address: www.sparklewash.com
Contact: Mr. Hans G. Funk, President

Description: SPARKLE WASH provides mobile power-cleaning and restoration, providing broad market opportunities to our franchisees for the commercial, industrial, residential and fleet markets. SPARKLE WASH franchisees can also provide special services, including wood restoration, all using our environmentally-friendly products.

# Franchised Units:	171 Units
# Company-Owned Units:	1 Units

Total # Units:	172 Units
Founded In:	1965
1st Franchised In:	1967
Average Total Investment:	50K
Franchise Fee:	15K
On-Going Royalty:	3-5%
Advertising Fee:	0%
Financial Assistance:	Yes(B)
Site Selection Assistance:	N/A
Lease Negotiation Assistance:	N/A
Contract Terms (Init./Renew):	Continual

Initial Training Provided: 1 Week Headquarters; 3 Days Franchisee Location; 3 Days National/Regional Meetings.

This section has been prepared to give you an idea of how much you could make by owning and operating a Sparkle Wash franchise. The following portion of the forecast is based on the responses to a survey of the past performance of Sparkle's United States franchises. 26 of our domestic franchise owners (about 30 percent) responded to the survey. The respondents based their figures on operations from January 1, 1998 to December 31, 1998. In the preparation of this forecast we have relied solely on the responses of our franchisees and have made no material assumptions. The following chart indicates the average amount spent by the franchisees, as a percentage of sales, on each of the categories listed.

Expense Category:	Percentage of Sales:
Payroll Tax	2.84%
Employee Benefits	1.61%
Cleaning Products	6.13%
Operating Supplies	3.24%
Equipment Parts & Maintenance	4.88%
Motor Vehicle Payments	6.05%
Fuels	3.94%
Insurance	3.88%
Uniforms & Laundry	0.62%
Telephone	2.40%
Professional Fees	0.75%
Rent or Lease	2.59%
Utilities	1.01%
Travel, Meals & Convention	0.62%
Royalties	3.11%
Advertising	2.67%
Other	1.94%

Expense Category:	Percentage of Sales:
Total Percent of Sales Spent on Expenses	48.25%
Profits, Includes Wages of Owner & Employees	51.75%

As the chart above indicates, our average franchise owner spends 48.25% of their sales on expenses before paying employees. This means that you could expect 51.75% (100–48.25%) of your sales to be retained as profits if you choose to perform all of the work yourself, less if you hire employees. 15 of the survey respondents had profits of greater than 51.75% before paying themselves or employees.

The following is the average sales volume of the top 10, 20, 30 and 40 percent of our franchise owners who reported sales for the full 12 months of 1998 as of February 1, 1999. Some of the franchisees own more than one franchise territory.

Franchisee Ranking:	Avg. Sales/Franchisee:
Top 10%	$746,444
Top 20%	$495,544
Top 30%	$384,290
Top 40%	$321,213

Actual results vary from franchise to franchise, and we cannot estimate the results of a particular franchise. There are risks in starting a business and no express or implied promises are made about the income or sales of this business.

Packaging & mailing

AIM MAIL CENTERS
20381 Lake Forest Dr., # B-2
Lake Forest, CA 92630
Tel: (800) 669-4246 (949) 837-4151
Fax: (949) 837-4537
E-Mail: mherrera@aimmailcenters.com
Internet Address: www.aimmailcenters.com
Contact: Mr. Michael R. Herrera, VP of Franchise
Development

Description: AIM MAIL CENTERS take care of all business service needs. AIM's services include renting mailboxes, buying stamps, sending faxes, notary, making copies and passport photos. AIM is also an authorized UPS and FedEx Shipping Outlet. It's like having a post office, office supply store, gift shop, and copy shop all rolled into one. We are so confident of our franchise program that we offer a money-back guarantee.

# Franchised Units:	58 Units
# Company-Owned Units:	0 Units
Total # Units:	58 Units
Founded In:	1985
1st Franchised In:	1989
Average Total Investment:	75-95K
Franchise Fee:	23.9K
On-Going Royalty:	5%
Advertising Fee:	2%
Financial Assistance:	Yes(I)
Site Selection Assistance:	Yes
Lease Negotiation Assistance:	Yes
Contract Terms (Init./Renew):	15
Initial Training Provided:	2 Weeks Corporate Headquarters; 3 Days In Store.

The information set forth in this document is a report of (1) total and average gross sales of AIM Mail Centers® Franchisees based on the weekly gross sales reported by AIM Mail Centers® Franchisees, as part of their normal weekly royalty reports to Amailcenter Franchise Corporation, for each Franchisee who filed reports during the periods covered, and (2) total and average gross sales for a unit owned and operated by the Franchisor throughout the same period. This information covers 36 franchised units, and 1 Franchisor-owned unit, which were open and in operation from January 1, 1998, through December 31, 1998. (Other AIM Mail Centers® [both franchised and Franchisor-owned] were open during calendar year 1998 but were not open for the entire period and, therefore, their reported gross sales are not included in the figures presented.)

Franchised Units — Reported Gross Sales — Totals and Averages

For the period from January 1, 1998, through December 31, 1998, the 36 units reporting weekly gross sales to Amailcenter Franchise Corporation for such entire period reported a total of $7,591,732 in gross sales, for average reported gross sales of $210,881 per unit for the 12 months covered. These figures do not include gross sales for any units which were not open and in operation for the entire January 1, 1998, through December 31, 1998, period (12 months) and do not include amounts received by AIM Mail Center® Franchisees with respect to gross American Express® money transfers or money orders, but do include actual commissions earned by AIM Mail Center® Franchisees with respect to such transactions. During the period from January 1, 1998, through December 31,1998, 14 (or 39%) of these 36 units had results which attained or surpassed the 12-month average of $210,881.

During the period from January 1, 1998, through December 31, 1998, 27 of the 36 franchised units had been open for 2 years or more and reported $6,660,301 in gross sales, for average reported gross sales of $244,211. During the period from January 1, 1998, through December 31, 1998, 19 (or 33%) of these 27 units had results which attained or surpassed the 12-month average of $244,211.

Franchisor-Owned Unit — Reported Gross Sales

For the period from January 1, 1998, through December 31, 1998, the one AIM Mail Center® owned and operated by the Franchisor throughout that period reported gross sales of *$344,177 for that Franchisor-owned unit*. These figures do not include amounts received by AIM Mail Center® Franchisees with respect to gross American Express® money transfers or money orders, but do include actual commissions earned by AIM Mail Center® Franchisees with respect to such transactions. This figure was subject to the annual independent audit performed in connection with the Franchisor's audited financial statements. During this period, one (or 100%) of this one unit had results which attained or surpassed the average of $344,177.

CAUTION: SOME OUTLETS HAVE SOLD THIS AMOUNT. THERE IS NO ASSURANCE YOU'LL DO AS WELL. IF YOU RELY UPON OUR FIGURES, YOU MUST ACCEPT THE RISK OF NOT DOING AS WELL.

A NEW FRANCHISEE'S INDIVIDUAL FINANCIAL RESULTS ARE LIKELY TO DIFFER FROM THE RESULTS SET FORTH IN THIS DOCUMENT.

Actual results will vary from unit to unit and Amailcenter Franchise Corporation cannot estimate or project the results of operation of any particular franchise. We are unable, and do not attempt, to predict, forecast or project future performance of any AIM Mail Centers® unit and the information presented herein should not be used to predict, forecast or project any such future performance. *The information presented should not be considered or used in estimating or projecting actual, probable or possible financial results for any current or future franchised unit and Amailcenter Franchise Corporation specifically and expressly disclaims any representation that the results reported will, are likely to or can be achieved by any current or future franchised unit at any time in the future. You should consult with appropriate financial, business and legal advisors in evaluating the information in this document.*

As of December 31, 1998, there were 43 AIM Mail Centers® units open and operating. Of the 43 units open and operating as of December 31, 1998, the 36 units whose gross sales are presented for the period from January 1, 1998, through December 31, 1998, make up 84%.

Substantiation of the data used in preparing the results set forth in this document will be made available to the prospective franchisee on reasonable request.

The information presented *has not been* audited and is (except for the gross sales reported for the AIM Mail Center® owned and operated by the Franchisor throughout the period reported) based on weekly gross sales as reported by AIM Mail Centers® Franchisees to Amailcenter Franchise Corporation for purposes of royalty computation and payment. Amailcenter Franchise Corporation has assumed that such reports are accurate and that the Franchisees have not overstated their weekly gross sales.

Prospective Franchisees should note that the AIM Mail Centers® who have supplied the data used in this document are located in California and Nevada, generally in urban or suburban areas. Many of the units whose results are reported are located in major metropolitan areas. The areas in which AIM Mail Centers® are located typically have a relatively high level of socioeconomic and demographic makeup, as well as business activity, which can contribute to a greater need for, and ability to afford, the products and services of the type offered by AIM Mail Centers® and accompanying possible higher sales. Revenues will also be affected by such factors as competition, population, numbers of consumers and businesspersons visiting and resident in the area of a unit and general economic conditions in the area. *The prospective Franchisee should independently verify whether such factors and conditions in his/her intended area of operation are comparable to those in existing Franchisees' areas.* Amailcenter Franchise Corporation has no experience with franchised or company-owned units in other areas and can make no prediction or estimation of the results that might be experienced by franchised units in other areas.

Prospective Franchisees should also note that the figures presented are averages, that they include results from some AIM Mail Centers® who have been in business for a substantial period of time and that *new AIM Mail Centers® Franchisees should not necessarily expect to achieve such results.*

Prospective Franchisees should, prior to making any investment decision, research the need in their proposed area of operation for the products and services of the type offered by AIM Mail Centers® Franchisees, including actual and potential competition and the socioeconomic and demographic background of their area. *In this regard, prospective Franchisees are strongly encouraged to speak with existing AIM Mail Centers® Franchisees and to make an independent judgment as to whether their experience may or may not be transferable to the Prospective Franchisee's proposed area of operation.*

Prospective Franchisees should further note that the information presented relates only to gross sales and that no information is presented, nor does Amailcenter Franchise Corporation have information, regarding the costs of operation of existing AIM Mail Centers® Franchisees or their profits, losses or cash flows.

PAK MAIL.
CENTERS OF AMERICA®

PAK MAIL
7173 S. Havana St., # 600
Englewood, CO 80112
Tel: (800) 833-2821 (303) 957-1000
Fax: (800) 336-7363
E-Mail: sales@pakmail.com
Internet Address: www.pakmail.com
Contact: Mr. Chuck Prentner, Licensing Manager

Description: PAK MAIL is a convenient center for packaging, shipping and business support services, offering both residential and commercial customers air, ground, and ocean carriers, custom packaging and crating, private mailbox rental, mail services, packaging and moving supplies, copy and fax service and internet access and related services. We ship anything, anywhere.

# Franchised Units:	400 Units
# Company-Owned Units:	0 Units
Total # Units:	400 Units
Founded In:	1983
1st Franchised In:	1984
Average Total Investment:	70-115K
Franchise Fee:	28K
On-Going Royalty:	5% Sliding
Advertising Fee:	2%
Financial Assistance:	Yes(I)
Site Selection Assistance:	Yes
Lease Negotiation Assistance:	Yes
Contract Terms (Init./Renew):	10/10

Initial Training Provided: 10 Days in Englewood, CO; 3 Days in Existing Center; 3 Days In New Center at Opening.

Report of Gross Sales of Franchised Pak Mail Centers

CAUTION: THE FOLLOWING DATA SHOULD NOT BE CONSIDERED AS THE ACTUAL OR POTENTIAL INCOME OR RESULTS OF OPERATIONS OF ANY PARTICULAR FRANCHISE. WE DO NOT REPRESENT THAT YOU CAN EXPECT TO ATTAIN THESE GROSS SALES LEVELS. A FRANCHISEE'S FINANCIAL RESULTS ARE LIKELY TO DIFFER FROM THE FIGURES PRESENTED. SEE ATTACHED NOTES.

	Number of Centers	Average Sales
Average Annual Sales: Top 10%	23	$417,467
Average Annual Sales: Top 30%	68	$321,560
Average Annual Sales: Top 50%	114	$274,781
Average Annual Sales: All Centers	228	$200,878

Explanatory Notes (Containing Summary of Factual Data and Significant Assumptions)

1. The data set forth above represents the reported gross sales of 228 franchised Pak Mail Centers that were in operation at least two years before the reporting period of December 1, 1997 through November 30, 1998. Not included are three non-traditional Centers (2 located within Von's Supermarkets and 1 located in a Hallmark Super Store), as these do not reflect typical results of a Pak Mail Center.

2. Aside from geographical and demographic differences and managerial emphasis, there are no material differences in the products, services, training or support offered to any franchisee. Differences in sales volumes are attributable to the amount of time a Pak Mail Center has been open, geographical and demographic differences, and a franchisee's ability and willingness to follow system guidelines.

3. The sales of products and services made by franchised Pak Mail Centers include those which reflect higher revenue margins such as freight, business services, custom packaging, etc. and those which reflect little or no revenue margins such as postage stamp sales. The mix of products and services varies at the discretion of each franchisee.

4. The above information was prepared from royalty reports provided by each individual franchisee. A franchisee pays us a royalty based on sales. However, we know of no instance, and have no reason to believe that, any franchisee would overstate its level of sales receipts in its royalty report.

5. This information represents aggregate results of sales reported to us and should not be considered the actual or probable sales which will be achieved by any individual franchisee. We do not represent that any prospective franchisee can expect to obtain these results. A franchisee's results are likely to be lower in its first year of business. We recommend that the prospective franchisee make his or her own independent investigation to determine whether or not a franchise may be profitable. We further recommend that prospective franchisees consult with professional advisors before executing any agreement.

6. Actual results may vary from franchise to franchise and are dependent on a variety of internal and external factors, many of which neither we nor any prospective franchisee can estimate, such as competition, economic climate, demographics, changing consumer demands, etc. A franchisee's ability to achieve any level of gross sales or net income will depend on these factors and others, including the franchisee's level of expertise, none of which are within our control. Accordingly, we cannot, and do not, estimate the results of any particular franchise.

Substantiation for the above data will be made available for inspection at our headquarters and will be provided to all prospective franchisees upon request.

EXCEPT FOR THE INFORMATION IN THIS ITEM, NO REPRESENTATIONS OR STATEMENTS OF ACTUAL, AVERAGE, PROJECTED, FORECASTED OR POTENTIAL SALES, COSTS, INCOME OR PROFITS ARE MADE TO FRANCHISEES BY US. WE DO NOT FURNISH OR MAKE, OR AUTHORIZE OUR SALES PERSONNEL TO FURNISH OR MAKE, ANY ORAL OR WRITTEN INFORMATION CONCERNING THE ACTUAL, AVERAGE, PROJECTED, FORECASTED OR POTENTIAL SALES, COSTS, INCOME OR PROFITS OF A FRANCHISE OR PROSPECTS OR CHANCES OF SUCCESS THAT ANY FRANCHISEE CAN EXPECT OR THAT PRESENT OR PAST FRANCHISEES HAVE HAD, OTHER THAN AS SET FORTH IN THIS ITEM. WE DISCLAIM AND WILL NOT BE BOUND BY ANY UNAUTHORIZED REPRESENTATIONS.

PARCEL PLUS

PARCEL PLUS
2661 Riva Rd., Bldg. 1000, Suite 102
Annapolis, MD 21401-8405
Tel: (800) 662-5553 (410) 266-3200
Fax: (410) 266-3266
E-Mail: staff@corp.parcelplus.com
Internet Address: www.parcelplus.com
Contact: Ms. Kelle Barchanowicz,

Description: Our five-year commitment to integrate logistics with the internet has created http://www.netship.com. Visit our site and you will quickly see that we are far more than a retail pack-and-ship chain.

# Franchised Units:	129 Units
# Company-Owned Units:	0 Units
Total # Units:	129 Units
Founded In:	1986
1st Franchised In:	1988
Average Total Investment:	45-80K
Franchise Fee:	22.5K
On-Going Royalty:	4%
Advertising Fee:	1%
Financial Assistance:	Yes(I)
Site Selection Assistance:	Yes
Lease Negotiation Assistance:	Yes
Contract Terms (Init./Renew):	10/10

Initial Training Provided: 1 Week Orientation at National Support Center; 2 Weeks Cargo Training; 2 Weeks at Stores.

Representations Regarding Earnings Capability

Gross Sales of Franchised Units in Operation at Least One Year as of December 31, 1998

Number of Units in Sample:	99
Arithmetic Average Annual Sales:	$226,352
Range of Sales for Top Ten Stores:	$640,551–385,508
Range of Sales for Bottom Ten Stores:	$102,251–64,375
Average Annual Sales Top 10% (Ten Stores):	$469,772
Average Annual Sales Top 30% (Thirty Stores):	$369,800
Average Annual Sales Top 50% (Fifty Stores):	$310,006

Notes:
1. The above data represents the actual operating results of the 99 Parcel Plus franchised units that were in operation at their present retail locations at least one year as of December 31, 1998. Stores moved by the franchisee to a different center are included after they have had one year in the new location to build market awareness of the new location. The 99 units included represent approximately 77% of the total number of franchised units operating fully (in retail locations) as of December 31, 1998. Average annual sales in each category above were determined by averaging total sales during the reporting period. 36 (or 36%) of all Franchised Businesses met or exceeded the average sales figure. Also, 4 (or 40%) of the Franchised Businesses in the top 10% met or exceeded the average sales figure for their group; 12 (or

40%) of the Franchised Businesses in the top 30% met or exceeded the average sales figure for their group; 22 (or 44%) of the Franchised Businesses in the top 50% met or exceeded the average sales figure for their group.

2. Aside from geographic differences, there are no material differences in the products, services, training or support offered to any franchise. Differences in sales volumes are attributed to geographical and managerial differences.

3. The sales of products and services made by franchised units include those which reflect high margin revenue such as UPS ground, Internet services, facsimile, copies, etc., and those which reflect little or no revenue or margin such as postage stamps sales. The service mix for both transportation and business support services offered to the public by each individual franchised unit varies at the discretion of each franchisee and because of competitive pressures. The sales volume attainable by you is largely dependent upon the type and quality of service offered to the public as well as individual sales and marketing efforts and your ability to build a high margin mix of profit centers.

4. The above information was prepared from royalty reports submitted to us by each franchised unit. You pay us a royalty based upon your gross sales less postage stamp revenue. We know of no instance in which, and have no reason to believe that, any franchised unit would overstate its level of gross sales in its royalty report.

5. The above information reflects the aggregate results of sales and should not be considered the actual or probable sales that will be realized by any individual franchisee. We do not represent that you can expect to obtain these results. In particular, your initial financial results are likely to be lower for the same product offerings. (We have recently developed several new products or services to be offered at the Franchised Businesses [e.g. Cargo Plus and Netship], but it is unknown what effect the new Cargo Plus and Netship products will have). We recommend that you make your own independent investigation to determine whether or not the franchise may be profitable, and consult with an attorney and other advisors prior to executing any agreement.

6. Substantiation for the above data will be made available by us to you upon reasonable request.

7. Except for the information in this Item 19, we do not make information available to prospective franchisees concerning actual, average, projected, or forecasted sales, profits, or earnings. We do not furnish or authorize our salespersons to furnish any oral or written information not contained in this offering circular concerning the actual, average, projected, forecasted sales, costs, income, or profits of a franchise. We specifically instruct our sales personnel, agents, employees, and officers that, other than as in this Item 19, they are not permitted to make any claims or statements as to the earnings, sales, or profits, or prospects or chances of success, nor are they authorized to represent or estimate dollar figures as to a franchisee's operation. Any representations as to earnings, sales, profits, or prospects or chances for success, other than as set forth above, are unauthorized. Accordingly, we disclaim any unauthorized representations as to earnings, sales, profits, or prospects or chances for success, and we urge you to disregard any such representations.

Actual results vary from franchise to franchise and are dependent on a variety of internal and external factors, some of which neither we nor any franchisee can estimate, such as competition, taxes, the availability of financing, general economic climate, demographics, and changing consumer preferences. Accordingly, we cannot estimate the results of a particular franchise.

POSTAL ANNEX+
7580 Metropolitan Dr., # 200
San Diego, CA 92108
Tel: (800) 456-1525 (619) 563-4800
Fax: (619) 563-9850
E-Mail:
Internet Address: www.postalannex.com
Contact: Mr. John Goodell, Director Franchise
Development

Description: Retail business service center, providing: packaging, shipping, copying, postal, mail box rental, printing fax, notary, office supplies and more.

# Franchised Units:	238 Units
# Company-Owned Units:	0 Units
Total # Units:	238 Units
Founded In:	1985
1st Franchised In:	1986
Average Total Investment:	108.9-158.4K
Franchise Fee:	27.9K
On-Going Royalty:	5%
Advertising Fee:	2%
Financial Assistance:	Yes(I)
Site Selection Assistance:	Yes
Lease Negotiation Assistance:	Yes
Contract Terms (Init./Renew):	15/15
Initial Training Provided: 2 Weeks San Diego, CA.	

Gross Sales of Franchised Units in Operation at Least 1 Year as of Fiscal Year End September 30, 1998

Number of Units in Sample:	161
Average Annual Sales:	$224,000
Median Annual Sales:	$197,000
Range of Sales for Top 10 Stores:	$570,000 to $391,000
Range of Sales for Bottom 10 Stores:	$105,000 to $54,000

Explanatory Notes:

The data above represents the actual operating results of 161 franchised businesses that were in operation at least 1 year as of September 30, 1998. These 161 franchised businesses represent all of the franchised businesses that were in operation at least 1 year as of September 30, 1998. Of these businesses, 42% achieved the average annual sales level and 50% achieved the median annual sales level.

There are no material differences between the operations of, or the services or products offered by, the franchised businesses whose results are reported above, and the franchises we currently offer.

The sales of services and products made by franchised businesses include those that reflect high margins such as UPS ground, facsimile and copies, and those that reflect lower margins such as postage stamps sales. Money order sales, electronic transfer of funds sales and utility collections are not included in the sales figures presented here. The mix of postal, photocopying, packaging and shipping, and business support services offered to the public by each individual franchised business varies at the discretion of each franchisee. The sales volume attainable by a franchisee is largely dependent on the type and quality of service offered to the public, individual sales and marketing efforts.

We prepared the information above from royalty reports submitted to us by each franchised business. Franchisees pay us a royalty based on their "Gross Receipts", as defined in Item 6. We know of no instance in which, and have no reason to believe that, any franchised business overstated its level of Gross Receipts in any royalty report.

The information above reflects the aggregate results of sales that were realized by 161 franchised businesses. Your individual financial results likely will be lower initially. We recommend that you make your own independent investigation to determine whether or not a franchised business may be profitable, and consult with your advisors before signing our franchise agreement.

We will substantiate the information above available to you on reasonable request.

Beyond the information contained in this Item, we do not furnish or authorize our salespersons to furnish any oral or written information on the actual or potential sales, costs, income or profits of a Postal Annex+ franchised business. Actual results may vary from unit to unit, and we cannot estimate the results of any particular franchised business.

CAUTION: THE SALES FIGURES ABOVE SHOULD NOT BE CONSIDERED AS THE ACTUAL OR POTENTIAL FIGURES THAT WILL BE REALIZED BY ANY PROSPECTIVE FRANCHISEE. WE DO NOT REPRESENT THAT YOU CAN EXPECT TO ATTAIN ANY OF THE FIGURES INDICATED.

UNISHIPPERS ASSOCIATION

746 E. Winchester St., # 200
Salt Lake City, UT 84107
Tel: (800) 999-8721 (801) 487-0600
Fax: (801) 487-0623
E-Mail:
Internet Address: www.unishippers.com
Contact: Mr. Tom Jones, Franchise Development

Description: UNISHIPPERS, the largest reseller of transportation services in the United States, is looking for goal-oriented Master Franchisees as it expands into the global market. UNISHIPPERS combines the shipping volumes of thousands of businesses to obtain discounts and benefits from major overnight express and other transportation service carriers. These discounts and benefits, usually available only to large corporations, are then passed on to our customers, primarily small-to medium-sized businesses.

# Franchised Units:	301 Units
# Company-Owned Units:	0 Units
Total # Units:	301 Units
Founded In:	1987
1st Franchised In:	1987
Average Total Investment:	10-100K
Franchise Fee:	10-50K
On-Going Royalty:	16.5%
Advertising Fee:	1% Gross
Financial Assistance:	Yes
Site Selection Assistance:	N/A
Lease Negotiation Assistance:	No
Contract Terms (Init./Renew):	5/5

Initial Training Provided: 1 Week Salt Lake City, UT; 2 Days at Franchisee's Location.

Actual results may vary from unit to unit. Unishippers cannot estimate the results of any particular franchise. Unishippers provides certain limited information regarding actual average past monthly sales of franchised units. Unishippers is providing it to you as part of its earnings claim. The information is based on monthly reports from 284 of the 292 Unishippers franchisees in operation in 1997. The information covers the period from January 1, 1997 through December 31, 1997. Data for months franchisees failed to report or were not in business is not included. The resulting monthly averages were as follows:

a. Average number of new accounts enrolled per month by the franchise: 30.9. The highest number by a single franchise was 348. The low was 0. The standard deviation was 37.8. The median was 21.6

b. Average number of franchisees' customer accounts that were active: 28.2%. The highest rate for a single franchise was 81.4%. The low was 7.9%. The standard deviation was 13.9%. The median was 25.0%.

c. Average number of shipments per active customer account: 14.1. The highest number by a single franchise was 109. The low was 1. The standard deviation was 9.0. The median was 12.9.

d. Average gross profit margin per shipment: $4.94. The standard deviation was $1.16. The median was $4.86.

Several material assumptions were made in deriving these figures. First, it assumes the franchisees were not new. The average number of months in operation for those franchisees reporting was 41.1 months. Second, the results assume the franchisee devoted full time and effort to the success of the franchise business. Third, the franchisees were, in large part, fully trained. It is assumed that they applied the principles, policies and requirements imposed by Unishippers, including those related to methods for identifying prospective customers, handling customer service concerns, making follow-up calls to customers, and others. Fourth, in most cases the franchisees likely sold their services to customers at the higher rates suggested by Unishippers. Fifth, the results assume that the shipments were primarily domestic, that they were made through the present Unishippers carrier, that they were at current carrier rates, and that the shipment weight distribution was approximately 49% letters and 51% packages weighing over 1 pounds or international shipments. Sixth, the franchisees were located across the United States in approximately 47 different states. Seventh, these figures do include Unishippers officer owned franchises.

A NEW FRANCHISEE'S INDIVIDUAL FINANCIAL RESULTS ARE LIKELY TO DIFFER FROM THE RESULTS STATED IN THE EARNINGS CLAIMS.

SUBSTANTIATION OF THE DATA USED IN PREPARING THE EARNINGS CLAIMS WILL BE MADE AVAILABLE TO YOU ON REASONABLE REQUEST.

alphagraphics®

DESIGN ■ COPY ■ PRINT

ALPHAGRAPHICS PRINTSHOPS OF THE FUTURE

3760 N. Commerce Dr., Suite 100
Tucson, AZ 85705
Tel: (800) 528-4885 (520) 293-9200
Fax: (520) 887-2850
E-Mail: opportunity@alphagraphics.com
Internet Address: www.alphagraphics.com
Contact: Mr. Tom Camplese, VP Global Development

Description: Businesses across the United States and around the world trust ALPHAGRAPHICS PRINTSHOPS OF THE FUTURE® stores as their one-stop source for designing, copying, printing and digital publishing services. With over 350 locations in more than 23 countries, our core expertise is helping business customers to easily and effectively communicate in any publishing medium…anywhere in the world… anytime.

# Franchised Units:	352 Units
# Company-Owned Units:	1 Units
Total # Units:	353 Units
Founded In:	1970
1st Franchised In:	1980
Average Total Investment:	311.4-532.7K
Franchise Fee:	25.9K
On-Going Royalty:	8-1.5%
Advertising Fee:	2.5%
Financial Assistance:	Yes(I)
Site Selection Assistance:	Yes
Lease Negotiation Assistance:	No
Contract Terms (Init./Renew):	20/20
Initial Training Provided:	4 Weeks Tucson Service Center; 1 Week Field Location.

Statement of Actual and Average Gross Sales for Calendar Years 1996 through 1998.

The following compares unaudited annual sales information reported by franchisees owning a full service Printshop for each of the 12 month periods ending December 1998, December 1997 and December 1996. A "full service printshop" is one in which high speed duplicating, basic bindery, Design Services, Hub Services and offset printing are performed on the premises. A description of the material assumptions and bases for the unaudited annual sales information for the full service printshops included in the comparison appear in the footnotes below. IT IS IMPORTANT THAT YOU REVIEW THIS INFORMATION VERY CAREFULLY.

1. Stores Open and Operating for 3 Years or More:

Sales	Number of Printshops		
	1998[1]	1997[2]	1996[3]
Under $300,000	0	1	2
$300,000–400,000	8	4	10
$400,000–500,000	7	8	13
$500,000–750,000	37	38	41
$750,000–1,000,000	45	40	38
Over $1,000,000	58	57	50
Total Number of Printshops Operating 3 Years or More	155	148	154
Average Annual Sales	$1,049,177	$1,038,722	$957,164
Percent of Printshops Meeting or Exceeding Average Annual Sales	35%	33%	36%

Average annual sales for Printshops 3 years or older increased 10% from December 31, 1996 to December 31, 1998.

2. Stores Open and Operating for 2 Years or More:

Sales	Number of Printshops		
	1998	1997	1996
Under $300,000	1	1	2
$300,000–400,000	8	7	11
$400,000–500,000	9	11	17
$500,000–750,000	47	45	45
$750,000–1,000,000	49	43	40
Over $1,000,000	60	59	53
Total Number of Printshops Operating 2 Years or More	174	166	168
Average Annual Sales	$1,013,476	$1,000,181	$939,462
Percent of Printshops Meeting or Exceeding Average Annual Sales	33%	36%	35%

Average annual sales for Printshops 2 years or older increased 8% from December 31, 1996 to December 31, 1998.

3. Stores Open and Operating for 1 Year or More:

Sales	Number of Printshops		
	1998	1997	1996
Under $300,000	8	3	6
$300,000–400,000	12	10	14
$400,000–500,000	12	14	23
$500,000–750,000	60	56	52
$750,000–1,000,000	51	46	41
Over $1,000,000	64	61	53
Total Number of Printshops Operating 1 Year or More	207	190	189
Average Annual Sales	$948,397	$949,477	$888,657
Percent of Printshops Meeting or Exceeding Average Annual Sales	35%	37%	35%

Average annual sales for Printshops 1 year or older increased 7% from December 31, 1996 to December 31, 1998.

YOUR INDIVIDUAL RESULTS ARE LIKELY TO DIFFER FROM THE RESULTS STATED ABOVE.

WE PREPARED THE ANNUAL SALES SHOWN ABOVE BASED ON FRANCHISEE SALES INFORMATION REPORTED TO US. WE HAVE NOT INDEPENDENTLY INVES-TIGATED THE AMOUNTS REPORTED. PROSPECTIVE FRANCHISEES OR SELLERS OF FRANCHISES SHOULD BE ADVISED THAT NO CERTIFIED PUBLIC ACCOUN-TANT HAS AUDITED THESE FIGURES OR EXPRESSED HIS/HER OPINION WITH REGARD TO THEIR CONTENT OR FORM. The amounts have not been audited or reviewed for reasonableness by independent auditors. We offered substantially the same services to all of the Printshops described in this Item 19. These Print-shops offered substantially the same products and services to the public as, and are all substantially similar to, the type of Printshop to be operated under the Franchise Agreement.

Net profits or earnings vary from Printshop to Printshop depending on a number of factors, including rent and other charges, construction costs, financing terms and conditions, utility rates, insurance rates, local and state taxes, wage rates, costs of goods sold and supplies used and the par-ticular franchisee's efficiency and business acumen.

Substantiation of the data we used in preparing this Statement will be made available upon reason-able request.

Statement of Average Gross Sales for ALPHA-GRAPHICS® Printshops Which Began Opera-tions between January 1, 1996 and December 31, 1998
Set forth below is a table identifying average gross sales data gathered from ALPHAGRAPHICS® Printshops which began operating between January 1996 and December 1998. 70 new ALPHA-GRAPHICS® Printshops opened between January 1996 and December 1998. The results of 48 of the 70 new ALPHAGRAPHICS® Printshops are included in Table 1. 22 ALPHAGRAPHICS® Printshops were not included in Table 1 because we had not received complete financial statements when we prepared the Table.

All of these shops offer essentially the same prod-ucts and services. The training for all franchisees, and the support provided for all shops, were essentially the same.

The results in the Table are based on unaudited financial statements submitted to our Financial Services Department. The financial statements have not been audited or reviewed for reasonableness by independent auditors.

The gross sales stated in the Table are average sales of all reporting ALPHAGRAPHICS® Print-shops, beginning with their first month of operation. Therefore, in the month designated #1, the total of all sales for the first operating month of the reporting ALPHAGRAPHICS® Printshops is divided by the total number of reporting ALPHAGRAPHICS® Printshops. The number of reporting ALPHAGRAPHICS® Printshops in a given month ranges from 48, which had operations for at least one month, to 22, which had operations for 24 months.

Table #1 Average Sales (Unaudited)

Months in Operation	Average Sales $/Month	Number of Printshops Participating	Percent Meeting or Exceeding
1	$8,762	48	27%
2	$16,111	48	40%
3	$19,999	48	35%
4	$23,990	48	42%
5	$26,453	48	44%
6	$29,015	45	40%
7	$29,329	45	38%
8	$34,731	43	35%
9	$35,695	43	44%
10	$37,967	38	39%
11	$39,214	36	44%
12	$40,587	32	47%
13	$44,888	31	52%
14	$47,173	31	55%
15	$48,326	30	43%
16	$50,856	29	48%
17	$50,745	29	48%
18	$54,564	27	37%
19	$54,016	24	54%
20	$49,039	24	50%
21	$51,494	23	57%
22	$49,841	22	36%
23	$51,185	22	50%
24	$51,237	22	45%

The reporting ALPHAGRAPHICS® Printshops are located in a variety of different areas and include all types of ALPHAGRAPHICS® Print-shops (for example, downtown metropolitan locations, rural locations and locations in university towns). Sales associated with hours of operation, staffing and other intangibles will vary.

YOUR INDIVIDUAL RESULTS ARE LIKELY TO DIFFER FROM THE RESULTS STATED ABOVE.

We offered substantially the same services to all of the Printshops described in the Table. The Printshops described in the Table offered substantially the same products and services to the public as, and are all substantially similar to, the type of Printshop to be operated under the Franchise Agreement.

Substantiation of the data we used in preparing the table will be made available upon reasonable request.

Except for the information in this Item 19, we do not authorize our salespersons to furnish any oral or written information concerning the actual or potential sales, costs, income or profits of an ALPHAGRAPHICS® Printshop. Actual results vary from unit to unit, and we cannot estimate the results of any particular Franchise.

AMERICAN WHOLESALE THERMOGRAPHERS/ AWT

12715 Telge Rd.
Cypress, TX 77429-0777
Tel: (888) 280-2053 (281) 256-4100
Fax: (281) 256-4178
E-Mail: awtsales@awt.com
Internet Address: www.awt.com
Contact: Mr. Bob Dolan, VP Franchise Sales

Description: Wholesale printing, providing next-day raised-letter printed materials to retail printers, copy centers and business service centers. Products include quality business cards, stationery, announcements and invitations.

# Franchised Units:	20 Units
# Company-Owned Units:	0 Units
Total # Units:	20 Units
Founded In:	1980
1st Franchised In:	1981
Average Total Investment:	340-352K
Franchise Fee:	30K
On-Going Royalty:	5%
Advertising Fee:	NR
Financial Assistance:	Yes(B)
Site Selection Assistance:	Yes
Lease Negotiation Assistance:	Yes
Contract Terms (Init./Renew):	25/25
Initial Training Provided:	2 Weeks Headquarters; 2 Weeks Operating Store; 2 Weeks On-Site.

There are twenty AWT Centers total. Four (4) of these centers are in Canada. Information about the Canadian centers are not included in this report.

Sales Analysis
All sixteen (16) US AWT Centers were in business for one year or more prior to the twelve month period from January 1997 through December 1997. All sixteen centers are represented in the following "Sales Analysis by Age of Center" chart. All centers are required to report their monthly gross revenue to us according to their franchise agreement, and it is on the basis of these reports that

the information in the "Sales Analysis by Age of Center" chart was compiled. This information was not audited by us. Calculation of the averages reported was made in accordance with generally accepted accounting principles.

The information presented in the "Sales Analysis by Age of Center" chart is for the twelve month period from January 1997 through December 1997. During this period, overall average (mean) sales for the sixteen U.S. AWT Centers were $976,598, and median average sales were $800,175 based upon the reports submitted by the AWT Centers.

Sales Analysis by Age of Center
(Based Upon Sales Reports of 16 U.S. AWT Centers)

Age	# of Centers	Mean Average Sales	Median Average Sales
2–4	3	$547,839	$684,009
5–9	3	$597,015	$570,982
10+	10	$1,219,100	$974,694

Cost of Sales and Labor Expense Analysis

The information presented in the following "Cost of Sales and Labor Expense Analysis (By Sales Volume and By Age of Center)" charts was obtained from financial statements from ten U.S. AWT Centers which responded to our request for financial statements. Financial statements were requested of all sixteen U.S. AWT Centers. Of the six centers which did not respond, there is no discernable trend or commonality as to age, geographical region or level of revenue.

The information supplied by nine of the ten responding Centers is for the calendar year January 1, 1997 through December 30, 1997. The tenth Center reported for its fiscal year of February 1, 1997 through January 30, 1998.

The financial statements of the ten responding Centers were not audited by us. Seven of the ten financial statements received from responding centers are unaudited, although prepared by outside professional accountants, and the other three financial statements are unaudited and prepared in-house (by bookkeepers and not certified public accountants).

All ten centers reported on an accrual, and not cash, basis. Charts of Accounts differ among some centers. (Although we provide a Chart of Accounts which we recommend our franchisees follow, many opt to change it to meet their own particular requirements in running and analyzing their business.)

In selecting those terms to include within the categories "Cost of Goods Sold" and "Labor" for purposes of preparing the following charts, we relied on the following criteria:

- *Cost of Goods Sold* includes: paper, chemicals, plate materials, rubber stamp materials, powder and ink.

- *Labor* includes: production and administrative employees (press operators, slitters, bindery, drivers, customer service, pre-press, sales). The figures also include the employee taxes, but do not include the owner's compensation or additional benefits (like health insurance).

Cost of Goods Sold and Labor amounts reported by franchisees have been modified by us based upon the definitions above in order to arrive at more consistent information as among the centers represented in the report.

Cost of Sales and Labor Expense Sales Analysis by Volume
(Based Upon Financial Statements of 10 AWT Centers)

Annual Sales Volume	# of Centers	Mean Average Cost of Sales	Mean Average Labor	Median Average Cost of Sales	Median Average Labor
$500,000–$800,000	3	20.7%	34.7%	19.8%	32.4%
$800,000–$1,000,00	3	18.2%	33%	22.2%	30.9%
$1,000,000–$4,000,000	4	21.9%	33.6%	21.7%	33.6%

Cost of Sales and Labor Expense Analysis by Age of Center
(Based Upon Year End 1997 Financial Statements of 10 US AWT Centers)

Age of Center	Number of Centers	Mean Average Cost of Sales	Mean Average Labor	Median Average Cost of Sales	Median Average Labor
2–4	1	21.3%	32.4%	21.3%	32.4%
5–9	2	20.4%	36%	20.4%	36.4%
10+	7	21%	33.5%	16.9%	28.4%

Other Center Characteristics

During 1997, fifteen of the sixteen U.S. AWT Centers were single unit centers. The other was a multiple unit center which combined the costs of sales and costs of labor in its financial statement provided to us. This one multiple unit center had a production facility in one city and a satellite office in another.

All centers have similar assigned territory as that term is described in Item 12 of this offering circular. All centers are located in major metropolitan areas. The location of the ten Centers which provided financial statements ranged across the United States.

These Centers vary among each other in some ways that may be material to their individual performance. These variations include:

- The number of customers who are considered mail order business. Mail order business customers are customers who are not on the center's local pick-up and delivery routes.

- Amount of area covered by delivery routes. Some centers may have only 4 delivery routes, while other centers have as many as 8 to 12 delivery routes. The number of routes a center develops depends on the ambition of the Owner, and how well the Owner is able to grow his business and still maintain profitability.

- Products and services offered. Some centers have more diverse product lines while others may stay very close to just thermographed business cards, stationery and rubber stamps.

- Dedicated sales person on staff or the owner calling on prospective and existing clients. We currently recommend that a center be staffed accordingly, but for the time period reported, only two centers had a dedicated sales person.

Assumptions Made about Centers' Operations

We assume that the majority of the responding centers operated according to the following business practices and that these business practices may have materially contributed to their performance during the time period reported and could contribute to future performance:

Marketing
- Centers use a catalog as the primary marketing/selling tool.
- Centers send out statement stuffers and direct mail pieces to advertise AWTs products and services.
- Centers send out newsletters of interest to their customers.
- Centers are beginning to offer ordering through the Internet on their Center's home pages.

Operations
- Of the 10 responding centers, 5 centers offer a 24-hour turnaround period on the majority of jobs ordered each day (Monday through Friday). The other 5 centers offer 48 hour service on the majority of jobs ordered each day (Monday through Friday).
- All centers offer free local pick-up and delivery and mail order service.

Equipment/Computerization
- The minimum amount of equipment and computerization needed or required is what is currently offered in our initial equipment package to support production of sales levels up to

379

$500,000 to $800,000, with additional equipment required to further develop the business.

Owner's Role

❧ The Owner's role is to manage all operational, marketing and administrative tasks to accomplish these sales.

❧ From time to time, the Owner may be required to step in and help with the production and delivery of the orders.

Financial criteria necessary

❧ Establishing profitable pricing for products and services.

❧ Maintaining a consistent cashflow by collecting all amounts due in a consistent and timely manner.

❧ Most centers need to offer a 30 day billing period and a limited credit line to customers.

❧ It is important to have these same terms with their vendors.

All initial franchises receive the same services from us. Substantiation of the data used in preparing this sales average report will be made available to you upon reasonable request. The identity of individual centers will not be disclosed in order to maintain the confidentiality of those franchisees unless we are able to obtain their consent.

SALES, COST OF SALES AND LABOR EXPENSE AVERAGES WERE CALCULATED TO AID YOU IN EVALUATING THE EXPERIENCE OF EXISTING AWT CENTERS DURING A SINGLE YEAR. THE INFORMATION IS NOT A PROJECTION OR FORECAST OR GUARANTY, IN ANY WAY, OF WHAT YOU MAY EXPERIENCE.

In preparing financial projections and an overall business plan for your franchise operation, it is important to keep in mind that each individual franchisee's experience is unique, and each individual franchise will experience sales and expenses different from all other franchises in the system due to the many factors which will impact the franchise. These factors include general economic conditions of the area, competition in the market, physical location, availability of supplies and labor,

expenses or levels of expenses peculiar to the area, effectiveness of the franchisee in the management of the business and the overall efficiency of the operation. A franchisee's energy and dedication to the business will also effect the results of the operation. The following factors should also be considered as potentially impacting sales, cost of goods and business expense.

Factors that may increase labor percentages:

❧ Shortage of workforce in the market

❧ Long term employees

❧ Having too many employees

❧ High turnover of employees

Factors that may affect sales positively and/or negatively:

❧ Developing customers through sales calls

❧ Development of routes

❧ Quality of products produced in house

❧ Customers going out of business

❧ National contracts with printing/copying companies

Factors that may increase cost of sales:

❧ Paper costs increase significantly

❧ Poor quality control

❧ Prices are too low

Factors that may increase Operating Expenses:

❧ Variable and fixed costs are high such as utility companies, rent, vendors, taxes, equipment maintenance and repair, technology upgrades, training and advertising.

❧ Buying/Leasing equipment that can not be cost justified (unneeded equipment).

A NEW FRANCHISEE'S INDIVIDUAL RESULTS ARE LIKELY TO DIFFER FROM THE RESULTS STATED IN THIS ITEM 19. JUST BECAUSE SOME EXISTING AWT CENTERS ATTAIN OR EXCEED THESE SALES AVERAGES DOES NOT MEAN THAT YOU WILL. A VARIETY OF FACTORS, AS WE HAVE DESCRIBED IN THIS ITEM 19, MAY CAUSE YOUR FINANCIAL RESULTS TO BE DIFFERENT THAN THE REPORTED CENTERS' FINANCIAL RESULTS.

BCT
3000 NE 30th Pl., 5th Floor
Fort Lauderdale, FL 33306
Tel: (800) 627-9998 (954) 563-1224
Fax: (954) 565-0742
E-Mail: rsa@herald.infi.net
Internet Address: www.bct-net.com
Contact: Mr. Robert S. Anderson, Franchise Development Director

Description: Join the 24-year old industry-leading wholesale, manufacturing franchise with the competitive advantage. We are recession-resistant, high-volume, quick-turn around, wholesale only manufacturers, specializing in next-day delivery of thermographed and offset-printed products and rubber stamps to retail printers, mailing centers, office supply stores and other retailers. Comprehensive training, excellent support and nationally praised.

# Franchised Units:	92 Units
# Company-Owned Units:	1 Units
Total # Units:	93 Units
Founded In:	1975
1st Franchised In:	1977
Average Total Investment:	354-441K
Franchise Fee:	35K
On-Going Royalty:	6%
Advertising Fee:	N/A
Financial Assistance:	Yes(I)
Site Selection Assistance:	Yes
Lease Negotiation Assistance:	Yes
Contract Terms (Init./Renew):	25/10

Initial Training Provided: 2 Weeks Ft. Lauderdale, FL; 1 Week Pre-Opening at New-Site; 2 Weeks After and Ongoing.

THERE IS NO GUARANTEE THAT ANY NEW FRANCHISE WILL ATTAIN THE AVERAGE ANNUAL GROSS SALES FIGURES OF ANY EXISTING FRANCHISE, AND YOUR FINANCIAL RESULTS ARE LIKELY TO DIFFER FROM THE FOLLOWING FIGURES. NO INFERENCE AS TO EXPENSES, COST OF GOODS OR PRODUCTS RELATING TO EXISTING OR FUTURE FRANCHISED BCT PLANTS SHOULD BE DRAWN FROM ANY CHART OR TABLE. SUBSTANTIATION OF THE DATA USED IN PREPARING THE FOLLOWING WILL BE PROVIDED TO YOU UPON REASONABLE WRITTEN REQUEST.

Calendar Year Sales Statistic Calculations
Includes only U.S. Plants reporting for a full 24 months

Network	Calendar Year 1998	Calendar Year 1997	Calendar Year 1996
Total Sales	$98,803,684	$88,795,637	$78,342,677
Average Sales	$1,250,680	$1,096,242	$1,017,437
Number and Percentage of Plants Included	79 (100%)	81 (98%)	77 (90%)
Percent of Plants Above Average Sales	39%	38%	38%
Percent of Plants Below Average Sales	61%	62%	62%
Number of Plants 2–5 Years Old	12	15	12
Number of Plants 5–10 Years Old	10	8	11
Number of Plants Over 10 Years Old	57	58	54

The above calculations are based on sales figures submitted by franchisees for reporting and Royalty Fee payment purposes. BCT has assumed that all franchisees have accurately reported their Gross Sales, but is not able to guarantee the accuracy of franchisees' reports. All BCT franchisees sell substantially the same products and services.

LAZERQUICK
27375 SW Parkway Ave., # 200
Wilsonville, OR 97070
Tel: (800) 477-2679 (503) 682-1322
Fax: (503) 682-7816
E-Mail: mhart@lazerquick.com
Internet Address: www.lazerquick.com
Contact: Mr. Michael Hart, Vice President of Franchising

Description: LAZERQUICK centers are complete, one-stop printing and copying centers. All centers feature state-of-the-art electronic publishing, digital graphics and imaging services that support our range of quality, fast-service offset printing, high-speed copying and related bindery and finishing services. The LAZERQUICK franchise is based on value and performance. Affiliates benefit from our unique and innovative programs.

# Franchised Units:	25 Units
# Company-Owned Units:	22 Units
Total # Units:	47 Units
Founded In:	1968
1st Franchised In:	1990
Average Total Investment:	172.5-275K
Franchise Fee:	25K
On-Going Royalty:	3-5% / $500
Advertising Fee:	1.5%/$250
Financial Assistance:	Yes(I)
Site Selection Assistance:	Yes
Lease Negotiation Assistance:	Yes
Contract Terms (Init./Renew):	7/7/7
Initial Training Provided:	5-7 Weeks at Corporate Headquarters.

GISI does not provide you with a forecast or estimate of the sales or earnings that you might expect to receive from the operation of the franchised business. You may, however, refer to information about GISI's current print/copy and copy centers that follows.

Included in Exhibit A are GISI's audited financial statements with information concerning the sales and profitability of GISI's Centers during the most recent fiscal year.

Fiscal Year Ending 12/24/98
In 1998, GISI had net sales totaling $19,935,186. Average sales per (GISI-owned) Center operating the entire year were $617,508 (after miscellaneous administrative sales adjustments). Of Centers similar to a franchise operation and operating the entire year, the average sales per Center were $596,346. 29% of GISI owned Centers achieved or exceeded this average sales volume. Centers ranged in age from 1½ years to 30¼ years of operation.

The audited company statements of the most recent year available (see Exhibit A) disclose the average net income/loss (before taxes, other income/expense, management bonuses, and management stock bonuses), for the previous year. Reflected in this are costs, which due to the nature of the GISI organization, are costs that might not be pertinent to a franchise. Costs to administer the multiple Center network of GISI, including fully staffed departments for Personnel, Marketing, Sales, Operations Management, Training, Delivery and Warehouse requirements, Headquarters and Training facilities, and research, testing and development of products and services at an administrative level, are costs pertaining to the multiple Center nature of GISI which might not be applicable to you in your franchise business. Many of these functions may provide benefit to you and are reflected as costs to you through the payment of initial franchise fees and on-going royalties. Also reflected in this profit/loss is the expense to GISI for its manager's payroll and incentives. GISI pays its managers a base salary and incentives on sales and on gross operating profit of the Center. GISI's managers' payroll and incentives ranged from $23,525 to $66,369 for those Centers that are similar to a franchise operation, operating the entire year in 1998. GISI anticipates that franchised Centers, except for Multiple-Center franchises, will be directly managed by the Franchise Owner.

This information is generated from the audited financial statements of GISI which have been prepared according to accepted accounting practices, and GISI's supporting subsidiary financial records for the most recent fiscal year. There are no guarantees that any franchised Centers will achieve similar results. Performance of any franchise is based upon the Franchise Owner's management of its business along with the economic or market conditions where you are located, equipment configuration, purchasing, sales and marketing decisions and various other external factors, all of which may determine actual performance of the franchise.

Material Assumptions: The financial statements and notes to financial statements in Exhibit A state the material assumptions underlying the computation of the figures on the sales schedule attachments. We make these assumptions in accordance with generally accepted accounting principles. There are, however, other factors that you should take into account when viewing these attachments. First, there may be geographic differences between the GISI Centers, which are generally in the Seattle, Washington, Portland, Oregon, or Salem, Oregon metropolitan areas, and the franchised Center. If the franchised Center is in a smaller metropolitan area, it is possible that your sales might be lower, depending upon traffic flow, population density, competition and demographics.

In addition, Franchise Owners who execute a Franchise Agreement (all franchisees except Joint Venture Multiple-Center franchisees) submit monthly reports of sales to GISI to support the calculation of their monthly royalty payments. Based upon these sales reports:

- For all LAZERQUICK® franchises operating at year-end in 1998, franchise Centers reported sales ranging from $1,080 to $682,770, totaling $6,260,947. These Centers ranged from 1 month of operation to 8½ years of operation as a franchised LAZERQUICK® Center.

- The average annual sales of all franchised LAZERQUICK® Centers in 1998 (total reported franchise sales divided by number of centers operating at year end) was $313,047 per franchise Center. 45% of franchised centers achieved or exceeded this annual average of sales.

- The average monthly sales per franchise Center in 1998 (total sales at year-end divided by actual months of operation in 1998 for each location) was $26,115. 45% of franchised centers achieved or exceeded this monthly average of sales.

- The average annual sales of those franchised LAZERQUICK® Centers operating the entire year in 1998 was $363,083. The average monthly sales per franchise Center operating the entire year in 1998 were $30,257. 47% of these franchise Centers achieved or exceeded both of these monthly and annual averages of sales.

A schedule of the individual LAZERQUICK® Franchise Center sales for the most recent fiscal year is included with GISI's financial statements, which are in Exhibit A.

Material Assumptions: The franchise sales reports were submitted monthly by Franchise Owners. These sales reports were checked each month by GISI to verify that the royalty payments are accurate, based on the Franchise Owner's reported sales for the month, and then checked annually against the annual profit and loss statements and copies of federal tax forms submitted by Franchise Owners. In 1997 GISI did not audit its franchise Centers nor did GISI contract with any person or company to provide independent audits of its franchised Centers; however, GISI assumes that the 1997 sales information reported by its Franchise Owners is accurate.

Economic and market conditions generally or in the specific market in which you are located may affect sales. GISI cannot predict these market or economic factors. GISI Centers receive services that are available to you, as well as receiving services that are not available to you, including the direct supervision of all Center personnel by GISI's management. Although you must provide these personnel, payroll, and other employment services, as well as general business management of your own Center, you do not incur the costs that GISI has incurred for these operations as stated above. You will have expenses which GISI Centers do not have, i.e. less group purchasing, markup on goods purchased from GISI, (see ITEMS 6, 8 and 9 above, and royalty payments).

A new Franchise Owner's individual financial results are likely to differ from the results stated above in this Item 19, due to start-up costs and other factors characteristic of new businesses.

These sales, profits or earnings are averages of GISI owned Centers currently operating, and franchised Centers currently operating as of the date of this document, and should not be considered as the actual or potential sales, profits or earnings that will be realized by any franchise. GISI does not represent that any Franchise Owner can expect to attain these sales, profits or earnings.

We will make available to you upon any reasonable request, substantiation of the data used in preparing the Earnings Claim.

MINUTEMAN PRESS INTERNATIONAL
1640 New Highway
Farmingdale, NY 11735
Tel: (800) 645-3006 (516) 249-1370
Fax: (516) 249-5618
E-Mail: MPIHQ@aol.com
Internet Address: www.minuteman-press.com
Contact: Mr. Robert Titus, President

Description: Full-service printing and graphic centers, specializing in multi-color commercial printing at instant print prices. A one-stop printing and graphics business.

# Franchised Units:	890 Units
# Company-Owned Units:	0 Units
Total # Units:	890 Units
Founded In:	1975
1st Franchised In:	1975
Average Total Investment:	100-120K
Franchise Fee:	44.5K
On-Going Royalty:	6%
Advertising Fee:	0%
Financial Assistance:	Yes(I)
Site Selection Assistance:	Yes
Lease Negotiation Assistance:	Yes
Contract Terms (Init./Renew):	35/10
Initial Training Provided:	3 Weeks New York; On-Site As Needed.

Gross Sales
The average gross sales of Minuteman Press Printing Centers in the United States in business for one (1) year prior to the study was $444,093 for the twelve month period of January, 1998 through December, 1998. This figure is based on the monthly sales reports we received during that period from 522 centers. These centers represent 60% of the U.S. centers operating at that time. The number of centers whose sales were used to calculate the average that attained or surpassed the average sales is 184 centers, or 35.2% of the centers used to calculate the average.

We did not use the sales reports from owners in calculating average sales if the owner had been in business less than one (1) year or did not report all twelve consecutive months during the time period.

Sales Study by Geographic Region

Region	Number of Centers	Percentage of Centers out of Whole	Monthly Sales Average	Yearly Sales Average
Northeast (1)	145	27.8%	37,983	455,798
South (2)	145	27.8%	34,855	418,270
Midwest (3)	118	22.6%	37,441	449,295
West (4)	114	21.8%	38,055	456,666

1. ME, NH, VT, MA, RI, CT, NY, NJ, DE, PA, WV, KY
2. MD, VA, NC, SC, GA, FL, AL, MS, TN, LA, TX
3. IL, IN, WI, IA, MN, OH, MI, NE, MO, KS, ND, SD
4. AZ, CO, UT, WY, MT, ID, NV, GA, OR, WA

EXCEPT FOR THE FOREGOING INFORMATION, THE COMPANY DOES NOT AUTHORIZE ITS SALESPERSONS TO FURNISH ANY ORAL OR WRITTEN INFORMATION CONCERNING THE ACTUAL OR POTENTIAL SALES, COSTS, INCOME OR PROFITS IN REGARD TO A MINUTEMAN PRESS FRANCHISE. MINUTEMAN ENCOURAGES PROSPECTIVE FRANCHISEE TO OBTAIN COSTS AND ASSOCIATED INFORMATION FROM CURRENT FRANCHISEES.

The services offered by Minuteman to its' franchisees are materially similar throughout the country. The services offered by the franchisees may vary somewhat as to type and extent depending on a number of factors. The franchisee's sales volume is dependent on the type and quality of the services it offers to the general public. Furthermore this volume will also be greatly influenced by the individual franchisee's sales and marketing efforts. It has been Minuteman's experience that there is no substitute for diligent marketing efforts by the franchisee.

Advisory Committee
(Presidents Million Dollar Circle)
In an effort to better assist the franchisees and to improve the system as a whole, we have created an advisory committee known as the Presidents Million Dollar Circle. Membership is predicated on the franchisee attaining gross sales over one million dollars in the past fiscal year. Presently Circle members' gross sales range from one million to over four million dollars annually. The club gives its

input as to various matters that affect the Minuteman franchise, system such as advertising, equipment, personnel and product vendors. There is a scheduled meeting once a year in addition to the various surveys and questionnaires that are proposed to the members. Members also serve as panelists on various issues at the franchise conventions. The membership fluctuates from year to year but a list of members is available upon request. Currently there are thirty-eight (38) members of the Presidents Million Dollar Circle.

It should be noted that the gross sales of the Presidents Million Dollar Circle are not representative of the system as a whole. Nor are their sales typical or average of a Minuteman store.

MINUTEMAN IN NO WAY MAKES ANY REPRESENTATION AS TO WHAT A SPECIFIC FRANCHISE CAN EARN OR REASONABLY EXPECT TO EARN. NET PROFITS AND EARNING VARY FROM FRANCHISE TO FRANCHISE BASED ON A NUMBER OF VARYING FACTORS, INCLUDING BUT NOT LIMITED TO RENT, FINANCING TERMS AND CONDITIONS, ELECTRIC RATES, LOCAL AND STATE TAXES, WAGES, AND COST OF GOODS. FURTHERMORE, THE AMOUNT AND TYPE OF EQUIPMENT IN EACH STORE VARIES ACCORDING TO THE AGE OF THE STORE AND THE AMOUNT OF OPTIONAL EQUIPMENT PURCHASED BY THE FRANCHISE. MINUTEMAN CAN GIVE NO ASSURANCES THAT A FRANCHISEE WILL ATTAIN THE GROSS SALES

LEVELS CONTAINED IN THIS STATEMENT.

Substantiation of the data used in preparing this earnings claim is kept at the Franchisors main office located at 1640 New Highway, Farmingdale, New York 11746. This data is available for inspection by a prospective franchisee on reasonable request and at the prospective franchisee's cost.

Signal Graphics. PRINTING

SIGNAL GRAPHICS PRINTING
6789 S. Yosemite St., # 100
Englewood, CO 80112
Tel: (800) 852-6336 (303) 779-6789
Fax: (303) 779-8445
E-Mail: SAMPACORP@ aol.com
Internet Address: www.signalgraphics.com
Contact: Mr. Michael Latham, Director Franchise Development

Description: A full range of services places SIGNAL GRAPHICS PRINTING ahead of the competition. Our franchising program will enable the owner having no previous printing experience to market quick printing, copying, desktop publishing, digital services, typesetting and high-quality commercial printing to a wide range of customers in the business community. Just the right size system to offer prime locations and personalized support.

# Franchised Units:	47 Units
# Company-Owned Units:	2 Units
Total # Units:	49 Units
Founded In:	1974
1st Franchised In:	1982
Average Total Investment:	190-230K
Franchise Fee:	18K
On-Going Royalty:	0-5%
Advertising Fee:	$100/Mo.
Financial Assistance:	Yes(I)
Site Selection Assistance:	Yes
Lease Negotiation Assistance:	Yes
Contract Terms (Init./Renew):	25/25
Initial Training Provided:	3 Weeks Headquarters; 2 Weeks On-Site.

We have compiled the following information regarding Gross Sales at existing SIGNAL GRAPHICS Centers:

SIGNAL GRAPHICS franchised Centers open for more than one year averaged $462,496 in Gross Sales for the 12 month period ending October 31, 1998. This average is based on 44 reporting franchises.*

The following is a more detailed breakdown of the average Gross Sales for the 43 reporting Centers during the 12 month period ending October 31, 1998:

Category	# of Centers	Average Gross Sales for the Period
Top 7%	3	$1,336,782
Top 16%	7	$1,049,314
Top 25%	11	$888,448
Top 50%	22	$661,213

We have not undertaken an independent investigation to verify the amounts reported.

The products and services offered by each Center, although essentially the same, may vary to some degree based on the individual franchisee's direction. The sales volume attainable by each Center depends on many factors including, but not limited to, geographic differences, competition within the immediate market area, the quality and service provided to customers by the Center, as well as their own marketing and sales efforts.

*Reported as of December 1, 1998. Forty-four franchises represent 85% of the total number of franchised SIGNAL GRAPHICS Centers open as of October 31, 1998. Those Centers not included in this figure had been open for less than one year.

YOUR ACTUAL FINANCIAL RESULTS ARE LIKELY TO DIFFER FROM THE FIGURES PRESENTED.

THE SALES FIGURES ABOVE ARE AVERAGES OF HISTORICAL DATA OF SPECIFIC FRANCHISES. THEY SHOULD NOT BE CONSIDERED AS POTENTIAL SALES THAT MAY BE REALIZED BY YOU. WE DO NOT REPRESENT THAT YOU CAN EXPECT TO ACHIEVE THESE SALES LEVELS. ACTUAL RESULTS VARY FROM CENTER TO CENTER AND WE CANNOT ESTIMATE THE RESULTS OF ANY PARTICULAR FRANCHISE.

SUBSTANTIATION OF THE ABOVE AVERAGES IS AVAILABLE TO YOU AT OUR HOME OFFICE IF YOU REQUEST IT, PROVIDED IT DOES NOT REQUIRE THE DISCLOSURE OF THE IDENTITY OF ANY CENTER OWNER

OTHER THAN THE ABOVE INFORMATION, WE DO NOT FURNISH OR AUTHORIZE OUR SALESPERSONS TO FURNISH ANY ORAL OR WRITTEN INFORMATION CONCERNING THE ACTUAL OR POTENTIAL SALES, INCOME OR PROFITS OF A SIGNAL GRAPHICS CENTER.

Cost Categories to Develop Projections
PERCENTAGES GIVEN ARE CONSIDERED ACCEPTABLE RANGES. YOUR ACTUAL RATIOS MAY VARY BASED ON MANY FACTORS INCLUDING THE SELLING PRICE OF PRODUCTS AND EFFICIENCY OF OPERATIONS. THESE ACCEPTABLE RANGES WERE DEVELOPED BASED ON OUR EXPERIENCE. THE EXPERIENCE OF OUR FRANCHISEES AND NATIONAL QUICK PRINTING INDUSTRY STUDIES.

Cost of Sales — For analysis, sales are broken down into three main elements: production sales (approximately 65% of total), copier sales (approximately 25% of sales), and brokered sales (approximately 10% of total). Your actual mix will vary. Therefore, the costs associated with those sales should be separated also. Production cost consists of all the consumable raw materials and supplies for the production of offset printed material and associated bindery functions but excludes labor and equipment costs. An acceptable range for this cost is 27% to 30% of production sales. Copier cost includes the supplies along with the maintenance charges associated with producing copies but excludes paper, labor and the cost of leasing the copier equipment. The range is usually between 22% and 28% of copier sales. Paper cost is included with production cost. Brokered cost is the expense associated with using an outside vendor and usually ranges between 60% and 70% of brokered sales.

Accounting — Expenses incurred for basic monthly financial statement preparation and business tax accounting by an independent accounting firm. Cost may increase as sales volume increases or based on services rendered. Estimated cost is between $2000 and $3000 per year.

Advertising — National Advertising Fee is 1% of sales capped at $150 per month. Initial local advertising in the first year is subsidized by the Initial Promotion Fee. Total advertising expenditure including Yellow Page ads, direct mail, Local Advertising Fee and National Advertising Fee is budgeted at a minimum of $9,000 per year.

Automobile — Based upon estimated business miles, expensed according to the appropriate Internal Revenue Service regulation.

Copier Leases — Based on a 5 year FMV lease for one convenience, one high volume and one laser color copier. Various models and taxes may affect cost of approximately $900–1,000 per month.

Equipment Payments — Original equipment package ($109,000) excluding copiers is approximately $1,558 per month plus tax when financed over ten years at an interest rate of 11%.

Equipment Repair — Cost to maintain newly purchased equipment other than copiers (included in copier cost). This may vary greatly based on the care and experience of the equipment operators. First year approximately 0.13% of total sales. Following years range from approximately .25% to 1% of total sales based on age of equipment.

Insurance — Business and general liability insurance. Additional equipment may affect this. Range may vary greatly based on location and insurance market conditions (approximately $1,800 to $2,500 per year depending on coverage).

Office Supplies — Cost of miscellaneous supplies used in operating the business.

Rent — Approximate monthly rent of a new center ranges from $1,500 to $3,300 per month including CAM (common area maintenance, taxes, insurance, etc.) charges depending on the location of the center. This will vary based on the leasing market and available locations. Some areas may be higher.

Royalty Fees — 5% of Gross Sales. A Royalty Waiver and Cap Program and a Royalty Rebate Program are offered.

Salaries and Wages — Salary figures should reflect the staffing requirements for press operation, counter sales, etc. and should range from 24% to 30% of sales, including employer's share of FICA. FUTA, SUTA taxes, and Workers Compensation insurance, provided the center is above the break-even level of gross sales. This may vary greatly based on the efficiency and effectiveness of the center operations and management. Owner's compensation for one working owner is not included in this range.

Taxes/Personal Property — Varies depending on individual state, county and city in which your center is located.

Telephone — Expenses associated with having two business lines and 1 separate fax line, plus increases related to levels of sales activity. This will vary depending on location. (approximately $3,000 to $4,000 per year — some areas may be higher)

Utilities — Expenses associated with operating the various equipment, etc.

Miscellaneous — Various minor expenses for help wanted ads, bank charges. cleaning, etc.

Note: If you finance the Franchise Fee and Start Up Fee, your ten-year monthly payment will increase approximately $400 per month.

THE ABOVE COST CATEGORIES ARE CATEGORIES WE SUGGEST YOU TAKE INTO ACCOUNT IF YOU DESIRE TO DEVELOP YOUR OWN PROJECTIONS FOR A SIGNAL GRAPHICS CENTER. NOT ALL OF THESE CATEGORIES MAY APPLY TO YOUR CENTER AND YOUR CENTER MAY INCUR MATERIAL COSTS NOT LISTED ABOVE. WE COMPILED THESE COST CATEGORIES BASED ON OUR EXPERIENCE WITH FRANCHISED CENTERS, BUT COSTS VARY FROM CENTER TO CENTER AND WE CANNOT PROJECT THE RESULTS OF ANY PARTICULAR FRANCHISE.

OTHER THAN THE ABOVE INFORMATION, WE DO NOT FURNISH OR AUTHORIZE OUR SALESPERSONS TO FURNISH ANY ORAL OR WRITTEN INFORMATION CONCERNING THE ACTUAL OR POTENTIAL SALES OR COSTS OF A SIGNAL GRAPHICS CENTER.

SIR SPEEDY
26722 Plaza Dr.
Mission Viejo, CA 92672
Tel: (800) 854-3321 (949) 348-5000
Fax: (949) 348-5068
E-Mail: fdelucia@sirspeedy.com

Internet Address: www.sirspeedy.com
Contact: Mr. Frank A. de Lucia, VP Franchise Development

Description: A Monday through Friday business-to-business service. it provides copying, printing, digital communication and graphic design for a diverse range of corporate clients. It's global digital link facilitates instantaneous communication and transfer of material between all centers in the group.

# Franchised Units:	755 Units
# Company-Owned Units:	17 Units
Total # Units:	772 Units
Founded In:	1968
1st Franchised In:	1968
Average Total Investment:	316-391K

Franchise Fee:	20K
On-Going Royalty:	4-6%
Advertising Fee:	1-2%
Financial Assistance:	Yes(I)
Site Selection Assistance:	Yes
Lease Negotiation Assistance:	Yes
Contract Terms (Init./Renew):	20/10
Initial Training Provided:	3 Weeks in Mission Viejo, CA; 6 Weeks at franchisee's site.

SIR SPEEDY MAKES NO REPRESEN- TATIONS AS TO ACTUAL, AVERAGE, PROJECTED OR FORECASTED PROFITS, EARNINGS OR SALES YOU MAY EXPECT FROM THE OPERATIONS OF A SIR SPEEDY CENTER.

United States Sir Speedy Centers in business over 1 year averaged $635,253 in gross sales for the 12 month period ending December 31, 1998. This average is based on 432 reporting franchises.*

The 1998 figures reveal that 28% or 123 of the 432 Centers actually attained or surpassed the $635,253 average; 25% or 106 Centers exceeded $700,000; 19% or 82 Centers exceeded $800,000; 15% or 66 Centers exceeded $900,000; 13% or 57 Centers exceeded $1,000,000; and 3.7% or 16 Centers exceeded $2,000,000.

Of the 432 Centers in this report, 58 had been opened and operating for 1 to 3 years; 41 Centers had been opened and operating for 4 to 5 years; 36 Centers had been opened and operating for 6 to 7 years; and 297 Centers had been opened and operating for over 7 years.**

*Reported as of February 17, 1999. 432 represents approximately 70% of the domestic Sir Speedy Centers, in business for more than 1 year as of December 31, 1998. Those Centers not included were either in business less than 1 year, non-domestic Centers, Copies Now Centers, or Sir Speedy Centers that did not report the total years' information as of February 17, 1999.

**Specific locations available upon reasonable request.

The sales figures, although unaudited, are based upon the actual reported sales volumes of the 432 Franchisees.

Sir Speedy offers substantially the same services to each of its Franchisees. The type and extent of services offered to the public by each individual Franchisee may vary somewhat with each Franchisee. The sales volume attainable by a Franchisee is largely dependent on the type and quality of service offered to the public as well as individual sales and marketing efforts.

THESE SALES ARE AVERAGES OF SPE-CIFIC FRANCHISES AND SHOULD NOT BE CONSIDERED AS THE ACTUAL OR POTEN-TIAL SALES THAT YOU WILL ACHIEVE. SIR SPEEDY DOES NOT REPRESENT THAT YOU CAN EXPECT TO ATTAIN THESE SALES.

SUBSTANTIATION OF THE ABOVE AVER-AGES IS AVAILABLE UPON REQUEST TO PROSPECTIVE FRANCHISEES.

Assumptions That May Be Used in Developing Projections (Percentages given for cost of sales and for salaries and wages are recommended ranges)
Cost of Sales — Includes consumable raw materials and supplies for the production of offset printed material (where applicable), copying, preparation and bindery, as well as the cost of goods purchased for resale such as business cards and rubber stamps. Cost of sales optimally should range from 28% to 32% for efficiency.

Accounting and Legal — Expenses required for basic monthly bookkeeping and financial statement preparation. Fees may increase as sales volumes increase (paid for by Sir Speedy in first year of operation).

Advertising — 1% of gross sales for network advertising fee for the first year of operation and 2% of gross sales after first year, plus costs associated with yellow page advertisement, direct mail and a dedicated full-time salesperson each year.

Automobile — Based upon estimated business miles, expensed according to the appropriate IRS regulation.

Depreciation — Original equipment cost depreciated over a 5-7 year period using the straight line method with additional equipment added as necessary to meet sales demands.

Insurance — Avenge cost of coverage under Sir Speedy's group business liability offered to all Franchisees is approximately $1,000.00 to $1,500.00 per year.

Office Supplies — Cost of miscellaneous supplies used in operating the business.

Rent — Approximate monthly rent of a new Center ranges from $1,200.00 to $3,500.00 per month depending on the location of the Center. Some areas may be higher.

Repairs and Maintenance — Costs associated with operating presses and cameras at various sales volumes, approximately 1% (Offset Equipment Upgrade Option only). Monthly costs of copier maintenance agreements.

Royalty Fees — 4% of gross sales for the first year of operation and 6% of gross sales after the first year. (See Exhibit "II" of the Franchise Agreement for royalty rebates).

Salaries and Wages — Salary figures should reflect the staffing requirements for press operation (if applicable), counter sales, etc. and optimally should range from 20% to 25% of sales for efficiency, including employer's share of FICA, FUTA and SUTA taxes. Owner's compensation is not included.

Taxes/Personal Property — Varies depending on individual state, county and city laws.

Telephone — Expenses associated with having two business lines, plus increases related to levels of sales activity.

Utilities — Expenses associated with operating the various equipment, etc.

Real estate inspection services

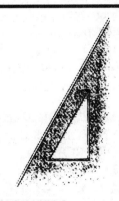

CRITERIUM ENGINEERS
650 Brighton Ave.
Portland, ME 04102
Tel: (800) 242-1969 (207) 828-1969
Fax: (207) 775-4405
E-Mail:
Internet Address: www.criterium-engineers.com
Contact: Mr. Peter E. Hollander, Director Marketing/ Development

Description: CRITERIUM ENGINEERS is a consulting franchise available to licensed professional engineers. Company specializes in building inspection and evaluation services for buyers, investors, corporations, attorneys, insurance companies, lenders and government. Services include pre-purchase inspections, insurance investigations, due diligence, maintenance planning, expert testimony, reserve studies, environmental assessments, design and construction review.

# Franchised Units:	66 Units
# Company-Owned Units:	0 Units
Total # Units:	66 Units
Founded In:	1957
1st Franchised In:	1958
Average Total Investment:	25K
Franchise Fee:	21.5K
On-Going Royalty:	6%
Advertising Fee:	1%
Financial Assistance:	Yes
Site Selection Assistance:	N/A
Lease Negotiation Assistance:	No
Contract Terms (Init./Renew):	15/5
Initial Training Provided:	1 Week Headquarters.

The table below represents the billings reported to us by Criterium Engineers franchisees. The results reported are for the total number of offices in business at the end of their first, second and third years in business. In putting together this information, we relied exclusively on information provided to us.

	First Year		Second Year		Third Year	
	Billings	Jobs	Billings	Jobs	Billings	Jobs
Number of Offices	50		42		35	
Average Annual Billings	$41,789	112	$83,610	222	$109,290	312
Median Annual Billings	$37,481	106	$71,142	191	$106,195	222
High Annual Billings	$121,883	322	$202,680	116	$231,152	810
Low Annual Billings	$2,513	9	$19,978	73	$27,466	76

The information provided is based on all franchises established after November, 1989. The information provided was based on the franchisee's monthly report, due on the 10th of the month following. The size of the territories vary, and no attempt was made to segregate the date by any other variables. Average, median, high and low billing levels were determined by examining the reports of all franchisees in business for the entire period of examination (one year, two years, or three years). We assume that this information is correct, but we have no guarantee that it is. We assume that this information is accurate because it is the basis for which we verify the amount of service and communication fees owed to us.

Your individual results are likely to differ from the results stated in the chart above. We make available to you substantiation of the data used in preparing this chart upon reasonable request. We offer substantially the same services to you as we provided to the franchisees we used in compiling these numbers. All of these franchisees offer substantially the same consulting engineering services to the public we expect you to offer although the proportionate mix of services does vary and we expect that you will offer additional, related services.

Although average fees from jobs can be easily calculated from the above information, performing such a calculation can be misleading. In the first year, average fees per job ranged from $227 to $1,041, depending on the type of engineering services pursued. In year 2, the range was $222 to $1,747. In year 3, the range increased from $226 to $2,448.

THESE STATEMENTS OF ANNUAL BILLINGS SHOULD NOT BE CONSTRUED AS THE ACTUAL OR PROBABLE AMOUNT OF BILLINGS THAT WILL BE REALIZED BY ANY FRANCHISEE. WE DO NOT REPRESENT THAT ANY FRANCHISEE CAN EXPECT TO ATTAIN SUCH BILLINGS, NOR DO WE IMPLY ANY SPECIFIC LEVEL OF PROFITABILITY WITH REGARD TO THESE REPORTED BILLINGS.

Rental services

Aaron's

AARON'S RENTAL PURCHASE
309 E. Paces Ferry Rd., N. E.
Atlanta, GA 30305-2377
Tel: (800) 551-6015 (404) 237-4016
Fax: (404) 240-6540
E-Mail: toddevans@aaronsfranchise.com
Internet Address: www.aaronsfranchise.com
Contact: Mr. Todd Evans, VP Franchise
Development

Description: AARON'S RENTAL PURCHASE is one of the fastest-growing rental purchase companies in the U.S., specializing in furniture, electronics and appliances. AARON'S RENTAL PURCHASE offers franchisees the expertise, advantages and support of a well-established company, plus the opportunity to realize a significant financial return in a booming market segment.

# Franchised Units:	156 Units
# Company-Owned Units:	213 Units
Total # Units:	369 Units
Founded In:	1955
1st Franchised In:	1992
Average Total Investment:	207-439.9K
Franchise Fee:	35K
On-Going Royalty:	5%
Advertising Fee:	2.5%
Financial Assistance:	Yes(I)
Site Selection Assistance:	Yes
Lease Negotiation Assistance:	Yes
Contract Terms (Init./Renew):	10/10

Initial Training Provided:3 Weeks Corporate Headquarters; 2 Weeks Minimum On-Site; On-Going Varies.

Exhibit A to this Offering Circular sets forth certain historical revenue and expense information for ARI-operated Aaron's Rental Purchase® stores. THE SUCCESS OF YOUR FRANCHISE WILL DEPEND LARGELY UPON YOUR INDIVIDUAL EFFORTS, AND THE FINANCIAL RESULTS OF YOUR FRANCHISE ARE LIKELY TO DIFFER, PERHAPS MATERIALLY, FROM THE RESULTS SUMMARIZED IN EXHIBIT A.

Exhibit A
To Franchise Offering Circular

Analysis of Average Revenues and Expenses for ARI Operated Aaron's Rental Purchase Stores

This Exhibit sets forth certain historical information on revenues and expenses for ARI operated Aaron's Rental Purchase stores and does *not* include revenues and expenses for franchisee operated Aaron's Rental Purchase stores. ARI has not included the information on franchised stores because

ARI cannot verify and control the level or type of expenditures made by individual franchisees. However, ARI recommends that you contact the franchisees listed on Exhibit E to the Uniform Franchise Offering Circular ("UFOC") regarding the operations and financial performance of their Franchised Businesses.

This Exhibit contains two Tables. The Tables reflect the arithmetic mean (average) annual revenues and expenses, as well as the highest, lowest, median, and number and percent of stores higher than the mean, of the stores included therein.

Table 1:
Table 1 contains the average revenues and expenses of ALL ARI operated stores which (i) have operated under the "12 Month Rental Purchase Plan" since their inception, (ii) were not converted Aaron Rents or Aaron Sells stores, (iii) were not acquired stores and (iv) have been operating one full year (89 stores), two full years (80 stores), three full years (67 stores), four full years (56 stores) or five full years (34 stores), respectively, as of December 31, 1998. ARI has closed some stores or acquired some competitor stores and has merged their revenues into existing revenues with other ARI stores operating in contiguous markets (see item 20). Stores that had not been in operation for at least a full year as of December 31, 1998 are not included, because annual figures were not yet available as of such date. The average revenue and expense information provided in Table 1 by year is also shown by month (by age or store).

Table 2:
Table 2 contains the average revenues and expenses for the year ending December 31, 1998 of ALL ARI operated stores which have been open for at least two full years as of January 1, 1998 and that were still open as of December 31, 1998 (98 stores). Figures are presented for those stores within the following ranges of annual gross revenues: under $800,000 (4 stores); $800,000 to $1,100,000 (34 stores); $1,100,001 to $1,400,000 (42 stores); and over $1,400,000 (18 stores). ARI has closed some stores or acquired some competitor Stores and has merged their revenues into existing revenues with other ARI stores operating in contiguous markets. This Table includes stores that

were converted at least two full years prior to January 1, 1998 into Aaron's Rental Purchase stores from Aaron Rents, Aaron Sells or acquired competitor stores (see Item 20).

ARI accrues certain expenses from time to time for internal recording purposes. Thus, in some instances, all of the expenses reflected in a given month may not have actually been paid as of the end of such month. Also, except for depreciation, the expenses listed in the Tables do not reflect any start-up expenses that you may incur (see Item 7 of the UFOC).

The ARI operated stores for which information is included in this Exhibit are substantially similar to franchisee operated stores in appearance, and in the products and services offered. Most of the ARI operated stores included in this Exhibit are located in metropolitan markets where expenses are frequently higher than non-metropolitan markets and those stores generally have to achieve relatively higher revenues to cover higher expenses. The amount of revenues and expenses incurred will vary from store to store, whether ARI operated or franchisee operated and whether located in a metropolitan market or a non-metropolitan market. In particular, the revenues and expenses of a franchise store will be directly affected by many factors, such as: (a) geographic location; (b) competition from other firms in the market; (c) the presence of other stores opened under ARI's Marks; (d) whether the franchise owner assumes the position of store manager or designates a store manager; (e) lease payments for exterior sign(s); (f) the payment of Continuing License Fees, Ad Production Fees and Regional Media Fees; (g) contractual arrangements with real estate lessors; (h) the extent to which the franchisee borrows working capital and finances inventory purchases, and applicable interest rate(s) on such borrowings; (i) vendor prices or distribution center prices on merchandise; (j) the franchisee's merchandise rental rates and merchandise prices; (k) whether the franchisee purchases or leases a delivery vehicle; (l) the cost of any other vehicles used in the business; (m) other discretionary expenditures; (n) the quality of management and service at the Franchised Business; (o) the franchisee's legal, accounting and other professional fees; (p) federal, state, and local income and other taxes; and (q) accounting methods, particularly the rate of depreciation for rental merchandise. In addition, a franchisee likely will not realize certain benefits and economies of scale that ARI realizes as a result of operating several stores in a single market. Therefore, the information contained in this Exhibit should be used by you only as a reference in conducting your own analysis and preparing your own projected income statements, balance sheets and cash flow statements. ARI strongly suggests that you consult your own financial advisor or personal accountant concerning any financial projections and federal, state, local income taxes or any other applicable taxes that you may incur in operating an Aaron's Rental Purchase franchise.

The revenues and expenses contained in this Exhibit should not be considered to be the actual or potential revenues and expenses that you will realize. ARI does not represent that you can or will attain such revenues and expenses, or any particular level of revenues and expenses. Moreover, ARI does not represent that you will generate income which exceeds the initial payment for, or investment in, the Franchised Business. THE SUCCESS OF THE FRANCHISE WILL DEPEND LARGELY UPON YOUR INDIVIDUAL ABILITIES, AND THE FINANCIAL RESULTS OF THE FRANCHISE ARE LIKELY TO DIFFER, PERHAPS MATERIALLY, FROM THE RESULTS OF ARI OPERATED STORES SUMMARIZED IN THIS EXHIBIT. Substantiation of the data used in preparing the information in this Exhibit will be made available to you upon reasonable request.

The following notes generally define each line item category shown on the attached Tables, identify some of the reasons why your results may differ, and highlight certain factors that you should be aware of. You should review the attached Tables only in conjunction with the following notes, which are an integral part of the numerical information.

Note 1: Rental Revenue
Defined: Rental Revenue is the sum of all revenues received from: all rental fees (for electronics, appliances, furniture, jewelry, pagers and other items),

renewal fees, damage fees, delivery fees, service plus fees, full rental agreement buyout payments, NSF checks net of NSF collections, and other fees, whether paid in cash, check or credit. Rental Revenue also includes revenue on pager air service which is pager service income (revenue derived from the service fee for pager air time only).

Variances for Franchisee: Within ARI guidelines, you will determine the merchandise rental rates, pager service rates and other fees for products and services rented and sold from the Franchised Business. Some states have statutes governing merchandise rental rates and fees. The cost associated with activating and maintaining air time for pagers varies from market to market.

Note 2: Other Revenue
Defined: Other Revenue consists of revenue for all retail sales of both new and used inventory, revenue from early buyouts of rental agreements, gain or loss on sales of fixed assets, cell phone commissions, pass code and access revenue, and any other miscellaneous charges or fees, whether paid in cash, check or credit.

Variances for Franchisee: Within ARI guidelines, you will determine the retail sales price and other fees for products sold from the Franchised Business, as well as the price for early buyouts of rental agreements. Sonic states have statutes governing early buyout amounts.

Note 3: Total Revenue
Defined: Total Revenue is the sum of Rental Revenue and Other Revenue.

Variance For Franchisee: Within ARI guidelines, you will determine the merchandise rental rates and other fees charged by the Franchised Business. Some states have statutes governing merchandise rental rates and fees.

Note 4: Cost of Sales
Defined: Cost of Sales is the net book value of all new and used inventory sold on a retail sale, the net book value of inventory sold on both early and full buyouts of rental agreements, pager service fees and cell phone air time and access fees.

Variances for Franchisee: You may elect to depreciate your inventory or fixed assets on a different basis than that used by ARI for tax purposes. Also, certain vendors offer purchase discounts to ARI for quick payment (i.e., a 2% discount on payments made within 10 days). You may not be able to obtain payment terms that are as favorable as those offered to or obtained by ARI. If you are able to obtain quick payment discounts, you must make payments by the early date in order to take advantage of them. You may also elect to depreciate your fixed assets on a different basis than that used by ARI.

Note 5: Personnel Cost
Defined: Personnel Cost is the sum of all store personnel costs, including: salaries and wages for full-time and part-time employees, employer contributions for FICA taxes, federal unemployment taxes, state unemployment taxes, workers' compensation, group health insurance, long term disability, cancer care, 401k, wages for contracted labor, expense of "help wanted" ads, employment agency fees, employee training expenses, and new hire physical examinations. ARI operated stores generally open with three to six associates.

Variances for Franchisee: ARI store managers are compensated on a draw plus bonus program. The draw ranges from $30,000 to $70,000, with an average draw of approximately $40,000. Personnel Cost also includes ARI's group health insurance cost. These expenses will vary considerably for you, depending on whether you hire a manager and their compensation program, prevailing wage rates in the area of the Franchised Business, and the types and amounts of non-salary benefits, if any, you provide to employees.

Note 6: Selling Cost
Defined: Selling Cost is the sum of all advertising expenses, including; yellow page ads, radio commercials, TV commercials, direct mailings, handbills, circulars, brochures, giveaways, sales floor signage, agency fees, exterior sign repairs and exterior sign depreciation.

Variances for Franchisee: You will conduct independent advertising programs and will pay an Ad Production Fee of 0.5% of your weekly Gross Revenues (if the Ad Production Fund is established by ARI). You may also pay a Regional Media Fee of $250 or 2% of weekly Gross Revenues, whichever is greater (if the Regional Media Fund is established by ARI). You must spend an amount equal to at least 4.5% of your Gross Revenues on advertising (this includes the payment of any Ad Production Fee and any Regional Media Fee).

ARI purchases the exterior wall sign and any exterior pole sign faces for each of its stores and depreciates its signs on a straight-line basis over 5 years. Therefore, the depreciation of signs is included in the calculation of this expense. ARI will purchase the exterior wall sign and any pole sign faces for the Franchised Business and will lease it to you over the first five years of the Franchise Agreement. See Item 7 of the UFOC for estimated lease payments for the exterior sign(s).

Note 7: Occupancy Cost
Defined: Occupancy Cost is the sum of all leased building expenses, including: rent, depreciation of leasehold improvements, depreciation of fixtures and equipment, building maintenance, common area maintenance, real estate commissions, real estate taxes, security systems, real estate insurance and utilities.

Variances for Franchisee: The stores used in this Exhibit vary in size from approximately 4,000 to 20,000 square feet. ARI's recommended square footage for the Franchised Business is between 7,000 and 12,000 square feet. ARI's lease rate per square foot varies from $4.00 to $10.00 and ARI's common area maintenance charge (CAM) varies from $0.30 to $1.00 per square foot. The cost per square foot in a strip-type shopping center and free standing buildings varies considerably, depending on the location and the market conditions affecting commercial property.

ARI operated stores typically pay in full for any portion of leasehold improvements it is responsible for and depreciate the improvements on a straight-line basis over the remaining life of the lease. Therefore, some depreciation of leasehold improvements is included in the calculation of this expense. Occasionally, the landlord will completely build (i.e. carpet, tile, counters, offices, etc.) the space out and increase the rental rate to cover the cost of such build-out. See Item 7 of the UFOC for an estimate of the cost of leasehold improvements.

ARI generally negotiates for deferred rental payments. Therefore, the Occupancy Cost may reflect several months with either no rental payments or reduced rental payments.

Note 8: Inventory Carrying Cost
Defined: Inventory Carrying Cost is the sum of all of expenses associated with carrying inventory, including: insurance for inventory in the store and in transit, an allocation of personal property tax on store inventory (on hand at year end), interest expense on inventory financing, depreciation of rental merchandise, repair cost and the cost of replacement parts for repairs or refurbishing, clearance center charge backs and freight charges absorbed by the receiving store on inventory redistribution. Also included in this item is depreciation on office furniture, which is depreciated over 36 months with a 0% salvage value. ARI generally begins depreciating its rental inventory the month after it is received in a store.

Variances for Franchisee: For internal and SunTrust Bank compliance reporting, ARI uses an eighteen month straight line depreciation (with no salvage value) for franchise calculations. Certain high end electronics (i.e. big screen t.v.'s) that are normally on twenty four month agreements are depreciated on a twenty four month straight line method (with no salvage value). This method is used mostly to reconcile SunTrust disposition book values with SunTrust amortization schedules. For company operated stores (prior to January 1, 1996), ARI paid in full for its rental inventory and depreciated most rental inventory generally over 14 months with a 5% salvage value, and depreciated office furniture over 36 months with 50% salvage value. For company-owned stores (effective January 1, 1996), ARI continued to pay in full for its rental inventory but prospectively changed its depreciation method on inventory purchased after that date to a method that depreciates the inventory over

the agreement period, generally 12 months, when on rent, and 36 months when not on rent, to a 0% salvage value (a method often referred to as income forecasting in the rental purchase industry) In addition, ARI extended the depreciable lives of inventory purchased prior to December 31, 1995 from generally 14 months to 18 months. ARI adopted the new method because it believes that it provides a more systematic and rational allocation of the cost of rental inventory over its useful life

The depreciation schedules used by ARI are for ARI's internal book purposes and SunTrust compliance reporting only. You should seek advice on depreciation from your financial advisor or personal accountant. ARI makes no recommendation as to the method of depreciation to be used by you for tax purposes.

Prior to February 1, 1996 each ARI store paid interest to ARI of 0.25% per month (i.e., an annual rate of 3%) on the total inventory cost for such store. Effective February 1, 1996 ARI began allocating total interest cost to the ARI operated stores based on the total inventory cost per store. ARI believes that this arrangement is substantially different from the arrangement you will have with your financial institution(s) for inventory purchases. ARI believes that your interest rate will be substantially higher, depending on the financing source, the collateral and your credit-worthiness.

Note 9: Delivery Cost
Defined: Delivery Cost is the sum of all expenses incurred in delivering and picking up rental inventory, including: vehicle depreciation or lease payments, rental of extra trucks, pro-rata share of vehicle insurance, truck decals, mechanical repairs, washing expense, parking expense, fuel and oil cost, mileage charged on extra trucks, vehicle repair costs incurred as a result of any accident, including insurance deductibles and taxes and vehicle registrations. Delivery cost also includes payments made to freight companies for the shipment of products from distribution centers operated by ARI.

Variances for Franchisee: You may, but are not obligated to, participate in ARIs fleet leasing or fleet purchasing programs. See Item 7 of the UFOC for the estimated cost for a delivery vehicle. ARI depreciates delivery vehicles that it purchases on a straight-line basis over 3 years with a 35% salvage value. Some delivery vehicles are leased and the monthly lease amount appears in this line item. Insurance rates for delivery vehicles will vary depending on the state and type of area (metropolitan or rural) in which the Franchised Business is located, and the amount and types of insurance coverage you maintain.

Note 10: Inventory Write-Offs and Collection Fees

Defined: Inventory Write-Offs are the net book value of all inventory write-off due to: customer skips, inventory shortages, inventory that is not picked up when rental agreements are not renewed and inventory that is damaged beyond repair. All fees paid to outside collection agencies for collections on bad debts and all expenses incurred outside of the normal course of business in collecting extremely delinquent rental fees are included in this line item. When calculating cash flow for its internal purposes, ARI does not consider fees that have been paid to outside collection agencies, which range from $500 to $2,000 per store per year, to be a cash expense (see Note 17).

Variances for Franchisee: You may be required to pay to your financial institution any outstanding loan amount on inventory that is written off at the time it is written off, and you may also utilize an outside collection agency more or less frequently than ARI.

Note 11: General Operating Cost

Defined: General Operating Cost is the sum of all operating expenses, including: telephone, office supplies, postage, general liability insurance, bank charges, credit card charges, miscellaneous charges, petty cash shortages, miscellaneous legal expenses, local business licenses and permits, store personnel errand and travel expense and generally a division allocation (beginning February 1996) and generally a regional allocation (beginning July 1995). The division/regional allocation is generally determined by calculating ARIs division/regional cost, and allocating it to ARI's stores pro-rata, based on the respective amount of revenues generated by such stores.

Variances for Franchisee: Your general liability insurance coverage will vary depending on the state(s) in which the Franchised Business operates, and the amounts and types of coverage you maintain. See Item 7 of the UFOC for an estimate of insurance costs. You will not be required to pay a division/regional allocation. However, you must pay to ARI a Continuing License Fee of 5% of weekly Gross Revenues.

Note 12: General Office Allocation

Defined: ARI operated stores are generally charged a General Office Allocation of 4.5% to 6.5% by the ARI home office. The current General Office Allocation is 5%.

Variances for Franchisee: You will not be required to pay a General Office Allocation. However, you must pay to ARI a Continuing License Fee of 5% of your weekly Gross Revenues.

Note 13: Miscellaneous Other Costs

Defined: Miscellaneous Other Costs includes bedding transfer cost and excess freight cost. The bedding transfer cost is the sum of the net book value of bedding shipped back to ARIs affiliate, MacTavish Furniture Industries ("MacTavish"), for rework, less credits paid by MacTavish for the raw salvage value of the bedding. The excess freight charge is the difference between allocated MacTavish freight charges and actual charges.

Variances for Franchisee: Depending on the proximity of the Franchised Business to MacTavish or other non-ARI bedding manufacturers, arrangements on the salvage value from non-ARI bedding manufacturers, and the potential freight charges, you may elect to dispose of old mattresses. You will have no allocation adjustment similar to excess freight because you will pay the actual freight charges on all merchandise ordered from MacTavish.

Note 14: Pre-Tax Earnings

Defined: Pre-Tax Earnings is Total Revenue minus the sum of: Cost of Sales, Personnel Cost, Selling Cost, Occupancy Cost, Inventory Carrying Cost, Delivery Cost, Inventory Write-Off and Collection Fees, General Operating Cost, General Office Allocation and Miscellaneous Other Costs.

Note 15: Depreciation

Defined: Depreciation is the total of all depreciation of rental inventory and fixed assets associated with store operations. The depreciation methods and periods are listed under the note for each expense described above which includes a depreciation component. This item does not include the net book value of inventory write-offs. The depreciation schedules used by ARI are for internal book purposes only. You should seek advice on depreciation from your financial advisor or personal accountant. ARI makes no recommendation as to the method of depreciation to be used by you for tax purposes.

Variances for Franchisee: You may elect to amortize intangible and depreciate rental inventory and fixed assets on a basis different than that used by ARI (for tax purposes).

Note 16: Net Inventory Purchases

Defined: Net Inventory Purchases is the sum of all electronics, appliances, furniture and other rental inventory purchased. These items are reflected in the month the merchandise is received in the store, not when the invoice is paid. These numbers also represent the net of book value of inventory transferred between ARI operated stores and inventory transferred from certain ARI operated stores to ARI operated distribution centers or clearance centers for disposal.

Variances for Franchisee: You may, but are not obligated to, participate in ARI's combined purchasing power, and to purchase inventory from ARI's furniture manufacturing division, MacTavish, for inventory pricing benefits. Your inventory purchases may vary if you have multiple locations and you transfer inventory to and from those locations.

If you utilize the SunTrust Bank inventory financing program, you will pay one eighteenth of your monthly inventory purchases as a principal payment, and interest on the total outstanding balance, to your financial institution(s) on a monthly basis (see item 10). These payments should be considered in any pro forma income statements, balance sheets, and cash flows for the Franchised Business.

Note 17: Pre-Tax Cash Flow

Defined: Pre-Tax Cash Flow is the sum of Pre-Tax Earnings, plus Depreciation, less Net Inventory Purchases, plus Cost of Sales, plus Inventory Write-Offs & Collection Fees (see Note 10).

Variances for Franchisee: Pre-tax cash flow assumes cash purchase of inventory. You may elect to finance your inventory purchases over a period of time through various lenders (including the eighteen month SunTrust loan program available for qualified franchisees described in Item 10. In determining cash flow, you may consider other cash payments made that are not directly expensed in the period in which the expenditure occurred.

Table 1

Statement of Average Revenues and Expenses for All Aaron's Rental Purchase Company-Operated Stores (As Defined) Opened Under the "12 Month Rental Purchase Plan." 1st, 2nd, 3rd, 4th and 5th Full Years of Operation

	Year 1		Year 2		Year 3		Year 4		Year 5	
	Average	%	Average	%	Average	%	Average	%	Average	%
Rental Revenue (Note 1)	$474,230	95.7%	$860,830	95.5%	$928,746	95.8%	$998,775	95.6%	$1,100,414	95.6%
Other Revenue (Note 2)	21,358	4.3%	40,395	4.5%	40,837	4.2%	46,145	4.4%	50,656	4.4%
Total Revenue (Note 3)	$495,588	100.0%	$901,225	100.0%	$969,583	100.0%	$1,044,920	100.0%	$1,151,070	100.0%
Operating Expenses:										
Cost of Sales (Note 4)	$14,610	2.9%	$49,549	5.5%	$53,622	5.5%	$56,467	5.4%	$56,670	4.9%
Personnel Cost (Note 5)	141,119	28.5%	186,507	20.7%	193,631	20.0%	201,026	19.2%	220,102	19.1%
Selling Cost (Note 6)	31,304	6.3%	34,229	3.8%	34,383	3.5%	33,492	3.2%	32,987	2.9%
Occupancy Cost (Note 7)	75,598	15.3%	92,905	10.3%	93,923	9.7%	91,051	8.7%	86,874	7.5%
Inventory Carrying Cost (Note 8)	204,781	41.3%	352,789	39.1%	356,841	36.8%	386,593	37.0%	421,336	36.6%
Delivery Cost (Note 9)	25,824	5.2%	32,234	3.6%	32,746	3.4%	35,344	3.4%	38,742	3.4%

	Year 1		Year 2		Year 3		Year 4		Year 5	
	Average	%	Average	%	Average	%	Average	%	Average	%
Inventory W/O & Collection Fees (Note 10)	17,356	3.5%	26,151	2.9%	27,540	2.8%	28,777	2.8%	28,049	2.4%
General Operating Cost (Note 11)	27,533	5.6%	32,501	3.6%	35,758	3.7%	40,541	3.9%	44,617	3.9%
Gen. Office Allocation (Note 12)	27,347	5.5%	47,229	5.2%	49,654	5.1%	51,900	5.0%	56,515	4.9%
Miscellaneous Other Costs (Note 13)	224	0.0%	579	0.1%	745	0.1%	851	0.1%	894	0.1%
Total Operating Costs	$565,696	114.1%	$854,673	94.8%	$878,843	90.6%	$926,042	88.6%	$986,786	85.7%
Pre-Tax Earnings (Note 14)	($70,108)	-14.1%	$46,552	5.2%	$90,740	9.4%	$118,878	11.4%	$164,284	14.3%
Number of Stores in Sample		89		80		67		56		34
Cash Flow Summary:										
Pre-Tax Earnings (Note 14)	($70,108)	-14.1%	$46,552	5.2%	$90,740	9.4%	$118,878	11.4%	$164,284	14.3%
Depreciation (Note 15)	210,424	42.5%	352,423	39.1%	353,445	36.5%	373,920	35.8%	402,375	35.0%
Net Inventory Purchases (Note 16)	(510,090)	-102.9%	(406,520)	-45.1%	(440,347)	-45.4%	(459,538)	-44.0%	(472,643)	-41.1%
Cost of Sales (Note 4)	14,610	2.9%	49,549	5.5%	53,622	5.5%	56,467	5.4%	56,670	4.9%
Inventory W/O & Collection Fees (Note 10)	17,356	3.5%	26,151	2.9%	27,540	2.8%	28,777	2.8%	28,049	2.4%
*Pre-Tax Cash Flow (Note 17)	($337,808)	-68.2%	$68,155	7.6%	$85,000	8.8%	$118,504	11.3%	$178,735	15.5%

*Assumes Cash Purchase of Inventory — Inventory Financing Available for Qualified Franchisees (See Item 10).

Note: The UFOC provides a detailed breakdown of revenues, costs and cash flow items by month for years 1–5. It also provides additional detail broken out by annual revenue breakdowns. Because of space limitations, this detail is not included.

Table 2
Statement of Average Revenues and Expenses of Aaron's Rental Purchase Company-Operated Stores for Year Ending December 31, 1998 for All Stores (As Defined) Open at Least Two Full Years Before January 1, 1998

	Annual Revenue Under $800,000		Annual Revenue $800,000–1,100,000		Annual Revenue $1,100,000–1,400,000		Annual Revenue Over $1,400,000		All Stores Annual Revenue	
	Average	%	Average	%	Average	%	Average	%	Average	%
Rental Revenue (Note 1)	$679,847	94.7%	$907,646	96.3%	$1,180,786	96.1%	$1,514,283	96.5%	$1,126,796	95.9%
Other Revenue (Note 2)	37,931	5.3%	45,178	4.7%	48,392	3.9%	54,601	3.5%	47,990	4.1%
Total Revenue (Note 3)	$717,778	100.0%	$952,723	100.0%	$1,229,178	100.0%	$1,668,884	100.0%	$1,174,786	100.0%
Operating Expenses:										
Cost of Sales (Note 4)	$35,138	4.9%	$41,041	4.3%	$45,711	3.7%	$61,935	3.9%	$46,639	4.0%
Personnel Cost (Note 5)	154,923	21.6%	182,723	19.2%	435,310	19.1%	296,723	18.9	225,065	19.2%
Selling Cost (Note 6)	32,010	4.5%	31,914	3.3%	32,218	2.6%	33,040	2.1%	32,255	2.7%
Occupancy Cost (Note 7)	101,012	14.1%	94,959	10.0%	96,080	7.8%	108,060	6.9%	98,093	8.3%
Inventory Carrying Cost (Note 8)	286,979	40.0%	372,733	39.1%	464,551	37.8%	584,083	37.2%	447,403	38.1%
Delivery Cost (Note 9)	34,169	4.8%	34,215	3.6%	40,007	3.3%	46,459	3.0%	38,944	3.3%

	Annual Revenue Under $800,000		Annual Revenue $800,000–1,100,000		Annual Revenue $1,100,000–1,400,000		Annual Revenue Over $1,400,000		All Stores Annual Revenue	
	Average	%	Average	%	Average	%	Average	%	Average	%
Inventory W/O & Collection Fees (Note 10)	29,509	4.1%	32,554	3.4%	29,662	2.4%	43,069	2.7%	33,121	2.8%
General Operating Cost (Note 11)	38,050	5.3%	48,261	5.1%	50,133	4.1%	55,758	3.6%	50,024	4.3%
Gen. Office Allocation (Note 12)	35,267	4.9%	46,985	4.9%	60,426	4.9%	77,296	4.9%	57,835	4.9%
Miscellaneous Other Costs (Note 13)	385	0.1%	759	0.1%	847	0.1%	1,367	0.1%	896	0.1%
Total Operating Costs	$747,442	104.1%	$886,144	93.0%	$1,054,945	85.8%	$1,307,810	83.4%	$1,030,275	87.7%
Pre-Tax Earnings (Note 14)	($29,664)	-4.1%	$66,579	7.0%	$174,233	14.2%	$261,074	16.6%	$144,511	12.3%
Number of Stores within the Range		4		34		42		18		98
Cash Flow Summary:										
Pre-Tax Earnings (Note 14)	($29,664)	-4.1%	$66,579	7.0%	$174,234	14.2%	$261,072	16.6%	$144,512	12.3%
Depreciation (Note 15)	288,143	40.1%	357,331	37.5%	437,848	35.6%	555,611	35.4%	425,433	36.2%
Net Inventory Purchases (Note 16)	(285,943)	-39.8%	(389,166)	-40.8%	(488,503)	-39.7%	(601,520)	-38.3%	(466,530)	-39.7%
Cost of Sales (Note 4)	35,138	4.9%	41,041	4.3%	45,711	3.7%	61,935	3.9%	46,639	4.0%
Inventory W/O & Collection Fees (Note 10)	29,509	4.1%	32,554	3.4%	29,662	2.4%	43,069	2.7%	33,121	2.8%
*Pre-Tax Cash Flow (Note 17)	$37,183	5.2%	$108,339	11.4%	$198,952	18.2%	$320,167	20.4%	$183,175	15.6%

*Assumes Cash Purchase of Inventory — Inventory Financing Available for Qualified Franchisees (See Item 10).

WHAT'S RIGHT FOR YOU.™

COLORTYME
5700 Tennyson Pkwy., # 180
Plano, TX 75024
Tel: (800) 411-8963 (972) 608-5376
Fax: (972) 403-4936
E-Mail:
Internet Address: www.colortyme.com
Contact: Mr. Pat Sumner, Director Franchise Develop.

Description: The nation's largest rental-purchase franchise company, specializing in electronics, furniture, appliances and computers. We help our customers find what's right for them and give our franchisees the support needed to be successful, at the best profit margins in the industry.

# Franchised Units:	293 Units
# Company-Owned Units:	0 Units
Total # Units:	293 Units
Founded In:	1979
1st Franchised In:	1981
Average Total Investment:	264-475K
Franchise Fee:	25K
On-Going Royalty:	4%
Advertising Fee:	$250/Mo.
Financial Assistance:	Yes(I)
Site Selection Assistance:	Yes
Lease Negotiation Assistance:	Yes
Contract Terms (Init./Renew):	5-10/5-10
Initial Training Provided: 3 Weeks Varied Training.	

1. Summary of Revenues and Cash Expenses of Colortyme, Inc.'s Franchised Rental Stores During their Last Fiscal Year

Income	Arithmetic Average per Rental Store	Percentage of Total	Aggregate Results of All Rental Stores	Percentage of Total
Rental Revenues	$538,822	87.7%	$121,234,880	87.7%
Reinstatement Fees	11,265	1.8%	2,534,585	1.8%
Waiver Fees	25,246	4.1%	5,680,448	4.1%
Store Sales	13,814	2.2%	3,108,112	2.2%
Misc. Income	23,069	3.8%	5,190,607	3.8%
Service Income	2,268	0.4%	510,294	0.4%
Total Revenues	$614,484	100.0%	$138,258,927	100.0%

Cash Expenses	Arithmetic Average per Rental Store	Percentage of Total	Aggregate Results of All Rental Stores	Percentage of Total
Accounting	$2,461	0.4%	$553,758	0.4%
Advertising	24,190	3.9%	5,442,785	3.9%
Building Repairs/Maintenance	2,371	0.4%	533,410	0.4%
Building Security	430	0.1%	96,650	0.1%
Licenses	588	0.1%	132,290	0.1%
Dues and Subscriptions	332	0.1%	74,635	0.1%
Interest	19,136	3.1%	4,305,574	3.1%
Insurance — All	12,956	2.1%	2,915,035	2.1%
Leased Equipment	3,159	0.5%	710,864	0.5%
Legal/Collection Expenses	1,893	0.3%	425,898	0.3%
Trash/Janitor	437	0.1%	98,250	0.1%
Misc. Expenses	12,198	2.0%	2,744,583	2.0%
Office Supplies	6,410	1.0%	1,442,172	1.0%
Postage/Freight	1,869	0.3%	420,424	0.3%
Rent	36,929	6.0%	8,309,052	6.0%
Repair — Parts/Service	12,316	2.0%	2,771,087	2.0%
Royalty Fees	15,904	2.6%	3,578,307	2.6%
Salaries (Includes Officers and Administrative)	172,983	28.2%	38,921,230	28.2%
Payroll Tax	12,284	2.0%	2,763,833	2.0%
Taxes — Property	2,581	0.4%	580,717	0.4%
Telephone	8,568	1.4%	1,927,870	1.4%
Travel — Training	5,382	0.9%	1,211,010	0.9%

Cash Expenses	Arithmetic Average per Rental Store	Percentage of Total	Aggregate Results of All Rental Stores	Percentage of Total
Utilities	7,515	1.2%	1,690,846	1.2%
Vehicle Expense	12,657	2.1%	2,847,684	2.1%
Total Expenses	$375,547	61.1%	$84,497,966	61.1%
Income before Debt Service, Depreciation and Taxes	$238,938	38.9%	$53,760,960	38.9%

2. Statistical Analysis of Revenue Range Summary

Arithmetic Average Annual Revenue: $614,484

Actual Store High and Low Annual Revenue:

High	$1,662,313
Low	$127,246

Range of Annual Revenue (see following table):

Average Annual Revenue	Percentage of Rental Stores Within Range	Aggregate Percentage of Rental Stores Equaling or Exceeding Revenue Range
More than $1,000,000	8%	8%
Between $700,000 and $999,999	21%	29%
Between $480,000 and $699,999	40%	69%
Between $300,000 and $479,999	25%	94%
Less than $299,999	6%	100%

Explanatory Notes to Summary:

1. This Summary is based upon information submitted by 225 of the 252 franchised Rental Stores (89%), which, as of December 31, 1998, had been open for business for at least 1 fiscal year.

2. We permit franchisees who have more than 1 franchised Rental Store to submit a financial report which reflects the aggregate results of all of their Rental Stores, rather than a separate report for each Rental Store.

3. As indicated in Item 11 of this offering circular, we have the right to require franchisees to contribute up to 3 % of Rental Store gross sales (Franchise Agreement Section 9.3) to the National Advertising Fund. In 1998 and continuing through the present time, each Rental Store contributed $250 per month to the National Advertising Fund, and our current intention is to continue this policy. Nevertheless, we have the right, at any time, to discontinue this policy and require a greater contribution in accordance with Section 9.3 of the Franchise Agreement.

4. The royalties paid by the Rental Stores whose results are reflected in this Summary vary, depending on the franchise agreement under which the Rental Store operates. The royalty percentage payable under our current Franchise Agreement requires a higher royalty percentage than that required under previous forms of franchise agreements.

5. This Summary was prepared from and based upon data submitted by ColorTyme franchisees for their most recent fiscal year. We believe that franchisees used the retail method of accounting in reporting their Rental Stores operations. The records and financial statements upon which this summary is based may not have been compiled in a manner consistent with generally accepted accounting principles and the underlying data may or may not have been audited. Except with respect to royalties as described above, we are unaware of any material differences between the Rental Stores whose results are reflected in the Summary and any Rental Stores that may be opened in the future.

6. The prospective franchisee is responsible for developing its own business plan for a Rental Store, including capital budgets, financial statements, projections and other appropriate factors, and is encouraged to consult with its own accounting, business and legal advisors in doing so. The business plan should make necessary allowances for changes in financial results to revenues and/or expenses that may arise during periods or in areas suffering economic downturns, inflation, unemployment, or other negative economic influences.

7. The Summary should not be considered to be the actual or probable revenues or expenses that will be experienced by any franchisee. We do not represent that any franchisee can expect to obtain the results set forth in this Summary. Actual results vary from franchise to franchise and we cannot estimate the results of any particular franchise. Significant variations in revenues and expenses exist among franchisees for a variety of reasons, such as the length of time the Rental Store has been operating, geographic region, the Rental Store's location, the franchisee's prior business experience, competition, and other factors. Moreover, historical revenues and expenses may not correspond to future revenues and expenses because of factors such as inflation, changes in minimum wage laws, and changes in the local labor market, among other factors. AS WITH MANY BUSINESSES, THE INITIAL FINANCIAL PERFORMANCE OF THE FRANCHISEE'S BUSINESS IS LIKELY TO DIFFER. Except as set forth in the Summary, we do not furnish or authorize any salespersons to furnish any oral or written information concerning the actual or potential sales, costs, income or profits of a franchise, and we will not be bound by allegations of any unauthorized representations as to earnings, sales, expenses, profits or prospect or changes for success.

8. Substantiation for the data set forth in this summary will be made available by us to all prospective franchisees upon reasonable request.

GINGISS FORMALWEAR

2101 Executive Dr.
Addison, IL 60101-1482
Tel: (800) 621-7125 (630) 620-9050
Fax: (630) 620-8840
E-Mail: gingiss@gingiss.com
Internet Address: www.gingiss.com
Contact: Mr. Tom Ryan, VP of Franchise Development

Description: GINGISS FORMALWEAR specializes in the rental and sale of men's and boys' tuxedos and related accessories. GINGISS is the leader in the formalwear wedding industry that does not go out of style, and is the only national formalwear chain that can coordinate groomsmen from coast to coast. GINGISS manufactures its own proprietary lines of formalwear, including exclusive designers such as Oleg Cassini.

# Franchised Units:	189 Units
# Company-Owned Units:	49 Units
Total # Units:	238 Units
Founded In:	1936
1st Franchised In:	1968
Average Total Investment:	98.7-242.7K
Franchise Fee:	15K
On-Going Royalty:	6%
Advertising Fee:	2%
Financial Assistance:	Yes(I)
Site Selection Assistance:	Yes
Lease Negotiation Assistance:	Yes
Contract Terms (Init./Renew):	10/10
Initial Training Provided:	1 Week Corporate Heaquarters; 1 Week Company Operated Store; On-Going on Location.

This earnings claim consists of two parts: the first describes average Gross Retail Revenues for all Stores open at least 12 months, and the second describes Gross Wholesale Revenues of those franchisees who engage in wholesale operations.

A. Statement of Average Gross Retail Revenues

We prepared the annual Gross Retail Revenues shown below based on franchisee information for the 12 months ended December 31, 1998, reported to us by franchisees owning 185 Stores, which are all of the franchised Stores which were open for at least 12 months at December 31, 1998 and which had reported all 12 months' volumes. These Gross Retail Revenues only include revenues reported to us for royalty purposes on which royalties are payable and do not include revenues from sub-rentals to other franchisees and other revenues where royalties are not payable. We have not independently investigated the amounts reported. Independent auditors have not audited or reviewed the amounts for reasonableness. We offered substantially the same services to all of the Stores. These Stores offered substantially the same products and ser-

vices to the public as, and are all substantially similar to, the type of Store you will operate under the Franchise Agreement.

We will substantiate the data we used to prepare this statement if you reasonably request.

We believe that the statement is relevant to the type of franchise we offer in this offering circular as to the geographic area as well as the shopping center locations and to the size and type of Gingiss Store for which we currently grant the franchises.

Average gross rental revenues	$278,070	87.0%
Average sales of merchandise	41,650	13.0%
Average Gross Retail Revenues	$319,720	100.0%

Of the 185 Stores included above, 83 Stores exceeded the average Gross Retail Revenues and 102 Stores did not exceed the average Gross Retail Revenues.

Below is a summary of the actual number of Gingiss franchised Stores at various levels of Gross Retail Revenues:

Gross Retail Revenue Levels	Number of Gingiss Stores in Each Gross Retail Revenue Level	% of Gingiss Stores in Each Gross Retail Revenue Level
Under $100,000	5	2.7%
$100,000–200,000	43	23.2%
$200,001–300,000	45	24.3%
$300,001–400,000	39	21.1%
$400,001–500,000	25	13.5%
Over $500,000	28	15.2%
Total:	185	100. 0%

B. Statement of Average Gross Wholesale Revenues

Some franchisees try to maximize their utilization of rental inventory by sub-renting to other formalwear providers. We endorse this type of revenue activity and will provide operational guidance and collateral materials. We prepared the annual Gross Wholesale Revenues shown below based on franchisee information for the 12 months ended December 31, 1998, reported to us by

9 franchisees. These Gross Wholesale Revenues only include those revenues reported to us for royalty purposes. Several of the franchisees reporting Gross Wholesale Revenues own and operate several Stores and/or own and operate off-site plants. We have not independently investigated the amounts reported. Independent auditors have not audited or reviewed the amounts for reasonableness.

For the year 1998, the following charts describe the range of Gross Wholesale Revenues and the number of Gingiss franchisees at each Gross Wholesale Revenue Level:

Wholesale Revenue Levels	Number of Franchisees in Each Revenue Level
$1,500–4,500	3
$4,500–49,999	4
$50,000–300,000	0
$300,000–1,000,000	1
Over $1,000,000	1

YOUR INDIVIDUAL RESULTS ARE LIKELY TO DIFFER FROM THE RESULTS STATED IN A. AND B. ABOVE. THE INFORMATION PROVIDED IN THESE STATEMENTS DOES NOT CONSTITUTE OUR PROMISE OR REPRESENTATION THAT YOU WILL EXPERIENCE A CERTAIN REVENUE LEVEL. WE DO NOT GUARANTEE THAT YOUR FINANCIAL RESULTS WILL MATCH THE RESULTS IN THESE STATEMENTS.

Retail: home furnishings

Decorating Den
INTERIORS

DECORATING DEN INTERIORS

19100 Montgomery Village Ave., # 200
Montgomery Village, MD 20886
Tel: (800) DEC-DENS (301) 272-1500
Fax: (301) 272-1520
E-Mail:
Internet Address: www.decoratingden.com
Contact: Ms. Alice Flester, Marketing Manager

Description: Established in 1969, DECORATING DEN INTERIORS is the oldest international, shop-at-home interior decorating franchise in the world. Our company-trained interior decorators bring thousands of samples including window coverings, wallcoverings, floor coverings, furniture and accessories to their customers' homes in our uniquely equipped COLORVAN ©. Special business features include: home-based, marketing systems, business systems, training, support and complete sampling.

# Franchised Units:	551 Units
# Company-Owned Units:	1 Units
Total # Units:	552 Units
Founded In:	1969
1st Franchised In:	1970
Average Total Investment:	19.9-59K
Franchise Fee:	9.9-23.9K
On-Going Royalty:	7-11% (Sliding)
Advertising Fee:	2%/$100 Min
Financial Assistance:	Yes(B)
Site Selection Assistance:	Yes
Lease Negotiation Assistance:	N/A
Contract Terms (Init./Renew):	10/10
Initial Training Provided:	10 1/2 Days in Montgomery Village, MD.

The following is a tabulation of the Average Monthly Gross Retail Sales for all operational Decorating Den Interiors Franchise Owners in business for more than twelve months in the year ending December 31, 1998. All Franchise Owners on whom we have based this information were in operation for the entire 12 months of 1998. The figures below are based upon the actual operations of Decorating Den Interiors Franchise Owners in nine Districts of the United States. The list of states in the 9 Districts excludes the states of Alaska and Hawaii where we have no Franchise Owners.

All Gross Sales figures are compiled from the data contained in the sales reports submitted by Franchise Owners as required by the standard Decorating Den Interiors Franchise Agreement. Our Franchise Owners are not required to keep their financial records under any uniform format or on any accounting basis, although the definition of Gross Sales to be reported to us and the time periods subject to reporting is specified by the Franchise Agreement. For this study, we added the monthly Gross Sales reports for 1998 of each Franchise Owner in the District who operated for the full year and divided the total by 12. We then organized and listed Franchise Owners in each District according to their levels of Average Monthly Gross Sales, and mathematically divided them into the top 25% percentile of the Franchise Owners in the District with the highest Average Monthly Gross Sales, the middle 50% percentile, and the bottom 25% percentile. We totaled the Average Monthly Gross Sales figures for the Franchise Owners in each percentile, divided by the number of Franchise Owners in the percentile, and included that percentile average in the following District by District presentation.

We have not undertaken to specifically substantiate the accuracy of the data reported by each individual Franchise Owner. The Gross Sales set forth are of specific franchises and must not be considered as the actual or potential Gross Sales that you will obtain. We do not represent that you can expect to attain these Gross Sales, and we do not have any method of estimating the results of operations of any particular franchise. YOUR

INDIVIDUAL FINANCIAL RESULTS ARE LIKELY TO DIFFER FROM THE RESULTS SET FORTH IN THIS ITEM 19.

Except for the foregoing, neither we, the Regional Director nor any of our respective sales personnel, officers, agents or employees are authorized to make any claims or statements as to the success that you can expect or that existing or former Franchise Owners have had. We and the Regional Directors explicitly instruct our sales personnel, officers, agents and employees that they are not permitted to make any such claims or statements as to the earnings, sales or profits or your chances of success of any franchise, nor are they authorized to represent or estimate any dollar figures except those specifically contained in this Item 19. Applicants for a Decorating Den Interiors franchise should make, and are encouraged to make, their own full and complete investigation to determine whether or not to purchase a Decorating Den Interiors franchise. Substantiation of the data used in this Item will be made available to you upon reasonable request; however, in order to protect the privacy of our Franchise Owners, we shall not disclose the identity of any specific Franchise Owner.

District 1

District 1 includes the states of Maine, New Hampshire, Vermont, Massachusetts, Connecticut, Rhode Island, New York, New Jersey and Pennsylvania. **The average number of months in business for the owners in this district who were included in this study is 80 months. The total number of franchisees in this District as of December 31, 1998 was 68.**

Percentile (%)	Average Monthly Sales in Percentile	Number of Franchises in this Percentile	Number and Percentage (#/%) of Studied Franchisees in District Who Met or Exceeded This Level of Average Monthly Sales
Top 25%	$19,333	15	5/8%
Middle 50%	$6,790	31	29/48%
Bottom 25%	$1,494	15	53/87%

District 2

District 2 includes the states of Delaware, Ohio, Maryland, West Virginia, Virginia, the District of Columbia and Kentucky. **The average number of months in business for the owners in this district who were included in this study is 82 months. The total number of franchisees in this District as of December 31, 1998 was 69.**

Percentile (%)	Average Monthly Sales in Percentile	Number of Franchises in this Percentile	Number and Percentage (#/%) of Studied Franchisees in District Who Met or Exceeded This Level of Average Monthly Sales
Top 25%	$22,530	15	6/10%
Middle 50%	$9,990	32	28/45%
Bottom 25%	$2,749	15	56/90%

District 3

District 3 includes the states of Tennessee, North Carolina, South Carolina, Georgia and Alabama. **The average number of months in business for the owners in this district who were included in this study is 69 months. The total number of franchisees in this District as of December 31, 1998 was 68.**

Percentile (%)	Average Monthly Sales in Percentile	Number of Franchises in this Percentile	Number and Percentage (#/%) of Studied Franchisees in District Who Met or Exceeded This Level of Average Monthly Sales
Top 25%	$21,336	15	4/7%
Middle 50%	$6,159	30	29/48%
Bottom 25%	$706	15	50/83%

District 4

District 4 includes the state of Florida. **The average number of months in business for the owners in this district who were included in this study is 75 months. The total number of franchisees in this District as of December 31, 1998 was 35.**

Percentile (%)	Average Monthly Sales in Percentile	Number of Franchises in this Percentile	Number and Percentage (#/%) of Studied Franchisees in District Who Met or Exceeded This Level of Average Monthly Sales
Top 25%	$37,398	8	3/9%
Middle 50%	$10,248	17	13/39%
Bottom 25%	$1,551	8	28/85%

District 5

District 5 includes the state of Michigan, Wisconsin, Illinois and Indiana. **The average number of months in business for the owners in this district who were included in this study is 94 months. The total number of franchisees in this District as of December 31, 1998 was 79.**

Percentile (%)	Average Monthly Sales in Percentile	Number of Franchises in this Percentile	Number and Percentage (#/%) of Studied Franchisees in District Who Met or Exceeded This Level of Average Monthly Sales
Top 25%	$20,284	18	7/10%
Middle 50%	$6,783	36	38/53%
Bottom 25%	$1,185	18	63/88%

District 6

District 6 includes the states of Minnesota, Iowa, Nebraska, North Dakota and South Dakota. **The average number of months in business for the owners in this district who were included in this study is 72 months. The total number of franchisees in this District as of December 31, 1998 was 34.**

Percentile (%)	Average Monthly Sales in Percentile	Number of Franchises in this Percentile	Number and Percentage (#/%) of Studied Franchisees in District Who Met or Exceeded This Level of Average Monthly Sales
Top 25%	$34,138	4	1/5%
Middle 50%	$7,022	11	10/53%
Bottom 25%	$1,647	4	17/89%

District 7

District 7 includes the states of Texas, Missouri, Mississippi, Kansas, Louisiana, Arkansas and Oklahoma. **The average number of months in business for the owners in this district who were included in this study is 78 months. The total number of franchisees in this District as of December 31, 1998 was 64.**

Percentile (%)	Average Monthly Sales in Percentile	Number of Franchises in this Percentile	Number and Percentage (#/%) of Studied Franchisees in District Who Met or Exceeded This Level of Average Monthly Sales
Top 25%	$14,127	16	7/11%
Middle 50%	$5,719	32	34/53%
Bottom 25%	$439	16	55/86%

District 8

District 8 includes the states of Montana, Idaho, Colorado, Nevada, Arizona, Utah, New Mexico and Wyoming. **The average number of months in business for the owners in this district who were included in this study is 90 months. The total number of franchisees in this District as of December 31, 1998 was 17.**

Percentile (%)	Average Monthly Sales in Percentile	Number of Franchises in this Percentile	Number and Percentage (#/%) of Studied Franchisees in District Who Met or Exceeded This Level of Average Monthly Sales
Top 25%	$12,663	4	1/6%
Middle 50%	$3,950	9	9/53%
Bottom 25%	$459	4	14/82%

District 9

District 9 includes the states of Washington, Oregon and California. **The average number of months in business for the owners in this district who were included in this study is 73 months. The total number of franchisees in this District as of December 31, 1998 was 25.**

Percentile (%)	Average Monthly Sales in Percentile	Number of Franchises in this Percentile	Number and Percentage (#/%) of Studied Franchisees in District Who Met or Exceeded This Level of Average Monthly Sales
Top 25%	$29,926	5	3/13%
Middle 50%	$9,202	13	11/48%
Bottom 25%	$948	5	20/87%

NORWALK - THE FURNITURE IDEA
815 Crocker Rd., # 5
Westlake, OH 44145
Tel: (888) NORWALK (419) 668-4461
Fax: (440) 871-6057
E-Mail: nfi turbo@aol.com
Internet Address: www.norwalk-furniture.com
Contact: Mr. Mike Turbeville, Vice President of Franchising

Description: Retail specialty stores, offering up-scale consumers an unparalleled selection of fashionable, upholstered furniture. Stores show samples of 2,000 fabrics and leathers, all available on hundreds of styles (30-40 groupings on display) with delivery in just 35 days. Stores are typically 5,000 square feet. The franchisor is the manufacturer.

# Franchised Units:	71 Units
# Company-Owned Units:	9 Units
Total # Units:	80 Units
Founded In:	1902
1st Franchised In:	1987
Average Total Investment:	200-300K
Franchise Fee:	35K
On-Going Royalty:	0%
Advertising Fee:	0%
Financial Assistance:	Yes(I)
Site Selection Assistance:	Yes
Lease Negotiation Assistance:	Yes
Contract Terms (Init./Renew):	20/5

Initial Training Provided: 1 Week Cleveland; 1 Week Memphis; 1 Week Another Store Opening; 1 Wk. Your Store Opening.

We provide historical sales data below for company-owned and franchised stores. Please review the following information in conjunction with your review of the historical sales data.

Except for the historical sales data listed below, we do not make any representations or statements of actual, average, projected, or forecasted sales, profits, or earnings to franchisees with respect to our franchises. We do not furnish or authorize our salespersons to furnish to you any oral or written information concerning the actual, average, projected, forecasted, or potential sales, costs, income, or profits of a franchise.

Except for the historical sales data listed below, we specifically instruct our sales personnel, agents, employees, and officers that they may not make claims or statements as to the earnings, sales or profits, or prospects or chances of success, nor are they authorized to represent or estimate dollar figures as to a franchisee's operation. Actual results vary from franchise to franchise, and we cannot estimate the results of a particular franchise. We recommend that you make your own independent investigation to determine whether or not the franchise may be profitable, and consult an attorney and other advisors before executing the Agree-

ment. We recommend that you consider the management and sales staff qualifications as significant factors in determining the sales performance of a franchised facility.

The results listed below should not be considered as the actual or probable sales results that may be realized by any franchisee. Actual results are dependent on a variety of internal and external factors, some of which neither we nor you can estimate, such as competition, taxes, general economic conditions and demographics.

Aside from geographical differences, there are no material differences in the products, services, training, or support offered to any franchises. Differences in sales volumes are attributed to geographical and managerial differences, competition, mix of products sold at store, taxes, general economic conditions, demographics, and one or more other variables noted above.

The information listed below reflects the aggregate results of sales and should not be considered the actual or probable sales that will be realized by an individual franchisee. We do not represent that you can expect to obtain these results. In particular, your initial financial results may be lower as a new

411

store. We recommend that you make your own independent investigation to determine whether or not the franchise may be profitable, and consult with an attorney, accountant, and other advisors before executing any agreement.

Historical Sales Information
The following information is considered an integral part of the historical sales data that follows, and should be read in conjunction with the data in the chart that follows.

1. The following information is based on our experience with our own stores and our franchisees. *Expect that your results will vary from the attached list of stores.*

2. The following information is based on 59 stores that operated under a franchise agreement (or are company-owned stores) for a full 12 months (for the respective years listed). We believe that adding additional stores without a full year's operating history may affect, or result in a difference with respect to, the information set forth below. Note: licensed stores are not included in this exhibit.

3. Of the 59 stores listed, 9 are company-owned stores (and are marked with an asterisk), and 50 are franchised stores.

4. This chart does not reflect any expenses which you should expect to incur. We believe that franchised stores incur many of the same expenses as company-owned stores, except that franchised stores will also incur the initial franchise fee, advertising payments, and other payments and fees noted in Item 6 above. Also, there will be other expenses, which are likely to be significant, and may vary widely among franchisees. These may include the costs and expenses described in Item 7 above, as well as ongoing costs, such as lease expenses; insurance; property taxes, business taxes and licenses, and income taxes; accounting, legal, and other professional fees; depreciation/lease payments on property and equipment; and interest or financing charges on any borrowed funds. In addition, some of the expenses may be influenced by our economies of scale.

You are strongly encouraged to consult with your financial advisors in reviewing this chart and, in particular, in estimating the categories and amount of expenses which you will incur in establishing and operating a Store.

5. This listing is for informational purposes only. Sales projections should be made independent of this listing considering the following variables:
    - economic or market area conditions
    - staff strengths and weaknesses
    - store location
    - consistency/efficiency of operations
    - franchisee capitalization level
    - franchisee business experience
    - store design
    - local costs and operational expenses
    - local advertising media & costs
    - store display

6. Sales reported are actual data reported by franchisees or company-owned stores to us for purposes of a sales awards program. Substantiation of data is available upon reasonable request.
    - Arithmetic Average Annual Sales (1998): $1,256,910
    - Median Annual Sales (1998): $1,105,114

Historical Sales Information

Store	Date Opened	Annual Written Sales 1996	Annual Written Sales 1997	Annual Written Sales 1998
1	6/90	$1,557,541	$1,566,290	$2,146,028
2*	5/90	1,195,551	1,279,369	1,032,013
3	3/88	1,515,610	1,853,400	2,130,332
4*	7/88	1,459,780	1,869,665	2,112,375

Store	Date Opened	Annual Written Sales 1996	Annual Written Sales 1997	Annual Written Sales 1998
5*	11/90	1,035,974	943,381	982,694
6	9/87	1,477,990	1,498,090	1,256,558
7*	7/96	N/A	946,089	1,100,235
8	11/90	1,440,201	1,909,876	1,918,300
9	11/96	N/A	764,499	945,619
10	10/90	1,329,202	1,440,043	1,488,278
11*	6/92	1,307,688	1,021,054	1,029,654
12	10/92	662,425	727,627	689,586
13	10/92	1,532,297	1,706,690	1,602,381
14	10/92	739,101	837,011	1,104,390
15	11/92	807,025	1,560,457	1,550,548
16	9/93	1,018,072	766,668	941,372
17	10/96	N/A	854,003	832,333
18	7/94	399,914	698,337	829,547
19	3/94	820,935	887,241	1,254,381
20	6/94	1,344,393	1,382,292	1,479,026
21	10/94	1,010,985	1,200,293	1,394,846
22	8/93	1,258,425	810,862	707,977
23	8/88	1,582,321	1,657,578	1,637,810
24	5/95	789,478	764,699	587,815
25*	12/94	809,146	1,013,840	851,911
26	10/95	1,433,066	1,436,135	1,340,300
27	1/96	824,823	915,437	1,043,073
28	6/95	1,064,539	1,243,398	1,544,640
29*	3/94	1,389,888	1,461,249	1,584,704
30*	9/95	1,178,030	1,286,090	1,375,267
31	1/96	783,812	1,117,237	1,262,224
32	12/95	1,600,581	1,482,603	1,411,565
33	7/95	1,754,336	2,028,556	1,309,610
34	4/95	2,296,468	2,249,746	2,461,601
35	11/95	1,426,334	1,637,346	2,197,169
36	10/96	N/A	571,207	590,990
37	12/96	N/A	985,265	946,714
38	9/96	N/A	567,549	795,815
39	11/96	N/A	1,487,227	1,727,063
40	7/96	N/A	1,678,468	1,794,630
41	6/96	N/A	649,753	676,410
42	5/96	N/A	1,412,029	990,714
43	12/96	N/A	1,062,205	1,332,298

Store	Date Opened	Annual Written Sales 1996	Annual Written Sales 1997	Annual Written Sales 1998
44	2/97	N/A	N/A	1,633,711
45	3/97	N/A	N/A	755,507
46	4/97	N/A	N/A	657,463
47	4/97	N/A	N/A	899,688
48	4/97	N/A	N/A	1,040,007
49	5/97	N/A	N/A	1,051,827
50	5/97	N/A	N/A	2,035,360
51	5/97	N/A	N/A	716,500
52	5/97	N/A	N/A	723,476
53	8/97	N/A	N/A	943,858
54	8/97	N/A	N/A	1,105,114
55	9/97	N/A	N/A	930,129
56	10/97	N/A	N/A	625,216
57	11/97	N/A	N/A	1,551,203
58*	11/97	N/A	N/A	2,435,184
59	12/97	N/A	N/A	1,062,665

Note: Our company-owned stores are marked with an asterisk in the chart above.

WINDOW WORKS
7167 Shady Oak Rd.
Eden Prairie, MN 55344-3516
Tel: (800) 326-2659 (612) 943-4353
Fax: (612) 943-9050
E-Mail: jspelbrink@windowworks.net
Internet Address: www.windowworks.net
Contact: Ms. Joanne Spelbrink, Vice President Operations

Description: WINDOW WORKS showroom and mini-plant concept retails custom window treatments and accessories all within a 1,000 to 1,500 SF facility. Designers offer in-home consultation service, selling top-quality drapery, shutters, cellular shades, wood blinds and verticals. Exclusive Windcom software tracks day-to-day business and generates 27 reports from marketing to sales tax.

# Franchised Units:	8 Units
# Company-Owned Units:	0 Units
Total # Units:	8 Units
Founded In:	1978
1st Franchised In:	1979
Average Total Investment:	39-67K
Franchise Fee:	17.5K
On-Going Royalty:	4%
Advertising Fee:	1%
Financial Assistance:	Yes(I)
Site Selection Assistance:	Yes
Lease Negotiation Assistance:	Yes
Contract Terms (Init./Renew):	15/15

Initial Training Provided: 1-2 Weeks Corporate Window Works — MN; Store Site, as Needed.

During the 1998 calendar year, our larger market franchisees achieved installed sales ranging from $329,168 to $830,951 and realized gross margins of 44–53%. By "larger market franchisees," we mean our franchisees who have been operating their Window Works businesses for at least two years and who are located in metropolitan areas with approximately one million people or more. During that same time period, our franchisees who have been operating Window Works businesses for at least two years in smaller market areas have attained installed sales ranging from $225,486 to $379,658 and realized gross margins of 44–53%. At the end of the 1998 calendar year, we had 11 franchisees, nine of whom had operated during the entire year. The respective sales ranges are based on the actual 1998 installment sales reported by our franchisees who operated during the entire 1998 calendar year, and we have assumed that those franchisees have fully and accurately reported their installment sales. In total, six of our franchisees who operated during the entire 1998 calendar year, three larger market franchisees and three smaller market franchisees, reported installment sales within the applicable stated ranges. Of the remain-

ing three franchisees who operated during the entire 1998 calendar year, one franchisee had been in operation for less than two years and the other two franchisees have not yet fully reported their 1998 installment sales. YOUR ACTUAL RESULTS, HOWEVER, MAY DIFFER FROM THESE SALES AND GROSS MARGIN CLAIMS DUE TO VARYING MARKET CONDITIONS AND UNFORESEEN EVENTS, CONDITIONS AND CIRCUMSTANCES. Information substantiating these sales and gross margin claims will be made available to you upon reasonable request.

Other than the sales and gross margin claims set forth above, we do not furnish any oral or written information concerning the actual or potential sales, costs, income or profits of a Window Works business.

Retail: pet products & services

PET VALU INTERNATIONAL
2 Devon Square, # 200, 744 W. Lancaster Ave.
Wayne, PA 19087
Tel: (888) 564-6784 (610) 225-0800
Fax: (610) 225-0822
E-Mail: petvalu@aol.com
Internet Address: www.petvalu.com
Contact: Mr. David J. Wheat, VP Franchise
Development

Description: Discount retailer of pet foods and supplies. 'Your Neighborhood Store With Superstore Prices.'

# Franchised Units:	333 Units
# Company-Owned Units:	95 Units
Total # Units:	428 Units
Founded In:	1976
1st Franchised In:	1987
Average Total Investment:	85.4-207.9K
Franchise Fee:	20K
On-Going Royalty:	N/A
Advertising Fee:	N/A
Financial Assistance:	Yes(B)
Site Selection Assistance:	N/A
Lease Negotiation Assistance:	Yes
Contract Terms (Init./Renew):	10/5/5
Initial Training Provided:	1 Day at Head Office, Wayne, PA; 3 Weeks at Head Office and Operating Store.

Subject to deductions and set-offs as provided in the Franchise Agreement, and subject to Our rights to terminate the Franchise Agreement (see Item 17), each of Our seventeen current U.S. franchisees will be paid a minimum of $40,000.00 or $50,000.00 per year (as applicable) in Base Royalties (payable at the rate of $1,538.46 or $ 1,923.08 every two weeks) in each of their first 3 Franchise Payment Years.

Although PVII does furnish demographic information as described in the paragraph below and in Appendix A, PVII does not furnish or authorize its salespersons to furnish any oral or written information concerning the potential sales, costs,

income or profits of a PET VALU store (except to the extent that such information relates to the $40,000.00 or $50,000.00 minimum Base Royalty payable during the first 3 Franchise Payment Years). Actual earnings will vary from unit to unit, particularly after the third year of operation, and We cannot estimate the results of any particular franchise. Because this demographic information consists of statistical information only, We do not believe that it needs to comply with the Standards for Accountant's Services on Prospective Financial Information.

In order to assist You in evaluating total expenditures on pet food and supplies within the trading area of a particular PET VALU location, We have compiled the information contained in Appendix A, which is based on data obtained from three sources: The 1990 United States Census; the 1996 American Pet Products Manufacturers Association ("APPMA") National Pet Owners Survey (a survey of 20,000 households selected from the national panel of NFO Research, Inc., with a 73% response rate); and the 1997 U.S. Pet Ownership & Demographics Sourcebook, prepared by the Center for

Information Management of the American Veterinary Medical Association ("AVMA") (a random survey of 80,000 households nationwide with a 75% response rate). PVII will make this underlying documentation available to You for review upon request. PVII makes no representation as to what percentage of this market You might obtain, nor do We warrant the accuracy of any of the numbers contained herein. You should do Your own investigation and research as to the market.

Petland

PETLAND

195 N. Hickory St., P. O. Box 1606
Chillicothe, OH 45601-5606
Tel: (800) 221-5935 (740) 775-2464
Fax: (740) 775-2575
E-Mail:
Internet Address: www.petlandinc.com
Contact: Mr. Drew Musser, Director of Franchising

Description: PETLAND is a full-service, pet retail store that features live animals, including tropical fish, marina fish, small mammals, reptiles, amphibians, tropical, domestically-bred birds, puppies and kittens. The PETLAND concept also features over 4,000 merchandise items to support the pets sold to or already in the homes of

its customers. Over 1,500 merchandise items are PETLAND brands, sold exclusively through PETLAND retail stores.

# Franchised Units:	166 Units
# Company-Owned Units:	4 Units
Total # Units:	170 Units
Founded In:	1967
1st Franchised In:	1972
Average Total Investment:	175-450K
Franchise Fee:	25K
On-Going Royalty:	4.5%
Advertising Fee:	N/A
Financial Assistance:	Yes(I)
Site Selection Assistance:	Yes
Lease Negotiation Assistance:	Yes
Contract Terms (Init./Renew):	20/20
Initial Training Provided:	1.5 Weeks Training Store, Chillicothe, OH; 1 Week Classroom; 2 Weeks New Store Location.

Set forth below are charts depicting the ranges of actual Gross Revenues (as defined in Item 6 of this offering circular) for the year ending December 31, 1998, for franchised stores located in the United States and central and western Canada which, as of December 31, 1998, had been in operation for more than one year. The revenues of those Canadian stores included have been reduced in a conversion to U.S. dollars.

The information presented in chart form in this Item 19 includes data for 99 stores in the United

States and certain Canadian stores which had been in operation for at least one year as of December 31, 1998. It does not include data for 39 stores in operation in Japan, France, Chile, Puerto Rico and stores located in the province of Quebec, Canada.

Following is information indicating the geographical breakdown of the stores included in the charts. We have divided the stores into 6 regions, which include the listed states/areas:

Region	States
East Coast	Connecticut, Delaware, D.C., Maine, Maryland, Massachusetts, New Hampshire, New Jersey, New York, Pennsylvania, Rhode Island, Vermont, Virginia and Toronto, Canada.

Region	States
Midwest	Illinois, Indiana, Iowa, Kansas, Michigan, Minnesota, Missouri, Nebraska, North Dakota, South Dakota, Wisconsin and Winnipeg, Canada.
Ohio Valley	Kentucky, Ohio, West Virginia.
Southeast	Alabama, Florida, Georgia, Louisiana, Mississippi, North Carolina, South Carolina, Tennessee, Puerto Rico.
Southwest	Arkansas, Colorado, New Mexico, Oklahoma, Texas, Utah, Wyoming.
West Coast	Alaska, Arizona, California, Hawaii, Idaho, Montana, Nevada, Oregon, Washington and western Canada.

The number of stores of each type with in each of the regions is as follows:

Region	Super Stores	Strip Center Stores	Mall Stores
East Coast	1	7	3
Midwest	2	16	7
Ohio Valley	3	8	9
Southeast	1	9	5
Southwest	1	4	5
West Coast	4	8	6
Total	12	52	35

The Gross Revenues figures set forth in these charts have not been audited by us. The figures reported were supplied by the individual franchisees through our uniform reporting system.

A. Super Stores

Range of Gross Revenues	No. of Stores	% of Total
$800,000–899,999	1	8.3
900,000–999,999	0	0.0
1,000,000–1,099,999	3	25.0
1,100,000–1,199,999	0	0.0
1,200,000–1,299,999	2	16.7
1,300,000–1,399,000	2	16.7
1,600,000–1,699,000	2	16.7
2,100,000–2,199,000	2	16.7
Total	12	100.0[1]

Average Super Store Gross Revenues: $1,391,602   Number of Stores Below Category Average: 8
Low Super Store Gross Revenues: $ 858,014   Number of Stores Above Category Average: 4
High Super Store Gross Revenues: $2,132,810

B. Strip Center Stores

Range of Gross Revenues	No. of Stores	% of Total
$200,000–249,999	1	1.9
250,000–299,999	0	0.0
300,000–349,999	1	1.9
350,000–399,999	4	7.7
400,000–449,999	1	1.9
450,000–499,999	3	5.8
500,000–549,999	1	1.9
550,000–599,999	5	9.6
600,000–649,999	7	13.5
650,000–699,999	5	9.6
700,000–749,999	3	5.8
750,000–799,999	3	5.8
800,000–849,999	3	5.8
850,000–899,999	1	1.9
900,000–949,999	1	1.9
950,000–999,999	1	1.9
1,000,000–1,049,999	5	9.6
1,050,000–1,099,999	2	3.8
1,100,000–1,149,000	1	1.9
1,150,000–1,199,999	1	1.9
1,200,000–1,249,999	1	1.9
1,250,000–1,299,999	1	1.9
1,350,000–1,399,999	1	1.9
Total	52	100.0[1]

Average Strip Center Store Gross Revenues: $732,430
Low Strip Center Store Gross Revenues: $215,968
High Strip Center Store Gross Revenues: $1,360,988
Number of Stores Below Category Average: 30
Number of Stores Above Category Average: 22

C. Mall Stores

Range of Gross Revenues	No. of Stores	% of Total
$200,000–249,999	1	2.9
250,000–299,999	2	5.7
300,000–349,999	3	8.6
350,000–399,999	5	14.3
400,000–449,999	5	14.3
450,000–499,999	6	17.1
500,000–549,999	2	5.7
550,000–599,999	2	5.7

Range of Gross Revenues	No. of Stores	% of Total
600,000–649,999	2	5.7
650,000–699,999	2	5.7
700,000–749,999	1	2.9
750,000–799,999	0	0.0
800,000–849,999	0	0.0
850,000–899,999	1	2.9
950,000–999,999	1	2.9
1,100,000–1,149,999	1	2.9
1,200,000–1,249,999	1	2.9
Total	35	100.0[2]

Average Mall Store Gross Revenues: $528,214
Low Mall Store Gross Revenues: $243,261
High Mall Store Gross Revenues: $1,239,585
Number of Stores Below Category Average: 22
Number of Stores Above Category Average: 13

THE GROSS REVENUE DATA SET FORTH ABOVE IS BASED UPON STORES THAT HAVE BEEN IN OPERATION FOR MORE THAN ONE YEAR. THE RESULTS OF EACH FRANCHISE WILL VARY BASED UPON MANY FACTORS INCLUDING THE LOCATION AND THE FRANCHISEE'S OWN ABILITY AND EFFORT. YOUR INDIVIDUAL GROSS SALES ARE LIKELY TO VARY FROM THOSE SET FORTH ABOVE AND NO ASSURANCES CAN BE GIVEN THAT ANY PARTICULAR LEVEL OF SALES OR PROFIT CAN BE ACHIEVED BY YOU.

Substantiation of the data used in preparing the charts set forth above will be made available to you upon reasonable request to us.

----

[1] Percentages when added may not total 100% due to rounding.
[2] Percentages when added may not total 100% due to rounding.

COMPUTER RENAISSANCE
4200 Dahlberg Dr.
Minneapolis, MN 55422-4837
Tel: (800) 645-7297 (612) 520-8500
Fax: (612) 520-8599
E-Mail: jleffler@cr1.com
Internet Address: www.cr1.com
Contact: Mr. John Leffler, Senior Franchise Sales

Description: COMPUTER RENAISSANCE stores buy previously-owned computers from a variety of sources. We then offer them to home users, small business and schools, who are looking for the most computing power for their dollar. Not all computer users need, want, or can afford brand new computer equipment. COMPUTER RENAISSANCE provides a way to meet these users' computing needs while spending less money than new. This dynamically growing concept is in the able hands of an established and proven franchise company.

# Franchised Units:	211 Units
# Company-Owned Units:	1 Units
Total # Units:	212 Units
Founded In:	1988
1st Franchised In:	1993
Average Total Investment:	180-225K
Franchise Fee:	20K
On-Going Royalty:	3%
Advertising Fee:	0.625%
Financial Assistance:	Yes(I)
Site Selection Assistance:	Yes
Lease Negotiation Assistance:	Yes
Contract Terms (Init./Renew):	10/10
Initial Training Provided:	2 Weeks at Minneapolis, MN; 2 Days in Store.

Representations Regarding Earnings Capability

An earnings claim entitled "Unaudited Statement of Average Annual Sales and Gross Profit" immediately follows this Offering Circular as *Exhibit A*. *Exhibit A* displays the average of 160 of the 164 franchised Computer Renaissance® Stores which had been in operation at least 1 year as of December 26, 1998. The figures shown are the actual unaudited results that these stores achieved during the 12 month period ended December 26, 1998.

THE GROSS SALES AND GROSS PROFITS STATED ON EXHIBIT A ARE AVERAGES GROW BIZ COMPILED OF SPECIFIC FRANCHISES. YOU SHOULD NOT CONSIDER THIS INFORMATION AS THE ACTUAL OR POTENTIAL GROSS SALES OR GROSS PROFITS THAT ANY OTHER FRANCHISE

STORE WILL REALIZE. GROW BIZ DOES NOT REPRESENT THAT ANY FRANCHISEE CAN EXPECT TO ATTAIN THESE GROSS SALES OR GROSS PROFITS. YOUR INDIVIDUAL FINANCIAL RESULTS ARE LIKELY TO DIFFER FROM THE INFORMATION STATED IN EXHIBIT A.

Grow Biz will, on reasonable demand, provide to prospective franchisees the supporting data for all information illustrated in *Exhibit A*. Grow Biz does not otherwise furnish to prospective franchisees any oral or written information concerning the actual or potential sales, costs, income or profits of a Computer Renaissance® Store. Actual results vary from unit to unit and Grow Biz cannot estimate the results of any particular franchise.

Exhibit A

Computer Renaissance® Unaudited Statement of Average Annual Sales and Gross Profit

The following statement of average sales and gross profits includes average gross sales and gross

profits during the 12 month period ended December 26, 1998 (Grow Biz' fiscal year) as reported by franchised Computer Renaissance® Stores that commenced operations in each of the years 1986 through 1997. This statement includes information from only those Computer Renaissance® Stores that had been in operation for the 12 month period ended December 26, 1998. No other Computer Renaissance® Stores are included in this statement due to insufficient history of operations (not in operation for the 12 month period ended December 26, 1998). There were 164 franchised Computer Renaissance® Stores which had been in operation for the 12 month period ended December 26, 1998. Only 160 out of the 164 Stores are reflected in the average, however, because Grow Biz did not have complete information on the remaining 4 Stores.

Statement of average gross sales and gross profits of the 160 of the 164 franchised Computer Renaissance® Stores for the fiscal year 1998:

Year Opened	#Stores Reported	Stores Attaining or Exceeding Average Gross Sales	Average Gross Sales[1]	Average Gross Profit[2]	Average Gross Profit Percentage[3]	Range of Sales
1997	68	33	$733,702	$288,629	39%	111,126–1,844,121
1996	57	30	884,790	353,857	40%	278,984–1,718,999
1995	24	12	831,276	338,794	41%	315,354–1,674,021
1994 & Prior	11	4	968,746	400,450	41%	251,717–2,568,268
Total	160	79	818,323	326,079	40%	

1. "Gross Sales" means all revenues the franchisee receives from the sale of goods and services, whether for cash or by check, credit card or trade, in connection with the Store, less sales tax and customer refunds and returns.

2. The Average Gross Profit equals Gross Sales less Cost of Goods Sold. Average Gross Profit does not reflect any expenses related to the

operation of a Computer Renaissance® Store other than the Cost of Goods Sold.

3. This figure represents Average Gross Profit as a percentage of Average Gross Sales.

The Statement of Sales Ranges for the 160 of the 164 franchised Computer Renaissance® Stores open at December 26, 1998 by quartile for the 12 month period ended December 26, 1998 are as follows:

Quartile[a]	1998 Gross Sales Range:
1st	$1,018,498–2,568,268
2nd	$798,731–1,018,466
3rd	$577,507–798,582
4th	$111,126–571,461

a. "Quartile" referees to that portion of the total number of Stores open that represents 25%.

For example, the first Quartile identifies those Stores which were in the top 25% of all Stores in Gross Sales.

These results relate to specific Computer Renaissance® Stores located in the United States and Canada and should not be considered as the actual or probable results that any franchisee will realize. Your individual financial results will likely differ from these results.

CONROY'S/1-800-FLOWERS
1600 Stewart Ave.
Westbury, NY 11590

Tel: (800) 557-4770 (516) 237-6000
Fax: (516) 237-6097
E-Mail: Aguinn@1800flowers.com
Internet Address: www.1800flowers.com
Contact: Mr. Brian McGee, Vice President of Expansion

# Franchised Units:	94 Units
# Company-Owned Units:	<u>24</u> Units
Total # Units:	116 Units

Summary of Operations

Conroy's provides you with the following summary of operations for the calendar year 1997 for Conroy's Flowers and Conroy's 1-800-Flowers Franchised Units in California and New Mexico operated by Conroy's franchisees who owned one Franchised Unit (a "Single Unit Operator") and Conroy's franchisees who owned more than one Franchised Unit (a "Multiple Unit Operator"). This summary does not represent a projection of the future sales and income of a franchisee, but, rather, provides a historical reference of past performance of the then-existing Conroy's, Conroy's Flowers and Conroy's 1-800-Flowers franchisees taken as a whole during a particular calendar year. The information was compiled from the results of operations for Conroy's Flowers and Conroy's 1-800-Flowers Franchised Units which had been open for an entire calendar year ended December 31, 1997, however, the Conroy's 1-800-Flowers Franchised Units, which are included in the compilation, operated as Conroy's Flowers units for the majority of calendar year 1997. Conroy's does

not include all Conroy's Flowers and Conroy's 1-800-Flowers units operating in 1997 in this summary since some stores were terminated, sold, re-acquired by Conroy's affiliate, Acquisition, or otherwise not in operation for the entire calendar year. Conroy's was not an affiliate of 1-800-Flowers, Inc. or Flowers before October 10, 1994. In May, 1993, 1-800-Flowers, Inc., formerly known as Teleway, Inc., assumed responsibility for the management of Conroy's and on October 10, 1994, Conroy's, Inc. was acquired by Bloomnet, Inc., a New York corporation which was liquidated and had its assets distributed to Retail in June, 1995, through the purchase of Amalgamated Consolidated Enterprises, Inc., a Nevada corporation, the parent corporation of Conroy's, Inc.

The source of this information is the unaudited statements of receipts and disbursements prepared from the detailed information provided to Conroy's by its current Conroy's, Conroy's Flowers and Conroy's 1-800-Flowers franchisees. No individual Conroy's, Conroy's Flowers or Conroy's 1-800-

Flowers Franchised Unit generated all the high or all the low cost percentages. The summary does not include any costs associated with depreciation, amortization, rent for the Franchised Unit or debt service, which are not costs generally reflected as a percentage of sales, but rather vary with the amount of a franchisee's investment and with characteristics of each Franchised Location. These costs are dependent on the amount of capital invested in the Franchised Unit, store size, landlord improvements, and real estate market conditions which vary greatly from area to area and landlord to landlord. Substantiation of the data used in preparing this summary of operations is made available to you on reasonable request.

Caution: Some outlets have sold or earned these amounts. There is no assurance you'll do as well. If you rely upon our figures, you must accept the risk of not doing so well.

Description	Single Unit Operators	Multiple Unit Operators	Total
Revenues: Units with sales			
> $1,000,000	3	1	4
> 850,000 < 1,000,000	3	3	6
> 700,000 < 850,000	8	2	10
> 550,000 < 700,000	15	10	25
> 400,000 < 550,000	2	4	6
< 400,000	1	5	6
	32	25	57

Cost Percentages (% based on unit sales)	Single Unit Operators		Multiple Unit Operators	
	High %	Low %	High %	Low %
Cost of Sales (1)	52.40%	30.50%	47.80%	34.40%
Labor (2)	28.60%	16.20%	33.90%	15.90%
Other Operating Expenses (3)	13.30%	6.40%	12.10%	7.70%
Gen. & Admin. Expenses (4)	21.40%	8.90%	19.30%	10.90%

See Notes 1–4 at the end of item 19 which are an integral part of this summary.

800-Flowers "Wire-In" Orders

As a franchisee of Conroy's, you are a member of the Network and are eligible to receive between 5% and 80% of the total 800-Flowers "Wire-In" floral orders sent by 800-Flowers for fulfillment to the zip code in which your Franchised Unit is located. The percentage of these orders which you are eligible to receive will be established by 800-Flowers and Conroy's at the time you execute your Franchise Agreement for your Franchised Unit and will be fixed for the 2 year period immediately following the opening of your Franchised Unit for business. 800-Flowers and Conroy's reserve the right to modify the percentage of the floral orders which will be sent to the Franchised Unit after the expiration of the 2 year period.

800-Flowers and Conroy's give you no assurance regarding the actual number or dollar amount of the 800-Flowers "Wire-In" orders which 800-Flowers will send to the Franchised Unit for fulfillment in the zip code in which the Franchised Unit is located since the actual number and dollar amount of 800-Flowers "Wire-In" orders sent to the Franchised Unit will vary and will depend upon many factors such as the number of 1-800-Flowers units in the trade area and in the zip code in which the Franchised Unit is located which also deliver to and within the zip code in which the Franchised Unit is located, the capacity of the Franchised Unit to fulfill the orders, the requirements of the 1-800-Flowers system to maintain satisfactory relationships with unaffiliated florists, general economic conditions, the extent, duration and effectiveness of marketing and promotional efforts conducted by 800-Flowers, seasonal fluctuations in the purchase of flowers and related products by consumers, wholesale and retail prices of flowers and related products offered through 800-Flowers, variations in disposable income and population, competition in the retail flower business, consumer preferences, and the like. 800-Flowers and Conroy's give you no assurance or guarantee regarding the profit, if any, or other benefits, if any, which you may receive or experience from 800-Flowers "Wire-In" orders sent to the Franchised Unit.

You must comply with all standard policies, procedures and requirements of Conroy's and 800-Flowers to receive 800-Flowers "Wire-In" floral orders for fulfillment in the zip code in which the Franchised unit is located. Franchisees with multiple Franchised Units may not use a centralized telephone system in the Franchised Units without the prior written consent of Conroy's. Inter-store and intra-store transmissions of "Wire-In-Sales" and "Wire-Out-Sales" at, from or to a Franchised Unit are prohibited without the prior written consent of Conroy's.

Notes:

1. Cost of Sales include flowers, plants, vases, ribbon and other supplies, and wire service costs (FTD, AFS, etc.). These costs fluctuate depending upon where and from whom items are purchased, delivery costs, inventory management, product pricing strategies, etc.

2. Labor includes all personnel wages (not including draws or salaries paid to the franchisee which are not reflected in this summary), payroll taxes (FICA, federal and state unemployment, etc.), outside labor and delivery expenses. These expenses fluctuate based on the number of employees, wage levels, level of involvement in daily operations of the franchisee, etc.

3. Other Operating Expenses include the following items:

    a. *Marketing Fees* — The fees paid to the Marketing Fund as described in Item 6.

    b. *Local Advertising and Promotion* — Additional advertising for a particular Franchised Unit which a franchisee may consider necessary, including Yellow Pages advertising.

    c. *Auto Expenses* — Expenses incurred in maintaining and servicing the van used for deliveries, including gasoline, oil, tires, tune-ups, etc.

    d. *Credit Card Expenses* — Expenses incurred for credit card charges, including the fee charged by the bank for the processing of credit cards.

    e. *Continuing Franchise Fees* — The continuing franchise fees paid to Conroy's as described in Item 6.

    f. *Shop Expenses* — Expenses incurred as the make-up and processing of flowers, including such items as processing materials, etc.

EXPENSES FOR RENT, DEBT SERVICE, AMORTIZATION AND DEPRECIATION ARE NOT INCLUDED IN THIS SUMMARY.

4. General & Administrative Expenses include the following items:

    a. *Utilities* — Electricity and gas for the Franchised Unit. This item may fluctuate based upon whether the store has air conditioning, the size and requirements of the cooler and the amount of signage using lighting.

    b. *Telephone* — The cost of telephone calls. This cost will fluctuate depending upon the volume of the business and the amount of wire sales at the Franchised Unit.

c. *Maintenance* — Maintenance of cooling systems, cleaning of the Franchised Unit, charges from the landlord for common area maintenance of the shopping center in which the Franchised Unit is located, and other miscellaneous maintenance items.

d. *Office Expenses* — Office expenses, including the cost of paper, forms, books and other office materials.

e. *Bank Charges* — Charges from the bank for the opening and use of a merchant's account which may vary from bank to bank and branch to branch.

f. *Insurance Expenses* — The cost of property, fire and all risk coverage on the improvements, general liability insurance on the business, worker's compensation costs as set by state law, and other insurance which is required pursuant to a lease. These costs fluctuate with the sales of the Franchised Unit, number of employees and wage levels and the replacement cost of the facilities.

g. *Professional Fees* — The cost of any outside legal and accounting or other professional services.

h. *Dues & Subscriptions* — Dues due to wire services and magazines which are used in the Franchised Unit.

i. *Cash Over/Short* — The amount which may vary from the cash register record of daily activity and a physical count of receipts caused by inaccurate handling or ringing up of the day's transactions.

j. *Bad Debts* — House account charges which are not collectable, plus Master Charge, Visa, American Express card charges which are returned unpaid by the customer regarding disputed items which are not resolved with the customer.

k. *Collection Expenses* — Expenses incurred in the collection of bad debts.

1. *General Taxes & Licenses* — Business taxes and licenses which are levied on the business by local, city, county and state governmental agencies.

m. *Disposal Services* — The cost of trash collection which may or may not be included in the common area maintenance provided by the landlord.

n. Protection Services — Due to the high volume of sales at certain holidays, some franchisees elect to have guard services on premises to protect the safety of the employees and the customers. Additionally, this includes costs of alarm services which may be hooked into the Franchised Unit.

o. *Contributions* — Contributions which a franchisee may make to local or national non-profit organizations.

p. *Entertainment & Travel* — Expenses incurred for business meals, entertainment and travel.

q. *Property Taxes* — The property taxes assessed by the county and city upon the Franchised Unit for personal property and/or real estate property and upon the franchisee's share of the landlord's property taxes as assessed pursuant to the lease for the Franchised Location.

r. *Miscellaneous Expenses* — Other expenses which may be incurred during the year which do not fit in the above classifications.

YOUR FINANCIAL RESULTS ARE LIKELY TO DIFFER FROM THIS SUMMARY OF OPERATIONS. CONROY'S RECOMMENDS THAT PROSPECTIVE FRANCHISEES CONTACT QUALIFIED PROFESSIONALS SUCH AS BANKERS, ACCOUNTANTS, ATTORNEYS AND BUSINESS CONSULTANTS REGARDING WHETHER OR NOT A FRANCHISE WILL BE PROFITABLE.

Gifts, Collectibles & Home Decor

COUNTRY CLUTTER

3333 Vaca Valley Pkwy., # 900
Vacaville, CA 95688
Tel: (800) 425-8883 (707) 451-6890
Fax: (707) 451-0410
E-Mail: ctryvision@aol.com
Internet Address: www.countryclutter.com
Contact: Mr. Terry Odneal, Vice President Franchise Dev.

Description: A charming country store for gifts, collectibles and home decor. A unique business that offers old fashioned quality, selection and customer service. A complete franchise program professionally designed, computerized and planned to sell a perfected blend of country merchandise made by primarily American manufacturers and crafters. Rich arrangements and displays of textures, colors and aromas make shopping at COUNTRY CLUTTER a true sensory delight.

# Franchised Units:	50 Units
# Company-Owned Units:	0 Units
Total # Units:	50 Units
Founded In:	1991
1st Franchised In:	1992
Average Total Investment:	155-307K
Franchise Fee:	25K
On-Going Royalty:	5.5%
Advertising Fee:	1%
Financial Assistance:	No
Site Selection Assistance:	Yes
Lease Negotiation Assistance:	Yes
Contract Terms (Init./Renew):	5/5

Initial Training Provided: 3-5 Days Headquarters; 3-5 Days On-Site; 40 Hours Home Training With Computer.

United States COUNTRY CLUTTER Stores in business over one year at the end of calendar year 1998 averaged $680,584 in gross sales for that year. The gross sales of 29 franchises and no company-owned operations are included in this average. The stores included represent 70% of all COUNTRY CLUTTER Stores in business as of December 31, 1998. The sales of 9 stores in operation less than one year were excluded from this average. Also excluded were sales for 2 stores that left the system in the first quarter of 1999.

Of those included, 20 stores (69%) attained or exceeded the $680,584 average gross sales for 1998, and of these, 5 stores (17%) exceeded $800,000 in gross sales and 3 stores (10%) exceeded $1,000,000 in gross sales. Nine of the stores included (31%) did not attain the gross sales average.

Of the 29 stores included, 19 had been operating 1 to 2 years at the end of 1998 and 10 stores had been operating for 3 years or longer at the end of 1998.

The gross sales amounts included in the 1998 average were compiled from franchisee royalty reports and were not audited or independently verified by COUNTRY VISIONS. Substantiation of the data used in preparing this earnings report will be available to you on reasonable request.

THE FOREGOING DATA IS NOT NECESSARILY INDICATIVE OF THE SALES LEVELS THAT MAY BE ACHIEVED BY A FRANCHISEE IN ANY MARKET AREA. YOUR RESULTS ARE LIKELY TO DIFFER FROM THE RESULTS REPORTED ABOVE. COUNTRY VISIONS DOES NOT REPRESENT THAT YOU WILL ACHIEVE THESE OR COMPARABLE SALES LEVELS.

Many factors can affect your sales, including the variety and amount of merchandise you carry, the quality of customer service you provide, your sales and marketing efforts, foot traffic at your location, whether the location is a tourist or "destination" shopping location, local advertising costs, number and financial resources of competitors, general economic conditions, how closely you follow our

System and your business acumen. You should bear in mind that these figures are of gross sales only, not profit. They do not account for expenses like royalties, advertising, salaries, inventory costs, rent, supplies, taxes, utilities, maintenance and repairs and oilier operating expenses, which may vary.

Except as stated above, COUNTRY VISIONS does not furnish or authorize its salespersons to furnish any oral or written information concerning the actual or potential sales, costs, income or profits of a Franchised Business. Actual results may vary from unit to unit, and COUNTRY VISIONS cannot estimate the results of any particular franchise.

GNC LiveWell.

GENERAL NUTRITION CENTERS
300 Sixth Ave.
Pittsburgh, PA 15222
Tel: (800) 766-7099 (412) 288-2043
Fax: (412) 288-2033
E-Mail: franchising@gnc-hq.com
Internet Address: www.gncfranchising.com
Contact: Director of Franchising,

Description: GNC is the leading national specialty retailer of vitamins, minerals, herbs and sports nutrition supplements and is uniquely positioned to capitalize on the accelerating self-care trend. As the leading provider of products and information for personal health enhancement, the company holds the largest specialty-retail share of the nutritional supplement market. GNC was ranked

America's #1 retail franchise in 1998/1999 by Entrepreneur International.

# Franchised Units:	1563 Units
# Company-Owned Units:	<u>2825</u> Units
Total # Units:	4388 Units
Founded In:	1935
1st Franchised In:	1988
Average Total Investment:	118.2-173.0K
Franchise Fee:	32.5K
On-Going Royalty:	6%
Advertising Fee:	3%
Financial Assistance:	Yes(D)
Site Selection Assistance:	Yes
Lease Negotiation Assistance:	Yes
Contract Terms (Init./Renew):	10/5

Initial Training Provided: 1 Wk. On-Site in Local Corporate Store; 1 Wk. in Pittsburgh, PA; 1 Wk. opening assistance.

We furnish the following information about the actual or potential sales, costs, income, or profits of the General Nutrition Center stores.

We base the financial information used in preparing the following statement of Average Store Sales and Earnings on financial results and the average sales numbers that appear in our Parent Company's Annual Report. We base our material assumptions on the operations of company-owned GNC Stores open for more than 1 year. The Parent Company and its predecessors have been operating retail stores for over 60 years.

The method we use to calculate the weighted average of General Nutrition Center company-owned stores is as follows: The sum of the number of stores operating each period divided by the Company's 13 financial periods provides the "weighted

average" number of GNC Company-owned stores open for the year. We divide the actual Parent Company operating results by the weighted average number of stores to develop the Average Store Sales and Earnings.

The numbers related to the 2,496 Company-owned domestic stores are as of our fiscal year-end, February 6, 1999, and indicate the number of retail locations open at that specific point in time. Except as explained in Notes 4 through 15 [on the following pages] on pages 84, 85 and 86 [refers to GNC UFOC] the GNC franchised stores are not materially different than Company-owned GNC stores.

Your expenses will vary from the Company-owned domestic stores as we describe below and in notes 4 through 15 in this Item:

  🙠 Royalty — Company-owned stores do not pay a royalty.

  🙠 Advertising — We may require that you spend up to 5% or more of gross sales on advertising and may spend more depending on your needs.

  🙠 Accounting Services — The Parent Company's internal accounting and payroll services are performed by its in-house financial staff. You will contract with us to receive certain of these financial services.

  🙠 Insurance — The Parent Company is self-insured with casualty and liability insurance. You will have to purchase casualty and liability insurance through an independent insurance company.

  🙠 Debt Service — You may decide to finance a portion of the initial costs. You will pay principal and interest on the amount you finance.

General Nutrition Corporation Statement of Actual Sales & Pretax Earnings
Average Store Sales & Earnings — Company Stores for the Period January 31, 1998 to February 6, 1999

	Amount	Percentage of Sales
Sales	$406,673	100.0%
Cost of Goods Sold	164,867	40.5%
Gross Margin	241,806	59.5%
Transportation & Distribution	10,440	2.6%
Adjusted Net Margin	231,366	56.9%
Salaries & Benefits	61,371	15.1%
Occupancy	54,886	13.5%
Operating Expenses	7,052	1.7%
Average Corporate Store Profit	$108,057	26.6%

Footnotes:

1. The Statement presents the actual, rounded unaudited operating results for sales and selected costs of the 2,413 of the total 2,496 GNC Stores owned and operated by our affiliate during the entire period January 31, 1998 through February 6, 1999. The 83 military base stores were not included in this breakdown. Because some of these Stores may have been open only part of the year, the average shown as a weighted average based on the number of months a Store was open during the period. Of the 2,413 stores whose results are included in the Statement, 375 stores did not have a full 12 months' results.

2. This Statement reflects the results of GNC company-owned Stores only. No results of franchised Stores are included in this Statement. No results of military base Stores are included in this statement.

3. This Statement was prepared from information compiled in the ordinary course of business by GNC employees, and is unaudited.

4. The sales and adjusted net margin figures shown for GNC company-owned Stores may not be representative of the net margins of franchisee-owned Stores due to material differences in: (i) the size and location of GNC company-owned Stores; (ii) retail prices at which GNC company-owned Stores offer and sell their products (which may include higher retail prices); and/or (iii) higher or lower retail prices or other discount programs. Our affiliate, General Nutrition Distribution Company ("GNC") sells GNC branded products and other products to your Store and other franchised and corporate General Nutrition Center Stores. GNC derives revenue from the sale of products whose prices may affect the gross margin percentage for the Store. (GNC company-owned Stores typically operate in locations within larger malls and shopping centers).

5. Other than as set forth in footnotes 4 and 11, we are not aware of any other material differences between the operations of the Stores

being franchised by us and the GNC company-owned Stores whose results are reflected in this Statement.

6. The averages reflected in this Statement are weighted averages.

7. The expense category "Salaries & Benefits" includes expenses such as salaries, wages, bonuses, and incentives for all store employees, including the store manager, as well as payroll taxes. Not included in this category are expenses such as health insurance which franchisees are likely to incur.

8. The expense category "Occupancy" includes expenses such as rent, utilities, mall association charges, common area maintenance, and personal property taxes. These costs are heavily influenced by the size and geographical location of a Store and, therefore may vary significantly among Stores. Not included in this category are expenses such as depreciation, which franchisees are also likely to incur.

9. The expense category "Operating Expenses" includes expenses such as telephone, maintenance and repair, extermination and cleaning services, supplies, banking and credit card expenses and postage. Not included in this category are expenses such as amortization, travel and entertainment, licenses and permits, which franchisees are also likely to incur.

10. The average GNC company-owned Store whose results are reflected in this Statement has been open approximately 14 years. In our experience, corporate Stores require at least 2 years of operation to reach their normal profit percentage.

11. This Statement does not reflect all expenses which a franchisee should expect to incur. Additional expenses, which are likely to be significant, will vary widely among franchisees, and may include the following: (i) royalty fees; (ii) advertising contributions; (iii) insurance; (iv) property taxes; (v) accounting, legal and other professional fees; (vi) depreciation/

amortization; (vii) interest or finance charges and/or repayment of principal on any borrowed funds. In addition, some of the expenses reflected in this Statement may be influenced by our economies of scale and therefore may be lower than a franchisee's expenses for the same categories. We strongly encourage you to consult with your financial advisors in reviewing this Statement and, in particular, in estimating the categories and amount of additional expenses which you will incur when you establish and operate your Store.

12. We will provide you with substantiation for the data set forth in this Statement upon reasonable request.

13. The information set forth in this Statement reflects the aggregate results of sales and selected costs of individual GNC company-owned Stores. You should not consider these results to be the actual or probable sales or cost results that any franchisee will actually realize. We do not represent that any franchisee can expect to obtain the results set forth in this Statement. As indicated in footnote 10, a new franchisee's individual financial results are likely to be lower.

14. Actual results vary from franchise to franchise and depend on a variety of internal and external factors, some of which neither we nor you can estimate, including competition, taxes, differences in management skills and experience levels, the availability of financing, general economic climate, demographics, the Store's location, size and type, discounting and changing consumer preferences. Therefore, we cannot estimate the results of a particular franchise. We recommend that you make your own independent investigation to determine whether or not the franchise may be profitable, and consult with an attorney and other advisors before executing any agreement.

15. Except for the information in this Item 19, we do not furnish or authorize our salespersons to furnish any oral or written information

about the actual, average, projected, or forecasted sales, costs, margins, income, or profits (the "earnings capability") of a Store. We specifically instruct our sales personnel, agents and employees that they are not permitted to make any claims or statements concerning a specific franchisee's earnings capability or chances for success, and we will not be bound by allegations of any unauthorized representations as to earnings capability or chances for success.

HobbyTown USA

HOBBYTOWN USA
6301 S. 58th St.
Lincoln, NE 68516
Tel: (800) 858-7370 (402) 434-5050
Fax: (402) 434-5055
E-Mail: sales@hobbytown.com
Internet Address: www.hobbytown.com
Contact: Mr. Ray Burney, Franchise Sales Manager

Description: HOBBYTOWN USA stores are full-line hobby stores, featuring hobby trains, models, radio-controlled vehicles, games, collectible cards, diecast toys, gifts, accessories and much more! The HOBBYTOWN USA system provides store owners with a comprehensive package of systems and services to be competitive in the hobby and entertainment industries.

# Franchised Units:	128 Units
# Company-Owned Units:	1 Units
Total # Units:	129 Units
Founded In:	1969
1st Franchised In:	1986
Average Total Investment:	120-250K
Franchise Fee:	19.5K
On-Going Royalty:	2.5%
Advertising Fee:	N/A
Financial Assistance:	Yes(I)
Site Selection Assistance:	Yes
Lease Negotiation Assistance:	Yes
Contract Terms (Init./Renew):	10/10
Initial Training Provided: 1 Week Home Office; 2 Weeks On-Site.	

This information is based on the last full calendar year for 80 HobbyTown USA® franchises that were open for the entire twelve month period. A new Franchisee's individual financial results are likely to differ from these results. The Company makes no representations, guarantees, or warranties, express or implied, with respect to actual volume. Substantiation of the data used preparing the data listed on the exhibit will be made available to you upon request. See Exhibit F, 1997 Sales Analysis and 1997 Actual Operating Results.

Exhibit F
HobbyTown USA ® 1997 Sales Analysis

Inventory Level	Avg. Inv.	Avg. Sales	Avg. Turns
Under 75,000	58,281	283,924	4.87
75,000 to 100,000	87,273	358,397	4.11
100,000 to 125,000	115,006	442,114	3.84
125,000 to 150,000	138,815	573,955	4.13
Over 150,000	185,700	713,457	3.84
Overall Average	117,015	474,369	4.05

THE ABOVE INFORMATION IS BASED ON ACTUAL SALES VOLUME FOR CALENDAR YEAR 1997.

HOBBY TOWN UNLIMITED, INC. MAKES NO REPRESENTATIONS GUARANTIES OR WARRANTIES, EXPRESS OR IMPLIED, WITH RESPECT TO ACTUAL VOLUME. ACTUAL RESULTS MAY VARY SUBSTANTIALLY.

HobbyTown USA®
1997 Actual Operating Results

	1997		Top 25%	
	Average	%	Average	%
Sales:	517,208	100.00%	697,420	100.0%
Cost of Goods Sold:	330,357	63.87%	436,417	62.6%
Gross Profit:	186,851	36.13%	261,003	37.4%
Operating Expenses:				
Advertising	9,827	1.90%	10,097	1.4%
Alarm	531	0.10%	637	0.1%
Auto	1,330	0.26%	1,629	0.2%
Bank Service Charges	2,027	0.39%	2,155	0.3%
Credit Card Charges	4,050	0.78%	5,271	0.8%
Insurance	3,160	0.61%	3,704	0.5%
Miscellaneous	1,275	0.23%	1,658	0.2%
Payroll	45,046	8.71%	56,177	8.1%
Postage	682	0.13%	656	0.1%
Professional Fees	1,235	0.24%	1,313	0.2%
Rent	41,884	8.10%	41,415	5.9%
Repairs & Maintenance	1,002	0.19%	1,186	0.2%
Royalty Fee	14,582	2.82%	18,057	2.6%
Supplies	3,913	0.76%	5,376	0.8%
Taxes & Licenses	1,465	0.28%	1,348	0.2%
Telephone	2,555	0.49%	2,840	0.4%
Travel	868	0.17%	1,575	0.2%
Uniform	194	0.04%	213	0.0%
Utilities	4,564	0.88%	4,324	0.6%
Total Operating Expenses	140,190	27.11%	159,629	22.9%
Operating Income	46,661	9.02%	101,374	14.5%
Other Income and Expenses				
Asset Retirement	154	0.03%	15	0.0%

	1997		Top 25%	
	Average	%	Average	%
Cash (Over) & Short	(240)	-0.05%	(681)	-0.1%
Interest Income	(113)	-0.02%	(158)	0.0%
Obsolete Inventory	545	0.11%	1,106	0.2%
Other Income & Expenses	(110)	-0.06%	(299)	-0.1%
Total Other Inc. and Exp.	237	0.05%	(18)	0.0%
Net Income (Loss)	46,424	8.98%	101,391	14.5%
Average Inventory	131,148		150,165	
Inventory Turns	3.94		4.64	

*EXCLUDES INTEREST EXP., OWNERS PAY, AND DEPR & AMORT

THIS INFORMATION IS BASED ON CALENDAR YEAR 1997 RESULTS FOR 80 HOBBYTOWN USA® FRANCHISES THAT WERE OPEN FOR THE ENTIRE YEAR.

HOBBY TOWN UNLIMITED, INC. MAKES NO REPRESENTATIONS, GUARANTEES OR WARRANTIES, EXPRESS OR IMPLIED, WITH RESPECT TO POTENTIAL OPERATING RESULTS. ACTUAL RESULTS MAY VARY SUBSTANTIALLY.

LITTLE PROFESSOR BOOK CENTERS

405 Little Lake Dr., # C
Ann Arbor, MI 48103
Tel: (800) 899-6232 (734) 994-1212
Fax: (734) 994-9009
E-Mail: lpbchome@aol.com
Internet Address: www.littleprofessor.com
Contact: Ms. Christi M. Shaw, Franchise Development Manager

Description: Full-line, full-service, community-oriented general bookstore.

# Franchised Units:	65 Units
# Company-Owned Units:	0 Units
Total # Units:	65 Units
Founded In:	1964
1st Franchised In:	1969
Average Total Investment:	300K-1.5MM
Franchise Fee:	37K
On-Going Royalty:	3%
Advertising Fee:	0.5%
Financial Assistance:	Yes(I)
Site Selection Assistance:	Yes
Lease Negotiation Assistance:	Yes
Contract Terms (Init./Renew):	10/10

Initial Training Provided: 1 Week
Ann Arbor, MI (Home Office), 1-2 Weeks On-Site, LPBC Coventions Once a Year

General Explanation

To help our franchise candidates evaluate our franchise opportunity, we are providing certain information for the 1998 calendar year (the most recent data available to us) about the sales per square foot of selling space at Little Professor Stores, based on information that our franchise owners reported to us. We provide this information for 5 categories of franchised Little Professor Stores:

1. All Little Professor Stores that were open for the entire 1998 calendar year (we exclude Stores which opened during 1998 or after from the survey), or a total of 40 reporting stores;

2. Mature Little Professor Stores that opened before December 31, 1994, or a total of 31 reporting Stores;

3. Mature Little Professor Stores that opened before December 31, 1995, or a total of 34 reporting Stores; and

4. Mature Little Professor Stores that opened before December 31, 1994 that are between 2,100 and 14,000 selling square feet (the current size range available for the past several years), or a total of 22 reporting Stores

5. Mature Little Professor Stores that opened before December 31, 1995 that are between 2,100 and 14,000 selling square feet (the current size range available for the past several years), or a total of 22 reporting Stores.

We have also prepared two statements ("Statements") reflecting certain operating statement information that certain Little Professor Stores reported for 1998. The first Statement in Table A reflects the results that Little Professor Stores (including both Little Professor Book Center and Little Professor Book Co.) that had been in business since before December 31, 1997 reported. The second Statement in Table B reflect results that little Professor Book Co. Stores opened before December 31, 1997 reported. You should review the Statements with all of the information in Item 19 and the rest of this offering circular. They are intended to help you and your professional advisors evaluate the types and levels of expenses that Little Professor Stores have recently experienced. The Statements do not reflect the actual past experience of any single Little Professor Store nor predict the future performance of any particular Little Professor Store or group of Stores. The actual results experienced by a particular Little Professor Store can and will differ from the statistical results shown in the Statements.

The actual performance of a particular franchised Store will depend on a number of factors specific to local market conditions and the individual franchise owner, including the following factors: amount of time in business; location of the Store; the nature and extent of competition in the local market; level of inventory; sales mix between periodicals and books; lease terms and costs of improvements; financing costs; local property taxes; labor conditions and costs in the local market area; skill of Store personnel; and the franchise owner's management skills and personal decisions and efforts.

Statement or 1998 Calendar Year Sales Per Square Foot of Selling Space and Value of Each Customer Transaction

Listed below are the average and median sales per square foot of selling area that our franchise owners reported during the 1997 calendar year. All figures are net of sales tax.

	Sales Per Square Foot of Selling Space	
	Average	Median
All Little Professor Stores (40 reporting) open for the entire 1998 calendar year	$222	$201
Mature Little Professor Stores (31 reporting) open before December 31, 1994	$236	$230
Mature Little Professor Stores (34 reporting) open before December 31, 1995	$229	$218
All Little Professor Stores (22 reporting) open before December 31, 1994 that are between 2,500 and 14,000 selling square feet the current size range now being offered	$241	$233
All Little Professor Stores (25 reporting) open before December 31, 1995 that are between 2,500 and 14,000 selling square feet, the current size range now being offered	$231	$221
Value of average customer transaction for all Little Professor Stores	$14.86	

Historical Operating Statements

The following Statements show the net sales and expense items that certain Little Professor Stores reported for 1998. The figures given are information that Little Professor Stores reported as of March 31, 1999 in response to a survey of all our franchise owners. We requested our franchise owners to provide all information according to generally accepted accounting practices (GAAP). We have not independently audited the information supplied by our franchise owners that was used in preparing the Statements. **Since this data has been provided to us by Little Professor franchisees and we have not audited the data, the data may contain errors that we are not aware of. You should use this information as only a part of your decision making process and should take additional steps to confirm the accuracy of the data contained here. In all events, the Statements are not a prediction of the results that you or any Little Professor Store is likely to achieve.**

In the following Statements, expenses that typically fluctuate as sales increase or decrease (for example, bags, credit card expense, payroll) are marked with an asterisk (*). Fixed expenses, including rent and electricity, depend upon the specific site under consideration and will vary by region of the country, type of market and site.

Table A represents the actual averages performance for all reporting Little Professor Stores opened before December 31, 1997. In preparing Table A, therefore, we included results reported by both Little Professor Book Center Stores, including

a number of Stores less than 2,100 square feet in size, and the Little Professor Book Co. Stores described in Table B. Of the 65 Stores open since December 31, 1997, 40 Stores, had responded to the survey as of March 31, 1999, and we used the results of all those Stores in preparing Table A. Table A presents both the average dollar figures reported in each category shown and the average of each expense category as a percentage of average net sales. In addition to these averages, Table A provides certain information about Little Professor Stores at the 25th percentile, median (50th) percentile and the 75th percentile as ranked for the percentage of each Store's category of expense to each Stores net sales (the percentage figures given do not reflect the performance of any single Store across all categories). You should note that, because each line item reported in the range of percentages is calculated independently and each percentage represents the results for a different Store as ranked for that line item, the percentages will not "add up."

Table B represents the actual average results reported for 1998 by selected Little Professor Book Co. Stores opened before December 31, 1997. Of the 8 Little Professor Book Co. Stores opened before December 31, 1997, 3 Stores in the category had responded to the survey as of March 31, 1999. We used the results of these 3 Stores in preparing Table B. While Table B presents the average results reported by Little Professor Book Co. Stores, it does not include range percentile information; providing this information would result in disclosing results of individual Stores.

Table A
Statement of 1998 Sales and Selected Expenses Reported
by Little Professor Stores Opened Before December 31, 1997

	Averages		Range of Percentiles		
	Amount	Percentage	25th Percentile	50th Percentile Median	75th Percentile
Net Sales (excluding sales tax)(1)	$761,938	100.0%	100.0%	100.0%	100.0%
Cost of Goods Sold (2)	$480,633	63.08%	66.5%	64.3%	62.4%
Gross Operating Margin (3)	$281,305	36.92%	37.6%	35.7%	33.5%
Expenses:					
Occupancy (4)	$69,033	9.06%	11.2%	8.6%	7.8%

	Averages		Range of Percentiles		
	Amount	Percentage	25th Percentile	50th Percentile Median	75th Percentile
Payroll* (5)	81,777	10.73%	12.1%	9.7%	7.9%
Advertising* (6)	17,495	2.30%	2.3%	1.7%	1.2%
Bank Charges* (7)	7,165	0.94%	1.1%	0.9%	0.7%
Royalties* (8)	16,761	2.20%	3.0%	2.7%	1.6%
Professional Fees (9)	4,633	0.61%	0.7%	0.4%	0.2%
Telephone Expenses	3,577	0.47%	0.6%	0.4%	0.3%
Supplies* (10)	7,763	1.01%	1.3%	0.8%	0.6%
Other Expenses (11)	11,952	1.57%	2.0%	1.4%	1.0%
Other (Income) (11)	(7,859)	1.03%	0.0%	0.7%	1.0%
Total of Listed Expenses	212,297	27.86%	34.3%	25.9%	20.3%
Return to franchise owners (12)	$85,131	11.17%	3.9%	9.7%	13.7%

Table B
Statement of 1998 Sales and Selected Expenses Reported by Selected Little Professor Book Co. Stores Open Before December 31, 1997

	Averages	
	Amount	Percentage
Net Sales (excluding sales tax)(1)	$2,737,779	100.0%
Cost of Goods Sold (2)	$1,734,299	63.35%
Gross Operating Margin (3)	$1,003,479	36.65%
Expenses:		
Occupancy (4)	$207,202	7.57%
Payroll* (5)	331,233	12.10%
Advertising* (6)	104,235	3.80%
Bank Charges* (7)	27,594	1.01%
Royalties* (8)	64,192	2.34%
Professional Fees (9)	22,723	0.83%
Telephone Expenses	11,448	0.42%
Supplies* (10)	37,648	1.38%
Other Expenses (11)	52,715	1.93%
Other (Income) (11)	(17,216)	0.63%
Total of Listed Expenses	841,774	30.75%
Return to franchise owners (12)	$256,087	9.35%

1. Net Sales reflect actual 1998 performance for reporting Stores opened before December 31, 1997. Median net sales dollars for 1998 were $578,041.

2. The overall Cost of Goods percentage reflected in Table A is typical of mature Little Professor Stores. A number of younger Stores (not shown on this table) have a lower cost of goods percentage and a higher gross operating margin because their product mix includes fewer magazines. Generally speaking, books are purchased at a 40% discount off of the list price, magazines at a 20% discount and sideline items like book marks, book plates, greeting cards and audio tapes at a 50% discount. There is no inbound freight charge on most books and other items purchased through the major suppliers. In addition to the actual price of the products the franchise owner will be selling, in-bound freight from certain suppliers and freight costs for returns, other expenses which affect the cost of goods are restocking charges assessed on book returns and the level of discounting which the market requires. While we are a full price retailer, we do recommend certain promotional discounting by our franchise owners, including discounting best sellers to meet market conditions, discounting to schools and certain other business accounts and discounting based on volume purchases by your preferred customers.

3. The Gross Operating Margin is the amount of money available after product cost to pay for the Store's operating expenses.

4. Occupancy Costs include base rent, "triple net" charges (the tenant's share of common area maintenance, taxes and insurance), utilities (including heat, electricity and water), real property taxes paid directly by the tenant and insurance. Insurance includes the annual insurance premium for fire, liability, comprehensive and extended coverages paid to the insurance carrier. All of these occupancy costs can vary significantly by region of the country. We suggest that franchise candidates contact a local insurance agent to obtain an estimate based on the initial investment being contemplated. Base rents vary widely with location, market conditions, length of lease and leasehold improvement allowances negotiated in a final lease. Before signing a lease and Franchise Agreement, a franchise candidate should be able to determine the occupancy expenses applicable to the specific site under consideration.

5. Payroll expense reflects using both full-time and part-time booksellers to staff the Store at appropriate levels. A Little Professor Book Co. Store typically keeps longer hours than a Little Professor Book Center Store and requires a higher level of staffing. Payroll expenses do not include compensation and benefits for a franchise owner who works in the Store, even though most franchise owners manage the Store full time. The prospective franchisee should consider that under the descriptions provided the net income of the Store does not include a separate salary for the franchise owner.

Little Professor Book Center Store. A Little Professor Book Center Store typically might be open from 10 a.m. to 9 p.m. 6 days a week and 5 hours on Sunday, and an additional hour per day for opening and closing activities should be staffed (a total of 78 hours per week). Typical staffing of the Store for these hours (except for the holiday season when staffing needs are

greater) might require 144 person-hours per week (in addition to the franchise owner).

Little Professor Book Co. Store. A Little Professor Book Co. Store typically might be open from 9 a.m. to 11 p.m. 7 days a week. Including an additional hour per day for opening and closing activities would lead to 105 hours per week to be staffed. About 563 person-hours per week (in addition to the franchise owner) might be scheduled outside of the holiday season when staffing needs are greater.

General. The actual average wage rates a franchise owner pays depend on local market conditions and the franchise owner's choices. We recommend that each prospective franchise owner survey retailers in its market area to determine a competitive hourly rate far its staff. Because the staffing needs discussed above assume the franchise owner's full-time management, they do not include any allowance for a non-owner manager.

Payroll Taxes and Benefits. Payroll taxes and benefits include the franchise owner's share of FICA on wages paid to staff (excluding the franchise owner), workers' compensation insurance, unemployment taxes and voluntary benefits (which may vary widely). Little Professor Book Co. Stores typically provide some benefits to full time staff, while Little Professor Book Center Stores typically do not. We recommend that each franchise candidate consult with advisors before making organizational and payroll decisions.

6. While we require the franchise owner to spend at least 2% of the Store's gross revenue on advertising and promoting the Store (including the required contribution to our Advertising Fund), we recommend that, during the first 3 years of operation, the franchise owner spend between 3% and 3.5% of gross sales on advertising and promotion to establish a market presence. This figure includes monies assessed by landlords for promoting the shopping center in which the Store is located, yellow pages, direct mail (including postage), media

purchases and materials to support in-Store promotions.

7. Bank charges include the service fees charged by local banks on checking and savings accounts and the fees charged for processing credit card purchases (Master Card, VISA and American Express).

8. The current annual franchise royalty fee for a new franchise is 3% of sales. The rate here is lower due to the effect of a reduced royalty rate beyond a certain sales threshold, lower rates under some franchise agreements granted earlier and some reduced renewal rates.

9. Professional Fees generally reflect the franchise owner's use of professional counsel for tax purposes, with bookkeeping handled by staff.

10. Supplies include gift wrap, business forms, bags for customers' merchandise and computer paper and diskettes.

11. Other Expenses include donations, dues and subscriptions, cash short/over, travel, entertainment, personal property taxes, transportation and miscellaneous costs. Other income includes display allowances, program participation credits, and volume rebates from various rebate programs.

12. Return to Owners reflects the income available to the franchise owner before certain other expenses. Depreciation and amortization are non-cash expenses and are not included. Interest expense will depend on the amount and terms of financing used by the franchise owner, is not an indication of operating performance and may be avoided by using sufficient owner investment. Taxes on Store income will depend on the Store's taxable income and the particular tax circumstances of the franchise owner. A franchise owner's benefits include salary, draw or other distributions to the franchise owner and any associated payroll taxes and other benefits to, and personal expenses the business pays for, the franchise Owner.

Relevance of Reported Data

Although the sales per square foot of selling space, historical operating statements and other information in this Item are furnished to help franchise candidates and their professional advisors evaluate our franchise opportunity, this information should not be viewed or used as an indication of the actual or likely performance of any particular Little Professor Store, including a Store you operate. Some of the factors that will affect a Store's performance are discussed above.

THE STATEMENTS DO NOT REFLECT ALL EXPENSES OF A LITTLE PROFESSOR STORE OR ALL EXPENSES THAT A FRANCHISE OWNER WOULD INCUR IN OPERATING A FRANCHISED STORE. EXPENSES THAT ARE NOT REFLECTED IN THE STATEMENTS, BUT WHICH A FRANCHISE OWNER WOULD INCUR AND SHOULD BE TAKEN INTO CONSIDERATION, INCLUDE THE FOLLOWING:

A. Depreciation of property and equipment.
B. Amortization of franchise fee and organizational costs.
C. Interest on debt.
D. Income taxes.
E. Discretionary expenses and expenses of attending training away from the Store.
F. Salary or draw and other benefits for the franchise owner, salary and other benefits for a Store manager and any associated payroll taxes.

THESE EXPENSES WILL AFFECT THE NET INCOME AND CASH FLOW OF A FRANCHISED STORE AND MUST BE CONSIDERED AND EVALUATED BY THE PROSPECTIVE FRANCHISE OWNER. THE ACTUAL PERFORMANCE OF A STORE WILL DEPEND ON A NUMBER OF FACTORS SPECIFIC TO THE STORE, INCLUDING THE STORE'S EXPENSES FOR THE ITEMS DESCRIBED ABOVE.

Franchise candidates also should note that the Statements do not include initial expenses associated with opening a Little Professor Store (although these expenses are reflected in the initial investment tables in Item 7) and that gross sales of a new Store during its first 12 months of operation are likely to be lower than gross sales in later years, absent unusual circumstances.

We also encourage each franchise candidate to meet with existing Little Professor franchise owners to discuss the franchise opportunity.

Substantiation
Substantiation of the data used in preparing this Item will be made available to prospective franchise owners upon reasonable request, although we will not disclose the identity or location of any specific franchised Store.

Caution and Disclaimer
The gross sales per square foot of selling space, value or each customer transaction and sales and expenses shown in the Statements should not be considered as the actual or probable results that will be realized by a franchise owner. A franchise owner's individual financial results are likely to differ from the figures shown in this Item. We do not represent that any franchise owner can expect to attain the sales or operating results reflected in this Item 19.

WE DO NOT MAKE, OR AUTHORIZE OUR SALESPERSONS TO MAKE, REPRESENTATIONS OR GUARANTEES ABOUT THE SALES, EXPENSES OR INCOME THAT A PARTICULAR FRANCHISE OWNER WILL OR IS LIKELY TO ACHIEVE.

MUSIC-GO-ROUND
4200 Dahlberg Dr.
Minneapolis, MN 55422-4837
Tel: (800) 645-7298 (612) 520-8419
Fax: (612) 520-84501
E-Mail: jschwitzer@growbiz.com
Internet Address: www.musicgoround.com
Contact: Mr. Jim Schwitzer, National Franchise Development

Description: MUSIC GO ROUND is a franchised, retail music store that buys, sells, trades and consigns used and new musical instruments, gear and equipment. Our success formula is based on buying and selling used products, aggressive marketing, retail site selection and support of franchises.

# Franchised Units:	72 Units
# Company-Owned Units:	8 Units
Total # Units:	80 Units
Founded In:	1986
1st Franchised In:	1994
Average Total Investment:	186.4-254.9K
Franchise Fee:	20K
On-Going Royalty:	3%
Advertising Fee:	$500/Yr.
Financial Assistance:	Yes(I)
Site Selection Assistance:	Yes
Lease Negotiation Assistance:	Yes
Contract Terms (Init./Renew):	10/10
Initial Training Provided:	11 Days at Home Office.

Exhibit A

Music Go Round® Unaudited Statement of Annual Sales and Gross Profit
The following statement of annual sales and gross profits includes annual gross sales and gross profits as reported by 4 Grow Biz-owned and 35 franchised Music Go Round® Stores that commenced operations during the years 1986 through 1997.

This statement includes information from only those franchised Music Go Round® stores that had been in operation for the 12 month period ended December 26, 1998 and those Grow Biz-owned Stores that had been in operation for the 12 month period ended December 26, 1998. No other Music Go Round® Stores (Grow Biz-owned or franchised) are included in this statement due to insufficient history of operations (not in operation for the 12 month period ended December 26, 1998 (franchised Stores) or December 26, 1998 [Grow Biz-owned Stores]). There were 36 franchised Music Go Round® Stores which had been in operation for the 12 month period ended December 26, 1998. Only 35 out of the 36 Stores are reflected in the average, however, because Grow Biz did not have complete information on the remaining Store.

Statement of annual gross sales and gross profits for 35 franchised Music Go Round® Stores for the fiscal year 1998:

Year Opened	# Stores Reported	Stores Attaining or Exceeding Average	Average Gross Sales[1]	Average Gross Profit[2]	%	Sales Range
1997	17	8	449,234	206,333	46%	335,672–773,840
1996	14	6	565,882	267,175	47%	278,155–1,046,565
1995 & Prior	4	1	597,883	286,547	48%	426,011–814,828
Total Store Average	35	15	512,882	239,837	47%	

Statement of average gross sales and gross profits for 4 Grow Biz-owned Music Go Round® Stores for the year ended December 26, 1998:

Year Opened	# Stores Reported	Stores Attaining or Exceeding Average	Average Gross Sales	Average Gross Profit	%
1997	0	0	0	0	0%
1996	1	1	451,091	196,187	43%
1995 & Prior	3	1	1,072,015	432,626	40%
Total Store Average	4	2	916,784	373,516	41%

1. "Gross Sales" means all revenues the franchisee receives from the sale of goods and services, whether for cash or by check, credit card or trade, in connection with the Store, less sales tax and customer refunds and returns.

2. The Average Gross Profit equals Gross Sales less Cost of Goods Sold. Gross Profit does not reflect any expenses related to the operation of a Music Go Round® Store other than the Cost of Goods Sold.

These results relate to specific Grow Biz-owned or franchised Music Go Round® Stores and should not be considered as the actual or probable results that any franchisee will realize. Your individual financial results will likely differ from these results.

1-800-229-1792

PAPER WAREHOUSE/PARTY UNIVERSE
7630 Excelsior Blvd.
Minneapolis, MN 55426-4504
Tel: (800) 229-1792 (612) 936-1000
Fax: (612) 936-9800
E-Mail: mikeanderson@paperwarehouse.com
Internet Address: www.paperwarehouse.com
Contact: Mr. Mike Anderson, Vice President of Franchising

Description: PARTY UNIVERSE is a specialty retailer, featuring party supplies, balloons and greeting cards at everyday discount prices. Single and multiple unit markets are available. PARTY UNIVERSE provides the following support: site selection and leasing, store planning, classroom and in-store training, store set-up, pre-opening team, extensive merchandise selection with factory direct purchasing, comprehensive print, direct mail and electronic advertising programs.

# Franchised Units:	46 Units
# Company-Owned Units:	97 Units

Total # Units:	143 Units
Founded In:	1985
1st Franchised In:	1987
Average Total Investment:	165.4-430K
Franchise Fee:	19-25K
On-Going Royalty:	4%
Advertising Fee:	N/A
Financial Assistance:	Yes(I)
Site Selection Assistance:	Yes
Lease Negotiation Assistance:	Yes
Contract Terms (Init./Renew):	10/10

Initial Training Provided:4 Nights, 5 Days in Minneapolis, MN.

Representations Regarding Earnings Capability

An earnings claim immediately follows this Offering Circular as *Exhibit A. Exhibit A* displays ranges of actual gross sales and sales per square foot of 59 Paper Warehouse® Stores, which have been in operation at least 12 months as of January 29, 1999. Paper Warehouse, Paper Warehouse Franchising's affiliate, owns these Stores.

THE RANGES OF ACTUAL GROSS SALES AND SALES PER SQUARE FOOT STATED ON EXHIBIT A ARE BASED ON SPECIFIC COMPANY (AFFILIATE)-OWNED STORES. YOU SHOULD NOT CONSIDER THIS INFORMATION AS THE ACTUAL OR POTENTIAL GROSS SALES OR SALES PER SQUARE FOOT THAT ANY FRANCHISEE WILL REALIZE. PAPER WAREHOUSE FRANCHISING DOES NOT REPRESENT THAT ANY FRANCHISEE CAN EXPECT TO ATTAIN THESE GROSS SALES OR SALES PER SQUARE FOOT. YOUR INDIVIDUAL FINANCIAL RESULTS ARE LIKELY TO DIFFER FROM THE INFORMATION STATED IN EXHIBIT A.

Paper Warehouse Franchising will, on reasonable demand, provide to prospective franchisees the supporting data for all information illustrated in *Exhibit A.* Paper Warehouse Franchising does not otherwise furnish to prospective franchisees any oral or written information concerning the actual or potential sales, costs, income or profits of a Store. Actual results vary from unit to unit and Paper Warehouse Franchising cannot estimate the results of any particular franchise.

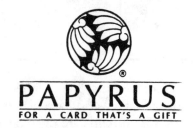

PAPYRUS
954 60th St.
Oakland, CA 94608
Tel: (888) 922-9555 (510) 428-0166
Fax: (510) 428-0615
E-Mail:

Internet Address: www.papurus-stores.com
Contact: Ms. Kathleen A. Low, Director Franchise Development

Description: A unique concept, featuring fine greeting cards, stationery, designer gift wrap and associated products in fine paper. Merchandise mix emphasizes superior design, style and quality.

# Franchised Units:	90 Units
# Company-Owned Units:	40 Units
Total # Units:	130 Units
Founded In:	1973
1st Franchised In:	1988

Average Total Investment:	205-417K	Site Selection Assistance:	Yes
Franchise Fee:	29.5K	Lease Negotiation Assistance:	Yes
On-Going Royalty:	6%	Contract Terms (Init./Renew):	10/5/5
Advertising Fee:	1%	Initial Training Provided:9 Days Corporate	
Financial Assistance:	Yes(l)	Headquarters.	

The following chart showing sales data is based on the 75 franchised PAPYRUS stores that have been open for more than one year as of the date of this circular:

Average Sales by Type of Location and Number of Years Open

Number of Years Open Type of Location	1	2	3	4	5
Regional Mall (61 Stores)	$434,282	$489,995	$535,924	$542,062	$597,360
Percentage of Stores in Category That Met or Exceeded Stated Sales During Last Fiscal Year (Rounded to nearest whole number)	49%	45%	49%	44%	47%
Annual Sales Per Square Foot (Rounded to nearest dollar)	$483.00	$569.00	$642.00	$687.00	$759.00
Percentage of Stores in Category That Met or Exceeded Stated Sales During Last Fiscal Year (Rounded to nearest whole number)	47%	41%	46%	52%	47%
Street Locations (14 stores)	$359,486	$405,886	$406,760	$355,507	$345,568
Percentage of Stores in Category That Met or Exceeded Stated Sales During Last Fiscal Year (Rounded to nearest whole number)	36%	36%	34%	50%	38%
Annual Sales Per Square Foot (Rounded to nearest dollar)	$462.00	$520.00	$539.00	$437.00	$438.00
Percentage of Stores in Category That Met or Exceeded Stated Sales During Last Fiscal Year (Rounded to nearest whole number)	36%	43%	42%	50%	38%

Notes:

1. The foregoing numbers have not been audited by our accountants. Substantiation of the data used in preparing the foregoing table will be made available to you on request. If you want to see this data, you must examine it in our office and must not make copies of the material since it constitutes a trade secret.

2. While mall locations may have higher per square foot sales, they also have higher occupancy costs. We currently are opening larger mall locations than we did in the past. The average mall location we are currently taking is approximately 932 square feet while our average mall location in 1990 was approximately 712 square feet.

442

3. The past performance of other PAPYRUS stores is no guarantee of the performance that you can expect. Many factors can affect an individual store's performance. Your results are likely to differ from the results stated in this earnings claim.

4. Other than for the material set forth above, we do not furnish or authorize any of our sales people to furnish any oral or written information concerning the actual or potential sales, costs, income, or profits of a PAPYRUS store. Actual results vary from store to store. We cannot estimate the results of any particular PAPYRUS store.

PLATO'S CLOSET

4200 Dahlberg Drive
Minneapolis, MN 55422
Tel: (612) 520-8480
Fax: (612) 520-8410

E-Mail:
Internet Address: www.platoscloset.com
Contact: Mr. John Lessler, Franchise Development Dir.

Representations Regarding Earnings Capability

Grow Biz will, on reasonable demand, provide to prospective franchisees the supporting data for all information illustrated in *Exhibit A*. Grow Biz does not otherwise furnish to prospective franchisees any oral or written information concerning the actual or potential sales, costs, income or profits of a Plato's Closet® Store. Actual results vary from unit to unit and Grow Biz cannot estimate the results of any particular franchise.

Exhibit A

Plato's Closet® Unaudited Statement of Gross Sales, Gross Profit and Net Income Results

The following statement of Gross Sales, Gross Profit and Net Income contains information derived from the unaudited financial statements of the Plato's Closet® store operated by Grow Biz' predecessor, Once Upon a Child, Inc. that had been in operation at least 12 months as of March 31, 1999. This store, located in Ohio, commenced operations in 1998. No other Plato's Closet® stores are included in this statement due to insufficient history of operations (not in operation for the 12 month period ended March 31, 1999). The financial statements for this store are unaudited and neither the preparer of the financial statements or Grow Biz expresses an opinion regarding the statements. The Gross Sales reported from this store was $649,818, the Gross Profit (Gross Sales less Cost of Goods Sold) was

$407,561 and the Net Income Before Taxes was $109,651.

Historical costs do not necessarily correspond to future costs due to factors such as inflation, changes in minimum wage laws, location, financing, real estate related costs and other variables. All information should be evaluated in light of current market conditions.

The services Grow Biz offers to prospective franchisees cannot be equated with the services provided to this store as Grow Biz' predecessor developed the Plato's Closet® concept and directly operates this store. The Plato's Closet® store reporting sales and income statement data included herein offers substantially the same merchandise and services to the public as a prospective franchisee may offer at a typical Plato's Closet® franchise.

THE GROSS SALES, GROSS PROFITS AND NET INCOME RESULTS STATED BELOW WERE SUPPLIED BY GROW BIZ' PREDECESSOR AND YOU SHOULD NOT CONSIDER THE FIGURES AS THE ACTUAL OR POTENTIAL SALES, EXPENSES, INCOME OR PROFIT THAT YOU WILL REALIZE. GROW BIZ DOES NOT REPRESENT THAT YOU CAN EXPECT TO ATTAIN THESE SALES, EXPENSES, INCOME OR PROFITS. YOUR INDIVIDUAL FINANCIAL RESULTS ARE LIKELY TO DIFFER FROM THE INFORMATION STATED BELOW.

**Plato's Closet® Store Gross Sales, Gross Profit and Net Income
Results For the 12 Month Period Ended March 31, 1999 (Unaudited)**

Gross Sales (1)	$649,818	100.00%
Cost of Good Sold	242,257	37.3%
Gross Profit (2)	$407,561	62.7%
Operating Expenses		
Salary & Wages (3)	135,257	20.8%
Payroll Taxes & Benefits (4)	16,719	2.6%
Rent (5)	40,149	6.2%
Advertising (6)	37,852	5.8%
Continuing Fees(7)	25,993	4.0%
Supplies (8)	9,329	1.4%
Repairs & Maintenance (9)	1,900	0.3%
Computer Supplies (10)	3,013	0.5%
Depreciation (11)	13,413	2.1%
Utilities	6,531	1.0%
Insurance (12)	1,900	0.3%
Bad Debt	897	0.1%
Credit Card Fees (13)	2,257	0.3%
Miscellaneous (14)	2,700	0.4%
Total Expenses	297,910	45.8%
Pre-Tax Income	$109,651	16.9%

1. "Gross Sales" means all revenues the franchisee received from the sale of goods and services, whether for cash or by check, credit card or trade, in connection with the Store, less sales tax and customer refunds and returns.

2. The Gross Profit equals Gross Sales less Cost of Goods Sold.

3. The Salary and Wages expense for this Store includes the following base salaries and bonuses (paid in the corresponding 12-month period): (i) Store Manager — Salary of $21,800 and bonus of $31,419 (based on Gross Sales of 649,818); (ii) 2 Assistant Managers — Salaries totaling $30,692 and bonuses totaling $14,578; (iii) Associates — Salaries totaling $27,462 and bonuses totaling $3,585; and (iv) Part-time Staff — $1,857 in wages. The owners/franchisees did not receive a salary.

4. The payroll taxes and benefit expenses reflect that portion of Once Upon A Child, Inc.'s total payroll taxes and benefits that were allocated to the Store (based on total compensation of the 9 Store employees).

5. The rent expense is based on total square footage of 2,750 with selling square footage of 2,600, including 3 fitting rooms. Each franchised location will vary significantly in its occupancy costs based on various factors, including the geographic location of the Store.

6. The advertising expense included $5,000 to produce a television advertisement. Franchisee must spend at least 4% of Store Gross Sales on local and cooperative advertising.

7. A Continuing Fee of 4% of Gross Sales is used in this statement because each franchisee must pay a Continuing Fee of 4% under the Franchise Agreement.

8. Some of the supply expenses reflect a portion of Once Upon A Child, Inc.'s total supply expenses that were allocated to the Store (based on Gross Sales of the Store).

9. This amount includes certain build-out expenses that were not capitalized.

10. This expense does not include the cost of computer hardware and software. The cost of Store's point-of-sale computers was capitalized based on a 4-year straight-line depreciation method and is included in the depreciation expense (see footnote 11). Franchisees tend to use various depreciation methods. Please contact an accountant or tax advisor to determine which depreciation/amortization method is best suited to your situation.

11. This amount is an estimated amount because Once Upon A Child, Inc. did not capitalize the cost of signs, build-out, fixtures and equipment. The estimate is based on the average cost of the items (as described in Item 7 of the Offering Circular), using a 4-year straight-line method of depreciation.

12. The Insurance expense is based on an allocated portion of several umbrella policies. The cost may not include all insurance coverage required for new franchisees, who must comply with the Franchise Agreement minimum requirements. Total premium costs will vary based on numerous factors, including the age and square footage of the facility, the insurance company and other risk factors specific to each location.

13. This amount reflects a portion of Once Upon A Child, Inc.'s total credit card expenses that were allocated to the Store (based on Gross Sales of the Store). This Store does not use check verification machines.

14. Items included in the Miscellaneous category of operating expenses include the following: business taxes and licenses, security system, postage, telephone, trash and recycling, uniforms, and legal and accounting fees. The business taxes and license fees and legal and accounting fees are estimated because Once Upon A Child, Inc. did not provide for these customary expenses. The actual costs for these items can vary based on many factors such as the extent to which franchisees rely on the services provided by independent legal and financial professionals.

THE FOLLOWING ITEMS ARE NOT INCLUDED IN THE PRECEDING FIGURES AND, IF INCLUDED, WOULD REDUCE THE NET INCOME SHOWN.

Interest/debt service costs are not included, since there is no consistent pattern as to average funds borrowed or repayment schedules. Please contact your banker to review the various types of financing which may be available to you.

Optional items such as automobile lease and expenses, donations, miscellaneous dues and subscriptions, and travel and entertainment are not included in the operating expenses. These items are not required for the successful operation of a "Plato's Closet" store, but are left to the franchisee's discretion.

THERE WILL BE SIGNIFICANT VARIATIONS IN SALES, AS WELL AS LABOR AND OPERATING EXPENSES AND COSTS, DEPENDING ON THE LENGTH OF TIME THE STORE HAS BEEN OPERATING, WHETHER OR NOT THE FRANCHISEE OWNS OTHER STORES AND OTHER FACTORS.

TINDER BOX INTERNATIONAL
Three Bala Plaza East, # 102
Bala Cynwyd, PA 19004
Tel: (800) 846-3372 (610) 668-4220
Fax: (610) 668-4266
E-Mail: tbiltd@ix.netcom.com
Internet Address: www.tinderbox.com
Contact: Mr. Fred Haas, Director Franchise
Development

Description: The world's largest and oldest chain of premium cigar, tobacco, smoking accessory and gift stores, with 70 years' experience as the undisputed industry leader.

# Franchised Units:	128 Units
# Company-Owned Units:	3 Units
Total # Units:	131 Units
Founded In:	1928
1st Franchised In:	1965
Average Total Investment:	175-250K
Franchise Fee:	30K
On-Going Royalty:	4-5%
Advertising Fee:	3%
Financial Assistance:	Yes
Site Selection Assistance:	Yes
Lease Negotiation Assistance:	Yes
Contract Terms (Init./Renew):	10/5

Initial Training Provided: 5 Days Home Office; 3-5 Days at Franchisee's Store; Follow-Up Store Visit within 30 Days.

TBI has surveyed the sales during its most recent fiscal year ended January 31, 1999 reported by the 97 licensee and franchisee-owned Stores which operated during that entire year. Stores which were not in operation the entire year were not included in the survey. The sales for these Stores were provided by TBI's licensees and franchisees and have not been audited. The following is the average sales of these Stores during that year. These calculations were not prepared in accordance with generally accepted accounting principles, however, the amounts represented do not exceed the sales reported to TBI by its licensees and franchisees.

Average Sales: $507,294

The figure of $507,294 is the average of these Stores. The actual sales of these Stores ranged from $109,708 to $1,917,623. Forty-five (45%) percent of these Stores achieved or exceeded the average; eighty-three (83%) percent of these Stores exceeded $250,000 and seventy-six (76%) percent of these Stores exceeded $300,000.

All of these Stores specialize in the sale of tobacco products, smokers' accessories and supplies, gifts and/or collectibles. These Stores are generally located in shopping centers or malls servicing geographic areas having populations between fifty thousand and over one million parsons and were managed by the owners or their managers. These licensees and franchisees received services from TBI that are available generally to you, and no others.

THE STORE SALES SHOWN IN THIS ITEM 19 ARE AVERAGES OF SPECIFIC STORE FRANCHISES AND SHOULD NOT BE CONSIDERED AS THE ACTUAL OR POTENTIAL SALES THAT WILL BE REALIZED BY YOU OR ANY OTHER STORE FRANCHISEE. YOUR SALES WILL MORE LIKELY THAN NOT DIFFER FROM THE AVERAGE SALES SHOWN IN THIS ITEM 19. TBI DOES NOT REPRESENT THAT YOU CAN EXPECT TO ATTAIN THESE SALES, OR ANY OTHER LEVEL OF SALES, PROFITS OR EARNINGS.

SUBSTANTIATION OF STORE SALES WILL BE MADE AVAILABLE TO YOU ON REASONABLE REQUEST.

Wicks'n'Sticks™

WICKS 'N' STICKS
P. O. Box 4586
Houston, TX 77210-4586
Tel: (888) 55-WICKS (281) 874-3642
Fax: (281) 874-3678
E-Mail:
Internet Address: www.wicksnstick.com
Contact: Mr. William McPherson, VP Franchise Development

Description: Nation's largest and most respected retailer of quality candles, fragrancing and related home decorative products. Franchisees are offered outstanding name recognition, comprehensive training and extensive start up and on-going support. Rated #1 franchise in category by Entrepreneur Magazine 7 years in a row. Rated a top franchise by both Success Gold 100 and Income Opportunities Platinum 200.

# Franchised Units:	218 Units
# Company-Owned Units:	4 Units
Total # Units:	222 Units
Founded In:	1968
1st Franchised In:	1968
Average Total Investment:	153.6-249.3K
Franchise Fee:	25K
On-Going Royalty:	6%
Advertising Fee:	1%
Financial Assistance:	Yes(I)
Site Selection Assistance:	Yes
Lease Negotiation Assistance:	Yes
Contract Terms (Init./Renew):	10/5/5/5

Initial Training Provided: 2 Weeks Corporate Office, Houston, TX.

Representations Regarding Earnings Capability

Except as described below, the Company does not furnish or authorize its representatives to furnish any oral or written information concerning the actual or potential sales, costs, income or profits of the Wicks 'n' Sticks stores. Actual results vary from store to store and the Company cannot estimate the results of any particular franchise

At the end of the calendar year 1998, there were 217 Wicks 'n' Sticks stores. The sales figures included in the Statement of Gross Sales ("Statement") included as part of this Item XIX are for the calendar year 1998 and are based upon 198 franchised Wicks 'n' Sticks stores which were in operation for the entire calendar year of 1998 and therefore qualified for this Statement. These stores will be referred to as "Comparable Stores" throughout this Statement. Nineteen stores did not qualify for the following reasons: Seven stores were not included because they were Company-owned and operated in 1998. Twelve stores were not included in the Statement because they opened in 1998. Of the 198 Comparable Stores, the 13 stores were not included in the Statement for the following reasons: One store operated as a "discount" store and is not a typical Wicks 'n' Sticks store. One store was not open for all 12 months of 1998. Eleven stores did not report a full year's sales to the Company.

The following data was compiled from sales information reported to the Company by the Franchisees of the stores. The Franchise Agreement requires the Franchisee to maintain records in accordance with generally accepted accounting principles, but the Company provides no assurance that all records were maintained accordingly. The numbers actually reported to the Company by the Franchisees may vary from those numbers reported on each Franchisee's individual financial statements due to, for example, different reporting periods, and different accounting methods. Therefore, no reconciliation of these numbers to the individual financial statements is available to the Company. Each store offered similar products and services as would generally be offered by a typical new franchised store.

A NEW FRANCHISEES INDIVIDUAL FINANCIAL RESULTS ARE LIKELY TO DIFFER FROM THE RESULTS STATED IN THE STATEMENT.

THESE SALES ARE AVERAGE OF SPECIFIC FRANCHISEES AND SHOULD NOT BE CONSIDERED AS THE ACTUAL OR POTENTIAL SALES THAT WILL BE REALIZED BY ANY OTHER FRANCHISEE. THE COMPANY DOES NOT REPRESENT THAT ANY FRANCHISEE CAN EXPECT TO ATTAIN THESE SALES. NO PERSON HAS ANY AUTHORITY TO MAKE ANY REPRESENTATION THAT ANY LEVEL OF SALES OR PROFITS WILL BE ACHIEVED BY ANY FRANCHISEE.

SUBSTANTIATION OF INFORMATION CONTAINED IN THIS ITEM WILL BE MADE AVAILABLE TO PROSPECTIVE FRANCHISEES AT THE COMPANY'S HEADQUARTERS UPON REASONABLE REQUEST.

Sales Summary 1998 Comparable Gross Sales As Reported To Wicks 'n' Sticks		
Gross Sales	Number of Franchised Stores	Percentage
Over $900,001	2	1%
$800,001–900,000	3	2%
$700,001–800,000	4	2%
$650,001–700,000	5	3%
$600,001–650,000	9	5%
$550,001–600,000	11	6%
$500,001–550,000	15	8%
$450,001–500,000	15	8%
$400,001–450,000	17	9%
$350,001–400,000	24	13%
$300,001–350,000	26	14%
$250,001–300,000	29	16%
$200,001–250,000	18	10%
Under $200,000	7	3%
Totals	185	100%

Wicks 'n' Sticks, Inc. Statement of Average Sales and Expenses for Corporate Stores Opened All of 1998

Sales (a)	$534,691	100.00%
Cost of Goods Sold (b)	240,581	44.99%
Gross Margin	$294,111	55.01%
Operating Expenses:		
Employee Expenses (c)	62,266	11.65%
Supplies (d)	13,047	2.44%
Advertising (e)	3,059	0.57%
Rent and Other Lease Charges (f)	79,674	14.90%
Utilities (g)	4,121	0.77%
Telephone (h)	2,189	0.41%
Credit Card Charges (i)	5,679	1.06%
Office Supplies (j)	4,234	0.79%
Travel and Entertainment (k)	2,726	0.51%
Other Miscellaneous Expenses (l)	9,681	1.81%
Royalties (m)	32,082	6.00%
Total Operating Expenses	218,758	40.91%
Net Income Before Interest, Depreciation, Debt Service & Taxes (n)	$75,353	14.09%

Notes:

a. *Sales* — This figure represents the average gross sales for all four Wicks 'n' Sticks, Inc. Corporate Stores which were open the full calendar year of 1998.

b. *Cost of Goods Sold* — This figure was calculated based upon the percentage average cost of goods of 44.99% for all four stores. Our corporate stores receive the same pricing and discount structure from our approved vendors as our franchisees.

c. *Employee Expense* — This figure is the average employee employee (does not include manager's salary) for all four stores.

d. *Supplies* — This figure represents the average cost of supplies (e.g.: bags and boxes) for all four stores.

e. *Advertising* — This figure represents the average advertising expense for all four stores.

f. *Rent and Other Lease Charges* — This figure represents the average expense for rent, percentage rent, and also includes CAM, trash removal, merchant association dues, promotional expense, and real estate taxes paid to the landlord for all four stores.

g. *Utilities* — This figure represents the average utility expense for all four stores.

h. *Telephone* — This figure represents the average telephone expense for all four stores.

i. *Credit Card Fees* — This figure represents the average credit card expense for all four stores.

j. *Office Supplies* — This figure represents the average office supply expense for all four stores.

k. *Travel and Entertainment* — This figure is the average travel and entertainment expense for all four stores and includes expenses for travel to the two Wicks 'n' Sticks Buying Shows held in 1998.

l. *Other Miscellaneous Expenses* — This figure comprises all other expenses not previously listed and includes bad debts, prop expense, repairs and maintenance, machine rentals, cash over and short, property taxes, and miscellaneous selling expenses, but does not include depreciation or amortization.

m. *Royalties* — This figure was calculated based upon the royalty fee of 6% of gross sales.

n. *Net Income* — This figure is calculated using the above sales and expense numbers which reflect the averages for all four corporate stores.

Certain expenses are not included in the above amounts that may be incurred by a franchised store including, but not limited to, professional fees, business insurance and dues.

A NEW FRANCHISEE'S INDIVIDUAL FINANCIAL RESULTS ARE LIKELY TO DIFFER FROM THE RESULTS STATED IN THE STATEMENT.

THESE SALES, PROFITS, OR EARNINGS ARE AVERAGE OF THE COMPANY-OWNED STORES AND SHOULD NOT BE CONSIDERED AS THE ACTUAL OR POTENTIAL SALES, PROFITS, OR EARNINGS THAT WILL BE REALIZED BY ANY FRANCHISEE. THE COMPANY DOES NOT REPRESENT THAT ANY FRANCHISEE CAN EXPECT TO ATTAIN THESE SALES, PROFITS, OR EARNINGS. NO PERSON HAS ANY AUTHORITY TO MAKE ANY REPRESENTATION THAT ANY LEVEL OF SALES OR PROFITS WILL BE ACHIEVED BY ANY FRANCHISEE.

SUBSTANTIATION OF INFORMATION CONTAINED IN THIS ITEM WILL BE MADE AVAILABLE TO PROSPECTIVE FRANCHISEES AT THE COMPANY'S HEADQUARTERS UPON REASONABLE REQUEST.

WILD BIRDS UNLIMITED
11711 N. College Ave., # 146
Carmel, IN 46032-5601
Tel: (888) 302-2473 (317) 571-7100
Fax: (317) 571-7110

E-Mail: pickettp@wbu.com
Internet Address: www.wbu.com
Contact: Mr. Paul E. Pickett, Director Franchise Development

Description: WILD BIRDS UNLIMITED is North America's original and largest group of retail stores catering to the backyard birdfeeding and nature enthusiast. We currently have over 240 stores in the U. S. and Canada. Stores provide birdseed, feeders, houses, optics and nature-related gifts. Additionally, stores provide extensive educational programs regarding backyard birdfeeding. Franchisees are provided an all-inclusive support system.

# Franchised Units:	263 Units	Advertising Fee:		NR
# Company-Owned Units:	0 Units	Financial Assistance:		Yes(I)
Total # Units:	263 Units	Site Selection Assistance:		Yes
Founded In:	1981	Lease Negotiation Assistance:		Yes
1st Franchised In:	1983	Contract Terms (Init./Renew):		10/5
Average Total Investment:	75-125K	Initial Training Provided:5 Days in Indianapolis,		
Franchise Fee:	18K	IN; 1 Day at Store Site.		
On-Going Royalty:	4%/$8K Min.			

Provided below is certain information regarding Gross Sales and Cost of Goods Sold as reported by our franchisees.

Schedule 1 is a summary of fiscal 1998 Gross Sales for those Wild Birds Unlimited franchises open and operational for at least 12 full months as of December 31, 1998. Schedule 2 is an analysis of the information presented in Schedule 1, broken down by years of operation. Schedule 3 is the average first year sales for all Wild Birds Unlimited franchises which had been open and operating for at least 12 full months as of December 31, 1998. Schedule 4 is the historical average Cost of Goods Sold for products offered by the Stores and the historical average of Advertising expenses incurred by first year stores that completed their first year of operation in 1997 and 1998.

You should consider the following material factors in reviewing and determining whether to rely on this data:

1. We have compiled the Gross Sales information in this survey from our Franchisees' monthly sales reports. The stores included in this survey range in age from 1 to 18 years of operation. The survey excludes all stores which had not been operational at least 12 full months as of December 31, 1998. This information is unaudited and we are unable to verify or warrant its accuracy or the method used by each Franchisee in its computation.

2. The stores included in this survey represent a variety of geographic and demographic circumstances. These variations in circumstances include: 1) the total population of the city in which the store is located ranges from over 700,000 to less than 1,000; 2) stores are located

in a diverse variety of locations throughout the United States and Canada; 3) a number of the cities in which the stores are located are suburbs of larger metropolitan areas; and 4) some stores located in areas with small populations are in areas with a substantial amount of "tourist" traffic.

3. The stores listed in this survey are generally located in neighborhood or regional strip shopping centers or free-standing buildings. We make no representations regarding the relative level of first year sales which the various types of locations have experienced.

4. While we grant each Franchisee an exclusive territory within which we will not grant another franchise or operate another store, the city in which the franchise is located may be geographically smaller or larger than the exclusive territory granted under the Franchise Agreement (see "Item 12, Territory").

5. Several of the stores included in the survey operate temporary seasonal kiosks. These sales are included in this survey as part of our Franchisees' Gross Sales. Sales derived from kiosks have, in some cases, represented a substantial portion of those stores' annual Gross Sales.

6. Definition of Gross Sales: the sales price of all merchandise and services sold, including cash and charge sales of every kind made at the store, and mail or telephone orders received or taken at the store.

THE FOLLOWING ACTUAL STATEMENTS OF GROSS SALES AND COST OF GOODS SOLD REFLECT THE OPERATION OF SPECIFIC FRANCHISES AND SHOULD NOT BE

CONSIDERED AS THE ACTUAL OR PROBABLE GROSS SALES OR COST OF GOODS SOLD THAT WILL BE REALIZED BY ANY GIVEN FRANCHISE. WE DO NOT REPRESENT THAT ANY GIVEN FRANCHISE CAN EXPECT TO ATTAIN SUCH GROSS SALES OR COST OF GOODS SOLD. A NEW FRANCHISEE'S FINANCIAL RESULTS ARE LIKELY TO DIFFER FROM THE RESULTS STATED IN THIS ITEM 19. THERE IS NO ASSURANCE THAT YOU'LL ACHIEVE THE GROSS SALES OR COST OF GOODS SOLD RESULTS SET FORTH BELOW IN THIS SURVEY. IF YOU RELY ON OUR FIGURES, YOU MUST ACCEPT THE RISK OF NOT DOING AS WELL.

Substantiation of the data used in preparing the following information is available upon request.

Schedule 1
System Wide Fiscal Year 1998 Gross Sales

As of December 31, 1998, 227 Wild Birds Unlimited franchises had been open and in operation for at least the previous 12 full months. Set forth below is a summary of the 1998 Gross Sales for these franchised stores.

Summary of Gross Sales

a. Total number of stores operating at least 12 full months as of December 31, 1998 and included in the Survey: 227
b. Total Number of Franchised stores included in the Survey: 227
c. Period covered by Survey: 1 year period beginning on January 1, 1998 and ending on December 31, 1998
d. System wide Average Gross Sales: $320,444
e. System wide Median Gross Sales: $281,386
f. System wide Range of Gross Sales: $55,223–1,273,299
g. Percentage of Stores Exceeding the Average: 40.53%

Schedule 2
Fiscal Year 1998 Gross Sales by Years of Operation

Each of the stores included in the following survey has been grouped into one of four categories based on the age of the store as of December 31, 1998. The period covered by Survey is the 1 year period beginning on January 1, 1998 and ending on December 31, 1998.

1. Stores Operational At Least 1 Full Year (and up to 23 months)
    a. Total Number of Stores In This Age Group: 19
    b. Average Gross Sales: $210,479
    c. Range of Gross Sales: $123,630–536,150
    d. Median Gross Sales: $168,058
    e. Percentage of Stores Exceeding the Average: 31.58%

2. Stores Operational At Least 2 Full Years (and up to 35 months)
    a. Total Number of Stores In This Age Group: 21
    b. Average Gross Sales: $216,826
    c. Range of Gross Sales: $99,362–434,415
    d. Median Gross Sales $197,012
    e. Percentage of Stores Exceeding the Average: 42.86%

3. Stores Operational At Least 3 and 4 Full Years (and up to 59 Months)
    a. Total Number of Stores In Group: 50
    b. Average Gross Sales: $295,356
    c. Range of Gross Sales: $103,590–783,189
    d. Median Gross Sales: $251,890
    e. Percentage of Stores Exceeding the Average: 36.00%

4. Stores Operational 5 to 18 Full Years
    a. Total Number of Stores In Group: 137
    b. Average Gross Sales: $360,735
    c. Range of Gross Sales: $55,223–1,273,299
    d. Median Gross Sales: $333,485
    e. Percentage of Stores Exceeding the Average: 40.88%

Schedule 3
First Year Gross Sales

Below is a Survey of average first year Gross Sales for franchised stores which had reported at least one full year of sales as of December 31, 1998 (excluding one conversion franchise operational before January 1, 1992). Prior to fiscal year 1988 we did not employ personnel exclusively for the purpose of franchise system development, therefore, only those stores opening after January 1, 1988, received first year assistance substantially similar to that which is currently provided to new franchise stores. Accordingly, stores opening before January 1, 1988 are included in one group and stores opening after January 1, 1988 are grouped and summarized by fiscal year of opening.

We in no way warrant, represent, promise, predict or guarantee that you can or will attain these financial results. New Franchisee's financial results will likely differ from the results stated in Item 19.

Summary of Stores Opened Before December 31, 1988
   a.   Number of franchised Stores Included in the Survey: 27
   b.   Average first year Gross Sales: $118,540
   c.   Median first year Gross Sales: $88,535
   d.   Range of first year Gross Sales: $34,822–298,355
   e.   Percentage of Stores Exceeding the Average: 37%

Summary of Stores Opened Between January 1, 1989 and December 31, 1990
   a.   Number of franchised Stores Included in the Survey: 29
   b.   Average first year Gross Sales: $156,823
   c.   Median first year Gross Sales: $142,666
   d.   Range of first year Gross Sales: $44,213–350,791
   e.   Percentage of Stores Exceeding the Average: 34%

Summary of Stores Opened Between January 1, 1991 and December 31, 1992
   a.   Number of franchised Stores Included in the Survey: 62
   b.   Average first year Gross Sales: $176,269
   c.   Median first year Gross Sales: $163,192
   d.   Range of first year Gross Sales: $68,040–379,235
   e.   Percentage of Stores Exceeding the Average: 45%

Summary of Stores Opened Between January 1, 1993 and December 31, 1994
   a.   Number of franchised Stores Included in the Survey: 68
   b.   Average first year Gross Sales: $180,897
   c.   Median first year Gross Sales: $164,004
   d.   Range of first year Gross Sales: $60,360–581,737
   e.   Percentage of Stores Exceeding the Average: 40%

Summary of Stores Opened Between January 1, 1995 and December 31, 1996
   a.   Number of franchised Stores Included in the Survey: 46
   b.   Average first year Gross Sales: $182,061
   c.   Median first year Gross Sales: $157,942
   d.   Range of first year Gross Sales: $77,518–547,942
   e.   Percentage of Stores Exceeding the Average: 33%

Summary of Stores Opened Between January 1, 1997 and December 31, 1997
   a.   Number of franchised Stores Included in the Survey: 20
   b.   Average first year Gross Sales: $182,013
   c.   Median first year Gross Sales: $158,689
   d.   Range of first year Gross Sales: $86,876–468,393
   e.   Percentage of Stores Exceeding the Average: 40%

Schedule 4
Cost of Goods Sold

Cost of Goods Sold is defined as the actual out of pocket expense to acquire merchandise held for resale, including shipping.

1.   Based on 1997 financial statements from 156 franchised stores in operation one year or more as of 12/31/97:
   a.   average Cost of Goods Sold: 51.99%
   b.   range: 43.26% to 63.70%
   c.   median: 51.45%
   d.   percentage of stores exceeding average: 43.59%

2. Based on survey of 1996 financial statements from 151 franchised stores in operation one full year or more as of 12/31/96, average cost of goods was 53.53%.

3. Based on survey of 1995 financial statements from 147 franchised stores in operation one full year or more as of 12/31/95, average cost of goods was 54.67 %.

We believe the decrease in Cost of Goods Sold from 1995 to 1997 was due to updated retail pricing strategies and advanced purchasing programs developed by the Wild Birds Unlimited Franchise Support Center staff.

The merchandise sold at Wild Birds Unlimited stores is classified into the following categories:

Birdseed: Consumable birdfeeding products, such as seed and suet.

Feeders: Birdfeeders, houses and baths, hanging hardware and other miscellaneous items used in delivering food products to birds and other wildlife.

Gifts: Nature related books, jewelry, apparel and figurines, thermometers, optics and other related decorative items featuring a nature theme.

The Cost of Goods Sold as a percentage of total Gross Sales will vary among the product categories and from product to product within each category, making the overall average percentage highly dependent on the specific product mix chosen by each franchisee. We make no representation as to the Cost of Goods Sold percentages applicable to each product category. It has, however, been our operating experience that, within the range of Cost of Goods Sold percentages a franchisee may experience, Birdseed products generally tend to be at the high end of the range. Gift items tend to be at the low end of the range and hobby products tend to fall in the mid-range.

First Year Advertising Expense

Advertising expense is defined as the out of pocket expense that Franchisees spend to market their store, including the cost of printing and mailing customer flyers; television, radio, newspaper and direct-mail advertising. Individual franchisees may decide to place other related expenses into this expense category.

Based on 1996 and 1997 first calendar year financial statements from 40 franchised stores who completed their first year of operation as of 12/31/96 or 12/31/97:

    a. average Advertising expense: 9.40%
    b. range: 3.27% to 19.68%
    c. median: 8.81%
    d. percentage of stores exceeding average: 40.00%

The Advertising expense as a percentage of total Gross Sales will vary from market to market depending on the cost of media advertising and the personal decisions of the individual franchisees. We make no representation as to the Advertising expense percentages applicable to each individual Wild Birds Unlimited franchise.

THE ACTUAL STATEMENTS OF GROSS SALES, COST OF GOODS SOLD, AND ADVERTISING EXPENSES SET FORTH ABOVE REFLECT THE OPERATION OF SPECIFIC FRANCHISES AND SHOULD NOT BE CONSIDERED AS THE ACTUAL OR PROBABLE GROSS SALES OR COST OF GOODS SOLD THAT WILL BE REALIZED BY ANY GIVEN FRANCHISE. WE DO NOT REPRESENT THAT ANY GIVEN FRANCHISE CAN EXPECT TO ATTAIN SUCH GROSS SALES OR COST OF GOODS SOLD. A NEW FRANCHISEE'S FINANCIAL RESULTS ARE LIKELY TO DIFFER FROM THE RESULTS STATED IN THIS ITEM 19. THERE IS NO ASSURANCE THAT YOU'LL ACHIEVE THE GROSS SALES OR COST OF GOODS SOLD RESULTS SET FORTH ABOVE. IF YOU RELY ON OUR FIGURES, YOU MUST ACCEPT THE RISK OF NOT DOING AS WELL.

FASTSIGNS.

FASTSIGNS
2550 Midway Rd., # 150
Carrollton, TX 75006
Tel: (800) 827-7446 (972) 447-0777
Fax: (972) 248-8201
E-Mail: Larry.Lane@fastsigns.com
Internet Address: www.fastsigns.com
Contact: Mr. Larry Lane, VP of Franchise
Devopment

Description: FASTSIGNS sign centers produce complete computer-generated signs and graphics for the business community. FASTSIGNS is the acknowledged leader of the quick sign industry. Rated #7 in Success Magazine's Franchisee Satisfaction Survey. Quality systems include comprehensive 3 week training, on-going support, unique marketing materials and National Accounts program. Site selection assistance and the latest industry equipment.

# Franchised Units:	432 Units
# Company-Owned Units:	0 Units
Total # Units:	432 Units
Founded In:	1985
1st Franchised In:	1986
Average Total Investment:	144.5-207.5K
Franchise Fee:	20K
On-Going Royalty:	6%
Advertising Fee:	2%
Financial Assistance:	Yes(I)
Site Selection Assistance:	Yes
Lease Negotiation Assistance:	Yes
Contract Terms (Init./Renew):	20/10
Initial Training Provided:	3 Weeks in Dallas, TX.

Analysis of Average Sales and Major Expense Items for Fastsigns Centers

This analysis sets forth average yearly gross sales for 325 franchised FASTSIGNS Centers located in the United States for the year ended December 31, 1998, based on sales reported by franchisees. On December 31, 1998, there were 421 FAST-SIGNS Centers open and in operation of which 68 were international. However, the average is based solely on the 325 Centers that were open in the United States and in continuous operation during the entire year ended December 31, 1998.

Based on gross sales reported by the 325 Centers, the average gross sales for such Centers for the year ended December 31, 1998, was $432,081. For purposes of this analysis, gross sales includes cash and credit sales as well as any goods or services received by the franchisee in exchange for goods and services sold at the Center. Gross sales does not include sales or use taxes.

Of the 325 Centers included in this analysis, 127 Centers reported gross sales above the average, ranging from $433,452 to $1,505,813, and 198 Centers reported gross sales below the average, ranging from $97,562 to $428,121. Overall, the Centers included in this analysis reported gross sales in the following ranges for the year:

Sales Ranges	Year the Center Opened						Total Centers	
	1997		1996		1995 or prior			
	# of Centers	Percentages	# of Centers	Percentages	# of Centers	Percentages	# of Centers	Percentages
$000,001–100,000	0	0.0%	0	0.0%	1	0.4%	1	0.3%
$100,001–200,000	18	45.0%	8	21.6%	13	5.2%	39	12.0%
$200,001–300,000	18	45.0%	14	37.9%	32	12.9%	64	19.7%
$300,001–400,000	2	5.0%	10	27.0%	57	23.0%	69	21.2%
$400,001–500,000	2	5.0%	2	5.4%	49	19.8%	53	16.3%
$500,001–600,000			1	2.7%	35	14.1%	36	11.1%
$600,001–700,000					23	9.3%	23	7.1%
$700,001–800,000			1	2.7%	17	6.9%	18	5.6%
$800,001–900,000					10	4.0%	10	3.1%
$900,001–1,000,000					3	1.2%	3	0.9%
$1,000,001–1,100,000			1	2.7%	3	1.2%	4	1.2%
$1,100,001–1,200,000					2	0.8%	2	0.6%
$1,200,001–1,300,000					0	0.0%	0	0.0%
$1,300,001–1,400,000					2	0.8%	2	0.6%
$1,400,001–1,500,000					0	0.0%	0	0.0%
$1,500,001–1,600,000					1	0.4%	1	0.3%
Totals	40	100%	37	100%	248	100%	325	100%

Of the 127 Centers reporting gross sales above the average, 34 Centers are located in the Southwest Region of the United States, 26 in the West Region, 14 in the Northeast Region, 26 in the Southeast Region and 27 in the Midwest Region. Included within the 34 Centers in the Southwest Region is one Center opened in 1985 that is affiliated with us; such Center reported gross sales of $731,766 for the year ended December 31, 1998. However, such Center is a franchised unit and is subject to the same obligations as all other franchisees under the System. Such Center pays us a monthly accounting fee for accounting services performed.

Of the 198 Centers reporting gross sales below the average, 33 are located in the Southwest Region, 43 in the West Region, 38 in the Northeast Region, 40 in the Southeast Region and 44 in the Midwest Region.

For use in making a comparison, provided below is an analysis of the average yearly gross sales for 290 franchised FASTSIGNS Centers located in the United States for the year ended December 31, 1997, based on sales reported by franchisees. On December 31, 1997, there were 387 FASTSIGNS Centers open and in operation of which 59 were international. However, the average is based solely on the 290 Centers that were open in the United States and in continuous operation during the entire year ended December 31, 1997.

Based on gross sales reported by the 290 Centers, the average gross sales for such Centers for the year ended December 31, 1997, was $416,813. For purposes of this analysis, gross sales includes cash and credit sales as well as any goods or services received by the franchisee in exchange for goods and services sold at the Center. Gross sales does not include sales or use taxes.

Of the 290 Centers included in this analysis, 112 Centers reported gross sales above the average, ranging from $417,559 to $1,474,291, and 178 Centers reported gross sales below the average, ranging from $90,862 to $416,356. Overall, the Centers included in this analysis reported gross sales in the following ranges for the year:

Sales Ranges	Year the Center Opened						Total Centers	
	1996		1995		1994 or prior			
	# of Centers	Percentages	# of Centers	Percentages	# of Centers	Percentages	# of Centers	Percentages
$000,001–100,000	0	0.0%	1	3.4%			1	0.3%
$100,001–200,000	20	50.0%	6	21.5%	11	5.0%	37	12.8%
$200,001–300,000	13	32.5%	11	37.9%	28	12.7%	52	17.9%
$300,001–400,000	5	12.5%	5	17.2%	59	26.7%	69	23.8%
$400,001–500,000	1	3.5%	4	13.8%	46	20.8%	51	17.6%
$500,001–600,000			2	6.9%	27	12.5%	29	10.0%
$600,001–700,000					24	10.9%	24	8.3%
$700,001–800,000					11	5.0%	11	3.8%
$800,001–900,000	1	3.5%			7	3.2%	8	2.8%
$900,001–1,000,000					2	0.9%	2	0.7%
$1,000,001–1,100,000					1	0.5%	1	0.3%
$1,100,001–1,200,000					2	0.9%	2	0.7%
$1,200,001–1,300,000					1	0.5%	1	0.3%
$1,300,001–1,400,000					1	0.5%	1	0.3%
$1,400,001–1,500,000					1	0.5%	1	0.3%
Totals	40	100%	29	100%	221	100%	290	100%

Of the 112 Centers reporting gross sales above the average, 26 Centers are located in the Southwest Region of the United States, 29 in the West Region, 12 in the Northeast Region, 17 in the Southeast Region and 28 in the Midwest Region. Included within the 26 Centers in the Southwest Region is one Center opened in 1985 that is affiliated with us; such Center reported gross sales of $776,222 for the year ended December 31, 1997. However, such Center is a franchised unit and is subject to the same obligations as all other franchisees under the System. Such Center pays us a monthly accounting fee for accounting services performed.

Of the 178 Centers reporting gross sales below the average, 26 are located in the Southwest Region, 48 in the West Region, 30 in the Northeast Region, 35 in the Southeast Region and 39 in the Midwest Region.

For purposes of this analysis, the Southwest Region consists of Arkansas, Louisiana, Oklahoma and Texas; the West Region consists of Alaska, Arizona, California, Colorado, Hawaii, Idaho, Montana, Nevada, New Mexico, Oregon, Utah, Washington and Wyoming; the Northeast Region consists of Connecticut, Delaware, Maine, Maryland, Massachusetts, New Hampshire, New Jersey, New York, Pennsylvania, Rhode Island, Vermont, Virginia, Washington, D.C. and West Virginia; the Southeast Region consists of Alabama, Florida, Georgia, Mississippi, North Carolina, South Carolina and Tennessee; and the Midwest Region consists of Illinois, Indiana, Iowa, Kansas, Kentucky, Ohio, Michigan, Minnesota, Missouri, Nebraska, North Dakota, South Dakota and Wisconsin.

All Centers included in the 1998 analysis are located in strip-shopping centers. 316 of the Centers are owner-operated; of such 316 Centers,

190 reported sales below the average yearly gross sales described above and 126 above such average.

We offer substantially the same services to all franchisees. Additionally, advertising and promotional materials developed by the NAC are available to all Franchisees. (See Item 11.) An individual Franchisee is not limited in the amount or type of advertising that it may conduct; provided, however, that all advertising materials developed by Franchisee must be approved in advance by us. (See Item 16.) Consequently, Franchisee's gross sales may be directly affected by the amount, type and effectiveness of advertising conducted by Franchisee.

The Franchise Agreement provides that Franchisees must offer and sell at the Center products and services required by us and may offer and sell such additional products and services approved by us. (See Item 16.) Franchisees offer substantially the same products and services to the public. In certain states, as noted in Item 1, Franchisees may be required to have a contractors license to perform certain types of sign installation work. In those states, if you do not have, or meet the requirements to obtain a license, then you may not be able to offer those installation services requiring a license. Additionally, although we may suggest prices for the products and services offered at the Center, Franchisees may offer and sell such products and services at any price it chooses. As a result, the products and services offered and the prices at which such products and services are offered to the public at the Centers included in this analysis may vary.

The average gross sales figures included in this analysis are based on sales reports submitted to us by each Franchisee. The figures in the sales reports have not been audited and we have not undertaken to otherwise independently verify (i) the accuracy of such information or (ii) whether such information was prepared in accordance with generally accepted accounting principles.

In addition to the average gross sales analysis, certain expenses, expressed as a percentage of Gross Revenues, have been provided based on the experience of certain of the foregoing FASTSIGNS Centers described below. The expense figures were extracted from the December 31, 1998 financial statements submitted by the FASTSIGNS Franchisees included in the 1998 analysis described above. As of the date of this Offering Circular, we have not been provided with expense data from 214 of the 325 Centers open and in continuous operation during 1998. This was primarily due to the close proximity of year-end to the time of compilation of these numbers and such 214 Centers were not included in the expense figures provided herein. Franchisee should note that with respect to the 111 FASTSIGNS Centers included in the compilation of the expense figures, the expense data relates to operations conducted during the one-year period ended December 31, 1998. Of the 111 Centers reporting expenses 1 opened in 1985, 2 opened in 1986, 3 opened in 1987, 3 were opened in 1988, 8 were opened in 1989, 16 were opened in 1990, 13 were opened in 1991, 12 were opened in 1992, 7 were opened in 1993, 7 were opened in 1994, 10 were opened in 1995, 14 were opened in 1996, and 15 were opened in 1997. These Centers are located in the following regions; 27 in the Southwest region of the United States, 18 in the West region, 14 in the Northeast region, 22 in the Southeast region and 30 in the Midwest region. The information relating to the operations expenses provided by the FASTSIGNS Centers and used by the us in determining the numerical values provided has not been audited and such information has not necessarily been prepared on a basis consistent with generally accepted accounting principles. In particular, we are unable to verify whether the expense data submitted by each FASTSIGNS Center for each separately provided expense item appropriately reflects the types of expenses which are ordinarily incurred by FASTSIGNS Centers and which should be included in the item according to generally acceptable accounting principles.

Each percentage given on this analysis reflects the mean average of the total percentages for the applicable expense item provided by the reporting FASTSIGNS Center (i.e., the aggregate sum of the expense percentages of all reporting FASTSIGNS Centers divided by the number of reporting Centers). The expense percentages for the various expense items provided by each reporting FAST-

SIGNS Center reflects that Center's expenses as a percentage of its Gross Revenues. No percentage given on this analysis is the actual expenses percentage experienced by any one FASTSIGNS Center and the actual expense percentages for the reporting FASTSIGNS Centers on any particular expense item may vary significantly. The following expenses represent the major expense items for a FASTSIGNS Center and should not be considered the only expenses that a FASTSIGNS Center will incur:

- *Cost of Sales* — Includes the cost of consumable raw materials and sub-contracting expense. Average cost of sales is 25.89%.

- *Advertising* — As set forth in Section 5, Advertising, of the Franchise Agreement, this includes yellow page placement, direct mail campaigns and general advertising. This does not include the advertising fee due to the NAC. Average advertising expense is 4.46%.

- *Salaries and Wages* — Includes compensation for production operation, customer service and sales (this does not include employee payroll taxes). Where indicated on the financial statements, the owner's compensation has not been included. Average salary and wage expense is 20.20%.

- *Rent* — Average rent expense of a Center is 5.69%, this is approximately $2,219.21 per month or $26,631 a year. New Franchisees may pay a higher rent depending on location of the Center.

- *Service Fees* — Based upon the current Franchise Agreement, a 6% of gross sales service fee is due to the Us.

- *Advertising Fee* — Based upon the current Franchise Agreement, a 2% of gross sales advertising fee is due to the NAC.

THE FRANCHISOR IS UNABLE TO VERIFY THE ACCURACY OF THE EXPENSE INFORMATION PROVIDED BY FASTSIGNS FRANCHISEES AND MAKES NO REPRE-SENTATIONS OR WARRANTIES REGARDING THE SAME.

The amount of gross sales realized and expenses incurred will vary from unit to unit. In particular, gross sales and expenses at Franchisee's Center will be directly affected by many additional factors not noted above, including, without limitation, the Center's geographic location, competition in the market, the presence of other FASTSIGNS Centers, the quality of management, the effectiveness of sales and marketing and the prices charged for products and services sold at the Center. Further, the franchise agreement to which each franchisee included in this analysis is subject is different from the Franchise Agreement attached to this Offering Circular as Exhibit B. Among other terms, the Franchise Agreement attached to this Offering Circular requires an initial franchise fee of $20,000 and a continuing Service Fee of 6%, while the franchise agreement applicable to each of the Centers included in this analysis required an initial franchise fee of $17,500, $18,500 or $20,000. Further, Franchisee may be required to participate in an Advertising Cooperative. This analysis, therefore, should only be used as a reference for Franchisee to use in conducting its own analysis.

Finally, Franchisee should particularly note the following:

EACH FRANCHISEE IS URGED TO CONSULT WITH APPROPRIATE FINANCIAL, BUSINESS AND LEGAL ADVISORS IN CONNECTION WITH THE INFORMATION SET FORTH IN THIS ANALYSIS.

THE AVERAGE SALES AND MAJOR EXPENSES REFLECTED IN THIS ANALYSIS SHOULD NOT BE CONSIDERED AS THE ACTUAL OR POTENTIAL SALES THAT WILL BE REALIZED BY ANY FRANCHISEE. WE DO NOT REPRESENT THAT ANY FRANCHISEE CAN EXPECT TO ATTAIN SUCH SALES. IN ADDITION, WE DO NOT REPRESENT THAT ANY FRANCHISEE WILL DERIVE INCOME THAT EXCEEDS THE INITIAL PAYMENT FOR OR INVESTMENT IN A FASTSIGNS FRANCHISE. NO INFER-

ENCE AS TO EXPENSES, COST OF GOODS SOLD OR PROFITS RELATING TO EXISTING OR FUTURE CENTERS SHOULD BE DRAWN FROM THE SALES INFORMATION REFLECTED IN THIS ANALYSIS. THE SUCCESS OF FRANCHISEE WILL DEPEND LARGELY UPON THE ABILITY OF FRANCHISEE, AND THE INDIVIDUAL FINANCIAL RESULTS OF A FRANCHISEE ARE LIKELY TO DIFFER FROM THE INFORMATION SET FORTH HEREIN. SUBSTANTIATION OF THE DATA USED IN PREPARING THIS ANALYSIS WILL BE MADE AVAILABLE UPON REASONABLE REQUEST.

THE ORIGINAL ONE DAY HI-TECH SIGN CO.

SIGNS NOW

4900 Manatee Ave. W., # 201
Bradenton, FL 34209
Tel: (800) 356-3373 (941) 747-7747
Fax: (941) 747-5074
E-Mail: terry@signsnow.com
Internet Address: www.signsnow.com
Contact: Mr. Terry A. Demarest, Director of Franchise Sales

Description: Founder of computer-generated quick sign industry. $1,000 marketing rebate. Only company with 14 regional managers, most having their own sign stores. Retail stores produce custom signs and graphics with the latest equipment and technology. SIGNS NOW operations system includes procedures; order-based POS with marketing support and tracking; proven sales and marketing; national accounts and vendor discount programs; free web page.

# Franchised Units:	324 Units
# Company-Owned Units:	0 Units
Total # Units:	324 Units
Founded In:	1983
1st Franchised In:	1986
Average Total Investment:	64.5-355.9K
Franchise Fee:	19.8K
On-Going Royalty:	5%
Advertising Fee:	2%
Financial Assistance:	Yes(I)
Site Selection Assistance:	Yes
Lease Negotiation Assistance:	Yes
Contract Terms (Init./Renew):	20/20

Initial Training Provided: 3-4 Weeks Regional Manager's Store or International Training Center; 1-2 Weeks Own Store.

Except for the sales figures provided below, we do not disclose profits or earnings levels of existing franchisees, nor do we project or forecast any particular level of sales, profits or earnings to prospective franchisees.

THE SALES FIGURES SET FORTH BELOW ARE COMPILED BY US FROM INFORMATION SUPPLIED BY OUR FRANCHISEES AND SHOULD NOT BE CONSIDERED AS THE ACTUAL OR POTENTIAL SALES THAT WILL BE REALIZED BY ANY OTHER FRANCHISEE. WE DO NOT REPRESENT THAT ANY FRANCHISEE CAN EXPECT TO ATTAIN THESE SALES. A NEW FRANCHISEE'S INDIVIDUAL FINANCIAL RESULTS ARE LIKELY TO DIFFER FROM THE SALES FIGURES PRESENTED BELOW.

THE SALES FIGURES OF THE FRANCHISED SIGNS NOW® STORES WERE OBTAINED FROM THE INFORMATION SUBMITTED TO US BY OUR FRANCHISEES FROM THE REQUIRED PERIODIC SALES REPORTS. NEITHER WE NOR AN INDEPENDENT CERTIFIED PUBLIC ACCOUNTANT HAS INDEPENDENTLY AUDITED OR VERIFIED THE PERIODIC SALES REPORTS.

ALL SIGNS NOW® STORES OFFER SUBSTANTIALLY THE SAME PRODUCTS AND SERVICES TO THE PUBLIC. NONE OF THE FRANCHISED SIGNS NOW® UNITS RECEIVED ANY SERVICES NOT GENERALLY AVAILABLE TO OTHER FRANCHISEES AND SUBSTANTIALLY THE SAME

SERVICES WILL BE OFFERED TO NEW FRANCHISEES.

WE DO NOT PROVIDE PROSPECTIVE FRANCHISEES WITH PROJECTIONS OR FORECASTS OF SALES, PROFITS OR EARNINGS. ACTUAL RESULTS MAY VARY BY REGION, MARKET POTENTIAL, THE FRANCHISEE'S MANAGERIAL SKILL, COMPETITION AND OTHER FACTORS BEYOND OUR CONTROL. THERE IS NO GUARANTEE THAT ANY NEW FRANCHISEE WILL ATTAIN THE AVERAGE SALES LEVELS ATTAINED BY THE EXISTING FRANCHISEES. SUBSTANTIATION OF THE AVERAGE SALES OF FRANCHISED SIGNS NOW® STORES WILL BE PROVIDED TO PROSPECTIVE FRANCHISEES UPON REASONABLE REQUEST.

The following chart shows the average sales, and the high and low, for franchised Signs Now® stores. The sales figures shown are for the twelve (12) month period from January 1–December 31, for the years 1987 through 1998. The sales figures are derived from periodic sales reports only from those franchised Signs Now® stores that were in operation for the entire period stated and that provided us with monthly statements of gross sales for the entire period stated.

THE FOLLOWING CHART CONTAINS INFORMATION RELATING SOLELY TO HISTORICAL SALES INFORMATION REGARDING EXISTING FRANCHISED SIGNS NOW® STORES. NO INFERENCE AS TO EXPENSES, COSTS OF GOODS OR PROFITS RELATING TO EXISTING OR FUTURE FRANCHISED SIGNS NOW® STORES SHOULD BE DRAWN FROM THE FOLLOWING SALES FIGURES.

Year	Number of Franchised Stores Open Full Period	Number of Franchised Stores Reporting Sales for Full Period	Total Sales of Reporting Stores	Average Volume of Reporting Stores During Reporting Period	% of Reporting Stores Meeting or Exceeding Average Volume	Highest Volume During Reporting Period	Lowest Volume During Reporting Period
Jan. 1–Dec. 31, 1987	7	7	$820,640	$117,234	57.1%	$164,695	$74,619
Jan. 1–Dec. 31, 1988	13	13	$1,900,136	$146,164	53.9%	$233,409	$96,862
Jan. 1–Dec. 31, 1989	20	20	$3,039,977	$151,999	40.0%	$275,531	$69,309
Jan. 1–Dec. 31, 1990	49	49	$6,568,465	$134,050	44.9%	$386,062	$47,694
Jan. 1–Dec. 31, 1991	98	98	$13,470,612	$137,455	45.9%	$384,247	$55,862
Jan. 1–Dec. 31, 1992	103	99	$15,450,625	$156,066	43.4%	$384,101	$54,302
Jan. 1–Dec. 31, 1993	104	101	$17,421,510	$172,490	41.6%	$446,504	$36,104
Jan. 1–Dec. 31, 1994	106	106	$21,239,965	$200,377	46.2%	$666,311	$27,377
Jan. 1–Dec. 31, 1995*	112	112	$24,097,425	$215,156	40.2%	$624,641	$42,642
Jan. 1–Dec. 31, 1996*	149	149	$32,998,659	$221,468	44.0%	$734,481	$38,801
Jan. 1–Dec. 31, 1997**	174	168	$39,897,130	$237,483	41.7%	$949,049	$31,593
Jan. 1–Dec. 31, 1998	203	201	$49,665,955	$242,119	41.0%	$1,321,944	$39,478

(*These figures do not include the Signery® stores converting to Signs Now® during 1995-1996.)
(**These figures do not include independent or Sign Express® stores converting to Signs Now® during 1997-1998.)

Travel

CRUISE HOLIDAYS INTERNATIONAL
9665 Chesapeake Dr., # 401
San Diego, CA 92123
Tel: (800) 866-7245 (619) 279-4780
Fax: (619) 279-4788
E-Mail: jflannigan@cruiseholidays.com
Internet Address: www.cruiseholidays.com
Contact: Mr. Jeffrey Flannigan, Dir. Franchise Development

Description: World's oldest and largest franchisor of cruise retail travel centers. Cruising is the fastest-growing and most dynamic segment of the travel industry. CRUISE HOLIDAYS INTERNATIONAL is at the forefront.

# Franchised Units:	208 Units
# Company-Owned Units:	0 Units
Total # Units:	208 Units
Founded In:	1984
1st Franchised In:	1984
Average Total Investment:	100-150K
Franchise Fee:	29.5K
On-Going Royalty:	1%/$525
Advertising Fee:	$275/Mo.
Financial Assistance:	Yes(I)
Site Selection Assistance:	Yes
Lease Negotiation Assistance:	Yes
Contract Terms (Init./Renew):	7/7
Initial Training Provided:	2 Weeks San Diego; 8-10 Days Miami.

We make no representations, express or implied, regarding potential earnings of your business and CHI has not suggested, guaranteed or warranted that you will succeed in the operation of a Cruise Holidays® Franchise or provided any sales or income projections of any kind to you.

No representations or statements of projected or forecasted sales, costs, income or profits, or other financial matters, are made to prospective Franchisees.

Other than as set forth in Exhibit "M" and its attachments *(which applies only to Standard Program franchises)*, we do not furnish or authorize our salespersons (or anyone else) to furnish any oral or written information concerning the actual or potential sales, costs, income or profits of a Cruise Holidays® Franchise. *Actual results vary from unit to unit and we cannot estimate or project the results of any particular franchise.*

We have specifically instructed our salespersons, agents, employees, and officers (and all other personnel) that they are *not* permitted to make any claims or statements regarding prospects or chances of success, actual or potential sales, costs, earnings, income or profits of, or other financial matters regarding, a Cruise Holidays® Franchise nor are they authorized to provide this information. We have not suggested or guaranteed that you will succeed in the operation of a Cruise Holidays® Franchise. We make no representations regarding any activities, items, matters or services to be engaged in or provided by us or with regard to any other matters, except as expressly provided in the Franchise Agreement. *If you believe that any promises, representations or agreements are or have been, at any time, made to you that are not expressly set forth in the Franchise Agreement or this Offering Circular, you must provide a written statement regarding this. If any information, promises, representations or agreements that are not expressly set forth in the Franchise Agreement or this Offering Circular have been provided to you, they should not be relied on, we will not be bound by them, and, if you do rely on anything not expressly set forth in the Franchise Agreement or this Offering Circular, you do so at your own risk. Please notify us in writing before you buy a franchise if any information, promises, representations or agreements that are not expressly set forth in the Franchise Agreement or this Offering Circular have been provided to you.*

Before signing any binding documents or making any investment, you should make your own independent investigation regarding the possible purchase of a Cruise Holidays® Franchise, including speaking with a significant number of current and past Cruise Holidays® Franchisees regarding their experiences and with independent advisors, such as an attorney and/or accountant, to assist your determination of the suitability of your possible investment in a Cruise Holidays® Franchise. See Item 20 and related exhibits regarding the names, addresses and phone numbers of current and past Cruise Holidays® Franchisees.

Exhibit M
Cruise Holidays International, Inc. Information Regarding Reported Franchisee Average Gross Sales — U.S. May, 1998, through April, 1999

The information set forth in this document is a report of average monthly gross sales of the 101 Cruise Holidays® Agencies located in the United States which were open, in operation and provided a minimum of 9 monthly sales reports for the complete period from May 1, 1998, through April 30, 1999. The factual basis for the information presented is the monthly gross sales reported by those Franchisees, as part of their normal monthly service fee reports to Cruise Holidays International, Inc., for such period. 63 other Cruise Holidays® Agencies were open for only a portion of the period or did not provide a minimum of 9 monthly sales reports, so their reports are *not* included in the figures presented. Nor do any figures presented reflect Cruise Holidays® Agencies located outside the United States, Affiliate franchisees' sales. The Affiliate Program was introduced in 1997.

For the period from May 1, 1998, through April 30, 1999, the U.S. Cruise Holidays® Agencies in operation throughout that 12-month period reported average sales of $1,438,626 per Agency for the 12 months covered. During the same period and for the same Agencies, reported sales for that same 12-month period ranged from $106,480 to $10,312,955 per Agency. These figures do not include gross sales for any Agencies which were not open and in operation for the entire May 1, 1998, through April 30, 1999, period nor for Agencies located outside the U.S., nor for Agencies from whom less than 9 months of sales were reported. Of the 101 U.S. Agencies covered by these reports, 39 Agencies (or 39%) reported average monthly sales above the stated average and 62 Agencies (or 61%) reported average monthly sales below the stated average. This information was compiled from monthly reports filed by such Franchisees, but has not been independently verified or audited.

CAUTION: SOME OUTLETS HAVE SOLD THIS AMOUNT. THERE IS NO ASSURANCE YOU'LL DO AS WELL. IF YOU RELY UPON OUR FIGURES YOU MUST ACCEPT THE RISK OF NOT DOING AS WELL.

A NEW FRANCHISEE'S INDIVIDUAL FINANCIAL RESULTS ARE LIKELY TO DIFFER FROM THE RESULTS SET FORTH IN THIS DOCUMENT.

Actual results will vary from franchised Agency to franchised Agency and Cruise Holidays International, Inc. cannot estimate or project the results of operation of any particular franchise. We are unable, and do not attempt, to predict, forecast or project future performance of any Cruise Holidays® Agency and the information presented herein should not be used to predict, forecast or project any such future performance. The information presented should not be considered or used in estimating or projecting actual, probable or possible financial results for any current or future franchised Agency and Cruise Holidays International, Inc. specifically and expressly disclaims any representation that the results reported will, are likely to or can be achieved by any current or future franchised Agency at any time in the future. *You should consult with your own independent financial, business and legal advisors in evaluating the information presented in this document.* Actual commission income for an Agency is, of course, only a portion of gross sales.

In particular, you should be aware that past performance is not necessarily a reliable guide to future performance or the results you may achieve, since *the most important qualities in success in the cruise agency business are personal to you* and include your energy, management skills, sales and marketing ability, financial and other resources and personality and desire.

For the period presented (May 1, 1998, through April 30, 1999), the results presented cover 101 of the 164 Agencies (62%) open and operating throughout such period in the U.S. 63 U.S. Agencies were not open and operating throughout the entire 12-month period and/or did not provide a minimum of nine monthly sales reports and therefore such 63 Agencies' results were not taken into account in calculating the average reported gross sales presented. In addition, no results for Agencies outside the U.S. or Affiliate Franchises are presented in this document.

Substantiation of the data used in preparing the information set forth in this document will be made available to the prospective Franchisee on reasonable request.

The information presented has not been audited and is based on monthly gross sales as reported by Cruise Holidays® Franchisees to Cruise Holidays International, Inc. for purposes of service fee computation and payment. Cruise Holidays International, Inc. has assumed that such reports are accurate and that the Franchisees have not overstated their monthly gross sales.

Prospective Franchisees should note that the Cruise Holidays® Franchisees who have supplied the data used in this document are located generally in urban or suburban areas. Many of the franchised Agencies whose results are reported are located in major metropolitan areas. The areas in which Franchisees are located typically have a relatively high level of socioeconomic and demographic makeup which can contribute to a greater need for, and ability to afford, the products and services of the type offered by Cruise Holidays® Franchisees and accompanying possible higher sales. Revenues will also be affected by such factors as level and nature of competition, years in operation, population, numbers of consumers visiting and resident in the area of a Cruise Holidays® Agency and general economic conditions (including disposable income) in the area. Prospective Franchisees should also note that the figures presented are *averages*, that they include results from some Cruise Holidays® Franchisees who have been in business for a substantial period of time and that new Cruise Holidays® Franchisees should not necessarily expect to achieve such results. *The prospective Franchisee should independently verify whether such factors and conditions in his/her intended area of operation are comparable to those in existing Franchisees' areas.* Cruise Holidays International, Inc. has no experience with franchised or company-owned Agencies in other areas and can make no prediction or estimation of the results that might be experienced by franchised Agencies in any areas.

Prospective Franchisees should, prior to making any investment decision, research the need in their proposed area of operation for the products and services of the type offered by Cruise Holidays® Franchisees, including actual and potential competition and the socioeconomic and demographic background of their area. *In this regard, prospective*

463

Franchisees are strongly encouraged to speak with existing Cruise Holidays® Franchisees and to make an independent judgment as to whether their experience may or may not be transferable to the Prospective Franchisee's proposed area of operation.

Prospective Franchisees should further note that the information presented relates only to gross sales and that no information is presented, nor does Cruise Holidays International, Inc. have information, regarding the cost of operation of existing Cruise Holidays® Franchisees or their commission income, profits, losses or cash flow. Commissions are determined by travel services providers and can vary over time or otherwise.

THE RESETTLERS, INC.

CENTREVILLE, DELAWARE
(302) 658-3414

RESETTLERS, THE
5811 Kennett Pike
Centreville, DE 19807
Tel: (800) 730-0090 (302) 658-9110
Fax: (302) 658-5809
E-Mail:
Internet Address: www.resettlers.com
Contact: Ms. Beth Lewandowski, Diector Franchise
Development

Description: The Resettlers offers a variety of services designed to assist older clients. Making the transition from the family home to an adult community or downsizing into smaller living quarters is, at best, stressful. In order to assist the ever increasing population of older Americans, we can provide a wide range of customized services that include move planning and coordination and setting the new household up. We also offer retail outlets for those excess items that are no longer needed.

# Franchised Units:	1 Units
# Company-Owned Units:	2 Units
Total # Units:	3 Units
Founded In:	1985
1st Franchised In:	1997
Average Total Investment:	85-200K
Franchise Fee:	20K
On-Going Royalty:	5%
Advertising Fee:	2%
Financial Assistance:	No
Site Selection Assistance:	Yes
Lease Negotiation Assistance:	Yes
Contract Terms (Init./Renew):	10/10
Initial Training Provided:	2 Weeks in Wilmigton, DE.

At the time of filing of this Offering Circular, The Resettlers, Inc. of Centerville, Delaware has four relevant operating departments specifically defined as three retail units and one moving department.

Factual Basis:
All retail facilities are within a 40 mile range from Centerville, Delaware. The gross size in square footage of the stores ranges from 1,600 square feet to 8,000 square feet.

- The Annex, located in Wilmington, DE occupies 8,000 square feet of warehouse space. The Annex was moved to its new location in 1997.
- The Resettlers Marketplace in Lafayette Hill, PA occupies 5,000 square feet of warehouse

space. The unit is a fully staffed office employing home visit and buyout coordinators for southeastern Pennsylvania. It also serves as a retail center and our prototype for this franchise offering.

- The Gallery located in Centerville, DE occupies approximately 1600 square feet of showroom space. Because the Gallery utilizes a different method of retail sales, we do not consider this to be the prototype of the franchise offered in this Circular; however, we are including the relevant financial figures.

- All three retail operations are located in densely populated, middle to high income areas, strategically placed near major thoroughfares, and all operations have strong competition. In our estimation, our existing geographic territories will be substantially similar to the demography of approved, proposed Protected Territories offered in this Circular.

- Our moving division is derived from all three retail units and occupies approximately 18% of gross sales.

Following are relevant financial figures for the year 1997:

Gross Sales	$1,880,640
Cost of Sales	710,310
Operating Expenses	616,231
Operating Profit	$553,244

THE FINANCIAL NUMBERS REPORTED ABOVE REFLECT OUR HISTORICAL ACTUAL NON-FRANCHISED OPERATIONS. WE MAKE NO REPRESENTATIONS OR WARRANTIES, OR OFFER ANY ASSURANCES THAT YOU WILL ACHIEVE THESE LEVELS OR ANY LEVELS. YOUR RESULTS ARE LIKELY TO DIFFER. SUBSTANTIATION OF THE DATA USED IN PREPARING THIS STATEMENT WILL BE MADE AVAILABLE TO YOU ON REASONABLE REQUEST.

TWO MEN AND A TRUCK
2152 Commons Pkwy.
Okemos, MI 48864
Tel: (800) 345-1070 (517) 482-6683
Fax: (800) 278-6114
E-Mail: halm@twomen.com
Internet Address: www.twomen.com
Contact: Mr. Hal McLean, Recruiting Director

Description: TWO MEN AND A TRUCK franchises provide local residential and commercial moving services, boxes and packing services and supplies. Our Stick Men University and First Gear Training program provide the most comprehensive initial and on-going training in the industry. We are the 7th largest moving company in the nation! The 'Company That's On The Move."

# Franchised Units:	95 Units
# Company-Owned Units:	0 Units
Total # Units:	95 Units
Founded In:	1985
1st Franchised In:	1989
Average Total Investment:	75K+
Franchise Fee:	28K
On-Going Royalty:	6%
Advertising Fee:	1%
Financial Assistance:	No
Site Selection Assistance:	Yes
Lease Negotiation Assistance:	No
Contract Terms (Init./Renew):	5/5

Initial Training Provided: 5 Days Lansing, MI at Stick Men University.

Graph 1 shows the number of TWO MEN AND A TRUCK® franchises that achieved sales volumes in each of the eleven sales volume categories during the 1st, 2nd, 3rd and 4th years of operation of the franchises. As used in the Graph, the 1st year of operation means the first 12 months of operation of the franchise, the 2nd year of operation means the 2nd 12 months of operation of the franchise, etc. Graph 1 also notes the range of ending dates for the 12 month periods represented in the Graph. The "1998" column in Graph 1 shows the number of Franchisees who have been in operation a minimum of 12 months at the end of 1998 who have achieved sales volumes in each of the eleven sales categories during the 1998 calendar year. Graph 2 (following Graph 1) lists the three lowest, three highest and average sales volume achieved for each year of operation represented in Graph 1. Graph 2 also notes the percentage of franchises that met or exceeded the average sales for each of those years of operation. The 1998 column only includes those Franchisees who were in business a minimum of 12 months at the end of 1998.

Graph 1

Range of Ending Dates (*)	First Year of Operation 04/86–12/98	Second Year of Operation 04/87–12/98	Third Year of Operation 04/88–7/98	Fourth Year of Operation 04/89–11/98	1998
$0–100K	22 (4)	4 (2)	2 (1)	2 (1)	0
$100–200K	17	11 (1)	5 (1)	3	4
$200–300K	9	8 (1)	5 (1)	2 (1)	2
$300–400K	7	12	5	3	3
$400–500K	3	6	9	7 (1)	10
$500–600K	0	0	6 (1)	3	4
$600–700K	2	3	3	2	3
$700–800K	0	1	4	2	4
$800–900K	0	1	0	2 (1)	2
$900–1 Mill.	0	1	1	2	4
>$1 Mill.	0	0	2	3	13 (3)
> $2 Mill.	0	0	0	0	1
Total Franchises (5)	60	47	42	28	50

*The ending dates for the 12 month periods represented in each year of operation in the table range by as much as 10 years. For example, in the 1st year of Operation, the earliest 12 month period represented ended in April, 1986, and the latest 12 month period represented ended in September, 1998. As a result, you must consider the effect of inflation, changes in economic conditions and other similar factors that could affect these numbers.

1. This number includes one unit operated by principals or members of the family of principals of the Company.

2. This number includes two units operated by principals or members of the family of principals of the Company.

3. This number includes three units operated by principals or members of the family of principals of the Company.

4. This number includes four units operated by principals or members of the family of principals of the Company.

5. The franchises listed under each year of operation in the graph include all franchises that operated for at least the number of months represented by that year of operation, even if those franchises are no longer in the system.

Graph 2

	First Year of Operation	Second Year of Operation	Third Year of Operation	Fourth Year of Operation	1998
First Lowest	$28,910	$46,684	$60,733	$58,990	$109,096
Second Lowest	$33,950	$51,552	$65,892	$73,126	$154,731
Third Lowest	$38,546	$53,103	$125,391	$154,268	$161,299
First Highest	$633,757	$990,061	$1,498,409	$1,744,832	$2,290,996
Second Highest	$617,285	$885,992	$1,262,558	$1,436,600	$1,780,662
Third Highest	$459,121	$707,124	$968,720	$1,010,166	$1,595,987
Average Sales	$187,535	$327,000	$461,487	$562,114	$762,315
% of Franchisees that met or exceeded the average	38%	49%	44%	35%	46%

These graphs are based on actual volumes reported to us by our Franchisees. These volumes have not been audited or verified by us. These Graphs should not be viewed as assurance that you will achieve any particular sales volume. Your sales volume will be affected by the condition of the economy, both locally and nationally, the status of the competition, your diligence and experience and many other factors beyond our control. Your individual financial results are likely to differ from the results stated in the Graphs.

Substantiation of the data used in preparing these Graphs will be made available to you upon reasonable request.

Other than the information contained in this Item and any substantiation of the information, we do not furnish or authorize our recruiters to furnish any oral or written information concerning the actual or potential sales, costs, income or profits of a TWO MEN AND A TRUCK® franchise. Actual results vary from unit to unit and we cannot estimate the results of any particular franchise.

Alphabetical listing of franchisors

Categorical listing of franchisors

Index

THE ONLY MINORITY FRANCHISING DIRECTORY

BOND'S MINORITY FRANCHISE GUIDE
2000 Edition

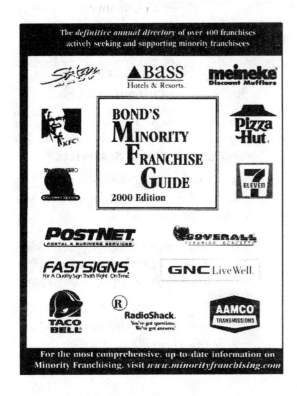

Key Features:

- Detailed profiles of over 400 forward-looking franchisors that encourage and actively support the inclusion of minority franchisees (See sample profile on back)

- Overview of franchising industry

- List of resources available to prospective franchisees

- 272 pages, 39 distinct business categories

- Direct comparability between franchise listings

JUST PUBLISHED

Yes, I want to order ___ copy(ies) of *Bond's Minority Franchise Guide* at $19.95 each. Please add $4.00 per book for shipping* & handling. California residents add appropriate sales tax.

Name _____ Title _____

Company _____ Telephone No. (_____)_____

Address _____

City _____ State/Prov. _____ Zip _____

❏ Check Enclosed or   Charge my: ❏ MasterCard ❏ Visa

Card #: _____ Expiration Date: _____

Signature: _____

Please send to:
Source Book Publications
P.O. Box 12488, Oakland, CA 94604

* Note: All books shipped by USPS Priority Mail (2nd Day Air).
Satisfaction Guaranteed. If not fully satisfied, return for a prompt, 100% refund.

For faster service, call (800) 841-0873 or (510) 839-5471 or fax (510) 839-2104

THE DEFINITIVE ANNUAL GUIDE OF INTERNATIONAL FRANCHISING

THE 1999 INTERNATIONAL HERALD TRIBUNE
INTERNATIONAL FRANCHISE GUIDE

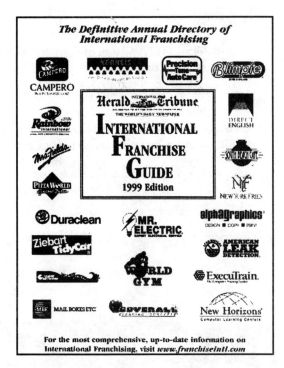

Key Features:

- The Most Comprehensive and Up-To-Date Directory of Committed International Franchisors.

- Profiles Are the Result of an Exhaustive 60-Point Questionnaire.

- 32 Distinct Business Categories.

- Listing of International Franchise Consultants, Attorneys and Service Providers.

- 192 Pages.

- Direct Comparability Between Franchise Listings.

Yes, I want to order ___ copy(ies) of the 1999 IHT *International Franchise Guide* at US$34.95 each, shipping included.

Name _____ Title _____

Company _____ Telephone No. (_____) _____

Address _____

City _____ State/Prov. _____ Zip _____

❏ Check Enclosed or

Charge my: ❏ MasterCard ❏ Visa

Card #: _____ Expiration Date: _____

Signature: _____

Please send to:
Source Book Publications
P.O. Box 12488, Oakland, CA 94604

Satisfaction Guaranteed. If not fully satisfied, return for a prompt, 100% refund.

For faster service, call (800) 841-0873 or (510) 839-5471 or fax us at (510) 839-2104.
Also check us out on the Internet at www.franchiseintl.com.

THE DEFINITIVE FRANCHISING DIRECTORY

BOND'S FRANCHISE GUIDE - 2000 (13th) Edition

(Previously Published as *The Source Book of Franchise Opportunities* - 7 Editions)

Key Features:

- The Most Comprehensive and Up-To-Date Directory of Franchise Listings

- All New Data Every Edition

- Over 2,150 Total Listings
  1,050 Detailed Franchisor Profiles
  ~ 1,800 American Franchisors
  ~ 350 Canadian Franchisors

- 51 Distinct Business Categories

- 496 Pages (425 Pages of Franchise Listings)

- Direct Comparability Between Franchise Listings

PUBLISHED ANNUALLY

Yes, I want to order ___ copy(ies) of *Bond's Franchise Guide* at $29.95 each ($42.75 Canadian). Please add $4.00 per book for shipping * & handling ($5.75 Canada; International shipments at actual cost). California residents add appropriate sales tax.

Name _____ Title _____

Company _____ Telephone No. (____) _____

Address _____

City _____ State/Prov. _____ Zip _____

□ Check Enclosed or   Charge my: □ MasterCard □ Visa
             Card #: _____ Expiration Date: _____
             Signature: _____

Please send to:
Source Book Publications
P. O. Box 12488, Oakland, CA 94604

* Note: All books shipped by USPS Priority Mail (2nd Day Air).
Satisfaction Guaranteed. If not fully satisfied, return for a prompt, 100% refund.

✂

For Faster Service, Call (800) 841-0873 or (510) 839-5471 or Fax (510) 839-2104